PIMLICO

626

THE MYTH OF DECLINE

George L. Bernstein was born and raised in the Washington, DC, area. He received his BA in Economics from Columbia University in 1968 and his PhD in History from the University of Chicago in 1978. He has taught at Tulane University in New Orleans since 1980, where he is currently Associate Professor of History, specialising in modern Britain. He is the author of *Liberalism and Liberal Politics in Edwardian England* (1986). He has lived in Britain twice for a year, as well as spending many summers there. Since July 2003 he has been Dean of Tulane College, the men's liberal arts college of Tulane University.

THE MYTH
OF DECLINE

The Rise of Britain Since 1945

GEORGE L. BERNSTEIN

PIMLICO

Published by Pimlico 2004

2 4 6 8 10 9 7 5 3 1

First published in Great Britain by
Pimlico 2004

Pimlico
Random House, 20 Vauxhall Bridge Road,
London SW1V 2SA

Random House Australia (Pty) Limited
20 Alfred Street, Milsons Point, Sydney,
New South Wales 2061, Australia

Random House New Zealand Limited
18 Poland Road, Glenfield,
Auckland 10, New Zealand

Random House South Africa (Pty) Limited
Endulini, 5A Jubilee Road, Parktown 2193, South Africa

Random House UK Limited Reg. No. 954009

A CIP catalogue record for this book
is available from the British Library

ISBN 1-8441-3102-5

Papers used by Random House UK Limited are natural,
recyclable products made from wood grown in sustainable forests.
The manufacturing processes conform to the environmental
regulations of the country of origin

Printed and bound in Great Britain by
Bookmarque Ltd, Croydon, Surrey

To Rose

to our English friends

Tracy and Peter

John and Jinny

Philip and Jane

Billie

and to the memory of our friend Brian Salmon

TABLE OF CONTENTS

PREFACE

In the spring of 1990, I taught a seminar in the Tulane Honors Program on Europe since 1914. Two of the assigned readings attributed Europe's peace and prosperity since 1945 to a division between East and West that was accepted by both sides as permanent. The authors, too, accepted its permanence.[1] Yet even as the students were reading these books, the Soviet domination of Eastern Europe was collapsing. Therefore, I asked in the final exam: if Europe's peace since 1945 depended on a permanent division and balance between a Soviet-dominated East and an American-dominated West, did we now have to resign ourselves to another major European war? Thus are the risks of analysing the present laid bare: as the scholar explains, the very bases of that explanation can be undermined. A second example further illustrates the dilemma of the contemporary historian. Walter Laqueur ended the revised edition of his *Europe since Hitler* with an 'Afterword' on the 1970s. It is a profoundly pessimistic chapter.[2] On the one hand, it reflects the years of unemployment and inflation that followed the OPEC oil-price increases of 1973 and 1979. On the other hand, it reflects the breakdown of East–West détente following the Soviet invasion of Afghanistan and the NATO decision to deploy medium-range missiles in Britain and on the Continent. Yet ten years later, not only had communism collapsed in Eastern Europe, but Western Europe, while entering a recession, was at the end of one of the most robust periods of economic expansion since the war.

Clearly, it is a dangerous business writing an overview of contemporary history. History is partly an attempt to describe and explain change over time, and such history requires a beginning and an end to provide the framework for that analysis. Yet a survey of the contemporary era has no end, except the arbitrarily imposed one of the year in which the historian writes. And it is impossible to know whether the present actually represents an appropriate end point, for that judgement requires the perspective that looking back on a more distant past allows. Even if the historian chooses to end the story at some date short of the present, it is difficult to judge which date represents an appropriate end for the purpose of defining and interpreting historical change.

As a final and explicitly British example, it is worth looking at the problem of evaluating the success or failure of Margaret Thatcher's policies in their aim of reviving the British economy. During the latter part of the Thatcher premiership, my father (a professional economist) would periodically tell me that the British economy performed better than any other in the European Community during the 1980s. I always replied that, if he measured from 1979 instead of 1980, he would get a different record for the British economy, which collapsed during the first year of Thatcher's government. My father needed no lessons from me on the slippery nature of economic statistics. He was not an expert on the British economy, however, and his information came from the pro-Thatcher *Economist*, while mine was from the anti-Thatcher *Manchester Guardian Weekly*. Of course, we were both right: everything depends on the selection of starting and end points when measuring economic performance. All that is left for the non-specialist historian who wants to be fair-minded (as I do) is to make both points. The problem with selecting an end date for evaluating Thatcher's record is especially difficult. One of the stated goals of Thatcherism was to effect a permanent reversal of Britain's economic decline by changing the mentality of the people to make them more entrepreneurial. Yet even if one accepts that part of Britain's economic problem was a failure of entrepreneurship (which is a subject of hot historical debate), it is impossible to evaluate whether a permanent change in the value system has occurred over such a brief period of time. Once again, the perspective of distance is essential. Hence, any judgement of the Thatcherite record must be partial and provisional.

These problems of chronology and evaluation have encouraged historians to shy away from contemporary history. This is not to deny that there are excellent monographic analyses of particular aspects of post-1945 Britain by historians. However, an awful lot of the work on specific issues and problems is still done by social scientists (economists, political scientists and sociologists) and journalists. There have been many thematic surveys by historians that have provided an overview of some aspect of the period, but the only attempt at a comprehensive analysis has been Kenneth Morgan's volume for the Oxford History of Britain. Morgan chose to break his work up into chapters covering three-to five-year periods. The effect is that, while it can be superbly analytical, the reader is overwhelmed by detail and loses a sense of the larger themes.[3] Other books that try to synthesise the period can be excessively 'presentist' – that is, the author assumes familiarity with the subject on the part of the reader. The people, the crises, the debates, even the scandals are all assumed to be part of the common discourse of writer and reader and so to require no explanation. Or, alternatively, there is excessive explanation of what was interesting at the time, even though it has little long-term significance – e.g. the personal divisions within the Cabinet, or the details of the budget. Revision does not necessarily rectify this problem. Revised editions might tack on a chapter dealing with the most recent period, without much or any revision of earlier chapters to take into account changing interests, new research or more recent information. Thus, both the original book and the new chapters end up being 'presentist'.

The purpose of this book is to try to counter this problem by writing the same kind of history that I would write if the period were 1845–1901 instead of 1945–2001. That means an attempt to be inclusive (not just providing a political narrative), but also an attempt to emphasise interpretation more than description, despite all the problems that this involves when writing about the present. In pursuing this goal, I have chosen to organise the book into relatively long time periods and to develop the narrative around the theme of decline. More specifically, I seek to analyse not only in what ways and to what degree there *was* decline, but also in what ways there was *not* decline. The larger objective is to question whether decline provides an adequate paradigm for understanding the period. My thesis is that it does not. Ordinary Britons and scholars alike, in focusing on Britain's economy and its role as a world power in the post-war era, have exaggerated the extent of Britain's decline. In particular, they have been preoccupied with change that often was inevitable and so represents no failure on the part of the British people. And the notion of failure – in the sense that the British did something wrong, and that if they had acted differently decline would not have taken place, or it would not have been so great – is implicit in the way almost everyone discusses Britain's decline.

At the same time, in focusing on Britain's economy and role as a world power, people have ignored revolutionary changes that occurred in Britain's society and culture. In using the word 'revolutionary', I am going out on a limb, for it implies that I accept the permanence, or at least a permanent impact, of the changes that I describe. Thus, I could easily fall victim to the dangers of writing contemporary history that I have described. I do not think it is much of a risk, however. There will be no going back on the changes that have occurred since the war – in the roles of and perceptions of women in society; in the prosperity of the society and the kinds of lives that prosperity has allowed people to live; in the extension of secondary and tertiary education to an enormously larger proportion of the population; in the contribution that immigration has made to a more diverse and energetic society; in the advent of a popular culture that has become universalised and commercialised; even in the nature of academic disciplines and methodologies that have helped transform elite culture and given due recognition to popular cultures. These changes and more may not define the future, but they will permanently affect it. That is what revolution means, and so in many ways Part III of this book, entitled 'Revolution', is its centrepiece. Whether or not all of these changes involve progress towards some better society is a subject of intense debate. Personally, I think they do. Thus, while I work hard to provide a balanced view of all the changes that have occurred since 1945, and to give equal time and equal credibility to those who believe that decline *is* the shaping paradigm for Britain in this period, or that there has not been much progress at all, my own belief is that Britain today is a more exciting, dynamic, diverse, prosperous, and so a better place than it was in 1945.

To summarise, then, there are three themes relating to decline that are developed in this book. First, even in the areas where it has occurred, the extent of decline has often been exaggerated by the British and outsiders alike. Second, Britain did a pretty good job of adapting to the radical changes of the twentieth century, most of which were beyond its control; so the implication of some sort of cultural or moral failing that accounts for decline is not justified. Finally, in focusing on decline, people have ignored a radical transformation of Britain since 1945 that has, on balance, been for the better and so represents progress rather than decline.

There are some other themes as well that shape the argument of this book. One is the rise and fall of consensus as a principle for understanding British politics, a theme that many political scientists and political historians have both developed and challenged. Like the theme of decline, it works especially well for a historical period that has Thatcherism as its chronological climax, for Thatcherism was an attempt to reverse decline, and one of the chosen methods of doing so was the rejection of consensus. Both Chapters 12 and 14 of Part IV (on 1979–2001) show how Thatcherism attacked consensus in an effort to effect radical change. Both conclude with the questions, how far did it succeed, and to what extent is a new consensus identifiable? As is appropriate when we are so close to the present, there is no clear answer. The ambiguous answer, however, is 'yes, but'. That is, there are clear areas of convergence between 'New Labour' and Thatcherite conservatism, but there are also areas where Tony Blair is trying to stake out a difference, while with no agreement on Europe, there can be no foreign policy consensus at all.

Another theme is the importance of the United States in shaping Britain's post-war history. America is central to all three of the major areas of contention concerning decline: economic, political (i.e. as a world power) and moral or cultural. The American influence is pervasive, and, as Chapter 1 shows, the differing attitudes of various British intellectuals and policy-makers towards the United States and the values it represents helped shape differing perceptions about decline. Writing as an American, and recognising all the flaws of my nation, I still cannot help but believe that increased American influence is one reason why Britain (and indeed Europe) *is* a more exciting, diverse and dynamic place. Thus, my view is opposed to that of those intellectuals in Britain (especially on the left) who bemoan the corrupting influence of American capitalism and racism on an implicitly pure British society and culture. While there is much wrong with the United States, it is not the source of all the evils that threaten Britain, and it has had much to offer the older societies of Europe. The United States has long reflected the influences of European culture (including embracing capitalism and racism). The more accelerated reverse flow across the Atlantic – even if it does include McDonald's, *Dallas* and Disneyland – has been healthy for Europe as well as for America in breaking down isolationism and provincialism on both sides. Thus, America plays a major role (though one capable of exaggeration) in influencing parts of the revolution I describe in Part III, and the narrative will selectively point out where parallels and differences exist between Britain and the United States – and also sometimes how both compare with the Continent.

The United States plays an important role in the rest of the book as well, defining the nature of the power and economic relationships that have shaped the world in general and Europe in particular since the Second World War. Even if there had been no cultural flow at all, the history of Britain since 1945 could not be written without the United States playing an important role, and that makes the modern period unique in European and British history. For Britain, this American role has created a special problem in its foreign relations: does it or does it not have a 'special relationship' with its American offspring? The belief in a 'special relationship' has been the source of difficulty for Britain: it has become excessively dependent on the United States for its defence, in shaping its foreign policy and even in developing its economy. A Briton is not necessarily anti-American to wish for greater independence, for the United States, like all nations, pursues its own interests, and those interests will not always converge with Britain's or anyone else's. Furthermore, this dependence on the United States has created an apparent trade-off between America and Europe in defining Britain's foreign policy almost from the beginning of this period. Hence, even in discussing Britain and the movement towards European economic and political union, there is an American influence that is inescapable (although not necessarily one initiated by the United States).

These, then, are the themes of interest to me as I seek to explain and interpret the history of Britain during the years since the end of the Second World War: in what ways there has or has not been decline; the rise and fall and perhaps rise again of political consensus; and the effects on Britain of the more intrusive political, economic and cultural role played by the United States in the affairs of Europe and the world. At the same time, I also try to avoid some of the other problems of writing contemporary history that I discussed earlier. First, I assume that the events being described are not part of the common knowledge of my readers, even those who are professional historians. This is partly because I am writing for an American as well as a British audience, and often I provide American comparisons as an aid.

Hopefully, however, this assumption applies also to Britons, who are not fully familiar with their contemporary history or with how Britain and the United States differ. As a corollary, since the events of 1945 did not occur in a vacuum, but grew out of a context that is important if they are to be understood, I try to situate what I discuss by giving some historical background as I go along, without weighing the narrative down too much. Too often, we historians treat what we describe in *our* period as something new and different, when some of it is very familiar to historians of an earlier period. Since I am myself a historian of an earlier past, I try to show the reader what is not new as well as what is, and just how long change has been going on – things that are especially important when we are talking about decline, which is by definition relative to the past.

I also do not assume a familiarity with the concepts that academics use in the ordinary course of their thinking and writing. This is most evident with my treatment of economic theory and relationships. Too often historians, and even more social scientists, simply assert these relationships without explaining them. I do my best to explain, either in the text or in notes – though, since I am not a professional economist, my best may fail more often than I would like. I do the same with some sociological concepts, like class and social mobility, and some cultural concepts like Modernism and Postmodernism. I also try to eliminate the kind of 'presentist' focus on detail that would burden the reader with the unnecessary and divert him or her from the broader themes that I want to be the focus of the book. It is difficult enough to keep a book on fifty-five exciting years of British history to a reasonable length without bombarding the reader with the details of every budget and every Cabinet reshuffle. Hopefully, the longer-term economic, political, social and cultural trends that are developed will illuminate what is crucial, so that the proverbial forest is not lost sight of for focusing excessively on the trees.

As part of this effort not to get too bogged down in detail, I have tried to keep references to a minimum. There are a few criteria that I have established for providing an endnote. I reference all data. I want others to be able to find where the numbers come from if they wish. I also reference any point or argument that seems to me to be counterintuitive, that is contrary to what we have come to believe or contrary to accepted interpretation, or that is subject to conflicting interpretations. Finally, I have provided a reference when I simply could not have written a narrative without the help of a specific author, or when a work is especially useful for anyone who wants to follow up on a subject. Because I am a political historian, this is the subject that I knew best going into writing this book. Since political history also involves the fewest statistics, the political history and foreign policy chapters have the fewest references. There are also times when I have provided some additional commentary or information which, while interesting (at least to me), cannot easily be incorporated into the narrative. Most of the time, I have used footnotes to provide this information. Occasionally, however, when I have thought the information of somewhat less importance, or when it is part of a larger historical debate, I have put it in endnotes. All my efforts to elaborate on economic definitions are in footnotes. My goal throughout has been to make the references useful rather than burdensome for the reader.

ACKNOWLEDGEMENTS

This book is based on secondary sources and newspapers. It could not have been written without the detailed research and analysis of an enormous number of scholars and journalists. Thus, my first debt is to all those people and newspapers listed in the bibliography. To single out a few, Kenneth Morgan and Peter Clarke were the first historians to provide first-rate analytical narratives of the period. They literally cleared the path in which the rest of us follow; I used them often to guide me, especially at the beginning. Social science is quantitative. Two books have been invaluable in providing the data and the analysis I have needed as I tried to get a handle on the British economy and British society: *The British Economy since 1945*, edited by Nicholas Crafts and Nicholas Woodward, and *Twentieth-Century British Social Trends*, edited by A. H. Halsey and Josephine Webb. Many tables based on both books appear in this one in some form or other; I am more grateful than I can convey for the work that all the contributors to both have done. David and Gareth Butler's *Twentieth-Century British Political Facts 1900–2000* also provides an enormous amount of useful data and information. Readers will note that the number of quotations goes up significantly in the chapters that deal with the arts, literature and culture. Being more ignorant on these subjects than others, I am more dependent on the words and analysis of others and so indebted to those authors.

Others who have written or edited works that have been especially helpful to me are B. W. E. Alford, C. J. Bartlett, Andrew Blake, Kevin Boyle and Tom Hadden, John Campbell, Susan Compton, John Darwin, John Davis, T. M. Devine, Michael Dintenfass, Simon Frith and Howard Horne, Richard Holt, Simon Jenkins, Dennis Kavanagh, Tariq Modood and his collaborators, Richard Pells, Ben Pimlott, Sidney Pollard, Bernard Porter, John Ramsden, David Reynolds, Peter Riddell, Eric Shaw, Richard Weight, Martin Wiener, Hugo Young and John W. Young. Finally, I must pay tribute to the *Guardian*. I started reading the *Manchester Guardian Weekly* in 1974, before I went to Britain for the first time to research my dissertation. I have stuck with it since then, with great benefit to myself. I have also read the daily when in Britain, though since the early 1990s it has shared time with the *Independent*. The quality of writing in both of these newspapers (and in the *New York Times* too) makes them a pleasure to read, and they have been essential sources for the more recent period.

Several friends and colleagues have read parts of this book, especially in its early stages. Meredith Veldman gave me early encouragement from a specialist in the post-1945 era that this was a worthwhile project. Lindsay Waters has been a friend since we were in graduate school together at the University of Chicago. He gave me the assurance of a trained editor that my approach and style had at least the potential to appeal to an audience beyond the academic one. Then, when I was finished, he suggested Will Sulkin of Pimlico as someone whom I might approach. My brothers Daniel and Alan both read chapters and so served as a test audience; both have shown unfailing belief in the value of this book. Nancy Maveety and Eric Gorham, both political scientists, pressed me to stay focused on the theme of decline. In a book this size, it is easy to lose sight of where one is going; I hope I have succeeded in keeping decline to the forefront as they have urged. I owe a special debt to my colleague Linda Pollock, who encouraged me to go ahead with a project of a kind that is not always looked upon favourably within the academic community.

THE MYTH OF DECLINE

Support from a scholar of her standing meant a lot to me. Several of my students helped to guide my thinking with their research on specific topics: Marta Starcevic on the Balkan crisis, Trey Hawkins on New Labour, Eric Marsteller on technical education, and most of all, David Simonelli on rock music. Finally, Ellah Allfrey at Pimlico prodded me to rethink and transform Chapters 9 and 10 in ways that have made them immeasurably better than they were when she got them. To the degree that they pass muster, she deserves a lot of credit.

Many changes have occurred in my life since I published my last book. My acknowledgements then opened by expressing the enormous debt I owed my mother and father. Now both of them have passed away – my father the year before I started this book, my mother the year before I finished it. Yet this book reflects both of them in many ways. As the chief economist in the American delegation to Bretton Woods and a participant in the negotiations of the British loan (as it is called on this side of the Atlantic), my father was associated with some of the events analysed here. A passionate lover of economics, he constantly impressed on his sons its pre-eminent importance to understanding the modern world. Since four chapters in this book are devoted to economic history, I clearly absorbed his message. My mother was of that generation of Americans who believed that Winston Churchill and the British people saved civilisation by standing up to the Nazis. Her memory of looking out over the ruins of London from the dome of St Paul's Cathedral in 1947, and weeping, has been permanently imprinted on my own. She periodically reiterated her view that the British people were worn out by the struggle to survive that war – thus providing my first introduction to 'declinism'. This book was written with both of my parents in mind, as they embodied one of the audiences that I wanted to reach. I only regret that they did not live to be able to read it.

Also gone is Brian Salmon. I first met Brian and Billie in 1974 when I went to London to research my dissertation. They welcomed me as the son of friends and then made me a friend in my own right – even to the extent of giving me a place in their home one summer when I was on a research trip. Brian loved to talk politics. He enjoyed quizzing me both on my work on the Edwardian Liberal Party and on the prospects of a Liberal revival in our own time – the latter, a subject on which he was much more qualified to have an opinion than I was. This book represents the best I can do in offering him my thoughts on the politics of his own era. Unfortunately, I haven't had the benefit of his combination of wit, penetrating questions and encouragement as I have worked my way through the subject.

Change has worked in the other direction as well. A year after my first book was published, I was introduced to Rose. Two years later, in the summer of 1989, she came to Britain to visit me for three weeks. She has transformed my life for the better in more ways than I can mention, but one is especially relevant here. She revolutionised my relationship with the country I study – a relationship which, until that time, was limited pretty much to London and Oxford. I hate to travel alone, but now I had someone to travel with. And so we saw the country as we took annual holidays – not just England, but Wales, Scotland and parts of Ireland as well. We have also lived outside London. Throughout the 1990s, we met lots of people who collectively put the lie to the myth that the British are not a warm and friendly people. Perhaps it is just the new, Thatcherite, service-oriented Britain, but I doubt it. We have been treated wonderfully everywhere we have gone. We also made new friends beyond the friends I already had in London and Oxford. Most memorably, we ended up one drizzly September afternoon at a somewhat obscure Scottish castle with a crazy couple from Leeds. They were hilarious. (Perhaps they thought we were too.) We spent half an hour talking in the rain after the tour. Thanks to a second accidental meeting six weeks later at Kew, we stayed in touch and now have become the closest of friends. It is to them and to our other English friends, who have done so much to make Britain a second home for both of us, that I dedicate this book. And most of all, I dedicate it to Rose; without her, it is just possible that it would never have come into being.

LIST OF ABBREVIATIONS

ANZUS	Australia, New Zealand, United States (alliance)
BBC	British Broadcasting Corporation
BMA	British Medical Association
BNP	British National Party
CAP	Common Agricultural Policy
CBI	Confederation of British Industry
CEMA	Council for the Encouragement of Music and the Arts
CIA	Central Intelligence Agency
CND	Campaign for Nuclear Disarmament
DEA	Department of Economic Affairs
EC	European Community
EEC	European Economic Community
ERM	Exchange Rate Mechanism (linking the exchange rate of European currencies)
EU	European Union
FA	Football Association
GATT	General Agreement on Tarriffs and Trade
GCSE	General Certificate of Secondary Education
GDP	Gross Domestic Product
GLC	Greater London Council
GNP	Gross National Product
GP	General Practitioner
IMF	International Monetary Fund
IRA	Irish Republican Army
ITV	Independent Television
MP	Member of Parliament
NATO	North Atlantic Treaty Organization
NEB	National Enterprise Board

LIST OF ABBREVIATIONS

NEC	National Executive Committee (of the Labour Party)
NEDC	National Economic Development Council
NHS	National Health Service
NUM	National Union of Mineworkers
OECD	Organization for Economic Cooperation and Development
OED	*Oxford English Dictionary*
OPEC	Organization of Petroleum Exporting Countries
PSBR	Public Sector Borrowing Requirement
R & D	Research and Development
RUC	Royal Ulster Constabulary
SALT	Strategic Arms Limitation Treaty
SDI	Strategic Defense Initiative
SDLP	Social Democratic and Labour Party (Northern Ireland)
SDP	Social Democratic Party (Britain)
SEATO	South-East Asia Treaty Organization
SERPS	State Earnings Related Pension Scheme
SNP	Scottish Nationalist Party
TGWU	Transport and General Workers' Union
TUC	Trades Union Congress
VAT	Value Added Tax

LIST OF TABLES

LIST OF PRIME MINISTERS OF THE UNITED KINGDOM (since 1868)

For coalitions, I have indicated the dominant party and the party of the Prime Minister in parentheses.

William Gladstone	1868–74	Liberal
Benjamin Disraeli	1874–80	Conservative
William Gladstone	1880–85	Liberal
Lord Salisbury	1885–6	Conservative
William Gladstone	1886	Liberal
Lord Salisbury	1886–92	Conservative
William Gladstone	1892–4	Liberal
Lord Rosebery	1894–5	Liberal
Lord Salisbury	1895–1902	Conservative
Arthur Balfour	1902–5	Conservative
Sir Henry Campbell-Bannerman	1905–8	Liberal
Herbert Henry Asquith	1908–15	Liberal
Herbert Henry Asquith (Liberal)	1915–16	Coalition (Liberal)
David Lloyd George (Liberal)	1916–22	Coalition (Conservative)
Andrew Bonar Law	1922–3	Conservative
Stanley Baldwin	1923–4	Conservative

Ramsay MacDonald	1924	Labour
Stanley Baldwin	1924–9	Conservative
Ramsay MacDonald	1929–31	Labour
Ramsay MacDonald (Labour)		
	1931–5	National Government (Conservative)
Stanley Baldwin (Conservative)		
	1935–7	National Government (Conservative)
Neville Chamberlain (Conservative)		
	1937–40	National Government (Conservative)
Winston Churchill (Conservative)		
	1940–45	Coalition (Conservative)
Winston Churchill	1945	Conservative
Clement Attlee	1945–51	Labour
Sir Winston Churchill	1951–5	Conservative
Sir Anthony Eden	1955–7	Conservative
Harold Macmillan	1957–63	Conservative
Sir Alec Douglas-Home	1963–4	Conservative
Harold Wilson	1964–70	Labour
Edward Heath	1970–74	Conservative
Harold Wilson	1974–6	Labour
James Callaghan	1976–9	Labour
Margaret Thatcher	1979–90	Conservative
John Major	1990–97	Conservative
Tony Blair	1997–	Labour

LIST OF PRESIDENTS
OF THE UNITED STATES
(since 1933)

American Presidents are elected in November, but they do not take office until January the following year (March for part of Roosevelt's presidency). The dates below are given for the year of inauguration rather than the year of election.

Franklin D. Roosevelt	1933–45	Democrat
Harry Truman	1945–53	Democrat
Dwight D. Eisenhower	1953–61	Republican
John F. Kennedy	1961–3	Democrat
Lyndon B. Johnson	1963–9	Democrat
Richard M. Nixon	1969–74	Republican
Gerald Ford	1974–7	Republican
Jimmy Carter	1977–81	Democrat
Ronald Reagan	1981–9	Republican
George Bush	1989–93	Republican
Bill Clinton	1993–2001	Democrat
George W. Bush	2001–	Republican

I

THE CHARACTER OF DECLINE

The Ambiguity of Decline

In the mid-1960s, the British people began to worry about national decline, as it became evident that, despite their unprecedented prosperity, their economy had not performed as well as the economies of other industrialised countries. With the apparent collapse of the economy in the 1970s, a national introspection that had begun as troubled questions became a pervasive sense of gloom. The fact that Britain's economic problems of inflation, unemployment and slow growth were shared by most of its competitors in the aftermath of the oil price increases of 1973 and 1979 made no difference to this mood of pessimism. However bad it may have been in West Germany or the United States, Britain's unique economic and social problems seemed to have made the crisis much worse there. The emergence and development of Thatcherism after 1979 was merely a further stage in this preoccupation with decline. Thatcherism was premised on its reality, and the politics of Thatcherism since the mid-1980s have been based on the claimed success of the new conservatism in reversing it.

In fact, Britain's decline has been far more ambiguous than such an analysis allows. For example, central to both British and foreign perceptions of decline has been Britain's shrinking influence as an international power. Yet even the character of this seemingly incontestable decline requires analysis. For in one sense Britain has never been more powerful: now it can destroy any country it chooses with a nuclear weapon – an exercise of power far beyond anything that it could have done in the nineteenth century. Clearly, then, a discussion of Britain's decline as a world power must distinguish between relative and absolute decline, and this is equally true of a discussion of economic decline. Furthermore, there is a tendency to see Britain's decline as a post-Second World War phenomenon – because the British themselves have been so fixated on decline in this period, and because it was after 1945 that the United States and the Soviet Union emerged as superpowers that dwarfed Britain's power. The reality, however, is that the British have been worrying about decline since the 1880s, even if they have not always been preoccupied with it, and the evidence of Britain's declining relative position as a world political and economic power dates back to that period. So any discussion of decline must look to the period before 1945 for its roots, which in itself may qualify the extent of the decline since 1945.

Britain's role as a world power has long reflected its economic development. Britain was the world's premier economic power by the second half of the eighteenth century, and it continued to be so in the first two-thirds of the nineteenth century. The sources of this power were Britain's domination of world trade and finance and its pioneering role as the first nation to develop a manufacturing sector based on technology and mass production – what historians have called the Industrial Revolution. The first two sources of Britain's economic power remained uncontested right up to the First World War, but the third came to be challenged in the last part of the nineteenth century with the emergence primarily of Germany and the United States, but also of France and Japan, as modern industrialising nations. It is no accident, then, that Britons first became concerned about economic decline in the 1880s. Historians, too, have been concerned about it, wondering if it reflected some failure in Britain itself. Among the subjects they have fought about are whether there was a failure to modernise the principal industries of the Industrial

Revolution and to expand into new ones; whether British entrepreneurs invested enough in research and development; whether British industry was too slow to take advantage of new forms of industrial organisation; whether capital that was exported (i.e. invested abroad) could or should have been employed at home; whether Britain was excessively reliant on the empire and less developed world for export markets; whether the education system and the broader culture were hostile to entrepreneurship; whether industry and the education system were too divorced from science.[1] Yet a basic fact remains: in 1914 Britain's economy was still larger than that of any other country except the United States. The only incontestable symptom of economic decline was that Britain was falling behind a country that was far larger in population and natural resources.

The period between the wars more clearly revealed problems with the British economy – most notably inefficiencies in the staple industries of the Industrial Revolution: coal, cotton, steel and shipbuilding. Yet the problems of the world economy were so great that it is difficult to tell how Britain's relative position may have changed over the period. After all, how does one compare Britain's economy with the performance of a German economy that collapsed due to hyperinflation in 1923, revived because of American loans after 1924, collapsed again with the Great Depression in the United States after 1929 and finally revived again because the Nazis broke every accepted rule of economic management (as they broke every other accepted rule)? In the 1920s, the United States was the world's dominant economy, but the Great Depression hit America harder than any other developed country, so once again it is difficult to arrive at an overall evaluation for the period. In fact, it is misleading to view the British economy as in a crisis during the whole period following the collapse of the post-war boom in 1921. While there were periods of genuine crisis, overall some regions prospered while others were in desperate straits. For the nation as a whole, the 1920s were worse than the 1930s, when the British economy actually outperformed the economies of both the United States and Germany, while from 1924 to 1937 Britain's annual average rate of growth equalled Britain's from 1856 to 1873 and exceeded that of 1873 to 1913.[2]

After the Second World War, there was no doubt of the overwhelming supremacy of the American economy. There was a new crisis of confidence in Britain in the 1960s, however, because for the first time since the 1880s there was a clear perception of economic decline relative to countries other than the United States. Yet for every piece of evidence of Britain's economic failure in the post-war period, there was counterbalancing evidence of economic success: relatively high inflation, low rates of growth of worker productivity and low growth rates for the economy as a whole compared with competitor nations were balanced by historically low unemployment, low poverty and (until the 1970s) high growth rates compared with Britain's past. Furthermore, Thatcherite efforts to reverse decline converted the successes into failures while attempting to convert the failures into successes. Thus while there was improvement in inflation and worker productivity after 1979, in the 1980s and early 1990s unemployment reached post-war highs, while poverty increased well beyond its position before 1979. Thus, the overall performance of the British economy since 1945 (or even in the twentieth century) is not one that justifies an unrelenting pessimism. Apart from the catastrophic decades of the 1920s and the 1970s, both linked to larger worldwide economic phenomena, the peacetime story has been one of growth and prosperity. Nor is the post-1979 revival more unambiguous than the pre-1979 decline. Indeed, in many ways the performance of the economy in the 1980s was comparable to that of the 1960s, although the strengths and weaknesses were different in the two decades. At the same time, the power economies of the 1960s and 1970s don't look so unstoppable any more. Japan has faced major economic problems for more than a decade, while the German and French economies have also been sluggish.

An evaluation of political decline hardly yields greater clarity than that of economic decline.[3] Britain may have been the world's dominant economic power between roughly 1750 and 1870, but it was not the world's dominant political power during those years. The word 'superpower' was invented for a reason – to convey a new level of power for the United States (and, more uncertainly, the Soviet Union) compared with other developed countries, because of their nuclear arsenals and their ability to exercise power and influence worldwide. In the eighteenth and nineteenth centuries, the phrase 'great power' was applied to a group of European states (later incorporating the United States and Japan), no one of which was able to exercise a dominating influence in Europe and the world. Britain may have had a worldwide empire, but it always needed allies if it was to exercise its power against any people except those with vastly inferior military technology. The first time it fought a major war without allies, it lost the American colonies. Britain needed all the other European powers as allies to defeat Napoleon's France between 1799 and 1815, and Britain and France together had no easy time defeating an economically backward Russia in the Crimean War of 1854–6. The relative decline of its economic power after 1870 merely made the situation worse, especially when combined with the escalating costs of naval technology in the age of steam and steel. Thus as Britain's empire and apparent power expanded from 1880 to 1914, its relative power declined. From the 1890s on, it was settling outstanding differences with the United States, France and Russia, while negotiating its first ever peacetime alliance, with Japan, all because it was overextended in defending its far-flung empire.

Clearly, the possession of the world's largest empire was not necessarily a source of strength for Britain, however central it may have been to Britain's prestige and image as a power. While the empire had been of great importance to Britain's emergence as the world's pre-eminent economy in the eighteenth century (though this is a controversial statement), its economic importance after 1850 was much less clear. The crucial possessions as markets, sources of food and raw materials, and targets for overseas investments were the self-governing dominions (Canada,

Australia, New Zealand and South Africa) and India.[4] India was uniquely important as the only part of the world with which Britain had a positive balance of trade in goods. By 1870, the trade deficit was insignificant, compared to the surplus of income from overseas investments, in determining Britain's overall balance of payments (in both goods and services). Nonetheless, the Indian trade surplus remained important in helping the Bank of England sustain the international role of sterling.[5] The rest of the empire was far less important to either trade or investment than the developed world. Indeed, the historian Eric Hobsbawm has argued that the empire hurt Britain economically after 1870. Because British industries could rely on the empire and other parts of the less developed world for markets, they could sell goods in these regions without having to modernise or compete with newly industrialising countries. As a result, these industries remained inefficient. At the same time, Britain failed to aggressively develop trade networks with the expansive markets in Europe and the United States, which offered the best opportunities for growth.[6]

Judging the empire's economic importance, however, is not identical to judging its importance to Britain's power. The empire had to be defended, and defending it was costly because navies were expensive and getting more so. In fact, for the period from 1870 to 1914, the British people were more heavily taxed than were those of other powers, and Britain spent nearly twice as much per capita on defence as did France and Germany, despite the fact that the continental powers had mass conscription armies.[7] Britain, for political and historical reasons, could neither maintain a large standing army nor resort to conscription. It could turn to the Indian army, however, which was paid for by the Indian taxpayer and was used outside India. Otherwise, the empire contributed little to the cost of defence. It provided virtually nothing for the British navy, except some key bases, while modernising and expanding the navy to assure its supremacy was by far the largest single cost to maintaining the empire. Given this reality, the new colonies added after 1880 not only did not increase Britain's power, they may well have reduced it. They meant more territory to defend without furnishing many more resources for defending it, apart from the new territories in South Africa. Thus by 1914, we are faced with a paradox: Britain claimed some quarter of the world's population within its orbit, and it was all the weaker for it.

During the First World War, the dominions and India really came through with troops to support the British. Britain literally could not have fought a world war without them.[8] Yet while all were technically subject to British rule, it is doubtful that Britain could have forced any but the Indians to fight if they had chosen not to do so. Arguably, the dominions were now simply paying Britain back for decades of providing for their defence at no cost to themselves. The war, however, had balanced the accounts, and in 1926 the independence of the dominions was formally recognised. Overall, the aftermath of the war merely made the underlying problem of overextension and British weakness worse. Under the peace treaties, Britain added more territory in Africa and the Middle East that it could not defend. Events in Ireland, Palestine and India all showed how limited Britain's ability was to mobilise military power to impose its will on its empire when there was determined resistance. At the same time, with the United States and the Soviet Union removed from the balance of power, Britain's position at home and overseas was more exposed than ever. The defence of the empire in the East was contingent on the goodwill of Japan; yet Britain's even greater dependence on the United States forced it to abrogate the Japanese alliance in order to stay on good terms with the Americans. In Europe, Britain's security interests were entirely dependent on the French army and France's willingness to use it. Thus, Britain's position between the wars was no different from its position before the First World War. Russian withdrawal, a broken alliance with Japan and French timidity changed the equation; however, Britain's dependence on other powers to protect its empire and its interests in Europe was the same. Since neither the French nor the Americans came through, both

Britain's position in Europe and its Asian empire collapsed before the onslaught of the Germans and the Japanese.

The situation after the Second World War simply made explicit what had been implicit since April 1917, when the United States entered the First World War: the US was the world's dominant power, should it choose to mobilise the resources and embrace the role. Because of its vast nuclear arsenal, its enormous army in Europe and its formal domination of Central and Eastern Europe, the Soviet Union eventually claimed a special status comparable to that of the United States. That superpower status has been compromised, however, by the break-up of the Soviet Union, the disarray of the Russian army and the loss of control over the Soviet European satellites. Thus, apart from the clear superiority of the United States, it is not obvious that Britain's position as a great power has declined since 1914. Russia has the potential to be a superior power, but its economic and political weaknesses mean now, as they did then, that its real power is well below that potential. Germany and Japan also may have the ability to be greater powers than Britain, but for political and historical reasons neither chooses to be so. China is in a position comparable to Russia's, without its nuclear stockpile. Thus, Britain and France – with nuclear weapons, an interest in exercising power worldwide and modern economies – are roughly the equal of any other power except the United States, until potential power becomes real.

Of course, there is the loss of empire. The two decades after the Second World War showed just how much that empire stretched Britain's resources beyond its ability to defend it. At the same time, a growing economic fixation on the empire since 1932 directed Britain's trade and investment relations away from the prosperous Western Europe that evolved after the war. In shedding its empire, therefore, Britain may well have lost an encumbrance rather than power. The loss of what little contribution the empire made to British security was more than compensated for by the formal commitment of the United States to defend Britain's European and Asian interests. It is certainly an interesting coincidence that the period of greatest prosperity in British history coincided with the end of empire. The loss of empire thus represented a decline only in how much of the world map was coloured red.

It is arguable, however, that in world politics image is as important as reality, and it was just this loss of territory that fatally undermined the perception of Britain as a world power, both by Britons themselves and by the rest of the world. Britons did not always identify the empire with their greatness, although they were proud of it. In the mid-nineteenth century, there was even a radical tradition that viewed the empire as an encumbrance; however, this 'little England' view represented a minority, even within liberalism. For most Britons, the empire was neither an encumbrance nor an irrelevance. Nonetheless, even those who valued the empire believed that Britain's real greatness lay not in territory, but in its economic strength: the technology of industrialisation, the cities that had grown with that technology and the worldwide trade that had followed from that technology. By 1900, however, a nation that was ceasing to be the most economically powerful country in the world was looking for some other way of defining its supremacy, and the fact that a large chunk of the world was British offered a means of reassuring its people that no nation was greater. In an era of social Darwinism, when many saw the world's powers competing in a struggle for survival and for racial supremacy, the empire was crucial in offering a criterion by which Britain's success in that struggle seemed secure. The fact that other states, including the United States and Japan, seemed to accept that criterion, rendered it all the more credible. Hence, from the 1890s on, generations of British children were educated to identify national pride and power with the empire. Those Britons who bought into this myth inevitably saw the loss of empire after 1945 as evidence of national decline. Yet the historian Bernard Porter doubts that either enthusiasm for the empire or a sense that it was important to Britain penetrated very deeply through the population, especially among the working class. This 'silent majority' were indifferent to its disappearance, as they were to the Commonwealth as a substitute.9

The more difficult adjustment was that, instead of Britain having its way with the weak of the world, it seemed now that Britain was being pushed around by every minor dictator playing to a domestic audience. Margaret Drabble captured this change in her 1977 novel *The Ice Age*. There her heroine Alison Murray reflected:

> England was a safe, shabby, mangey old lion now: anyone could tweak her tail. So the Indians imprisoned school-teachers and writers, the Ugandans threatened to execute British offenders, schoolgirls were tried for currency offences in Kenya, a mere child was jailed for drug smuggling in Turkey. Malice and justice united, to persecute the once so prosperous, once so arrogant, once so powerful of nations, the nation on whose empire the sun had never set.10

So the real character of Britain's decline was not relative to the other great powers at all, but to the rest of the world, and especially to the former empire itself. Gunboat diplomacy was a thing of the past, as the Suez Crisis of 1956 made abundantly clear. Yet in this respect, Britain again was no worse off than the other powers, even including the United States. For while America could throw its weight around more effectively than most, it too had to learn that it could not always have its way with the less developed countries of the world. It was not merely that its massive power was not easily mobilised against the likes of North Vietnam or Iran. Perhaps more importantly, the modern morality of international relations (a morality which the United States had helped promote) did not accept the arbitrary exercise of power by the strong against the weak in order to get their own way. So, once again, the character of Britain's decline is more ambiguous than it seems. First, it is not clear that the loss of empire represented any decline in real power at all; the decline was primarily a perception by Britons and others who had identified Britain's greatness with its empire. Second, while there was a clear loss in Britain's ability to exercise power arbitrarily when dealing with weaker peoples and states outside Europe, that loss applied equally to the other world powers, even including the great super-power itself.

If perceptions may differ when looking at Britain's economic and political decline, such variability of outlook is even more evident when evaluating cultural decline. For here, one person's decline can be another's progress. Recent views of cultural decline are clearly linked to events of the 1960s: the sexual revolution, the increase in divorces and the threat to the family that followed the influx of married middle-class women into the workforce, the decline of religion and the rise of secularism and moral rela-tivism, the apparent increase in crime coupled with the apparent decline in the quality of education. More broadly, there seemed to be a decline of standards, of self-discipline, of respect, of order, of morality – of all that was associated with Victorian values. Yet, not surprisingly, Victorian values began to decline during and immediately after the Victorian era. The advent of Modernism as it came to be shaped by Darwin, Nietzsche, Freud and Einstein (among others) affected Britain as it did the rest of the West. Any reader of George Gissing's 1890s novels *The Odd Women* and *New Grub Street* can see that moral relativism and the rejection of self-denial as a moral principle were part of the *fin de siècle* British intellectual scene. The decline of religion from its Victorian apogee was a continuous process during the twentieth century, not some sudden post-1945 collapse. The violence of the militant suffragettes from 1905 to 1914 as part of their campaign for female suffrage, the sexual liberation of middle-class women and their employment in two world wars and the changing attitudes towards female behaviour, work and dress that the wars brought, all launched a rethinking of what was appropriate in women's roles and ways during the first half of the twentieth century. Whether all of this represents decline is very much a matter of a person's point of view. Victorianism meant constraints on individual behaviour, so its rejection could be viewed as liberation. Liberation, as the word implies, was more likely to appeal to a liberal than to a conservative. To the former it was a freeing up of individual potential and creativity, as well as the rejection of a stifling moral code; to the latter it was the dissolution of traditional social and moral reference points, encouraging a society that was both immoral and amoral. So the perception of cultural decline seems to have a clear political connotation; perhaps perceptions of economic and political decline have one too, although it may be less evident.

The Politics of Decline

To what degree, then, does politics help to account for this British preoccupation with decline? Conservative perceptions of decline can be traced back to the aftermath of the American and French Revolutions and to the advent of the liberal state that they heralded. Ultimately, this liberal state was defined by democracy, the guarantee of rights, the rule of law, equality before the law and equality of opportunity – in other words, liberty and equality. Britain had been a state committed to liberty in principle before either of those revolutions occurred; indeed, both were partly inspired by the British example. Britain was not, however, a state committed to equality. It was a society based on a privileged aristocracy. Those privileges were not institutionalised by law, except politically through the House of Lords. However, there was a broader ideological claim, going back to the eighteenth century, that the aristocracy were the nation's natural rulers. Rule by the aristocracy was rule by the educated, the rational, the cultured, the best that society could produce; rule by democracy was rule by the ignorant, the emotional, the base, the worst that society could produce. The professional, financial and commercial classes were not excluded from positions of status and power in the eighteenth century, especially in their local communities, while the richest of them were part of the ruling elite. Nonetheless, their position was clearly subordinate, for their numbers were still limited – especially the number of those of great wealth.

That was changed by the Industrial Revolution and the broader capitalist expansion that came with it. Thus, throughout the nineteenth century, as this newly enhanced middle class began to assert its values of individualism and profit maximisation and to demand an equal role in the political system, the aristocratic and educated elite bemoaned the threat of political and cultural decline. In *Culture and Anarchy* (1869), Matthew Arnold explicitly established the opposition of middle-class notions of liberty – 'when every man may say what he likes' and is 'able to do as he likes' – to aristocratic conceptions of culture, which he defined as aspiring 'to make the best that has been thought and known in the world current everywhere'.[11] All one had to do was to look at the United States to see the danger. America was the home of a society based on liberty, equality and capitalism – a land without an aristocracy and so without culture. For Arnold, schooled by Tocqueville, Americanisation meant the triumph of vulgarity and banality over the aspiration to perfection. Indeed, America was no model for any of Britain's elite, except the most thoroughly democratic of the middle class. Yet the principle of equality continued its subversive expansion. The extension of the franchise, the broadening of the curriculum of Oxford and Cambridge beyond the study of the Classical world, and the opening of the civil service to appointment by examination, all threatened to introduce a standard based on equality and utility rather than quality and culture (and so, in modern parlance, a 'dumbing down'). All these changes were resisted, though futilely.

The danger posed by the rise of the middle class passed, however, as that class embraced many of the values of the aristocracy. These values were passed on to the children of both at the growing number of public schools and at Oxford and Cambridge. At the same time, the culture aimed at the middle class proved to be of a quality equalling any that Britain had begot before. For the class that had produced and embraced Dickens and Eliot, Trollope and Tennyson, the Brontës and the

Pre-Raphaelites could hardly be decried for undermining an aspiration to perfection. A new danger appeared, however. With the introduction of universal elementary education after 1870 and the creation of a majority working-class electorate in 1884, governance by the masses, and a culture aimed at them, now threatened. That threat came to be symbolised in the 1890s by the emergence of the popular press, written for what George Gissing's entrepreneur journalist Whelpdale called 'the quarter-educated . . . that is being turned out by the Board [i.e. state-provided primary] schools, the young men and women who can just read, but are incapable of sustained attention'.[12] The peril seemed to be confirmed by the perceived political power of the first 'press barons', Lords Harmsworth and Beaverbrook, during the First World War and between the wars. The traditional elite countered with their own attempt to control culture in the new democratic age. After the First World War, for example, the elitist and paternalistic BBC was established following the advent of radio. The masses might have had their own distinct culture, but its ability to expand beyond their own world and achieve any broader validity would be circumscribed. Once again, however, America was a contaminating influence. For nothing could be done to limit the influence of Hollywood, and American films helped define the fantasies and pleasures of people of all classes in Britain as well as in the United States during the Great Depression of the 1930s. F. R. Leavis took up the mantle of Arnold in decrying the 'levelling down' of British cultural standards that came with the influence of American movies and advertising. Culture, for Leavis, was defined by literature, not by anything that ordinary people were doing.

In the aftermath of the Second World War, the politics of the working class emerged triumphant in Britain. By the 1960s, prosperity, universal secondary education and a post-war baby boom had created the conditions for the emergence of a popular culture that could be universalised. The fact that this culture incorporated American imports, American marketing techniques and sometimes even British working-class influences hardly endeared it to the intellectual and social elite, even as their own children embraced it. These elites were now far more broadly defined than the old aristocracy, though they still incorporated it and many of its values. More than anything else, they came to be defined by education (public schools and Oxbridge) and profession (government service, the professions and finance, as well as land ownership). For some among this class, decline was real enough. They had had a stake in governing the empire and in the military and naval forces that protected it. The shrinkage of these positions harmed them. They were also threatened by efforts to reform education – the expansion of the number of universities and so of the population that received a higher education, the transformation of the university curriculum to incorporate new methodologies and disciplines and the end of educational tracking through the introduction of comprehensive schools which included students of all abilities and backgrounds. These social groups were not necessarily the defenders of threatened Victorian values, which were associated with the nineteenth-century middle class that was the target of Arnold's irony. Rather, they were the bearers of Arnold's and Leavis's concerns about maintaining standards, resisting the triumph of ideology over reason and common sense, and preserving a dominant culture that was defined by the intellectual and social elite. Here, then, was one group of people who had a stake in emphasising the dangers of decline in the post-war era. In doing so, they could build on a long cultural tradition that had helped to define their privileged status in the society.

In the late 1960s, however, there emerged a second group who embraced the mythology[13] of decline. They were conservatives, but the term 'neo-liberals' better conveys their association with the *laissez-faire* values of the Victorian middle class, as well as their opposition to the paternalistic conservative elite whose traditions derived from the Victorian aristocracy. Politically, they were represented by Margaret Thatcher and her followers; intellectually, their voice was the Austrian-born economist Friedrich von Hayek. For them, the source of decline was socialism, which promoted a false conception of equality because it undermined the rewarding of ability and effort. Like the aristocratic and intellectual proponents of decline, they identified a lowering of standards and the subordination of quality to quantity; unlike the former, however, they were not sceptical about the democracy, and they were not wedded to Oxbridge definitions of quality. Indeed, they were as suspicious of the traditional elite as they were of the socialists, for they believed the former had been fatally tainted by the latter. Indeed, paternalism and socialism seemed suspiciously similar. While the welfare state had long been with Britain (longer than Victorianism had been), and while socialism (and its liberal counterpart 'new liberalism') had been shaping government policy since the beginning of the twentieth century, the year 1945 had a special meaning for the neo-liberals in marking the advent of decline. First, the policies of the Labour government of 1945–50 represented the triumph of the socialist consensus that shaped Britain for the next thirty-five years. Second, the post-war era marked the triumph of Keynesian economics, with its corollary of government interference in the economy and so the disruption of the market as the arbiter of economic activity. Finally, it was only in the 1960s that the values of moral decline became pervasive. However long the forces for social and cultural change may have been at work, it was in the sixties that it became *good* to have sex outside marriage, that homosexuals were defined as normal, that women were *encouraged* to get divorces if they were unhappy in marriage, that personal happiness and self-gratification rather than self-discipline and self-denial became guiding moral principles of life.

While the neo-liberals and the elitists represented two different strains of what might be called a predisposition to see decline, there was some overlap between them. The most important was their attitude towards popular culture. The neo-liberals should have been attracted to popular culture: it was an expression of the democracy that was validated by the marketplace, while it weakened the hold of the elite on the values of the country. They could not embrace it, however, because socialists promoted different aspects of popular culture as an expression of the working class that was of equal validity with elite culture. It was another mark against the sixties that it was the decade in which popular culture first became pervasive. This phenomenon was another example of the decline of objective standards of quality which both groups so hated. More generally, their dislike of a broader compromising of standards in search of an impossible equality also linked the neo-liberals and the elitists. The supposed decline in the quality of British education came to embody all that was wrong with the socialist vision of society for both groups. It introduced trendy subjects instead of teaching students the basics that would prepare them for life; it substituted feeling good about oneself for self-discipline as the basis for learning; and it suppressed quality in favour of equality. Local authorities dominated by socialists, who wasted the public's funds to promote faddish methodologies in education (as well as popular culture), became the targets of the wrath of the neo-liberals in their effort to reverse moral decline.[14]

There was one more reason why Margaret Thatcher and her supporters saw socialism as the source of Britain's decline: as an anti-imperialist and pacifist ideology, it seemed in some ways responsible for Britain's decline as a world power. In this respect, socialism was the heir to the tradition of nineteenth-century liberalism represented by the free-trade radical Richard Cobden and by William Gladstone, the leader of the Liberal Party for most of the years 1868–94. Cobden saw empire as a burden to be shedded, wanted to reduce defence spending as low as possible, and thought all quarrels between states should be settled by arbitration. Gladstone believed that the principles of Christian morality should be applied to foreign policy and that decisions involving the European powers should be made collectively by a Concert of Europe rather than unilaterally by Britain and other states pursuing narrow national interests. Gladstone was not a pacifist and did not want to get rid of the empire, but he embraced the Cobdenite position on defence spending, while his moralistic approach to policy became the watchword for most Liberals. Some of the early leaders of the Labour Party, like Keir Hardie and

Ramsay MacDonald, came out of the left wing of the Liberal Party and carried its traditions to the new party. At the same time, socialism brought to the Labour Party its own traditions of anti-imperialism and pacifism, which were a product of its hostility to capitalism. Socialists saw imperialism as the result of capitalism's insatiable search for profits, based on an exploitation of other peoples abroad analogous to its exploitation of the working class at home. War, too, was the result of the competition for markets by capitalist states; it involved the workers dying to expand the profits of their masters. Marx had said that the workers knew no nation, that their common interests were stronger than any national identity they could have with the capitalists. Thus pacifism was an expression of the view that the workers had no stake in wars, which were fought in the interests of others while weakening a working-class movement that was supposed to transcend national boundaries.

The reality of working-class nationalism, however, became evident in all European countries during the First World War, and socialism everywhere had to adapt its foreign policy to reflect that reality. Nonetheless, there always remained a socialist left wing that stood by the pure ideology. As a result, conservatives were sceptical of the patriotism of the movement as a whole, and they found it politically useful to emphasise the influence of this 'unpatriotic' left wing. In Britain, the First World War allowed a complete fusion of the liberal and socialist pacifist traditions in opposition to the war and to the introduction of conscription by the British army. So the decline of the Liberal Party after the war made no fundamental difference in the foreign policy map of the left. Labour incorporated many of the same tensions and divisions as the Liberals had, with some differences of emphasis. Most importantly, anti-imperialism was much more central to all shades of socialist opinion than it had been to liberalism, and socialists had an interest in socialist solidarity in Europe that was irrelevant to liberalism. During the inter-war period, socialist foreign policy was based on internationalism as represented by the League of Nations, disarmament and a suspicion of the

Conservatives' hostility to the Communist Soviet Union. Following a Labour Party split in 1931, the pacifist George Lansbury was even leader for a few years; however, from 1935 to 1945 the centrists re-established their control of the party and its foreign policy. After the Second World War, Labour foreign, defence and colonial policies were not radically different from those of the Conservatives. Indeed, it was the Conservatives who unloaded most of the empire.

For the Thatcherites, however, this consensus was merely evidence of how much the socialist mentality had permeated the Conservatives' ruling establishment. For dating back to Benjamin Disraeli in the 1870s, identification with the empire as a central tenet of British patriotism had been a watchword of the Conservative Party. It is hardly a coincidence, then, that the fixation on decline by patriotic Conservatives coincided with the end of empire, and they saw a consensus defined by Labour as the culprit. Thatcher and others believed that such socialist influences were the source of a national tendency to apologise for Britain's past and to be embarrassed about asserting power to pursue British interests. This mentality was represented by Drabble's Alison who, after pondering how so many non-Europeans got away with tweaking the lion's tail, concluded, 'And it served it [Britain] right'.[15] Most dangerous to the Thatcherites was the sacrifice of the military to an expanding and bloated welfare state, which represented socialist priorities. If reversing Britain's decline was central to Thatcherism, then it had to involve an attack on the whole socialist approach to Britain's external interests as well as on socialist domestic policies.

Given this apparent conservative interest, dating well back into the nineteenth century, in promoting the view that Britain was in decline, it would seem reasonable to assume that the political left had an equal stake in rejecting that view. An alternative myth of progress can be traced back to the Enlightenment in France, and it certainly was central to the liberalism of the Victorian middle class. Progress was rooted in three sources: the Industrial Revolution and the wealth and technological innovation that it generated; the march of science as it better understood the natural world; and the spread of liberal democracy. The last was more an assertion of faith than an observed reality in the nineteenth century, but for those who held to its inevitability and its association with progress, the example of the United States was a source of hope and inspiration rather than a lesson of what was to be avoided. Socialism propagated its own myth of inevitability: the claim that the working class and the socialist state must triumph for historically determinable reasons. The inevitable triumph of socialism might also involve a march of progress, but especially for the pure Marxist, small gains were dangerous because they could postpone rather than facilitate the triumph of the working class. While most members of the Labour left after the Second World War were not Marxists, the left came to the conclusion that the policies of 1945–50 had had just this effect of postponing a more broadly based advent of socialism in Britain. Thus, they had no stake in arguing against decline. On the contrary, they had a stake in embracing economic decline in particular, for they had their own solution to it: a more radical socialisation of the British economy and of British society.

Radical socialists also offered no challenge to contentions of cultural decline, for they were not convinced that all that much change had occurred. Where the conservatives saw a decline in standards by the revamping of the education curriculum and the introduction of comprehensive schools, the socialists saw public schools and Oxbridge colleges that were as elitist as ever and which still defined privileged access within British society. Even the spread of popular culture was an ambiguous gain. On the one hand, government still channelled most of its money to elite institutions like the Royal Opera House and the National Theatre. On the other hand, popular culture was becoming suspiciously Americanised. The radical socialists distrusted the United States. They believed that it used the Cold War as a pretext to divide Europe, exploit the less developed world and to sustain an arms race that threatened a nuclear holocaust. All of this had negated the possibility of a genuinely socialist foreign policy, by undermining the benefits of decolonisation, blocking socialist solidarity and forcing Britain to waste enormous amounts of money in order to be a nuclear power and maintain its worldwide influence. Worst of all, the United States was the self-proclaimed home of un-restrained capitalism. Too much of popular culture seemed to socialists to be driven by the imperatives of American capitalism, replacing more genuine expressions of British working-class cultural identity. So while there was much socialist celebration of certain aspects of popular culture as an alternative to elite culture, there was less inclination to repudiate aggressively charges of cultural decline, especially by the socialist intellectuals who were themselves part of the elite.

Arguably, the centrist mainstream of the Labour Party should have had no stake in promoting arguments about Britain's decline. Yet by the early 1960s, Britain's 'deficient' economic performance when compared to other developed countries was a political issue that was too tempting to resist. After all, the Conservatives had been in power since 1951 and had proclaimed that Britons had never had it so good. Yet the 'objective' data showed nothing but failure relative to Britain's peers. What better issue was there for a party to unite on, when it had been in oppo-sition for more than a decade and had been riven by divisions for much of that time? So Britain's decline became the centrepiece of Labour's campaign in 1964. Thereafter, it remained at the centre of the political debate, as each party attacked the other for doing nothing about reversing decline, while claiming that it could do better. Thus, in every respect, politics was at the heart of percep-tions of Britain's decline – whether economic, political or cultural.

Decline was not merely a function of the British imagination. Britain had been the world's premier economic power for more than one hundred years. This position, however, was the result of Britain's development as the world's foremost capitalist state from 1714 to 1870, and especially of its being the pioneer of the economic revolution which came with the accelerating develop-ment of manufacturing technology after 1760. All the advantages of being first would inevitably disappear as other countries caught up, and indeed it has been argued that they became liabilities thereafter.[16] There was also a real element of political decline. While Britain was never the undisputed supreme power of Europe, there was no state anywhere that was greater in the nineteenth century. The rise of the United States as a supreme power may not have been inevitable, but it certainly was foreseeable, and many Britons did foresee it in the mid-nineteenth century, long before most Americans thought in these terms. As with the loss of economic supremacy, it was not something Britain could easily have done anything about, unless it wanted to try to help the South win the American Civil War. Finally, in terms of the territory it controlled worldwide, Britain *was* the world's greatest power until after 1945. In many ways, however, after 1850 this empire was more a symbol of power than a source of power.

Yet the rhetoric of decline implies something more than merely the loss of this economic and territorial supremacy through circumstances beyond Britain's control, or in ways that may even have been beneficial. It implies fault: that this loss of supremacy reflected some larger weakness in the British people, and if that weakness were corrected, decline would be reversed. This perception of weakness was largely because Britain's relative *economic* decline went well beyond its loss of supremacy to the United States. By the 1960s, it was falling behind other industrialised nations, as measured by gross domestic product (GDP) per head of the population, and that slide in the 'league tables' of economic performance continued in the 1970s and 1980s. Here there seemed to be a problem that the British could do something about. Yet always, in this process of self-analysis, Britons tended to focus on the glass that was part empty rather than part full. They saw what was wrong rather than what was right, weaknesses rather than strengths, failures relative to other nations rather than successes relative either to other nations or to their own past performance. The argument here has been that this tendency to focus on the negative rather than the positive was the result of several factors. One was a longer-term tendency, not just in Britain but in Western culture more broadly, especially on the part of the intellectual and social elite, to see decline as a product of democracy and capitalism.[17] Second, there emerged in Britain a group of conservative critics of socialism, the welfare state, decolonisation and the moral revolution of the 1960s, who identified decline with the triumph since 1945 of the values represented by all of these phenomena. These conservatives justified their own policies for reversing that triumph with the necessity of reversing decline. Finally, the post-1945 left was weak in its defence of the political, social, economic and moral changes that had occurred. On the extreme were those who thought reforms had not gone far enough and so were interested in attacking and denigrating them. But even the moderates in the Labour Party saw political gain to be made in promoting decline. As a result, there was a built-in bias in favour of decline in the political and intellectual rhetoric discussing the state of Britain since the Second World War.

PART I: 1945–1964
RECOVERY

2

THE HARD ROAD TO PROSPERITY

It all starts with the economy. This has been true of Britain for a long time – at least since the Industrial Revolution that began in the second half of the eighteenth century. The economic transformation that was wrought over the next one hundred years made Britain the world's leading economic power and shaped the nature of Britain's economy. Britain became the world's only free trade nation, while its manufactures were directed towards exports. By 1900, Britain's society was predominantly urban rather than rural, as the industrial and service sectors of the economy grew at the expense of agriculture. At the same time, the political system slowly became more democratic, as the old landed aristocracy yielded primacy of place to new middle and working classes whose wealth (in the former instance) and numbers were the product of nearly two centuries of capitalist expansion. New political ideologies – liberalism and socialism – were also a response to economic change, while conservatism redefined itself to win votes in a democratic age.

Since the end of the First World War, and especially since 1945, the economy has remained at the centre of Britain's history. No issue has preoccupied Britons and their political leaders more than the nation's supposed economic decline, as well as its decline as a major power, which the economy helped to explain. For the economy limited Britain's capacity to project itself throughout the world – including its ability to hold on to its empire – while it also helped drive Britain into the European Community. Social change since the war was also partly economically determined. The expansion of the welfare state, the changing role of women, the emergence of new kinds of popular culture, the rise and fall of trade union power and the changing nature of class were all shaped in part by the nation's unparalleled prosperity in the 1950s and 1960s and the more limited nature of that prosperity since then. So an analysis of Britain's history since the Second World War must start with the economy because so much follows from it.

Britain came out of the war with serious economic problems. Furthermore, the Labour government foresaw major new economic and social commitments which would cost money, while it was determined to maintain Britain's status as a power equal to the United States and the Soviet Union. Any notion, however, that Britain was one of a 'big three' in 1945 was vitiated by the near bankrupt state of the nation and the traumatised condition of an economy that had long been overstretched by the demands of total war. Indeed, while we hear much of the economic miracles of Germany and Japan in the aftermath of the war, it is something of a miracle that the Labour government was able to combine economic recovery with achieving its many policy goals. By the 1950s, the people of Britain were seeing the benefits in the form of an unparalleled prosperity that allowed standards of living to shoot up. Throughout the decade, however, there was evidence that the economy was not altogether equipped to take on the demands that were put on it. The government found that its two principal goals – maintaining full employment and preserving the value of the pound – came into conflict with each other. That is, the expansive economy that assured full employment led to a balance-of-payments deficit that threatened the value of the pound; while the tight economic policies that were necessary to defend sterling led to unemployment. This conflict was the origin of the government policies that came to be known as 'stop-go'. Yet few challenged the basis on which prosperity was built, except a fringe at each political extreme: the Labour left questioned the resources poured into defence and the Tory right questioned the resources poured into the welfare state. Only in the early 1960s, when it became evident that other countries were doing better that Britain, did a consensus develop that all was not well with the economy.

The Legacy of War

Britain's economic prosperity has been tied to a global economy since English merchants began to challenge Dutch domination of the Atlantic carrying trade (including the trade in slaves) in the second half of the seventeenth century. By the eighteenth century, Britain's position at the centre of that global economy – as an importer and exporter of goods, as a carrier of other people's goods and as an insurer of goods – helped secure it the position as the richest nation in the world. The Industrial Revolution then began to define more specifically the nature of Britain's role within that global economy. Initially British manufacturers exported their goods – especially cotton goods and machinery – in exchange for food and raw cotton. By the end of the century, as other countries industrialised, the exchange became more complex. Britain imported as well as exported manufactures, and exported coal while importing other raw materials and semi-finished goods. Such changes in the composition of British exports and imports over the course of the nineteenth century, however, did not alter one constant feature of the exchange: Britain could never export enough goods to pay for all the food, raw materials and other products that it had to import. Yet this negative balance of trade was not a problem because of Britain's other and even more important role in the world economy as a provider of services. As had been the case in the eighteenth century, Britain dominated the world's trans-oceanic carrying trade. Now, however, Britain also provided financial services for the rest of the world. These included not only insurance, as in the eighteenth century, but also the provision of loans by British banks and the flotation of capital issues on the London Stock Exchange, as well as an enormous range of other financial services. In effect, Britons were investing their surplus capital in foreign states. In the first half of the nineteenth century that meant primarily the industrialising states of Europe; after 1850 it also meant the United States, the self-governing dominions of the British Empire and India. The net income from overseas investments alone was larger than the entire deficit in the balance of trade for every year from 1907 to 1913, while net income from services and overseas investments together assured that Britain never had a deficit in the overall balance of payments after 1850.[1]

Because Britain's economic wellbeing was so dependent on the world economy, Britain suffered disproportionately when the world economy was in trouble or when Britain's ability to service that economy was disrupted. Such was the case during the era of world wars and depression from 1914 to 1945. The effect was to leave Britain with serious economic problems at the end of the Second World War. War disrupted the traditional patterns of overseas trade. Because all British production had to be for the war effort, the nation ceased to produce for export. The result was the loss of overseas markets, either to those who *could* produce for export (such as the United States and Japan before they entered the war) or to domestic producers, who now had the benefit of protection during and after the war. The diversion of manufacturing to wartime production also meant that many plants had to be reconverted to peacetime production after the war, which would make it hard to recover lost markets quickly. Reconversion was not the only handicap as Britain sought to return to pre-war levels of exports after 1945. The war had taken a toll on Britain's manufacturing capacity, which suffered from both bomb damage and the inability to replace outdated or rundown plants and machinery. The United States, by contrast, while also having to reconvert, had a far larger manufacturing economy which had suffered no bomb damage and had not been so run down during the war. So American manufacturers were better positioned to meet post-war demand immediately.

Since Britain depended on importing food and raw materials in the best of times, the limited ability to export manufactured goods to pay for those imports would accentuate Britain's chronic balance-of-trade deficit. For, during the period until the manufacturing sector could be up and running on a peacetime basis, Britain would also have to import manufactured goods. Furthermore, the war undermined Britain's ability to generate the surplus in income from services which historically had enabled it to cover the deficit in goods. Because of the increased risks involved in wartime, and because the world's richest countries were also engaged primarily in wartime production, the war raised the cost and reduced the volume of seaborne trade. Since Britain had earned money from carrying the world's trade, it lost income as trade shrank and as British ships concentrated on the task of keeping the nation supplied with food and munitions from overseas. Germany also waged a relentless submarine campaign against British shipping; so the stock of ships was reduced during the war, making it more difficult for Britain to recover its preeminence when the war was over. However, world trade was not going to recover rapidly from the war in any event. Winners and losers alike in Europe and Asia had devastated or severely disrupted economies; it would take time for them to become active participants again in the world market. So Britain's carrying trade would not quickly return to its old role as a net earner of money to pay for imports.

Britain's most important source of money to balance the deficit in foreign trade had been the income from overseas investments. The war reduced this income too. In proposing Lend-Lease in 1941, President Roosevelt sought to provide Britain with the credits it needed to buy food and munitions while avoiding the burden of the inter-allied loans that had caused so much friction after the First World War. The Americans, however, used their economic muscle to extract a substantial price from the British government for providing the supplies that it could not pay for – in part because the Americans had exaggerated notions of Britain's wealth. First, Britain had to pay for what it could. This meant running down its dollar and gold reserves and liquidating those foreign investments held by Britons that could easily be converted into dollars. As a result, virtually all British holdings of American investments, some of the most valuable they owned, had to be sold. At the same time, Britain had to accept severe restrictions on its ability to accumulate further reserves and to export to other countries.* Finally, the Americans sought British collaboration in building the kind of post-war economic world that the US government wanted – based on free trade (including no preferences within the British Empire) and a reduced role for sterling in the world economy. So the price America imposed on Britain for winning the war was to leave the British economy gravely weakened at the end of the war, while its ability to recover thereafter was severely handicapped.

There had been one final source of net income to pay for imports: the services that were provided by the banking, brokering and insurance industries in the City of London.† Except for insurance, there was little opportunity for the financial sector to earn much overseas income during the war. Moreover, its recovery after the war would be tied to the broader recovery of the world economy. The war, however, imposed a special burden on Britain which would hamper the recovery of the City's pre-eminent role in providing financial services to the world. As we have seen, while Britain's need to import food, raw materials and munitions did not decrease during the war, its ability to pay for those imports decreased substantially. How, then, was Britain to import what

---

* The level of distrust of the British by some Americans, even some who were Anglophile, remained extraordinarily high. So some people in the US Treasury and Congress were convinced that the British were cheating on Lend-Lease – either by re-exporting American goods or by diverting some domestic production away from military goods to exports. American demands relating to exports and reserves were intended to make such cheating impossible.

† The City is a shorthand term for Britain's financial services industry broadly conceived, wherever it was located. In this book, at times the term will imply those financial services that are international, many but not all of which historically have been centred in and around the old City of London, where the Bank of England and the Stock Exchange are located.

it needed? Lend-Lease was part of the answer. However, Britain also conducted trade, despite American efforts to limit it, with countries that had long been important trading partners. They included dominions like Australia and Ireland, semi-autonomous parts of the empire like India and Egypt, and the colonies. Their trading relations had become especially close in the 1930s when, as a defence against the Depression and American and European protectionism, they had linked their economies to Britain's in an increasingly closed sterling area, protected by tariffs. With the gold standard having collapsed in 1931, they kept the value of their currencies fixed relative to the pound, and they used sterling (in addition to gold) as a reserve to settle debts.* The sterling area was formalised during the war. Britain could not pay for many of its imports with goods, so these countries and their people loaned Britain the money by accepting sterling, which was invested in London. In some cases, their citizens were glad still to be able to sell to Britain and earn interest on what they received while waiting out the war. In the case of India and Egypt, they mostly had no choice. The result, however, was that Britain, for the first time, was in debt to its empire rather than the other way around. These debts were the sterling balances.

After the war there would be no obligation for these foreigners to stick with sterling. If the holders of sterling balances tried to cash them in, however, Britain would quickly be bankrupted. Its gold reserves and its supply of dollars would be exhausted buying up the pounds people no longer wanted.[2] Britain would be left with nothing with which to buy its own imports, and people's confidence in the pound as a currency and in London as a financial centre would be destroyed. American leaders would have been happy to see the sterling area liquidated; however, they were persuaded by the British that this could not happen quickly. So the Bretton Woods Agreement of 1944, which defined the structure for international finance after the war, made some

---

* Before the war, the sterling area had included Argentina and a number of European countries, like the Scandinavian countries and Portugal. Canada was not part of the sterling area because of its economic ties to the United States.

accommodation of the sterling problem. The purpose of Bretton Woods was to develop mechanisms that would assure an orderly means of ending trade imbalances and so prevent the competitive currency devaluations and financial instability that had prolonged the Great Depression. While American conservatism insisted on some form of the pre-1931 gold standard, which had tied national money supplies to gold, there needed to be more flexibility so that the money supply would not act as an impediment to growth by imposing an artificial limit on the expansion of trade. Hence, the dollar was now to serve as a reserve currency, with the same status as gold. Nations would settle their international debts in dollars, while the dollar itself could be exchanged for gold on demand, thus assuring some of the same discipline as under the old gold standard. Each country would define the exchange rate of its currency in terms of the dollar, and these exchange rates would remain fixed unless fundamental changes in a nation's economy forced an adjustment. In the immediate aftermath of the war, the United States would be the country best able to supply the manufactured goods that people wanted. So everyone would be glad to hold dollars as well as gold, and the recovery of world trade would not be so restricted by a shortage of money with which to pay for goods and services – although it would still be limited by a shortage of dollars, as everyone wanted them.

As part of the agreement, Britain was given a five-year transition period in which to adjust to the new regime by retaining controls over sterling assets. Thereafter, the survival of the sterling area would depend on the strength of the British economy and so the attractiveness of holding sterling. If it survived, then within the sterling area sterling rather than the dollar would be the reserve currency. For sterling to remain attractive, Britain's manufacturing sector had to recover relatively quickly, so that there would be goods to offer those people who held sterling balances. A revival of manufacturing exports would also enable Britain to eliminate the payments deficit, so that it could begin to accumulate reserves again. Since Britain's wartime damage, as bad as it was, was far less than that of major competitors like

Germany and Japan, such a recovery did not seem a forlorn hope. If Britain was to export, however, there also needed to be a revival of the world trading network that had been destroyed by two decades of depression and war. Ideally, such a revival would best be promoted by freer trade. For the first time in the nation's history, the American government supported tariff reductions, although the Republican Congress was hostile. Its price, however, was the end of imperial preference, and the British were not prepared to give way on this issue. Nonetheless, as a condition of a 1946 loan from the US, the British agreed to support American efforts to promote tariff reductions. The latter resulted in the General Agreement on Tariffs and Trade (GATT), signed by twenty-three nations in 1947 – but with imperial preference intact. Thus, by the end of 1947, an international framework had been worked out that offered some promise of facilitating the recovery of Britain as an export economy, with London providing the full range of financial services that had been its speciality since the nineteenth century. Only then would people be glad to have investments in Britain – i.e. to hold on to their sterling.

The dominions and other states in the sterling area had their own reasons for collaborating with Britain to preserve it during the post-war years. They certainly did not want to bankrupt Britain or see the value of the pound collapse; then their assets would disappear. Like the British, they were short of dollars and so could not easily purchase goods from the United States, while there were few markets outside the sterling area where they could sell their produce. They had long depended on Britain for capital, and the City gave them access to it on favourable terms.[3] Once the world economy returned to normal, however, the main Commonwealth countries would diversify their trade and end their dependence on Britain. Thereafter, the sterling area could survive only if the British maintained the value of the pound. Foreign national banks would hold sterling as a reserve, but they could turn to other currencies if the pound looked weak. Foreign commercial banks, corporations and individuals would hold sterling because they did business in Britain, or they did business where sterling was used to settle accounts, or they found London a useful place to hold funds for the short term. If they saw the value of their assets threatened, they would move the money else-where – first and foremost into the world's strongest economy, the United States, but from the 1960s to any country with a strong economy and so a strong currency.

There were two threats to the value of the pound. One was inflation. If prices in Britain went up faster than prices elsewhere, sterling would be worth less relative to the dollar in terms of the goods it could purchase. The second threat to the value of the pound was a devaluation of its exchange rate with the dollar.* Devaluation would be necessary if, over time, the British economy weakened in comparison with the American economy, so that eventually the exchange rate failed to reflect accurately the rela-tive value of goods in the two countries. Persistent differential rates of inflation might be one indicator of such a change. Persistent differences in worker productivity might be another.† For Britain, one of the most important indicators of the health of the economy came to be the balance of payments: a persistent deficit showed that Britain was not able to produce enough goods and services to pay for all the goods and services that its people consumed. As a nation, it was living beyond its means. Yet the excess goods and services had to be paid for somehow: either

---

* An example will make this clear. If the exchange rate is £1 = $4, then £1000 will buy $4000 worth of goods. If the exchange rate drops to £1 = $2.80 (as it did in 1949), then the same £1000 now will buy only $2800 worth of goods. The holder of pounds has suddenly seen the value of his assets, as measured by their purchasing power in the United States, fall by 30 per cent. All coun-tries in the sterling area tied their currency to the pound; so if Britain devalued, they did too.

† Worker productivity is the amount of output the economy gets from each unit of worker input. In effect, an economy with high worker productivity is getting more output for the same amount of work than an economy with low worker productivity. Initially, the exchange rate should reflect the relative rates of productivity for all inputs (capital as well as labour), but if worker productivity improves or deteriorates in one of the countries, then the exchange rate will no longer reflect the relationship accurately.

Britain had to pay in dollars or gold, which would reduce its reserves and weaken its ability to support the pound, or it would have to sell more government notes, which would increase the supply and so undermine the value of sterling. Either way, it signalled trouble for the holders of sterling and so was a sign to sell and move into assets in some other currency. Thus, if the British government wanted the City of London to return to its old role as a major centre of international financial services and a generator of income, it believed that it had to maintain the attractiveness of holding sterling. This, in turn, required it to keep inflation under control and to assure a balance-of-payments surplus in order to preserve the value of the pound.

The Advent of Socialism

This wartime legacy circumscribed what economic policies any British government could pursue in 1945. The new Labour government that was elected in July, however, had obligations that were defined in the party's election manifesto. Three commitments, in particular, had important economic implications: the promise to maintain full employment, the promise to expand the welfare state and the promise to nationalise certain key industries. The pledge of full employment was a direct result of the prolonged crisis of unemployment between the wars. Britain's socialists, in many respects, retained the same belief in the importance of work to individual self-respect and self-reliance that had characterised nineteenth-century liberalism. The depression of the inter-war years merely confirmed the devastating effect of unemployment on the character of the individual and the well-being of the family. Unemployment was also an important source of poverty, since the dole (unemployment benefit) could not possibly be maintained at the level of a living wage. A socialist party like Britain's, whose roots were much more liberal humanitarian than they were Marxist, could not allow such human suffering and waste of human resources to persist. Prior to 1914, Labour policy was based on the 'right to work'. In practice, this meant that government should use public works as a source of jobs in times of recession while providing adequate benefits for the unemployed. In the face of the mass unemployment of the inter-war years, the right to work became incorporated into a broader vision of government action that included public works, nationalised industries and economic planning.

This crisis of mass unemployment led the liberal economist John Maynard Keynes to an alternative solution in *The General Theory of Employment, Interest and Money*, which he published in 1936. Keynes demonstrated that government could secure full employment by managing its own taxing and spending so as to achieve that goal. In looking at the Depression, Keynes saw economists and policy-makers alike unnecessarily paralysed by the danger of government competition with the private sector, particularly for investment funds. In an economy as depressed as Britain's was, he argued, there was no private-sector demand. For, if there was no demand to buy more goods or services, there was no incentive for the private sector to invest. Government, therefore, could safely borrow money (i.e. run a budget deficit) in order to subsidise public works programmes to put people back to work. As these people earned wages, they would start to demand more goods and services, which in turn would lead to more production of goods and provision of services, and so the economy could gradually pull out of the depression. In *The General Theory*, Keynes worked this argument out theoretically in a way that divorced it from its Depression origins. He demonstrated that government could use its own spending, plus its control over the tax system (i.e. the amount of money its citizens had to spend) and its ability to influence interest rates (i.e. the terms on which firms borrowed money to invest in future production), to affect the nation's aggregate level of output of goods and services – what Keynes called the gross national product, or GNP. In theory, if government could evaluate the inter-relationship of all these factors accurately, it could adjust the variables to assure that GNP was at a level to support full employment. If there was excessive unemployment (there would always be *some*), government could encourage demand for goods and services by lowering taxes or interest rates, or by increasing its own spending. If, on the other hand, demand was beyond the capacity of the economy to meet it – resulting in inflation, or, in Britain's case, a turn to imports for the wanted goods, and so a balance-of-payments deficit – the government could dampen demand by raising taxes and interest rates, or by reducing its spending and running a budget surplus so as to remove spending power from the system.

During the Second World War, Keynes acted as an adviser to the Treasury, and over the course of the war his views gained some degree of acceptance there. Keynes's views in fact had much in common with those traditionally held in the Treasury. He was well aware of the dangers of deficits that gave excessive stimuli to consumer spending. He preferred to keep the current account budget in balance and see the government stimulate employment (when a stimulus was needed) by investing: thus his 1930s emphasis on public works. He was also quite realistic (even pessimistic) about the minimum rate of unemployment that could be achieved, guessing about 5 per cent.[4] The key, however, for post-war governments was that they apparently had the means to assure full employment without having to interfere with the free market or to involve themselves directly in the provision of goods and services, beyond what government always did – e.g. by public works or its demand for military equipment. Government's ability to do so depended on two things: accurate data on the many variables that influenced and contributed to supply and demand, and a correct understanding of the economic formulas that defined the relationship among those variables. In the decades that followed, governments, universities and international institutions all over the world threw themselves into the task of gathering data. Their accuracy was mixed, however, while the economic relationships have proved difficult to get a handle on.[5]

Keynesian economics helped put an end to the debate in the Labour government over whether it should embrace economic planning. For many in the party, planning was what socialist management of the economy was all about. However, it would have posed serious problems for the government. It was difficult to escape the association with Soviet-style planning, which abridged all freedom as it superseded the market. Since the United States was beginning to see everything in Cold War terms, planning would have generated friction with the US at a time when the British economy was especially dependent on the Americans. At the same time, planning implied the possibility that government would determine where people worked. For it must incorporate the allocation of labour as well as capital and other resources. Labour's own constituency among the trade unions had a long history of resisting any such dictation. During the war, Winston Churchill had circumvented this hostility by putting one of their own – Ernest Bevin, the leader of Britain's largest trade union – in charge of mobilising labour for the war. As much as possible, Bevin had relied on voluntary measures and incentives to direct workers into the industries where they were needed. Without the necessities imposed by a war of survival, however, most workers would not accept limitations on their freedom to work where they wished and to determine wages, hours and conditions of work by collective bargaining. Reconciling such freedoms with meaningful economic planning posed a serious problem. Keynesianism eliminated the problem. The market was left free of all government dictation. Government would simply use the influence that it always had on the economy (for it always employed people, bought goods and services and taxed) so as to assure full employment without inflation.

As important as full employment to Labour's social policy was its commitment to expand Britain's welfare state. The Second World War had produced the myth that it was a people's war. Since all Britons had contributed equally to achieve the common goal of victory, all should share the benefits of a better society now that victory was achieved. Labour's leaders believed that the war had, in fact, created a spirit of cooperation and mutual concern that laid the foundation for a fairer allocation of the product of the economy. For the working class, that meant a benefit system that assured a minimum standard of support above the poverty level for all citizens. It also meant the elimination of any implication of fault or failure on the part of the benefit recipients: there would be none of the humiliation that had been associated with the Victorian Poor Law and the dole of the 1930s. The most original innovation that Labour introduced was the creation of the National Health Service (NHS), which came into existence in 1948. Under the National Insurance Act of 1911, all working men whose annual income was below a defined level were required to contribute (with their employers and the state) to a health insurance fund. The insurance covered medical care by a participating doctor, plus a daily payment after a prescribed waiting period in lieu of income lost due to illness. The measure revolutionised health care for the insured. Wives and children, however, were not covered, while many workers fell between the cracks – including virtually all women, sweated labour (i.e. those industries in which employees were forced to work in poor conditions for low pay) and those who were employed irregularly. Finally, even the insured received no coverage for hospital costs or specialists' fees. The NHS closed all these gaps, providing comprehensive health care for all Britons who chose to use it. As under the old Insurance Act, individuals would be able to choose any doctor who participated in the system; a doctor would be paid an annual capitation fee for each patient on his (or her) list. Hospitals were nationalised. Prescription drugs were covered, initially at no cost, although later charges (co-payments) were introduced. Regional boards were expected to rationalise the whole system of health provision, assuring that the necessary services were provided and appropriately distributed in each region. There would be incentives to encourage doctors to settle in areas with shortages. Anyone who chose could stay outside the system: general practitioners would have to choose between public and private practice, but specialists (consultants) could have both NHS and private patients and hospitals could maintain private beds for paying patients.

The second pillar of Labour's welfare state reforms was comprehensive insurance, as had been recommended by the

Beveridge Report of 1942. Like the NHS, the National Insurance Act of 1946 (with supplemental legislation in 1948) built on earlier legislation: not only the 1911 Act that provided health and unemployment insurance for specified categories of citizens, but also the 1897 Workmen's Compensation Act, the 1908 Old Age Pensions Act, and the inclusion of widows and orphans in the pension scheme and the vast expansion of unemployment insurance after the First World War. All citizens would make payments into a contributory insurance fund that provided for all their social welfare needs. All were assured an income if they could not work because of unemployment, illness, disability or old age. In addition to payments to those who could not work or were retired from work, there were widows' and orphans' benefits, death benefits to help pay funeral costs and maternity benefits. A system of family allowances gave a payment for each child beyond the first – in theory, not only to allow for differential family size, but also to assure that children were properly fed and cared for.[6] As with health care, anyone with the resources could choose to supplement this state provision through private insurance.

Thus, Labour's welfare reforms did not try to create a level playing field in the competition between rich and poor for economic advantage. The private sector remained, and those who could afford to were free to take advantage of the services it provided. This approach also characterised the government's education policy, which left untouched the public schools which served the privileged. The 1944 Education Act introduced by R. A. Butler (a Conservative) had already implemented a radical reform to facilitate a society based on equal opportunity: universal secondary education. As the Act was implemented under Labour, the eleven-plus exam, which had been used by some local authorities since the 1920s to determine who would qualify for free places at grammar schools, became the universal means of identifying the most talented children (at the age of eleven). Under the new system, grammar schools were for those pupils going to university or into white-collar jobs. If they were under the local authorities, their fees were abolished. Many of the old independent grammar schools, however, chose to remain outside local control. They received grants directly from the government, continued to charge fees and were expected to increase their number of free places. Those who did not qualify for grammar school would either go to a school offering a terminal secondary degree (the 'modern' schools) or one providing technical (vocational) training. The approach was elitist, but it was not meant to be class-biased. The effect, however, was to reinforce privilege, for those from upper- and middle-class backgrounds were best positioned to qualify for the grammar schools – although this result was not immediately obvious. The Labour government was well satisfied with the new tripartite system. The leadership strongly supported the grammar schools, which they believed had served well as vehicles for working-class upward mobility. The government even initially blocked pupils at the new secondary modern schools from sitting for certification exams, and, when it relented, it set a high standard for passing that would be beyond the reach of virtually all such pupils.[7] Thus it was difficult for most pupils to leave school with meaningful qualifications. Labour thought it was more important, as a means of expanding working-class opportunity, to raise the school-leaving age to fifteen, which it did in 1947.

Thus, Labour's social welfare programme was not 'levelling' in the sense that it did not seek to eliminate the ability of wealth to buy a superior service. Labour's socialist assumptions, however, did mean that it was determined there should be no taint associated with taking publicly provided benefits and services. Since its origin in the nineteenth century, British socialism had assumed that most poverty was the consequence of structural inequalities embedded in modern capitalist society, which distributed the rewards of work very unevenly. Thus, because poverty was not the fault of the poor, there must be no stigma attached to the receipt of benefits. Labour's legislation therefore was based on the principle of universality. All people contributed to the insurance fund and all people received benefits; the NHS and state-provided education were available to all. Benefit was now a right, not something given as a matter of generosity to the poor by the state. There was another assumption underlying the Labour approach to welfare – one which long had provided the justification for the state provision of education. Society as a whole would benefit by this universal provision – first with a stronger and healthier (and so more productive) workforce, and second with a population which could begin to add its demand for those goods and services that defined life above the subsistence level, as the poor no longer had to worry about providing for every contingency or catastrophe. The economy would grow faster as it met this demand, helping the government's efforts to assure full employment.[8] Yet in one respect Labour was still to be guided by nineteenth-century Victorian assumptions about poverty. Since the introduction of National Insurance in 1911, the insurance principle had been viewed as a test of worthiness; benefits were received because the recipient had paid for (i.e. earned) them. Thus, while Labour may have believed that most poverty was the result of failures of society rather than failures of the individual, it still seemed to accept old liberal assumptions (which were very much Beveridge's assumptions) that a recipient had to prove self-reliance by work. Only then could the state be protected from the lazy and shiftless (the 'unworthy poor') who sought something for nothing by living off public handouts. The Labour government *did* make provision for the poor outside the insurance system, however. The National Assistance Act of 1948 assured that no one would fall below a minimum defined standard of wellbeing (though a very austere one). The targets were those who had no insurance benefits, whose insurance benefits had run out or whose insurance benefits were insufficient.

The government, however, probably assumed that there would be few such poor. Given the commitment to full employment, unemployment would be temporary – the result either of people changing jobs or of minor structural changes in the economy. Hence, there would be no need to provide benefits for long-term unemployed whose insurance coverage had run out, as had been the case during the Great Depression. Thus, people would mostly be making insurance payments; any drawing down of benefits would be temporary. Nor would there be many other long-term demands on the insurance fund that it could not provide for. Since the NHS would raise the national standard of health, there would be few who faced long-term disability for health reasons. Only the permanently disabled would have to be taken care of, so the insurance fund would be able to manage. The residual who would still require state assistance under the 1948 Act therefore was expected to be quite small. Yet, in fact, there were problems for the future that would make it difficult to keep benefit recipients above this implicit poverty level. The system made no allowance for rent. As a result, those who lived in high-rent areas like London were left in poverty by the flat-rate benefit. Eventually rent rebates (and rates rebates as well, to help with local taxes) had to be introduced as part of the welfare system to close this gap. There also was no built-in provision for the level of benefit to rise with prices. Thus, as the intermittent increases offered by government did not keep up with inflation, more people on benefit fell into poverty in the 1950s and 1960s and had to turn to national assistance (renamed supplementary benefit in the 1960s) for help.

The insurance principle had another important function. It made it easier for the government to finance its welfare reforms. Although the benefits offered were at little more than subsistence level, they were still significantly above those of the 1930s, while the NHS was potentially very costly. (Indeed, the government seriously underestimated its cost.) How was the government to pay for such a radical extension of the system (along with the rebuilding of Britain)? In part, the money would come from a restructuring of the economy after the war. However extensive Britain's post-war overseas commitments, they were tiny compared to the cost of the war itself; so the armed forces could be and were run down between 1945 and 1948. At the same time, little was done to modify the high wartime tax rates. On the contrary, they went up somewhat: the one levelling plank in the Labour platform was steeper taxation on the income and wealth of the rich. National insurance, however, offered another source of revenue. It required contributions from the individual and the employer (as well as the state), and full employment assured that almost everyone would be contributing. Indeed, full employment was essential if the system was not going to make politically unacceptable demands on taxation.[9] Nonetheless, even with insurance contributions, the welfare system that was introduced after 1945 was underfunded and somewhat contradictory. Because contributions were based on a flat rate rather than varying with income, they had to be at a level consistent with the wages of the poorest workers, which limited how much money was brought in by insurance payments. At the same time, universal benefits meant that overall costs would be high unless the benefit was kept fairly low, thus risking more people falling into poverty. Finally, if the underlying assumptions proved unfounded or if conditions changed, there was the potential for an increasing burden on the taxpayer, unless either universality or flat-rate contributions and benefits were compromised.

The welfare state was not the end of the new demands that Labour's programme placed on the budget. The third major election manifesto promise – to nationalise certain key industries – meant that the government had to compensate the private owners. Clause IV of the Labour Party constitution of 1918 had committed it to 'the common ownership of the means of production'.[10] While many party members took this statement seriously as defining their ultimate aspirations for a socialist state, most probably did not see full nationalisation as an attainable goal of practical politics, rather than a distant dream. Nor, in 1945, was it necessary in order to further other Labour goals of greater fairness and efficiency in the economy. By the end of the war, there existed a broad consensus as to the candidates for a first round of nationalisation. It was hardly controversial to nationalise the Bank of England, when no other country in the world allowed the institution that controlled the nation's money supply to be in private hands. The nationalisation of other industries – such as electricity, gas and telecommunications – could be justified on much the same grounds that municipal ownership of public utilities had been justified in the latter part of the nineteenth century: they were natural monopolies, so the public needed to be protected from the adverse effects of no competition. In a small country like Britain, even civil aviation seemed like a natural monopoly; only the United States was big enough to support competition among domestic airlines, and the industry there was regulated until 1980. Ownership seemed to have an important advantage over regulation: it would assure an integrated national system of production and distribution.

Two other industries had been viewed as candidates for public ownership for much of the twentieth century: the railways and coal. Before the First World War, Churchill had spoken approvingly of railway nationalisation.[11] The railways, like air transport, could be viewed as a natural monopoly. The industry had already been rationalised after the First World War: the government had taken over the railways during the war, and before it gave them back to private ownership the rail network was consolidated into four companies. Thus, it seemed a small step to complete this process after the next war. Nationalisation of the coal mines had also been part of the political debate since the end of the First World War, when the miners had proposed that the government should not return the mines to private ownership. Their case had been supported by judge Sir John Sankey, who headed a Coal Industry Commission in 1919; however, the Conservative-dominated coalition would not contemplate such a socialist policy. Between the wars, the industry, which suffered from overcapacity, was generally viewed as inefficient and in need of rationalisation, though at the time this meant the modernisation of technology more than the closing of inefficient mines. Partly because of the industry's problems, labour relations had been a disaster in the 1920s, culminating in the six-month strike of 1926 which had triggered the General Strike. The failures of the mine-owners either to improve the mines or their relations with their workers assured they had little public sympathy. At the same time, they seemed to undermine the claim that private ownership was more efficient than public management would be. Within the world of labour itself, the legacy of the industrial strife of the 1920s, culminating in the vindictive behaviour of the mine-owners after the 1926 strike, assured that nationalisation of the mines was a priority of the Labour government. Nothing that government did was more popular with its working-class constituency.

Generally, the public easily accepted all this nationalisation, and while the Conservatives never hid their preference for private over public ownership, they accepted it too. The same could not be said for the nationalisation of road haulage and iron and steel, both of which were far more contentious. In both cases, the government was breaking new ground, for neither a natural monopoly nor an inefficiency argument could be used to justify public ownership. The nationalisation of road haulage might be defended as part of an integrated transportation policy. Why bring the railways and the airlines under public control and not the road haulage industry? In the end, however, the government had to agree to exclude small operators, so the integrated system was sacrificed. There was no pragmatic argument at all for nationalising iron and steel. While many inefficient producers remained – protected by Depression-era tariffs and wartime demand – the industry was able to reorganise itself somewhat between 1946 and 1948 under the aegis of a government-appointed Control Board. Thus there was not the same compelling case for bringing the industry under public ownership that there was for coal. Nationalisation looked like an assertion of the socialist principle of public ownership for its own sake – which is exactly why the more extreme socialists in the Labour Party insisted on it. At the same time, however, steel nationalisation also mobilised industry against Labour, as businessmen feared it was a prelude to further nationalisation. Thus, the Tories made steel nationalisation and socialist dogma more generally a centrepiece of their election campaign in 1951, and they returned steel to the private sector soon after their victory.

Socialists expected all nationalisation – whether justified on grounds of natural monopoly, inefficient performance under private ownership or ideology – to offer public benefits. The industries would be run to improve public wellbeing rather than for private profits. For example, plants could be sited in areas of high unemployment. Telephone, rail or electricity services could be provided to (or continued in) rural areas at a financial loss. Most important of all, gains in efficiency due to the economies of scale that resulted from a single nationwide industry, or to planned reorganisation and rationalisation, would go to consumers in the form of lower prices and to workers in the form of higher wages rather than to shareholders in the form of higher dividends. Because there would be no incentive to exploit workers, labour relations would be harmonious. Since the day-to-day management would be by businessmen, there seemed every reason to believe that the publicly owned businesses would be as efficient as privately owned ones – perhaps more so, as the managers could look to long-term benefits rather than short-term profits in their decision-making. Finally, nationalisation would weaken the political power of capitalism and capitalists.

Never So Good

Thus, Prime Minister Clement Attlee and his team had to reconcile a complicated set of expectations and demands as they developed Labour's economic policies after the war. On the one hand, they had to promote economic recovery in a way that allowed for the reconstruction of British industry and the protection of sterling. On the other hand, they had to assure full employment and to pay for a significant expansion of the welfare state, as well as the cost of bringing a significant section of the economy under public ownership.* Two other factors further complicated policy-making, as the government sought to reconcile these potentially conflicting expectations. First, the

---

* Compensation for the nationalised industries was paid in the form of government stock. While that entailed no immediate outlay, it did mean an additional long-term burden on the budget in terms of the returns paid on that stock. The actual level of payment has been judged to be extremely generous.

worldwide devastation created by the war had left the United States as the principal provider of manufactured goods. Since the United States was also a major supplier of food, everyone wanted dollars with which to make purchases from America. Even before the First World War, Britain had had a substantial trade deficit with the United States, which had imported little in the way of manufactured goods. Now, with Lend-Lease terminated as soon as Japan surrendered, Britain had an acute need for dollars. Just as bad, so did the holders of sterling balances. Thus, the post-war situation assured a constant pressure on the pound. Second, as part of the post-war settlement, Britain became one of the occupying powers in Germany. This not only required supporting a large British army there, but also to some degree providing for the German people in the British zone. This and other overseas commitments meant an additional demand for resources from Britain which would add to the balance-of-payments deficit. All these factors assured that, at least initially, it would be difficult to support the pound.

The government had no choice but to delay the return to free market conditions; but it preferred some element of economic planning anyway. Since the government envisaged a major role for the sterling area in Britain's recovery, exchange controls were necessary to limit how much foreign exchange holders of pounds could convert at any one time. Controls assured that there would be no large-scale exodus from the pound that would undermine the value of the sterling balances. For the same reason, Britain's net external payments needed to be balanced as quickly as possible, for a persistent deficit would undermine the stability of the pound. The key component of earlier payments surpluses – income from overseas investments – could only increase slowly under exchange controls. In fact, it would never return to anything like its old preeminence. Financial services more broadly conceived, however, *would* continue to be important, as many new kinds of services would develop in the years ahead that had not existed in the first half of the century. However, growth could only come with the recovery of the world economy.

Shipping, by contrast, would fade as a significant source of income. In the post-war environment, nations increasingly provided their own carriers or turned to poorer countries which could provide a cheaper service than Britain could. Thus, the whole composition of Britain's balance of payments was going to change in the post-war period.

In the short term, however, there was little in the way of 'invisible exports' (i.e. those other than goods) to help the balance. Government policy, therefore, had to focus on the reconstruction of Britain's export industries so as to eliminate the deficit in the balance of *trade*. Thus, most wartime rationing and other restraints on consumption remained in place, in order to limit demand for imports or even for domestic goods that might be produced instead of exports. Wartime controls of industry were retained, as the government directed where raw materials went, what investment was undertaken, who could import goods and where they could import from. As much as possible, trade was directed within the sterling area, which pooled its dollar reserves under British management. Price controls were retained in order to limit inflation, contain costs and manage demand. Wages were kept down by bargaining with the Trades Union Congress (TUC), which was willing to cooperate as long as the government controlled prices and subsidised wages through its welfare policies. Finally, a loan from the United States in 1946 (which cancelled the remaining Lend-Lease debt) was expected to provide the extra cushion the economy needed as it adjusted to peacetime conditions – and especially to help cover the inevitable deficit in overseas trade.

Yet it was still difficult for the government to judge the right fiscal (i.e. taxation and spending) and monetary policies to pursue in order to reinforce its goals of a strong pound, a balance in the nation's external payments and full employment. The Chancellor of the Exchequer, Hugh Dalton, feared a return to the Great Depression of the 1930s, while remembering all too well the collapse of the boom after the First World War in 1921. Thus, the greatest danger appeared to come from unemployment, not from inflation, which had never been a problem. Dalton therefore kept interest rates low in order to encourage investment, and he cut taxes to encourage spending and (on the part of the rich) investment. By 1947, however, he faced a crisis. A coal shortage meant Britain had to increase imports where it was usually self-sufficient, while cuts in power led to a drastic, if temporary, drop in industrial production. At the same time, a rise in the prices of agricultural goods and raw materials because of a worldwide shortage meant the overall cost of imports was rising. With Dalton's expansionary fiscal and monetary policies, and the jump in government spending because of its social policies, there was a budget deficit, a balance-of-payments deficit and signs of inflation. The climax came in July, when Britain was forced (as a condition of the US loan) to end the exchange controls that had protected the pound and restore full convertibility – ahead of the time envisaged by the Bretton Woods Agreement.[12] The result was a massive exodus from sterling into dollars and a quick end to convertibility.

A radical change of course was necessary – a change that was symbolised when Sir Stafford Cripps replaced Dalton as Chancellor in November 1947. The government adopted a more deflationary policy, by increasing taxation, in order to restore confidence in the pound. It also imposed stricter import controls, tightened still further the rationing regime (although rationing never covered more than one-third of consumer spending),[13] increased incentives to channel more resources into export industries and negotiated a wage freeze with the TUC. Yet it still kept interest rates low in order to encourage investment, and its spending policies remained expansive in order to assure full employment. Finally, it looked to the colonies for more help in exporting raw materials to secure scarce dollars. It is unlikely that it could have continued this balancing act between deflationary and expansionary policies if the United States had not intervened decisively. The US government concluded that a much greater effort was needed to promote economic recovery, not only in Britain but in all Western Europe. Thus, virtually simultaneously with the convertibility crisis of the summer of 1947, the Marshall Plan was launched to channel American resources to Europe.

The Marshall Plan ended the dollar shortage. In Britain, it assured that the money was there both to meet Labour's many obligations and to protect sterling. In 1948, controls on business, and even to a limited degree on the consumer, could be relaxed somewhat. Yet the broader pressures on the budget and the pound remained, for the principal determinants of government spending at home and abroad had not altered. As a result, success was vulnerable to any change in the favourable circumstances of 1948. That change came early in 1949, with a decline in American demand due to the end of a domestic boom. Britain's balance of payments fell into deficit, and, as people speculated on the possible devaluation of sterling, a run on the pound began. While Cripps felt a strong commitment to support the pound, the even tougher spending cuts and deflationary measures that would be necessary were politically unacceptable, given the restrictions already being imposed on the British people. In the end, the Cabinet opted for a radical devaluation from $4.03 to $2.80 to end the speculation once and for all. It succeeded, as British exports to the United States immediately leapt up, and the balance of payments came back into surplus.

While the economy was bouncing back from the crisis of 1949, an observer at the end of that year might be forgiven for being pessimistic about the future. The British economy seemed to be perpetually on the edge of crisis, while the people seemed doomed to a regimen of self-denial as part of the effort to ward off such crises. Yet ten years later, the Prime Minister, Harold Macmillan, ran his general election on the theme that the people had 'never had it so good'.[14] How was such a rapid transformation possible? The devaluation of 1949 helped. Speculation against the pound stopped and an important source of instability was removed for the time being. At the same time, with the help of Marshall aid, the British had achieved much on the road to recovery between 1946 and 1949. By 1950, industry was producing and exporting far above 1938 levels and seemed well positioned to benefit from a broader European recovery that also was underpinned by Marshall money.

Much more important, however, were circumstances beyond anyone's control. First and foremost was the more broadly based recovery of the world economy. Just as the Great Depression had created an environment of low trade, low demand and low investment which helped lock the world economy into the Depression, so the post-war recovery created an expansionist environment that encouraged investment and helped promote further recovery. There was an enormous backlog of demand for consumer goods, going back not merely to before the war, but even to before the Depression, and there was a far wider range of goods available at prices that more people could afford. The expansive economies of the developed world facilitated a level of employment far beyond what might have been conceived possible in an earlier era, with Britain's unemployment rate usually hovering between 1 and 2 per cent.[15] As a result, people had money in their pockets and began to buy goods. Greater demand meant more trade and more investment, which in turn helped to sustain employment, income levels and so more demand. This recovery of the richest countries of Europe, Asia and America consolidated the recovery of Britain. Britain was also helped by a fall in the world prices of agricultural goods and raw materials. Since these goods were such an important component of British imports, a fall in prices meant Britons could buy many more imports with the same number of exports. It also kept prices low, relieved pressure on the balance of payments and made it easier for governments to pursue an expansionist economic policy.

Nonetheless, all was not plain sailing for the British economy in the 1950s. The policies known as 'stop-go' were a reflection of the balancing act that the governments of 1950–64 had to perform in order to protect the value of the pound while maintaining full employment. There were several sources of difficulty. First, there was Britain's enormous military commitments overseas; indeed, it was no coincidence that 'stop-go' was launched by the Labour

Chancellor of the Exchequer, Hugh Gaitskell, in 1950, when he sought to pay for the Korean War. Since Britain was already at full employment, the effect of wartime demand was to divert production from civilian to military goods, which meant away from exports. At the same time, prices went up worldwide because of the demands from rearmament. Finally, the end of price controls meant the end of wage restraint, as the shortage of labour gave workers leverage to push wages up. All these factors contributed to inflation and a balance of payments crisis, as Britain's defence spending as a percentage of gross domestic product (GDP)* rose from 5.8 per cent in 1950–51 to 8.7 per cent in 1952–3[16]. At the same time, Britain's enormous overseas commitments meant a net outflow of resources quite independent of the short-term crisis created by the Korean War. Throughout the 1950s, Britain theoretically was back where it had been before the First World War: the net income from services more than counterbalanced the deficit that usually (though not always) occurred in the balance of trade. In 1913, however, the income from these invisible exports had covered 40 per cent of British imports; in the 1960s, it covered only 5 per cent. Hence, any balance-of-payments surplus was much more precarious than it had ever been before 1914, and the deficit in military spending constantly threatened to push it into deficit (see Table 5.9).[17] This was one source of the resort to 'stop-go' policies. Given the Tories' desire to re-establish London's role as a major centre of international finance, a payments deficit – or, indeed, anything that called into question people's confidence in the economy – required a response to defend the value of the pound, especially as exchange controls were being relaxed in stages and ended in 1958.

Thus began the 'stop' phase of the cycle, as the government

---

* Gross domestic product is the total value of goods and services produced by a nation (gross national product) less the amount invested overseas, thus yielding the product that remains within the nation. As will be seen in later chapters, it is the measure now used most commonly by economists to measure the size of an economy, rather than GNP.

sought to restore a balance-of-payments surplus. It dampened demand for imports by reining in consumption and investment – raising taxes and interest rates and cutting the rate of growth of government spending. Eventually, however, the effect of these deflationary policies was an increase in unemployment. Since the government was committed to full employment, it had to reverse itself, returning to the 'go' phase of the cycle by lowering taxes and interest rates and increasing spending. In the prosperous 1950s, however, public demand for consumer goods eventually outran the ability of British industry to supply them when the economy was expanding. This insufficiency of domestic capacity was a second source of difficulty. Partly it resulted from the large commitment of domestic resources to military production rather than to the production of consumer goods. Partly it resulted from the high interest rates during the 'stop' phase, which discouraged corporate investment and the expanded capacity it would bring. More important than either of these factors, however, was the resistance of British industry to change that would make the manufacturing sector more efficient. The Labour government had been conscious of the need to increase the productivity of British industry by modernising technology, investing in research and development, improving marketing and workforce training and consolidation to create larger firms. Industry, however, was suspicious of Labour's intentions and was determined to return to an economy free of wartime government interference. Hence, even the most modest admonitions were resented, while there were limits to how much Labour was willing to interfere with free enterprise.[18] While there were important exceptions, therefore, too much of British industry continued as it had been before the war. The problem was not so much plant and equipment: there was plenty of investment in modern production technology (though there is debate about whether there was enough). Rather, it was the system of management, the organisation of production, and the allocation of labour that created inefficiency and raised prices. The effect was to leave important sectors of the economy unable to meet the demand that came with an expanding economy and to contend with more modernised European and Japanese competitors.

Thus, demand started to outstrip domestic supply during the 'go' phase of the cycle, and prices started to go up, while people turned to imports to provide the goods they wanted. At the same time, in conditions of full employment, trade unions were able to put pressure on employers for wage increases. They got what they asked for because management wanted to avoid strikes which reduced profits when demand was high. While trade union demands were not excessive, wage increases were often more than was justified by improvements in worker productivity, thus putting pressure on prices. Productivity was lagging because not enough was being done to improve production methods. Indeed, unions used their strength during the 1950s to consolidate the traditional practices that led to overmanning.[19] Nonetheless, the main source of price rises at this time was the demand for goods beyond what British industry could supply rather than excessive wage increases. The limited inflation that resulted, in addition to the balance-of-payments deficit resulting from the increase in imports, made holders of sterling nervous, which put pressure on the pound. So once again the government had to return to 'stop' policies to slow down the economy.

It might be thought that the Conservatives, who claimed to support freer markets and less government intervention, would have ended controls of every sort while cutting domestic spending so as to channel resources into defence or tax cuts. Churchill's government, however, was not as eager to return quickly to the rigours of the unrestrained market as their election rhetoric implied. Having inherited a balance-of-payments crisis and ebbing reserves, the Cabinet briefly in 1952 considered a plan to make the pound convertible right away and allow the exchange rate to float. There was too much opposition to such a radical measure, however, so instead governments proceeded cautiously towards economic liberalism. The pound was made convertible only in 1958, while private purchase of foreign currency was subject to controls until 1980. The removal of restraints on trade was just as slow. Half the nation's imports were still subject to control in 1953,[20] and some controls remained at the end of the decade. The whole move towards freer trade was subject to prolonged international negotiation through GATT, while Britain's desire to preserve imperial preference provided a counterweight.

Nor were the Conservatives eager to attack Labour's welfare state. Indeed, they expanded it, for the leaders wanted to dispel any lingering image from the inter-war years that they were a party hostile to the working class (just as Labour had wanted to dispel notions that it was hostile to capital). Conservative Party traditions made it easy to accept the welfare state. Since the emergence of modern conservatism in the nineteenth century, the party's leaders had emphasised their willingness to reform when legitimate grievances existed. They contrasted this pragmatic approach to reform to the Liberal (and later the Labour) approach, which was ideologically driven. In the 1870s and 1880s, Benjamin Disraeli and Lord Randolph Churchill (Winston's father) developed a mythology of Tory paternalism to justify social reforms. Tory paternalism was an effort to define the basis for an alliance between the landed and working classes by harking back to an era when a paternalistic landed aristocracy supposedly provided for the wellbeing of the rural labourers, while the latter deferred to the former as their natural leaders. Social reforms passed by modern Conservative governments were simply paternalism in a new form. They helped those in need without creating dependence or weakening those who created wealth. Furthermore, this paternalistic tradition gave the Conservatives another basis for distinguishing themselves from Labour: they were the party of the whole nation, which sought to promote social unity, while Labour was the party of a class, which emphasised and accentuated social divisions.

Pragmatic, paternalistic and one-nation: these were the qualities that Tory leaders sought to emphasise after the war. All the prime ministers – Churchill, Sir Anthony Eden and Macmillan – came out of this tradition. There need be no concern about socialism. If policies benefited the working class and the nation, the Tories would not reject them merely because someone called them socialist. The test would always be: was there a proven need for something to be done, and did the proposed remedy provide a practical means of meeting that need? The judgement of the party leadership in the 1950s was that the Labour policies generally met both of these tests, while, because they were excessively driven by ideology, they did not provide sufficient scope for private enterprise and the free market. The evidence of Labour's ideological bent was the nationalisation of steel and road haulage. Both unnecessarily interfered with the free market, with no countervailing benefit to the public; therefore, both were returned to private ownership. Other nationalisations remained in place, as did the welfare reforms and the commitment to full employment. At the same time, the prosperity of the 1950s allowed Churchill's government to move towards a domestic free market, with the last of the food rationing ending in 1954. Yet Tory governments were willing to intervene in other ways for social welfare purposes – e.g. by retaining both subsidies on the prices of staple foods and some forms of rent control.

Tory policy was especially expansive in two important areas. The first was house-building. Substandard housing had been a problem for the British working classes throughout the nineteenth century. Disraeli's government of 1874–80 had been the first to provide mechanisms to facilitate slum clearance, and one of the great social successes of the Conservative-dominated governments of the inter-war period had been the house-building programmes they had encouraged. The Second World War had, of course, left British housing a mess – both from bomb damage and from the failure to repair and replace when resources were limited. Much working-class housing that remained still was substandard – i.e. it was run down or did not provide basic amenities like hot water and indoor lavatories. The Labour government built some one million new houses, as well as undertaking the repair of many others, but with so much demand for scarce funds, resources and manpower, the achievement fell well short of the need. Furthermore, Labour's emphasis had been almost entirely on working-class houses built and owned by local councils, which let them out at subsidised rents. Thus, there was a clear opportunity for the Conservatives to promote a more broadly based housing programme, one that provided for all social groups and allowed for an end to restrictions and a return to the private sector as a major supplier. The Tory promise of three hundred thousand houses per year at the 1951 general election was more than met. From the mid-1950s on, it was assisted by the general prosperity that enabled building societies to provide low-interest mortgages to help fund private demand. Nonetheless, a large proportion of the building continued to be of council housing for rent, while funds also continued to be devoted to slum clearance and repair. The other major Tory initiative was an expansion in hospital building, beginning in the late 1950s, following a very favourable report in 1956 on the cost-effectiveness of the National Health Service. The NHS had already become the most popular of all the welfare programmes, and Tory policy recognised this reality.

Hence, when Tory governments faced the economic problems of the 1950s, social programmes were not specifically targeted for retrenchment. Instead, whenever a balance-of-payments crisis forced a resort to 'stop' policies, the government cut back on the *rate of growth* of its spending for both defence and social welfare. Because tax revenues were ample with the economy doing well, total spending did not have to be reduced at all, while the Conservatives could still plan for a balanced budget. The priorities set by Labour continued unchallenged until a crisis in 1957–8. There had been growing concern about inflation. Keynesians viewed it as the product of wage increases. Monetarists, however, led by the economist Lionel Robbins, thought it was the result of excessive government spending. As a result, government was borrowing too much from the banks and so encouraging an inflationary expansion of credit. The Chancellor of the Exchequer, Peter Thorneycroft, his Financial Secretary Enoch Powell, and the Prime Minister, Harold Macmillan, all leaned towards the monetarist view. Thorneycroft therefore proposed a more drastic deflationary policy in the autumn of 1957 and then again in early 1958. He sought a freeze on government spending, thus limiting investment and wage settlements in the public sector and cutting welfare and defence spending. This plan forced the Cabinet to re-examine its priorities. There was general agreement on the need to have it all – full employment, low inflation and a stable exchange rate. Thorneycroft, however, thought that it might be necessary to allow unemployment to increase to 3 per cent to control inflation,[21] and Macmillan was determined to do nothing that would interfere with the general prosperity. Everyone supported Thorneycroft's 1957 proposals, and the differences between the Chancellor and others in 1958 was not great, a mere £50 million. The Cabinet concluded that the extra spending posed little threat of inflation, while by increasing unemployment and cutting welfare provision Thorneycroft's cuts would undermine social cohesion and constitute a repudiation of the bases of Conservative policy since 1945. The status quo was reaffirmed, as Thorneycroft resigned. That year, the nation was hit by what would be the steepest post-war recession until the 1970s, so the next budget returned to expansion of the economy. 'Stop-go' continued as the Conservatives' policy of choice.

By the early 1960s, however, there was a growing sense that something was wrong. There is an irony in this perception, for the average rate of growth of Britain's economy was never to be higher than it was between 1960 and 1964.[22] The immense volume of statistics that economists were generating, however, had been showing for some time that this performance was not as good as that of other developed countries. (See Table 5.3.) In particular, the European Economic Community, which was launched in 1958, seemed to be doing dramatically better than Britain. Inflation was also becoming more of a concern, as there was a general upturn in world prices. Indeed, inflation was an endemic problem for the economy in a way that it never had been before. One reason was almost surely the definition of full employment that was adopted. Throughout the 1950s, the Tories' targeted maximum unemployment was around 500,000 to

600,000, a level that, judging by what economists now believe an economy can manage, was outrageously low.[23] At the same time, government borrowing created an inflationary bias that had never existed before. (See Table 5.11.) Inflation was still modest by comparison with what was to come, but even slight inflation had a grievous effect because of government's commitment to defend the value of the pound. After 1958, the pound became more difficult to defend, as it became convertible for foreigners. For the first time since the war, governments holding sterling could freely cash in their assets.

In 1961, the government concluded that Keynesian policies alone were not sufficient to manage the economy. With its new concern about inflation and growing public pressure to do something about Britain's 'inferior' economic performance, it resorted to direct controls – in the form of a pay freeze. An independent commission was then set up to promote the voluntary adherence of wage increases to a targeted norm. That norm was defined by the National Economic Development Council (NEDC), which was established in 1962. The NEDC was a step towards formalising what came to be called 'corporatism'. During the war, the government had incorporated the representatives of industry and labour into a consultation process. After 1945, such consultations continued on a more informal and haphazard basis, depending on the government and the circumstances. NEDC now brought together the representatives of both sides of industry and government to agree on policies that would assure faster growth – which economists were coming to look upon as the measure of national economic success. As its first task, NEDC tried to define what needed to be done to bring the annual growth rate up to 4 per cent and what obstacles stood in the way.

Taken together, these innovations represented a modest new level of direct government interference with the economy. Such interventionism, in conjunction with corporatist consultation, would increasingly become the norm of government economic policy-making over the next seventeen years, as both parties came to accept that some degree of government planning and management was necessary if economic decline was to be reversed. For the moment, however, the primacy of Keynesian policies remained. The Chancellor, Selwyn Lloyd, mostly did what all his predecessors had done, adjusting the levels of government spending, taxation and interest rates in an effort to dampen economic expansion and protect the pound. Macmillan was not happy; he wanted expansionist policies and searched for means to avoid having to put the brakes on every time economic growth started to pick up. He got his expansion in the autumn of 1963 when, with an election approaching and the economy sluggish, Lloyd's successor, Reginald Maudling, ended the pay freeze and introduced policies that would produce a 'dash for growth'. The aim was to stimulate demand and investment. The effect, it was hoped, would be to generate an increase in the rate of growth that would break through the bottlenecks in the economy during the 'go' phase and so avoid an increase in inflation. Yet the Prime Minister foresaw the likelihood that the result would be another balance-of-payments crisis. He and Maudling therefore toyed with the idea, when it occurred, of allowing the pound to float while selling off Britain's dollar assets so as to increase the reserves available to the Bank of England to defend the pound. Then there would be no need to deflate the economy to protect sterling.[24] Thus, just as the Conservatives' thirteen-year rule was coming to an end, they began to consider a fundamental rethink of the role of the pound as an international reserve currency. It seemed to be the only way to break free of the 'stop-go' policies that had dominated policy-making during those years, seemingly at the cost of constantly choking off more rapid economic growth.

3

THE STRAINS OF GREAT POWER STATUS

The rhetoric of a declining Britain usually implies that decline was a product of the period following the Second World War and so was linked to economic decline. After all, Britain in 1945 had successfully held off and helped to defeat the Nazi colossus. It was one of the 'big three' – the equal of the United States and the Soviet Union in determining the fate of Europe. Its power was rooted in a worldwide empire, by far the world's largest. Yet by the 1960s, it was clear that Britain was no superpower, while its empire was dissolving at breakneck speed. What could this be but decline? Yet the whole premise is wrong. It assumes that Britain had achieved a level of power in the nineteenth century comparable to the superpowers after 1945, and that the empire was the cornerstone of that power. Both of those are questionable assumptions. Britain had never had an ascendancy like that of the United States and the Soviet Union after the Second World War. And while the empire may have been crucial to Britain's rise as a great power in the eighteenth and early nineteenth centuries, by 1914 it had become a very questionable asset – except those parts that were already virtually independent nations – that was impossible to defend.

Britain's ability to project power around the world between 1689 and 1914 had been contingent on several fortuitous factors. First, Britain's great wealth enabled it to buy European friends that had armies. France was defeated from the time of Louis XIV to the time of Napoleon by some combination of Austrian, Prussian and Russian troops and British money. While Britain contributed its navy, plus a small (and even occasionally successful) army, to the many European wars from 1689 to 1815, it was also able to devote significant land forces to imperial battles. The second fortuitous factor was that no other power was able to mobilise the resources to challenge Britain in other parts of the world as it accumulated and defended its empire. The French had tried in the eighteenth century, but ultimately they had failed because, unlike Britain, they had to field a large army in Europe, and because (also unlike Britain) they did not have the financial means to fight a war in Europe and wars overseas simultaneously for an extended period of time. Even in the eighteenth century, however, Britain's European enemy and its enemy in the rest of the world was the same. It was never faced with multiple enemies until the twentieth century. The third fortuitous factor was cost. Britain was rich by eighteenth- and nineteenth-century standards. More importantly, it was the first country to work out how to use its wealth as collateral to borrow from its own people (through the national debt) in a way that would not bankrupt the state. Britain's wealth was not infinite, however, and the adequacy of its resources depended in part on naval technology being relatively cheap and simple enough so that merchant and naval ships and their sailors were at least somewhat interchangeable. With the advent of steam power, metal casing and ever more powerful gunnery in the second half of the nineteenth century, these favourable circumstances ceased. They ceased, moreover, at the same time that Germany, Japan, the United States and Russia had joined France as major powers capable of threatening Britain outside Europe. Furthermore, while Britain had commitments everywhere, most of these new powers only had localised interests. By 1900, Britain, which had always been overextended, was now desperately in need of friends – not merely to fight its wars in Europe, but to help protect its empire.

In fact, Britain made friends with everyone except Germany,

but at the cost of agreements that ceded predominance to the United States in the Americas and parity to Japan in Asia. After the First World War, however, Britain's network of friendships fell apart. The Communist takeover in Russia converted a friend into a potential enemy, while American distrust of Japan had the same effect by forcing Britain to end the Japanese alliance. Since the United States retreated into isolation, the British and French were left friendless in an ever more hostile world. Britain's long latent weakness was now exposed, as it could not afford to build up a military establishment capable of protecting it and its empire in every part of the world. The era of fortuitous circumstances was over, and Britain paid the price in the Second World War. The years after the war were much the same. Britain, with limited resources and vast commitments, struggled in vain to preserve its empire and its role as a power nearly on a par with the United States and the Soviet Union. The costs of holding on only increased. The expense of military technology soared ever higher, while the colonial peoples were no longer content to remain within the empire. So the process of retreat and reliance on others that had begun at the start of the century merely accelerated. Britain's efforts to remain somehow greater than the other non-superpowers were not only futile; they put additional strains on the economy that it could not comfortably bear.

Inventing a Special Relationship

Soon after Winston Churchill became First Lord of the Admiralty in September 1939, he received a brief letter from President Franklin Roosevelt inviting Churchill to feel free to communicate openly with him at any time. Thus began a correspondence that was to amount to some nine hundred letters on each side by the time Roosevelt died in April 1945.[1] Churchill, more than any other person, was the inventor of the special relationship between Britain and the United States, and his correspondence with Roosevelt was the physical embodiment of that relationship and of all the effort that Churchill put into cultivating it. Churchill was building, however, on a tradition that reached back at least to the 1830s. That tradition identified the ties of language and history, liberal values and institutions, Protestant religion and trade as the bases for a relationship between Britain and America that was unique in an era when authoritarian government was the norm. Britons who were sympathetic to the United States tended to view this relationship through the metaphor of a child's relationship with its parent after the child has grown to adulthood. This nineteenth-century association, however, had no political dimension. Indeed, through much of the century, American aggressiveness when asserting claims, first in disputes over the Canadian border and then over Central and South America, seemed to the British to make political relations between the two unnecessarily difficult. Nor were the Americans particularly susceptible to a parent–child analogy that was essentially patronising. The massive Irish immigration to the United States in the second half of the century assured a powerful source of anti-British sentiment there, while the even more massive immigration from elsewhere in Europe and Asia was indifferent to Britain. All was not hostility, however. The many marriages between American wealth and British aristocracy – with Churchill's own mother and father as a high-profile example – were merely one of many links between the social elites of the two countries, elites which included the Roosevelts on the American side. At the same time, there was much intercourse among intellectuals, as well as between more broadly based middle-class organisations with shared interests, such as the Protestant churches and the women's suffrage movements. Despite such links, however, America's foreign policy tradition was to remain divorced from Europe's affairs.

The First World War should have shown that America's political interests were linked to those of France and Britain. Yet for Americans, the lesson of the war, and more especially of the peace, was that it had been a mistake to intervene. The myth of American innocence threatened by European corruption and cynicism, first propagated by George Washington, re-emerged with new power in the aftermath to the Treaty of Versailles. It offered a useful pretext for Americans to wash their hands of European affairs and retreat into isolation and prosperity. In reality, however, isolation was no longer possible for a nation with an empire and worldwide trading interests. In the 1920s, American governments tried to have it both ways, intervening when they wanted to do so, while maintaining the fiction of isolation. The effect was to annoy the British, as American intervention involved issues – war debts, naval competition, interests in the Near and Far East – that generated the maximum friction between the two. With the advent of the Great Depression in the 1930s, however, the United States retreated much more firmly into isolation and left Europe to pay the price of its decadence.

For Churchill, the lesson of the inter-war period was clear: without American political involvement, the democracies of Western Europe did not have the resources to counter the threats to the east, whether from a vengeful Germany or from a Communist Soviet Union. Churchill himself had no doubt as to which of these two represented the greater threat in the 1930s: Nazism linked to Germany's economic and military power was much more dangerous than communism linked to Russia's economic weakness and uncertain military strength. Therefore, during the appeasement crises of the latter half of the decade, Churchill had pressed for some sort of accommodation with the Soviet Union, and he had embraced the Soviet alliance from the moment he learned of Germany's invasion in June 1941. Nonetheless, it was the United States that had to be the pillar of British security, not a Soviet Union whose communism was at best alien and at worst a direct threat to Britain and its worldwide interests.

So Churchill worked towards involving an isolationist America in Britain's war. Roosevelt collaborated with Churchill, hoping to preserve Britain and stop the expansion of Nazism while keeping America at peace. Pearl Harbor transformed the American position, but it did not change Churchill's long-term goals. With the United States now at war, he first convinced the Americans that

Europe had to be the primary focus of their war effort, and then he worked to assure that planning for a post-war Europe would keep the United States involved there. Once again, Roosevelt was a willing partner. With American isolationism shattered by the Japanese attack, he was able to give expression to his own liberal internationalism. However, an America involved in the war was a far different partner for Churchill than an America cheering from the sidelines. While Britain would be dependent on American supplies in either instance, Churchill would still be answerable to no one but his own Parliament in shaping wartime policies as long as the United States was not a belligerent. With the United States as an ally, however, it inevitably became the senior partner, and that posed problems. Churchill did not want Britain reduced to the role of a lesser power, and he believed that Britain's worldwide empire was fundamental to defining its unique status as a power. In dealing with the Americans, therefore, he had to work to assure the principle of equality between the partners and to assure that Roosevelt's liberal idealism did not threaten the British Empire.

Stalin, of course, also had no interest in a new world order based on liberal principles, so he could be a sort of ally in curbing Roosevelt's enthusiasm. Soviet involvement, however, presented its own problems for Churchill. The Soviet Union was bearing the brunt of the war in Europe and so was emerging as Europe's dominant military power. The effect was to encourage the Americans to look beyond the British to the Soviets as their only military equal and so relegate Britain to minor power status, as Roosevelt was already inclined to do to France. Given Britain's inherent weakness, Churchill did reasonably well in getting his way when it came to the determination of military strategy in the West and to securing a place for France as a victorious power. He failed, however, in any larger aim to get the Americans to pursue policies in Britain's interests or even to be guided by Britain in their thinking about the post-war world. Furthermore, the Americans imposed an enormous economic cost on Britain, as it strained to contribute more than its share to the war effort while mortgaging its future. Even so, after the invasion of Europe in June 1944, it became increasingly difficult for Churchill to counter American and Soviet preeminence.

By 1944, with the Red Army in Poland and heading westwards and the Western Allies hamstrung in Italy, the balance of danger in Europe was beginning to change. Russian imperialism, now with the ideological underpinnings of communism, was re-emerging as a major threat to Central Europe. Churchill's response was more confusing than he and his admirers later allowed. During an autumn trip to Moscow, he negotiated with Stalin as a fellow *realpolitik* politician, giving tacit acceptance of the Soviets' dominant interest in Romania and Bulgaria, while recognising their equal interest in Hungary and Yugoslavia. In return, Stalin confirmed British preeminence in Greece. By 1945, however, Churchill was urging the Americans to drive eastwards to block Soviet domination. The former approach was surely more in touch with the political realities of the time than the latter, however distasteful it may have been to recognise this fact. For with a Red Army of some five million men in occupation of Eastern Europe, there was little that Western armies could have done to secure democracy in states that had never known it, short of a war with the Soviets. Since neither American nor British public opinion would have endorsed such a war, the American inclination to negotiate with Stalin and hope that he would want to maintain the alliance after the war was the only practical policy. Churchill's alternatives (such as diverting Western troops to Prague to liberate Czechoslovakia) would have risked undermining post-war cooperation without changing the outcome in Eastern Europe. For Czechoslovakia was not the issue in 1945 – the Soviets did not remain there. Poland and Germany were the real bones of contention, and Churchill's alternatives would not have affected the fate of either one.

Clearly, then, there were tensions in the relationship that evolved during the war. Churchill and Roosevelt really did have a mutual respect that facilitated collaboration between their countries, and the level of military and diplomatic cooperation that was achieved was truly unique. However, neither the interests of the two nations nor their leaders' interpretation of events was the same. Given Britain's inherent weakness, Churchill did well to secure what he most wanted. Britain emerged from the war with its prestige greatly enhanced because it had held out against the Germans despite all the odds, and it was recognised by the Americans and Soviets as an equal power in shaping post-war Europe. The British Empire was reclaimed with the standing of the mother country severely shaken, but only in India (a psychologically important exception) was retreat obviously unavoidable. Finally, Britain had done well for its defeated ally, France, securing it the return of its empire too, as well as a place as an occupying power in Germany.

Redefining the Balance of Power

Yet even as Churchill was achieving so many of his aims, all was threatened when the foundation of the 'special relationship' was shattered. Roosevelt died in April 1945, while Churchill was defeated in the general election of July of the same year. The shape of the post-war world was going to be determined by two apparent novices in international affairs, who would have to deal with the wily and ruthless old pro, Stalin. At the same time, forces that might be hostile to Anglo-American cooperation were reasserting themselves in both countries. Clement Attlee, the new British Prime Minister, was in fact no neophyte. He had been instrumental in securing Churchill's elevation to Prime Minister in 1940 and had served in his coalition from its inception. Churchill had formally made him Deputy Prime Minister in 1942 and had kept him involved in all of the decision-making that had determined British foreign policy during the war. Labour's Foreign Secretary, Ernest Bevin, did not have the same experience. Bevin had led Britain's most powerful trade union, the Transport and General Workers' Union, during the inter-war period and had been responsible for labour allocation and labour relations during the war. This was a man whose focus clearly seemed to be domestic, not international. Yet in a Labour Party with a powerful pacifist and pro-Soviet wing that was suspicious of the United States, Bevin had strong credentials as an anti-appeaser in the 1930s. He also had fought vigorously against Communist influence within the British labour movement during the inter-war period. He was not going to look benignly on a possible Soviet threat to Europe or to oversee Britain's retreat from great power status. While he was not an uncritical believer in the United States, he did not join in the extremists' acute suspicion of the US either.

The new American President Harry Truman was much more of an unknown entity than his British counterpart. Truman had only become Roosevelt's Vice-President in 1944, which meant he took office in January 1945, less than three months before the President died. While Churchill had incorporated Attlee into his policy-making apparatus, Roosevelt had excluded Truman, who did not even know about the project to develop an atomic bomb until he became President. A former Senator from Missouri, Truman seemed to be a typical hack politician from the Midwest, the centre of American isolationism. His first Secretary of State, James Byrnes, was cast in the same mould – a former Senator from South Carolina who had been involved in organising the American economy during the war. In defining a post-war foreign policy for the United States, these two greenhorns would have to reckon with Congress, a notoriously difficult institution for a president to deal with, even when it was dominated by his own party.

Truman's political position was weak. This vulnerability required that he be firm in dealing with his British ally, whose imperialist aims had long been an object of American suspicion. The fact that Britain was now run by a bunch of socialists merely reinforced this distrust. With anti-British feeling as strong among some Americans as pro-British sentiment was among others, it was all the more important that the administration should not appear to be the instrument for holding the British Empire together. Actions which generated resentment in Britain – such as cutting off Lend-Lease aid as soon as the war with Japan was over (as required by law) and insisting that sterling be made convertible as a condition for the 1946 loan – reflected the views of those in the government who mistrusted Britain, as well as anti-British public opinion.* The administration, in any case, was eager enough to take advantage of Britain's weakness to push hard for economic policies deemed in the interest of the United States.[2] Such policies also helped it protect its flank among conservatives in Congress. As it was, many in Congress opposed the loan to a socialist government, and in the elections that November the Republicans captured both the House and the Senate. Now Truman had to carry the opposition with him as he got the United States increasingly involved in Europe's defence and recovery. The Republican party, like Britain's Labour Party, was divided over foreign policy. It was the home of American isolationism. However, it had a powerful internationalist wing centred in the Northeast, while a rabid anti-communism was emerging in areas of the country that had been isolationist before 1941. The chairman of the Senate Foreign Relations Committee after 1946, Arthur Vandenberg of Michigan, embodied all these tendencies – pre-war isolationism, post-1941 interventionism and post-war anti-communism. He was crucial in enabling Truman to develop a bipartisan consensus on policy in Europe.

Germany inevitably was a central preoccupation of the new American administration as the war in Europe drew to a close. Churchill, Roosevelt and Stalin had learned crucial lessons from the First World War and its aftermath that shaped their German policy between 1941 and 1945. No new Hitler would be allowed to claim that Germany had not lost the war – that its undefeated army had been stabbed in the back by weak-kneed civilians. As

---

* A 1945 Gallup poll taken prior to the negotiations found that 60 per cent of Americans opposed a post-war loan to Britain; a poll in June 1946, when the loan agreement had passed the Senate but not the House, showed 38 per cent supported and 40 per cent opposed the loan. Alan Bullock, *Ernest Bevin: Foreign Secretary, 1945–1951* (London: Heinemann, 1983), pp. 122, 272.

early as 1940, the Royal Air Force carried the war to the German people, making certain they understood that their armed forces were not invulnerable. By 1944 and 1945 Allied bombers were levelling Germany, while in 1945 and 1946 the Red Army carried out a systematic and horrendous revenge of its own for the atrocities committed against the Soviet people earlier in the war. The myth of German invincibility was shattered for good, and the German people were made to pay mightily for the transgressions of their military and political leaders. The need to defeat Germany decisively also determined that there would be no armistice and no Fourteen Points. Both had allowed the Germans after 1919 to claim that the Allies had tricked them into surrendering when they had not been defeated. The Allied conditions for peace during the Second World War were simple and unequivocal: unconditional surrender. The Allies would not haggle over terms; they wanted Germany prostrate before the victors. Finally, and most importantly, the Germans would not be entrusted with the enforcement of a peace treaty on themselves; the aftermath of the Treaty of Versailles had shown that they could not be trusted to do so.[3] Thus, the unthinkable of 1919 became the policy of 1945: Germany as a sovereign state would temporarily cease to exist, as it was carved up into occupation zones and administered by its victorious enemies. Occupation also assured that there would be no reparations dispute after the Second World War as there had been after the first: Allied administration was a guarantee that Germany paid appropriate reparations, both in kind and in money. With the onset of the Cold War in 1946, the Western Allies slowly and reluctantly retreated from this policy of punishing Germany for the war. While the war continued, however, there was no major disagreement among the Allies about it.

Instead, disagreement was over Poland. Poland had long been a focus of contest among the European powers. Once a major power itself, by the eighteenth century it was falling apart politically. France and Russia vied with each other to establish their influence through client-kings, but Russia, as always, had the advantage of proximity. Thus, France could do little as the Eastern powers (Russia, Prussia and Austria) carved Poland up in three partitions between 1772 and 1795. Britain had no interest in Poland, but it did want to keep Russia out of Central Europe. Hence, at the Congress of Vienna in 1814–15 it tried to limit Russia's attempt to appropriate all of Poland, and it even succeeded in getting an attenuated constitution for the expanded Russian Poland that was established. During the course of the nineteenth century, however, Russia annulled the Polish constitution and sought in every way possible to absorb Poland and suppress a separate Polish identity. France at times tried to revive its role as the patron of an independent Poland, but Britain, recognising the realities of geography and seeing no compelling national interest involved, offered no support to such efforts. The defeat of all of the partitioning powers (Russia as well as Germany and Austria-Hungary) in the First World War, plus the American commitment to national self-determination, transformed the situation. The peace settlements recreated an independent Polish state, but no one was satisfied with the territorial arrangement that resulted – neither the Poles nor the Russians nor the Germans. With the rise of Hitler and his repudiation of the Treaty of Versailles, the Poles were as eager for revision as the Germans were, while they were understandably more afraid of the Soviets than they were of the Nazis. In the end, however, their effort to play the role of a major European power balancing its giant neighbours failed. Germany and the Soviet Union divided the Polish state again in 1939, and the geographical realities that had blocked action by the British and French in the eighteenth and nineteenth centuries assured that the Western powers could do nothing to help Poland this time either.

Thus, Britain had a long history of indifference to Poland's fate, despite occasional French pressure in the other direction. All that changed, however, on 3 September 1939, when Britain went to war explicitly in defence of Poland. The Polish government moved to London, and the British felt honour-bound to secure its restoration at the head of a liberated Poland. The

Soviets, by contrast, had a long-standing interest in dominating Poland and a geographical advantage in imposing their wishes on the Poles, whatever the Western powers wanted. Stalin was not about to give up that advantage, especially since the evidence of two world wars confirmed for him that Poland was integrally linked to Soviet security. The Western powers recognised the Soviets' unique interest in a friendly Poland. Yet, given the Poles' well-founded fear of the Russians, they never admitted that the free and fair elections which they insisted on in all likelihood would have resulted in a Polish government that was suspicious of, if not hostile to, the Soviet Union. Presumably, the Western powers hoped for a solution like the one later developed by Finland: a democratic government whose foreign policy could not be fully independent, as it had to accommodate Soviet sensibilities. Stalin, however, had a very different solution in mind. The only government he considered reliably friendly was one under his complete domination, and the only way to assure Soviet security was to line its borders with such governments. Stalin was willing to play the game of elections if that was what the British and Americans wanted, but he was going to make very sure who won the elections. The result was a process of negotiation over Poland in 1944 and 1945, whereby Stalin made cosmetic concessions to Western demands for elections while exterminating all opposition and consolidating a Communist government in power answerable to him. The effect was to convince the Western powers that he could not be trusted.

Distrust bred distrust. On the one hand, the Western powers appeared hypocritical, cloaking their own self-interested policies in the language of morality. The United States and Britain, after all, were not about to allow Communists to come to power in France or Italy if they could possibly help it. To Stalin the geopolitical thinking of the two sides must have seemed much the same – a view seemingly confirmed by Churchill's 1944 Moscow trip. The Western powers, however, could not acquiesce in the control of Eastern Europe by an oppressive Communist dictatorship, having just fought a major war on the principle that Nazi dictatorial power could not be allowed to dominate Europe. There may be legitimate spheres of influence for major powers, but that influence must be exercised within a framework of democratic freedom.

Western suspicions of Soviet motives generated by the breakdown over Poland led to backtracking on German policy. Germany's industrial heartland was in the west and so under British and American occupation. The Soviets had expected to recover some of the reparations due them from these regions. The Western Allies, however, were willing to accept this principle only within a broader framework treating Germany as an economic unit. For the Soviet zone incorporated Germany's agricultural areas, and Germans were starving – so much so that the British diverted grain from their own hungry population and introduced bread rationing at home in order to help feed the Germans in their zone. Given that Britain and France had their own economic problems, while the Americans were not prepared to feed all of Europe, the only viable option seemed to be German economic recovery. Yet the Soviets blocked all proposals for economic consolidation, until finally the British and Americans concluded that they had no intention of giving up complete control over their zone. The Americans and the British then decided to create a single economic unit from their zones, which came into existence at the beginning of 1947, and the French (who were not keen on seeing Germany's economy rebuilt) eventually joined them. To the Soviets, it looked as if the Western powers were depriving the Soviet Union of its rightful reparations – rightful because of the disproportionate sacrifice the Soviets had made during the war – while promoting the revival of a powerful Germany capable of posing a security threat. The Western powers, however, were less likely to accommodate Stalin over Germany just because of their growing apprehensions about his broader intentions in Europe. In a way, each side was coming to the same conclusion. The West thought a stronger Germany might be a very useful barrier against Soviet expansionism; the Soviets saw the strengthening of Germany as a threat to their security.

This distrust was reinforced because each side started with the suspicion that the other wanted to destroy it. The proclaimed aim of communism was a worldwide revolution to destroy capitalism, and the West knew that Stalin had an organisation for the purpose of subverting other governments. For their part, the Soviets assumed that the capitalists had to try to destroy communism in order to survive. The policies of each side from 1945 to 1947 had seemed to confirm the other's apocalyptic interpretation. The climax of this process of cumulative distrust came in 1948. A Communist coup in Czechoslovakia, the one Central European nation that had a democratic tradition and was outside any plausible Soviet sphere of influence, confirmed the Western fear of Communist expansionism. A the same time, the decision of the Western powers to issue a new currency for their combined zone of Germany, as the next step towards economic recovery, confirmed Stalin's fear of a revived German threat aimed at the Soviet Union. Stalin's blockade of Berlin in an attempt to force the West to retreat on the single currency set up the first direct confrontation in a new Cold War, as the West organised an airlift to save its outpost on the front line of democracy.

What was Britain's role in this evolution of events towards the Cold War? British mythology used to claim that the British government took advantage of the special relationship with the United States to educate the Americans concerning the Soviet threat to Europe and so helped convince the Truman administration that the United States must remain engaged there. It is certainly true that, while the Americans recognised a Communist threat, some in the Truman administration still hoped that the United States could straddle Soviet and British imperialism and keep the wartime alliance alive. At the same time, residual American isolationism led the administration and Congress alike to underestimate the level of American commitment that Europe required, as they quickly initiated a drastic post-war demobilisation. Recent research, however, has shown that the Labour government was also reluctant to come to the conclusion that it was hopeless to work with Stalin. Nor were Attlee and Bevin eager to become dependent on the US, especially since the Americans were being so difficult when bargaining over economic issues, which was greatly resented in Britain. Bevin wanted to work with France to lead a 'third force' (both political and economic), consisting of Western Europe and its empires, that was independent of both superpowers and so free of economic subordination to the United States. Close cooperation was therefore slow to develop between Britain and the US, even as both became increasingly sceptical about Soviet intentions. Each government remained reluctant to completely forswear the possibility of a change in Soviet policy, while each was still worried about the domestic implications of closer ties with the other. Thus, the evolution of a stronger and more formal American commitment to Western Europe was slow, as was a return to the closer wartime relationship between Britain and the United States. Furthermore, this hesitant process reflected British preferences as much as American.[4]

Apart from Europe, the region that most concerned the British in 1946 was the eastern Mediterranean, an area they had contested with the Russians since the nineteenth century. Communists had played a central role in the anti-Nazi resistance in Greece, as they had in most of Europe, so with liberation they were well-positioned to seize control of the government. Churchill's one gain from his trip to Moscow in 1944 was Stalin's recognition that Greece was within Britain's sphere of influence. As long as he thought he had an agreement, Stalin did nothing to aid the Greek Communists, so the British were able to establish a friendly government there through elections in 1946. As the Communist insurgency resumed, however, Stalin began giving it aid. By early 1947, the British economy was not able to sustain further drain on its resources, with defence spending for the fiscal year at the astonishing level of 18.8 per cent[5] of national income.* Britain was already mired in a messy conflict in

---

* By contrast, the United States was spending 10.6 per cent of national income on defence. Nearly 20 per cent of adult British men were in the armed forces, compared to 10 per cent of American men.

Palestine and a potentially explosive situation in India. Given the enormous financial demands placed on Britain's armed forces worldwide, Attlee had never shared others' fixation with the Middle East as an area of crucial importance to a British Empire without India. Now he was able to secure retreat from Greece as part of a larger process of reducing Britain's commitments to a more manageable level. The result was the Truman Doctrine promising American aid to Greece, Turkey and more generally to any country resisting an internal Communist threat. The same process of targeted British retreat also resolved the tension between the British and Americans in Palestine. There, the British faced a guerrilla war and Arab and Jewish populations that would not compromise with each other. To Bevin's fury, the Americans kept pushing for a Jewish state while refusing to get involved on the ground. He believed the Democrats were driven entirely by political considerations at home rather than any larger moral principles. American actions undercut his futile efforts to find some basis of agreement, while leaving the British to face the military consequences alone. Indeed, fear of the effects on American opinion limited the measures the British could employ in their efforts to suppress Jewish terrorism. The Americans also undermined Bevin's attempts to maintain good relations with the Arabs – even to the point of courting Arab nationalists – so Britain could retain influence in the region. The British finally gave up and got out – preserving limited influence in the Arab world as they secretly supplied arms in the war against Israel. Following Israel's victory, however, there remained considerable Arab resentment against the British, and it exploded in Egypt in the early 1950s and in Iraq in 1958.

Western Europe, however, was Britain's main concern. An American military presence was assured as long as the United States was part of the occupying force in Germany and Austria, but the US had cut the numbers drastically since the end of the war. Furthermore, the very nature of such an obligation was temporary; a final peace treaty would bring it to an end. Increasingly concerned about the Communist threat, Bevin saw the need to reconstruct Britain's security arrangements, with or without the United States. He therefore initiated negotiations with France, resulting in the March 1947 Treaty of Dunkirk directed against Germany, which was still France's principal security preoccupation. The real threat to Europe in 1947, however, came from continuing economic dislocation, which assured that governments in all the continental states were fragile. Following the catastrophic winter of 1947, Europe was an economic mess. There seemed to be an acute shortage of everything. As Communist parties withdrew from coalition governments and went into opposition, the danger of Communist subversion seemed all too real. By now, the US State Department recognised this danger. The new American Secretary of State, General George Marshall, had been the Army Chief of Staff during the war, and his appointment early that year was an unambiguous statement of America's interest in Europe. The Marshall Plan was initially simply a public hint by Marshall that the United States would be willing to provide aid to Europe if the Europeans could cooperate to assure that the aid would promote recovery. While the British resented being treated like any other devastated European state, they could not do without American assistance; therefore, Bevin took the lead in mobilising the rest of Western Europe to develop the kind of joint recovery programme that the Americans wanted. Although many American politicians resented subsidising socialism in Britain, Congress, shaken by the Czech coup and now fully in Cold War mode, approved the first aid package in 1948. It helped that much of the money would be spent in the United States; indeed, one of the purposes of the programme was to help American exports by relieving Europe's dollar shortage.

Bevin did not allow matters to rest there. Now persuaded that there would be no early change in Soviet behaviour, he used European collaboration over the allocation of Marshall money to promote an expansion of the Treaty of Dunkirk into a broader treaty of mutual defence. The Czech coup and word of Soviet pressure on Finland and Norway increased his sense of urgency.

The Brussels Treaty was signed in March 1948 by Britain, France, Belgium, Luxembourg and the Netherlands. The signatories of the treaty were in no condition to defend themselves, however. With 1948 an election year, the Truman administration still wanted to remain outside any formal alliance, hoping a promise of military aid would be sufficient. However, the Czech coup, the Berlin blockade and European insistence on a formal American commitment all provided the impetus necessary to bring the United States into the alliance. The result was the North Atlantic Treaty Organization (NATO) of 1949, in which the United States recognised its own security interest in the defence of Western Europe. The immediate symbol of this new departure in US policy was the establishment of American air bases in Britain for its strategic nuclear bombers.

For the moment, isolationism had been marginalised in the United States. At the same time, the relationship between Britain and the US had been strengthened. Bevin had taken the lead on the European side in promoting the reforms that integrated America into European affairs, even as he had sought vainly for some way to avoid dependence on the United States. Ultimately, the recognition that Britain and France alone could not provide an adequate check on a power as great as the Soviet Union triumphed. So the defence of Western Europe now depended on the United States; the great powers of the past – not just Britain, but France, Germany and Italy – had been reduced in status as a result.

The Rocky Road of the Special Relationship

It would be dangerous to assume that there was an identity of interests between Britain and the United States. The conceptualisation of a 'special relationship' had been rooted in history and culture, not political interest. Though the recognition of common interests was essential before it could take on a political form, there was no obvious reason why the interests of the United States should be closer to Britain's than they were to France's or

West Germany's. Already, when British and American interests were in conflict, the United States had shown no inclination to give Britain preferred treatment. Indeed, in negotiations over economic issues such as Lend-Lease, the 1946 loan and trade liberalisation, the Americans had proved to be aggressive pursuers of their own long-term interests, imposing a significant cost on Britain when assistance was given. The Truman administration ultimately saw the danger of being too self-serving in providing economic assistance, so no strings were attached to Marshall aid. The United States also backed away from pushing some of its pet projects so relentlessly – such as the end of imperial preference and of the sterling area. Still, in the 1950s the US and Britain did not have the same economic objectives. While the Americans in theory wanted a world based on free trade and the free flow of capital, in practice American governments proceeded slowly in reducing the United States's substantial trade barriers. The British were even less eager for free trade. The Tories throughout the twentieth century had been the party of protection, and were not even convinced that competition was all that good. Thus, in the 1950s they were still determined to defend trade patterns based on preference within the empire, while they saw little reason until the end of the decade to impose a free trade regime on British industry.[6] The British and the Americans were closer in wanting the full convertibility of sterling; however, the crisis of 1947 had shown that Britain could not move in that direction as fast as the United States wanted. Thus, British and American economic interests only somewhat overlapped, while both felt the need to proceed cautiously.

In other respects, too, the Anglo-American relationship was a rocky one. Inevitably, the interests of two independent states could not always coincide, however much their general security interests converged. Whenever those interests did differ, the United States tended to try to use its superior power to prod (even bully) Britain in the American direction. Britain, however, still had pretensions to great power status. Pride, self-interest and the continued respect of the international community all dictated that

British governments could not appear to be the lackey of the United States. At the same time, the British never quite lost their patronising view of America as a child of inferior experience in the ways of the world, who combined a naive belief that morality should be the predominant influence on foreign policy and an appalling boorishness in its approach to diplomacy.7 Furthermore, as in the nineteenth century, American diplomacy still seemed excessively driven by the dictates of domestic politics. In the 1950s, this meant the imperative of not appearing soft on communism; therefore, American leaders could not risk the pragmatic approach to issues that was natural to the Europeans. Thus, not only did the British resent it when the Americans rather crudely threw their weight around in pursuit of American ends, but there was some contempt when those ends seemed excessively out of touch with the real world, or even seemed dangerous. Yet in the end, whatever the Americans did, British governments saw pursuit of a special relationship with the United States as a policy goal in itself – which often led them to bend to the American will. By contrast, the Americans usually refused to admit that there was any special relationship at all; hence accommodating the British was almost never a goal.

One of the first sources of tension in the 1940s and 1950s was nuclear weapons. The development of the atomic bomb during the war, while centred in and dominated by the United States, had been a collaborative effort, as Britain's leading scientists moved to America to contribute their intelligence and expertise. Yet once the bomb was developed, the Americans refused to share the technology with their ally as they had promised – a policy that was ossified in law by the McMahon Act in 1946. If Britain was to remain one of the 'big three', it had to develop its own nuclear weapons without American help. The decision to do so partly reflected a fear of American isolationism. Even more, however, it reflected the determination of Britain's political leaders to aspire to a substantial place in international affairs, whatever the economic cost. The Americans simply would not take the British seriously unless they were a nuclear power.

This indifference to the price of power marked a real break with the past, for Britain had been very cost-conscious in the nineteenth century. In the second half of that century, defence spending tended to be around 2 per cent or less of gross domestic product (GDP). It had ratcheted up to between 3 and 3.5 per cent of GDP during the naval race with Germany prior to the First World War.[8] Even then, however, rearmament had stayed within the country's economic means, as all construction was paid for from taxation. One of the reasons for appeasement in the 1930s was the politicians' acute consciousness of the fragility of the economy. Now, however, with the economy in even worse shape and a whole array of new domestic programmes and military obligations to be paid for, the government was prepared to damn the consequences in the name of international prestige. The increased burden that resulted over the next twenty-five years was enormous. Between 1932 and 1937, British defence spending had averaged 3.1 per cent of GDP; by 1948–50 it had doubled to 6.6 per cent; by 1952–4 it had tripled to 9.6 per cent; and it was still at 6–7 per cent in the 1960s.[9] No numbers better illustrate that we are not really talking about British decline after 1945, because the environment was so radically different. Never before had Britain been required to commit such a massive level of resources to maintain its interests worldwide. It is doubtful that it could have sustained a rate of defence spending of 6–10 per cent of GDP any better in the 1850s or the 1900s than in the 1950s. Certainly no government of those eras would have been willing to contemplate spending on such a scale; on the contrary, all would have been appalled at the thought. It was the cost of defence and the nature of the world facing Britain that had changed, far more radically than Britain's capabilities if it could have operated at traditional levels.

The decision to launch itself into the nuclear age demonstrated the problems facing Britain if it was to compete in this new environment. It had to devote an enormous quantity of financial and scientific resources to developing nuclear technology that might have been invested in civilian economic innovation. Furthermore, constant innovation meant that the British always remained behind. Thus, even as Britain was detonating its atomic bomb in 1952, the Americans and Soviets were about to detonate much more powerful hydrogen bombs. Then, while Britain was developing a hydrogen bomb, the technology of delivery was changing from bombs to missiles. The economic burden of developing both its own missile or submarine system and the weapons to go with it was too great for Britain. By the early 1960s, the British were buying Polaris missiles from the United States, and they were back where they started – dependent on the US and so not really an equal power. A new rhetoric emerged which claimed that nuclear interdependence was itself a manifestation of the 'special relationship'. In the late 1950s, the Americans relaxed the restrictions on sharing nuclear technology, giving the British unique access to American secrets as well as weapons (and the United States equal access to the results of British research). None of this altered the reality of dependence. The decision early in the 1950s to locate American nuclear weapons in Britain as part of the NATO alliance reinforced this subordination. The ambiguity concerning what authority, if any, the British had over their use, when their presence made Britain a front-line target in a nuclear war, was an important factor in the emergence of the anti-nuclear Campaign for Nuclear Disarmament (CND) in 1958. That ambiguity was never clarified in the decades ahead.

Britain's nuclear programme was just one example of how its aspirations to great power status exceeded its resources, with potential adverse effects on the economy. As Table 5.8 shows, Britain was second only to the United States between 1950 and 1975 in the percentage of its GDP that it spent on defence. Maintaining an army of occupation in Germany,[10] significant forces in Singapore and other major bases, its role as a naval and nuclear power and its presence in traditional spheres of influence like the Middle East, while trying to prevent internal insurrections in its colonies, involved an enormous military commitment. Indeed, it was an impossible one, and the retreats from Greece and Palestine in 1947 and 1948 were merely the first evidence

that Britain would have to figure out a more economically efficient way to allocate its scarce military resources. Yet there was
no major reassessment of what Britain's military strategy outside
the NATO area should be, or whether it had the ability to sustain
the same worldwide imperial defence structure that had existed
before the war. On the contrary, conscription was reintroduced in
1946 in order to provide the necessary manpower when faced
with the loss of the Indian army. Hence, there were some three
hundred thousand military personnel outside Europe when
the Korean War broke out in 1950.[11] Then, under pressure from
the United States to increase its defence spending, the Attlee
government committed troops and weapons that it could not
afford to the war effort. The result was an immediate economic
crisis and a reduction of the unsustainable levels of military
spending by the Conservatives in 1952. Yet in 1954 Britain had
to accept a substantial increase in the ground forces that it
stationed in West Germany. By the late 1950s, Britain was again
looking to scale back its defence spending. A 1957 defence review
decided to concentrate Britain's efforts on nuclear weapons (both
long-range and tactical) as the means of getting the most defence
for a price that it could afford. Conscription was to be ended by
1962 and the commitment to Germany reduced, as the total
armed forces manpower was to be nearly halved. Apart from
Britain's NATO contribution, a mobile professional force would
be created that was prepared to fight local conflicts. More extensive cutbacks were limited, however, by Britain's continued use
of military force to influence events in the Middle East and Asia.
Indeed, the emphasis on local conflicts made these regions even
more important as the most likely sites of action. So more than
one hundred thousand men remained there.[12] At the same time,
the cost of new weapons and equipment and the development of
bases east of Suez to support the strategy of mobility ate up the
savings achieved by retrenchment. Thus, overall there was no
dramatic reduction of defence spending as a percentage of GDP
in the aftermath of the 1957 review, while Britain's military
commitments remained as widespread as ever.

The Middle East, more than any other region, was an area where the British still saw themselves as a major player. Throughout the nineteenth century, Britain, France and Russia had competed to dominate (or carve up) the decaying Ottoman Empire that straddled the Mediterranean from the Balkans to Morocco, while Britain and Russia had sparred over Persia (Iran). For Britain, the principal justification for its role in the region had been the protection of the routes to India, and it was for that reason that it had occupied Egypt in 1882. The defeat of Russia and Turkey in the First World War had assured the supremacy of Britain and France, just when Middle Eastern oil was being exploited and beginning to replace coal as the fuel of choice. Egypt, Palestine, Transjordan, Iraq, the Gulf states and Iran all became either British mandates or autonomous states with regimes amenable to British influence. The early years of the Second World War had threatened Britain's position, as potential Nazi sympathisers emerged in governments in Iraq, Iran and Egypt. The British had acted decisively then to suppress any effort to throw off their domination. While the independence of India in 1947 removed the original pretext for British involvement in the region, they were more dependent than ever on its oil; moreover, in the 1950s, 30 per cent of British overseas investments were in the Persian Gulf and Iran.[13] At the same time, the Suez Canal remained the means through which Britain communicated with its base in Singapore and so sustained its power in the Far East. Finally, Britain's bases in the eastern Mediterranean were the means for projecting air and naval power in many directions, including towards the Soviet Union.

Britain's weakened position after the war assured a fitful but ongoing pattern of retreat from the region before the advance of American influence. Events in the Persian Gulf in the early 1950s showed some of the problems Britain faced. In 1951, the government decided not to intervene in Iran following the nationalisation of the Anglo-Iranian Oil Company – in part because of the cost, but also in response to American pressure. With the advent of the Eisenhower administration in 1953, the Americans came around to the British view and used the CIA to restore the shah. The Foreign

Secretary, Sir Anthony Eden, then brought Iran into the Baghdad Pact of 1955, his major initiative to influence events in the Persian Gulf and the Muslim world. Originally launched by Turkey and Iraq as a defence against communism, the pact included Pakistan as well as Britain and Iran by the end of the year. Yet Eden saw that if the pact was to be effective, it needed the United States to join. The Americans, however, believed that their influence in the region depended on not being associated with British imperialism; so the US remained aloof. The alliance finally collapsed because no other Arab state would attach itself to the British imperialists. In other words, the Americans had been right! For the failure of the Baghdad Pact was the result of anti-British feeling that was being fuelled by a surging Arab nationalism centred in Egypt.

Egypt, the first Arab state brought within the British orbit in the nineteenth century, had been a hotbed of anti-British feeling since the war. Even the British client, King Farouk, demanded the withdrawal of British troops from the Suez Canal Zone, Britain's principal military base in the Middle East. In 1952 Farouk was deposed by nationalist military officers, and eventually Gamal Abdel Nasser emerged as leader. Churchill was reluctant to vacate Suez – and especially to appear to be driven out by Egyptian pressure, which would be taken as a sign of British weakness. Yet everyone recognised that thermonuclear weapons were changing the whole strategic situation and making such bases less important. Furthermore, Britain needed to stay on friendly terms with Arab regimes if it was to continue to influence events. Eventually, the Cabinet accepted Eden's arguments for conciliating Arab opinion. Under the 1954 agreement, British troops would be withdrawn gradually, until none were left by the end of June 1956. Nasser, however, did not respond as Eden had expected. His Arab nationalism only seemed to get more virulent and, as he appealed to Arabs in other states still under British influence, more threatening to British interests.

During the course of 1955, Eden (who became Prime Minister in April) became convinced that Nasser, who was playing the Soviets and Americans off against each other, had dangerous pro-Soviet leanings. Anthony Adamthwaite has described Eden this way: 'Living on his nerves, jumpy, constantly interfering, Eden was temperamentally unsuited to the premiership.'[14] He began to see Nasser as another Mussolini: a leader who had to be stopped, not appeased, or he would destabilise all the regimes in the Middle East. The crisis came in July 1956, when Nasser responded to America's withdrawal of aid for his Aswan Dam project by nationalising the Suez Canal to secure its revenues.* Eden concluded that the time had come to eliminate Nasser before the Canal (and British trade) became a hostage to his foreign policy, with the Soviet danger lurking in the background. Yet even as the British and the French set in motion plans for a military campaign to seize the Canal, they were never clear as to how they were going to bring Nasser down or who would succeed him if he did fall. Immediately before the operation was launched in late October, the Chiefs of Staff warned the Cabinet that success would result in an extensive occupation of a hostile country, requiring the withdrawal of a division from Germany. Still they went ahead.

The messages from the Eisenhower administration – which had come to power in January 1953 – during the Suez crisis were mixed. Facing an autumn re-election campaign and fearful of alienating Arab opinion, it did not want any action that would tarnish the President's image as a man of peace and might drive the Arab world into the Soviet camp. Eisenhower himself was hostile to Nasser, but insisted that the Canal was not the issue on which to take him on. He was therefore consistent and unambiguous in his opposition to military action at this time.

* The Suez Canal had been built by a Frenchman, Ferdinand de Lesseps, and the company he set up was based in Paris. In law, however, both the company and the Canal were Egyptian. The company held a lease from the rulers of Egypt to operate the Canal for ninety-nine years, that is, until November 1968. In 1876, Disraeli had bought the shares in the company that had been allotted to the Khedive of Egypt. Thus, ownership of the Suez Canal Company rested partly with the British government and partly with French and British financial interests. See Keith Kyle, *Suez* (New York: St Martin's Press, 1991), pp. 12–14, for the legal status.

Secretary of State John Foster Dulles, however, could be read both ways – toeing the Eisenhower line, but implying that force might be necessary as a last resort. In meetings that the Chancellor of the Exchequer, Harold Macmillan, had with the President and key cabinet members in Washington that September, he came away uncertain about the strength of American opposition to intervention. Perhaps he wanted to be uncertain. In fact, Britain's leaders did not read American opinion accurately because they were convinced that the US would never desert its closest allies in an area of such strategic importance.[15]

Yet they took American hostility seriously enough to reject the preferred French policy of a direct military assault to topple Nasser and take control of the Canal. Instead, to prove their desire to resolve the crisis peacefully, the British hosted two conferences of Canal users in London and then engaged in negotiations with the Egyptians at the United Nations. Indeed, the last were productive, and by October the parties seemed close to an agreement. Eden, however, was drawn back to his first choice of military action when the French came to him with a proposal for Israel to invade Egypt, enabling Britain and France to intervene to protect the Canal and force some sort of international control. The plan was kept secret; only a few in the Cabinet knew of it. Hence, Britain would retain a cloak of moral respectability, as it would appear to world opinion as the peacemaker acting defensively in the interests of all, rather than simply making a naked grab for the Canal while trying to overthrow Nasser by force.*

When the campaign was launched by Israel on 29 October, however, it quickly turned into a catastrophe. Eisenhower was furious. He felt that he had been deceived by the British, when

---

* The French had none of the British government's concerns about either American or world opinion, or about providing a moral justification for military action. The French government wanted to end Nasser's support for the growing rebellion in Algeria. It viewed both the British and the Americans as hypocrites, and if it hadn't been held back by the British, it would have sent troops much sooner. David Carlton, *Britain and the Suez Crisis* (Oxford: Basil Blackwell, 1988), chaps 3 and 4.

he had counted on them not to rock the boat during the election. The whole operation was a reversion to old-fashioned colonialism. The effects would be to weaken the United Nations, alienate the Arab world (and beyond) from the West and drive them into the arms of the Soviets. The Americans not only insisted on an immediate cease-fire, but also, after it occurred on 7 November, a complete withdrawal of British troops from Egypt and the Canal. When the British resisted the latter demand, the Americans encouraged a run on sterling, while blocking Britain from securing aid from the International Monetary Fund to which it had a right. Eisenhower refused to communicate further with Eden, while the British embassy was shut out from all but the most formal communications in Washington. At the same time, the US led the charge in criticising its allies in the United Nations. Finally, in early December, the Cabinet (with Eden packed off to Jamaica because of a breakdown in his health) reluctantly agreed to an evacuation. All of this alienated the French and drove them closer to the Germans, but the British had no doubt that the American terms for renewing support of the pound involved a complete surrender on their part. Having stood up to Anglo-French neocolonialism, Nasser emerged with his prestige enhanced. Britain and France were universally condemned, with their credibility weakened among the emerging independent nations of the 'third world'. The whole fiasco showed how much Britain's world had been transformed. Despite unprecedented economic growth, the pound was so vulnerable that it limited the government's freedom to act independently of the United States. Furthermore, despite the 'special relationship', the Americans had actively promoted the humiliation of Britain.

Still, as the Iranian coup of 1953 had shown, the Americans did not reject interventionist action as a matter of principle. Because of the vulnerability of sterling, however, America could assure that British gunboat diplomacy occurred only with the concurrence of the United States, which it believed represented the broader interests of the free world rather than a narrow colonial interest.[16] The Eisenhower administration had always been convinced of the dangers posed by Nasser's pretensions as the leader of the Arab world while flirting with the Soviet Union. In 1958, therefore, it took strong action when the union of Egypt and Syria, as the United Arab Republic, plus a rebellion in Iraq, seemed to presage a nationalist threat to friendly regimes in Lebanon and Jordan. In response to requests for help from these governments, the Americans and British collaborated in a joint intervention: the United States sent troops to Lebanon while the British dispatched paratroopers to Jordan. As long as there was oil and the Cold War, the Middle East would be an area where the West sought to impose its influence; however, the United States would determine when action was necessary. Events there in the 1950s only confirmed how difficult it was for Britain to sustain a role as a world power that could act independently of the United States.

The one area of foreign policy where Britain did succeed in fending off American pressure was its relations with Western Europe. In the United States, the mentality of the Marshall Plan dominated: anything that strengthened its European allies would block the westward expansion of communism and so was in America's interest. Economic cooperation among the former wartime enemies was an important step in this direction. Hence, the Truman administration had been enthusiastic about the proposal in 1950 by French Foreign Minister Robert Schuman for pooling coal and steel resources in a supra-national organisation. What to do about Germany's heavy industry in the Ruhr and Saar had been a point of friction between Britain and France since the end of the war. The Schuman plan was France's solution to the problem of how to allow German economic recovery without threatening France's security. The aim was to pool sovereignty in order to bind Germany. The Attlee government, however, did not share France's acute fear of a revived German nationalism, while it did fear that European collaboration might threaten the Atlantic alliance. At the same time, the British would not compromise national sovereignty, especially when Labour had just established government authority over the coal and steel industries.[17] Finally, many Britons probably still felt some contempt for the continental countries. All of them had succumbed to Nazism during the war, while Britain alone had withstood the onslaught. Thus a sense of national pride and of racial (i.e. ethnic) superiority inclined many to stay aloof from unnecessary involvement in the affairs of Europe.[18] As a result, after some hesitation and despite American urging to the contrary, the government decided to stand aside when France, West Germany, Italy and the Benelux countries formed the European Coal and Steel Community.

The return of the Conservatives did nothing to warm Britain towards participation in European ventures, despite Churchill's supportive rhetoric when in opposition. After all, they were the party identified with British power and imperialism. With the outbreak of the Korean War, the US began pressing for a European defence community that could provide a cover for the rearmament of West Germany and so reduce the American defence commitment there. The Tories, however, had no intention of integrating Britain's defence forces into a European army, and without a firm British commitment the French (who really did not want German rearmament) were not interested either. Eden was able to save the day with the Americans by developing an alternative solution. West Germany signed the Brussels Treaty (now known as the West European Union), which became the vehicle for it to contribute to European defence with some external supervision, while it also joined NATO. The cost to Britain was a firm commitment to maintain four divisions in Germany, while France had to accept West German sovereignty.

The United States had secured some of what it wanted, but Britain's relationship with its European allies had been uncertain and ambiguous. This attitude remained evident when, in the wake of the frictions created by these defence negotiations, the six members of the Coal and Steel Community decided to go forward with negotiations for a broader customs union. The British government never believed the negotiations could succeed; it was inconceivable that the French and Germans would willingly compromise their freedom of independent action. It did not want to alienate the Europeans, however. So British observers were active participants in the first stage of negotiations in 1955, hoping they could steer the proposals away from a common market. The government understood full well that successful negotiations with Britain on the outside could only harm British interests. There would be enormous economic costs in a customs union that was likely to be protectionist, while it would have much more political weight with the United States. British participation, however, might destroy sterling as an international reserve currency and the Commonwealth as an economic entity. In balancing these considerations, Eden and R. A. Butler (the leader of the House of Commons) were hostile to British participation, while Macmillan was only interested on terms that were unacceptable to the six. In December 1955, therefore, Eden and Macmillan withdrew Britain from the talks and tried to sabotage them. The result was to alienate the Europeans, who saw exactly what the British were doing. The British were left on the outside and without any influence over events. Following the Suez fiasco, Macmillan, now the Prime Minister, was preoccupied with relations with the United States – even though throughout the negotiations the American government had been enthusiastic about European economic integration and wanted Britain in. The six thus signed the Treaty of Rome in 1957 without Britain. By then, the government was working to negotiate a free trade area involving the new EEC, Britain and several other European countries – one which excluded agricultural goods so as to protect imperial preference. The French vetoed that proposal at the end of 1958.

These debates over closer European cooperation, like the crises in the Middle East, showed how much the United States in the 1950s interpreted events in all parts of the world in terms of the evolving Cold War. The Cold War had helped to forge the relationship between Britain and the United States. Yet perhaps surprisingly, the Churchill government began to redirect Britain's policy somewhat away from that of its American ally. Under the pressures of McCarthyism and the prolonged Red Scare that it generated in the United States, the Eisenhower administration was uncompromising in its hostility to Communist states. Churchill, however, hankered after the old wartime summits where Britain could be perceived as the peer of the Soviet Union and the United States. Furthermore, Eden as Foreign Secretary was not inclined to see Britain so closely tied to the United States. Thus, both men could visualise a role for Britain as a moderator of Cold War tensions. Attlee had already taken on this role during the Korean War, as he had worked to prevent both a widening of the war with China and the use of nuclear weapons. By 1954, the danger of nuclear war seemed, if anything, greater. Both the Americans and the British had come to the conclusion that the threat of nuclear retaliation was the only means of deterring a Soviet military attack in Europe, given the Soviets' overwhelming superiority in conventional weapons. Thus, the use of nuclear weapons was now becoming part of Western military strategy. Given this reality and Dulles's belligerent rhetoric, Eden and Churchill saw a real benefit in trying to reduce the decibel level on the part of the superpowers. Following the death of Stalin in 1953 and the stalemate of the Korean War, they believed that the Soviets were no longer interested in a military challenge westwards. They therefore tried to use the special relationship to restrain the Americans, employing (as they saw it) Britain's experience in pragmatic diplomacy to guide its more emotional and ideological friends towards an understanding with the Soviets.

Eden's success at the 1954 Geneva Conference perfectly reflected his view of Britain's world role. There he brokered an agreement to secure France's withdrawal from its colonies in Indo-China on the basis of the creation of a Communist state in North Vietnam and a free state in South Vietnam, along with the neutral states of Laos and Cambodia. Following the recent settlement in Korea, which had also been pressed on the Americans by Eden, the accord seemed to prevent a new ideological war in Asia that once more would pit the United States against China. The Americans, however, were not happy with any of this. They were already suspicious of British weakness because the Attlee government had insisted on recognising the Communist regime in China rather than the government of Chiang Kai-shek in Taiwan. Attlee and Bevin had rejected the American view of a monolithic Communist threat and saw the possibility of using China as a counterweight to Russia in the East, a view that both Truman and Eisenhower dismissed. The disagreement over Indo-China was merely one more source of tension between the allies in Asia.

In 1954, the Americans and Chinese faced off again, this time over Taiwan's claims to Quemoy and Matsu, two islands near the mainland. The US government feared that intensified Chinese shelling of the islands was a prelude to an attack on Taiwan. Dulles told Eden that the United States would use nuclear weapons against China if that occurred and resisted all British efforts to find a compromise that would give the islands to China in return for guarantees of the security of Taiwan. The British were appalled that the Americans were ready to risk a nuclear war over two insignificant islands that were irrelevant to Taiwan's defences, while the Americans were irritated by the constant British nagging. The British once more appeared 'soft' on communism, as the shadow of appeasement reared its ugly head. Indeed, some Americans thought there was a broader effeteness that characterised the British people, especially the ruling elite, after having been worn down by two world wars. A series of spy scandals in the early 1950s, which exposed Britain's leading nuclear scientist and several Cambridge-educated public servants as Soviet agents, merely reinforced such perceptions of British decline. Thus, the influence that British governments could exercise over American relations with the Communist world was strictly limited.

These limitations were as evident in Soviet-American relations as they were in Sino-American relations. Summit diplomacy produced few gains either before or after Suez. Macmillan was able to achieve some lowering of the temperature of the rhetoric; but then events always scuppered his efforts. The 1960 summit, for example, ended as a fiasco when an American spy plane was shot down over the Soviet Union. The Cuban missile crisis followed two years later. President John Kennedy talked regularly with Macmillan and the British ambassador. Both served something of the role of a therapist, as people whom the President felt comfortable talking to. While he listened to their views, however, he did not consult about policy.[19] Perhaps the 1963 treaty banning nuclear tests above ground reflected Macmillan's mediating influence on America; he certainly had been propagandising for something of the sort in recent years. The Soviet premier Nikita Khrushchev, however, was the key figure in moving towards an agreement, and Macmillan's influence with him was limited. In the end, the treaty came about because it served everyone's political needs, including Macmillan's.

Overall, British leaders had enough to do merely to keep the relationship with the United States in good repair. After Suez, Macmillan patched things up with Eisenhower during a meeting in Bermuda in 1957, and he did it again with Kennedy in Nassau after the Cuban missile crisis. The central issue at both conferences, however, had nothing to do with Soviet-American relations. Rather, it was nuclear weapons, as Britain became increasingly dependent on the United States for its own weapons, while the Americans expanded their nuclear presence in Britain. Each agreement enhanced Britain's nuclear capability with the assistance of American technology. Perhaps the best evidence of a special relationship between Kennedy and Macmillan, who genuinely appreciated each other, was that the President agreed in 1962 to sell Polaris missiles to Britain, even though the US would have been happier if it had no nuclear deterrent at all. The American cancellation of the Skybolt rocket, which Eisenhower had promised to Britain in 1960, had come as close to provoking a rupture as Suez itself. With a Franco-German axis emerging in a protectionist EEC, however, the US could not afford to dispense with a British ally who could still project power around the world and shared some of its views on the international economy. So perhaps something of a special relationship was developing after all, as America began to recognise some benefit in having a 'special' friend in Europe. It is not clear what Britain was gaining from it, however, apart from nuclear weapons which increased its dependence on the United States.

The Setting Sun

For two centuries, the empire was central to virtually everyone's conception of Britain as a major power. The reality of its contribution to Britain's power, however, is open to contention. Historians cannot agree on what role the empire had in either Britain's emergence as the world's premier economic power or its ability to sustain that position in the nineteenth century. Amidst this often politicised debate, it seems clear that, by the second half of the nineteenth century, the settlement colonies of Canada, Australia, New Zealand and (later) South Africa, plus India, were far more important economically than any others, both as outlets for British investment and as trading partners. Beginning with Canada in the late 1840s, the custom emerged for the white populations in the settlement colonies to be self-governing. While these dominions had full control over domestic matters, however, they still looked to Britain for their defence. They all had small armies, and Australia and New Zealand had rendered Britain some assistance during the Boer War of 1899–1902. Despite British pressure after 1900, however, the dominions contributed little to the navy which protected them all.

Among the other colonies, India was unique. Indian taxpayers supported the British army in India – the principal means, apart from the navy, by which Britain exercised power in the East. Furthermore, in the first half of the nineteenth century, India developed as a major market for Lancashire cotton goods; as a result it was one of the few parts of the world with which Britain had a trade surplus. By the end of the century, a couple of million pounds added to the trade surplus did not make that much difference to the overall balance of payments. The surplus, however, was still important to the international financial system that was centred in London.[20] At the same time, British imperialists now saw India as the keystone of the empire: without it, Britain would be a second-rate power. This in itself was a commentary on how little the rest of the empire was worth, except as a matter of prestige. Given the high cost of the navy that was needed to defend it, the empire in Africa, East Asia and the Caribbean almost surely was a money-losing proposition – although key colonies like Singapore, Hong Kong and Egypt (not technically a colony) had important strategic or commercial roles. The British absorbed these costs for a number of reasons. First, the navy was far more than an instrument for holding on to the empire. It was Britain's principal means of exercising power worldwide, and so an important reason why it carried weight among the other powers. Britain would have devoted substantial resources to its navy even without such a far-flung empire. At the same time, the administrative costs of the colonies were born primarily by the colonies themselves, not by British taxpayers. Finally, the colonial peoples accepted British rule, in that they generated little resistance. This did not mean that there was no unrest – merely that disorder was sporadic and politically unfocused. So the military cost of holding on to the colonies was slight.[21]

The British Empire expanded as a result of the First World War, as it added some of the Ottoman territories in the Middle East and German colonies in Africa. The cost of holding on, however, also went up with the emergence of a more politicised resistance in some colonies. India had developed its first constitutional nationalist movement in the 1880s, with the founding of the Indian National Congress, which represented a Westernised elite. As a result of its pressure, British governments had introduced limited representative institutions at the provincial level by 1914. After the war, however, those institutions no longer satisfied. Congress initially had demanded self-government within the empire, but following the violence of 1919 – culminating in the massacre of Indian civilians by the British army at Amritsar – only complete independence was acceptable.

More dangerously for the British, Mohandas K. Gandhi emerged as a leader who could mobilise the masses in support of independence. By the 1930s, both British parties were committed to eventual dominion status for India, which meant *de facto* independence. A substantial group of Conservative die-hards continued to resist, however, led by Churchill.

Nationalism was also a source of difficulty in the Middle East. The British had created the problem during the war, when they had promised the Arabs independence to lure them into rebellion against the Turks, while promising the Jews a homeland in Palestine with the Balfour Declaration. The promises to the Arabs were ignored, as Britain and France divided the Arab territories between them. Egypt, Iraq and Transjordan became autonomous kingdoms subject to Britain's domination through its military presence, while Palestine was put directly under British rule as a League of Nations mandate.* Throughout the inter-war period, the British sought to reconcile the irreconcilable demands of Jews and Arabs over Jewish immigration to Palestine. No plan could satisfy, however; the result was growing violence on both sides after 1930. During the Second World War it exploded into a Jewish independence movement, with the violence directed against the British as well as the Arabs.

While India and Palestine were the most intractable colonial problems between the wars, nationalist movements emerged elsewhere as well – most notably in West Africa. As in India, the initial demand by the Westernised leaders was for self-government, not independence. All they asked was that the British apply their liberal principles to Africa. For the moment, however, the British conceded little. While there was occasional violence in Africa or Asia, there was nothing that the British military could not handle with the forces on the spot. Britain's hold over most of the colonies therefore remained firm. However, the government had to concede full

* Iraq and Transjordan were also League mandates, but by the 1930s Britain had formally withdrawn and recognised their independence, while assuring that the new kings were pro-British.

independence to the dominions, which were joined with Britain in a Commonwealth of Nations. Their economies were linked to Britain's after 1932 by a system of preferential tariffs and the emergence of the sterling bloc as the only way any of them could conduct international business in the protectionist 1930s. Thus, by 1939 the *de facto* acceptance of British rule which had characterised the pre-war era was beginning to break down. The empire, however, including the dominions, was tied to Britain economically as firmly as ever.

The Second World War was a disaster for Europe's two great colonial powers, Britain and France. The collapse of their armies in France before the Germans and the overrunning of their Asian empires (except India) by the Japanese destroyed any aura of invincibility they may have had, and the prestige that came with it. In the wake of such a fiasco, and with their cause seemingly lost, the British needed to persuade the colonial peoples to fight with them. So they presented the war as a struggle for liberty and equality against Japanese and German tyranny and racism. The peoples of Asia and Africa – long subject to the less tyrannous and brutal but nonetheless oppressive effects of British racism – did not altogether buy it. Many fought anyway, either because they recognised that the Germans and Japanese offered something far worse, or because they had no choice. Some did not. Many Congress leaders were thrown into prison for preaching non-cooperation, while some forty thousand Indians fought with the Japanese. When the war was over, the Westernised colonial elite were determined to hold the British accountable to the values they had preached. Hence, colonial nationalist movements were stronger and far more determined. The era of relatively passive acceptance of British rule was over, which meant the cost of preserving the empire was bound to rise. And while the British could hold on if resistance was limited to a couple of colonies, they could not suppress it everywhere simultaneously. Britain had never had the economic resources to keep all of the colonial peoples down by force.

Local pressures for independence were sporadically reinforced by the United States, which had a long-standing anti-imperialist tradition and was now willing to throw its weight around to secure its political goals. Although the Cold War led American leaders to look more benignly on the British and French empires, which could serve as barriers to Communist expansion, the Americans also feared that too tenacious an insistence on the status quo might drive colonial nationalists into the arms of the Communists. So residual American hostility to the empire burst forth at times to create additional problems and new pressures for Britain to retreat, as happened in Egypt before and during the Suez crisis.

The Labour Party had long been opposed in principle to imperialism. While it was not a Marxist-Leninist party, it had some sympathy with the argument that imperialism was simply another means by which capitalism exploited the weak. Its own idelogy of equality assured that there would be some support for colonial liberation, and the liberal humanitarian tradition pushed it in the same direction. On the other hand, many in the Labour Party shared the assumption of white superiority that characterised most Europeans in the first half of the twentieth century. Imperial issues had a low priority with the rank and file, while the empire was important to the Labour government's plans for Britain's economic recovery.

The policies that Labour implemented reflected a consensus that had evolved among progressive imperialists in both parties during the war, but modified by post-war economic exigencies. In theory, exploitation would stop, as economic, social and political reforms were introduced that would benefit the colonial peoples. Yet simultaneously, for the first time ever British governments were trying to construct a genuine imperial economy as part of a broader strategy to preserve Britain's place as a world power – which meant using the empire for British purposes. For example, the intention was for Britain to invest more in the economic improvement of its colonies so that they could be viable states. The colonies would have stronger economies, while Britain would benefit because they would be able to raise enough tax revenues to pay for government and service foreign debts. Yet to assure appropriate complementarity with the British economy, new investment focused on agriculture and raw materials, with few development funds going to industry. The result was to create economies that were excessively dependent on a single product and so more vulnerable to a downturn in world prices. At the same time, all dollars earned from exports were controlled by Britain. While the dominions were strong enough to secure some share for their own purposes, relatively little was reallocated to the colonies. So the whole system of post-war economic development was more exploitative than Labour would have liked to admit. Another goal was to provide more for basic health and educational resources; however, this goal too was compromised, because funds were limited by what the Treasury said the nation could afford. A final goal was to begin a gradual transition to self-government and, more distantly, independence. Representative institutions were to be introduced gradually starting at the local level, as had been done in India – allowing Westernised elites trained at newly established colleges of higher education to be schooled in the ways of democratic government and competent administration. The whole reform programme, it was hoped, would keep the empire together as a source of strength for Britain, so that it would be a power that the United States took seriously.

While the intent was to go slow, change could not wait in India. India was not as valuable as it once had been. After the First World War, the value of Britain's trade with India declined substantially; by the 1930s, Britain was running a trade deficit and India's industries were protected by tariffs. During the Second World War Britain became a debtor to India, which was the largest holder of sterling balances in 1945. At the same time, the war intensified the pressure for immediate independence. Since, after 1939, Britain was bearing an ever increasing share of the costs of the army there, the financial burden of holding on shot up. By 1945, therefore, the problem was how to get out in a way that would keep India within the British financial network as a member of the Commonwealth, and without India exploding in sectarian strife. Since the turn of the century, the Muslim League had rejected a single democratic state, which it feared would be an instrument for Hindu domination. By 1940, its leaders insisted on partition into two states, one with a Hindu majority and one with a Muslim majority. Gandhi and Jawaharlal Nehru, however, wanted a non-sectarian liberal state incorporating all Indians. The disagreement was irreconcilable, and communal violence increased after the war as it became clear that independence was imminent.

Labour's sympathies were with Congress, whose aspirations for a secular state were much more consistent with European socialist principles. Yet the Labour Cabinet was crippled by its own misconceptions about India, while it faced a wartime legacy of Indian hostility and distrust. Until the end of 1946, the government tried to broker a settlement that would avoid partition, yet it always seemed to be one step behind the reality of conditions in India. By 1947, it had to accept that it was unable to influence events there. British interests now dictated getting out as quickly and painlessly as possible so as not to be responsible for the escalating violence that was threatening a complete breakdown of order. The Cabinet devised a formula for retreat that would save face: a deadline for the Indian parties to agree on a settlement, plus the assertion that the denouement was what British policy in Indian had intended all along.[22] Under Lord Mountbatten as Viceroy, the independent states of India and Pakistan came into existence in August 1947, and the British managed to avoid blame for the violence that followed as the religious communities sorted themselves out. Burma and Ceylon became independent states the following year, completing a relatively amicable retreat from South Asia.

By contrast, there was nothing amicable about Britain's withdrawal from Palestine. By 1945, the British had a guerrilla war on their hands like the one that had driven them out of Ireland in 1919–21. The principal aggressors were Jewish terrorists fighting for an independent Jewish state. At the same time, the Jewish and Arab communities directed violence against each other, as the Jews pressed for increased Jewish immigration which the Arabs opposed. The Holocaust transformed this struggle between Jews and Arabs, which had been going on for the life of the mandate. Most importantly, it mobilised American Jews, and so the American government, on behalf of an independent state of Israel. As a result, all British efforts to devise a compromise acceptable to both communities were subject to constant criticism from the Truman administration. European opinion also now moved behind the Zionist goal. Like the Americans, the Europeans could assuage their guilt over the extermination of six million Jews by supporting an independent Jewish state. British public opinion did not quite flow with this tide. The British people resented Jewish acts of terrorism against Britons. There were also many Arabists who spoke for the Arab cause in Britain, as well as important strategic and economic interests in the Arab Middle East. Nonetheless, the Labour Party had long been sympathetic to Zionism, and there were Zionist sympathisers in the Cabinet. On the Tory side, Churchill had been one of its earliest proponents among the ruling elite. So both political and public opinion tended to be divided.

Bevin had no sympathy with Zionist immigration demands, which would undermine British influence in the Arab world. He wanted Britain to try to conciliate moderate nationalist opinion. The Chiefs of Staff agreed. They wanted to hold on to everything Britain had in the Middle East as a base from which to project power. Palestine, in particular, was a fall-back if Britain had to give up its Suez base. They feared that a Jewish state would undermine friendly relations with the Arabs, which were crucial for military purposes. Bevin therefore tried to negotiate a settlement that would reconcile Jewish, Arab and British interests – an impossible task. With the economic crisis reaching an acute stage in 1947, Palestine became a place to retrench. Attlee always had questioned the strategic benefit of the Middle East now that India did not require protecting any more. Once the United States plumped for partition, which the British were certain would be a catastrophe, he and Bevin decided to hand the mandate back to the United Nations. Over the remaining months of the mandate, the British tried to prevent an Arab-Israeli war while secretly supplying arms to the Arab states. At the same time, Bevin successfully lobbied for the incorporation of the Arab portion of post-partition Palestine into the British client state of Jordan. Despite these gestures of sympathy by the British, the Palestine crisis and the creation of an independent Israel was a disaster for Britain's relations with Arab states. It paid a heavy price for failure over the next decade.

Palestine was the messiest of Britain's retreats from empire, but it was not the only messy retreat. In 1952, the Mau Mau insurrection began in Kenya. It was a resistance movement by the Kikuyu, Kenya's largest tribe, directed against British land policies favouring the white settlers and their own tribesmen who collaborated with the British. It required a patient and substantial military response over the next three years to suppress it. So did the Communist rebellion in Malaya, which began in 1948 and was not brought under control until the mid-1950s. In this case, the Malay majority was against the rebels, who were primarily Chinese, so there was no question of the British resisting the popular will.* In Cyprus, the British once again were faced with two mutually hostile peoples – a Greek majority and a Turkish minority. The Greek guerrillas wanted union with Greece, leading the British to imprison the nationalist leader, as they also did in Kenya. In all three instances, the British armed forces were successful in defeating the insurgency, but inevitably with the expenditure of much money and some British lives. The British no longer had the stomach for such things, however, so the long-term tendency was to give way rather than fight.

Paradoxically, this trend evolved under the Conservatives, who long had been the party of empire. India had been the keystone

---

* Malaya was especially important to Britain because its rubber and tin exports to the United States were an important and rare source of dollars for the sterling area – meaning for Britain, as dollars earned in the sterling area were pooled in London.

of the Tory empire. With Indian independence now an accomplished fact, the Tories moved the psychological centre of British power westwards to the Middle East, including East Africa. At the same time, they accepted Labour's policy of colonial economic development, which they could associate with the Conservative philosophy of 'constructive imperialism'. When first articulated in the late nineteenth century by the likes of Joseph Chamberlain (Neville Chamberlain's father), it had meant that British investment would provide the colonies with a suitable infrastructure, while the colonies would be developed to complement Britain's industrial economy. Constructive imperialism had not been tested as a policy then, for imperialism went out of favour after the traumas of the Boer War. Between the wars, when the Conservatives dominated government, there was no money (either public or private) to implement a constructive programme beyond a few infrastructure projects in the 1920s.

The post-war vision of the empire gave constructive Conservatives an opportunity to prove that imperialism could work to the benefit of both the colonies and the mother country. Economic development would strengthen the sterling area, as Britain could buy more goods with sterling and the colonies could buy more British goods in return. Exports from the colonies also offered a means for Britain to get more dollars. In many ways, it was just a modernised version of Chamberlain's vision, as the Conservative governments promoted export-based agricultural or mining industries in the colonial economies. Projects of economic development, however, involved British officials telling Africans what to do while encroaching on entrenched interests. The effect was to generate resentment and give nationalists a means of broadening their base of support in the fight to end British rule. In the early 1950s, Kwame Nkrumah showed other nationalist leaders how to organise a mass political party that could tap into these discontents. The effect was to force the British to concede eventual independence to the Gold Coast (Ghana), with its dollar-earning cocoa exports, rather than risk internal disorder or a drift over to the Communist side.

The Conservatives also tried to build more viable colonial states by consolidating territories. In Africa, in particular, one of the aims was to protect the position of white settlers. After 1945, however, the British would not simply turn the blacks over to unfettered white domination, as they had done in South Africa in 1910. Instead, Labour articulated the principle of 'partnership'. All races (including Indians) would participate in new representative institutions that were to be the basis for a transition to independence. These proposals, however, looked suspiciously like efforts to consolidate white rule; certainly the white settlers took them that way. The effect, therefore, was to provide a stimulus to black nationalist movements which had been weak. Plans to federate Kenya, Uganda and Tanganyika were never consummated because of black resistance in the two latter colonies. The Central African Federation – which combined Northern and Southern Rhodesia and Nyasaland – lasted for about a decade. Viewed by whites in the Rhodesias as a means to create a dominion on the South African model, it fell apart in the early 1960s when blacks in Northern Rhodesia and Nyasaland insisted on independence with majority rule.

Beyond these attempts to use federation to secure multi-racial states, the British grafted together territories whose only link sometimes was geographical proximity. They thought that larger states would have a better chance to succeed, both politically and economically. Almost every African state was an artificial creation of this sort, bringing together regions or peoples who disliked or distrusted each other, or who simply did not want to be dominated by 'foreigners'. Although European tribes had been fighting each other for centuries, and had just tried to exterminate one of their number (the Jews), politicians in London ignored the danger that African tribes would be similarly incompatible under a single government. The results were often disastrous when independence came, starting with the bitter civil war in Nigeria in the late 1960s. Even the West Indian Federation failed, despite initial support from West Indian leaders. The larger islands were not inclined to support the smaller and poorer ones, while local politicians in all the islands did not want to see their power eroded by a federal government.

By 1960, the Conservatives were losing interest in reconstructing the colonies according to Western views. Everywhere, they had created representative institutions, hoping that such concessions would conciliate the local elite and preserve British influence. These institutions, however, provided the means for those who disliked British policies to generate resistance to British rule. At the same time, it was becoming evident that the empire was not going to prove a successful foundation around which to develop the British economy. The Tories were not yet looking to unload the colonies; however, coming out of the 1959 general election, the costs of promoting a prolonged and gradual transition to independence were going up. Faced with crises in Kenya and Nyasaland, where atrocities by white governments had raised the moral temperature at home, Harold Macmillan saw that policy in Africa needed to be revamped. The urgency of making reductions in military spending pushed him in the same direction. Most importantly, with the Cold War turning into a competition between the Communist powers and the West for influence, the imperative became to assure that independence meant new states that were friendly to the West. The danger was driven home by the violent crisis in the Congo from 1960 to 1962. It gave a further impetus to independence sentiment in Africa, while making manifest the opportunities for the Soviets to cause trouble if the British procrastinated. Kenya embodied the dilemma that Macmillan believed he faced: 'If we have to give independence to Kenya, it may well prove another Congo. If we hold on, it will mean a long and cruel campaign – Mau Mau and all that.'[23] There was no way that the government was prepared to contemplate the latter, however distasteful it might be to turn Kenya over to the 'bloody butcher [Jomo] Kenyatta'. And if it could be done in Kenya, it could be done everywhere else in Africa.

While the Colonial Office tried to assure that representative institutions were in place and to secure a handover to moderate leaders who would be friendly to British interests, its main concern was to get out before internal frictions exploded in disorder that Britain would have to suppress. Somehow, the British managed to pull it off with an impression of goodwill that had a beneficial political effect, as between 1960 and 1970 most of the remaining colonies became independent nations. Old enemies like Kenyatta in Kenya and Kenneth Kaunda in Zambia became valued statesmen, and they in turn were willing to forgive former persecution and join the Commonwealth. The only hitch was in (Southern) Rhodesia, where the whites who had dominated government since the 1920s would not accept majority rule. Following the break-up of the Central African Federation and the granting of independence to Rhodesia's two former partners under majority rule, they declared independence in 1965 and became a pariah state. Other African nations wanted the British to intervene militarily, but that had ceased to be economically or politically feasible. Having given up what they had wanted to keep, the British were not about to devote the resources necessary to reconquer a Rhodesian colony in which they had no interest.

One reason the Macmillan government gave way so easily was the hope that independence did not mean the end of British influence. Nearly all the new states, beginning with India and Pakistan (but not Israel or the Arab states), joined the Commonwealth, which had become a vehicle for securing British economic interests. Britain and the old dominions had agreed to a system of preferential tariffs in the 1930s. As Table 3.1 overleaf shows, imperial preference reflected the pattern along which British trade had been evolving since the First World War. That trend continued during and after the Second World War. The empire was never more important than in the 1940s. During the war, it enabled Britain to purchase (or requisition) goods paid for in sterling; after the war, the sterling area provided a crucial cushion for Britain until the world economy returned to normal. The British hoped that this relationship would continue after normality was restored. The empire and Commonwealth would

Table 3.1. Portion of Trade with and Overseas Investments in the Empire, 1910–1960

	Imports (%)	Exports (%)	Overseas Investments[a] (%)
1910–14	25	36	46
1925–9	28	42	59
1935–9	39.5	49	–
1946–9	48	57.5	–
1955–9	47	51	60

[a]Figures on the portion of overseas investments going to the empire are for the periods 1911–13, 1927–9 and 1958–60.

Source: Porter, The Lion's Share, pp. 267, 327.

be the principal basis for the development of British trade – providing Britons with cheap food, offering protected markets for their manufactured goods and contributing dollars from their exports to the rest of the world. While the most important trading partners were still the richest states, poorer Commonwealth members supplied specific food products (like sugar and tea) and key raw materials (like rubber and copper). The empire would also be a safe outlet for British investment overseas. Thus, the British had a stake in trying to preserve the imperial economic relationship in the age of colonial independence; it would give Britain the economic muscle to continue to count in world affairs. The gradual transition of African, Asian and West Indian territories from colonies to members of the Commonwealth would assure that their economic role remained unchanged. At the same time, regular meetings of Commonwealth heads of government would provide British prime ministers with a forum where they could try to mobilise opinion in support of British policies.

At least that was the hope – that the Commonwealth would

enable Britain to continue to punch above its weight in the ring of world politics. In practice, it did not work that way. As American independence had shown nearly two hundred years earlier, Britain's economic relationship with a former colony did not require a formal connection if both had an interest in maintaining it. So neither trade nor investment required the Commonwealth relationship, while that relationship could harm British economic interests if capitalists saw reasons to move elsewhere. Arguably, the Commonwealth and empire had done such harm in the 1950s by diverting Britain away from an expanding Europe. During the next decade, British trade turned decisively towards that Europe. At the same time, the newly independent states were not inclined to have the old colonial relationship prolonged by submitting to British leadership. Indeed, domestic politics demanded that they prove their independence by standing up to Britain, while the United States became at least as important to their foreign policy calculations. Even the older white-dominated dominions found their interests being defined as much by their relationship with the United States or with the new states of Asia and Africa as by that with Britain.

Nor did the British themselves prove to be very good Commonwealth members when their interests dictated otherwise. Crucially, the Suez campaign was undertaken without any prior consultation with the Commonwealth. In response, the Commonwealth was nearly unanimous in condemning the venture. There were divisions again over the explosive issue of relations with the apartheid regime in South Africa. In 1961, Britain was outvoted as South Africa was forced out of the Commonwealth. Britain was similarly hammered by the new member states of Asia and Africa over its failure to bring Rhodesia to heel. Despite the tensions, however, no one wanted to get rid of the Commonwealth. Indeed, it established a permanent secretariat in London, and in the years ahead many were eager to join – including some states that had never been part of the British Empire. Clearly, governments believed that it had a useful function as a vehicle for discussing issues and projecting themselves on the world stage. It was useless, however, as a means of increasing Britain's influence, as it ceased to be a British institution altogether.

In retrospect, it seems hardly credible that British leaders believed that a group of countries as economically and geographically diverse as the Commonwealth could have a common interest that the British could mobilise for foreign policy purposes. Such a triumph of wishful thinking was simply one more example of how much British governments wanted to retain a powerful independent influence in world affairs. They exaggerated Britain's real position in 1945, even though they were fully aware of its economic weakness. Thereafter, policy-making seemed to be a series of rearguard actions by political leaders as they were forced to retreat from the ambitious positions they had defined for Britain. The 'special relationship' with the United States brought with it British dependence and subordination; it was a heavy price to pay for a limited influence on superpower relations. The Commonwealth could not have much influence as an institution that carried diplomatic weight; it represented too many diverse and even conflicting interests. So as both the United States and the Commonwealth turned out to be considerably less than British leaders had hoped for, they had to begin to look to Europe as an alternative way of making British influence felt in international affairs.

4

THE AGE OF CONSENSUS

The Return to Politics as Usual

Far more than in the American political system, Britain's depends on two parties whose constitutional function is to criticise each other. Because the executive under the British constitution is the leadership of the largest party in the House of Commons, the incentives for party discipline are extraordinary. The very survival of the government depends upon it. By contrast, Congress is independent of the executive, with its own substantial powers. It has an institutional suspicion of the executive which makes it an effective scrutiniser and critic of executive action, independent of party. Indeed, Congress's autonomous power assures that, on any issue, there may be cross-party alliances which threaten the President's ability to enact his programme, even when his party controls Congress. In Britain, by contrast, Parliament is sovereign; it can enact any policy it wants. While the House of Lords has some residual powers to delay, the real sovereign power rests in the House of Commons, which can always override the Lords. Party discipline further narrows effective sovereign power to the government, which can implement its programme without any real constitutional check. This is why the role played by the opposition party is so important. For the only check on the government's power to do what it wants is popular opinion, and the job of the opposition is to make sure that the public understands all that is wrong with any policy the government may propose. Thus, far more than in America, there always is an identifiable opposition, and its function is clearly defined by usage as opposing and criticising everything the government does. For the lack of an effective opposition removes an important constraint on the power of the government to do as it likes.

Yet between 1915 and 1945, the norm in Britain was coalition government: the wartime coalitions of 1915–18, the Lloyd George coalition of 1918–22, the National Government of 1931–40, and the Churchill coalition of 1940–45. The fact that coalitions governed Britain for twenty-one of thirty years was a sign of abnormal times. They *were* abnormal, of course, with two world wars and a great depression. A more important explanation of this propensity towards coalition, however, especially during the years of peace, was the weakness of the left. The decline of the Liberal Party and the rise of the Labour Party assured that the vote on the left was divided, both in the country and in the House of Commons. Thus, the dominant Conservative Party could do what it liked without fear of the only retribution that could effectively check it: the possibility of losing the next election. Oddly, this pre-eminent position did not make the Conservatives more radical; rather, it made them more cautious.[*] Especially in the 1930s, after Labour had split following the formation of the National Government in 1931, a controversial policy risked providing an opening for Labour to rally the opposition and so re-establish its credibility as a viable alternative to the government. One result of this caution was the paradox of a Conservative Party pursuing a foreign policy of appeasement, criticised by an opposition that was also Conservative.

There is no surprise, however, that Winston Churchill was the leader of the opposition to appeasement, for he was not much of a party man. Like his mentor David Lloyd George, Churchill was most at home when the traditional party system broke down.

---

[*] The contrast with the radical behaviour of the Conservatives in the 1980s, when a split on the left again allowed them to dominate government with little fear of retribution at the polls, is striking.

These men, each one in his own way a political genius, saw the rituals of party warfare as constraints on implementing policy, even though each could be a brilliant (and often controversial) warrior when engaged in party combat. The constraints resulted because parties were prevented from pursuing policies that commanded a broader base of support for fear of their own extremists, who saw every item in the party programme as a matter of principle and therefore every concession to the opposition as a sacrifice of fundamental beliefs. It was not just the fanatics, however, who were sceptical about Lloyd George and Churchill. All party politicians were suspicious of them because of their tendency to prefer coalition government. It seemed as if they did not want to play by the rules because those rules hampered them in the struggle for political power. Thus, what Lloyd George and Churchill saw as an effort to get things accomplished, others saw as political opportunism, and one did not have to be a zealot to question the commitment of both men to principle. Churchill, in particular, was susceptible to such charges, as he had changed parties twice at very opportune moments for his career: in 1904, when he abandoned a Tory Party about to lose power to join the Liberals; and in 1922–3, when he abandoned a Liberal Party that was fading as a credible party of government to rejoin the Conservatives. Ordinary Conservative MPs never quite trusted Churchill, and there was probably much relief when the leader, Stanley Baldwin, was able to marginalise him in the 1930s, first on the issue of Indian self-government and then on appeasement. Similarly, when the war came, there was no rush to Churchill by either the party leadership or the rank and file. Only the crisis created by the Nazi victories in the spring of 1940, and so the absolute need to bring Labour into a coalition, forced his ascension to the premiership, while he was not elected party leader until after Neville Chamberlain's death at the end of 1940.

Getting Labour into a coalition was no easy task, for the party had its own reasons to distrust both coalition government and Churchill. The formation of the National Government in 1931 turned the Labour rank and file against coalition, as a matter of ideology. They believed the party leaders who joined that government, Ramsay MacDonald and Philip Snowden, had abandoned principle (by agreeing to cut unemployment benefits) and caved in to the capitalist elite (the London bankers) in order to hold on to power. The lesson was that Labour should stop trying to conciliate the capitalists by moderating its programme, as MacDonald had done during his two terms as Prime Minister. Hereafter, Labour should live or die by implementing its socialist policies, which meant it should not share power with any other party. The outbreak of war in 1939 changed nothing. Everyone understood the value of a national coalition to conduct the war; however, Labour had no liking for Chamberlain, whose efforts to bring them into the government were at best half-hearted. The military crisis of the spring of 1940 finally convinced everyone that there could not be business as usual in conducting the war. A national coalition was essential, and Labour, holding the whip hand, insisted that it would only serve under Churchill.

There is an irony that Labour was second in importance only to Hitler himself in bringing Churchill to power, for the trade unions had long distrusted him. There was a mythology about Churchill's hostility to labour, going back to a Welsh mining strike in 1910, when as Home Secretary he had sent troops to the village of Tonypandy in case they were needed to suppress disorder. Later, after the First World War, Churchill was at the forefront of those who sought to tar domestic socialists with the Bolshevik brush. The climax came with the General Strike of 1926, when Churchill was among the ministers who opposed all compromise, insisting that the strike was a challenge to constitutional government. To the workers, he seemed to be deliberately provocative in his words and actions during the strike, while Tory policies after the strike seemed to be aimed at breaking the trade union movement and the Labour Party. Yet Churchill's record as an opponent of appeasement was unmatched. More importantly, the experience of the Lloyd George government during the last two years of the First World War had shown the importance of decisive, energetic and imaginative leadership in winning a war, when morale at home was as important as the military wherewithal abroad. In 1940, domestic morale was all that remained between Britain and defeat, so Labour accepted Churchill as the only leader with the qualities to mobilise the people for the effort.

While the wartime coalition was a generally harmonious collaboration between the Conservative and Labour leaders, it did not leave Labour's rank and file any more reconciled to Churchill. On the contrary, as the war in Europe neared its end, distrust re-emerged. Churchill wanted to keep the coalition together until Japan was defeated, which was expected to be at least a year away. The workers, however, remembered the post-war Lloyd George coalition of 1918–22, which they believed had forsaken its promises of a better life for them at the bidding of the capitalist interests that dominated the Conservative Party and the coalition. Why should a post-war Churchill coalition be any less susceptible to the same pressures, especially with Churchill's supposed anti-labour record? Attlee and the other Labour Party leaders, however much some may have preferred to continue the coalition, could not risk a repeat of the 'betrayal' of 1931. The impetus from below was to end the coalition and to run the general election on the socialist platform that the party had been developing over the previous ten years. The Tory grass roots were equally unhappy with coalition government, which many thought had hogtied conservatism since 1931. Thus, party activists on both sides were ready for a return to partisan politics.

The election that followed seemed in every way to confirm Labour's judgement. On the one hand, Churchill reverted to his old role of the anti-socialist warrior of the 1920s, associating Labour policies indiscriminately with the Nazi Gestapo and Soviet communism. On the other hand, Labour embodied for many voters their aspirations for a more egalitarian and more economically secure society after the war. While the Conservatives were also committed to social reforms, they had no specific policies to offer. Their election strategy was geared primarily to promoting Churchill as national hero, while emphasising the dangers of socialism and their unique ability to protect Britain's worldwide interests. Social reform was marginal to their campaign. By contrast, social security and social justice were integral to Labour's ideological purpose and so to its vision for the nation, while the party had a series of very specific proposals to offer the electorate. At the same time, Labour's campaign had a clear underlying message: if people were determined that there should be no return to the miseries of the 1930s, Labour was their party, not the Conservatives who had seemed so grudging in relieving the distress then. Millions of Britons were just so determined, and they were not only from the working class. By-election and polling evidence in the last years of the war had shown the Conservatives to be unpopular. Similarly, opinion polls showed Labour ahead throughout the campaign. So it should not have been a surprise that they won. Yet it *was* a surprise – in part, because no one could quite believe the voters would reject Churchill, the war hero, but more because of the sheer size of Labour's victory. With 393 MPs returned to 213 for the Conservatives, it was the largest electoral landslide between the Liberals' triumph in 1906 and Labour's in 1997.[1]

The Tories Embrace Consensus Politics

It is the nature of political parties to incorporate people of differing views. Even Nazi and Communist parties contain differing visions of what the party stands for; it is just that a Hitler or a Stalin destroys all who dissent from his party line. In a democratic party, such dissent cannot be so easily suppressed, though party leaders try – especially in Britain, where party discipline is so integral to the system. A British party leader's job is made easier, however, because, whatever the internal differences, all are held together by a shared ideological purpose which distinguishes them from the opposition, as well as by a desire to get and keep power. Yet from 1945 to 1964, it sometimes seemed as if a political consensus had evolved that left the greatest differences within the two major parties rather than between them.[2]

In principle, Labour was united by an ideological commitment to socialism, while the Conservatives were united by an ideological commitment to the free market. Yet in practice, Labour accepted the free market, while the Tories accepted socialism as embodied in the legislation of 1945–50 – that is, a mixed economy of nationalised industries and private concerns, heavily weighted towards the latter; the NHS; and universal state-provided insurance. Both also accepted Keynesian management of the budget as the means of maintaining full employment. Similarly, while there was a difference in emphasis, both parties accepted a foreign policy based on a commitment to NATO and the American alliance, while preserving Britain's role as a world power. So general elections after 1950 were fought on which party could best achieve the common aims of social and national security. While each party emphasised their differing visions for the country, once a party was in power, policy changes occurred only at the margins – in contrast to the transformative policies of 1945–50 and 1979–90.

Pragmatic electoral concerns dictated that the Conservatives move towards this consensus position. They had been humiliated in the general election of 1945, in which they had placed great emphasis on the return to a free enterprise economy. Hence, they had to adapt to bring themselves more into line with popular aspirations. Churchill, who had little interest in policy, resisted formulating specific alternatives to Labour until closer to a general election. The rank and file, however, wanted policy statements, as did leading members of the shadow Cabinet. Churchill finally gave way after the 1946 party conference, thus unleashing R. A. Butler to oversee a complete rethink of Conservative policy. Butler headed the Conservative Research Department that was reconstituted in 1945, and he mobilised talented young Conservatives like Iain Macleod, Reginald Maudling and Enoch Powell to work out a new Tory approach to policy. Over the next few years, they and others (like Harold Macmillan) developed policy statements that integrated the reforms of the 1940s with a reassertion of basic Conservative principles. For example, while accepting the principle of a welfare state based on the provision of an adequate safety net, they rejected any notion that either the tax or the benefit system should be used to redistribute wealth and promote egalitarianism. Their preference was for targeted (i.e. means-tested) rather than universal flat-rate benefits, so that spending could be kept down and tax rates lowered. Similarly, while they accepted the 'mixed economy' with the relatively small public sector on offer by 1949, there must be no government planning. The free market must shape economic activity, with all the incentives and rewards for individual initiative that followed in its wake. In the realm of foreign policy, Labour arguably was pursuing Tory policies. The only possible difficulty was India. Churchill and a group of hard-line imperialists, constituting about one-third of the party in the 1930s, had been consistent opponents of Indian independence, and back-bench opinion had never really accepted it. After the war, however, independence was inevitable. Although Churchill sometimes tried to revive the glory days of 1930s opposition, the front benches mostly collaborated to remove India from partisan politics. Otherwise, Labour's colonial policy did not involve a wholesale withdrawal from empire, so the Tory imperialist right was quiet.

Thus, when the Conservatives contested the general elections of 1950 and 1951, they did so accepting most of what Labour had done, while pointing to the very different emphases that would underlie Tory policy-making. Their promise to reverse the nationalisation of steel and road haulage perfectly highlighted the ideological differences between the parties, while reinforcing a growing sense that Labour was being too socialist. Labour's eccentric proposals for further nationalisation in the 1950 election – such as meat wholesaling, cement making and sugar refining – contributed to the impression that it was more driven by ideology than what was best for the country. The Conservatives, by contrast, emphasised their commitment to the free market and the end of controls. What they were offering, they hoped, was an alternative and more satisfying means of consolidating and expanding optimal social welfare for all. At the same time, they appealed to the popular desire to be rid of the socialist ethic of sacrifice. Their 1951 election promise to build more houses underscored the Tory ideal of a property-owning democracy as an alternative to Labour's austere version of socialism. Labour responded by emphasising its achievements and the danger that a Tory government would reverse all that had been done since 1945, with a return to 1930s unemployment.

While Labour held on to its working-class electorate, the Conservative message appealed to many of the middle-class voters, a portion of whom had helped produce the landslide of 1945. Labour had taxed them a lot, and they felt as if they had gained very little in return (which was not true). Many resented the redistributive effects of 1940s policies and the new power of the trade unions. Finally, they were tired of austerity and sacrifice. The Labour government had some understanding that people felt this way. It organised the Festival of Britain in 1951, which extolled British culture and the British way of life, to celebrate Britons' survival of more than a decade of war and hardship while hinting at a brighter future ahead. The middle class wanted that future now, not more self-denial. So it swung back to the Tories, who barely lost the 1950 election and barely won in 1951.[3]

The 1951 election was a very close-run contest. Since Labour had done its best to persuade the electorate that the gains of 1945–50 were in danger under a Conservative government, the Tories had a powerful incentive to prove that the welfare state was safe in their hands, especially since they were having difficulty attracting working-class voters. Their biggest immediate asset was Harold Macmillan's ability to deliver on the promise to build lots of new houses, for many voters saw housing as Labour's biggest failure. The lower middle class, in particular, was attracted by the broader Tory vision of a property-owning democracy. Prosperity eventually became another asset in enabling the Conservatives to consolidate their position after 1951, but prosperity did not come right away. It was not until 1953 that Butler, as Chancellor of the Exchequer, was able to reduce taxes, and only in 1954 did he end remaining food rationing. By then there was enough money to increase pensions and channel some resources into the NHS. Given the continuing fluidity of the political situation, however, Churchill was adamant that there should be no opportunity for Labour to paint his government as hostile to the worker. He therefore gave his Minister of Labour, Walter Monckton, a brief to avoid conflict with the unions. Indeed, throughout the period of Conservative rule, there seems to have been an implied understanding with the unions that the government would leave them to manage their own affairs, including wage bargaining, in return for wage restraint on their part.4 If there was the threat of a strike, the government promoted conciliation, if necessary by setting up a formal inquiry to investigate the union's claims and recommend a settlement. These inquiries tended to be sympathetic to the demands of labour – in part because trade union leaders kept their demands moderate, but also because the government wanted them to be so. Some Cabinet ministers were not pleased with this approach, and there was even greater hostility to it in the constituencies. The parliamentary party, however, never pushed the issue to the point where it created a crisis. This weakness on the right was to characterise the whole period of Tory rule from 1951 to 1964. While at various moments there was considerable discontent with both domestic and foreign policy, there was little the right could do to change its direction.

By 1954, the principal source of tension in Churchill's government was Churchill himself. He was now an old man, and since suffering a stroke in June 1953 (if not before) he was unfit to run a government. The Cabinet wanted rid of him before the next election. Indeed, many had wanted to be rid of him before the 1950 election. Anthony Eden's relationship with Churchill was particularly tense, as the two jockeyed over who would be in charge of foreign policy. Churchill did not want to go, however; so he kept procrastinating. It finally took threats of resignation to force him out. Since the 1945 general election, it had been understood that Eden would be his successor. Eden had made his reputation when he resigned as Foreign Secretary in 1938, following Hitler's annexation of Austria. Although he had been involved in the government's foreign policies since 1931, and had been Foreign Secretary since the end of 1935, he now managed to free himself from the taint of appeasement – unlike Butler, who supported Munich. Churchill thus made him Foreign Secretary again at the end of 1940, and thereafter Eden operated in Churchill's shadow. He was respected as a diplomatist, but had no experience as a parliamentary manager, and he was ignorant of domestic affairs. While his colleagues were aware of his weaknesses, no one challenged his right to the succession. Eden consolidated his position by calling a general election. With the economy strong and Labour weak and divided, the outcome was never in doubt, and the Tories increased their majority to nearly sixty over all other parties. Yet all was not happy in the new government. Butler and Macmillan, who both had an eye on the succession, did not get along with Eden or each other. Macmillan, in particular, had little respect for Eden and was particularly resentful when Eden moved him from Foreign Secretary to Chancellor so the Prime Minister could manage foreign policy. Eden, however, meddled excessively in the details of all departments, not just the Foreign Office, while colleagues found him too indecisive, unpredictable and sensitive to press criticism. By 1956, he was generally seen as a weak and vacillating leader, and even the Tory press grew hostile. With the economy suddenly in trouble and the party's rank and file restless after four years of 'socialist' economic and labour policies, Eden's popularity plummeted.

The Suez crisis erupted in this unsettled political environment. Initially, it was not clear that Suez would present a problem. Following Nasser's nationalisation of the Canal, everyone – the Cabinet, the party, the press, the Labour opposition – favoured a vigorous response. Eden was certainly convinced that Britain's standing as a great power depended on strong action, and his colleagues saw it the same way. For example, Alan Lennox-Boyd (the Colonial Secretary) wrote to the Prime Minister, 'If Nasser wins, or even appears to win, we might as well as a government (and indeed as a country) go out of business.' Earlier in the year, one junior member of the government had claimed, 'Ministers – led by the PM . . . [are] mad to land British troops somewhere to show that we are still alive and kicking.'[5] So all agreed that this was the moment to draw the proverbial line in the sand and stop Britain's decline.

Yet they had great difficulty in agreeing on exactly what to do, and the Cabinet evaded the issue of whether to proceed if the United States opposed a military operation. Eisenhower was bombarding Eden with letters that made clear that he *was* opposed to the use of force. Furthermore, as the weeks passed and the Canal continued to function smoothly, the consensus behind a decisive response collapsed. Labour indicated that it would only support action that was endorsed by the United Nations. The government understood that they were treading on dangerous ground if they adopted a policy contrary to the ideals that Britain had fought for in the war: the rule of law and national self-determination. It was harder to flout Gladstonian principles of foreign policy than it had been a hundred years earlier. For just this reason, they turned to negotiations at the United Nations and then embraced the French plan to bring in the Israelis. The Cabinet needed moral cover both with the Americans and with domestic opinion. The plan of invasion that was finally concocted, however, was morally dubious, and several members had doubts that it would do the job.*

The government's one unambiguous source of support was the Conservative Party. The party's right wing had not been happy with Eden's earlier backpedalling in the Middle East. Following

---

* There may also have been some thirty Conservative MPs who were critical of the invasion. The key figure was Butler, who had his doubts. If he had given a lead, a far stronger Tory opposition would have emerged. However, he was inhibited by a combination of loyalty and his appeaser past, which would have made doubts look like weakness rather than conscience or principle. John Ramsden, *The Age of Churchill and Eden, 1940–1957* (London, New York: Longman, 1995), pp. 308–12.

the 1954 treaty to withdraw British troops from the Canal Zone, they had organised a 'Suez Group' of MPs critical of imperial retreat. Now they mobilised in earnest. At the party conference in October, they made it very clear that they expected forceful action to secure international control over the Canal, and they carried the party with them. American interests in restraint carried little weight with them. The Tory right had no love for the United States, which seemed to be superseding British influence in every part of the world while covering its self-interested actions in a cloak of moralism. Once the Suez operation was launched, they were furious with the Americans for deserting and humiliating Britain and opposed the policy of cut and run that the US imposed.[6] Yet the position of the right was a weak one. Much of the world attacked Britain's actions. With Commonwealth states like India and Canada at the forefront of Britain's critics, the Commonwealth was not proving to be the bulwark of British worldwide influence that Tory imperialists had dreamed of. Labour, too, was outraged that Britain was pursuing a policy of aggression rather than restraint and opposed the government in Parliament from the moment of the invasion. Among the broader population, there was an enormous patriotic response in support of the government and a wave of anti-American sentiment. Yet a large segment of public opinion, including many Conservatives, condemned such a flagrant violation of the UN Charter and all that Britain claimed to stand for. Centrist establishment organs like *The Times, The Economist* and the *Observer* all were among the government's critics. Thus, the country was more bitterly divided by Suez than at any time since Munich, when it was just the memory of Munich that Eden had been hoping to purge.

Faced with so much criticism and pressure to withdraw British forces, Eden's health (always precarious since a series of operations in 1953) broke. In mid-November he retreated to Jamaica, leaving the rest of the Cabinet to pick up the pieces. Macmillan took the lead in pressing for capitulation to American terms. Macmillan's position during the crisis had not been a noble one.

He had been a leading hawk in September and October. He had been untroubled by warnings since early September concerning the effects on sterling if Britain acted without American support. He did not even alert the Cabinet of the danger until 26 October, just before the invasion. He had also misled Eden about Eisenhower's attitude following his meeting with the President in September, even though the two had hardly discussed the crisis. Once Eden was out of the way, however, he took the lead in pressing for complete surrender to the US rather than risk a devaluation of the pound.[7] He and Butler, who was acting Prime Minister, struggled to hold both the government and the party together through the latter part of the crisis. They also maintained constant contact with the American ambassador in London, even implying that Eden was on the way out.

Eden would have been happy enough to continue as Prime Minister. Yet he had little credibility left with the party. Not only had he presided over a fiasco in British foreign policy that had exposed the nation's dependency and weakness, but he had deserted his post at the crucial moment. Randolph Churchill, Winston's son and an unrelenting critic of Eden, said that 'even Hitler did not winter in Jamaica' as the German army was being pounded at Stalingrad.[8] Furthermore, on his return from Jamaica, he had lied to the House of Commons, denying that the British had planned to attack Egypt or had known in advance of the Israeli invasion.[9] Finally, it was likely that his health would break again. So Eden was finished. Butler, who had overseen Britain's withdrawal while Eden was recuperating, was too unpopular with the parliamentary party to succeed him. Many still did not forgive him for his past as an appeaser, while his persistent hints at his dissent from the Suez action reinforced a perception that he was too weak and left wing. Macmillan, who was equally left wing, came off better simply because he had been an enthusiastic supporter of Suez. Thus, he had near unanimous support and became Prime Minister. Apart from keeping Butler out, however, the Tory right had been powerless to shape events once the invasion of Egypt was launched. The voice of assertive imperialism was irrelevant in the face of forces outside Britain's control – like American power, the weakness of the pound and the universal condemnation of a world opinion that now counted for something.

The new Prime Minister had first come on the scene in the 1930s as a Keynesian critic of unemployment before Keynes had become economic orthodoxy. During the war he had served brilliantly as the British government's liaison with the American armies in North Africa and Italy. In Africa, in particular, he had successfully negotiated the figurative minefields of American and French sensibilities while increasing British influence with Eisenhower. After the Labour landslide in 1945, he had been one of the people behind the reshaping of Tory policy towards accepting the welfare state. He was still not a major figure in the party, however, until he made his reputation in the early years of Churchill's government as the successful builder of houses. His record during the Suez crisis had been pragmatic and opportunistic: pushing for intervention against Nasser, yet recognising the reality of failure once American support was lost. Initially, Macmillan's position was weak; he even questioned whether the government would survive for long. Within a year, however, he had consolidated his power – by cultivating the Tory backbenchers and the press and winning them to his side and by dominating the Commons. At the same time, he developed a public image that reassured the country: calm, sensible, civilised, worldly, slightly aloof and always in control – in short, the qualities of the aristocracy. As his position strengthened, he could more easily ignore a right wing that remained bitter over Suez.

Almost immediately, Macmillan faced a Cabinet crisis over what to do about inflation. His difference with the Chancellor of the Exchequer, Peter Thorneycroft, later took on the look of a conflict between left and right. In fact, both Macmillan and Thorneycroft took a monetarist view, which in the 1950s meant balancing the government's budget so that it would not have to borrow. The Cabinet went far towards providing the expenditure reductions that the Chancellor wanted – including defence cuts and the end of national service. Thorneycroft, however, insisted on paring social welfare spending more. By 1958, there was considerable resentment about his stubbornness and his ideological Financial Secretary, Enoch Powell. The Cabinet saw little to gain and much to lose from cutting the additional £50 million he was insisting upon. For limits on money for pensions, family allowances and the NHS would hurt the party's middle-class constituents, as well as the upper working class that it aimed to attract. So the Cabinet dug in its heels and Thorneycroft and Powell resigned.[10] The issue was ultimately rendered irrelevant by the 1958 recession, which allowed a return to a more expansionist budget leading up to the 1959 general election.

Perhaps the most difficult of Macmillan's policies for Conservatives to swallow was decolonisation, which accelerated after 1960. Once again, however, the right was unable to make the leadership's position too uncomfortable. Many Tories had lost interest in the empire, while the dictates of larger economic and international forces, as well as party loyalty, assured that those who did care mostly remained quiet. Nor was it easy to mobilise a united front on any particular colonial issue. For example, Sir Edward Spears, a Conservative MP and chairman of Ashanti Goldfields, could do nothing to stop the movement towards independence of the Gold Coast (Ghana), where the company's holdings were, between 1951 and 1957. Although many Tory MPs had business concerns in Africa, the imperialist right had little interest in the Gold Coast and just wanted to see a peaceful transfer of power.[11]

East and Central Africa were far more controversial politically than was West Africa because they had substantial white settler populations. Macmillan's approach throughout was pragmatic rather than ideological. He would have preferred to slow down the pace of independence in order to accommodate the right, but Iain Macleod, the Colonial Secretary, was brought in to 'get a move on Africa'. He insisted on pushing forward, and he had considerable support from the younger generation of MPs.[12] The crisis came over Kenya and Northern Rhodesia in the summer of 1961.* Kenya had a significant but not enormous white minority, many of whom had been encouraged to emigrate there by British governments. At the same time, the Mau Mau movement of the 1950s seemed to imply a threat of violence to Europeans. The key issue was the release of Jomo Kenyatta from prison. Macmillan feared it would cause a revolt in the party just when he had decided to apply to join the European Common Market, which would also be resented by the right. When Macleod threatened to resign, however, Macmillan caved in. The same thing happened when the Colonial Secretary insisted on black–white parity in a new constitution for Northern Rhodesia. The Central African Federation was in danger of falling apart. Its Prime Minister, Roy Welensky, was almost hysterical in resisting a change that would hasten the process. For years Welensky had been an active and effective lobbyist in London, so he could command significant support from Tory backbenchers. Lord Home, the Foreign Secretary, and others in the British government also opposed the proposed change. Macmillan stood by Macleod in the short run, but replaced him with Reginald Maudling in the autumn, while in March 1962 he gave Butler responsibility for overseeing a settlement in Central Africa. All these changes served to conciliate the centre of the party and leave the right isolated, while hardly slowing the progress towards the break-up of the Federation and black majority rule in Northern Rhodesia (Zambia).

It may be that the party imperialists were becoming disenchanted with the empire anyway. The rank and file long ago had turned against immigration from the Caribbean and Asia. Furthermore, the Commonwealth was showing that it would not be a tool of British policy and power. For example, in 1961 the

---

* There had been an earlier crisis over the release from prison of the Nyasaland nationalist leader, Hastings Banda, and there was a concurrent crisis linked to the attempt of Katanga province to secede from the newly independent Congo. In these instances, as in the cases of Kenyatta and Northern Rhodesia, the government's policies were contrary to the wishes of the right.

new non-white nations overrode Britain's opposition to push for South Africa's expulsion because of apartheid. This was merely the final nail in the coffin of the old white Commonwealth which the Tory right most cherished. The most Anglophile of all the old dominions, Australia and New Zealand, had already been drawn into the American defence network with the ANZUS alliance of 1951. Their support of the Vietnam War in the 1960s would reflect the same kind of loyalty to the United States that they had previously shown in supporting Britain's wars in 1899, 1914 and 1939. So the imperialist right reluctantly accepted retreat from empire, while its effort to protect the interests of the white settlers in Africa was eventually narrowed to defending the secessionist regime in Southern Rhodesia.

The Labour Left Challenges Consensus Politics

The strongest challenge to the consensus came from the Labour left, not from the Tory right. The parties of the left had a long history of internal division. Nineteenth-century radicalism seemed so antipathetic to party discipline that historians cannot agree when the Liberal Party came into existence, while one has questioned whether the post-1870 Liberals were a party at all, rather than a collection of special interest groups each pursuing its own cause.[13] Historians have been kinder to the Labour Party, under the illusion that socialism embodied a shared ideology in a way that liberalism had not. Yet Labour did not formally embrace socialism until 1918, eighteen years after the founding of the party, while splits in 1931 and 1981 indicate that Labour was not much more successful than the Liberals in containing the inherent centrifugal forces within it. Two problems always beset the party of the left in Britain. First, how fast should it proceed with its reform programme? Moderates want to be certain that public opinion will accept the policies implemented, so they do not want to go too fast; while radicals believe the party was elected to implement its programme, so they see no reason to conciliate the views of the defeated opposition. Secondly, the left is usually divided on external (i.e. foreign, defence and colonial) policies. Moderates have much the same view of the policies required to assert and defend the national interest as mainstream Conservatives; while radicals believe external policy embodies party principle just as much as domestic reform does. Both of these sources of division have troubled the Labour Party of the twentieth century just as much as they did the Liberals of 1830–1914.

The leaders of the Labour government in 1945 came from the moderate wing of the party. Clement Attlee's background was middle-class professional – the group that provided many of Labour's socialists before the First World War. He had joined the Fabian Society, the home of socialist intellectuals, in 1907, soon after he graduated from Oxford. He established himself politically in London's East End, where he was engaged in settlement house work[*] with the poor. He held minor positions in the two Labour governments, but broke with MacDonald in 1931, thus catapulting himself to the top of the hierarchy as deputy leader. He succeeded George Lansbury as party leader in 1935, with the purpose of restoring Labour's credibility by moving it in a more realistic direction on foreign and defence policies. As Prime Minister, Attlee had the perfect temperament for promoting consensus. He had a strong commitment to the principles of fairness and justice that underlay Labour's programme, but that was the limit of his socialism. He was a listener, which meant he was good at brokering agreements when necessary. At the same time, he was not afraid to be decisive and to take the lead in imposing a kind of Christian abstinence on the nation in the interests of all.

Ernest Bevin, the Foreign Secretary, was the other dominant influence in the government. His background, as one of the premier trade union leaders between the wars, was completely different from Attlee's. He was driven, however, by similar

---

[*] Settlement houses were houses in deprived areas of a city where social workers lived and worked with the poor.

principles of loyalty and concern for the workers' wellbeing. He had always been a pragmatist rather than an ideological socialist in his approach to politics and foreign policy. He had helped push Lansbury out in 1935 because the leader's pacifism meant that Labour could not take a strong stand against fascism. From 1945 until his death in 1950, he was an unswerving source of support for Attlee. For example, in the spring and summer of 1947, with the economy a mess and British power in the eastern Mediterranean seemingly collapsing, there was a real sense that the government was floundering and they were on the verge of another 1931. Attlee was criticised for the weakness of his leadership and Bevin seemed to be the one man with the strength that the situation called for. Yet Bevin vetoed any change and so squelched the nascent rebellion. Instead, Attlee reshuffled the Cabinet, bringing Stafford Cripps in as Chancellor to take charge of the economic crisis, and ultimately emerged with his position strengthened and his reputation enhanced.

Five years of helping to shoulder the responsibilities of government during the war had reinforced a cautious approach to policy for all of Labour's leaders. They were supported in this by a trade union leadership that was dominated by right-wingers, some of whom identified almost any expression of left-wing opposition with Communist influence. The most plausible representatives of the left in the Cabinets of 1945–51 were Aneurin Bevan, the architect of the National Health Service, and Emmanuel Shinwell, the Minister of Fuel and Power and then Secretary for War. Neither was a major power-broker in the party. Furthermore, there was a strong consensus behind the party's domestic programme and a reservoir of support that a Labour government could draw upon when pressed. Therefore, despite considerable left-wing strength in the constituency parties, the left could not easily broaden its base in the Commons. Hence, when the 'Keep Left' group was formed in 1947 to press for more aggressive socialist planning in the face of the economic crisis that winter, it included only fifteen MPs.[14]

Perhaps the issue that best embodied the weaknesses of the

left was nationalisation. During the crises of 1947, it demanded the immediate nationalisation of iron and steel. Very quickly, however, the terms of the debate were transformed as the left had to fight to keep iron and steel nationalisation on the government's agenda at all, as moderates sought to drop it. While the left succeeded in saving this touchstone policy, it was disappointed in the limited promises of further nationalisation included in the party's next election manifesto. Nor was it happy with the programme that had been implemented. By 1949, it had developed a critique: nationalisation policies had provided excessively generous compensation, did not involve meaningful government control or planning and did not include workers' participation in management. These were the criticisms of the trade union left, where there was considerable support for industrial democracy. The mainstream of the TUC, however, was more comfortable viewing management as something to be opposed and so showed little interest in workers' participation. Nor did the government, which did not want workers interfering with policy-making in the nationalised industries. The story of nationalisation was the story of the influence of the left on domestic policy from 1945 to 1950 in general. It was almost nil, leaving many on the left feeling that a golden moment for a really radical transformation of British society had been squandered by timidity at the top.

The left was far more active in opposing the government's foreign and defence policies. There was much hope for the possibilities of a 'socialist foreign policy', though what this meant was never very clear. In part, the left was suspicious of hostility to the Soviet Union. Between the wars, such anti-communism seemed to be driven by the interests of international capitalism and by Tory political opportunism rather than by a genuine threat. After the war, the left hoped that Britain, and indeed Western Europe, could become a moderate third force between capitalist America and Communist Russia. The left also drew on the long pacifist tradition within liberalism and socialism. This tradition was rooted partly in their suspicions of an elite that sought to identify its own interests with those of the nation, and partly in an inter-nationalism that characterised both movements. It saw arms races as driven by capitalist weapons producers and an aristo-cratic officer corps which had an interest in war, while the 'balance of power' was an artificial construct of Foreign Office mandarins (also from the aristocracy) rather than a genuine necessity for European peace. The First World War had proved the failure of a foreign policy built around an arms race and the balance of power. Both the liberal and the socialist left claimed it was the product of secret diplomacy and chauvinist anti-German para-noia rather than real British interests. After 1945, the socialist left wanted the Labour Party to promote international disarma-ment, while socialist internationalism implied working with other European socialist parties or acting through international organ-isations like the United Nations to encourage international coop-eration and the arbitration of conflicts to preserve peace. Socialist anti-imperialism was shaped by many of the same concerns. The competition for empire, again driven by capitalist and aristocratic rather than national interests, was a prime cause of arms races and wars. With the end of empire, an important source of European and international conflict would disappear, while the socialist character of the Indian Congress Party under Jawaharlal Nehru hinted at new possibilities for socialist cooperation.

The Cold War exposed, as appeasement had before it, some of the contradictions in the Labour left's approach to foreign policy. Mostly, the Labour left was not Communist. Yet in 1945, many still hoped that the wartime 'popular front' of Communists and democratic socialists could be continued as the basis for re-building Europe. After all, there was much admiration for Stalin's success in industrialising the Soviet Union and defeating the Nazi onslaught. There was no sympathy, however, with Stalin's totalitarian state. The suppression of free trade unionism alone assured the hostility of the broader labour movement. Could Britain and a Labour government be friendly with such a state? The left was divided. Many fairly quickly came to the conclusion that Stalin could not be trusted. Reluctantly, they began to support

Bevin's foreign policy, although they still saw it as too hostile to Russia and too friendly to the United States. Some, however, wanted a more active cooperation with the Soviet regime, though they attacked British friendship with right-wing authoritarian governments and were fully aware of the threat of Russian imperialism. Such a position was, at the very least, somewhat contradictory.

These people were initially willing to give the Soviets the benefit of the doubt because of their suspicions of the United States, the home of unbridled capitalism. They saw American foreign policy as a vehicle for promoting the interests of business and finance and stopping the spread of socialism (as opposed to communism), rather than in any larger strategic terms. At the same time, the United States seemed to be promoting the Cold War in pursuit of its own interests. Thus, as early as November 1946, left-wing MPs introduced a motion calling for a socialist foreign policy between American capitalism and Soviet communism. It was signed by fifty-seven MPs, and while in the end no one voted for it, some one hundred abstained. The left was united in opposing the Truman Doctrine in 1947. With the launching of the Marshall Plan, however, it began to divide in its view of the US. Many became more sympathetic to American policy, although some saw it as a plot to entrench American-style capitalism in Europe. The Communist coup in Czechoslovakia and the blockade of Berlin in 1948 further consolidated the shift of most of the left to the more moderate position. Nonetheless, there remained enough nervousness about being tied to the United States for more than one hundred Labour MPs to abstain in the 1949 vote on establishing NATO.[15]

It was in Asia that the Cold War finally began to play out in a way that helped reduce the political isolation of the left. In 1949, the British resisted American pressure and recognised Communist sovereignty over China rather than support the American fiction that Chiang Kai-shek's regime in Taiwan was the legitimate government there. Yet when the Korean War broke out in 1950, Britain was America's most loyal ally as it joined the fray. To satisfy the Americans, the government had to increase defence spending well beyond what Britain's economy could comfortably afford. The Chancellor of the Exchequer, Hugh Gaitskell, therefore insisted on introducing charges for spectacles and false teeth in his 1951 budget in order to reduce non-defence spending.[*] Aneuran Bevan now emerged as the leader the left wing had lacked – one who was capable of mobilising a broader opposition within the party to the moderate leadership. A free NHS was Bevan's child, and the proposed fees were tied to a ballooning defence budget that was already troubling him. Hence, he attacked the decision to charge working people so that Britain could support a war which, after American bombing had brought in China as a combatant, was beginning to look like a dangerous crusade against communism. When Gaitskell would not budge and the Cabinet supported him, Bevan and Harold Wilson resigned. For Bevan, a free NHS symbolised the socialist achievements of 1945–50. Now the welfare state was being sabotaged by the war. In theory, this way of framing the issue should have had considerable appeal within the party. In practice, however, many still could not accept the left's view of the Cold War. People feared communism, and North Korea *had* invaded South Korea without any provocation, so that fear seemed justified. The main effect of the Cabinet resignations, therefore, was to divide Labour and help erode its credibility as a party of government. The government's policies also hurt the party with the electorate. Gaitskell's effort to counter the expansionary effects of defence spending with deflation meant that people got both rising prices and a tighter rationing regime. Both made the government more unpopular. Thus, the Bevan–Gaitskell split was also the first step in the transition of power to the Conservatives that occurred in the general election of 1951.

As was often to be the case over the next half century,

---

[*] Charges did not mean that patients paid the full cost of a pair of spectacles or a pair of false teeth, only a portion of the cost. They were like a present-day co-payment demanded by an American Health Maintenance Organization.

opposition opened the floodgates for the always simmering dissension in the Labour party – disagreements which had been contained by the necessity of supporting a Labour government. The emerging division between right and left was reinforced because the Conservatives accepted most of Labour's policies, domestic as well as foreign. So there was little for the moderate leaders of the party to attack. Indeed, they had expected the Tories to undo the welfare state and allow a return of high unemployment; when neither happened, they had no alternative strategy and thus nothing on which to fight the 1955 general election. The Labour left, however, was not enamoured of the consensus. It embraced the role of an opposition that was as much to its own leadership as it was to the government.

This division provided a stage for the continuation of the political struggle between Gaitskell and Bevan. The Cabinet battles of 1950–51 had left the two deeply suspicious of each other. Bevan did not think Gaitskell was a real socialist, while Gaitskell thought Bevan was irresponsible. Gaitskell was sensitive to criticism, especially when his integrity was impugned, and Bevan too often did just that when he attacked those he opposed. So a legacy of hostility and resentment accumulated over the years. Each thought the other would be a disaster for the party if he succeeded to the leadership, and each tended to see conspiracies by the other to seize the leadership when Attlee resigned. Conspiracy theories had some credibility because each was supported by a group of MPs who were at least as virulent in their hostility to the other side as the leaders were. Many of those involved were younger MPs who would be prominent in the party over the next thirty years – Michael Foot, Richard Crossman and Barbara Castle among the Bevanites and Roy Jenkins, Tony Crosland and William Rodgers among the Gaitskellites. They would come out of these struggles in the 1950s with a deep distrust of their opponents and an instinct to try to undermine their position in the party whenever the going got tough. The effect was to weaken Labour right up to the party split in 1981, when Jenkins and Rodgers (among others) led a secession after Foot had succeeded to the leadership of a party now dominated by the left.

Some key issues of principle divided the left and the right in the 1950s. Bevan, for example, interpreted the crisis of 1951 in terms of the Treasury's stranglehold over all policy-making, which blocked a more thoroughgoing implementation of socialism. He looked to economic planning as a means for a Labour government to break free from Treasury control. The right, by contrast, had little interest in the left's view that nationalisation was the route to socialism. In foreign policy, the left remained acutely suspicious of the United States, while Gaitskell thought that Britain had no choice but to follow the Americans as the anchor of European security. A typical issue was the American proposal to rearm West Germany in 1954. Attlee followed Churchill's lead in endorsing the American policy of incorporating West Germany more fully into the Western defence system. The left, however, was able to generate considerable opposition from a broader cross-section of the party because of the fear that the Americans were heating up the Cold War in a manner provocative to the Soviets by bringing Russia's traditional enemy into NATO.

The left's most potent issue in the 1950s was nuclear weapons. The Labour government had taken the decision to develop an atomic bomb, which was finally exploded in 1952. Britain's nuclear deterrent and the role of the American nuclear umbrella in NATO's defence strategy were part of the cross-party consensus on foreign policy. Here was a cause with which the left could attack that consensus, for nuclear disarmament had an obvious appeal to those bred in socialism's pacifist and disarmament traditions. Bevan was not opposed to Britain's nuclear deterrent; it was essential if British foreign policy was to be independent of the United States. He was appalled, however, by the prospect that a hydrogen bomb might actually be used. In 1955 he was temporarily deprived of the party whip after seeming to challenge Attlee in the Commons on the use of nuclear weapons in response to a ground attack. This crisis followed disagreement over Britain's accession to SEATO (the South-East Asia Treaty

Organization) – an attempt to replicate NATO in Asia to protect against the threat of Chinese aggression. Bevan saw SEATO as an effort to encircle China. It confirmed his fear that Britain was being tied to the whims of a fanatical American anti-communism which could foresee the use of nuclear weapons in support of conventional warfare.

The crisis over nuclear retaliation provided a pretext for Gaitskell and his allies (urged on by right-wing trade union leaders) to try to get Bevan expelled from the party. Bevan's tendency to rant against those who opposed him and to publicly embarrass the leadership alienated many MPs who would have been happy to stay out of the internal party struggle. He was saved, however, because of Attlee's opposition to expulsion and evidence that Bevan commanded significant support in the constituencies.[16] Nonetheless, four years of public bickering undoubtedly weakened the party and was one reason for its defeat in the general election in 1955. When Attlee resigned soon afterwards, the struggle between Bevan and Gaitskell came to a head. Their styles were entirely different, though neither of them had great skill in the arts of political compromise and conciliation. Bevan was the man of passion and emotion. He could not always control his emotions, however, and then he let them cloud his judgement. Gaitskell, by contrast, was an intellectual pragmatist. He was reserved and distant, though on the right occasion he could speak with feeling and conviction. Bevan was Gaitskell's senior in age and experience. Yet Attlee had chosen Gaitskell to replace Cripps as Chancellor in 1950. Bevan's image as a left-wing extremist would upset the international financial world (and the Americans), while Attlee had feared his tendency to fly off the handle. By contrast, Gaitskell had been Cripps's number two for some time, so Attlee trusted his judgement on economic issues. However neither Bevan nor the left fully accepted that Gaitskell had jumped over him in the party hierarchy.

The same factors that had weighed against Bevan in 1950 remained true in 1955. Gaitskell's easy victory in the leadership election showed that calm judgement and centrist views were what the parliamentary party most valued. Bevan immediately made his peace with Gaitskell in an attempt to close ranks. Furthermore, Bevan's line during the Suez crisis, which strongly condemned Nasser as well as the government's use of force, coincided with Gaitskell's own views while dividing him from his left-wing supporters. That division became wider when, at the 1957 party conference, he spoke decisively against a resolution for Britain to renounce its nuclear weapons.

Yet it soon became apparent that the loss of Bevan's leadership was irrelevant. Fears about American intentions, the explosion of Britain's hydrogen bomb and the doctrine of massive nuclear retaliation as the basis for national defence all were behind the founding of the Campaign for Nuclear Disarmament (CND) in 1958. CND was a non-political movement, with plenty of middle-class intellectuals, pacifists and young people as well as Labour activists and leftists of various hues at its core. It appealed to the fear of a nuclear holocaust that seemed frighteningly plausible to ordinary Britons in the late 1950s. To CND's idealists, the use of nuclear weapons was immoral, indeed criminal. They hoped that if Britain unilaterally renounced its own weapons and assured that there were no American weapons on its soil, it would re-establish its moral position as a world leader in the aftermath of the Suez embarrassment. The effect would be to bring worldwide pressure on the superpowers to negotiate an end to the nuclear arms race. The movement was really a reassertion of nineteenth-century Gladstonian liberalism: foreign policy should be determined by Christian morality. Indeed, Christian activists were well represented in both the leadership and the rank and file. More pragmatically, there was an underlying hope that if Britain had no nuclear weapons, it could escape devastation in the event of some American folly – since the presence of American weapons assured that Britain would be a target of any Soviet strike.

However non-partisan CND intended to be, though, its policy could only be implemented through political action, and the only political vehicle available was the Labour left. For the left, nuclear disarmament offered a means to broaden its base of support by taking advantage of an issue that troubled many ordinary party members. It was a way of parading its anti-American colours without pursuing a policy that was overtly anti-American, which would have turned off the moderates it was seeking to woo. It also enabled the left to attack the right-wing leadership of Gaitskell in a way that could win support from trade unionists and others who were not normally on the left wing of the party.

The battle over unilateral nuclear disarmament was part of a broader fight between Gaitskell and the left for the soul of the party. His opponents saw Gaitskell as arrogant and divorced from the moral vision that had underpinned the labour movement from its inception. With his deep commitment to equality, however, Gaitskell resented the left's insistence that theirs were the only true socialist policies. He was contemptuous of their pacifism and socialist purity when such policies were so evidently politically impossible. The effect was to turn off the non-socialist middle-class voters who had given the party its majority in 1945 and who seemed to have condemned it to permanent opposition since then. He was not alone; many serious commentators were wondering if Labour could ever win another election. For Gaitskell, the self-defeating effect of this narrow ideological purity was embodied in Clause IV of the party's constitution, which committed it to the nationalisation of all the means of production, distribution and exchange.

Tony Crosland had made the case for revising Labour's policies in his 1956 book, *The Future of Socialism*. Crosland argued that the nature and structure of capitalism had changed radically. It was no longer as irresponsible as socialist myth portrayed it, while government interventionism and strong trade unions together provided effective checks on the actions of capitalists. At the same time, a thriving private sector was not incompatible with socialist ideals of justice. On the contrary, it was necessary if there was to be economic growth, and thus both the goods that were improving people's lives and the resources to be redistributed to make a more just society. Crosland's revisionism was different from the New Labour version that would emerge in the 1990s because equality and a classless society were the central goals. Those ideals would be best approached not by nationalising industry, however. Indeed, Crosland was suspicious of nationalisation because it had created centralised monopolies, which were an inefficient way to deliver services. Instead, let the private sector produce the goods people wanted, while redistributive taxation financed adequate levels of social welfare and public investment. As the historian Jose Harris described Crosland's views, 'State provision of education, rented housing and healthcare should be raised to such a quality that the private market in these sectors would wither away from want of custom.'[17]

As a matter of practical politics, no Labour government had any intention of nationalising everything anyway. Gaitskell believed that to enshrine such an unattainable and indeed undesirable aspiration in the party's constitution merely had the effect of scaring away the vast majority who were not socialists, but who might well be attracted to the humanitarianism and egalitarianism that socialism stood for. The devastating political effect seemed clear in the party's electoral failures of the 1950s. The Conservative share of the vote remained relatively constant over the three general elections that Labour lost, fluctuating between 48 per cent and just under 50 per cent. The Labour share, however, dropped from 48.8 per cent in 1951 to 46.4 per cent in 1955 and 43.8 per cent in 1959; as a result, the Conservative majority over all parties increased from 17 in 1951 to 58 in 1955 and 100 in 1959.[18] The evidence seemed clear that the voters were not so much voting for the Conservatives as refusing to vote for Labour, even though Labour's policies in 1959 were hardly radical. Part of Labour's problem may have been a reluctance (especially on the left) to adapt to the changes in society that were coming in the late 1950s with increased prosperity. The party was too wedded to traditional modes of thinking about politics and presenting political issues. There was an excessive tendency to patronise the electorate and to moralise – telling people what they should want and what was good for them. Conservative political campaigns proved much more willing to embrace the changes brought by the emerging consumer society and advertising – changes that many on the left did not like.[19]

This resistance to change was starkly revealed when Gaitskell proposed to revise Clause IV as a signal to the electorate that Labour was no longer a class party driven by ideology. With Clause IV now gone in the wake of a more recent effort to make Labour electable, Gaitskell's campaign may seem to be little more than good sense and an appreciation of practical necessity. At the time, however, good sense could point equally in the opposite direction. For the Labour Party was steeped in myths of triumphs and betrayals. Those myths were tied to its socialist identity, and they had an appeal far beyond the left wing in defining the party's sense of itself and its mission. The adoption of the constitution of 1918, with its unambiguous commitment to socialism, coincided with Labour's emergence as the principal party of the left. The watering down of that commitment by the MacDonald governments of 1924 and 1929–31 coincided with the failure of those governments, climaxing in the 'great betrayal' in the summer of 1931. The return to a more full-blooded socialism after 1935 had been vindicated by the triumph of 1945. Thus socialism seemed to be identified with the party's success, not with its failure. What is more, many activists, both in the trade unions and in the constituencies, believed that Labour's identity as a party with a moral purpose was inextricably linked to its identity as a socialist party, and no party was going to win elections without the support of its activists. As Harold Wilson later put it, 'We were being asked to take Genesis out of the Bible. You don't have to be a fundamentalist to say that Genesis is a part of the Bible.'[20] What Wilson did not add was that the fundamentalists would desert if Genesis *were* taken out of the Bible. Gaitskell did not always understand this kind of emotional and even irrational appeal. He had been warned early that the trade unions were unalterably opposed to such a change. The breadth of opposition became unmistakable at the party conference in November 1959, while it opened up a new opportunity for the left to attack him for not being a true socialist. With the left mobilising against him the next year on the nuclear issue, Gaitskell backed away rather than weakening his position by pushing for revision and failing to secure it.

Thus, the real showdown came over nuclear disarmament. For the left, the issue seemed to offer an opportunity to remove Gaitskell, whose standing, especially with the unions, had been weakened by the Clause IV conflict. The fact that the new leader of the TGWU, Frank Cousins, was on their side merely strengthened their position. The success of their strategy became evident at the 1960 Labour Party conference, when some of the large unions helped pass a resolution in favour of unilateral nuclear disarmament by a narrow majority. It was a triumph that Gaitskell was determined to reverse. Once again, the battle was between his pragmatism and the left's idealism. This time, however, Gaitskell's position was stronger than it looked. There was broad public support for NATO (though less for the American bases), and the extremists on the left who supported unilateral nuclear disarmament envisaged a neutralist Britain outside the Cold War. Consequently, it was easy to argue that they were undermining the alliance and Britain's security. Furthermore, the alternative proposal of negotiating for multilateral disarmament, while trying to persuade NATO to be less reliant on nuclear weapons, was so reasonable, especially in the face of a Soviet threat that most people accepted as real, that Gaitskell's position was surely the more popular one with the electorate. Lastly, Gaitskell himself was gaining in stature by standing up to the left. Many people, even unilateralists, resented the personal attacks on him by his enemies in the party and wanted an end to the internal bickering. Gaitskell therefore was able to secure a reversal of the 1960 resolution at the next party conference in 1961 by a decisive majority, although even then the conference voted against an American Polaris base in Scotland.

At the same time, CND began to fade from the scene. While a crowd of one hundred thousand joined the annual march from the Aldermaston nuclear research centre to London in 1961, the more radical wing wanted a strategy of civil disobedience. Some 12,000 people participated in a sit-down demonstration in Trafalgar Square that September, resulting in prison sentences for many of the leaders. The next year, the Cuban missile crisis showed that the superpowers were not going to fight a nuclear war. Thereafter, left-wing activists turned their attention to other issues – like opposing British entry into the EEC and the Vietnam War.

Christine Keeler and Harold Wilson

Between 1958 and 1961, Labour was behaving very much like a party that was falling apart. Neither for the first time nor the last, it seemed unable to define a common vision of socialism that would unify the party. And a divided party lacked credibility with the electorate as a party of government. Yet it was the Conservatives rather than Labour who actually self-destructed over the next few years. Suddenly, the master politician Harold Macmillan lost his touch. In part it was because, having led the Tories to an increased majority in 1959 – an unheard of achievement for a party coming off two consecutive election victories – Macmillan became more aloof and divorced from his back-benchers. More importantly, however, policy-making started to go wrong. The Conservatives always claimed that they had two advantages over Labour: they were more prudent and competent managers of the economy, and they were more effective custodians of Britain's overseas interests. Yet having won in 1959 on the basis that things were never so good, they now had to face up to the mounting evidence that Britain was not doing as well economically as the rest of Western Europe. As Tory chancellors vacillated between contraction in 1961–2 and expansion in 1963–4, they seemed to have no notion of how to remedy the situation. Tory foreign policy, too, appeared to be a failure. For, having rejected participation in the movement towards European economic integration throughout the fifties, the government now reversed itself and sought to join the new and obviously successful

EEC. Indeed, membership was the centrepiece of the government's new economic strategy. President de Gaulle's veto of British entry in 1963 merely confirmed the impression that somehow the Tories had misjudged the whole situation in Europe and thus had left Britain weakened compared to France and West Germany.

In an attempt to reverse this image of failure, Macmillan decided on a major Cabinet reshuffle in July 1962. He substituted Reginald Maudling for Selwyn Lloyd as Chancellor, while sacking a slew of older ministers and replacing them with a new generation. His aim was to re-energise the government and give it the appearance of being directed more towards the future than the past. Yet this so-called 'night of the long knives', in which Macmillan replaced no fewer than one-third of his Cabinet (the largest turnover in a Cabinet shake-up in British history), was quickly judged a failure. It was carried out in a particularly brutal way, as Macmillan dumped several long-time friends with no warning. Thus, it further discredited his leadership, as his image of aristocratic unflappability was shattered. Yet the whole fiasco probably made little difference to the standing of the party. When Cabinet reshuffles work, they are a sign of strong, decisive leadership; when they do not, they are a sign of panic.[21] The Conservatives' record of by-election losses in 1962 continued unabated both before and after the reshuffle, indicating that it hardly mattered.

The immediate beneficiary of these Tory problems, however, was not the divided Labour Party, but a revived Liberal Party that had been on the margins of British politics since its final split in 1932. The Liberal representation had declined since the war from twelve MPs in 1945 to six in the general elections of the 1950s, with much of it centred in Wales. Evidence of change began in 1961 and 1962, with a small stream of municipal election victories and second-place finishes in parliamentary by-elections. In March 1962 the Liberal candidate only just lost a by-election in the solidly Conservative seat of Blackpool North, and the next day another Liberal won the even more solidly

Conservative seat of Orpington in Kent. Voters in these traditionally Tory constituencies clearly viewed the Liberals as the alternative to the Conservatives when the Labour Party was divided or seemed too much under the influence of its left wing. This would continue to be the Liberals' role in the future, as their fortunes to some degree fluctuated inversely with those of Labour – at least until 1997.

The climax to the Tory collapse was the Profumo scandal of the summer of 1963. John Profumo, the Minister for War, had been having an affair with a call girl, Christine Keeler, who had also been sleeping with a Russian diplomat. When the scandal was first breaking, Profumo denied in the House of Commons that there was any sexual relationship between himself and Keeler. It was this lie, rather than any hint of a security leak, that cost Profumo his job. The real damage, however, was to the image of the Tory elite, who now were associated in the public mind with a call-girl racket supposedly run by the bisexual osteopath Stephen Ward, who committed suicide following his conviction for living off the earnings of prostitutes. The smell of aristocratic decadence could hardly have been stronger. These men certainly did not look like the natural governors of the nation. And the Prime Minister had been unaware of the whole thing! Macmillan's reputation for political canniness had already suffered numerous hits from the problems of the past three years, and the Profumo scandal seemed to confirm the impression that he was out of touch. The press, with whom Macmillan had been waging a war of attrition for several years, went after him with a vengeance, while party discontent came close to forcing his resignation.

Macmillan hesitated. He was tired, but the party's standing in the polls was rallying by September. His hand was forced when he required emergency surgery in October, on the very eve of the party conference. Butler was the obvious successor. He had been deputising for Macmillan while he was in the hospital, had been the number two man in the government for years and was almost surely the preference of the majority of the Cabinet. Macmillan, however, never thought he would do as party leader, reflecting a lack of generosity for years of loyal support. Butler could never escape a perception that he was weak – a perception that is reinforced by his failure to put up any sort of fight as Macmillan manipulated and used him over the many years of their relationship. Furthermore, he was *persona non grata* on the right: he had been associated in recent years with a leftish management of the Home Office and the break-up of the Central African Federation. Finally, he did not generate much enthusiasm; his very longevity of service meant that he represented no significant break from the past when one seemed to be needed. Macmillan's preference was Lord Hailsham, but he flubbed this advantage at the party conference. Thereafter, Macmillan constructed a consultation process that came down in support of his new preferred successor, the Foreign Secretary the Earl of Home (who was not even publicly a candidate). Home, who forswore his peerage and became Sir Alec Douglas-Home, had no background as a party leader in the Commons, no experience of working on domestic political issues and limited skills as a public speaker. The argument offered in his favour was that he could unite the party because he was the candidate whom the fewest people disliked. The secrecy of the process by which he was selected alienated many, however, and he was hardly known at all to the public. Two potential young stars, Enoch Powell and Iain Macleod, refused to serve under him, thus undercutting the claim that he was a unifier, while at sixty he hardly represented the coming generation.[22] Yet all of the leadership candidates except Hailsham seemed dull. It looked as if the Tories had nothing exciting to offer the electorate after thirteen years of power.

The contrast with Labour could not have been more striking. This, in itself, was something of a shock, since the party had spent so many years in the political wilderness, many of them knifing each other. Signs of a Labour revival began to appear in 1962, when the party gained its first seat in a by-election since the general election in 1959. However, while Gaitskell's leadership clearly had been strengthened by his battle over nuclear

THE AGE OF CONSENSUS

disarmament, it is difficult to escape the impression that his sudden death in 1963 was an important factor in transforming Labour's fortunes. Gaitskell, like his great antagonist Bevan, had been a divisive figure. The left never forgave him for his triumph at their expense when he was elected leader and was always on the lookout for an opportunity to pounce on him. At the same time, Gaitskell's own actions had undermined his attempts to be a conciliator and had contributed to the tumultuous politics of 1959–61. The death of Bevan in 1960 and Gaitskell in 1963 offered Labour the opportunity for a fresh start with fresh men.

Like Gaitskell, the new leader, Harold Wilson, was an Oxford economist, but otherwise the two differed radically. Wilson had resigned with Bevan in 1950 over the introduction of NHS charges and the expansion of defence spending required by the Korean War. As a result, he always retained the image of a man of the left. In reality, however, he was part of the pragmatic centre of the party. He followed Bevan in reconciling with Gaitskell's leadership; however, he thought Gaitskell's handling of the Clause IV and unilateral disarmament issues was a disaster. Wilson therefore challenged him for the party leadership in the autumn of 1960, securing one-third of the votes. Thus, he was well positioned to win the contest to be Gaitskell's successor. Although the right wing saw him as an opportunist, their own candidate, George Brown, was unacceptable to many MPs because of his temperament. Thus, Wilson was able to defeat him on the second ballot.

Wilson turned out to be just the person to pull the Labour Party back together. Gaitskell had lacked the political skills to deal effectively with those whom he did not like. Wilson, on the other hand, was a master politician who sought to smooth over the rough edges of political debate in a party whose members always seemed to be looking to fight among themselves over ideology. No one in British politics since Lloyd George had been so assiduous at promoting agreement by obfuscating the real points of difference between two sides in a dispute. Furthermore, Gaitskell had never been a great speaker, while Wilson was a superb performer who could energise his parliamentary following with the apt sarcasm at the expense of the opposition. Finally, he looked the part of a leader. John Kennedy had shown the importance of image (especially television image) to political success; so, in his own way, had Macmillan. The middle-class Wilson could convey simultaneously the folksiness of the working man with the Yorkshire accent and the intellectual weight of the former Oxford don without the snobbery of Gaitskell. Thus, unlike Attlee, he was not an aloof figure, distanced from the people; he was one of them.

The contrast between Wilson, the man of the people, and Home, the aristocrat, was even starker than that between Wilson and the previous generation of Labour leaders. At forty-six, Wilson exuded youth and energy; yet having been President of the Board of Trade in the Labour government of 1945–50, he had administrative as well as political experience. Home, by contrast, seemed far removed from the knock-about world of party politics, although he had been a backbencher representing a Highland constituency for many years before he succeeded to his title. His administrative experience, in foreign and colonial affairs, was also more divorced than Wilson's from the economic problems that were becoming the preoccupation of the 1960s.

Labour exploited the differences between them in the 1964 election campaign. For the first time since the war, Britain's decline was placed at the centre of a general election. Labour offered science and technology plus a managerial revolution as solutions to Britain's economic problems. On the one hand, this modernisation campaign evoked the image of a Conservative Party and leadership that were bound by generation and tradition to an obsolete past and class which had left British industry hamstrung. On the other hand, the images it projected of the Labour Party and its leadership connoted youth, the energy of the classes who were excluded from authority and all that was modern. Thus, only Labour had the ability to mobilise the most up-to-date methods of planning, economic organisation and technological innovation that were needed to propel Britain's economy out of the doldrums of the past and into a dynamic future. A second set of images contrasted a Labour Party relying on scientific and economic expertise to revitalise the economy with a Tory Party whose resources were limited to Eton-educated amateurs. These images not only highlighted all the Tories' problems of recent years; they also conveyed a radical break with Labour's own recent past – with its fixation on issues like nationalisation and nuclear disarmament that were marginal to both the concerns of ordinary voters and the economic problems which everyone accepted were at the heart of the nation's wellbeing.

With all of these apparent advantages, however, Labour was only barely able to eke out a victory, with a margin of thirteen over the Conservatives and of only four over all parties combined. Labour's vote was actually smaller than it had been in 1959, for many of those who deserted the Tories voted for the Liberals. In part, the Conservatives' respectable showing was because Home had done well in establishing his credibility with the electorate as a man of integrity. As a result, Labour's big lead in the polls faded away before the dissolution, as it had in 1959. Given the enormous burden of having been in power for thirteen years (no party in the modern era had won four consecutive elections until the Tories did it from 1979 to 1992), the party of Home was hardly a discredited band. It failed, in the end, because too much had gone wrong after 1960, and it had nothing new to offer the electorate when something new seemed desperately to be needed to reverse the nation's perceived economic decline. All this was part of the Macmillan legacy. The Conservatives looked and acted like a party whose time had run out, and this was not an image that Home was well suited to combat.

PART II: 1964–1979
CRISIS

5

UNDERSTANDING ECONOMIC DECLINE

Progress or Decline?

In the 1960s, the British began to believe that their economy was not performing as well as it should. The resulting national angst steadily increased over the next two decades, as people worried about what was wrong and what needed to be done to get the economy back on track. Yet all government efforts seemed to have no effect. So the problem of economic performance increasingly came to be identified with a broader sense of Britain's decline. After all, this was the economy that had once dominated the world. If it could no longer compete effectively, surely there could be no more powerful evidence of long-term national decline! The very concept of 'national decline' as it evolved in this context implied a failure of character, and so the British began to ask what was wrong with themselves. The answers focused on human failures – of entrepreneurs, of workers, of politicians, of a population worn out by war and now seeking comfort and security.

Yet the very evidence of decline is partial and ambiguous. It is shaped by the judgements of economists first and foremost, and by politicians following in their wake, who define certain data as fundamentally important in evaluating an economy. The starting point for almost everyone is economic growth. By the historical standard of Britain's past growth, however, it is not clear what all the fuss was about, for the British economy had never performed as well as it did in the twenty-five years after the Second World War. Table 5.1 below shows Britain's economic performance from 1856 to 1979, as measured by the average annual growth rate of gross domestic product (GDP). However that average is calculated, the post-war era was one of unique prosperity. Furthermore, the story would not change if we went

Table 5.1. Average Annual Growth Rates, 1856–1979

	GDP (%)	GDP/person (%)	GDP/ employee (%)
1856–73	2.2	1.4	1.3
1873–1913	1.8	0.9	0.9
1924–37	2.2	1.8	1.0
1951–73	2.8	2.3	2.4
1973–9	1.3	1.3	1.1

Source: N. F. R. Crafts and N. W. C. Woodward, 'The British Economy since 1945: Introduction and Overview', in Crafts and Woodward, *The British Economy since 1945*, p. 7.

back earlier. A different set of estimates, for example, puts the average growth rate of real GDP at 2 per cent from 1801 to 1831 and 2.5 per cent from 1830 to 1860.[1]

It may seem counterintuitive that Britain's economy was performing better during this period of perceived failure than during the heyday of the Industrial Revolution. Yet it is not! The Industrial Revolution occurred in just a few industries: the spinning and weaving of cotton goods and then of all textiles; the smelting and refining of iron ore; and the movement of goods and people by railway. The rest of the British economy was still relatively backward – that is, it still used pre-industrial methods of production, even such 'modern' industries as coal mining and the making of engines. Even British agriculture, which was very advanced by the standards of the period, had low levels of productivity; and in 1851, agriculture still employed a quarter of the adult male population. Since the average growth rate of GDP is an annual *average* of the whole economy, during the early years of British economic expansion the fast growth rates in the rapidly industrialising sectors were being counterbalanced by the slow growth rates in those parts of the economy that were still untouched by mechanisation. As more and more of the economy was modernised, however, the drag of traditional sectors was reduced, while growth in the sectors that industrialised early slowed down. Thus we are left with the paradox that, even though the British economy suffered from prolonged unemployment in the old industries of the Industrial Revolution between 1924 and 1937, the strength of the rest of the economy assured that the average annual growth rate during that period of depression was the same as during the heyday of Victorian prosperity from 1856 to 1873, and only slightly lower than during the railway boom of 1830–60.

There was a second factor which slowed down the ability of Britain's economy to grow from 1780 to 1850 when compared with today's economy. The rest of the world was economically backward then, which limited the foreign demand for British goods. So it is hardly surprising that Britain after 1950 was able to achieve historically high growth rates. Many more parts of the world were in a position to buy a much wider range of goods than a hundred years earlier, and the number of competitors was limited because of the war. As a result, even the 'sick' industries of the Industrial Revolution were able to prosper for a while. The modern economy was so strong that, even during the tumultuous 1970s, its performance was no worse than it had been before the First World War.[2]

The human benefits of this prosperity were unprecedented, and it is just this pay-off that economists sometimes discount when measuring economic performance. Most important was the low level of unemployment. Table 5.2 overleaf shows the unemployment rates for the United Kingdom in selected years between 1929 and 1979. Between 1950 and 1966, the rate fluctuated between 1 and 2.1 per cent, while even in 1979, after a decade of economic

Table 5.2. United Kingdom Unemployment Rate, 1929–79

1929	1937	1951	1964	1973	1979
9.7%	10.1%	1.3%	1.7%	2.0%	4.7%

Source: S. N. Broadberry, 'Unemployment', in Crafts and Woodward, *The British Economy since 1945*, p. 217.

crisis and industrial turmoil, the rate was still far lower than during the inter-war years. Furthermore, once again, if we went back even further, the unprecedented nature of the post-war era would be confirmed. While specific years between 1870 and 1920 would show the low levels of unemployment of the period from 1945 to 1970, the long-term tendency in the earlier period was for radical fluctuation.[3] Economists attribute this long period of steady full employment to the expansive nature of the world economy, which meant that British industry could sell its exports, and this in turn helped stimulate an investment boom.

The effect of low unemployment, in conjunction with the revamped welfare state and the general level of prosperity, was to reduce poverty radically. Poverty is notoriously difficult to measure. Should we use an absolute measure, based on someone's judgement of what is necessary to maintain a minimum standard of living (or should it be an *adequate* standard of living)? Or should we use a relative measure, based on the number of families whose income falls a defined percentage below the national average family income? Whatever measurement is used, the tendency has been for the norm to increase over the decades in industrialised countries, as the overall standard of living has gone up – and with it either the national average family income or the general conception of what is an acceptable minimum. So the standard of living of those in poverty in a later era will usually be higher than that of those in poverty in an earlier era. Indeed, the modern poor surely have a higher standard of living than many of the employed working class of the beginning of this century, who would have been judged then to be above the poverty level. Attempts to measure urban poverty at the turn of the century, based on a minimum standard of subsistence, concluded that at any one time, about 10 per cent of the population lived in acute poverty, and another 20 per cent lived on the verge of acute poverty, usually slipping into it several times in their lives. So we can take as a very rough guess a poverty rate around 30 per cent before the advent of the modern welfare state, though many more would fall into poverty at some time in their lives. By the 1960s, that rate had dropped to somewhere between 5 and 10 per cent, or even lower, and it remained there in the 1970s.[4] This represented a staggering improvement on anything that the British economy achieved in the era of world domination.

Given this astonishing record of success, where does the perception of failure come from? First and foremost, it is the result of the fact that the rest of the industrialised world seemed to be doing even better. Table 5.3 below compares Britain's growth

Table 5.3. Comparative Annual Average Growth Rates, 1950–73

	GDP (%)	GDP/person-hour (%)
France	5.1	5.0
Italy	5.5	5.5
Japan	9.7	7.6
UK	3.0	3.2
USA	3.7	2.4
West Germany	6.0	6.0

Source: Crafts and Woodward, 'The British Economy since 1945: Introduction and Overview', in Crafts and Woodward, *The British Economy since 1945*, p. 8.

rate with that of some of the other major industrialised nations. The shocking part of these statistics for Britons was not their economic weakness compared to Japan and West Germany, but their weakness compared to France and Italy, two countries long deemed Britain's economic inferiors. As a result, Britain's comparability with the United States tended to be ignored. Britain's relatively slow growth rate ultimately affected its international standing among the wealthiest nations of the world. In 1950, only the United States, Switzerland, Canada and Australia – all countries untouched by war damage – surpassed Britain in GDP per person. By 1973, Denmark, France, the Netherlands, Sweden and West Germany also equalled or surpassed Britain.[5] Yet these statistics may exaggerate how poorly Britain did. For if one looks at real GDP per person-hour (thus taking into account how much work people were doing), Japan ranked 16 in 1950, 1973, and 1997. While Britain's ranking fell from 5 to 11 between 1950 and 1973, it stayed there in 1997.[*] In other words, Japan's spectacular growth was achieved partly because workers were willing to work longer hours for less return.[6] One could say this reflected the fact that the British workers were lazy and did not want to work (something which *was* said). Leisure, however, is a product that people demand like any other, and we have seen in the 1990s that Japan's economy was not able to sustain growth based on demanding more from its workforce without compensating benefits for them.

Britain's decline was also signalled by its poor performance in manufacturing exports. Its role as the first industrial nation and its domination of the world economy in the nineteenth century had been symbolised by the worldwide reach of its export industries. Its pre-eminent position inevitably declined with the emergence of other industrialising countries, but it was artificially restored by the Second World War, which wiped out the productive capacity of most of them. These competitors were

---

[*] The country that improved the most by this measurement was France, which was ranked 10 in 1950 and 1 in 1997.

bound to revive after the war, and the number grew, as developing countries in Asia and Latin America appeared on the scene. Still, none of the other major industrial powers was quite so adversely affected by this competition as Britain. Table 5.4 below tracks Britain's performance, as it retreated from a position of near parity with the United States to one of near parity with a French economy that historically had not been very export-oriented.[7] By the 1970s, Britain's manufacturing weakness was also evident in the inability of key industries – like cars and steel – even to compete in the home market. By the 1980s, for the first time since the Industrial Revolution, Britain was importing more manufactured goods than it was exporting. So there were problems in British industry that need to be explained.

Table 5.4. Share of World Manufactured Exports, 1950–79

	1950 (%)	1960 (%)	1970 (%)	1979 (%)
France	9.9	9.6	8.7	10.5
Japan	3.4	6.9	11.7	13.7
UK	22.5	16.5	10.8	9.1
USA	27.3	21.6	18.5	16.0
West Germany	7.3	19.3	19.8	20.9

Source: Crafts and Woodward, 'The British Economy since 1945: Introduction and Overview', in Crafts and Woodward, *The British Economy since 1945*, p.12.

Britain's relative economic decline came to be especially identified with its performance in two linked areas: inflation and labour productivity. In neither case was Britain's performance as bad as later mythology came to portray it – or at least not until the crisis years of 1973–9. Table 5.5 overleaf shows that until 1964, Britain's inflation record compared very well with that of

Table 5.5. Comparative Inflation Rates, 1950–81

	1950–64 (%)	1965–73 (%)	1974–81 (%)
France	6.0	5.0	11.0
Japan	4.2	6.2	7.0
UK	4.0	5.9	16.0
USA	2.2	4.3	8.4
West Germany	3.2	4.5	4.7

Source: Crafts and Woodward, 'The British Economy since 1945: Introduction and Overview', in Crafts and Woodward, *The British Economy since 1945*, p. 6.

its competitors – once again showing that, as with unemployment, in the short term the 'stop-go' economic policies worked fairly well. Even in the period from 1965 to 1973, Britain's inflation performance was better than that of the high-powered Japanese economy. It was only following the two gigantic oil price increases of 1973 and 1979 that Britain's policy-makers clearly failed, just as it was in this period that West Germany's revealed themselves as the stars of inflation control.

Britain's inflation problem was at least partly the result of poor productivity. Yet the record for worker productivity was also somewhat ambiguous. The usual comparative measure used is the rate of growth of output per worker. Table 5.6 opposite shows that Britain's growth rates tended to be below those of its chief competitors, dating all the way back to the 1870s. Worse still, the gap between Britain and the others (except the United States) increased after the Second World War, even though Britain was achieving record rates of growth in productivity.[8] Yet this whole mode of comparison places Britain at a disadvantage; for Britain's biggest gains in productivity had taken place between 1760, when the Industrial Revolution in textiles began, and 1873. In fact, if we look at real GDP per hour worked (i.e. not the rate of growth,

Table 5.6. Comparative Average Annual Growth of Real Output per Worker Employed, 1873–1979

	1873–99 (%)	1899–1913 (%)	1924–37 (%)	1951–64 (%)	1964–73 (%)	1973–9 (%)
France	1.3	1.6	1.4	4.3	4.6	2.8
Japan	1.1	1.8	2.7	7.6	8.4	2.9
UK	1.2	0.5	1.0	2.3	2.6	1.2
USA	1.9	1.3	1.4	2.5	1.6	-0.2
West Germany	1.5	1.5	3.0	5.1	4.4	2.9

Source: N. F. R. Crafts, 'Economic Growth', in Crafts and Woodward, *The British Economy since 1945*, p. 261.

but the absolute level), then Britain was ahead of France, Germany and Japan prior to the outbreak of the Second World War, while it was well behind the United States. Inevitably, after the war Britain was even further behind the United States and ahead of the other three. So the three countries that were catching up after the war saw their worker productivity grow faster than Britain and the United States. Yet when comparing the actual levels of productivity, Japan's remained strikingly low compared to Britain's. If the British level is given an index value of 100, Japan's had an index value of 36 in 1938 (i.e. it was about one-third the level of Britain's); because of the war, it was only 34 in 1960; but it was still only 64 in 1973 and 69 in 1984. In other words, the star of industrial production achieved a worker productivity level that was about two-thirds of Britain's in the 1970s and 1980s. By contrast, West Germany and France had surpassed Britain by 1973, though not by a lot.[9] Britain, however, was closing its productivity gap with the United States. Thus, the trend since the war was towards a convergence among the industrial countries, while Britain's productivity clearly was not as pathetic as the economic literature would lead us to believe.

One reason why Britain's competitors could achieve bigger productivity gains, even after they had made up for their devastation after the war, was because they could transfer resources from agriculture, which has low productivity, to manufacturing, which has high productivity. In other words, in West Germany, France and Japan, the agricultural sector was shrinking between 1950 and 1979, and the manufacturing sector was growing. This transfer had taken place in Britain between 1760 and 1914; agriculture couldn't be shrunk much more. Furthermore, Britain's problems were not universal throughout the economy. For example, it is not clear how much Britain's relative decline in productivity was in manufacturing, as opposed to transportation, utilities, communications or social overhead sectors of the economy.[10] Even within manufacturing, the difficulties were concentrated in a few industries: cars, iron and steel and shipbuilding, as well as coal mining. These industries will come up over and over again as the focus of many of Britain's problems, including bad industrial relations, weak management and inadequate research and development.

All these statistics show how difficult it is to measure the success or failure of an economy. The United States, supposedly the economic superpower of the world, hardly performed better than Britain, if the measure is average annual growth per person-hour or average annual growth of worker productivity. Yet the United States was way ahead of Britain in overall worker productivity. Japan had staggeringly high average annual growth rates of GDP and worker productivity, but with relatively high inflation until the late 1970s and persistently low absolute levels of worker productivity. Britain's own performance, while not quite up to the level of the other four powers that are measured in the above tables, was very respectable on a comparative basis until 1973–9. Furthermore, Britain's performance in providing for the well-being of its people – as measured by employment, a safety net that kept them out of poverty, and improved standards of living – was outstanding. There are two reasons why Britain's economic decline in this period has been exaggerated. First, when evaluating economic performance, economists discount measures of social wellbeing compared with what they judge to be more important purely economic measures. Second, the critics of socialism and purveyors of decline found it politically useful to treat the years 1973–9 as representative of the nation's performance for the whole era from 1945 to 1979.

One aspect of decline *was* unambiguous: the performance of Britain's manufacturing industries, as reflected by their decreasing competitiveness. By the 1980s, France's industrial production was double Britain's, and West Germany's was three times as large.[11] This decline was a product of the problems evident since the end of the First World War of those industries that were at the heart of Britain's Industrial Revolution. Decline in these industries was inevitable, though not the extent of the decline. In all industrialised nations, textiles, steel and shipbuilding were subject to increased competition by the 1970s from new competitors which had far lower labour costs. It might be possible for a European country to continue to compete, as Italy has done in shoes and clothing, by aiming at specialised markets – usually at the richer end of the trade. British textiles did not make this adjustment any better than American manufacturers did, and by the 1980s both were being overrun by Asian competitors. Coal had been subject to competition since the First World War, first from oil and later from natural gas as well. While Britain was able to limit the decline in domestic demand through the 1970s (partly because of artificial subsidies), coal was hammered as a major exporter in the inter-war years and never recovered thereafter. Thus, far more than for later competitors, the shape of Britain's economy had been defined in the nineteenth century, so it was going to be staggered by the emergence of a different world economy in the twentieth century. Furthermore, for all the economically most advanced nations the long-term trend since the 1960s was towards a decline in the manufacturing sector in the face of new competitors, and so the restructuring of their economies away from industry towards services. This trend began earlier in Britain, partly because of the long-term problems of the 'sick' industries of the Industrial Revolution. More importantly, however, Britain's historic strength in providing financial services and, more recently, its role as a magnet for tourists made it easier and less costly to move into service sectors than into new and risky industrial ventures. It is important to keep these long-term trends in mind as we turn to the explanations for decline and try to judge whether and how it might have been slowed or reversed.

Culture and Entrepreneurship

Whatever the strengths of the British economy between 1950 and 1973, and however ambiguous the character of economic decline, the fact remains that by the mid-1960s there was a general perception that the British economy was failing compared to its peers. Much of the next fifteen years (and since) was given over to trying to understand the reasons for that failure. The rest of this chapter will explore the explanations that have been offered. In doing so, it will inevitably adopt the language of decline and failure, since they are what is being explained. Thus, the previous section must be taken as an assertion of the qualified nature of the economic decline that is being analysed hereafter.

Given the impression of failure, it is not surprising that many cultural explanations for decline were offered. The search was for something about the British people themselves that would account for their inability to compete effectively in the international marketplace. Generally economists do not like cultural explanations. Economic theory premises a rational 'economic man' who acts in a way to maximise economic wellbeing. If the economy is not performing as well as it should, this failure is not because people do not behave like 'economic man'. Rather, it is because obstructions with the market lead the rational economic actors to make decisions which contribute to a less than optimal performance by the economy as whole. Yet if Britain's government, welfare state and trade unions were part of the problem because they interfered with the market, the reasons they did so were themselves culturally determined. So we are left in the contradictory position of implicitly accepting cultural explanations for the behaviour of politicians, civil servants and workers, but not for businessmen and entrepreneurs. The historian, who is an interdisciplinary animal, tends to be sceptical that one set of explanations is correct to the exclusion of all others, and so is uncomfortable with the complete rejection of cultural explanations for economic phenomena. And indeed, some economists have begun to turn to them – even blaming businessmen who showed little interest in change, stuck with outdated management organisations and made insufficient effort to provide customers with what they might want.[12]

Between 1960 and 1980, explanations for Britain's economic failure tended to focus on one of two problems: inadequate investment or high inflation. Explanations focusing on investment were concerned with the supposed failure of British industrialists to modernise the old nineteenth-century industries, the apparent failure of British entrepreneurs to move into new industries aggressively enough and the seeming inability of British industrialists to compete effectively internationally and finally at home. The first two failures assumed insufficient investment in British industry; all three assumed some failure of entrepreneurship. Inflation-related explanations saw the reason for any failure of British competitiveness in prices that were too high by the standards of the world market. These explanations blamed politicians and trade unions (though sometimes businessmen too) for policies that led to inefficient production methods that kept prices high.

The explanations that posit a failure of entrepreneurship are most obviously cultural, since they are not based on economic actors responding to market conditions. Historians have been looking at possible entrepreneurial failure from the period of the so-called 'Great Depression' of 1873–96 on. Their explanations have started with the structure of British society as it evolved in the nineteenth century. There are two central premises: the value system of the Victorian elite represented a fusion of the values of the eighteenth-century landed aristocracy and those of the middle class that emerged during the Industrial Revolution; however, it was the values of the aristocracy that shaped attitudes towards status and making money.[13] The aristocracy was not against making money. On the contrary, many aristocrats were just the kind of profit maximisers that economists love, financing the modernisation of agriculture and transportation that were so important to the Industrial Revolution. Nonetheless, while making the family rich was a good thing, there was a status hierarchy that defined the most acceptable ways to earn a living and bring in income. Roughly, that status hierarchy was as follows: land, the professions (including government service and the clergy), finance, trade and manufacturing. Thus, to the degree that British upper and middle classes accepted this hierarchy, there would be a status disincentive to going into industry – even among those who wanted to be capitalists rather than landowners or professionals. Thus Britain's 'best and brightest' in general – inevitably there would be a large number of exceptions – would opt to be civil servants, lawyers and bankers rather than entrepreneurs.

Furthermore, these values were reinforced by Britain's education system, for they were taught at the public schools where the upper class had long sent their sons. The number of these schools expanded radically in the Victorian era to accommodate the many middle-class capitalists and professionals who were joining Britain's economic and political elite, and the new public schools propagated much the same value system as the older and more prestigious ones. These values emphasised the importance of public service and discounted the value (and status) of profit maximisation. While significant numbers of school-leavers went into business, status went with service to the state, not making lots of money. The same values were taught at Cambridge and Oxford. These became the values of Britain's ever-expanding professional classes over the next century, including those who went into business.[14]

In Britain, unlike the United States, business was not considered a profession until very recently. When American students think of professional schools, the big three since the Second World War have been law, medicine and business. Britain did not have the American system of professional schools. After the Butler Act, British education encouraged early specialisation at undergraduate level, even for aspiring lawyers and doctors. The professional supplemented the undergraduate degree by a combination of advanced degree and/or apprenticeship. Businessmen did not even pursue an undergraduate degree. They learned on the job, just as they had in the nineteenth century. Indeed, there was a real hostility within the business community to the formal training of managers, which was shown in the 1950s and 1960s as they resisted American pressures to introduce business training into the universities. Managers believed that business was an art, a skill one was born with and then honed by experience on the job. The pressure for change came from politicians, not businessmen. Even after the first business schools were launched in Manchester and London in the mid-1960s, and other universities and polytechnics created departments of management, business showed relatively little interest. At the same time, these programmes were viewed within the university communities as second class, and so commanded little respect and carried a low status. As a result, those who went into manufacturing in the 1950s and 1960s had no professional training for the job – not as managers, as in the United States, nor as engineers, as on the Continent. On the contrary, those at the top were chosen by boards dominated by men who were educated at the public schools and Oxbridge but who had no business education at all. Thus, it was the norm in smaller firms for managers to have no degree, and it was not uncommon at large corporations.[15] The messages in this system were clear: business did not carry professional status; business did not require higher education; therefore, those who aspired to a status defined by education and profession should not go into business.

How much did such status disincentives affect the quality of people who went into industry? It is difficult to tell how many talented men chose to go into a profession rather than business because all the signals they received from their family and their peers, as well as from the social environment in which they grew up, indicated that status attached to the former but not to the latter – and indeed, that wanting to make a lot of money was a bit 'common'. Looking at the question from the other side, it is difficult to tell whether those who went into business, and especially into industry, were an inferior lot. For plenty did go into business. The number of Oxford graduates going into industry and commerce increased substantially over the course of the century – from 16 to 20 per cent from 1900 to 1939 to 42 per cent in 1960–70. Yet by the 1960s, while an awful lot of Britain's ruling elite everywhere – in politics and the civil service, press and broadcasting, finance and education – came out of the most prestigious public schools and/or Oxford and Cambridge, the manufacturing sector provided a relatively small portion of that elite.[16] Much economic policy was being articulated and implemented by that elite, especially those at the Treasury and the Bank of England. Yet these people were no better trained to manage an economy than to manage a business. As a result, the economic historian B. W. E. Alford thinks that this higher civil service has much to answer for in explaining Britain's economic failures.[17]

The education argument that has been developed thus far pertains to the sons of the elite. Presumably, the sons of everyone else would still find business an attractive way to make money and improve status, and there should have been many more talented people among this enormous segment of the population than among the still narrowly defined group at the top of society. Once again, however, the British education system seemed to work against encouraging entrepreneurship. For the 11-plus exam, which had the effect of determining at the age of eleven whether a child would eventually go on to university, cut off the vast majority from opportunities to improve themselves. For example, higher education in Britain remained extremely limited. Even with the expansion of university places in the 1960s, the percentage of students between eighteen and twenty-two in higher education remained tiny compared to the United States for another two decades. While many American college students do not belong in higher education when judged by British standards, the American system has the benefit of flexibility. Although there is an advantage in attending an elite college, the prospects for success remain enormous for able students who did not go to those colleges. Furthermore, students are given much more opportunity to reveal their energy and talent by prolonging their schooling through a wide range of non-elite options.

The British secondary education system may have handicapped economic performance in another way. There is evidence that Britain's industrial workforce suffered from an inadequate education compared to competitors. Perhaps the secondary education of British children was not teaching them the necessary adaptability to be productive workers; perhaps they simply were not getting enough secondary education; perhaps there was not adequate training in mathematics and technical skills that would be useful to them as industrial workers. Certainly, the technical education option originally envisaged by Butler was not developed very fully. By the late 1970s only about 5 per cent of British eighteen-year-olds (apart from those in higher education) were getting some form of technical or vocational education, compared to over half of Germans of the same age. As a result, two-thirds of Britain's industrial labour force had no vocational qualifications, compared to one-third of Germany's. Whatever the specific reason, the productivity of skilled and semi-skilled manual workers suffered because of educational deficiencies.[18]

The failure to develop technical education has been a criticism of the English education system since the nineteenth century. It reflects another aspect of the cultural interpretation of the failure of British industry: it did not sufficiently mobilise science and technology in the interests of business. Britain has always produced more than its share of outstanding pure scientists. The lacking is claimed to be in applied science and the development of constructive links between science and industry. Two causes have been suggested. First, engineering, like business, was a relatively low-status profession, so the education system did not develop high-powered universities to train engineers. In America, by contrast, colleges like the Massachusetts Institute of Technology (MIT) and the California Institute of Technology (Caltech) carried the same status as Harvard and the University of California at Berkeley; their graduates (even at undergraduate level) moved immediately into well-paid jobs that carried status within society. There are problems, however, with focusing on higher education, for Britain did better at university level than the criticisms allow. Prior to the First World War, nearly 10 per cent of Cambridge graduates had engineering degrees. (Oxford remained way behind.) During this period, there seems to have been enough graduates in science and technology; but there was not sufficient demand for such degree holders by business – a problem that remained in the 1960s.[19] Thus, critics have focused on a second issue, claiming that business did not cultivate ties to the university scientific community, as American and German universities did, in order to promote research and development. Such criticism again tends to focus on Oxford and Cambridge. Universities like Manchester, Leeds and Birmingham were founded in the nineteenth century in part to serve local industry. Still, by 1890 Germany had many more academic scientists with much closer relations to business than Britain had.[20] Between the wars, the record was also mixed. Many provincial universities were providing what industry needed in some areas of science and engineering but not others, while overall the bias of their education was increasingly moving towards the arts, as they aspired to a more elite status.

How might all of this have affected the performance of British industry? Perhaps no myth is more pervasive about the British of the last two centuries than the cult of 'muddling through'. Originally, it was a military metaphor: however many battles the British lost at the beginning of a war (and they always seemed to lose at the beginning), they invariably worked out a way to muddle through and win in the end. Ultimately, however, 'muddling through' came to incorporate a set of attitudes that disdained expertise, education and professional training in favour of common sense and learning by experience. The rejection of business as a profession requiring expertise and higher education tied it to the approach of 'muddling through', as would any indifference to harnessing engineering skills to the production process. In practice, however, business as it evolved after the Second World War required both – the expertise of professional training and the flexibility and adaptability that come from a general education and from experience (i.e. the ability to muddle through). To the degree that British business relied on the latter without the former, it hampered itself competitively. To the degree that it cut itself off from the specialised training of scientists and engineers, it may have isolated itself from important sources of technological innovation and so competitive advantage, while failing to optimise production processes.[21] The evidence is that many industries did both – i.e. they showed little interest in having either trained managers or trained scientists and engineers on board.[22] Finally, to the degree that British businessmen incorporated a more general value system that was satisfied with a comfortable income and an adequate rate of return rather than seeking to maximise profits, they may have been indifferent to innovation and averse to risk and so may not have been sufficiently entrepreneurial.

Finance Versus Industry and the Costs of Great Power Status

From the late 1950s through the 1980s, one of the favoured explanations for the 'under performance' of Britain's economy was insufficient investment in new industries and new technologies. More recently, economists have become doubtful that a lack of investment explains slower growth; rather, they see slower growth as an explanation for insufficient investment. There was plenty of British investment during the 1950s and 1960s; however, Britain did not get as much out of its investments as did its principal competitors.[23] Why was there such a fixation on investment?

Keynes had taught that investment stood out among the possible contributors to economic growth because investment would have a more powerful 'multiplier effect' than ordinary consumption.* Furthermore, investment implied new technology, and there was a sense that part of the problem was that British industry was too slow to modernise. Thus Keynesians looked to investment as a means of improving economic performance, and to the failure to invest to explain underperformance. If entrepreneurs were acting rationally, then insufficient investment meant that market conditions must be discouraging it – or, to accept the more modern view, they were discouraging the kind of investment that would most help Britain's industrial sector.

Table 5.7 opposite shows that Britain did, in fact, invest a smaller percentage of its GDP than did its principal competitors, except the United States. Here was the basis for the perception of under investment. Economic historians agree (for the moment) on two points about British investment in the 1950s and 1960s: there was no shortage of capital, but there are plenty of kinds of investment apart from that in new plants or equipment – such as business reorganisation and the development of new product lines – which businessmen did not undertake and which would have made firms more profitable. Some of this failure was attributable to a conservative management that was not inclined to change old ways. Some of it, however, may also have been due to the uncertain investment climate that was partly the result of government 'stop-go' policies. The constant raising and lowering of the interest rate, taxes, national insurance payments, etc, made it more difficult for businessmen to project the costs and the expected returns of any change they wanted to undertake. Thus, these policies increased the risk of investments, which meant

---

* The 'multiplier' was Keynes's attempt to quantify how much increase in demand for goods and services would be generated for the economy by an increase in spending. He claimed that spending on investment would create more economic activity than spending on consumption – i.e. the multiplier would be larger. Nowadays, economists tend to focus more on consumption because it accounts for a much larger part of the total national economy.

Table 5.7. Comparative Investment as a Percentage of
GDP, 1950–79

	1950–59 (%)	1960–67 (%)	1968–73 (%)	1974–9 (%)
France	17.5	23.2	24.6	23.6
Japan	23.3	31.0	34.6	31.8
UK	14.6	17.7	19.1	19.3
USA	17.4	18.0	18.4	18.7
West Germany	20.7	25.2	24.4	20.8

Source: Crafts and Woodward, 'The British Economy since 1945: Introduction
and Overview', in Crafts and Woodward, *The British Economy since
1945*, p. 10.

managers required higher expected returns. At the same time,
they acted as a drag on the economy as a whole by slowing down
the rate of growth, which itself would act as a disincentive to
invest.

It is difficult to know how much weight to give to 'stop-go'
policies as an explanation. Not only is there no evidence of insufficient investment, but long-term factors may have been more
important in determining investment decisions than short-term
fluctuations in interest and tax rates. For example, Nick Tiratsoo
and Jim Tomlinson claim that the predictability provided by
government's commitment to full employment swamped the
unpredictability resulting from such policies. Nonetheless, from
the early 1960s, industry was constantly criticising 'stop-go'
policies as harmful to investment and growth. Since then, it has
been among the explanations on offer for Britain's comparatively
weak economic performance, one that would be latched on to by
anti-Keynesian politicians in the 1970s.[24]

The use of 'stop-go' policies reflected a broader priority of
government – the primacy of London's role as a financial centre

over the needs of manufacturing, and especially of exports. For the 'stop' phase was dictated by the necessity of preserving the value of the pound and its role as a reserve currency, which were threatened by balance-of-payments deficits. As a result, the bias of policy was to keep interest rates higher than in competitor countries so that holders of sterling balances would want to keep their money in Britain. The priority of finance over industry had a venerable history in British economic management after 1918. Perhaps the first clear instance came in 1925 when, after having gone off the gold standard during the First World War, the British government returned to it at a deliberately overvalued exchange rate with the dollar. The aim was to restore London's role as an international centre of financial services and source of capital, but another effect was to cut off a tentative recovery in the coal industry and lead to the General Strike of 1926. The same mentality dominated thinking in the 1950s and 1960s. The economist Peter Oppenheimer thinks that this was purely a matter of prestige and a futile attempt to capture past glory: the British economy and the British people gained nothing from this fixation on sterling.[25] The effect, however, was to give preserving the value of the pound equal weight with full employment in driving government policy.

After the devaluation of the pound in 1967 and the end of the Bretton Woods system of fixed exchange rates in 1971–2, the formal role of a reserve currency no longer existed, although the sterling area survived until the end of the decade, when the Thatcher government ended all remaining restrictions on capital flows. Nevertheless, the City continued to have a stake in a strong pound. For in the 1960s London emerged as a centre of what came to be called the Eurodollar market (to be followed quickly by markets in other 'Euro-currencies'). These were dollars accumulated by foreigners – the result of America's chronic balance-of-payments deficit and of transactions in dollars (like the sale of oil) – that were deposited outside the United States to avoid American regulations. The City served as a vehicle for channelling these dollars as loans to foreign countries and international corporations. So as much as ever, it was acting as a centre of international finance; indeed, the Eurodollar market was crucial in re-establishing London as *the* centre of international finance. For the numbers involved were enormous: the whole of the Euro-currency market grew from £1 billion in 1959 to about £800 billion in 1978. At the same time, and because of the Euro-currency market, foreign banks set up shop in London. Between 1967 and 1978, the number went from 113 to 395.[26] The banks established new branches in London for the same reason the Euro-currency market was established there: they saw a favourable economic environment for doing business, including a minimum of government regulation.

While the Euro-currency market was new, London's role in supplying traditional financial services continued to pull in money from all over the world. For example, by 1978 income from insurance premiums totalled over £13.5 billion, accounting for nearly one-third of the City's income from overseas.[27] Yet there was a paradox in this apparent bias of government policy in favour of finance: the many other ways in which the government regulated finance between 1945 and 1979 – especially with the continued use of exchange controls – harmed the City's international role and hampered its competitiveness.[28] For just this reason, the Conservatives ended exchange controls in 1979, and policies thereafter continued to give greater importance to finance than industry. As a result, Britain's manufacturers complained about the high interest and exchange rates in the mid-1980s, while in 1998 they were again screaming because the Bank of England raised interest rates when exports were being creamed due to an overvalued pound. It still seemed as if the needs of the City superseded those of manufacturers trying to export their goods.

Since a balance-of-payments deficit was the signal of trouble for the pound, why did Britain have a chronic problem? One reason was governments' insistence upon maintaining Britain's role as a world power (quite apart from the role of sterling), when it no longer had the economy to support that role. Table 5.8

below shows that Britain spent a larger portion of GDP on national defence than the other major European powers, though less than the United States. Furthermore, as we saw in Chapter 3, Britain's spending (when measured as a percentage of GDP) was far beyond anything it had attempted in the nineteenth century or between the world wars. Japan had a unique advantage over other competitors in having its defence provided by

Table 5.8. Comparison of Percentage of
GDP Spent on Defence, 1950–75

	1950 (%)	1955 (%)	1960 (%)	1965 (%)	1970 (%)	1975 (%)
France	5.5	6.4	6.5	5.2	4.2	3.8
Japan	–	1.8	1.1	0.9	0.8	1.0
UK	6.6	8.2	6.5	5.9	4.8	4.9
USA	5.1	10.2	9.0	7.6	8.0	5.9
West Germany	4.4	4.1	4.0	4.3	3.3	3.6

Source: Sked, *Britain's Decline*, p. 33.

America. Still, the disparity between Britain on the one hand and France and West Germany on the other is not that enormous. The real difference is that while France and especially West Germany mostly spent their resources on defence at home, Britain spent its resources in West Germany and other parts of the world. In fact, spending overseas accounted for about half the defence budget in the 1960s.[29] Thus, defence spending added substantially to Britain's balance-of-payments problems. Indeed, it has been calculated that without the adverse balance in the government sector, the structure of Britain's balance of payments was not much different from what it had been before the First World War: a deficit in trade was made up by a surplus in invisible exports – although the surplus was small compared to the norm before 1914.[30] Table 5.9 below shows that it was mainly the government sector that accounted for the persistent crisis in Britain's balance of payments; in 1966, about three-quarters of the 'services and transfers' was defence spending. Thus, without the deficit in defence spending, Britain would not have had a balance-of-payments problem until the crisis brought on by the oil price increase in 1973.[31]

Table 5.9. British Balance of Payments, 1961–78[32] (£ million)

	Private Sector Balance			Public Sector Balance			Overall Balance
	Trade	Invisibles	Balance	Income on Capital	Services, Transfers	Balance	
1961	−153	554	401	−164	−332	−496	−95
1964	−519	688	169	−119	−432	−551	−382
1967	−557	886	329	−168	−462	−630	−301
1971	190	1658	1849	−204	−520	−724	1125
1974	−5351	3272	−2079	−352	−842	−1194	−3273
1978	−1542	5497	3955	−615	−2401	−3016	939

Source: Pollard, *British Economy 1914–1990*, p. 307.

Britain, of course, had had overseas military commitments before the First World War, but the largest, the Indian army, was paid for by India and so did not represent a financial outflow from Britain. Indeed, one of the most obvious costs of the loss of empire, if Britain was going to continue to try to be a world power, was the expense of overseas bases which no longer were paid for by the colonial peoples. More important still, the army in Germany was primarily paid for by the British after 1954, since the Germans were supporting their own army. Although the Germans made a contribution to British costs, it was nowhere near enough, thus creating a source of tension between the allies. On balance, Germany was the gainer: in 1966 it had a net inflow of some £437 million from military expenditures. If it had had to bear the same relative outflow as Britain, the result would have been a deficit of £250 million – a turnaround of £687 million that would have converted an overall balance-of-payments surplus of £92 million into a deficit of £595 million.[33] Britain's balance of payments did gain (as Germany's did) by the presence of American forces, but it lost again from the cost of weapons purchases from the United States.

Balance-of-payments problems were not the only cost to the economy of retaining Britain's role as a world military power. It also affected spending on research and development (R & D). British industry was way behind its American counterpart in its spending on R & D in the first half of the twentieth century. This lag was partly the result of the continued prevalence of small, family-owned firms, with their traditional nineteenth-century management structure, and partly because engineering did not develop as a research-based discipline in the universities with strong ties to industry.[34] While there was a tremendous increase in money spent on R & D immediately after the war, a disproportionately large share of that money was channelled into defence rather than into civilian industries. Table 5.10 opposite shows the comparison of Britain with the other major economic powers. It is striking how closely the British figures approximate to those of the United States, even surpassing them in the 1970s. Of course, this money was not necessarily ill-spent from an economic standpoint. First, if the result was military products that could be exported, then it would be good for the balance of payments. Second, if the research resulted in innovations which could then be applied to civilian use, the consumer would benefit from new or better products. Malcolm Chalmers, however, judges that such spin-off benefits were minimal, while Britain did not perform as well as France or Italy as an arms exporter from 1979 to 1983.[35] The costs, on the other hand, may have been substantial. First, by diverting R & D money and scientists away from

Table 5.10. Comparison of Percentage of Research and
Development Budgets Spent on Defence

	1963–5 (%)	1966–70 (%)	1971–5 (%)	1976–9 (%)
France	26.2	22.5	18.4	19.6
Japan	0.9	0.9	0.7	0.6
UK	34.5	25.6	28.9	29.3
USA	40.6	31.2	27.7	25.4
West Germany	10.8	10.3	6.9	6.2

Source: Sked, *Britain in Decline*, p. 34.

the civilian sector, this concentration on defence hampered innovation in that sector. Second, government investment in non-defence industries focused on those having some association with defence: aerospace and nuclear energy. The effect of this focus may have been ultimately to discourage R & D in other parts of the economy. The amount spent by the private sector as a percentage of output actually declined from 1967 to 1975. Furthermore, while British industry spent more on R & D between 1945 and 1965 than did industry in Japan, France and West Germany, Britain's rate of increase in spending from 1967 to 1983 was the slowest of the ten leading industrial nations.[36] So the evidence indicates a real tailing off. Britain's most successful industries – especially chemicals and pharmaceuticals – spent a lot of money on R & D, so it seems to have made a difference in how well industry competed. Yet if it made such a difference, it is not clear why Britain did not do better from 1950 to 1965, when it outspent competitors.

Where, then, do we stand in assessing the influences on investment in the domestic civilian economy between 1950 and 1979? There are three overlapping and related considerations: the primacy of financial over industrial considerations in government policy-making; the 'stop-go' economic policies that followed from this prioritising; and the efforts by British governments to maintain the nation's role as a major military power, which helped create the persistent balance-of-payments problems that led to the 'stop-go' policies. One effect of all this may have been to encourage British investors to look overseas rather than invest their surplus capital at home. Until 1980, there were controls on capital exports outside the sterling area to protect the pound. The government did not like to discourage the export of capital, however, as it had long contributed positively to Britain's balance of payments through the income it yielded. Hence, there was always some capital exported outside the sterling area, while investment within the sterling area was positively encouraged. By the early 1960s, British investment in the Commonwealth and empire had grown to something like pre-1914 levels. Investors at times must have been choosing between projects of roughly equal return. In particular, British multi-national firms were making decisions about whether to undertake direct investment (i.e. in plants and equipment) in Britain or overseas. Foreign firms were making the same decisions. In some cases, the uncertainties in Britain resulting from periodic balance-of-payments crises and 'stop-go' policies might have tipped the balance away from British investment for these firms. Yet for the moment (given that there are economic historians on each side), the balance lies towards not giving *too much* weight to investment as an explanation for Britain's economic problems. There was not a shortage of capital for investment projects, while direct investment by American firms was pouring into Britain during the period when 'stop-go' policies predominated. Rather, the real problem was, according to Nicholas Crafts, Britain's 'relatively weak capacity for innovation and for making use of technological change'. In other words, it was the kinds of investment undertaken and how that investment was used that 'lie at the heart of disappointing British economic growth'.[37]

Inflation, Trade Unions and the Welfare State

Labour, in particular, was attracted to investment-related explanations for Britain's economic problems. If only businessmen would invest more, or undertake more of the right kinds of investments to modernise the industrial plant, then all would be well. For the left wing of the party, such arguments could even be used to justify further nationalisation or government direction of industry's policies. By the 1970s, however, inflation-related explanations were becoming ascendant, and these appealed to Conservatives. This change reflected the broader movement away from Keynesian analysis and towards monetarism in the 1970s and 1980s. The Keynesian ascendancy resulted from the unemployment crisis of the inter-war years and the political determination not to allow such a social catastrophe to happen again. The revival of monetary explanations was a response to the great inflation of 1973–82, which was worse in Britain than in other industrial countries. Inflation rather than unemployment now seemed the primary enemy of a healthy economy and a stable society. Monetarists taught that inflation was the signal that the money supply was growing too quickly. They believed that a steady and slow growth of the money supply was necessary for optimal economic performance, so inflation explained underperformance. Yet just as insufficient investment does not quite work as an explanation, so there is a problem with attributing underperformance from 1950 to 1973 to inflation: Japan's inflation rate was even higher (see Table 5.5), and Japan, of course, was the star performer in economic growth.

Those who saw inflation as the source of Britain's economic problems targeted the trade unions as the primary culprits. Judgements on Britain's trade unions have been highly politicised.[38] Yet it is important to note one point at the outset: virtually all the arguments developed below apply to the period after 1950. It is nearly impossible to use union power and labour intransigence to explain Britain's economic problems between 1880 and 1939.[39] From 1950 to 1980, however, it is argued that unions increased the costs of industry in many ways. They imposed work rules that blocked an efficient production process. They insisted on defining the demarcation of jobs (i.e. which workers performed which job) and even which unions represented which workers, thus increasing the cost of industrial relations. They had an unusual propensity to strike compared with unions in other industrialised nations. Finally, they used their power to force up wages and other benefits faster than was justified by increases in worker productivity. Indeed, by resisting technological innovation, the reorganisation of tasks and the redefinition of rules, any of which might lead to a reduction in jobs, the unions were supposedly a barrier to the kinds of improvements in productivity that were essential to justify the wage increases they were demanding.

Initially, defenders of the unions concentrated on the issue of strikes, showing that Britain did not lose any more worker-days to strikes (i.e. the sum of all days for all workers on strike) than did its competitors. These statistics, however, hid the radical differences between Britain and other countries in their industrial relations, and so the more destructive nature of British strikes. A comparison of the British and American motor car industries illustrates these differences. In the United States, there was a single union representing all car workers. The union contract with the 'Big Three' automobile companies (General Motors, Ford and Chrysler) came up for renegotiation once every three years, when the union targeted one of the companies for bargaining. If bargaining broke down, the workers at that company went on strike, while those at the others kept working. Since all these companies were enormous, a strike of any length at once involved the loss of many worker-days. When the strike was settled, however, there was a three-year contract that was enforceable under the law. The other companies usually accepted the agreement negotiated by the target company, with variations. There were rarely wildcat strikes about specific plant grievances. Thus, the result of the process was relative stability and predictability over the next three years. The situation in Britain was very different. Because British unions had developed around crafts and skills rather than industries, workers in the British motor car industry were represented by many unions. So the bargaining process for management was inefficient, and there was no assurance that an agreement with one union would secure industrial peace with the others. British agreements were for one year rather than three, so as soon as a bargaining round was over, both sides were jockeying for position in the new year's negotiations. Finally, British collective bargaining agreements were not enforceable under the law. This did not result in unions breaking the agreements they had made. Rather, it increased the risk of wildcat strikes at specific plants over specific grievances, with the national union leadership unable to impose discipline on the local union.

Indeed, the trend of industrial relations by the 1960s was towards supplementing national agreements with informal bargaining and agreements at the plant level, thus strengthening factory shop stewards. In part, this trend was a shop-floor response to archaic and oligarchic trade union structures that had become increasingly cut off from the rank and file, leading to distrust of the leadership. In part, it was a flexible improvisation, given that the workers at a factory were often represented by more than one union and that issues came up that were not covered by collective bargaining agreements. Shop stewards and factory committees offered a means of cutting across multi-union representation to deal with day-to-day issues, and as such they were welcomed by management. This new assertiveness at the grass-roots level was one reason for the shift to the left in the unions in the 1960s, which was eventually reflected back at the top in a new generation of union leaders. At the same time, however, the whole process meant that the centre was losing control and so increased the probability of unofficial strikes.

The effects of such strikes were potentially devastating. Assume, for example, that workers at a Chrysler plant making doors for all Chrysler cars in Britain had an unauthorised strike over a minor issue. The notorious stereotype of the kind of issue involved was the length of the tea break, which was certainly no luxury given the harshness and tedium of some of the work in heavy industries.[40] It could as easily be about work rules, however, or a demarcation dispute between two different unions in the plant, or the disciplining of a union member. The effect would be to bring production at all Chrysler plants in the United Kingdom to a halt. When the strike ended, a minor issue would be settled, but there would be no assurance of long-term industrial peace in the British motor car industry. Another strike could happen the next day, with equally disastrous effect, and its settlement also would contribute nothing towards peace and predictability. This is not an arbitrary example, especially once labour relations turned bad in the 1960s. From 1969 to 1973, 94.5 per cent of the strikes outside the coal industry were unofficial, resulting in 55.7 per cent of the workdays lost due to strikes.[41] Thus, even though in some years the United States may have lost more worker-days to strikes than Britain did, American strikes achieved something by settling outstanding issues for all workers in an industry over a period of years and so assuring an interval of industrial calm. British strikes achieved none of this. The effect was to raise costs, and these higher costs were passed on to consumers in the form of higher prices.

The behaviour of the unions sometimes seems irrational and destructive to the outside observer. Why should so much weight be given to which union represents which workers, to how jobs are defined, to nit-picking rules about who does what work when? The answers are historical. We should never forget the extent of exploitation of workers in the nineteenth century before unions were able to protect them. If unions abuse work rules now, employers abused work rules in the early decades of the Industrial Revolution to reduce the wages they had formally agreed to. Unions that have had to fight for recognition, and so for their very lives, will fight to retain and expand the membership that assures their survival. These battles were thus a form of re-enactment of historic class conflicts. Indeed, the workers may have seen such actions as a means of re-establishing some form of control over their work in the conditions of the modern factory. *They* rather than the bosses would define who would negotiate for them or the conditions in which they worked. Historical memory worked in another way, too. It was not so long ago that employers had used their power in a sluggish market to squeeze workers. This was exactly what happened to the miners at the time of the General Strike of 1926, when employers took advantage of weak export markets to force down wages and victimise strikers. In the 1950s and 1960s, the power relationship was reversed. Demand was buoyant, and employers did not want to lose production and sales. Unions were simply using their power to their advantage, as employers had done and would do again in the 1980s. It is the job of the union to get the best deal it can for its members, just as it is the job of management to get the best deal it can for its shareholders. Britain's industrial relations problems were concentrated in a few key industries: cars, iron and steel, shipbuilding, and, in the 1970s, coal. These were all industries in trouble, so the unions were fighting to protect jobs and standards of living. Their bad industrial relations, however, had a disproportionate effect on the economy because of their continued economic importance.

Other countries dealt with this inherent conflict in different ways from Britain – ways that reflected their own history and culture. In particular, West Germany and Japan sought to mute the conflict between management and labour by creating conditions for consensus bargaining. America had much the same system of confrontation as Britain's, but with weaker unions. It had developed in a way that gave management greater predictability, but, as Table 5.6 shows, with the result of similarly low growth rates for worker productivity. For whatever reasons, the Germans and the Japanese were able to make deals with their labour force that preserved rather than sacrificed productivity.[42]

Why, then, didn't British management resist more effectively or respond more constructively? First, the message from government was ambiguous: it wanted efficiency and competitiveness, but it also wanted full employment. The confusion was evident in the policies of the nationalised industries. Each of them was technically a public corporation independent from direct government interference (along the lines of the BBC), and governments did not usually intervene directly in managerial decisions. Mostly, they were in terrible shape when they were taken over after the war, suffering from underinvestment and inefficiency. There was some improvement in the 1950s, but managers were uncertain what criteria should guide their decision-making, while they were not fully free from government interference. In particular, prices were kept low as a benefit to consumers, while investments were squeezed whenever the economy was in a 'stop' phase of the cycle. In the 1960s, the government opted to treat the nationalised industries like commercial enterprises. Since they were mostly natural monopolies, however, and the intent certainly was not for them to maximise profits, it was never clear how this should be done. They did achieve a significant improvement in productivity over the decade. Yet they were still expected to take their social obligations into account. Hence, they faced pressure to keep prices down (especially under the Heath government from 1970 to 1973), both as part of the fight against inflation and as a subsidy for consumers, while social considerations might slow down the closing of coal mines or branch railways. By the 1970s they were running substantial deficits, and after 1974 the Labour government was so concerned with preserving jobs that it poured money into them. By then, the nationalised industries had become something of an extension of the welfare state, with overmanning, underinvestment and prices that were too low. Yet with all their problems, the nationalised industries did not perform worse than those in the private sector from 1945 to 1979, probably including even in the 1970s.[43]

Clearly, then, the private sector was an important part of the problem. In the 1950s, the message private industry received from the Conservative governments was to avoid confrontation with the trade unions. Times were good, and new competitors were only just beginning to emerge to challenge Britain's exports. Wage increases could therefore be passed on relatively easily in the form of higher prices, while bad labour relations could hurt business and profits. So management gave in to union demands – demands which, in the 1950s, were not very great. By the late 1960s and 1970s, when inflation began to be a serious problem and foreign competition was cutting into British export markets, it proved difficult for employers to reverse direction. Faced with an increasingly aggressive and intransigent trade union movement, management often still found it preferable to conciliate labour and raise prices. Many executives did not want a return to the 1930s, with high unemployment and low wages. These would be the inevitable result if wages and manning levels were cut, and they would bring low demand and reduced profits in their wake.

Moreover, British businessmen had their own reasons for being satisfied with the status quo. In the 1950s, when large chunks of the British private sector still looked shockingly primitive, they did not want radical change. Keith Middlemas has described the decade as characterised by 'the continued survival of a mass of small firms, reliant on sheltered domestic markets, which were unable or unwilling to reform their practices or their low productivity'.[44] In this environment, many executives were comfortable with the old ways of doing business, as long as they could continue to make a sufficient profit (which is quite different from profit maximisation). Throughout the decade, there were efforts to persuade industry to adopt 'American' practices that would improve productivity. Examples include reforming the layout of the factory, improving the flow of materials through the production process, using work-study evaluations to see how jobs could be done more efficiently, standardising product lines and using sampling techniques of quality control. Many of these innovations would have cost relatively little money to implement, and workers were not necessarily hostile to such changes. Indeed, the Americans were urging resistant British managers to include unions in discussions about improvement. While some notable firms did adopt reforms, more commonly British management resisted change.[45] Management was equally slow to take up industrial training, for fear of losing highly trained workers to other firms. Hence, managers were content to leave training to the old apprenticeship system, which left workers with a low level of skills. Some of this changed in the 1960s, when the Wilson government promoted mergers on the principle that larger was better. Mostly, however, it did not make much difference. The traditional indictments of British management continued to apply. It showed little interest in what customers wanted and so was unimaginative in creating new product lines, tailoring service to demand and developing effective marketing strategies. It also did little to modernise the structure of corporate management itself. The overall picture, then, is that businessmen were content to leave things as they were. Furthermore, the reasons were partly cultural: 'British executives aspired to be relaxed and patrician, capable of enjoying other refined pursuits. They judged that Americans were overcommitted to their companies and ultimately rather vulgar in matters of taste.'[46]

Along with labour and management, government too has been blamed for Britain's inflation problems from 1950 to 1979. Keynesian policies may have tended towards that result. To begin with, the aim of policy was too ambitious: the level of unemployment aspired to was simply too low for the economy to sustain without inflation. Between 1960 and 1968, for example, the unemployment rate ranged between about 1.5 and 2.5 per cent, when it probably should have been from 2.5 to 2.7 per cent to prevent inflation. Even in the 1970s, when the situation was deteriorating, unemployment only averaged 3.8 per cent.[47] Because of this stringent definition of full employment, 'stop-go' policies erred in favour of expansion rather than contraction. And error there must have been! For even with the most accurate statistics, governments cannot tell exactly when economies are beginning to slow down or speed up, when recessions begin or end. Furthermore, statistics cannot be *that* accurate, and Britain's certainly weren't in the 1950s and 1960s. So it is necessary to keep revising the statistics (say for growth) later, as better information becomes available. Even now, economic historians do not produce exactly the same statistics for the period from 1950 to 1973.[48] Nor do economists know the relationships among multitudinous parts of the economy well enough to predict exactly what increase in interest rates or taxes is necessary to slow down the economy just the amount necessary to reduce inflation without causing too much unemployment. Given the combination of ignorance and error with the importance of full employment, there was probably a tendency to stop too late and go too soon. Political considerations sometimes reinforced this tendency, as chancellors opted for inflationary giveaway budgets preceding general elections.

While there is debate over whether mistakes in policy-making *systematically* accentuated Britain's business cycle fluctuations (i.e. by making recessions or expansions greater than they would otherwise have been), there certainly were specific moments when policy made things worse – such as in 1959, 1963–4, 1971–3, 1979–81 and 1987–9. In each of these instances, the government's mistakes were inflationary, while the 1979–81 policies also (paradoxically) made a recession worse than it would otherwise have been. At the same time, there may have been an inflationary bias in post-war policies that was independent of 'stop-go'. Table 5.11 overleaf shows the growth of Britain's national debt over the past 160 years, and the distribution of spending in what economists call the current account. In the nineteenth century, even though government spending grew, public finance was deflationary, as governments balanced their budgets and reduced the debt. As a result, from 1820 to 1913 the national debt declined by about 25 per cent. Even after the First World War, and despite the depressed economy, there was a substantial cut in government spending, and government borrowing was kept down so as to keep the debt from growing. The period after the Second World War, by contrast, saw government spending keep growing, and with it the size of the national debt. Thus, for the first time in peacetime, the bias of government policy was expansionary rather than deflationary. Table 5.11 also shows how everything got out of control in the 1970s, as government spending (especially

Table 5.11. Government Spending and the
National Debt, 1820–1980
(£ millions, with percentage of total spending)

	Total Spending	Civil Spending	Military Spending	Interest on Debt	Total Debt
1820	57.5	5.4 (9.4)	16.7 (29.0)	31.3 (54.4)	840.1
1880	81.5	16.9 (20.7)	25.2 (30.9)	28.1 (34.5)	737.8
1913	184.0	54.6 (29.7)	72.5 (39.4)	19.9 (10.8)	625.0
1920	1,665.8	574.5 (34.5)	604.0 (36.3)	332.0 (19.9)	7,809.5
1934	770.5	368.3 (47.8)	107.9 (14.0)	216.3 (28.1)	7,810.2
1950	3,530.6	2,069 (58.6)	740.7 (21.0)	499.7 (14.2)	25,802.3
1970	12,822	9,812 (76.5)	2,204 (17.2)	513 (4.0)	33,079.4
1980	61,007	46,456 (76.1)	9,139 (15.0)	4,143 (6.8)	95,314.2

Source: Mitchell, *British Historical Statistics*, pp. 587–93, 600–603.

spending for civilian purposes) and the debt leapt up by a factor usually associated only with wartime spending. Still, there was always a current account surplus in the budget: i.e. current receipts always covered current expenditures for the year. The source of the deficit was the government's investments – whether it was in building roads or building a new factory in the nationalised steel industry. And yet it could not invest enough; the infrastructure and nationalised industries began to be run down in the 1960s and 1970s in the effort to control spending. It seems clear that British government took on more than it could handle after the war, with all the usual responsibilities of government – including a defence effort that was far beyond what heretofore had been the norm – plus a vastly expanded welfare state and the nationalised industries.

However, the same trend towards increased government spending in the post-war era was evident among Britain's European competitors. Table 5.12 below shows that British government expenditure as a percentage of GDP was comparable to that of France and West Germany, once recovery in those two countries was complete by 1960. Indeed, given Britain's greater commitment of resources to defence (Table 5.8), British governments actually spent a smaller percentage of GDP for civilian purposes than did the other two. In fact, both countries had passed Britain in their spending on social security as a percentage of GDP by 1952.[49] Furthermore, both showed the same expansion of spending as Britain between 1968 and 1979; so the crisis of the 1970s produced a similar effect on all three countries.

Table 5.12. Comparative Average Annual Government Expenditure as a Percentage of GDP, 1950–79

	1950–59 (%)	1960–67 (%)	1968–73 (%)	1974–9 (%)
France	32.1	37.4	38.9	43.3
Japan	14.9	18.7	20.5	28.4
UK	35.1	34.7	39.6	44.3
USA	26.4	28.3	31.0	32.6
West Germany	30.9	35.7	39.8	47.5

Source: Crafts and Woodward, 'The British Economy since 1945: Introduction and Overview', in Crafts and Woodward, *The British Economy since 1945*, p. 10.

While Japan spent significantly less than the Europeans, Japan had both the highest average annual growth rate of expenditure on social services and the highest average annual growth rate of GDP between 1960 and 1981 among OECD countries. Britain had the lowest growth rate in both categories over the same period.[50] Thus, the welfare state and the size of the public sector more generally do not seem to offer an explanation for any difference in Britain's economic performance compared with other developed countries.

Where is Decline?

The attempt to analyse Britain's post-war economic performance shows how politicised contemporary history is. This is true of the assessment of Britain's economy from 1950 to 1979, and it will be equally true of the assessment of the economy after 1979. Does the earlier period reflect success or failure, progress or decline, or something more ambiguous? The answer, in part, is shaped by one's attitude to the welfare state and towards the Keynesian economics that dominated those years. To the degree that Britain had economic problems, who was to blame – entrepreneurs, or unions, or the nation's great-power ambitions, or government? Again, politics helps determine where an individual comes down in the debate. Is it possible, then, to draw any conclusions that are divorced from *my* political outlook? The point with which this chapter opened is incontestable: the period from 1950 to 1973 was one of unparalleled success, when compared to Britain's past performance. Even when Britain is compared with the other major industrial powers, its economic performance was still respectable. This is especially evident in comparisons with the United States, the economic superpower of the post-war era. Comparisons are difficult, however, for the goal posts keep moving in contemporary history. Thus, the Japanese economy was the unquestioned star performer of the 1970s and 1980s. Yet its problems in the 1990s revealed some of the costs of its earlier success, rendering long-term comparisons with Britain less certain than they seemed ten years ago. As one further example of the difficulty of such comparisons, inflation was supposedly Britain's great economic failure: yet Britain held its own when compared to Japan and France until 1974–81. Thus, from 1950 to 1973 Britain's comparative economic performance was quite good; however, the years from 1974 to 1981 do seem to mark an era of economic catastrophe and so failure.

The one unambiguous area of decline over the whole period was manufacturing competitiveness. This is the reason analysts paid so much attention to the performance of management and labour in the industrial sector and to the effects of government policies on the actions of both. Any or all of the many factors that have been discussed could have had some influence on the performance of industry. For whatever reasons, British management did not perform as well as management in other countries, and there is some agreement that part of the blame rests with the businessmen themselves. Thus, in the motor car industry (a particularly bad one for Britain), American plants in Britain outperformed the plants of British motor car companies. Since the labour and the government policies were the same, there seems nowhere else to turn but to management for an explanation, and cultural factors surely contributed to the problem. Nonetheless, British management was also operating under a unique handicap: the determination of British governments to maintain Britain's position as a world military and financial power while reducing unemployment to extraordinarily low levels. Supporting finance at the expense of industry may have had an economic justification – if international financial services rather than manufacturing exports were where Britain's real advantage lay when compared to other economic powers. The military spending, however, had no *economic* justification. The two together led to government policies that put a heavy burden of uncertainty on entrepreneurs who were trying to make judgements about the future. While there is debate over the exact relationship between Britain's slower growth rates compared to other countries and its tendency to invest less, there is considerable agreement that there was not enough

research and development (R & D) in many sectors of industry –
and what there was was excessively driven by defence considerations. Since R & D is an investment decision, investment clearly
was affected at least to that degree. Britain's labour relations were
also uniquely bad, for reasons which had deep historical and
cultural roots. As a result, the fear of labour (or, perhaps, the desire
to compensate for its past suffering) meant Britain was less able
than its competitors to mobilise the possibilities for improved
worker productivity. After 1968 there was a breakdown in British
industrial relations unlike anything experienced by the other major
industrial powers. Finally, at the moment there is some consensus
that Britain's labour force was undertrained compared to
competitor countries, and that Britain's education system was a
handicap to more rapid economic growth. Thus, cultural factors
do have something important to offer in explaining Britain's
economic performance since the Second World War.

6

ECONOMIC UPHEAVAL

From the early 1960s, the nature and causes of Britain's economic problems preoccupied political debate. It was a rare person who questioned whether or not there was a problem. The only question was what to do about it. As politicians grappled with that question, their solutions reflected some of the explanations for economic decline discussed in the last chapter. As a very broad generalisation, Labour looked to explanations based on insufficient investment, while Conservatives moved from investment-based explanations to those based on inflation. As a corollary, Labour was more likely to see the problem in terms of a failure of entrepreneurship, while Conservatives focused more on the excessive power of the trade unions. It is important not to treat such generalisations too rigidly, however. Harold Wilson, the Labour Prime Minister from 1964 to 1970, saw trade unions as part of the problem and toyed with legislation to limit their power. Similarly, Margaret Thatcher, the Conservative Prime Minister from 1979 to 1990, accepted cultural explanations for a failure of entrepreneurship and therefore tried to transform the whole value system to encourage venture capitalism. Despite such exceptions, however, the above generalisations are useful, for they reflect the biases with which each party approached the problem of bringing Britain's economy up to scratch.

During the last couple of years of the Macmillan–Home

governments, the focus of Tory economic policy had begun to change towards promoting growth. That became the preoccupation of governments for the next ten years. Both Wilson and his Conservative successor, Edward Heath, struggled to find ways to free themselves from the constraints of 'stop-go' policies and to accelerate Britain's economic growth so that it would be comparable to the growth rates of competitor nations. Although the 1960s were perhaps the most successful decade of the century in terms of high growth, low unemployment and low poverty, you would never know it from the narratives of Britain's economic history – and you won't know it from this chapter either. For all efforts to improve Britain's economic performance were swamped by new signs of failure: the end of the pound's role as a reserve currency, the accelerating rate of inflation, the increasing number of damaging strikes, and finally, in the 1970s, the collapse of growth and full employment. As a result, the story of the years 1964–73 reads like a chronicle of futility. The climax came under the Labour governments of 1974–9. Inflation pushing an annual rate of 30 per cent in the first half of 1975 set one record, while a wave of strikes in the winter of 1978–9 set another. Britain and its economy were beginning to look unmanageable. Yet these last years also saw the beginning of change. The Bretton Woods system of fixed exchange rates collapsed in the early 1970s, while the government of James Callaghan took strong action from 1976 to 1979 to rein in inflation, even at the risk of more unemployment. Thus, the post-war economic priorities of full employment and a stable pound faded away, to be replaced by ending inflation and limiting the power of the trade unions.

The End of 'Stop-Go'

Labour's election campaign, based on 'the white heat of technology', encompassed a view of what was needed for Britain's economic regeneration. Wilson was determined to break out of the 'stop-go' cycle, much as Maudling had tried to do the previous year with his dash for growth. Since underinvestment was the

problem, a programme of modernisation was required –
including not only technological innovation and investment in
industry, but also a radical reform of higher education to increase
the number of universities and give science greater importance,
and the professionalisation of management. The Labour revolution thus involved nothing less than the substitution of expertise
for 'muddling through'. But how could Britain underwrite a
massive programme of investment without generating inflationary pressures that would require the government to slam on
the economic brakes and so short-circuit the whole process? The
government assumed that a continuation of the wage restraints
introduced by the Conservatives would provide the time needed
to allow the new investment and modernised technologies to
work. Then industry would be able to produce the goods people
wanted to buy, while the higher growth rate would assure that
the rate of inflation remained at a tolerable level. Hence, there
would be no balance-of-payments crisis or run on the pound.
Since left-wing economists also thought that insufficient demand
was one of the reasons for slow growth, they believed that the
expansion resulting from all this investment would actually be
good for the economy rather than a problem.

Wilson proposed to create a Department of Economic Affairs
(DEA), free from the conservative restraints of Treasury control
and staffed by university economists, to develop the plan to do
the job. At the same time, a new Ministry of Technology would
prod the private sector to modernise, disseminate information so
that private firms would be more informed about best practice,
organise all of Britain's research and development efforts
(including the armed forces'), and provide more funds to support
those efforts in civilian industries. This programme reflected what
Labour understood to be the planning model that had produced
France's economic transformation in the 1950s and early 1960s.
The French planning system had evolved over many years,
however, with much learning from trial and error. Furthermore,
France's economy had been given a big boost by a huge devaluation of the franc, while growth had been accompanied by

relatively high inflation (see Table 5.5). The Labour leadership ignored these facts, if it thought about them at all. In fact, Wilson and his team, like Macmillan's before them, did not really understand what was necessary to improve growth, and particularly what was required to improve productivity. At the same time, the Labour leadership gravely underestimated the power of Britain's international finances to become the engine driving all economic policy-making. Thus, while they were committed to the pound, they did not understand all that its defence entailed. They would learn soon enough.

In the year following the election, Labour had to work out the specifics of its economic plan while it was getting the DEA up and running. Something that was very complicated, involving much that was still not fully understood, was done in a hurried way. The plan was generated from the top, with little meaningful consultation with either management or labour in individual industries in setting its targets. At the same time, James Callaghan, the Chancellor of the Exchequer, was struggling with an economy that was in trouble. The legacy of the expansionary budget of 1963 was a balance-of-payments crisis as soon as Labour came to power. Furthermore, after thirteen years in opposition, Labour was committed to increasing the benefits of the welfare state as well as renationalising the steel industry. All of this would cost money and make deflationary policies to defend the pound more difficult, though the proposed introduction of capital gains tax and increases in corporate income tax offered some counterweight. Finally, Wilson and his Defence Secretary, Denis Healey, were committed to preserving Britain's worldwide military role. So Callaghan had a variety of policies that he had to juggle without thwarting a new dash for growth before it was out of the starting blocks.

It could not all be done. The new economic plan was launched in 1965, but it was merely a statement of aspirations – a set of economic targets that was internally consistent. There was no blueprint of how to get there. Nor was there any flexibility built in that would allow for the adaptation of targets in the light of

changing circumstances. Finally in 1966, in the wake of the deflation required by a balance-of-payments crisis that summer, it
collapsed and disappeared. While the DEA hung on for several
more years, its functions eroded away as short-term concerns
dominated Labour's policy-making. The Ministry of Technology
did somewhat better. Labour had been discussing a science policy
intermittently since 1956, and Wilson had been part of those
discussions since 1960. So the general headings of an investment policy had been worked out prior to the election. Focusing
on a few industries (including defence industries) that were
deemed to have growth potential and were dependent on
technology, the Ministry promoted research and development and
encouraged improved links between industry and the universities. Yet it found firms troublingly uninterested in its programmes. Its most famous (or notorious) project was Concorde,
the supersonic commercial aeroplane built with the French.
Concorde, however, showed the problem with the whole
approach. The cost was enormous, and the result was a commercial flop. Overall, since the small amounts of money involved
made only a marginal contribution to economic growth, the
Ministry could have little effect on the short-term performance
of the economy.

Callaghan's task was equally difficult. He raised a variety of
taxes to finance the promised increases in welfare spending, and
he even experimented with direct controls on imports. At the
same time, Labour embraced the Conservative experiment with
direct wage controls, while it added price restraint to the remit
of a new Prices and Incomes Board. Initially, as under the
Conservatives, the policy of controls (known as an 'incomes
policy') was based on voluntary compliance. In other words,
exhortation would persuade workers to restrain their wage
demands and businesses to limit rises in prices and dividends.
A seamen's strike in the summer of 1966, however, drove Labour
to take radical new steps: it imposed a six-month freeze, followed
by a period of severe restrictions on increases in the first half of
1967. Under the revised law, all wage, price and dividend

increases could be referred to the Prices and Incomes Board, and the mechanism of referral gave the government the means to delay an increase it thought was too great.

Incomes policies brought the Labour government into conflict with the trade unions, which hated any limitation on their freedom of action. The right they most prized was the negotiation of wages and working conditions with employers. This fixation on free collective bargaining reflected the history of the union movement. The very existence of trade unions had depended on getting employers to recognise them as the sole bargaining agents for employees. An incomes policy negated this central defining function of unions by imposing the government into the negotiating process. In a world of government dictation, unions would be irrelevant – this was the principal reason they had always opposed any systematic government economic planning. In addition to opposing controls as a matter of principle, unions also did not like the way incomes policies worked in practice. Experience proved that wage restraint was more effective than price restraint. Thus, as inflation continued, the real purchasing power of those who limited their wages eroded. Furthermore, regulation could not work fairly. Given Britain's system of annual negotiations, some categories of workers inevitably got an increase just before new controls were imposed. It was also easier to force public-sector workers to adhere to targets for wage increases, since the government literally was the paymaster. So they tended to fall behind those with comparable skills in the private sector. All these potential inequities played havoc with the wage differentials among workers of different skill. Socialist egalitarianism did not extend to the narrowing of pay differences between skilled and unskilled workers, so when those differences eroded, the skilled workers exerted pressure to restore them. The fastest expansion in union membership since the war was among white-collar workers, many of whom (like teachers) had education and skills. Since many of them were public employees, they were just the ones who suffered most from the inequities of wage controls. Not surprisingly, then, the public-sector unions were the source of much labour discontent as incomes policies became the norm from the mid-1960s to 1979. They were not alone, however. Any skilled manufacturing worker was hostile to the erosion of wage differentials and to the distinctions which gave him status over the unskilled.

The unions' response to Labour's more stringent incomes policy was slow to develop. The impression that somehow the 1960s were a strike-prone era is misguided, as Table 6.1 below shows. The years from 1964 to 1968 actually had fewer stoppages

Table 6.1. Strike Activity, 1954–69

	Number of Stoppages	Days Lost to Strikes (000)	% Strikes Less than 3 Days
1954–8[a]	2,508.9	4,039.0	81.7
1959–63[a]	2,425.6	3,778.6	75.3
1964–8[a]	2,261.8	3,015.4	67.7
1969	3,116	6,846	62.3

[a]Average of the annual figures over the five-year period.

Source: Robert Price and George Sayers Bain, 'The Labour Force', in A. H. Halsey, ed., *British Social Trends since 1900: A Guide to the Changing Social Structure of Britain*, 2nd edition (Basingstoke: Macmillan, 1988), pp. 195–6.

on average, and fewer working days lost to strikes on average, than did the previous ten years. This relative stability was probably because the new incomes policy, while statutory, was not backed up by legal penalties. In other words, the leaders of trade unions and managers of firms were not threatened with the sanction of the law if they failed to abide by what the Prices and Incomes Board told them to do. It may also have been due to the fact that inflation was still relatively modest for most of the 1960s, even though it was going up. Thus, by one calculation, the average annual rate of retail price inflation from 1956 to 1962 was 2.5 per cent, while from 1962 to 1968 it was still only 3.8 per cent. By contrast, from 1968 to 1973 it was 8.7 per cent.[1] So the pressure to push for ever larger wage increases did not become acute until 1969.

Why, then, did contemporaries think that strike activity was getting worse? The answer may lie in the last column of Table 6.1. There was a steady trend towards longer strikes: by 1964–8, one-third of all strikes were three days or longer, as compared to less than one-fifth from 1954 to 1958. Strikes in the 1950s were often at plant level and unofficial; the product of specific grievances, they were quickly settled. By the 1960s, however, more strikes were national, were about wages and so took longer to settle. Such national strikes had a higher national and international profile, as did the resulting wage settlements, which would be seen as inflationary if they could not be justified by increases in labour productivity. Given the acute sensitivity of the financial markets to anything that would produce a run on sterling, even a small increase in inflation was dangerous. The result was a growing government paranoia about the trade unions, for the pound was becoming more and more difficult to defend.

Wilson and Callaghan were determined not to devalue the pound, for Labour had to fight the perception in the City that it was not a reliable manager of the economy. This distrust by the financial powers that be had destroyed the Labour government of 1929–31, and the post-war problems culminating in the devaluation of 1949 again seemed to taint Labour as unsafe – although that very sensible devaluation had helped the 1950s recovery. Their determination was bolstered by the American government. After the war, American leaders had not been keen on the survival of the pound as an international competitor of the dollar. By the 1960s, however, the United States had its own chronic balance-of-payments deficit, so the dollar was now vulnerable. The US administration feared that a devaluation of the pound would weaken the dollar, as people fled sterling and accumulated ever more dollar assets (thus increasing the liabilities of the US

Treasury), which in turn would threaten the whole Bretton Woods system of fixed exchange rates. President Lyndon Johnson also feared that protecting the pound would force the British government to cut defence spending. He did not want to see Britain's military role in Europe or the Far East undermined when the United States was getting ever more deeply embroiled in Vietnam. The United States therefore exerted constant pressure on Wilson and Callaghan not to cut Britain's commitments in Singapore, the Indian Ocean and the Persian Gulf; while at the same time, the US Federal Reserve was generous with assistance to stop any speculative run on sterling, as long as the British pursued the necessary deflationary policies to support these efforts.

It was in this international context that Wilson faced the labour unrest. His relations with the unions had been chummy enough from 1964 to the 1966 general election, as the government followed the Tory precedent of trying to promote acceptable wage settlements. There was a growing sense, however, that Labour's very reputation as a credible party of government was at stake: it could not devalue the pound again. Thus, Wilson became increasingly edgy about union demands. He finally cracked during the seamen's strike in the summer of 1966, which crippled British exports and led to a run on the pound. When the union leadership rejected a compromise, Wilson hinted at conspiratorial elements among extremists who sought to undermine the political system. Thus a Labour prime minister confirmed the bogey of Communist influence that was so often used against the trade unions. It shows how perilous the position of the pound had become.

In retrospect, it seems clear that the effort to prevent devaluation was a futile one. It was just another example of the destructive effect of the fixation on preserving Britain's status as a major power. During the crisis of the summer of 1966, about one-third of the Cabinet swung in favour of devaluation – including Callaghan (for a moment), plus Wilson's closest political friends, Richard Crossman and Barbara Castle. Wilson would not budge, however, and so the opponents of devaluation prevailed. Callaghan did what had to be done to stop the haemorrhage. In addition to the new policy of wage controls, he introduced the most severe deflationary package yet, imposing the usual higher taxes and interest rates, plus spending cuts – cuts that had to include nationalised industries and social services as well as defence. Yet increasingly, the effort to prop up the pound depended on the willingness of the United States and the central banks of Western Europe to provide stand-by loans to the Treasury to meet any speculative run. The measures taken in 1966 succeeded, but it only needed some new confluence of events to provoke the fears of sterling-holders and generate a new crisis. Those events occurred the next year. The Arab-Israeli War in June closed down the Suez Canal; an economic downturn in the United States began over the summer; and a rash of dockers' strikes hit Britain in October. The effect was to increase the cost of imports and hurt exports, leading to a new balance-of-payments deficit and a new run on the pound. The United States, the West German Bundesbank and the International Monetary Fund were all willing to help with new loans, but the government was not prepared to accept the terms that would have been attached. Finally, it admitted defeat, devaluing the pound in November from an exchange rate of $2.80 to one of $2.40.

The devaluation alone, however, solved nothing: the owners of sterling balances still held the British economy hostage with the threat of a run. To make the devaluation effective, the new Chancellor of the Exchequer, Roy Jenkins, introduced a dose of deflationary measures far more severe than any that had been seen since the late 1940s – including substantial defence cuts, with an end to Britain's military commitments east of Suez by 1971.[2] Even so, it required two years of pain and further deflationary policies before the economy began to turn around at the end of 1969. Jenkins's job was made all the more difficult because 1969 saw an explosion of strike activity. The strikes followed the easing of the government's incomes policy, which had imposed some modest restraint on wage and price increases.

In an increasingly inflationary environment, workers scurried to regain lost ground, with the initiative sometimes coming at plant level. Public-sector unions, in particular, struck to restore wage comparability with the private sector and the wage differentials between skilled and unskilled workers. More strikes for higher wages, however, merely made holders of sterling jittery again, leading to renewed pressure on the pound. Britain was now caught in a new kind of 'stop-go' cycle. Inflation, which triggered demands for higher wages, was now being pushed along by those wage increases. The strikes that forced these increases led to pressure on the pound, so the government had to adopt deflationary policies, including wage and price controls. Yet as soon as the economy turned around, the unions, feeling that they had lost out under controls, demanded higher wages to catch up and resorted to strikes to get what they wanted. So once again, there was pressure on the pound.

The collapse of this cycle finally came in 1972. Following the 1967 devaluation, the sterling area began to break up, and sterling's importance as a reserve currency waned. The final push came from the United States. The Americans were suffering from their own inflation problems – due to spending on new social welfare programmes and the Vietnam War. People were therefore less inclined to hold dollars, the reserve of choice since the end of the war. Gold was beginning to look like a better hedge against inflation. Under the Bretton Woods Agreement, the US Treasury was obliged to exchange gold for dollars on demand. Hence, pressure on American gold reserves began to increase. Unlike the British, President Richard Nixon did not believe that national prestige was tied to preserving the international role of the dollar at all costs. In 1971 he abandoned the obligation to buy dollars, much to the fury of America's allies, whom he did not even bother to consult. With the mighty dollar brought down, and the whole concept of a reserve currency as it had existed over the past twenty-five years rendered irrelevant, the tattered logic of tying the British economy to a specific exchange rate – whatever the cost to the rest of the economy – was gone. When the next balance-of-payments crisis hit Britain in the first half of 1972, the Conservative government abandoned the fixed exchange rate, and the Americans did the same in 1973. The Bretton Woods system and the age of 'stop-go' economic policies to defend sterling were both dead.

The War Against the Trade Unions

The same inflationary pressures that finally brought down the pound also launched the war between British governments and the trade unions that dominated the 1970s. Ironically, it was a Labour government that struck the first blow, and the fact that Wilson had to retreat in humiliating defeat was a transforming event that shaped the course of battle over the next ten years. By the late 1960s, British public opinion, like foreign investors, was becoming increasingly disturbed by the power of the unions. The source of the problem appeared to be several conventions that had evolved in British industrial relations: the system of annual negotiations, the authority of the leadership of most unions to call a strike without the approval of the members, the fact that many union leaders never had to be re-elected, the fact that national negotiations were increasingly being supplemented or vitiated by informal negotiations at the plant level, the fact that collective bargaining agreements were not legally binding and the legal immunity of unions for any actions by the union or its members during a strike. The resulting impression was that the unions were above the law and were potentially subject to manipulation by a narrow group of leaders who were not formally answerable to the rank and file. Or, contradictorily, they were at the mercy of shop stewards who ignored the leadership and pursued their own agendas. In either case, unions could and did behave in ways opposed to the interests of the community at large and even to the interests of their own members. The Liberals had given the unions legal immunity in 1906 because they believed that trade unions provided a means of imposing order on industrial relations while giving workers some rough equality in the bargaining process. By 1969, both the order and the equality appeared to be gone. Now, the power seemed to rest with the unions. Furthermore, when they defied the government and the law by ignoring wage controls, unions hardly looked like a force for order in the system of industrial relations.

By 1969, Wilson saw union legislation as a means of winning popularity for the government. More surprisingly, his newly appointed Secretary of State for Employment and Productivity, the left-winger Barbara Castle, also favoured reform. Castle did not see why industrial relations alone should be exempt from socialist planning and left to market forces – a view which was pure heresy among the unions. Both Wilson and Castle thought the unions would go along because the projected legislation also sought to strengthen unions and enhance some of their rights, while the threat of more stringent Tory legislation would make the mild dose they proposed seem acceptable. Early in 1969 the government published a planning document, *In Place of Strife*, which outlined its proposals. Those that the unions disliked gave new powers to the government: to impose a twenty-eight day 'cooling-off period' in certain disputes, to impose a settlement when two unions had a jurisdictional dispute (an important cause of wildcat strikes) and to call for a strike ballot. Furthermore, a new Industrial Relations Court would enforce some of these provisions, with the power to impose legal sanctions if the law was broken. The proposals hardly seem radical. Yet the trade union movement was almost unanimous in its opposition, and it had powerful support in the parliamentary party. Wilson finally recognised that he could not get such a bill through the House of Commons and dropped the whole thing.

The weakness of the Labour government was never clearer. The need for trade union legislation seemed obvious, as there was a level of strike activity in 1969 well beyond any that had been known since the war (see Table 6.1). Yet having apparently conceded that the unions were part of Britain's problem, the government had backed away from dealing with the issue. This failure encapsulated the barrenness of Labour's economic policies under Wilson. Economic planning had been buried beneath the crises of 1966–8. In 1967, Wilson had reluctantly concluded that Britain had to be attached to that powerful engine of growth, the EEC (by now known as the European Community), as a means of economic regeneration. Macmillan had tried the same thing in 1961, and, like Macmillan, Wilson failed because President de Gaulle of France vetoed Britain's application. Now Labour had tried trade union reform, and again it had failed.

The Conservatives under Edward Heath, by contrast, had developed a new analysis of Britain's economic problems and a new set of policies that reflected that analysis. Like Labour, they took a failure of entrepreneurship and insufficient investment as their starting point; however, they did not look to the debilitating effects of 'stop-go' policies to explain weak economic performance. Rather, it arose from heavy taxation that discouraged income accumulation and investment; from excessive government interference with the market through wage and price controls and the mediation of labour disputes; and from trade union power, which resulted in excessive wage settlements that pushed up inflation. What were the policies that followed from this analysis? All of them aimed to solve Britain's economic problems by using the market to force more efficient operations on firms. First, the government would stop interfering in collective bargaining, leaving both firms and workers to pay the price imposed by the market for excessive wage settlements and price increases. Not only would this force greater efficiency on management; it would also push workers towards greater productivity if they wanted higher wages. Second, there should be no government bail-outs and subsidies to nationalised industries. These too undermined efficiency. Limits on government spending would force all industries that were losing money to look for ways to cut costs, while reduced taxes would provide new incentives for investment and entrepreneurship. Third, Britain must enter the European Community (EC). Then British firms would have to compete with the successful firms of the EC to survive, while the big EC market would allow them to benefit from the economies that came from producing on a larger scale and so would encourage investment. Finally, the Conservatives wanted to limit the expansion of the welfare state, though without attacking the welfare system. Rather, they intended some selective cutting and redirecting of benefits away from universalism towards those in need. The whole programme was similar to the one that would later be associated with Margaret Thatcher, but it was not as stringent. Heath was merely trying to modify the post-war consensus by changing the balance in favour of market forces, individual initiative and less government interference, rather than rejecting it altogether.

Thus, like Labour in 1964, the Conservatives came to power in 1970 with a programme to improve the performance of the British economy. Over the next two years, however, that programme was shattered by the same forces that had destroyed the credibility of the Wilson government, though after 1972 without the albatross of the pound hanging over policy. The central problem was rising costs, which were destroying the competitiveness of inefficient industries. The point was driven home when Rolls-Royce – long a byword for quality in British manufacturing – went bankrupt in 1971. The company's failure seemed to illustrate the larger problem of British entrepreneurship, since it was managed by engineers rather than businessmen. The government could not allow such a famous name, major employer and important engine manufacturer for the Ministry of Defence to go under, so it took over the firm. Suddenly, nationalisation was taking on an entirely new role – the rescuing of sick firms in order to preserve jobs. The same message was sent again when the government bailed out the Upper Clyde Shipbuilders with a subsidy. The shipbuilding industry – one of the great industries of the nineteenth century – was now in terminal decline. After the war, it had failed to adapt to the advent of greater standardisation of products and mass production techniques, which required much larger firms. In the 1960s, Labour had resorted to mergers, grants and loan guarantees in an attempt to modernise the industry, but the Tories were supposed to stop such largesse. However, the government was not prepared to let so many jobs disappear in an area of high unemployment. Full employment remained the goal, and by 1972 unemployment was getting desperately close to the politically unacceptable one million mark.³ Furthermore, British industry had to be ready within a year to compete inside the EC. So the government went further. It passed an Industry Act to promote industrial expansion and investment, stopped the running down of the coal industry and planned to invest more money to modernise the steel industry. This was not merely reacting to a crisis; it was a complete reversal of policy.

Inflation also undermined the government's attempt to cut spending. Any cuts imposed in the welfare state (and there were some) were overwhelmed by rising prices. At the same time, spending was driven up by the jump in unemployment and the need to increase pensions and other welfare payments to keep up with inflation. As a result, between 1970 and 1974 government expenditure went up by over £7 billion, an average annual increase of nearly 14 per cent.⁴ Inevitably, the budget deficit ballooned. The government's policy of lowering taxes only made matters worse; over the three-year period 1971–3 tax revenues as a percentage of GDP fell by an unprecedented 7 per cent.⁵ The rise in unemployment seemed to justify the decision of Heath and his Chancellor, Anthony Barber, to offer an enormous tax cut in 1972 on top of the more modest one of the previous year, despite the increasing inflation. It was intended to be another 'dash for growth', like that of 1963. The result, however, was an even bigger disaster than its predecessor. The budget deficit soared, as did the money supply, since the government made no effort to put a lid on credit. Along with the falling value of the pound, once it was allowed to float in 1972, it all gave an impetus to inflation.

So did wage increases. The Tories had abolished Labour's Prices and Incomes Board, daring the market to do its worst. The market duly obliged. Rising prices and a growing sense of their own power drove the unions to push for settlements that kept wages ahead of prices; but such settlements only further fed the inflation. The result was a record increase in strike activity during the Heath years (see Table 6.2 below). The government's decision to limit the power of the unions only made matters worse. Trade union reform had been a central plank of the government's 1970 election campaign. While the Tories insisted ever afterwards that their intention was not to confront the unions, but to rationalise the system of labour relations in ways that offered benefits as well as imposing obligations, few at the time had any doubt that the government was throwing down the gauntlet. There was virtually no consultation about the Industrial Relations Act, which was forced through the Commons in 1971. It did what Labour had proposed in 1969, giving government the power to demand a strike ballot and to enforce a cooling-off period of sixty days in key industries. These powers would be exercised by an Industrial Relations Commission and enforced by an Industrial Relations Court, which could impose penal sanctions if its rulings were ignored. The Act, however, went well beyond Labour's proposals. Unions were required to register to retain

Table 6.2. Strike Activity, 1969–74

	Number of Stoppages	Days Lost to Strikes (000)	% Strikes Less than 3 Days
1969	3,116	6,846	62.3
1970	2,906	10,980	59.4
1971	2,228	13,551	50.7
1972	2,497	23,909	48.5
1973	2,873	7,197	49.1
1974	2,922	14,750	42.8

Source: Price and Bain, 'The Labour Force', in Halsey, *British Social Trends since 1900*, p. 196.

their immunity under the law, and registration meant that they accepted restrictions on what constituted a legal industrial action. Agreements could be made enforceable under the law if both sides agreed, and the Industrial Relations Commission was given the power to adjudicate jurisdictional disputes between unions. The aim of the legislation was to enhance the authority of union leaders, giving them the means to block wildcat strikes and limit intimidating picketing. Heath never admitted that it could be seen as an attempt to weaken the unions. Yet the unions themselves had little doubt about it. They were virtually unanimous in opposing the Act and refused to register, thus not coming under its provisions. Furthermore, every industrial dispute now became a political challenge to an act of Parliament and to the government.

The most important battle in this phase of the war between the government and the unions was fought in the winter of 1972, even before the Industrial Relations Act became law, when the miners went on strike. The strike immediately took on political overtones because both the Vice-President and the Secretary of the National Union of Mineworkers (NUM) were Communists, increasing fears about the sinister influence of Communists in the trade union movement. Yet these men were not elected to leadership positions because of their politics, but because of their success in representing the interests of the rank and file.[6] The miners wanted larger wages, for they had fallen behind both inflation and the wage increases of other workers from 1966 to 1971. The strike of 1972 delivered the wage increases they wanted, thus reinforcing the message to all workers that a more aggressive leadership, like that associated with the Communists, succeeded. But did the Communists have a goal beyond getting the best deal possible for their members? Did they have political aims, like bringing down the government or destroying capitalism? In 1972, the only political aim of all union leaders was to destroy the Industrial Relations Act. The 1972 miners' strike, however, did introduce a more confrontational approach. The most threatening manifestation of this new radicalism was 'flying pickets' – the mobilising of large numbers of miners (in one instance as many as 15,000) from around the country at a single location to prevent the movement of coal. This tactic reinforced a public perception that the union was no more averse to a war than the government, and was just as inclined to use the threat of force to achieve its aims.

The miners' strike was a public relations disaster for the government. Polls indicated much public support for the miners. They had a case, based on comparability with other workers, for better wages, while everyone recognised that they had a miserable, difficult job on which the nation depended. So they should be adequately compensated. Furthermore, the public was suffering. In the midst of winter, there was a shortage of coal, while power shutdowns meant large layoffs for workers. Although coal's importance was declining (the number of miners had fallen from over 700,000 to under 300,000 over the previous fifteen years),[7] it was still a key fuel, especially for electrical power stations. The government finally had to give way, granting a wage increase that ranged from 17 to 24 per cent and other concessions as well.[8] This success by the miners gave a further impetus to union militancy. In this regard, the dramatic reduction in days lost to strikes in 1973 is deceptive. In part, the big increase in 1972 was due to the miners' strike, so there was bound to be a substantial fall-off the next year. By 1973, however, the Industrial Relations Act was not being enforced any more, while several unions adopted a work-to-rule,* which disrupted services and secured a favourable settlement without a strike.

Nonetheless, the agreement with the miners did not immediately lead to higher wage settlements elsewhere. Renewed pressure came only with an acceleration of inflation over the summer of 1972, which was triggered by the expansionary

---

* This means that the members would only work according to the rules defined by the collective bargaining agreement, eliminating all of the rule-breaking conventions (like overtime) that had been adopted to give flexibility to employment arrangements.

policies of the government and the decision to float the pound. Heath then decided to return to an incomes policy – thus once more retreating from a reliance on market forces. He tried to negotiate an agreement with the Confederation of British Industry (CBI) and the TUC for voluntary controls, but talks broke down over the unions' insistence on a statutory price freeze (without a corollary statutory wage freeze). The government therefore resorted to legislation in November. Like Labour in 1966, it started with a freeze on wages and prices, with subsequent stages setting a ceiling on increases, and it created a Pay Board to enforce the controls. Initially, the new policy did not lead to a major showdown with the unions, but it also did not do much to limit inflation. Then, in October 1973, Britain was hit by a new catastrophe. The Yom Kippur War between Israel and the Arab states led to an oil embargo, followed by a large increase in the price of oil imposed by the producers' cartel OPEC (Organization of Petroleum Exporting Countries). Every Arab–Israeli War had been a disaster for Britain, and this one was no exception. A fourfold increase in the price of a commodity that was a necessity for industry and individual consumers alike was inevitably going to precipitate a dramatic increase in inflation, as well as a serious deterioration in the balance of payments. Furthermore, the leap in the price of oil gave new leverage to the miners, for coal became more attractive as a cheaper alternative fuel. Once more, Heath faced a possible confrontation with the NUM.

The government had been bargaining with the NUM during the summer in the hope of avoiding a showdown over the next stage of wage controls. No agreement was reached, however, and the new legislation was introduced virtually simultaneously with the outbreak of war in the Middle East. In November, the NUM published wage demands far in excess of the limits imposed by the new incomes policy. At the same time, it began a ban on overtime to put pressure on the government to settle. The conflict escalated over the next two months. The overtime ban was supported by action by the power plant engineers and the railwaymen, so coal supplies were running down by the end of the year. The government responded by introducing a three-day working week on 1 January and limiting the use of heat and electricity on commercial premises. The intention was to minimise the inconvenience to the home consumer, but the policy put the burden of dislocation on industry and the economy. Negotiations continued throughout January. The TUC tried to break the deadlock by promising that its members would recognise the miners as a special case; therefore, any concessions made to them would not be used by other unions as a basis for their own demands. For ten years, however, the TUC had failed to make good on promises of voluntary wage restraint, so the government was sceptical that, even with the best intentions, it would be able to deliver this time either. In any case, Heath was not prepared to accept an agreement outside the statutory wage controls, while the NUM insisted on such an agreement. The impasse was complete.

Far more than in 1972, it looked as if a radical union was holding the public hostage and trying to coerce the government, and on that basis Heath called an election in February 1974. Yet this was no Communist ramp. The NUM was one of the few unions in the country to require a strike ballot, and 81 per cent of those voting supported the strike. Furthermore, they had the whole of the TUC behind them – most of whose leaders were not Communist. Nor had the government's management of the unions and the economy over the past three years inspired much confidence. If the unions were unpopular, the government was too. Finally, people were inconvenienced, if not suffering, under the three-day week, and Labour promised that its special relationship with the unions would bring industrial peace and restore normality to life. Nonetheless, the British people were as sceptical of Labour as they were of the Tories. Neither party seemed to have the slightest idea how to resolve the country's economic problems. Indeed, it is arguable that an economy that had been doing quite well in 1964 was now a mess, and while some of the causes were structural or even beyond anyone's control, political mismanagement had contributed mightily to the decline.

So while Labour won the election, it did not have a majority in the Commons over all other parties. The result was hardly a popular vote of confidence in the new government.

The Failure of the Social Contract

When Harold Wilson returned as Prime Minister in February 1974, he was faced with an economic crisis that could only get worse. Britain's high underlying rate of inflation – which was proving difficult enough to get under control – was now going to be pushed higher. First, not only was there the rise in the price of oil; commodity prices as a whole had increased by 50 per cent in 1973 and by nearly 160 per cent over the period from 1971 to 1974.[9] Second, the end of fixed exchange rates in 1972 meant that any such inflationary pressure would be more diffi-cult to control. Whereas previously signs of inflation had forced governments to deflate the economy in order to preserve the value of the pound, now they could let the exchange rate fall, which would encourage exports and so preserve jobs. This is exactly what Wilson chose to do;[*] however, as a result, imports became more expensive, thus contributing to further inflation. A third factor contributing to inflation was Britain's entry into the European Community in 1973. Over the rest of the decade, Britain was obliged to phase out its food subsidies, as well as the system of preferential tariffs with the Commonwealth which had reduced the price of food imports. At the same time, the government had to introduce the EC's Common Agriculture Policy, which would raise food prices. Entry into the EC also required Britain to introduce a value added tax in place of Britain's own purchase tax, with uncertain effects on prices.[†] Thus, even if there were brilliant economic management,

---

[*] Sterling's exchange rate fell from one pound equalling $2.34 in 1974 to $2.22 in 1975 and $1.80 in 1976, based on annual averages. Butler and Butler, *British Political Facts 1900–2000*, p. 418.

[†] The Common Agriculture Policy and value added tax are discussed in detail in the next chapter.

Britain's economy faced built-in inflationary pressures for several years.

Labour's policy for dealing with this crisis was the 'social contract'. This was an agreement between Wilson, as leader of the opposition, and the TUC concerning Labour's policies when it returned to power. Wilson promised to repeal the Tories' Industrial Relations Act and end statutory wage and price controls. The TUC promised to press its member unions to exercise restraint in wage demands, if the government pursued a more aggressive socialist policy based on expanded welfare provisions and more nationalisation of industry. In other words, once again Labour was relying on the failed policy of voluntary restraint, just when inflation was going to take off. Furthermore, Labour's new promises could provide yet another push to inflation if they led to a larger budget deficit. In effect, the government was turning its fate over to the trade unions – relying on their interest in preserving a Labour government to push them towards wage restraint and a reduction in strikes.

The government delivered on its part of the bargain. The objectionable Tory legislation was repealed, while a new act in 1975 strengthened the trade unions. The Chancellor of the Exchequer Denis Healey's first budget increased pensions and other benefits, along with food and housing subsidies, to help the poorest people cope with inflation. He tried to cover these increases with higher taxes and cuts in defence spending, but effective budget control was impossible, especially because of the soaring wage settlements in the public sector. As a result, there was a dramatic increase in budget deficits as government expenditures outstripped revenues over the next three years (see Table 6.3 overleaf). The government's industry policy also contributed to this deficit. Under the social contract, the government promised to expand its control over industry. In 1975 it created the National Enterprise Board (NEB), which, as the left saw it, was supposed to invest in firms (not just the sick, but also the profitable), impose planning on them, and so help them modernise and become more competitive. The government would become a shareholder

Table 6.3. Government Budget Deficit, 1974–8 (£ million)

	Gross Income	Gross Expenditure	Deficit
1974	18,226	19,965	1,739
1975	23,570	26,803	3,223
1976	29,417	36,047	6,630
1977	33,778	39,372	5,594
1978	38,773	43,989	5,521

Source: Mitchell, *British Historical Statistics*, pp. 586 (income), 592 (expenditure).

in the firms it assisted and use its leverage to influence their policies in socially desirable directions. Wilson, however, ensured that the NEB simply acted as another vehicle for rescuing sick firms which would otherwise have gone under. Most notably, Britain's utterly inefficient car giant, British Leyland, which was threatened with bankruptcy but employed some 170,000 people, came under the Board in 1975. The NEB was also able to channel money to smaller start-up firms, and it did so with some success. Finally, in 1976 the government nationalised the shipbuilding industry and British Aerospace. The objective of this activist policy was to preserve jobs when unemployment, which permanently breached the million mark in 1975, was becoming a politically explosive issue (see Table 6.4 opposite). All these policies cost money, however. The government gave these industries large subsidies to preserve jobs, and it did the same for the old nationalised industries. Hence, its whole industrial policy helped to swell the deficit.

In part, the trade unions also delivered what was expected of them. Following the 1974 miners' strike, the days lost to strikes dropped precipitously over the next two years (see Table 6.4). As an instrument for checking inflation, however, the social contract was a disaster, as one union after another scrambled to get a

Table 6.4. Unemployment and Strike Activity, 1974–9

	Unemployment (Maximum for Year)	Number of Stoppages	Days Lost to Strikes (000)	% Strikes Less than 3 Days
1974	628,000	2,922	14,750	42.8
1975	1,152,000	2,282	6,012	40.6
1976	1,440,000	2,016	3,284	46.7
1977	1,567,000	2,703	10,142	41.0
1978	1,608,000	2,471	9,405	42.4
1979	1,464,000	2,080	29,474	42.0

Source: Butler and Butler, *British Political Facts 1900–2000*, p. 401 (unemployment); Price and Bain, 'The Labour Force', in Halsey, *British Social Trends since 1900*, p. 196 (strike activity).

wage settlement that kept its members ahead of ever more rapidly rising prices. As a result, after an average annual increase of 9.3 per cent from 1970 to 1973, prices went up by 16 per cent in 1974 and 24 per cent in 1975. At its peak, inflation was nearing an annual rate of 30 per cent, while wage increases were over that rate. These were rates of inflation rarely seen in an economically developed nation.[10] Clearly, something had to be done. Healey pushed for a statutory incomes policy, but Wilson would do nothing without union support.

Jack Jones – the General Secretary of the Transport and General Workers' Union (TGWU) and one of the most powerful of the left-wing union leaders – finally took the lead to resolve the crisis. Jones had been in regular contact with Wilson and Healey from the moment Labour returned to power. He trusted the government because, with Michael Foot as Employment Secretary, it consulted with the unions and had delivered on its promises to them. Now he feared that continuing inflation and economic crisis would destroy it. Then the unions would be faced with a Tory backlash. The unions therefore had to act to save the policies they valued. Jones agreed that the unions should accept a maximum wage increase of £6 per week for the 1975–6 bargaining season, thus assuring that the lowest paid workers got the most protection (i.e. the largest percentage wage increase). The TUC General Council approved the flat rate in June (though only by a vote of 19–13), and the annual conference did so in September. At last, the unions had accepted the importance of reducing inflation and, more importantly, a mechanism for limiting wage increases.

The replacement of Wilson by James Callaghan as Prime Minister in April 1976 assured that the government, too, was fully committed to defeating inflation. Healey, who continued as Chancellor, incorporated a 3 per cent target as a maximum for wage increases in 1976–7 into his 1976 budget (the agreement actually reached was somewhat higher). Thus, while voluntary restraint remained the policy in theory, the government was now setting a stringent target for wage increases and building its economic assumptions around that target. Furthermore, employers who breached the target were not allowed to pass on the higher wages in price increases. The effect of the new wage restraint was immediately evident, as inflation fell back to 16.5 per cent in 1976.[11] It might have done even better, except the government still could not get a handle on its finances. Healey had vacillated between mildly deflationary and inflationary budgets in 1975 and early 1976. The continuing rise in unemployment meant there were enormous pressures to pursue expansionary policies to bring it down. Demands that pensions and other welfare payments keep up with inflation had the same effect. The result was a ballooning deficit in 1976 (see Table 6.3). As long as the deficit continued to be large and inflation high, there was pressure on the pound. The Treasury welcomed some devaluation, but it was unable to control the collapse of the exchange rate that occurred, from $2.22 in 1975 to $1.70 in May

1976 and $1.50 in October.[12] This fall was yet another source of inflation, increasing import prices. The Treasury was able to secure a short-term loan from other central banks to prop up the pound, but the Americans made it clear that no more would be forthcoming. The government had to rein in the budget deficit and inflation or see Britain's reserves disappear.

By November, the government felt that it had no choice but to turn to the International Monetary Fund (IMF) for a loan. Since the IMF imposed strict deflationary conditions, it gave Healey extra leverage to impose drastic cuts in expenditure (with capital spending taking the biggest hit), and Callaghan backed him up. Furthermore, IMF supervision finally satisfied the financial markets and the US government that Labour was putting its house in order. The tide now began to turn for the British economy. Deflationary budget policies (which imposed far more severe cuts than Margaret Thatcher would attempt in the 1980s), reasonably successful wage restraint and a worldwide recession in the aftermath of the oil price increase all contributed to a reduction in the rate of inflation to about 7 per cent by mid-1978.[13] At the same time, sterling recovered in value and the balance-of-payments problem disappeared. During the IMF crisis, Callaghan arranged with the Americans to run down the sterling balances and end sterling's role as a reserve currency. Thus, this artificial constraint on the exchange rate and on government policy was finally removed. At the same time, oil from Britain's wells in the North Sea began to come ashore in large quantities. By 1980, Britain would be self-sufficient in oil, thus eliminating an expensive import and making sterling more attractive to hold. By 1978, the economy seemed to be doing well. Healey felt sufficiently confident to introduce a modestly expansionary budget.

Yet recovery was a signal for renewed trouble from the unions. Even Jack Jones had accepted wage limitation as a distasteful necessity. Like virtually all trade unionists, he was committed to free collective bargaining. Only his enormous prestige within the movement had enabled him to drag the unions after him in accepting voluntary wage restraint from 1975 to 1977. He had come under constant personal attack for his efforts, and in the autumn of 1977 his own union turned against another year of forbearance. Furthermore, the very policy of wage restraint created pressures for ending it. First, the wages of many workers fell behind the rate of inflation, so they lost purchasing power. Second, in relative terms, the biggest losers were the most skilled, as the wage differentials between skilled and unskilled workers were eroded. Public employees like nurses and teachers especially suffered, as Healey forced small increases on them by imposing strict cash limits on the relevant ministries. Since steel workers, coal miners and railway workers were also public employees, wage differentials narrowed in industry as well. While the government had a sanctions policy to try to force wage discipline on the private sector, it was ineffective, as private sector employees were able to do better in wage negotiations. So a third grievance was the erosion of wage comparability between workers of similar skill in the public and private sectors. Yet another source of resentment was the government's willingness to give large pay increases to public employees with professional status (like doctors, judges and high ranking civil servants), or to those in vital services (like policemen and soldiers). The message from the government to most public employees and industrial workers, therefore, seemed to be twofold: what they did was less important to the public than the contribution of (say) the police, while there was no ethic of equal sacrifice during the economic crisis, given the raises for professionals working for the state. Comparability with the private sector was the criterion for professionals, but not for the rest.

Ultimately, such differences in treatment made it impossible to contain trade union discontent. They gave radicals built-in grievances that they could appeal to. The government and the more moderate leaders had barely managed to keep the lid on wage increases during the 1977–8 bargaining year. Now, in 1978, Jack Jones, the man who seemed to have held it all together, retired as leader of the TGWU. His successor, Moss Evans, was elected in part because he had been a vocal opponent of the social contract. Callaghan ignored the clear warnings from the unions that another year of voluntary restraint was impossible. He was determined to impose a 5 per cent target for wage increases in 1978–9, a figure that even Healey thought was overly stringent. So the stage was set for a confrontation. All the cumulated resentment over three years of self-denial exploded in an inundation of strikes during the autumn and winter of 1978–9, which was quickly dubbed the 'winter of discontent'. The private sector led the way, with the TGWU securing a 17 per cent wage increase after a two-month strike at Ford during the autumn. Ultimately, however, it was public sector strikes – such as those by hospital workers (like orderlies), school employees (like janitors and cooks) and dustmen – that came to symbolise the unions' willingness to impose suffering on the public for selfish ends. The stories in the press multiplied of garbage that remained uncollected in the streets (with a plausible risk to public health), sick people who could not get to hospitals because there was no ambulance to take them and bodies that could not be buried because no one would dig the graves. A lorry drivers' strike had the same effect on the public, as it threatened fuel deliveries to schools, hospitals and the population at large. Whatever the merits of any individual wage claim (and the public employees all had a strong case), the trade union movement as a whole was completely discredited by the 'winter of discontent'.

So was the Labour Party. Far more than its leaders realised, its credibility as a party of government since 1974 had been based on the special relationship with the trade unions. That relationship was supposed to prevent the kinds of crippling strikes that had occurred under Heath. Now it had been exposed as a fraud. Labour could not control the unions any better than the Tories could, and the British public was unforgiving. The government and the TUC tried to cobble together a new version of the social contract, but Labour actually had nothing new to offer to deal with the economy or the trade unions. Later, those writing on the Thatcher years made much of the fact that many economic policies associated with Thatcherism were first introduced by

Healey and Callaghan between 1976 and 1978. These could not be the policies of the Labour Party, however, for they were repudiated by the trade unions and the Labour left. So Labour had no policy, while the Conservatives had a better articulated version of the free market, neo-liberal policies first floated by Heath in 1970.

Once again the pendulum swung back to the Tories, as the British people searched for someone to end the sense of crisis that had beset the economy since the late 1960s. Things were not as bad as they seemed: both the average annual growth of GDP and the average annual growth of worker productivity were roughly 1.2–1.3 per cent from 1973 to 1979 (see Tables 5.1 and 5.6); there had been no actual decline. Nonetheless, when inflation could approach an annual rate of 30 per cent, as it did in 1975, and when the trade unions seemingly could bring the country to its knees, something was wrong that needed to be faced. People were worried about the possibility of a renewed conflict between a Tory government and the unions; they did not want a repeat of 1972–4. However, at least the Conservatives had a clear policy for limiting trade union power which seemed reasonable. Similarly, while the electorate claimed to trust Labour more than the Tories on the key issues of inflation and unemployment,[14] Labour's policies had been discredited by the 'winter of discontent'. Again, people claimed that they did not want tax cuts if those cuts meant a cut in public services, but they were still attracted by the income tax cuts that the Conservatives promised. So while the electorate seemingly distrusted the Tories on a whole range of economic issues that they cared about, they voted the Conservatives back in anyway because Labour had no credibility any more for having a strategy capable of overcoming the nation's economic problems.

7

POLITICAL FAILURE

European political parties look radically different from American parties. First, parliamentary government imposes a degree of party discipline that is alien to the American system. At the same time, European parties are more explicitly defined by ideology. Because most European countries have some form of proportional representation, there is no disincentive to organising parties around even narrow ideological positions, for they can still secure representation in the legislature. Thus, there is no impetus towards the centre in European parties, as exists in American parties, which traverse the political spectrum. Democratic compromise occurs during the process of negotiating coalition governments rather than within the political parties themselves. While this model is less true of Britain, which does not have proportional representation, British parties still appear to be defined by ideology. For the Conservatives and Liberals, the ideology was expressed in the name of the party; for Labour, it was embodied in the 1918 constitution, which committed the party to a socialist programme.

Yet it is easy to exaggerate these differences. British parties have always been coalitions of diverse interests and ideological viewpoints, far more than their names would indicate. The various sections of the nineteenth-century Liberal Party were constantly fighting with each other and dividing the party, while the historian D. A. Hamer has denied that liberalism as a political ideology existed at all.[1] The Conservatives, on the other hand, never projected themselves as a party based on ideology. They were the party of pragmatism; that, they claimed, was what distinguished them from an ideologically driven liberalism. The advent of socialism looked as if it tightened the ideological bases of the parties. Socialism claimed to be rooted in a reasonably coherent theoretical view of society, and its triumph in the Labour Party appeared to impose a kind of ideological struggle on the British party system. In fact, little had changed. Labour inherited many of the divisions that had bedevilled the Liberals, while socialism turned out to be as difficult to pin down as liberalism. The Conservatives continued to promote themselves as the party of pragmatic reform and sought to contrast themselves with a Labour Party which threatened to uproot the whole system in the name of abstract theory. All three parties incorporated a range of ideological viewpoints, and there was substantial overlap between the Liberal or Labour right and the Conservative left – just as there was between the Democratic right and Republican left in the United States.[2]

Nonetheless, some impetus to ideological unity has been enforced in Britain by the exigencies of party discipline within the parliamentary system. As a result, British parties have been more brittle than their American counterparts – with periodic splits or threats of splits shaping the course of politics. As early as 1846, Sir Robert Peel split the Conservative Party over the repeal of the Corn Laws. Peel's disciple William Gladstone split the Liberals in 1886 over granting Ireland Home Rule. Ironically, Peel and Gladstone, who crippled their parties for twenty years or more as a result of their actions, are viewed as two of the greatest political leaders of the modern era. By contrast, leaders who have successfully fought to hold their party together in the face of the centrifugal forces of ideological struggle have not been viewed so favourably. The bias of history (and the historians who interpret it) has favoured those leaders who stood by strong beliefs (especially beliefs which historical hindsight seemed to validate) and against those leaders who were willing to sacrifice ideological purity (read as principle) in the name of expediency.

This has certainly been the judgement of Arthur Balfour, the Conservative Prime Minister from 1902 to 1905 and leader of the party until 1911. Balfour faced a potential split over proposals by Joseph Chamberlain to reintroduce tariffs. Believing Peel had committed the unforgivable sin in dividing his party, Balfour prevaricated, limited the number of defections and held the party together. The tariff issue left the party weakened, however, and Balfour's indecisive and inconsistent leadership was blamed when Tory policies led to two more election defeats, the end of the House of Lords' veto over legislation and the imminent prospect of Irish Home Rule. So he was forced to resign. Twice since 1945, political leaders have been faced with the same problem as Balfour: when radicals try to impose a test of ideological purity on the party, should the leader seek to obscure differences and promote compromise, or should he purge the radicals and risk dividing the party? First, Harold Wilson and his successors as leader of the Labour Party from the late 1960s to the late 1980s were confronted by Labour's left wing on a whole range of political issues. Then John Major, the Conservative Prime Minister from 1990 to 1997, was challenged by those in his party who opposed closer ties with Europe, and specifically the single European currency. Wilson and Major, like Balfour, managed to prevent the kind of major split that had occurred under Peel and Gladstone. The result, however, was (as with Balfour) an overwhelming opposition triumph which allowed it to dominate government for as long as the party divisions lasted. As a result, both (like Balfour) have been perceived by contemporaries and historians alike as weak because of their failure to deal more effectively with those divisions.[*]

---

[*] There is another similarity among the cases: the leaders who were left to pick up the pieces (Andrew Bonar Law, Neil Kinnock and William Hague respectively) were politicians of relative obscurity at the time, and each had difficulty establishing his credibility with the public.

The divisions of the Labour Party, already important to the political history of the 1950s, became one of the driving forces of politics in the 1970s and 1980s. They helped change Wilson from a confident and accomplished political leader into a timid and ineffectual one. Wilson's transformation came at an unfortunate time for Britain. For as the nation's economic ills came to be the paramount issue of politics, it sorely needed a prime minister who was more than a political manipulator. It certainly was not getting what it needed from the Conservative side. On the contrary, Edward Heath was a bigger disaster than Wilson. Heath was so lacking in political savvy that it remains a source of amazement that he could have risen to the top of a major political party at all. Far more than Wilson, he completely lost the confidence of the electorate, and, unlike Wilson, he lost the confidence of his party as well. Yet even after three electoral defeats in four elections, he would not retire gracefully. As a result, he allowed a person whose views he had contempt for to triumph as leader of his party, and he then threatened to divide the party by waging a campaign against her for the next fifteen years.

Thus, while Rome burned, the politicians on both sides fiddled. Neither party seemed to have a clue as to how to stop a decline that both agreed was *the* paramount problem facing Britain. One result was a fracturing of the political scene. Not only did the Liberals come back from the dead. More significantly, Celtic nationalist parties which had not even been taken seriously up to now suddenly did well enough in the 1974 general elections to make devolution (or modified home rule) for Scotland and Wales practical politics. Thus, to all the other evidences of British decline, one could add the breakdown of the political consensus that had governed since 1945 and the threatened end of the United Kingdom.

The Trials of Harold Wilson

Harold Wilson has never been considered a weak man. He had held his own very well in the internecine warfare of the 1950s

Labour Party as he worked his way to the top. Furthermore, during his first stretch as Prime Minister from 1964 to 1966, he was an effective leader. After re-election in 1966, however, he was increasingly reacting to events. Indeed, sometimes he seemed to be mainly concerned with thwarting feared plots against his leadership. So policy initiatives took a back seat. The devaluation in November 1967, the crisis over trade union reform in 1969 and the election defeat in 1970 all took a heavy toll on Wilson's standing in the country. Following that defeat, Wilson's one preoccupation (beyond protecting himself) was party unity. As a result, he was incapable of giving a strong lead on any issue that was potentially divisive. Thus, when he became Prime Minister again in 1974–6, he could not control the trade unions and was paralysed in the face of the nation's intractable economic problems. The record now was one of failure.

A key factor in Wilson's transformation was his reluctance to try to master Labour's divisions on two key issues when they first threatened party unity: trade union reform in 1969 and Britain's entry into the European Community in 1971. In both instances, he backed away from the risks of splitting the party that a showdown would have entailed. In doing so, however, he also repudiated policies that he had supported. These retreats helped to shape a view of Wilson as a man of no principles. While this judgement is not entirely fair, it is clear that preserving the unity and so the political viability of the Labour Party transcended all other issues for him. It was in itself a matter of principle. Two other factors have contributed to the image of Wilson as a failed leader. First, his prevarications did not succeed in securing his immediate goal. Making concessions to the trade unions and the left did not dampen their divisive pressures; on the contrary, those pressures continued to build until they split the party in 1981. Second, to the degree that historical judgement reflects the views of posterity concerning where right lies, Wilson comes out poorly. For the power of the trade unions *did* need to be limited, and Britain *did* belong in the European Community. Wilson had the opportunity to help promote both goals, but he backed away from doing so. He thus left a legacy of greater difficulties for his successors as leader of the Labour Party and as Prime Minister to deal with.

The Wilson era started hopefully. During their first two years in office, Wilson and his team projected an image of energy, competence and excitement. While they had little administrative experience, they were the names that were going to dominate both government and the party for the next fifteen to twenty years, and they were an able group: James Callaghan, Denis Healey, Roy Jenkins, Barbara Castle, Richard Crossman and Tony Crosland. As they kept up a constant flow of new measures and new ideas, the contrast with the last years of Tory rule could not have been starker. The continued weakness of the Conservatives remained an asset. Sir Alec Douglas-Home was an ineffectual leader. Many Tories wanted someone who would be more aggressive and would take the fight into the socialist camp. At the same time, polls showed he was not matching up well against Wilson. In 1965 he resigned to enable the party to regroup, and under a reformed system for selecting the leader, a ballot of Tory MPs chose Edward Heath. In recent years, Heath had been an increasingly visible and effective debater in the Commons. Conservatives thought that he had just the abrasive style that was necessary to take on Wilson. He had none of Wilson's flair for public presentation or speech-making, however, so he did not catch on with the electorate. Moreover, like many new party leaders (it would be true of Margaret Thatcher and Neil Kinnock in the years ahead), he found that success as a lieutenant did not easily translate into effectiveness as the leader of the opposition in the cut and thrust of parliamentary questions and debate when going up against an experienced prime minister. In reality, Wilson could cut him to pieces. Thus, the Conservatives did not gain by the change; it merely confirmed Wilson's dominant position in the Commons and the country. Wilson and Labour perhaps also benefited from the mood of excitement and optimism in the mid-1960s, represented by the success of the Beatles in capturing America and the world and by England's World Cup victory over

West Germany in 1966 – which prompted the most widespread outpouring of popular patriotism in England since VE Day. Labour still embodied youth and energy and newness after thirteen years of Tory rule.

By the time of the World Cup victory, Labour had already consolidated its political position. Because the result of 1964 had been a narrow margin of four seats, the Cabinet had always understood that there would be a new general election as soon as the time was right. The first year or two were, in effect, a trial period, whereby the government would prove (or rather prove again) Labour's fitness to govern. With confidence in Wilson never higher (especially since Heath was the alternative), the government held the new election in March 1966 and increased its majority to ninety-six over all other parties. Yet by 1966, the hollowness of Labour's economic programme was becoming evident, while the increasingly troubled economy began to undermine Wilson's position with his party's left wing. First, Callaghan as Chancellor of the Exchequer had to impose deflationary policies that halted further steps on the road to socialism (not that Wilson had much interest in taking more such steps). Second, and more importantly, increasing inflation forced Callaghan to extend the policy of wage and price controls inherited from the Tories, which brought the government into direct conflict with the trade unions. Since the war, the unions had sided with the moderate leadership of the party. That alliance began to break down in the late 1950s, however, and now a new generation of leaders was moving some of the more powerful unions to the left. This strengthening of the left, and the divisions in the trade union movement that resulted, made both the unions and the party much more difficult for the Labour leadership to manage. The first signal of this more vexatious relationship was Wilson's outburst during the seamen's strike in the summer of 1966 about conspiratorial elements in the union.

Foreign policy, and especially the Vietnam War, also made Wilson's relations with the left troublesome. Britain's reliance on the United States to support the pound and to support sanctions against Rhodesia made it awkward for the government to criticise the war. Wilson had no particular commitment to the special relationship with the United States; however, he recognised America's leadership role in the West and Britain's military dependence on the US. He also agreed with the Americans about the Communist threat in Southeast Asia, although he had doubts about the Johnson administration's constant expansion of the war. With American military resources getting sucked ever deeper into Vietnam, Johnson was eager for Britain to make a token commitment of troops as a symbol of support. Wilson was able to fight off the Americans on Vietnam, but at the cost of increasing the tensions in his relationship with the President. Another source of strain between them was Wilson's desire to take on the British role of mediator between East and West. The Americans were cool to his efforts, which went nowhere. Wilson *was* willing to oblige Johnson by preserving Britain's military forces east of Suez, for Wilson was just as determined to maintain Britain's position as a world power as his predecessors had been. This commitment remained substantial, with some sixty thousand men in Singapore and Hong Kong and another seven thousand in the Persian Gulf.[3] Even before November 1967, however, Britain was planning a run-down of its presence in the East. The devaluation crisis merely accelerated a decision that had already been made. The result, though, was a further dip in Anglo-American relations, as the US had wanted Britain to hang on until the Vietnam War was over.

The Labour left was not much interested in Wilson's difficulties managing a particularly prickly period in the special relationship. It simply did not like foreign and defence policies which it found to be too right-wing. With Labour's increased majority following the 1966 general election, plus a loosening of party discipline on dissident backbenchers, the discontents had greater freedom to demonstrate their dissent by voting against the government. There was much for them to dislike. For Wilson was determined to prove that Labour was just as firm as the Tories in protecting British interests and projecting British power abroad. He had therefore backtracked on the manifesto promise to cancel the purchase of Polaris missiles from the United States. Britain would remain a nuclear power under Labour. Indeed, until 1968 the government seemed to be going out of its way to spare defence as it looked for places to slash the budget. Wilson also seemed to be doing nothing to bring the white-supremacist government in Rhodesia to heel. Most importantly, while the left all over Europe and America was mobilising in opposition to the Vietnam War, he was offering tacit support by refusing to criticise it. The left's very vision of socialism as an ideology based on morality was being flouted by the Prime Minister's pragmatism. That moralism, however, was being reaffirmed at the same time by Roy Jenkins as Home Secretary, who helped enact a radical agenda of social reforms – including abolishing the death penalty, ending censorship, decriminalising homosexuality, legalising abortion and broadening the grounds for divorce. While all these non-party measures were passed on the initiative of back-benchers, the government made time for them in part because it knew they were popular with its supporters. Thus, there were compensating gains for the left in having a Labour government.

While both Vietnam and social reform helped shape the relationship between the government and the left between 1966 and 1968, it was the economic crisis, with the ever more stringent incomes policies and budget cuts it required, that was central. From 1966, Wilson's authority as Prime Minister was weakened, with the collapse first of the national plan, then of Britain's application to join the EC and then of the pound. For a moment in 1966, when both the left and the right in the Cabinet combined to support devaluation, his very control over his government seemed to be threatened. Wilson saw conspiracy in the combination – as he tended to do in general, thus keeping the Cabinet constantly on edge. More likely, it was just an alliance of convenience against a policy that each side now had reason to believe had failed. Wilson was able to weather that storm; however, when devaluation finally did come, and it was followed by the draconian deflationary policies of 1968 and 1969, left-wing MPs saw the final abandonment of any effort at a socialist policy. Increasingly disillusioned, they began to defect from the government more frequently on specific votes.

The climax of disaffection came in 1969, with the government's proposed trade union reforms. Wilson saw them as a vote-winner – a way to outflank the Tories and to appeal to the ordinary voter at a time when Labour was unpopular in the polls. Yet the proposals were the ideal issue for the left to mobilise around because so much of the labour movement hated them. The trade unions were virtually unanimous in their opposition. Any MP who was sympathetic to the unions (not to mention those who were union nominees for their seats) would hesitate to oppose them on an issue which union leaders considered so fundamental. Criticism focused on the possible use of penal sanctions against those who might be convicted under the proposed law. What Labour member in good conscience could support throwing a trade unionist in prison for striking? Not many! Labour's National Executive Committee (NEC) came down against the bill. The government was divided. There had been rumblings against Wilson for more than a year, and the trade union proposals gave potential adversaries an ideal pretext on which to challenge him. Callaghan, who had seen Jenkins emerge as the heir apparent following the devaluation crisis, recovered his standing in the party as he led the opposition. Since he had stronger ties to the unions than either Wilson or Barbara Castle, the bill's sponsor, his opposition was a serious matter. But the consensus against the proposed legislation was broad once it was clear that the trade unions were opposed. When the Chief Whip told them that he could not secure a Commons majority for the legislation, Wilson's colleagues gradually deserted him, until finally he had to drop the measure.

Wilson never recovered from the humiliation of 1969. For a moment, his leadership seemed to be at risk. More permanently, his confidence as a leader and his public image as a man of strength were both shattered. Never again would he take on the trade unions. Indeed, he would never let another subject become so contentious within the party as to threaten the kind of division that blew up in 1969. For Wilson, no issue was worth the kind of showdown that Gaitskell had forced over unilateral nuclear disarmament in 1961. As a result, hereafter Wilson reacted to events. He sought to manipulate people and policies so as to contain problems and prevent their reaching a crisis stage. But this meant he could never again provide a strong lead to the party or the nation; all he could do was patch together compromises that looked increasingly barren, if not downright hypocritical. At the same time, the left got a tremendous boost to its own prestige from the battle against trade union reform. New left-leaning leaders like Jack Jones of the Transport Workers and Hugh Scanlon of the Engineers had taken the lead in opposing the government. Their power within the trade union movement was enhanced, and the ties between the unions and the political left were strengthened. This was the alliance that Wilson and his successors would face throughout the 1970s. The first test for Wilson was Britain's entry into the European Community.

The Battle over Europe

The Labour left had never warmed to the European Economic Community (EEC). The left feared that, in attempting to assure a fair competitive market among its members, the EEC could impose policies that would limit the freedom of a Labour government to implement a socialist agenda. The EEC in any case looked as if it existed primarily for the benefit of business. For this reason, the trade unions shared the left's suspicions. In the 1960s, there was no evidence of an EEC interest in the conditions of workers, while the Commission (the EEC executive) had the power to impose regulations that British trade unionists did not like. Finally, there was probably more residual dislike of both the French and the Germans (especially the Germans) than anyone cared to admit publicly. Thus, when Macmillan applied for entry, in a 1962 broadcast Gaitskell expressed his suspicion of 'a kind of giant capitalist, catholic conspiracy, our lives dominated by

Adenauer and de Gaulle, unable to conduct any independent foreign policy at all'.4 Gaitskell was not unsympathetic to joining if the terms were right. However, he was coming off the bruising battles over Clause IV and nuclear disarmament, and he saw that the EEC had the potential to revive these divisions in the party. Thus he sat on the fence for as long as possible. The federalist enthusiasms of Community leaders, with which he had no sympathy, and the terms agreed to by the government (especially relating to the Commonwealth) finally turned him against joining at this time. It was a decision that bought him peace by assuring there would be no new conflict with the left.

Nonetheless, Wilson applied to join in 1967. He did so for the same reasons that Macmillan had in 1961: to assure that Britain was not eclipsed as a power by the new European bloc, and to attach the British economy to one of the most prosperous and fastest growing economic regions in the world. Britain's trade with Europe had been steadily growing in importance, while that with the Commonwealth was declining. Membership would give British producers full access to the large West German and French markets. At the same time, competition within the EEC would hopefully impose greater efficiency on British firms. There was another reason to join – a fear that the United States would give more weight to a powerful EEC than to Britain as a political partner. Perhaps the only way that Britain could count in the affairs of the world was as part of the EEC. Both times, however, the British application was killed off by President de Gaulle, who wanted the EEC to be an instrument of Franco-German power in Europe, independent of the United States. He rightly feared that Britain's primary ties were with America rather than Europe, so that Britain would be a voice for US interests within the Community. Since one of the functions of the EEC was to protect European agriculture, he would also not consider British partici- pation as long as Britain insisted on preferential treatment for Commonwealth agricultural imports. De Gaulle's vetoes assured that EEC membership in the 1960s never became an issue of practical politics to divide the Labour Party.

Wilson was no true believer in the European ideal, any more than Macmillan was. Both had opted for the EEC for pragmatic reasons. Heath, by contrast, *was* a true believer – not in the ideal of a united Europe, but in the conviction that Britain could not have a meaningful influence in the world except through Europe. He was not indifferent to good relations with the United States; no responsible leader could be. That relationship, however, was looking less attractive in the 1970s – with the US trying desperately to extricate itself from Vietnam while the Nixon administration tried to dig out from the Watergate crisis. America was also beginning to show some of the same inflationary problems that Britain had. Those problems had led to the end of the special status of the dollar as a reserve currency in 1971, and so, it seemed, of the era when the United States stood alone astride the world economy. While not yet America's equals, the (after 1967) European Community (EC) and Japan were challenging the US economically. It seemed to many that Britain would benefit by being part of one of the big three players in the world economy, rather than remaining a relatively weak outsider trying to straddle Europe, the US and the Commonwealth. Thus, while Heath maintained proper relations with the United States, there was not a lot of warmth in them, and Heath insisted on acting as much as possible with the other members of the EC. The Nixon administration was not happy with this coolness. It was especially dissatisfied with Heath's response to American policy initiatives during the Arab–Israeli War of October 1973 – in part because Heath did not want to step out of line with broader European policy.

For those who embraced it, the European ideal was more than just a policy for economic prosperity. It was a policy for peace. The EC had ended the great power struggle for supremacy between France and Germany and had created a common interest for its members. Perhaps it could also create a common identity for its peoples as well. One did not have to believe in a United States of Europe, however, to see the possibilities for closer collaboration among members and so the EC evolving into an independent force on the international stage – in fact, de Gaulle's vision. By the 1970s, EC members were making intermittent (though not very successful) efforts to coordinate their foreign and even their defence policies. Heath was sensitive to this aspect of community relations. As British membership edged towards reality, he was careful not to do anything to give credence to Gaullist fears that Britain would simply be America's voice in the EC. Indeed, whenever possible he sought to represent European opinion in conversations with Nixon.

It was the retirement of de Gaulle in 1969 that made Britain's membership in the EC possible. With Heath's election in 1970, negotiations could be launched over the terms of British entry with a real prospect of success. Membership would have a very substantial cost, however. The rules had been drafted between 1957 and 1970, with West Germany and France as the principal influences in determining the structure of the Community. France wanted to protect its farmers, whose holdings were relatively small and inefficient. This goal was ultimately embraced by virtually every member state that had high-cost agriculture, including West Germany. Indeed, with Denmark and Ireland negotiating to join at the same time as Britain, the number of members with a stake in agricultural protection would be growing. The means of protection was the Common Agriculture Policy (CAP), whereby the EC guaranteed prices for many agricultural goods. Whatever EC farmers could not sell on the free market would be bought by the EC at the guaranteed price. Thus, there was no penalty for inefficient farming. The incentive was for farmers to produce as much as possible at any cost below the floor price, knowing they could always sell what remained to the EC at that price. With agriculture thus protected from competition, consumers in member states faced very high food prices, while the EC accumulated 'mountains' of unsold grain and butter and 'lakes' of unsold wine that went to waste.

Britain had its own system of subsidies. The British farmer was a relatively efficient producer, having faced foreign competition under Britain's free trade regime from the 1840s until the 1930s. Even so, he could not match the low prices of America's subsidised farming. Rather than support prices, however, British policy allowed them to be determined by the market, and the government paid the farmers whatever was necessary to assure a sufficient return. This approach was consistent with Britain's policy, since the repeal of the Corn Laws in 1846, of keeping food prices low. Joining the EC meant the repudiation of that long tradition, as Britain would have to adopt the CAP, phased in over the rest of the decade, with food prices going up. Furthermore, as a member of the Commonwealth, Britain was part of a preferential tariff system that secured British consumers low-priced Commonwealth farm products. Membership of the EC meant Britons would also lose this source of cheap food. Given that Britain already had an inflation problem, the CAP assured that EC membership would have the maximum adverse impact on every single citizen of the United Kingdom. Only Britain's small population of farmers would benefit, since they would get the same high prices as other farmers, while they operated at lower costs.

There was a second cost of membership for the British. CAP had to be financed. (While there were other Community programmes, and the numbers would grow with the number of EC members, CAP overwhelmingly absorbed the largest percentage of the budget in the 1970s.) The formula for determining the EC budget was not finally agreed upon until 1970. Revenues came from two sources. The first was a percentage of each country's revenues from value added tax (VAT). VAT is a form of sales tax which is supposed to distort the market less because it is imposed at each stage of the production process (based only on the value added at that stage) rather than all at the end, like the sales tax. Everyone has to pay some tax, not just the retailer, as with a sales tax. From the point of view of the consumer, however, there is no difference. The cumulative value added taxes still appear in the final price of the goods. By taking on the obligation to introduce VAT, therefore, Britain was agreeing to increase prices beyond what they otherwise would have been at a time when it was struggling to control inflation.

(Food is not subject to VAT, so it did not increase food prices any more.) The second source of funds for the EC budget was customs revenues on food and manufactures imported from outside the Community. The purpose here was to encourage intra-Community trade by raising the cost of imports from outside. In that sense, the EC was protectionist, since there was an incentive to keep the common external tariff high enough to finance Community programmes like CAP. Such a system discriminated against countries that relied more on foreign imports as opposed to domestic production, and against those whose trade links were outside the EC rather than within it. Britain was the principal victim of such a system, since it had long relied on foreign trade far more than any other country, and it still had extensive trade links with the Commonwealth. As a result of the budget system and CAP combined, Britain would be contributing far more to the EC budget than it would be getting back from Community programmes. Britain would also be contributing far more to the EC budget than the relative size of its economy justified. And finally, CAP and VAT assured that EC membership would result in a substantial increase of prices in Britain.

Given the immediate and obvious costs involved, when weighed against the uncertain and distant gains, EC membership was always going to be a difficult sell to the British people. Heath had done what he could by securing a gradual transition before the full burden of CAP and of Britain's contribution bit, and before Commonwealth members (primarily New Zealand) lost all preference. He also pressed for an EC development fund from which Britain could benefit. There was no way, however, to hide the reality of the burdens that would fall on the British. Nonetheless, governments headed by each of the major parties had decided over the previous decade that it was in Britain's interest to join. If that kind of consensus could have been sustained as part of a concerted campaign to persuade the British people that the rather elusive benefits of membership were worth the immediate costs, then possibly the opposition to membership could have been minimised and so marginalised. Nor was the Labour left the only source of such opposition. A nationalist segment of the Conservatives, led by Enoch Powell, also fought a step that involved a major circumscribing of British sovereignty.

The Labour left, however, was by far the largest centre of resistance to the EC, and its hostility assured that a joint front to win the British public to Europe was never given a chance. For with Labour now out of power the left was unmuzzled, and the success of 1969 had shown that Wilson could be bullied. In any case, Wilson was not the kind of leader to take a strong stand in opposition that might split the party. That had been Gaitskell's mistake in 1960. The danger of a split now was at least as great as it had been then. Callaghan was leading the opponents of the EC and Jenkins the supporters, and both were looking to replace Wilson if he made a false step. Wilson therefore slowly trailed behind the majority that was consolidating against joining. He also followed the lead of others in directing his attack against the terms Heath had negotiated and in promising a referendum on EC membership by a Labour government. This focus on the terms and on a referendum gave Wilson a way out of his immediate dilemma. He could oppose entry for the moment, while claiming he would negotiate better terms and then allow the British electorate to decide. Thus, in theory, he was not retreating from the principle of British membership at all.

This approach was really a sham, however, for there were no significantly better terms to be had. Therefore, a kind of charade had to be played out when Wilson returned as Prime Minister in 1974. Negotiations were launched with the EC over new terms. The other members were good sports and made some concessions; most importantly, the Community negotiated favourable terms for imports from all of the members' former colonies in the developing world. However, the refund formula agreed on to reduce Britain's budget contribution was only temporary, while the CAP remained unaltered. Wilson duly declared the new terms a significant improvement over what Heath had secured; however, it was difficult for the ordinary observer to see much difference, beyond the continued availability of New Zealand butter for a little longer. In 1975, Britain's first ever referendum was held on whether it should remain in the EC. The new terms were irrelevant to the campaign; the debate was over the larger question of whether Britain's future should be inside or outside the Community. Though a significant majority in the Cabinet favoured staying in, the NEC, the parliamentary Labour Party and the trade union movement were all strongly against. So the government could not provide a lead in the referendum campaign. The pro-EC forces were headed by the Conservatives, the Liberals and the minority of Labour 'true believers'. The Prime Minister and the Foreign Secretary (Callaghan), while indicating their support, remained on the sidelines. The EC was not an issue that they were prepared to go to the wall for.

The referendum produced a decisive vote of two to one in favour of remaining in the EC. The outcome did not reflect enthusiasm by the British people for the European connection; rather, it was an expression of their fear of breaking it. Yet such a clear result would seem to have settled the matter. In fact, it did no such thing. The whole exercise had merely consolidated and accentuated the divisions in the Labour Party on EC membership, which were now played out and validated on a national stage. Paradoxically, despite the referendum result, the left was the winner in the struggle for the soul of the party. Wilson and Callaghan seemed to have no strong commitment one way or the other, while the supporters of the EC were marginalised – so much so that Roy Jenkins departed in 1977 to become President of the European Commission. There was no future for the likes of him at the top of the Labour Party. At the same time, the emboldened left made clear that it had no intention of accepting the referendum result as final. It would continue to fight to secure Britain's withdrawal. So the issue still divided Labour, while the dictates of party politics constantly drove Wilson and then Callaghan to be obstructionist in EC negotiations on issues ranging from energy to fishing rights. Furthermore, time seemed to be on the side of the opponents of the EC. For the costs of membership would begin to bite as prices (especially food prices) rose, while people would realise that the new terms of entry (like the old ones) had left Britain with a disproportionate contribution to the Community's budget at a time when its economy was reeling. Hence, disillusionment was sure to set in, and, with it, the possibility of reversing the verdict of the referendum. Wilson's prevarication therefore had left Britain's EC membership as a festering issue in British politics and increasingly a hostage to an ever stronger left wing in the Labour Party.

The Failure of Political Leadership

The election of Edward Heath as Prime Minister in 1970 was a complete surprise. At no time since the onset of sophisticated polling methods had the predictions for a general election been so badly off the mark. In retrospect, it seems amazing that Wilson could have seemed so clearly the frontrunner. After all, the government's record during its second term was not a happy one. The fight to save the pound had failed and had been followed by a savage retrenchment. The whole ambience was one of economic failure. The government's application to join the EC had been vetoed. It had been humiliated by its own rank and file on trade union reform. It had been forced to cut back further on Britain's role as a world power after 1968 by ending all military commitments east of Suez. Finally, it had come up with no satisfactory solution to the embarrassing problem posed by the declaration of independence by Rhodesia, one of Britain's last remaining African colonies, whose white rulers would not accept a transition to black majority rule. Wilson tried twice to negotiate an agreement with Ian Smith, the Prime Minister of the breakaway state, but to no avail. Some of the African members of the Commonwealth wanted Britain to intervene militarily, but nineteenth-century gunboat diplomacy was not an option. Britain did not have the power, the resources or the will to force states that challenged it to toe the line, even if force was acceptable to world opinion. Hence, Britain had no real alternative to the one chosen: to mobilise worldwide economic sanctions against the renegade state. The sanctions would always be porous because South Africa and (until 1975) Portuguese Mozambique would not cooperate, but in the long run they did help to isolate and weaken the regime.

Nonetheless, the picture could not possibly have been as bleak as this catalogue of failures implies, or Labour would not have looked as strong as it did. Two factors appeared to be in Labour's favour. First, in the second half of 1969 the economy began to turn around, and as the numbers for the balance of payments and the value of the pound got better, the Tories' lead in the polls disintegrated. Inflation was still high by the standards of the time, however, and incomes policy still sought to limit wage increases. These reminders of failure over several years surely made more of an impression than any recent improvement that hardly affected people's day-to-day lives. More importantly, Labour had no policy to offer for strengthening the economy and so ending the climate of perpetual crisis management, while the Conservatives did. It is important not to exaggerate the coherence of the Tory platform. Nonetheless, its promises to end government interference in the economy, reduce taxes and public spending (to encourage entrepreneurship) and limit the power of the trade unions were a clear alternative to what Labour offered. It was not quite the neo-liberalism of 1979 – it was still committed to full employment, and there was no attack on the mixed economy and the welfare state. Yet it seemed distinctively new.

Thus, the one factor remaining in Labour's favour was Wilson himself – or perhaps, more accurately, Heath. Heath had never been able to catch on with the electorate, partly because his performance as leader of the opposition against the adroit and accomplished Wilson was a dismal one. Wilson was a man who was comfortable in the public eye and comfortable in the world of politics. Heath was comfortable with neither. He had no knack for self-presentation and no taste for the politics of the stump and the television interview. Even his biographer describes his public persona as 'stiff, cold, tense and humourless'. Furthermore, as he continued to be criticised, he 'became more withdrawn, prickly and aloof'.[5] These are powerful negative adjectives to use to describe a politician, for they are hardly the qualities that will enable him to establish a strong position with the party or the electorate. Heath was ill at ease with both – especially with his party as a grammar school boy and rank outsider. It is difficult to escape the feeling that he had an inferiority complex among the world of self-assured Tory aristocrats and businessmen. There are other ways in which Heath's personality simply did not fit the mould. His mentality was more bureaucratic than political, which ultimately came to be translated to mean more rigid than flexible. His most important responsibilities in government had been outside the major Cabinet slots – first as Chief Whip from 1955 to 1959, charged with mobilising the party's forces for votes in the Commons, and then as negotiator for the first effort to join the EEC from 1961 to 1963. So his experience was not as a policy-maker, or even as an administrator. Yet he had done his assigned tasks well, was interested in policy and was willing to work harder than anyone else to master the details of a problem. At the same time, he seemed to believe that hard work and greater efficiency were all that were needed to improve Britain. It was hardly an inspiring vision.

Wilson, by contrast, radiated confidence, and his whole election campaign reflected a man who assumed he would win. But probably this presumed advantage, too, was something of an illusion. For Wilson had done nothing to enhance his reputation for leadership over the past four years and so to justify the confidence he sought to generate. On the contrary, his record gave voters little reason to expect better from him than from Heath. The Conservatives focused their campaign on inflation, which affected ordinary Britons, and the underlying weakness of the economy. They also benefited from the immigration issue and the fact that Wilson had alienated the Labour rank and file. Finally, Heath ran a strong and aggressive, if uninspiring, campaign, while Wilson hardly seemed to be campaigning at all. A combination of Labour supporters who did not bother to vote and swing voters who were unimpressed by Wilson's record, and so were willing to give Heath a chance, provided a decisive swing to the Conservatives and secured them a majority of thirty-one over all other parties.

The description of Heath as rigid may appear unfair. As Prime Minister, he was perhaps best known for the U-turns of 1971–2, which reversed the policies of economic *laissez-faire* on which the Conservatives had campaigned in 1970 and returned to the interventionism of the 1960s. Surely this was evidence of flexibility. Inflation was getting worse; unemployment was going up; Rolls-Royce could not be allowed to go under. Once it became evident that the new policies were not working, it was simply good sense to change course. That is the way he and his supporters portrayed the changes in policy. His critics in the Conservative Party, however, were later to characterise them as weakness and a failure to stand by principle. It is also difficult, however, to see Heath as a man without principle, though it is likely that the election manifesto of 1970 did not reflect his principles very accurately. He had a genuine belief in a Britain where class did not matter and tolerance prevailed. He had expelled Enoch Powell, whose intellectualism he distrusted, from the shadow Cabinet in 1968 for speeches on immigration that appealed to racist sentiments. He had supported the abolition of capital punishment and sanctions against South Africa. Most of the time, however, Heath was a pragmatic problem-solver with a bureaucratic mind, and both of those qualities predisposed him towards intervention from the centre as the economy deteriorated. He was also a rationalist, and some of his reforms – like the redrawing of local government boundaries and the introduction of a decimal money system – overturned centuries-old traditions. They confirmed the image of Heath as aloof and unable to empathise with ordinary party members and voters. This failure was at the heart of his weakness as a Prime Minister and a party leader.

Judgements about flexibility and rigidity often boil down to timing. All leaders must be both. Rigidity in the right circumstances is strength, staring down opponents and standing by principle. Flexibility is adapting to circumstances, holding the party together, or doing what is necessary to achieve something. The crucial skill is knowing what occasions call for which quality.

This was Heath's other failure. The U-turns may well have been right. Certainly at the time, most commentators and economists endorsed them, while Thatcher and her allies were not eager to condemn them.[6] Yet politically, they were a disaster. For if the Conservatives had no economic policies to offer the electorate other than what Labour had done, one of their main political advantages was dissipated.

Not getting the timing right was central to Heath's dealings with the trade unions. If there was one mandate that his government surely had, it was to limit the power of the unions. Yet at every step between 1972 and 1974, Heath seemed to misjudge what was called for. In the first confrontation with the miners in 1972, he first stood firm in resisting their wage demands, thus provoking a strike, despite substantial public support for the miners. Then, having drawn the line, the government caved in and gave them everything they demanded and more. The public had been forced to suffer for no good reason. In 1973 Heath worked hard to reach an accommodation with the unions; even the leaders recognised that he was sympathetic to their cause. Yet the scenario of 1972 was then played out again in the crisis of 1973–4. The NUM resisted the government's new incomes policy, while the Tory rank and file were eager for a showdown that would put the miners in their place. So the government did not give way. Indeed, it precipitated a sense of crisis by imposing a three-day working week in the new year. However, Heath was hesitant and inconsistent during the negotiations – first seeming to offer concessions, then backing away; first resisting submission of the case to the Pay Board, then doing so once a general election was under way. There was similar hesitation about going to the country. Since early in 1974, some Conservatives had urged an election on the issue 'Who governs Britain, the government or the trade unions?'. Heath hesitated a long time, preferring a negotiated settlement and not wanting to accentuate divisions in the country; but he refused to back down on the government's incomes policy. Finally, in early February, he agreed to an election. Even then, however, he was not prepared to fight it on the basis of a class war against the unions. He just couldn't think of anything else to do.

By the time of the general election, Heath was very exposed politically. His style seemed to many colleagues to discourage debate and dissent and, following the death of Iain Macleod soon after the election in 1970, he had no confidants of weight who could stand up to him. Thus, almost everything that happened over the next four years was identified with him personally. He showed no interest in backbench views and made no effort to cultivate ordinary Tory MPs. Too often, in fact, they perceived him as rude. His U-turns, especially the passage of the 1972 Industry Act, turned off many Tory supporters, as did his decision to allow Asians expelled from Uganda to settle in Britain. The result was a cleavage between the Conservative left and right that was far more visible than any that had existed in 1970. He had virtually been at war with the representatives of industry during the last two years of the government. They were bitter about his unpredictable economic policies and the seemingly endless confrontations with the unions, while he was furious that they were not investing more and so doing their bit to bail out the economy. With the electorate, too, Heath was exposed and isolated. He had no interest in public relations, and he could not speak in a way that would either energise or move ordinary people. It was his policies alone that had to sell him. It was his bad luck that his greatest successes – Britain's entry into the EC and the negotiation of a power-sharing arrangement between Protestants and Catholics in Northern Ireland at the end of 1973 – had little popular appeal and so did him no good. The government's failed economic policies were much more important, especially with the party's middle-class supporters who felt that they had lost out during the past four years. These policies were very much Heath's. When they failed, he was done for.

The inability of either major party to come to grips with the country's economic problems now led to growing cracks in the two-party system. The Liberal Party had appeared to be on its death bed in the 1950s, but it had refused to expire, and in the 1960s a minor revival began. The Liberals' initial appeal was in areas like the West of England and the Scottish Highlands, where people retained a suspicion of landlord and capital-based Toryism but were also turned off by Labour's ties to trade unionism. These were areas of small-scale agriculture, no large cities and no heavy industry. The Liberals in the 1960s had developed a gadfly mentality and even a sense of moral superiority that saw virtue in being excluded from the corrupting influences of power. It was an attitude that assumed permanent opposition, and many Liberals had no interest in being part of government, even if the opportunity were on offer. A new generation of activists, however, started to focus on local government and built a reputation for paying attention to community issues. As a result, by the mid-1970s, the Liberals were running Eastbourne and were the largest or second largest party on several other councils – the first time in decades that they were having a significant influence on any form of government.

At the national level, the Liberals sought to define a position between the Conservatives and Labour, claiming they were free from the vested interests attached to both, and so above divisive class politics. By the 1970s, however, they had become much more a party of the left that differed from Labour on some key issues. For example, they supported some form of devolution (self-government within the United Kingdom) for Scotland and Wales when Labour refused to consider such a reform. They were strong supporters of an incomes policy that had the force of law behind it. Most importantly, they were unambiguously and enthusiastically in favour of Britain's membership in Europe. On the welfare state, they endorsed the post-war consensus for as long as it lasted, but without Labour's ties to the trade unions and socialist ideology. Thus, they could appeal to Tory or swing voters who supported 'one-nation' policies and the EC.

The Liberals' most distinctive policy was their support of proportional representation. This policy was clearly in their own interest as the Liberal share of the vote in general elections was always well above their number of MPs. The Liberals claimed that true democracy required a parliament that accurately reflected the will of the voters; however, there were also potential costs to proportional representation. In Israel, for example, it allowed small parties of religious extremists to dictate policy opposed by the majority, and so actually undermined the will of the people. In Italy, it resulted in chronic political instability since the Second World War. Furthermore, proportional representation enabled extremists to re-emerge as a major political force. This happened in Austria in the 1990s, where the neo-fascists became the second most powerful party. One strength of the British system is that it marginalises extremism by forcing it to work within the traditional parties. Neither fascism nor communism made any headway there during the Great Depression, during the crisis of the 1970s, or during the 1990s, when neo-fascism exploded all over Europe as a movement of protest and discontent.

Proportional representation was an irrelevance for most voters except committed Liberals. The party could make a breakthrough in 1974 because it was untainted by the mess of the previous decade. Furthermore, its successes in local government were beginning to reassure people that it was not simply a party of political cranks. The Liberals were thus well-positioned to appeal to the Tories' dissatisfied middle-class constituency who were being creamed by inflation. By the early 1970s, therefore, they had become the party of protest in England and parts of Scotland: they won four seats from the Tories and one from Labour in by-elections in 1972 and 1973. In the Celtic countries, however, the more powerful vehicle for protesting the Westminster establishment was one of the nationalist parties.*

In Northern Ireland, independent Unionist parties emerged to combat the Catholic civil rights movement and Conservative weakness in assuring the Protestant ascendancy. At the same time, the Catholics' increasing political assertiveness generated their own parties. As a result, from 1974 the British parties were

* The emergence of Celtic nationalism will be discussed fully in Chapter 11.

not represented in Northern Ireland at all. In Scotland, too, there was a growing feeling among a significant portion of the population that the political system was not responsive to Scotland's needs. Those needs, as in Wales, were centrally tied to the decline of the staple industries of the Industrial Revolution. Unlike in Wales, however, there suddenly appeared a prospect of salvation for Scotland in the form of North Sea oil. Thus, the Scottish Nationalist Party (SNP) could appeal to the Scots' sense that *their* money should not be used for English purposes, especially when the government at Westminster was so obviously mismanaging the economy. The SNP won its first seat in a 1967 by-election. While there was a slide in 1970, the SNP was well-positioned to draw discontented Scottish voters away from the major parties as the economic situation worsened. Plaid Cymru, the Welsh nationalist party, was much weaker, for Welsh nationalism was less an expression of political dissatisfaction than an assertion of cultural identity. Nonetheless, it had some appeal in the Welsh-speaking counties, and its leader had won a 1966 by-election. There had been a couple of near misses thereafter, but Plaid Cymru did not have the same potential as the SNP to expand its base of support.

The general elections of 1974 revealed just how strong the discontent with the existing parties had become. The Liberals were able to field more than five hundred candidates (their most since 1924) and won 19 per cent of the vote in February and 18 per cent in October – well above their previous post-war high of 11 per cent in 1964. As usual, these votes did not translate into seats, so the 14 and 13 MPs were only a slight improvement on the party's previous best of 12 in 1945 and 1966. Nonetheless, a major breakthrough had occurred. The Liberals were now better entrenched as a third party than at any time since the 1920s. The performance of the Celtic parties was equally striking. The Northern Irish parties now commanded all 12 seats in the province's delegation, 11 of them won by Unionists opposed to any form of compromise with Catholics. In the October election, the SNP won 11 seats and Plaid Cymru won 3. Thus, a total of

37 seats representing 25 per cent of the vote in February, and 39 seats representing 24 per cent of the vote in October, had gone to parties other than the Conservatives and Labour.[7]

The Collapse of Consensus

Such results were a significant repudiation of the traditional parties. However, the February election was not a clear repudiation of Heath, with all his liabilities, and it was certainly no vote of confidence in Wilson. For the Conservatives actually won slightly more votes than Labour, although Labour ended up with four more seats. Heath wanted to try to form a coalition with the Liberals. Their leader Jeremy Thorpe, who had been one of the few stars of the election, was interested, but his colleagues would not let him pursue it without a firm commitment on proportional representation. Labour therefore returned to power with no mandate from the electorate. Its first task was to end the miners' strike to show that its special relationship with the unions could produce peace – which it did on very favourable terms for the miners. It also had to repeal the Industrial Relations Act, which had few friends left anyway. Otherwise, its brief was to prepare for a new election so that it could secure a working majority. In part, this meant giving the electorate a preview of the benefits contained in the election manifesto – an increase in pensions to adjust for inflation and a cap on rents. More importantly, however, it required showing that the divisions that had developed in the party during its years of opposition would not hamper it providing competent government. For the lesson of modern British politics over and over again – from the Liberals of 1886–1902 and the Conservatives of 1902–5 to Labour in the 1950s and 1980s and the Conservatives in the 1990s – has been that nothing undermines the voters' belief in a party's ability to govern like internal divisions that the leadership is unable to control.

This was the kind of political challenge that Harold Wilson thrived on, for circumscribing the left and preserving party unity were what he was genuinely devoted to, and he had the political skills necessary to achieve these aims in the short term. The left, however, had been greatly strengthened in the party since 1970. A shift to the left of the leadership of some of the largest unions from 1967 to 1969 was crucial in effecting this change, as was growing left-wing strength in the constituency parties. As a result, the NEC was now fairly evenly split between the left and right, and it was getting more difficult for the leadership to control either the content of the party's election manifesto or events at the annual party conference. Furthermore, in Michael Foot and Tony Benn, the left had quality leadership in the parliamentary party for the first time since Aneurin Bevan was in his prime. Foot's father had been a Liberal MP, but Michael entered Parliament in 1945 on the side of Labour. He edited the left-wing party paper *Tribune* and strongly supported Bevan, eventually writing a biography of him. He was active in CND and remained a strong advocate of nuclear disarmament. He was an equally strong opponent of Britain's membership in the EC. It was one of many issues on which he had broken with Wilson after 1965. In 1970, he was elected to the shadow Cabinet following Labour's defeat. In the early 1970s, he had worked to assure unity between the parliamentary and trade union leadership through a new liaison committee with the TUC. Wilson made him Secretary for Employment in 1974, with responsibility for negotiating a settlement with the miners and overseeing the social contract with the unions – the political equivalent of putting the fox in charge of the hen house. Since Wilson had no intention of resisting union demands, however, it was an easy means of securing their trust. Foot was not likely to make trouble for Wilson from inside the government. Like Bevan before him, he had a real commitment to the party, so he preferred to work with his colleagues rather than against them. Since Wilson had devised formulas that avoided confrontation on the two issues most likely to lead Foot to rebel – the referendum on the EC and the social contract to control wage claims – Foot would be a team player.

Tony Benn was a much more difficult problem. His pedigree

was elite: he was linked to the Wedgwood pottery family, while his two grandfathers and his father had all been Liberal MPs. His father had switched to Labour after the First World War and was eventually given a peerage. Benn had been a driving force for legislation to allow peers to repudiate their titles, which he did as soon as the act was passed in 1963. In the 1960s, Benn had been an uneasy protégé of Wilson's, but in the early 1970s he moved leftwards. He became the leader of a growing and more coherent left-wing movement directed at radically transforming the political, social and economic systems. This so-called 'hard left' claimed that Labour's failures in the 1960s and 1970s were attributable to its deviation from a pure socialist agenda. It rejected the kind of consensus politics that had characterised the party since its inception, as well as the specific post-war consensus based on Keynesian economics, the welfare state, NATO and an independent nuclear deterrent. In particular, it spurned the argument for revisionism that Crosland had put forward in the 1950s. It blamed the failure of Wilson's government on the power of international capital, supported by the financial interests of the City. The conclusion was that giant capitalism needed to be tamed if Labour's commitments to justice and equality were to be realised. So these left-wingers argued that the party should promote a much more comprehensive programme of nationalisation (to include financial institutions) and welfare provision than anything it had contemplated up to now. They were protectionist (one reason they opposed joining the EC) because the control of imports and capital movements was necessary to the economic management they envisaged. In external affairs, they were anti-American, while by the end of the decade they were pushing for unilateral nuclear disarmament and willing to contemplate withdrawal from NATO. Most were not Communists; however, their radical agenda meant that all kinds of Marxists within the Labour movement began to associate with them. A charismatic leader like Benn made such a group much more formidable. He gave their views a voice within the Labour hierarchy which could not easily be silenced or ignored. Once some of their views were enshrined as party policy in conference resolutions and the manifesto, Benn could portray himself as the voice of party democracy, fighting a timid, back-sliding party establishment which sought to ignore the wishes of the majority in the name of political expediency.

In the run-up to the February election, Wilson had managed to mute Labour's manifesto in just this way, excising many of the radical socialist policies approved by the party conference over the last two years. He had also done his best to persuade his colleagues that they had to tone down the socialist rhetoric if the party was to have a chance of winning. During the campaign, he projected an image of sensible moderation, supported by an experienced team who were similarly moderate and sensible. Once he was in charge, he tried to tame Benn by bringing him inside the Cabinet as Secretary of State for Industry. Hopefully, the exigencies of collective decision-making would limit Benn's ability to deviate too far from the party line. At Industry, Benn could implement Labour's agenda for the National Enterprise Board by helping lame-duck firms. It would be difficult for him to go further, by securing partial state ownership of profitable companies, because of the opposition of the Prime Minister and other right-wingers in the Cabinet. At the same time, the crisis of the economy assured that the money simply was not available for the kind of ambitious programme Benn wanted. Yet ultimately Benn proved beyond control; so Wilson moved him to Secretary of State for Energy, thus removing him from a department where he could use manifesto commitments to promote his brand of socialism.

While Wilson's own weaknesses in confronting the left had probably enhanced its credibility in the party and so helped strengthen its influence, he was also the leader best equipped to limit the damage. By balancing left and right in the Cabinet and fudging divisive issues to prevent them from exploding, he was able to keep the party a credible force with a second election impending. Wilson was aided in his task in 1974 because he was always able to convey an image of confidence and conciliation, while the Conservatives under Heath appeared weak and divisive. The symbol of Tory uncertainty was Heath's constant toying with the temptation of coalition, without ever quite being able to make up his mind what he wanted. All parties had to confront the possibility that a new election would merely result in another hung Parliament. Labour, ever mindful of the betrayal of 1931, was unambiguous in its rejection of coalition under all circumstances. The Liberals, recognising that they would never wield any influence without one, were tempted by a grand coalition of all the parties to deal with the economic crisis. That way they would not have to choose between Labour and the Tories, with the risk of alienating those supporters who found one of the major parties intolerable. Since Labour would not consider a coalition, however, this was a dead-end policy. By supporting a coalition in principle, the Conservatives could show their willingness to set aside party rivalries in the interest of national unity, as well as muting their confrontational image due to their recent battles with the trade unions. The hope was to contrast themselves with Labour's uncompromising commitment to the politics of class and its unwillingness to set the national interest above party concerns by joining a coalition. At a time of economic crisis, such a position might have played well with the voters. The main barrier to any coalition, however, was Heath himself, who was an unacceptable prime minister for the Liberals. The Conservatives ultimately chose to blur the issue by urging the need for national unity while skirting all talk of coalition until the last days of the election.

Thus neither the Tories nor the Liberals offered the voters a very persuasive alternative to Labour's social contract with the unions. The results of the October election reflected this fact. Labour increased its lead over the Conservatives from the 4 seats of February to 42 in October. However, the other parties were also able to do slightly better than in February. Thus, Labour's overall majority was a mere 3 seats – fewer than the 4 that had been considered an insufficient working majority in 1964. More than anything else, the October 1974 election confirmed the

February result. The voters saw nothing decisively attractive in either of the major parties, so the politics of protest and fragmentation were consolidated.

While Wilson's position was only marginally strengthened by the October election, he benefited over the next two years from the weakness of the opposition. For the October result finished Heath. He had never been very popular as a leader. He would have been dumped in 1970, but for his unexpected victory. Now he looked like a loser again, as he had been unable to capitalise on Labour's obvious weaknesses in two successive elections. He was not popular with the electorate and commanded little loyalty within the parliamentary party. The leader everyone appeared to want was William Whitelaw, who represented the post-1945 consensus and the 'one-nation' tradition. Whitelaw was the author of one of the Heath government's most impressive successes – the 1973 Sunningdale Agreement, which had created a power-sharing government in Northern Ireland. Although that government was brought down in 1974, Sunningdale survived as a model of what might be possible in that troubled province. It made Whitelaw's reputation as a statesman. Anyone able to bridge the divisions between Irish Protestants and Catholics, a task which no sensible British politician even wanted to take on, seemed the perfect person to deal with the trade unions and to pull Britain together in a time of economic crisis. Whitelaw, however, was a man of loyalty, as he was to prove many times over the next fifteen years. He did not have the ruthlessness that required a politician to abandon a sinking ship at the crucial moment (as Macmillan had done in the aftermath of Suez), or to stab a colleague in the back when necessary. Hence, he would not run against Heath, and Heath would not admit that he had become a major liability to his party, even though many of his advisers urged him to step aside.

It was therefore left to an outsider to take Heath on in the winter of 1975. At this time Margaret Thatcher did not represent either a decisive break with 'one nation' conservatism or an explicit right-wing challenge to the post-war consensus. Yet she did represent a desire from below for some sort of radical change – for a different way of looking at policy – as well as the real dissatisfaction that existed with Heath and his approach to leading the party. She was able to appeal to the Tory backbenchers because the nature of the parliamentary party had changed so much over the past twenty years. Party activists in the constituencies had long been agitating for a break with 'socialist' policies. These views were now much better represented in the Commons than they had been in the 1950s. Many fewer MPs came from the old landed establishment and the traditional public schools and professions, and many more were from middle-class backgrounds, the grammar schools and business. Thatcher was at one with the latter group, and for that reason she could identify with their aspirations for a more radical ideological outlook and their dissatisfaction with the party establishment.[8] The level of opposition became clear when, contrary to all expectations (except by Thatcher's own team), Heath finished second on the first ballot, forcing him to resign.* The parliamentary party then elected Thatcher over her better-known challengers (including Whitelaw) in the subsequent votes to replace Heath – showing both how much they appreciated her courage and their gratitude for ridding them of an unwanted leader.

The real break at this point involved choosing a relatively unknown quantity, and a woman at that, over the safe and predictable Whitelaw. Yet that break would prove decisive. It created a much more fluid environment within the party, with greater flexibility for it to redefine itself, than would have existed under someone like Whitelaw, who was so closely identified with the old guard. In the years immediately following Thatcher's election, however, it was not clear that the Tories had done themselves any good by the change. On the one hand, Heath was unreconciled to being dumped by the party, and he held Thatcher

---

* Because there was a third candidate, Thatcher did not get a majority of the Conservative MPs on the first vote, and new candidates were free to enter in subsequent rounds of voting. So there were, in fact, four new candidates in the second round, and Thatcher did not win her majority until a third vote.

responsible. He remained in the shadows – surly, uncooperative, a threat to the new leader and to party unity. On the other hand, while Labour's sorry performance in managing the economy meant that the Conservatives won a series of by-election victories, Thatcher was unable to establish herself in the Commons as the equal of Wilson or Callaghan. She did not yet look like a credible leader.

The Conservative position was further weakened when Wilson suddenly resigned as Prime Minister and was replaced by Callaghan in 1976. If he had been defeated in February 1974 (as had been predicted), Wilson would have gone then. Thereafter, he looked for the appropriate moment, and he chose his sixtieth birthday. His wife hated the political spotlight, while Wilson himself was tired and no longer found any fun in the job. Many in the Cabinet thought he was coasting. It is difficult to blame him if he was sick of coping with the constant tension between left and right in his party, the constant struggles with the trade unions and the intractable nature of Britain's economic problems when balancing party demands against the demands of foreign investors and lenders. Yet everyone was taken by surprise when his retirement was announced, even those friends and colleagues who knew in advance, and some thought he was up to something and hoped to be recalled in some way. Thus did Wilson's reputation for deviousness dog him to the end. In leaving when he did, Wilson also left himself with the further stigma of abandoning the party in the midst of crises which he had done little to resolve and had even helped to create. Certainly, the next few years would show that he had failed in his main goal of preventing the left and right wings of the party from tearing it to pieces as they struggled for the dominating position in shaping its future. The next step in that struggle came immediately, in the battle to succeed him. The surprise of the election was the performance of Foot. He had shown himself to be very effective, both as a parliamentarian in Commons debate and as a voice of reason against British membership in the EC. His success suddenly thrust him forward as a viable leadership candidate for the left, as well as for those dissatisfied with Wilson's dithering approach to the nation's problems. As a result, he actually got the most votes in the first round of the election, besting Callaghan, the representative of continuity, by 90–84. While Callaghan ultimately triumphed in a third round, Foot's showing revealed just how powerful the left had become in the parliamentary party.

It is ironic that Callaghan, who had been no great success as a minister in the 1960s, emerged as an effective leader in the 1970s. His initial associations had been with the trade union wing of the party as a union official, and he had been a leader of the opposition to reform in 1969. As Chancellor of the Exchequer from 1964 to 1967, he was tainted by the failed policy of fighting in the last ditch to protect the pound. Neither of these crises, however, had clearly defined his position along Labour's political spectrum. While his views were Gaitskellite, he had tried studiously to damp down party differences in the 1950s. Like Wilson, he was strongly committed to party unity, but he was much more the conciliator, while Wilson was the manipulator. As the unions became more militant and the left more aggressive in the early 1970s, Callaghan and Wilson were driven closer to each other politically. Thus it was natural for Wilson to appoint him Foreign Secretary in 1974. Though no fan of EC membership, he presided over the negotiations with Britain's EC partners with tact and skill, not allowing them to become a forum for British posturing. At the same time, he was now Wilson's closest confidant in the business of government. Callaghan's stint as Foreign Secretary thus redeemed his reputation as a minister. He was the same kind of calm, non-ideological pragmatist that Wilson was, but with an aura of statesmanship and principle that Wilson now lacked. At the same time, he encouraged discussion in a way that Wilson had not. As a result Foot, whom he made deputy leader of the party and leader of the Commons, found him easier to work with than Wilson and established a good relationship with him.

The new Prime Minister confronted the nation's economic problems with a determination to end the crisis. While Wilson had evaded issues, Callaghan seemed more intent on resolving them, even at the risk of straining party unity. And strain it he did, as left-wing MPs fought economic retrenchment every step of the way. He was able to pull it off for two reasons. Jack Jones, by far the most influential of the trade union leaders, was now fully committed to supporting the government, and he was willing to swallow almost any medicine as a result. At the same time, Callaghan showed a political touch that was far more sure than Wilson's. His performance when faced with the IMF's demands for budget cuts was masterful. He contacted foreign leaders in an attempt to secure modification of the draconian spending reductions initially demanded by the IMF, urged on by the US Treasury. Other Western leaders were sympathetic to Callaghan but could do little to help him in the face of their hostile central bankers. The Prime Minister finally took on the IMF directly to secure a compromise. At home, instead of trying to force the IMF package through the Cabinet, Callaghan allowed real debate, giving members ample time to talk through their differences. At the same time, he brought pressure on key colleagues behind the scenes to persuade them that there was no choice – waving the red flag of another 1931 catastrophe if the party did not unite behind him. The most important was the Foreign Secretary, Tony Crosland, the guru of socialist revisionism and a passionate opponent of giving in to IMF dictation. Ultimately, Crosland came around in the interest of party unity, and Callaghan was able to carry the Cabinet with no resignations, despite the left's dismay at the IMF policy. Finally, he kept the trade union leaders fully informed of what was going on, thus assuring that they acquiesced in budget cuts that went against all that they had been pushing for since Labour's return to power. As a result, Labour's uneasy coalition of left and right, politicians and trade unionists, weathered the storm of IMF-dictated retrenchment. With the help of another Callaghan success in arranging the end of sterling's role as a reserve currency, the international financial position settled down, allowing the economy to turn around. By 1978 Callaghan was the preferred choice of a clear majority of the people as Prime Minister, running well ahead of his party in popularity polls.

Callaghan was faced with a second major headache as Prime Minister: the government lost its paper-thin majority in the Commons as a result of a series of by-election defeats, including some seemingly safe Labour seats. In 1977 he took the radical step of negotiating a deal with the Liberals to remain in power. The Liberal leadership had changed in 1976, as Thorpe was forced to resign because of potential scandals over corruption and his homosexuality. His career was torpedoed for good when he was arrested in 1977 on charges of conspiring to kill the man who claimed to be his lover, a charge on which he was later acquitted. Thorpe's successor, David Steel, wanted to revive the Liberals' declining fortunes by driving home their new image as a party of government rather than a party of cranks. Therefore, his demands on Callaghan for Liberal support were minimal. The Prime Minister did not have to create a coalition (anathema to the Labour rank and file) or make concessions on proportional representation. The government only had to consult with the Liberal leaders and to move forward with its devolution policy for Scotland and Wales.

Labour had a much more ambivalent commitment to devolution than the Liberals. However, the importance of the SNP and Plaid Cymru was greatly enhanced by Labour's tiny majority after October 1974. In Scotland in particular, Labour had to do something to stem the apparent tide of support for the Scottish Nationalists. It therefore proposed to create elected assemblies in each country. The Scottish Assembly would have some legislative power, but the Welsh would be purely administrative. Both Scotland and Wales were Labour strongholds, however, so Labour activists were divided on devolution. On the one hand, national autonomy would almost surely weaken Labour both in the Celtic nations and at Westminster; on the other hand, to do nothing risked alienating a significant body of supporters who favoured some form of self-government. Thus, while the Cabinet was hardly committed, political necessity required that it push the reform through. After an initial defeat, the pact with the Liberals assured that the government had no choice but to introduce new bills for Scotland and Wales in 1977.*

One of the provisions that emerged from the committee required a referendum in each country, which had to be carried by the support of at least 40 per cent of the registered voters if devolution was to go forward. Given the Labour government's lukewarm attitude to its own legislation and the divisions in its ranks on the issue, it was not able to generate much of a campaign in support when the referenda finally took place in March 1979. Welsh nationalism had always been uncertain about autonomy, and the Welsh Assembly was overwhelmingly rejected. The potential financial cost seemed to outweigh any plausible gains in democratic accountability, while the government had become much more unpopular following the 'winter of discontent'. In Scotland, where there had been much stronger support for devolution, it waned in the face of the limited autonomy offered. The pro-devolution vote also suffered from the declining fortunes of the SNP and the increased unpopularity of the government. While the Scottish bill was approved, it did not secure the 40 per cent threshold necessary to enact it.

The failure of devolution was the end of a miserable six months for Callaghan, which finally discredited his government. Everyone had expected that he would call a general election in the autumn of 1978. The government apparently had the economic crisis under control, and his own standing against Thatcher remained very high. Yet Callaghan, who heretofore had acted with considerable confidence and decisiveness, now hesitated. He wanted certainty, and the polls gave a mixed reading of Labour's prospects. He therefore decided to postpone the election, a decision opposed by the majority of the Cabinet. Presumably he hoped that the continued turnaround of the economy would strengthen Labour over the next six months, while an impending election

---

* The government had introduced devolution bills earlier, but they had been defeated on a vote in committee just prior to the pact with the Liberals.

would restrain the unions. Yet even his strongest supporters among the trade union leaders were furious. Not only did they think Callaghan had misled them about the timing of the election, but he also was not listening to their warnings that the 5 per cent target for wage increases was impossible. So the nation got the 'winter of discontent', and the Prime Minister was incapable of framing any sort of response to it. The Liberals had already abandoned ship, and, with the failure of the Scottish referendum, the SNP did the same. The climax came when, for the first time since 1924, a sitting government was forced to resign because it lost a vote of confidence in the Commons.

More importantly, however, the government had lost the confidence of the people. Labour had nothing to offer them in the general election but Callaghan himself. While he should have been a badly tarnished asset in the wake of his paralysis facing the strikes, he still consistently rated much higher than Thatcher in the polls. So the campaign pushed his image as a moderate who was tough but fair, in contrast to Thatcher's image as an extremist who was removed from the concerns of ordinary people. The Conservatives seemingly played into Labour's hands by promoting their programme as radical. While the election manifesto had much in common with Heath's in 1970, the Tories portrayed their agenda as a decisive break with the past, emphasising the party's desire to change how things had been done. Labour wanted to give ever more responsibilities to the state, but the Tories stood for limiting the authority of the state and freeing the individual. Yet there was a paradox in this contest between the parties to construct a radical image for the Tories: it was Labour whom people saw as dominated by extremists. This was the first legacy of the industrial chaos of the 'winter of discontent'. The Conservatives were clear that they would deal with the unions, and that was sufficient for the public. Secondly, the strikes of 1978–9 discredited Labour's policies for limiting inflation and turning the economy around. For these policies, too, depended on the party's relationship with the unions, which was supposed to promote wage restraint. Thus, even though voters trusted

Labour more than the Tories on inflation and unemployment, they had no confidence that Labour's policies could work. Hence, these issues did not help Labour. Finally, the Conservatives were also able to take advantage of growing public anxiety about crime and so to capitalise on an issue that had long been one of the areas where they were preferred to Labour. Most of all, however, people wanted a change, and only the Conservatives could offer that possibility. The result was a substantial Conservative victory, with a margin of 70 seats over Labour and 43 over all parties combined.[9]

Britain seemed to be in a state of collapse from 1972 to 1979. The economy was a mess, and while economic problems were worldwide – brought on by the big oil price increase of 1973–4 and the recession that followed – all seemed worse in Britain. Britain's standing in Europe was low, as its politicians allowed domestic concerns to supersede Britain's clear interest in getting a handle on the economy and becoming a full-fledged member of the EC, in spirit as well as in law. Indeed, with American prestige also at a low, following Nixon's resignation and the weakness of Presidents Gerald Ford and Jimmy Carter, the lead in world affairs shifted to those countries that were most successful at weathering the economic storm – Japan and West Germany. Chancellor Helmut Schmidt in West Germany and French President Valéry Giscard d'Estaing, both former finance ministers, reconfirmed the Franco-German axis in the EC, now based on moderate liberal politics and prudent economic management. They viewed with considerable contempt the failure of the Anglo-Americans to provide their people with strong leadership on economic issues, and aspired themselves to be the world leaders in economic affairs. Wilson and Callaghan hardly counted in such calculations.

Domestically, the nation seemed to be fracturing. The trade unions appeared out of control, and the old image of class warfare, which had been buried in the aftermath of the Second World War and the prosperity of the 1950s and 1960s, now reasserted itself. At the same time, a new and nasty kind of violence was appearing, whether in the form of football hooliganism or neo-fascist attacks on immigrants. The United Kingdom itself resembled a dissolving state. Northern Ireland was spinning out of control as violence escalated, while a minority separatist nationalism had established itself with reasonable firmness in Scotland and less firmly in Wales. Britain's political leadership throughout had been weak, unable to confront crises and impose solutions. For a brief moment in 1977–8, Callaghan had reversed this impression of failure, but the 'winter of discontent' had reconfirmed it more strongly than ever. Writing from the United States in 1979, Isaac Kramnick discerned 'a general mood of malaise and stagnation on the one hand, and on the other the growth of unrest, discontent, and disorder'. The effect was a 'sense of crisis and accelerating decline'.[10] Indeed, much of the image of Britain in decline was established during this decade, along with a feeling that nothing could be done about it.

Yet to some degree, things were not as bad as the doom-sayers would have it. Mostly the British people were not suffering, despite all the problems of the decade. Many workers had managed to keep their wage increases ahead of inflation, although others (especially in the public sector) had fallen behind. The welfare state, too, had done reasonably well in keeping up with rising prices, at least until the IMF cuts. Increasing wages and welfare payments may have been contributing to the inflation problem, but they also assured that the percentage of the population in poverty remained fairly steady over the decade. The standard of living, however, did not hold up as well as statistics on real wages indicated, for rising taxes were part of the cost of the 1970s as much as rising prices were. Taxpayers therefore felt the pinch, and many lower income families were now paying income tax. Those on salaries also suffered, for their incomes often did not come close to keeping up with inflation, while their taxes went up.[11] Hence, many were losing out and blamed it on the high taxation to support the welfare state as well as on inflation. In addition, there were the growing numbers of unemployed, themselves the result of the inflation as well as of the inability of British industry to compete.

As a counterweight to these economic problems, however, Britain was a more dynamic and exciting place than it had ever been before. The advent of women's liberation, immigration and youth culture was contributing to a far more diverse and less stodgy and class-bound society than the one that had come out of the war. Even the emergence of a more assertive Celtic nationalism, which was forcing the British to rethink their highly centralised view of national identity, had the potential to create a more diverse British nation. It is to these revolutionary changes that we must now turn, in order to assess fully the extent or limits of British decline.

PART III: REVOLUTION

8

SOCIAL REVOLUTION

One of Margaret Thatcher's means for reversing Britain's decline was to create a more entrepreneurial society. To her, this meant changing the mentality of the British people so that they would place greater value on making money and so that those who succeeded economically would command greater respect in the society. Nothing, however, contributes to making a society entrepreneurial like opening it up to all the energy and talent that its people possess – and, if one takes the United States as a standard, as Thatcher did, opening it up to the energy and talent that people elsewhere possess as well. This is exactly what happened in Britain after 1945, in part because of a social revolution that Thatcher herself was ambiguous about, but also, in part, because of government policies which aimed to open that society up. Four major post-war trends helped to make Britain more accessible to people of talent: the influx of immigrants from the West Indies, Africa and Asia; the women's revolution, which brought women of all classes into the marketplace and multiplied their education and career options; the expansion of secondary and higher education to society as a whole, not just to women; and some breaking down of class as a barrier to mobility. All these changes helped to create a more fluid, skilled and competitive society, in which more people were in a position to do anything they chose. This is not to say that there is full equality of opportunity in Britain

– any more than there is in any other nation. It *is* to say, however, that Britain is far closer to that ideal than it has ever been before, and the changes that made this possible amount to a progressive revolution of major proportions.

Many of these changes were not limited to Britain. Its postwar social and cultural evolution reflected phenomena that were common to other Western European countries, as well as the United States and the rest of the English-speaking world. As was often the case, Britain sometimes found itself torn between these two poles – the more open societies of the United States and the former dominions on the one hand and the more traditional, hierarchical and paternalistic societies of its continental friends on the other. Despite the social and cultural convergences between Europe and America that occurred after 1945, most West European governments had no desire to see their countries become like the United States. While they became more open and less elitist, they also sought to define an alternative to an American society that seemed to have much weaker educational and cultural standards, greater inequalities of income and wealth and fewer welfare services for the poor. Drawn by the tie of the English language, it was harder for the British to push American social and cultural trends away. Thus American approaches to education and women's liberation, for example, probably had a stronger impact on Britain than on the Continent. Part of the story of this chapter will be about how Britain negotiated between the European and American poles as it committed itself both to improving the standards of life of its people and to creating a society that was more open to talent.

Demography

The same basic trends in population change characterised much of the economically developed West, though with inevitable variations by country. Britain's most rapid population growth had occurred in the nineteenth century. By the twentieth century, it was slowing down a lot, despite an intermittent baby boom between 1930 and 1970. Thus, between, 1901 and 1951 population increased from roughly 38 to 50 million; between 1951 and 1971 it increased to 55.9 million, a faster rate of increase; while by 1996 it was 58.8 million, a much slower rate of increase.[1] What accounts for this trend? The single most important factor in determining population historically was the age that women married. Early marriage enabled young women to start having children sooner and thus have more. This is exactly what happened in Britain, starting around 1740. In the nineteenth century, the norm was for a family to have lots of children, which counterbalanced the appallingly high child mortality rates, especially in the cities and especially among the poor. By the end of the century, some families were having fewer children. Improvements in nutrition and urban public health meant a reduction in the prevalence of some infectious diseases, so that more young people (though not more infants) were surviving, especially in the upper and middle classes.[2] These parents were able to choose to have fewer children and to invest more in each child, while increasing their own levels of consumption. Rising standards of living had much the same effect.

The twentieth century saw this reduction of family size spread throughout the society. Now the key factor was a general reduction in infant mortality, so that all parents could assume that most of their children would survive and could plan accordingly. As a result, the average number of children per family, which was six in the nineteenth century and about four at the beginning of the twentieth century, had fallen to around two by 1945.[3] While the average went up again from 1950 to 1970, it fell thereafter and is now less than two. What accounts for the mini-boom that occurred between 1930 and 1970, and especially from the mid-1950s to the late-1960s? Prosperity seemingly encouraged a fall in the age when women married for the first time, from an average of about 25 in 1931 to 22.6 in 1971.[4] In the 1930s, that prosperity was limited to the South and the Midlands in England, but after 1950 it was more broadly based. After 1970, however, the trend once more was towards later marriages (so that in 1995 the average age for women's first marriages was 26.9) and the postponement of the age when a woman had her first child in marriage. In part, this was because economic prosperity was waning; but also, far more married women were choosing to work. As a result, a record high percentage of births now are to women over the age of thirty.[5] It is unlikely that new forms of contraception made much difference to this new fall in the rate of population growth; the evidence indicates that contraception was common between 1940 and 1970, before the advent of the pill.

Clearly the ebb and flow of population growth was sensitive to two important external factors: the state of the economy and the more general state of public health. Improvements in the second half of the nineteenth century were benefiting the whole population, not just the most prosperous. The life expectancy for Britons increased from 41 years for men and 43 for women at mid-century to 51.5 for men and 55.4 for women by around 1910. The twentieth century saw this progress accelerate. Health care was more broadly available to the whole population, due to the introduction of national health insurance in 1911 and then of the National Health Service in 1948. Thus, most people could benefit as new vaccines, medicines and advances in medical technology became available. At the same time, higher standards of living, especially during and after the Second World War, meant greater food consumption for the poor, with the possibility of improved diets and better nutrition. Together, these improvements produced a dramatic drop in infant mortality: by the 1990s, deaths in the first year of life accounted for less than 1 per cent of all deaths, compared to 25 per cent in 1900. Since 1945, the biggest gains have been for those over 45 years old, and especially those over 75. Now, 59 per cent of deaths occur in this latter age group, compared with only 12 per cent in 1900. These improvements of survival chances at both the beginning and end of life yielded a sensational increase in life expectancy: in 1993–5, a male baby could expect to live to 74 and a female to 79.4.[6]

These changing patterns of birth and survival have changed

the age distribution of the population. In 1901, people aged 0–14 were 32.5 per cent of the population, while those 65 and over were only 4.7 per cent. By 1951 the percentages were 22.5 for youth and 10.9 for the elderly; in 1995 they were 19.4 and 15.7 respectively. The demands of youth, and especially the effect of the baby boom of 1950–70, will be evident in many sections of this chapter and Chapter 10, as we look at education, youth culture and crime. However, the long-term trend that was placing the greatest demands on community resources by the end of the century, in Britain as in the rest of the developed world, was the ageing population. It is a myth that elderly parents in Britain used to live with children as part of an extended household. In 1861, 47 per cent of households had no family member beyond the nuclear family of parents and children; the number was exactly the same in 1966. In 1861, 15 per cent of households included a relative of the head, the same number as in 1951; however, by 1966 that percentage had fallen to 10. The elderly tended to live alone in 1911, as they did in 1991.[7] In the nineteenth century, the elderly poor who could not afford to live alone were relegated to the Poor Law workhouses that Dickens made notorious. After the Second World War, local authorities took on this responsibility. The trend in the 1980s and 1990s was to try to provide services in the home rather than move people into institutions – both because it was less expensive and because the elderly preferred it. Elderly poverty continued to pose an enormous problem at the end of the century – the elderly were the largest single block of people below the poverty level. Yet they were surely better provided for than they had been in 1945 or earlier.

Not only has there been a change in the age distribution of the population since 1945; there has also been a change in its geographical distribution. The Industrial Revolution led to a relative increase in the population of the North of England, historically the poorest and most economically backward part of the country, as well as of the Scottish Lowlands, South Wales and Northern Ireland. The decline of the old industries of the

Industrial Revolution now led to a reversal of that trend, especially from the 1960s. Scotland's overall population actually declined between 1961 and 1991. Within England, the areas of greatest population growth were the Southeast (excluding Greater London), the Southwest and East Anglia, while the North stayed still and Greater London declined substantially. This shift did not bring any change in the level of urbanisation. On the contrary, Britain was so urbanised by 1901 that little further increase occurred over the whole of the twentieth century.[8] The real change was towards suburbanisation. The process began in the nineteenth century, when the new industrial middle class moved out of the urban centres that their industries had built, in order to get away from the pollution and the sanitation problems. Suburbanisation was facilitated by the development of the railways, which meant people no longer had to live near work. It made class segregation easier, as new developments aimed at very specific socio-economic groups sprang up outside the cities, even as the cities annexed older suburbs.

This whole process of dispersal and social segregation continued at an accelerated pace after 1918. Between the wars, a massive building programme offered new suburban homes to the expanding middle and lower middle classes. They were linked to the city centre by suburban railway (or London Underground) extensions or by bus. After 1945, a more widespread prosperity and, with it, the increased use of the car resulted in even more suburbanisation. The effect, however, was not to reduce urbanisation. Rather, as people moved ever further from the old nineteenth-century metropolitan areas (thus explaining the decline in the population of Greater London), they ended up in small and medium-sized cities on the periphery of or outside those areas – cities with populations between 50,000 and 200,000. The number of these cities increased from 61 in 1901 to 162 in 1961, while the percentage of the population living in them increased over the same period from 21.6 to 37.9. Those within the orbit of the old metropolitan areas were eventually integrated back into them as part of ever larger urban conurbations. The census recognised seven such conurbations in England, which together accounted for over 40 per cent of the population in 1961,[*] while another developed around Glasgow.[9] Except for Greater London, the centre of each was one of the great industrial cities of the nineteenth century. The booming economy of the South, by contrast, was built on light industry and services which could be accommodated in the smaller urban areas that accounted for so much of the population growth in this region. The areas around Edinburgh and Cardiff grew because of the same kind of economic growth. After the 1960s, however, the population in medium-sized cities and in urban conurbations declined somewhat, as the search by the upper and middle classes for open space, and with it the distance people were willing to commute, took them ever further afield. As a result, the population of rural England increased by 25 per cent between 1975 and 2000, even though agriculture employed only 4 per cent of the workforce in rural areas.[10]

After the war, the government sought to plan the process of dispersal by promoting the development of 'new towns', located outside urban centres that were surrounded by green belts protected from development. The first ten such towns were designated in an act passed in 1946. The legislation was inspired by an idealistic belief in the power of planning to preserve sociability based on neighbourhood and community. The ideal was a town of 50,000 subdivided into neighbourhood units of no more than 10,000 people, incorporating a mix of social classes. By the 1960s, however, when another twelve new towns were approved, these aims were being undermined by the demand for more housing and so the need to grow these communities. In 1991, there were 1.9 million people living in the twenty-eight new

---

[*] The seven conurbations are Greater London, Greater Manchester, the West Midlands (greater Birmingham), West Yorkshire (greater Leeds–Bradford), South Yorkshire (greater Sheffield), Merseyside (greater Liverpool) and Tyneside (later Tyne and Wear, greater Newcastle-upon-Tyne). Clydeside (greater Glasgow) is second only to Greater London in size.

towns.[11] No one, however, saw them as more desirable places to live than other towns of comparable size, while the social mix was limited.*

This massive dispersal in the context of continued high urban density would not have been possible without a transformation in the infrastructure of the country, as the railways were downgraded and roads were built. Between 1928 and 1997–8, the amount of track halved, while the number of passenger journeys fell from just over 1.25 billion to 800 million. Virtually the entire decline in track occurred after 1960, as lines were shut down to save money. The decline in passengers began during the Second World War and was over by 1970, as many people continued to use the train to commute and move around the country. Nonetheless, the trend was towards the roads. In 1923, there were about 38,000 miles of classified roads in Britain, all of them provided by local government. By 1997, there were over 100,000 miles of classified roads, 10,000 of them trunk roads provided by the central government. These roads served 187,000 private cars in 1920 and 21.7 million in 1997. Yet Britain still had significantly less road mileage per car than the European Union (EU) average, so it had more congestion. Indeed, because of years of underinvestment in public transportation and the railways, by 2000 Britons spent more time commuting and faced worse traffic jams than any other people in the EU. Congestion was made worse because roads also became the preferred means for transporting goods. In 1997, there were 98 billion ton miles of goods moved by road, compared with 11 billion moved by rail.[12]

Immigration

As the more prosperous middle and working classes moved out of the cities after the Second World War, immigrants from the

---

* The largest new towns are Basildon, Crawley, Harlow, Hemel Hempstead, Stevenage and East Kilbride (Scotland), all founded between 1946 and 1949; and Milton Keynes, Northampton, Peterborough, Redditch and Telford, all founded in the 1960s.

West Indies, Africa and Asia moved in. Immigration was not a new phenomenon, although the predominant flow of migrants was out of the United Kingdom in the nineteenth and twentieth centuries. The most important migration into Britain prior to 1945 was from Ireland, which meant that before 1922 it was simply a movement of people within the UK. While there are no statistics on Irish immigration, the census does indicate how many people there were of Irish birth. That number remained large throughout the century – about 630,000 in 1901, declining gradually to 505,000 in 1931, then increasing to 950,000 in 1961 and 1971, before declining to 835,000 in 1991.[13] The other major migration into Britain prior to 1945 was of Russian Jews, who came between 1880 and 1914, at the same time they were migrating to the United States.

Both the Irish and the Jews moved into run-down areas of London and some of the industrial cities of the North of England and, in the case of the Irish, Scotland. The British people tended to see both as inferior races; as a result, they were the victims of the same kind of racism and stereotyping that was directed against colonial peoples at the turn of the century. For example, *Punch* cartoons in the nineteenth century depicted the Irish in terms very similar to those used by American cartoons to depict blacks – giving them simian features that conveyed they were barely above the apes in development. The fears generated by Jewish immigration (resulting in a population increase of roughly 250,000 from 1880 to 1914)[14] led to the passing of the first Aliens Act in 1905, which restricted immigration to eight ports and defined 'undesirable' characteristics (such as the likelihood of going on the Poor Law) that would justify blocking disembarkation or later deportation. A much more restrictive measure was then enacted in 1919. Between the wars, hard economic times liberated virulent anti-Irish and anti-Semitic sentiments. The latter were reinforced by an influx of another fifty thousand Jewish refugees in the 1930s and helped the British Union of Fascists establish a toehold in the East End of London during the decade.[15] One notorious practitioner of racist politics was Alexander

Ratcliffe, who built a career stirring up anti-Catholic (which meant anti-Irish) feeling in Scotland through his Scottish Protestant League. By the late 1930s he was embracing anti-Semitism as well, and after 1945 he was a Holocaust-denier. In fearing and disliking those who were different, the British were like other peoples throughout the world, though with a distinctive anti-Catholicism which had deep historical roots in the sixteenth and seventeenth centuries and which characterised many Protestants in Europe and the United States.

The arrival of populations from the colonies of Asia, Africa and the Caribbean added a new dimension to this kind of racism – a legacy of white domination buttressed by claims of non-white inferiority. These racial hierarchies had been used to justify colonialism and were only beginning to be challenged systematically in Europe and America in the 1950s. There were already small populations of Indians, West Indians, Africans and Chinese in Britain prior to 1945. Many had been sailors who ended up in ports like London, Liverpool and Cardiff. In addition, by the turn of the century there was a student population, based mainly in London, numbering a couple of thousand, plus a few Indian businessmen. The Second World War brought more West Indians to work primarily at airfields. Still, even with the migration from the Caribbean that began in 1948, there were only about 80,000 non-white residents in Britain in 1951, primarily from the West Indies. By 1961, the number was 500,000; in 1971, it was 1.5 million, and in 1991 3 million, accounting for 5.5 per cent of the total population of Great Britain (excluding Northern Ireland). The 2001 census showed a minority population of over 4.6 million, comprising nearly 8 per cent of Britons and 9 per cent of the population of England and Wales. In 1991, about 500,000 were from the Caribbean; 840,000 were Indian; 475,000 were Pakistani; 160,000 were Bangladeshi; 210,000 were black Africans; 155,000 were Chinese.[16] They tended to be concentrated in the metropolitan areas of London, Manchester, Leeds–Bradford and Birmingham, plus some smaller cities like Leicester, Bristol and the Lancashire cotton towns. This large flow from the Commonwealth was supplemented by a significant post-war immigration of Poles and Italians.[17] Nonetheless, the ongoing exodus of Britons, especially from Northern Ireland and Scotland, meant that from 1950 to 1980 there was still a net out-migration of people.* After 1983, the increasing numbers claiming asylum helped to reverse the flow.

Immigration from overseas was a product of full employment after the war. West Indians were shut out of the United States by a change in the law in 1952 and so turned to Britain. They were supplemented in the late 1950s and 1960s by immigrants from India and Pakistan. Many of these immigrants did well, moving into the middle class either immediately (if they had enough education) or after years of hard work that enabled them to provide a good education for their children. For example, there was a significant entrepreneurial population among the Pakistanis, Indians and Chinese, who bought shops or ran small businesses. Indeed, they were replacing the native population as the nation of shopkeepers: by 2000, South Asians owned 70 per cent of independent grocery stores and newsagents.[18] Nor were they alone in constituting an immigrant middle class. Many West Indian women initially came to fill the shortage of nurses in the NHS, and there was a significant minority of West Indian men who were well educated and able to take white-collar jobs. By the 1990s, West Indian women as a group had slightly higher average earnings than white women who worked full time. They were as well educated as white women, except at the university level, and the younger generations were nearly equal at that level as well. However, it was the Indians who were expelled from East Africa in the late 1960s and 1970s who comprised the largest single influx of middle-class immigrants. Their families had lived for several generations in Africa, where they had established themselves as

---

* The net outflow numbered over three hundred thousand in both the 1960s and 1970s. Zig Layton-Henry, *The Politics of Race in Britain* (London, Boston: Allen & Unwin, 1984), p. 25. Mostly these emigrants went to the United States and the white-dominated members of the Commonwealth.

professionals and businessmen, so they simply carried their skills to Britain. By the 1990s, the job distribution among all Indians was comparable to that of whites, with a significant number of them self-employed. Overall, a larger percentage of those aged sixteen to forty-four had an A-level or higher qualification than whites, and the Indians were far ahead in terms of university degrees. Another immigrant group that did well was the Chinese, who came both from Hong Kong and other parts of Asia. They, too, were better educated than the white population. Even more than the Indians, by the 1990s they were disproportionately well represented among the upper and middle social strata, and much more than Indians or whites they were underrepresented among manual labourers and the unemployed.[19]

While there were significant numbers of immigrants in business and the professions, they were overrepresented in unskilled and manual labour. They were filling the jobs that white Britons had moved out of during the years of prosperity, with concentrations in transportation, hotels, restaurants, hospitals and manufacturing such as textiles and metals. In 1984, '83 per cent of Caribbean males, 73 per cent of Asian males and 58 per cent [of] white males were engaged in manual labour'.[20] The populations suffered terribly from the unemployment that followed the downturn in the economy in the 1980s. They were vulnerable because they were less skilled, trade union rules required that the last people hired were the first laid off and employers discriminated against them. Nor was unemployment evenly divided among the immigrant communities. In 1988, the overall rate for ethnic minorities was 20 per cent (compared to 10 per cent for whites); it was 31 per cent for Pakistanis and Bangladeshis, 22 per cent for West Indians and Africans and 16 per cent for Indians.[21] The combination of low skills, insufficient education and unemployment meant that many Pakistani, Bangladeshi and West Indian families were very poor, far more in number than their share of the population. Yet, despite these economic problems for non-whites, the possibilities for their contribution to the economy remained enormous. A couple of statistics drive home how important they had become. In 2000, Indian restaurants employed more people than coal mining and iron and steel together, while nearly a third of Britain's doctors and nurses had been born overseas.[22] With services replacing manufacturing as the engine of the British economy, such facts serve as a paradigm for its future.

British immigrants were citizens. The 1948 British Nationality Act, which conferred citizenship on all colonial residents (and those of the dominions, which were now independent nations), was seen as confirming what had always been the case. No one in 1948 expected an acceleration of non-white immigration. When it came, both parties in theory were committed to a vision of Britain as the leader of a multi-racial Commonwealth with a common citizenship. In practice, both Labour and Conservative governments sought to frustrate 'coloured' immigration (Europeans were just fine), despite the labour shortage. They looked to the governments of India and Pakistan to use the issuing of passports to discourage emigration, while colonial governments in West Africa and the Caribbean were pressured (not always successfully in the latter case) to adopt similar controls over travel. The Attlee government even produced a film for use in the West Indies depicting the miseries of an English winter and the prospects of unemployment for immigrants.[23] In 1954–5, the Conservative Cabinet seemed ready to legislate to limit immigration, but it could not agree on how to implement controls. It was unthinkable to curb immigration from Ireland and the old dominions; but some ministers resisted restrictions defined by race. There were real fears about the effect that discriminating between the white and 'coloured' citizens of the Commonwealth would have overseas. As a result, nothing was done.

The situation began to change following the 1958 white riots in Notting Hill – then a rather poor, working-class part of London – and Nottingham, each lasting several days. The resentment of immigrants that had always been there was now out in the open. There had been instances of anti-black violence in the late 1940s and early 1950s. With the much larger influx, there was now political capital to be made from the fears and prejudices of the native British. A May 1961 Gallup poll showed 73 per cent of the population favouring limits on immigration.[24] Yet in the immediate aftermath of the riots, Macmillan's government was determined not to be seen to be giving way to violence. However, a new surge of immigrants from the West Indies in 1960 and South Asia in 1961 signalled that indirect controls could no longer be relied on. The government therefore introduced the Commonwealth Immigrants Act of 1962, which provided the means to exclude the least educated and least skilled immigrants.

In theory, Labour was committed to the principle of equality and opposed to such discriminatory legislation; in practice, its MPs were more likely than Tories to represent constituencies with substantial immigrant populations and so resentful whites. The 1964 general election showed the danger of allowing 'coloured' immigration to be used as a campaign issue when Labour's shadow Foreign Secretary, Patrick Gordon Walker, was defeated by a campaign using the slogan, 'If you want a nigger neighbour, vote Liberal or Labour.'[25] As a result, Wilson's government passed two more measures in 1965 and 1968 to tighten the rules further. The 1968 act aimed to stop the upsurge of Indian immigrants who were being forced out of Kenya by limiting the annual intake. They held British passports and so had a right to enter, but it was an obligation that many of the British people, including the Labour government, were not inclined to honour. With all these changes, however, the steady stream of immigrants from Asia, Africa and the Caribbean continued – remaining between 30,000 and 50,000 in all but two years from 1963 to 1989.[26] The bias in the system was now weighted towards Asians, who were more likely to benefit from the family reunification provisions of the legislation and from the privileging of educated immigrants like doctors and people in technology.*

---

* West Indians were more likely to have arrived as families or already have brought their dependents over by 1962, while the more recent South Asian immigrants were predominantly men.

The message that racism was good politics was reinforced in 1968 when Enoch Powell became Britain's most popular politician after a speech warning of the dangers of immigration. Powell spoke of the strong sense of grievance of white Britons, who resented laws to protect immigrants when they themselves were the ones who were threatened. They feared that their neighbourhoods, their schools, their hospital beds and their jobs were in danger of being overrun by the influx. He evoked the danger of race riots like those occurring in the United States and implied that more immigration could lead to massacres of whites.[27] Powell's solution was the repatriation of immigrants – though at least initially it would be voluntary. Opinion polls over the next month showed that from 67 to 82 per cent of the British people agreed with Powell, and many felt that he was the first British politician who was actually listening to them. Powell made the Tories into the anti-immigration party, although Heath expelled him from the front bench team because of his speech. Hostility to immigration was one factor contributing to the Conservative victory in 1970, and Heath delivered on the promise to tighten up the rules further with a 1971 act which defined citizenship rights for future immigrants in terms of British descent.[28] Heath's efforts to bury the immigration issue, however, were undermined in 1972 by the expulsion of Indians from Uganda. Like the Kenyans before them, the Ugandan Indians were British passport holders, and this time Heath was determined to honour Britain's obligation to them. Not only did the government do nothing to bar their entry; it organised their evacuation from Uganda and found other countries that would take some of the refugees.

The rise of the neo-fascist National Front in the 1970s led Thatcher to adopt a tough stand on immigration in opposition. In 1981 she replaced the 1948 act with a new one that defined citizenship in terms of those who were legally resident in the UK. After 1973, the pressures were coming from the families of immigrants already in Britain rather than new immigrants. Over the next two decades, legislation and regulation narrowed which family members were eligible to enter and tried to prevent marriages of convenience as a vehicle for immigration. From the late 1980s, asylum seekers became a new source of immigrants. In an attempt to stop supposedly 'bogus' asylum seekers, potential immigrants were forced to get visas prior to their arrival in Britain. Government screening and the appeals process sought to assure that asylum seekers were genuine political refugees who faced persecution if they returned home. Those who were deemed 'economic' refugees, coming to Britain in search of greater opportunity, were to be deported. As had been the case all along, however, efforts to stop the flow of immigrants met with only limited success. Between 1991 and 1999, average annual immigration was virtually the same as the average annual net increase in the domestic population.[29]

Clearly non-white immigration brought to the surface the same kind of racism that had been evident in British responses to Irish and Jewish immigrants. Racism in Britain, as in the United States, was in part simply a reaction against people who were different and unknown. As with the Irish and the Jews, difference was partly defined by religion; however, now it was also defined by colour. Most white Britons were totally ignorant of the cultures that constituted their empire. In fact, they had been taught not to regard them as cultures at all, but rather as uncivilised societies that mirrored the backwardness of their peoples. At the same time, there was an underlying sense that somehow immigrants were threatening – for example, because they took jobs or were a source of crime. Thus, by the 1960s, the overwhelming majority of the British people thought there were too many immigrants in the country. Such hostility and prejudice led to substantial discrimination in employment, trade unions and rental housing (including public housing).

In 1965, Wilson's government passed an act to make discrimination in facilities serving the public illegal; however, cases brought under the act were subject to conciliation rather than criminal action. It served as a first official statement that discrimination was wrong, rather than as an effective deterrent. Another measure in 1968 expanded the areas where anti-discrimination legislation applied, but it did not do the job either. Finally, in 1976 Labour passed an anti-discrimination act that was the most comprehensive in Europe at the time. It outlawed racial discrimination (including indirect discrimination) in jobs, housing, trade unions, education, government programmes, etc, and created the Commission for Racial Equality as a vehicle both to enforce the law and to promote equality. The 1976 act and the Commission improved the environment for resisting racism and discrimination. For example, housing discrimination, while still substantial, declined over the next quarter of a century. Segregation remained the norm for the immigrant working class, especially in the industrial cities of the North, but it was significantly less than in the typical American city. The 1991 census showed that there were only three local government wards in England that were less than 20 per cent white, while a 2002 study of Leeds and Bradford found that upwardly mobile second- and third-generation Asians moved into mixed suburbs, just like everyone else.[30]

Nonetheless, discrimination persisted in the 1990s – not just job and housing discrimination against poorer Asians and blacks, but also discrimination in the professions, including accountancy, law, teaching, medicine and the civil service. For example, in 1997 non-whites constituted 2.3 per cent of solicitors, and there were only twelve non-white QCs. Similarly, it was estimated in 2001 that only 2 per cent of senior civil servants were from non-white minorities, while non-white doctors felt excluded from the high paying consultancies like surgery.[31] The Blair government therefore extended the 1976 act to the public sector in 2001. It required institutions like hospitals, schools and universities and public bodies to take positive steps to foster good race relations and end discrimination, and it gave the Commission for Racial Equality the power to take any such institution to court if it failed to do so.

The tenaciousness of racism and discrimination, even under improving conditions, provided an incentive for the West Indian and Pakistani communities, in particular, to organise politically. Despite Labour's anti-immigration legislation, it was the primary beneficiary of non-white support – because of its record legislating against discrimination and because most non-white voters were working class.[32] The issues of most concern in the 1980s, for example, were Labour issues – unemployment, housing, poverty and discrimination, though crime was also very important. By 1970, non-whites still had made little progress in getting even a toehold into institutions of power, apart from organisations dealing with race relations. Slowly, however, political activism led to minority representation. In 1982, there were 76 Labour Asian or West Indian councillors on London borough councils, and by the end of the 1980s several had immigrant leadership. In 1996, there were some 400 Asian and Afro-Caribbean councillors throughout Britain. In 1993, 21 of Birmingham's 107 councillors were from ethnic minorities (12 of them Muslims), while in 2001 Birmingham's council had 17 Muslims and Bradford's had 13 of 90.[33] Progress at the parliamentary level came more slowly still. In 1983, there were 6 Labour minority candidates, but only 1 was fighting a winnable seat. After the 1987 general election, there were 4 minority Labour MPs; after 1992 there were 5 and 1 Conservative. In 1997 all 9 of Labour's candidates from immigrant communities won, while the Tories fielded 10 minority candidates and the Liberal Democrats 15, all of whom lost.[34] Conservatives tended to do best among the Asian middle class in areas with relatively low minority populations. By 1992, for example, both Maidenhead and Leamington Spa had had Conservative Asian mayors.

At the same time, the minority communities deployed a wide range of voluntary organisations to press their concerns on issues like education, housing and employment, as well as working through established institutions like trade unions and, most important of all, their places of worship. For South Asians, in particular, their religion was central to their identity. Thus Muslims, Hindus and Sikhs created strong religious institutions that were their own, and they did relatively well in holding the younger generations. For the most part, Africans and West Indians were Christians; however, they sometimes found the local churches unwelcoming to people of colour, or they felt uncomfortable in institutions that were structured for white English society. Thus, while many stayed true to the religion they arrived with, others organised their own black evangelical churches, which appealed especially to the young. Whatever the faith, the religious institutions performed the same socialising and support functions for the new immigrants, especially among the poorer classes, that those of the Irish and the Jews had performed in the nineteenth century.

Overall, the record by the end of the century was a mixed one, with many examples of both success and failure in creating a society hospitable to racial diversity. The Notting Hill Carnival, which was originally launched in the aftermath of the riots of 1958 as an exuberant assertion of West Indian culture, had become a major national happening by the 1980s, drawing Britons and foreigners of all races. The city of Leicester embodied a similar sort of transformation. When Indians arrived from Africa in the 1970s, it had its National Front marches and 'Paki-bashing'. Asian entrepreneurship, however, created some thirty thousand jobs there. By the end of the century, it prided itself on being Europe's most diverse and tolerant city. Non-white school children did not see racism and bullying as a problem, while Asian migration to the surrounding countryside was tentatively welcomed for reviving village high streets, as it had done for Leicester's hosiery industry.[35] Bradford, too, had had its successes despite riots in 1995 and 2001; over the previous two decades, the city and the Muslim community had mostly managed to work out ways of accommodating Muslim sensibilities in the schools. There was evidence of success among West Indians and Africans too. A survey in 2000 showed them with growing confidence, both about their own culture and about living in Britain. Judging from the detailed study conducted by Tariq Modood and his associates in 1994, such confidence was justified not just for these groups, but for Asians as well. By almost every measurable standard – education, employment, earnings, mobility – conditions for non-whites had improved significantly since the 1970s, while the gap with whites had narrowed. Those who had been born in Britain might well have white friends, though perhaps not their closest friends.

Yet a substantial residual remained who were locked into insufficient education, low skills and poverty, and it was significantly larger than among whites. These disadvantaged were disproportionately concentrated among Muslim Asians. This group suffered from high male unemployment and low wages for those who did work. In addition, cultural factors increased the likelihood of poverty: women who chose not to work outside the home, large families and an ethic of sending money back to family in the home country when possible. At the same time, there remained a sense of exclusion. Most people of colour, even those who were second- or third-generation British, did not think of themselves as exclusively British – first and foremost because white Britons viewed them as foreign. They saw themselves first as (for example) Afro-Caribbeans or Pakistanis. Many also thought of themselves as British, though this was more likely among West Indians than South Asians.[36] White Britons saw this pattern as evidence of a refusal to assimilate; but then many of them, too, would think of themselves as Scottish, Welsh, Irish or even English first rather than British.

The Women's Revolution

Some of the most dramatic demographic changes after 1945 reflected a revolution in people's attitudes towards women and their role in society. The Victorians had constructed an ideal of the family, and with it the role of the woman, which had come to define the norm. It was based on the principle of separate spheres: while the man earned a living to support the family, the woman made the home a refuge – both by her character, as a deferential support to her husband, and by her duties overseeing the functioning of the household and raising the children.

Women of the upper and middle classes performed these duties through proxies – domestic servants whom they supervised. Working-class women did it all themselves. The woman also was to be the custodian of morality in the family, acting by example as a beacon of moral purity herself and raising the children to understand the values of the society. Two assumptions underlay this ideal: that all women would marry and that married women would not join the workforce as paid labour. Neither of these assumptions could be fully realised. Many working-class women had to work, even after marriage, and the poorest even after having children. Nonetheless, working-class wives who could manage it usually stopped working once they became mothers. Indeed, by the early twentieth century, it was a sign of status and respectability for a working-class wife to be able to stay at home, and, given the miserable conditions of much paid work, they found it the preferable option.[37] Some middle-class women, too, had to work, for there were more women than men, so not all could marry. The kind of work open to them was severely circumscribed by their class, however. Hence, many became a burden on male relatives or lived out their lives in poverty that was not always genteel. Beyond such instances of necessity, many middle-class women pushed against the Victorian ideal through voluntarism and participation in appropriately 'feminine' political causes involving moral issues.

This ideal began to break down in the first half of the twentieth century. During the decades before the First World War, the women's suffrage movement insisted on the vote for women, while women became eligible for election to a variety of local government positions.* There was also pressure for equal education for middle-class women, which meant the chance to go to university and receive a degree, with appropriate job options

---

* By 1914, women could be elected as Poor Law Guardians and members of City and County Councils. They had been eligible to be elected to School Boards from their inception in 1870 until their abolition in 1902. They got the vote in 1918, making them eligible to be elected as MPs.

afterwards. Two world wars then brought middle-class women more fully into the marketplace, while opening up new job opportunities for working-class women. As the latter fled from domestic service, more middle-class women were forced to take on household responsibilities directly: the number of female domestic servants fell from 2 million to 200,000 between 1931 and 1961.[38] Nonetheless, many worked for a few years before taking up their duties as a full-time wife and mother. The first half of the century also saw some challenges to Victorian sexual repressiveness and conceptions of feminine behaviour more broadly construed.

Yet the traditional ideals were still strongly held after 1945. There was a major public relations effort to repromote the importance of the family in the aftermath of the dislocation caused by the war, and to push women back into the home, as had happened after the First World War. Indeed, the principal purpose of introducing family allowances as part of the welfare state was to assure that mothers had the means to take care of their children, without having to work themselves. Furthermore, the size of those allowances was deliberately kept low, in order to reinforce the view that the male was the family's principal provider and to assure that employers would not be tempted to lower men's wages. In the 1950s, even feminists tended to accept that a woman's primary obligation was to her family. Everyone had absorbed the lessons of the new psychological thinking that was now mainstream: healthy children needed the full attention of a caring mother, while a marriage based on mutual respect still meant a wife at the centre of the home.

Many women, however, did not want to stop working. While they accepted that their first duty was to their family, middle-class women in particular had enjoyed the autonomy that war work had given them, as well as the sense of fulfilment that came with it. They also liked the extra income that they had earned for the household. With the post-war labour shortage, there were jobs available. Thus, while there was much agonising about the effects of working mothers on children, the number of employed women kept growing in the 1950s, with ever more working part-time. In the expanding public sector, the bars on the employment of married women, which had been relaxed during the war, now tumbled down. By the 1960s and 1970s, the small size of the family and the wide range of labour-saving appliances and new shopping options – such as supermarkets and frozen foods – made it even easier for married women to work and still perform their household duties, even if they took a few years off while their children were young. The new technologies were crucial for middle-class women who, unlike their grandmothers and perhaps their mothers, no longer had domestic servants to do the housework for them. From the late 1970s, the woman's income became even more important, especially in working-class families, as living standards began to stagnate and government payments were scaled back.

All these factors created a revolution in the level of female participation in the workforce, as middle-class women and married working-class women were fully integrated into it. In 1901, 35 per cent of women of school-leaving age or above worked; by 1951 the number had actually declined slightly; in 1998 it had doubled to 62 per cent. Most of this change was accounted for by married women: nearly 10 per cent of them worked between 1911 and 1931; over 20 per cent did in 1951; and 53 per cent worked in 1991, while for women aged 35–54 it was over 70 per cent. Thus, in 1991 only about one-quarter of women between 16 and 59 years of age were economically inactive, while in 1998 women accounted for 44 per cent of the workforce. This larger participation reflected a second phenomenon: the enormous growth in part-time work by women. In 1951, only about 10 per cent of women worked part-time; by 1971 the percentage had increased to one-third; by 1990 it was around 45 per cent.[39] At least initially, many of these women went into part-time work as a way of increasing family income, especially as hard times hit in the 1970s and 1980s. They then came to see work as a good in itself – that is, something they wanted to do, not something they had to do. Not only did it give them a sense of independence; it provided a social life outside the home.

As the number of women in the workforce expanded, so did the kinds of employment available to them – although most women were still likely to be in occupations dominated by females. The most radical change since the beginning of the century was in clerical work: in 1911 it was an overwhelmingly male occupation, whereas by 1951 it was mostly female. Clerical jobs exploded after 1945 with the advent of the welfare state, and many of these were in family-related or child-related programmes deemed appropriate for women. As a result, growing local government bureaucracies offered a burgeoning of female employment opportunities. This increase was at the expense of female participation in manual labour. Between these extremes, women continued to do very well at getting lower professional and technician jobs like teaching and nursing, as they had in 1911. While they significantly improved their share of higher professional jobs (in 1988 half the entrants to the legal profession were women, while from 1985 to 1995 their numbers doubled to 30 per cent of solicitors), they were still markedly underrepresented when compared to their numbers in society. This was especially true in science-based professions like engineering. They also faced discrimination in those positions that carried highest status (and pay). For example, while nearly half of medical graduates were women for much of the 1980s and 1990s, they made up only 4 per cent of surgeons. Similarly, they were poorly represented in high-status jobs in business and administration, with hardly any women in senior management or as directors in the 1990s.[40]

With women entering the workforce on such a scale, discrimination in pay, long a central concern of feminists, took on new prominence as an issue. Indeed, the hourly earnings of working women relative to those of men actually fell between the early 1950s and the mid-1960s. For decades, unequal pay had been justified because the woman supposedly was not supporting a family (even if she was); her income was seen as entirely supplemental. Still, equal pay was introduced in the civil service by the Tory government in 1954. It was not until 1970, 1975 and 1983, however, that equal pay and anti-discrimination legislation gave new weight to the principle of equality, both in hiring and in compensation. In 1970, the median earnings of all adult women working full time was 54 per cent of the male median; in 1983 it was 66 per cent; in 1997 (with a change of definition in 1983) it was 75 per cent. However, the gains after 1983 were primarily by the best paid women, while these figures excluded part-time workers, who were particularly poorly paid. Overall, Britain's pay gap was the worst in the European Union in 2000.[41] This differential was possible because so many women were still in jobs labelled as women's work. Women's pay was also held down because many married women interrupted their work during the early years of motherhood. When they returned to work, it was either part-time or they ended up in a lower-paying position than the one they had quit.

With the disappearance of manual jobs, women could not have entered the labour force in such numbers at the clerical level and above unless there had been a major expansion of women's education. Table 8.1 overleaf shows that a gradual improvement in women's qualifications had begun after the war (those born between 1930 and 1939 and so finishing school between 1945 and 1960), with the pace accelerating from the 1960s. By the time we get to those who went to school in the 1980s and 1990s, only 9 per cent had no qualification at all, and nearly one-third had A-levels – virtually the same as the percentage of men (see Table 8.2, p. 327).* The number of women with university degrees or professional qualifications also climbed significantly, although the percentage goes down for the younger generations. Many of these, however, have not completed their schooling because they are or will be involved in continuing education.

---

* In 1951, an examination system was created whereby pupils in England and Wales could take O-levels at the age of sixteen and A-levels at around eighteen, the latter being the standard examination for university admission. In the mid-1960s, a third level of certification, the Certificate of Secondary Education (CSE), was introduced below O-level. In 1988, O-level and CSE were combined into the General Certificate of Secondary Education (GCSE). Scottish schools had their own certification system, but it was roughly comparable.

Table 8.1. Highest Level of Qualifications Achieved by
Adult Females, by Date of Birth
(Percentage with Qualification)

	1910–19	1930–39	1940–49	1950–59	1960–69	1970–79
None	77.4	59.6	46.2	32.3	14.8	9.1
O-level, CSE, etc.	11.3	20.3	30.6	35.0	48.2	44.6
A-level	2.2	3.1	4.7	9.1	17.1	30.9
University/ Professional	9.1	17.1	18.4	23.6	19.9	15.3

Source: George Smith, 'Schools', in Halsey and Webb, *Twentieth-Century Social Trends*, p. 209.

The gap between men and women at this highest level of education peaked for the 1940–49 generation and then declined to a very small one for the youngest group. The shifting pattern clearly reflects the changing expectations of what a woman could and should do, and so what kind and level of education she should receive.

In the 1980s, girls started doing better than boys on A-levels throughout Britain, and the gap had widened significantly by the 1990s.[42] Girls were still directed more towards humanities and arts and away from maths and science in their A-levels, although by the late 1980s biology had become an exception. This dramatic increase in the number of girls achieving A-levels was reflected in the universities. In the early 1970s, women accounted for about one-third of the full-time students there, a small increase from something under one-quarter prior to the war. By 1997–8 the percentage was slightly over a half. Women had similarly come to constitute a majority of part-time students. They had not, however, done as well at Oxford and Cambridge, where they were about 30 per cent of the students in 1980–81 and 40 per cent in the late 1990s.[43] Reflecting the A-level pattern, women were underrepresented in degree programmes in applied science, engineering and pure science, while they predominated in arts and humanities degrees (including education). Women were grossly underrepresented among the teaching faculty of universities[44] – which is somewhat surprising, given the historic view of teaching as a 'woman's' profession and the supposed left-wing bias of university faculty.

Such dramatic changes could not have occurred without a fundamental rethinking of what it meant to be a woman and what a woman's role in society should be. It was the aim of the new feminism that emerged in the 1960s to force such a reconceptualisation. Feminists had been attacking traditional stereotypes for more than a century, and the feminist organisations that had been created between the wars were still active. The new feminism, however, was much more broadly based, and some versions of it were much more radical than the liberalism of the old order. Feminists now sought to politicise women's issues and develop a distinctive social and political theory that would explain and justify their goals. That theory challenged the whole Victorian model: the insistence on separate spheres for men and women; the claim that the role of wife and mother was central to female self-realisation; conceptions of femininity based on passivity, deference and chastity that were expressed in gender-specific dress and modes of behaviour. Some basic truths were told: the romantic ideal of love and marriage was an illusion, housework was boring, and neither could be the sole basis on which to construct a satisfying life. As it had for a long time, the liberal principle of equality infused feminist goals. Equality in education and work opportunities assured that each woman would have the freedom to choose what role worked for her self-fulfilment as a human being, including the choice not to marry. The law should treat women the same as men – in terms of property rights, in terms of the family and in terms of claims upon the state. Within the family itself, women should also have full equality with men: equality in family decision-making (including defining the sexual relationship within the marriage), equality in caring for children and doing housework, equal rights to divorce and an equal claim to custody of the children in the event of divorce (with equal responsibility for ex-husbands to provide for those children). Finally, women should be subject to the same moral codes as men.

The women's liberation movement that promoted these goals arose in Britain at the end of the 1960s, influenced by that in the United States. Its leaders came from the growing population of university-educated women who had married young. They were frustrated by the drudgery of being a housewife and by their inferiority within the marital relationship. Younger ones had become involved in student activism in the late 1960s, only to find that the men saw them as 'gofers' rather than fellow revolutionaries. Their call to arms came in 1970, with the first national women's conference at Ruskin College, Oxford, and the publication of *The Female Eunuch* by Germaine Greer. Greer embodied a radical feminism that went beyond the liberal demand for equality. For many, it was tied to socialism or even Marxism, with its analysis of exploitation. Yet socialists and radicals could not agree on priorities, because they could not agree on the principal source of exploitation, class or gender. So the movement remained divided. Radical women's libbers claimed that women were oppressed by men; therefore, the whole institutional structure of society that reinforced male authority and validated that oppression had to be dismantled. This meant an attack first on the traditional family – which implied the woman as subordinate, dependent and too often the object of sexual coercion by her husband – and second on society's treatment of women as sex objects. They insisted on women's own sexual liberation, demanding free contraception, abortion on demand and more (lots more) child care facilities. A minority took lesbianism as the ultimate statement of freedom from male domination. Along with others in the movement, they helped to redirect attention in the late 1970s to the culture of male violence against women, which society mostly ignored: assault, rape, sexual harassment and spousal coercion and abuse. Over the next decades, feminists organised and participated in a wide range of voluntary associations and community programmes designed to provide direct assistance to women and to put pressure on local authorities and the national government to deliver more services needed by women, and at more generous levels.

There were tensions between the liberal and radical wings of the women's movement. Should the focus be on asserting what was distinctively female or on insisting upon full integration into the larger society on a basis of complete equality with men? Should there be separate legislation for women (such as the acts protecting them at the workplace, which had been on the books since the nineteenth century), or did that reinforce paternalism and subordination? What degree of engagement should there be with male society? At the same time, it was not easy for many women outside the women's liberation movement to repudiate traditional attitudes and roles without some ambivalence, especially for the generation raised in the 1950s and early 1960s (if not earlier). For example, many women wanted *both* a career and a family. How was this to be done, when men did little to help with the housework, without giving one or the other insufficient attention? For many a woman the result was guilt – guilt that somehow she was not doing things right, that she did not want what she should want, that she was failing either her sex or her family or herself.

This ambivalence helps to explain both the extent and the limits of how much behaviour and attitudes were changed. For example, attitudes towards marriage, divorce and sex outside marriage changed radically. We have seen that women tended to marry young between 1930 and 1970. Furthermore, most women married. Thus in 1971, 60 per cent of women between the ages of 20 and 24 were married or had been; 87 per cent of those between 25 and 29 had married; and only 5 per cent of women never married. All this changed over the next thirty years. The number of young women who married fell precipitously: in 1972, 1.25 million women between 16 and 24 were married; in 1996 the number was 250,000. In 1995, the probability of a woman marrying before the age of 50 had fallen from its maximum of over 95 per cent in the 1960s to under 70 per cent. In 1992, only 59 per cent of women aged 18–49 were married, though, of course, many had been, but were divorced.[45] Divorce had been made easier by a series of reforms in the law, beginning in 1969. In the 1950s, the number of divorces in England and Wales had averaged about 40,000 per year; in Scotland, the average in the 1960s was a mere 2,000. In 1993 there were 183,000 divorces in England and Wales, though the number then started to decline. By the 1980s, about one-third of all marriages ended in divorce, while in 1984 over 70 per cent of petitions for divorce were initiated by women. Immigrants, however, were much less likely to divorce than whites.[46]

The counterpart to this decline in marriage and increase in divorce was an increase in extra-marital sex. Sex outside marriage had always been common enough among a minority of couples intending to marry. During the 1950s, new thinking about the nature of love and sex, much of it influenced by psychology, aimed to demystify sex and remove its Victorian association with sin. As it came to be accepted that sex was an important part of love and a successful marriage, a kind of ideological underpinning was provided that justified people sleeping together and even living together prior to marriage. At the same time, feminists saw a loosening of constraints on sexual behaviour (when there was no implication of marriage to follow) as central to ending the double standard which had accepted such sexual activity for men but not for women. The transformation in female behaviour that followed was extraordinarily rapid. A 1969 survey indicated that 63 per cent of women were virgins at the time of marriage, while another 26 per cent had married the man with whom they had their only sexual experience before marriage. Yet at virtually the same time, in 1970, only half the girls in their last year at Durham University were still virgins. A 1974–5 survey found that 42 per cent of girls aged 16–19 in England and Wales had had sexual intercourse. By the end of the century, teenage

English girls had the highest rate of sexual activity in the developed world: 86 per cent were sexually active by the time they were 19, and less than 1 per cent were virgins when they married.[47] The birth control pill facilitated this freedom by giving women a sense of being in control that they had never had before. To most women, it seemed much more natural than existing devices, while it made birth control much easier for the inhibited to discuss with their partners.[48] All this change reflected the new attitude that women did not have to feel guilty about sex any more – either about wanting it, having it or liking it.

There were two demographic consequences of this loosening of sexual morality. One was implied above: cohabitation became morally acceptable. In 1996, 39 per cent of women aged twenty-five to thirty-four were cohabiting, while only 19 per cent were married. As with divorce, the rates of cohabitation were much lower among immigrant communities (except those from the Caribbean) than among whites. Yet cohabitation was usually a precursor to marriage rather than a substitute for it. In the 1990s, 60 per cent of first marriages and 75 per cent of remarriages were preceded by some period of cohabitation.[49] The second and more controversial result of greater sexual freedom was more births outside marriage. In the 1950s, fewer than 5 per cent of births in Britain were illegitimate. By 1996, more than 35 per cent of births in England and Wales were to unmarried women, with the rate highest among Caribbean women. In Scotland, it was nearly as high as in England and Wales. Many of these births, however, were to couples living together: in 1986, 70 per cent of births outside marriage in England and Wales were registered to both a mother and a father. Because the stigma of having a child out of wedlock was disappearing, more unmarried women chose to have a child and keep it, when earlier they would not have done so. At the same time, the combination of more single women having children and more divorces meant another radical demographic change: the number of families headed by one parent more than doubled between the early 1970s and the mid-1990s, with the proportion highest among Caribbeans and smallest among South Asians, who among all Britons were least inclined to accept the sexual revolution of the 1960s.[50]

An unmarried woman who did not want to have her child had two options in the 1950s: put the child up for adoption or get an abortion. Even before abortion was legalised in 1967, some twenty thousand legal abortions took place – if the woman was in danger, either physically or psychologically. At the same time, estimates of illegal abortions ranged from 15,000 to 100,000.[51] The movement for legalisation gained momentum as people came to believe that sexual and family matters were personal and so should be outside the regulation of the state. The potentially large number of 'back street' abortions also enabled reformers to present a change in the law as necessary to protect the health of the woman. Legalisation was accompanied by the first official support for the provision of contraceptives through the NHS, which it was hoped would reduce the demand for abortions. In the 1970s, the number of abortions was roughly comparable to the pre-1967 number of legal abortions plus the highest estimates for illegal abortions. The number increased further in the 1980s, until it stabilised at around 160,000 per year.[52]

All these changes add up to a revolutionary transformation in people's views of acceptable sexual behaviour, acceptable behaviour by women and the nature of the modern family. At the same time, however, there were clear limits to the progress of the women's revolution in the home, just as there were limits to its progress in the workplace. The law was changed in 1970 to recognise that the work of a housewife entitled her to an equal share of the family property if there was a divorce. Yet it was still work that husbands and male partners were not inclined to do, as conceptions of masculinity remained tied to the view that housework was women's work. The only chores that substantial numbers of men helped with were shopping and washing dishes – apart from home repairs, which had always been the man's responsibility. There was also a significant minority of men who helped wives who worked full-time with the cooking and cleaning, though not washing and ironing. Furthermore, while men now helped more with the children, caring – for elderly parents as well as children – was still primarily the woman's job and was integral to women's own conceptions of femininity. Where did this leave the family? A mid-1980s survey found that the vast majority of women were basically satisfied with the amount of work their husbands did;[53] however, those who were least happy in marriage were women who had to stay home with the children. Clearly work outside the home contributed something fundamental to a satisfying marriage for many women, even if there was not equality in doing housework. At the same time, marriage had become more 'companionate' (a sociologist's term) – meaning that the man recognised a responsibility to be as sensitive to the wife's wishes and needs as she was to his, that there was better communication between wife and husband, and that more time was spent together and more activities were done together as a couple or as a family.

The Standard of Living

As we have seen, one reason that more women could go to work in the 1960s and 1970s was that rising standards of living enabled them to do their household chores more quickly and easily. They stayed there, and were joined by others, in order to maintain their family's standard of living as economic times got worse. Nothing so epitomises how dramatically life got better for most of the British people after the war than the increase in the standard of living, which affected everyone, including the poor. Yet even this trend was not new. Living standards improved significantly between around 1850 and 1896 and again between 1921 and 1939. In both periods, falling prices had meant that the value of wages (real wages) went up on average; since wages did not fall as much as prices, people could buy more goods with what they earned. Even the large numbers who were out of work after 1921 were better off with lower prices. The Second World War resulted in a further significant improvement in living standards. First, everyone was employed. Then, with wage and price controls, real wages went up by about 80 per cent, as wages increased more than prices.[54] Finally, rationing had a dramatic effect on health. For example, infant mortality in Scotland fell 27 per cent from 1939 to 1945, while the average height of thirteen-year-olds in Glasgow increased almost two inches over the same period. This improvement accelerated after the war; by 1953, the average income of a Scottish working-class home was roughly 2.5 to 3 times greater than it had been in 1938.[55]

The trend continued over the next three decades. Between 1951 and 1974, real wages roughly doubled, despite the accelerating inflation of the last decade of the period. Real wages for men went up another 20 per cent from 1973 to 1986, though for manual workers the increase was only 10–11 per cent. Women did better, with their real wages increasing by about 40 per cent.[56] That was not the end of it, however. The hours of labour shrunk somewhat; or, more accurately, the standard working day for unionised workers went down to forty hours per week. Most in manufacturing worked overtime, however, thus adding to the weekly wage packet. At the same time, workers' holiday entitlement went up. In 1950, virtually all workers had the right to a paid holiday. By 1960, most got two weeks per year; it had increased to three weeks by the 1980s and four weeks by the 1990s. Finally, workers now had the full benefits of the welfare state.

The most important state-provided benefit was the NHS. Health services included medical care by a personal doctor, specialist care (including dental and eye care), hospital care, drugs at subsidised prices and mental health care. Given the demand for and the cost of health care, the NHS was consistently under-funded all through the 1960s and 1970s. Its customers were basically satisfied, so it was treated as a low priority by governments that were looking to keep public spending under control. The lack of adequate funding, however, meant that doctors, nurses and staff became demoralised. At the same time, governments were unable to come up with an administrative system that was flexible and efficient. With medical costs just going up, by the 1980s there was a growing sense that the NHS was ceasing to provide the kind of service that was needed, and some means had to be found to increase resources while using them more efficiently.

Other welfare provisions could also help improve living standards. Many of these went disproportionately to the poor, but payments were usually kept low, so they did not necessarily raise recipients above a poverty level. The system that was introduced in the 1940s was modified and added to at various times. Ultimately, payments included family allowances (later renamed child benefit), which were paid for all children after the first until 1977, and then all children; several widows' benefits; more extensive unemployment insurance than had existed before 1945, with means-tested benefits available for the long-term unemployed; supplements for the families of low-paid workers; more extensive sickness and disability benefits than had existed before 1945; and more generous old-age pensions. In addition, there was a system of income support for those whose payments were insufficient. Earnings-related supplements were added piecemeal to some of these benefits, and in 1975 the Labour government extended this reform to the old-age pension. At the same time, it improved child benefit and added a single-parent benefit. After the Conservatives returned to power in 1979, however, they ended earnings-related increases, eroded their value by slowing the rate of increase, started to tax benefits, tightened eligibility requirements and introduced more means-testing. Yet even as the Tories tried to limit traditional social security benefits, spending on personal social services was exploding. Although a lot of these services were provided in institutions, government policy sought to reduce the numbers in homes and hospitals. Instead, local authorities were encouraged to provide services to the elderly, the disabled and the mentally ill in their homes, and to provide for children either with their families or in foster homes. Taking welfare provision as a whole, by far the largest amount of money (nearly half) went to the elderly, with the sick and disabled, the unemployed (during periods of high unemployment) and family support benefits accounting for much of the rest.

Thus, the economy and the welfare state were putting more money in people's pockets. Families therefore spent more: total real spending tripled between 1948 and 1989.[57] At the same time they diversified their consumption, spending a smaller proportion of their income on food, clothing, alcohol and tobacco, while spending more on housing, transportation, communication and services. Housing was by far the most important of these. Ever since the population revolution began in the latter half of the eighteenth century, housing had not been able to keep up with the rate of population growth and urbanisation. As a result, there was always a deficit of adequate housing. The two world wars made it all the more difficult to close this gap, as all building stopped, while houses were destroyed in the Second World War. Thus, despite the massive building that occurred between the wars, the deficit in 1945 was as bad as ever. The population boom of 1950–70 then added new pressure on housing. So did the trend after 1970 towards more one-person households, as young adults married later or did not marry at all, more couples divorced and the elderly lived longer. The cumulative effect was an extraordinary demand over much of the post-war era.

Government began to get involved in building after the First World War. Between the wars, councils in some of the largest cities built housing estates (usually comprising small, semi-detached houses) in new suburbs. Much of the new building was of relatively high quality, but it was far removed from work, which meant the break-up of old neighbourhoods, and was beyond the means of most unskilled workers and pensioners. After 1945, government became even more involved as a builder. Now there was greater interest in diversifying public housing. Large tower blocks were added to the mix for the poorer groups who still were not accommodated. These high-rises offered a way to clear slums, reduce the housing shortage and upgrade the housing stock relatively quickly. Clearing, however, often was indiscriminate, as planners wanted to build anew, even when the existing stock could be renovated and when clearance meant the end of old neighbourhoods. Furthermore, when new high-rises resulted, they were usually ugly – as were the rebuilt city centres, new road networks and private sector development projects (such as shopping centres and office buildings) that were the aim of much slum clearance in the 1950s and 1960s. The high-rises also offered little sense of community, and there was a shortage of nearby shops and other amenities. Some of the blocks built in the 1960s were pretty appalling and were run down quickly over the next two decades. The people themselves certainly did not want them, preferring a house with a garden. By the end of the decade, there was a greater interest in renovating older buildings and in historic preservation, but the poor among the working class were not the beneficiaries. They needed rent subsidies even to benefit from the new council houses, which tended to be more expensive than the housing they replaced.

All told, the boom in council building meant that the share of the housing stock owned by local authorities jumped from one-tenth in 1938 to a bit under 30 per cent (including new towns) by the late 1970s. Thereafter, as the Thatcher government sold off council houses throughout the 1980s and slowed new building by councils to a trickle, it fell to 20 per cent in 1991.[58] The sale of public housing continued in the 1990s. What was left was the least desirable, which meant it was the most run down, with the most social problems like drugs and crime. The public sector had thus become a vehicle for providing the poorest class with slum housing, as Thatcherite policies blocked councils from using the proceeds from sales to renovate and upgrade what was left. At the same time, those policies had reduced the supply of rental properties and eliminated government rent subsidies, thus forcing up rents. Housing allowances had to be expanded to help the poor pay the market rents, while the number of homeless increased dramatically, especially with the onset of the recession in 1989. Councils literally had no means to build for them.

All the building by local authorities between 1919 and 1979 was more than matched by the private sector. The result was a drastic reduction in Britain's overcrowding problem. In 1911, about 17 per cent of households in England and Wales lived in overcrowded housing; the percentage between the wars was even larger. The situation in Scotland was worse than that in England, and it was worse in the North of England than in the South. Glasgow was the worst, with half of its population in 1911 living in housing of two rooms and one-eighth in a single room. But London was not that much better: in 1931, only 37 per cent of families there had their own house or flat. By 1971, the percentage in overcrowded housing in England had fallen to 6 per cent, and by 1991 it was 3 per cent. The overcrowding that remained was concentrated in a few large cities, and immigrant populations (especially Pakistanis and Bangladeshis) were the ones most likely to be stuck in such substandard housing. Even for these ethnic populations, however, overcrowding had decreased significantly since 1980.[59]

The new housing had basic amenities, while older houses were also renovated to add them. As a result, by the 1990s virtually all houses had running hot water, an indoor toilet and a bath or shower. By contrast, in 1947 4.8 million houses (about 40 per cent) in England and Wales lacked a bath or shower and 7.4 million (nearly 65 per cent) did not have hot water. While there are no figures for those without toilets in 1947, it is reasonable to assume that the percentage fell somewhere in that range. The British were much slower to treat central heating as a basic amenity, but eventually they did. In 1961 only 800,000 houses (about 5 per cent) in England and Wales had it, compared with 16.5 million (under 85 per cent) in England alone in 1991.[60] Similarly, new housing included appliances like stoves, refrigerators and washing machines, while workers could afford to buy others. By 1987, virtually everyone had a refrigerator, 83 per cent of houses had a washing machine and 39 per cent had a separate dryer.[61] Still, in 1991 7.6 per cent of dwellings in England were deemed unfit, with the number in Scotland 4.7 per cent and in Wales 13.4 per cent.[62]

No greater social revolution occurred in the twentieth century than the rise of home ownership as the norm. In the nineteenth century, most people rented, even the fairly wealthy among the middle class. While there are no reliable figures for home ownership before the First World War, a very rough estimate of 10 per cent is probably reasonable. By 1938, nearly one-third of all housing in England and Wales was owner-occupied, and nearly half of those houses had been built since 1918 with the encouragement of government subsidies. The percentage was the same in 1951, but then it gradually climbed to two-thirds in 1991. This increase was subsidised through the right of purchasers to write off mortgage interest payments on their income tax and (from 1965) the exemption of home sales from capital gains tax. There was already evidence after the war that workers wanted to own their own home, and growing prosperity made this possible for more of them. Conservatives encouraged this trend when possible, and workers were the principal beneficiaries of the sell-off of council housing in the 1980s. By the end of the decade, half of the working class were homeowners. This transition to private ownership, however, was far less extensive in London and the big cities of the North, while in Scotland, owner-occupiers accounted for only 43 per cent of housing in 1987.[63] The expansion stopped in the 1990s with the collapse of the housing market in the South. Indeed, many people who had bought houses in the 1980s lost out in the recession of 1989–92, which brought record repossessions.

After housing, the second great object of redirected consumer spending was transportation, as more and more people could afford to purchase a car. The bicycle had revolutionised life for working people at the beginning of the twentieth century. For the first time, they had a means of personal transportation that was relatively cheap, apart from walking. Cars, by contrast, are expensive and costly to run. Yet they vastly increase mobility, while they also give pleasure and status. Car ownership therefore came to be a measure of just how far down the social ladder the improvement in living standards had spread. In 1951, 14 per cent of households had a car; by 1970 that number had grown to 52 per cent; and in 1996 it was 70 per cent, with 25 per cent having two or more cars. Among unskilled manual workers, 38 per cent of households had a car in 1985–6. The single most popular item of consumption, however, was the television. Television ownership went from near zero at the end of the war to virtually 100 per cent by the 1970s. Other consumer goods followed the trend of the television in becoming nearly universal. Telephone ownership spread more slowly – from less than half of households in 1973 to 95 per cent in 1997. Nearly half the households had a video recorder in 1987, while 90 per cent did in 1997. Two-thirds had a CD player in 1997, while one-third had a computer.[64]

There was a whole range of other technological innovations which increased the diversity of goods available to the British people, and often at prices that meant the working class could afford them. The chemicals industry, for example, developed an enormous assortment of products such as plastics, artificial fibres, pesticides and fertilisers (which could benefit the weekend gardener as well as the farmer), detergents and medicines. The sale of food was revolutionised in a variety of ways. Regulation meant that food and water were purer than before the war. Frozen foods were of much higher quality than tinned foods; by the last decades of the century, whole meals of good quality could be purchased frozen or refrigerated. The supermarket increased the range of goods (not just food) available in a single place, and at a lower price (and eventually at more convenient hours) than was offered by the local shop – although sometimes with some loss of quality. Similarly, department stores started to sell food. Supermarkets did not, however, always drive the local market, butcher or greengrocer out of business, so the option of convenience, personal service and sometimes better quality, but at higher prices, remained. Shopping centres and malls centralised all shopping. All these changes made life infinitely easier, especially for the burgeoning suburban middle class and for working women.

Yet technology had its costs. The degradation of the environment had been ongoing for at least as long as the Industrial Revolution. In the nineteenth century, factories, railways and homes poured coal dust into the air, while human waste and a variety of chemical pollutants were dumped in the rivers. London's notorious fogs were the result of the former, while the Thames may easily have become one of the world's most polluted rivers. By 1945, people were more conscious of the need to preserve what was left. The National Parks and Access to the Countryside Act, passed in 1949, designated ten mountain and coastal areas as national parks (though areas in which people would continue to live and work), while also seeking to assure that 'green belts' would remain around the major metropolitan areas in the face of growing suburbanisation. In the 1960s, an improved environment was beginning to be identified with a better quality of life and so a higher standard of living. Clean air and beaches, safe food and water, an unblemished and scenic countryside for walking and holidaying were all becoming items of consumption demanded by a more prosperous society.[65] At the same time, others questioned the values of a society that was based so completely on economic growth and consumption that it was indifferent to the effects of both on the environment. These people became the base for environmental activism, which blossomed as a major political force over the next decade.

Much was achieved in the post-war years. The use of coal was cut in both the factory and the home, pollution controls were placed on the coal-burning furnaces and generators that remained, and the railways were converted to electricity. The dumping of human waste in rivers had long since ceased; now efforts were made to stop pollution by industry and clean up the rivers. By 2001, they were cleaner than at any time since the Industrial Revolution. Yet the prevalence of the car and the lorry substituted new forms of air pollution that led to global warming. It is likely, too, that carbon monoxide and exhaust emissions contributed to health problems. The British were initially slow to convert to unleaded petrol and to require catalytic converters on vehicles, but by 1997 they ranked way ahead of the United States and slightly ahead of Germany and Japan in keeping down carbon emissions.[66] Even such improvements, however, were overwhelmed by the sheer increase in numbers. The car was not the only invention which brought an environmental sting with its consumer benefits. Refrigeration and air conditioning contributed to global warming, while many of the chemical inventions mentioned earlier – plastics, fertilisers, pesticides and detergents – carried with them health and environmental problems, the latter in the form of toxic waste and pollution of rivers and beaches. Finally, there was nuclear energy. Britain's first nuclear power plant was built at Windscale in Cumbria; the first electricity generated by nuclear power came on line in 1956. It became a polluter of the Irish Sea, however, while no one has yet worked out how to dispose of the nuclear waste that it and others like it around the world produce.

In addition to spending their extra money on goods, Britons spent it on leisure – and with the slightly shorter working week and much longer holidays than before the war they had much more time available for leisure activities. As a result, the percentage of the population employed in leisure services nearly doubled between 1939 and 1997, from 4.4 to 8 per cent.[67] The post-war era saw the decline of cinema and of attendance at football matches by working men. The villain in both instances was television, which by the 1970s was well established as the most popular form of leisure for all classes. Other forms of leisure, like visiting friends or going for a walk, were free or low-cost. The most common activity for people to spend money on, apart from the television, was to go out to dinner. By the 1980s, the restaurants they ate at were providing a higher quality meal than ever before, and if they did not serve foreign cuisine they were influenced by it. The pub, too, was more than ever a place to dine as well as to drink. For the suburban middle class, clubs, charities and organisations like the Rotary Clubs all provided a means of socialising outside the workplace, as did politics and sports. Participation in sport and exercise went up substantially for the middle class in particular, as people became more health-conscious, but they were not alone. Working-class men had long been playing football, and, with greater leisure, it boomed after the war. Thus, the number of clubs affiliated with county football associations increased from nearly 18,000 in 1948 to over 40,000 in 1985. In 1979, it was estimated that 20 per cent of males between sixteen and twenty-four participated in organised football, usually in clubs associated with the workplace or the local pub.[68] But most of all, as increasing numbers of people became homeowners, Britons of all classes spent their time improving those homes and working in their gardens.

None of this necessarily cost a lot of money, depending on the choices of individual families. By the 1950s, therefore, many workers could invest in a summer holiday. Those skilled labourers who got a week off in the summer had been taking their holiday at the seaside since the latter part of the nineteenth century. Now increased incomes and time off opened up the option of travelling abroad. In the 1960s, a major business developed in packaging European holidays for the working class, primarily to Spain – although most people continued to take their holiday in Britain. In 1978, for example, the British people took 48 million holidays (an increase from 27 million in 1951); 9 million of these were taken abroad and 30 per cent of those were to Spain. Nonetheless, not everyone could afford to travel. Only about half of unskilled workers did so during their holidays.[69]

Over the post-war era, therefore, people had more money to spend on what they wanted and more leisure time to do a greater variety of things. Yet even with all this improvement, Britons at the end of the century were not doing as well as their peers in other developed countries. In the 1990s, the average hourly compensation for production workers in Britain was less than half of the average in Germany, and was 20–25 per cent less than in France and the United States. At the same time, workers had a substantially longer working week than their counterparts in France and Germany, though a shorter one than those in the US. The advent of 'labour flexibility' meant that the stress level at work went up and job satisfaction went down, as everyone from the shop floor to the supervisor's office was subject to more pressures on the job, worked more overtime and felt less job security. For middle-class managers and professionals, this extra work in the evenings and over the weekends was unpaid and made major encroachments into their family life. In these respects, too, Britons were worse off than their peers in Europe, though not necessarily those in Japan and the United States.[70]

Poverty and Inequality

People did not benefit equally from the vast improvements in the standard of living that prosperity and the welfare state made possible, and some hardly benefited at all. Nonetheless, the booming economy of 1945–73 meant a reduction of poverty to levels so low that they literally could not have been conceived of before 1939. We have already referred to the evidence of the poverty that existed when discussing other changes that occurred in the century: the high infant mortality and low life expectancy, the prevalence of a wide range of infectious and childhood diseases – all of these affected the poor disproportionately. For example, even in 1942 (after much improvement), both the infant mortality rate and the childhood death rate were 50 per cent higher in South Wales and the North of England than they were in Southeast England, the richest part of the country. In 1944, the death rate for children aged one to fifteen from measles was four times greater in the former.[71] The poor were more vulnerable because of the overcrowded housing and the inadequate diets already referred to. The miserable existence of poor working-class housewives during the Great Depression is described by Michael Anderson for Scotland:

> [Their] lives remained a constant grind. Keeping homes and husbands and children clean, carrying and heating water, preparing meals with few convenience foods and almost no domestic appliances, systematically starving themselves to

allow their husbands and young children an adequate diet, last to bed and first to rise . . . [they were] worn out and old before their time . . .[72]

Yet, according to the only comparative measure we have, poverty between the wars was actually less than it had been in 1900. Seebohm Rowntree's study of York in 1899 had found nearly 28 per cent of the population living in poverty. When Rowntree conducted his study again in 1936, using a higher standard of subsistence to define the poverty level, the number had fallen to a little below 18 per cent – although it was over 30 per cent of the working class. The reasons for this fall are simple: unemployment and low wages were the principal causes of poverty. York did not suffer as much unemployment as more industrialised towns in the North, while low prices meant that people could buy more with the wages they got. In the South, where a lot of new jobs paid a living wage, by Rowntree's definition poverty would be even less. In the old industrial areas, by contrast, unemployment (and so poverty) could reach staggering levels. For example, 71 per cent of men in Northeast England and 45 per cent in the Rhondda Valley of South Wales had been unemployed for more than five years in 1938. Using Rowntree's still minimal standard, the poverty rate for the Liverpool region was 30 per cent in 1928–32, which meant, of course, it was much higher among workers.[73] Numbers like these meant that every shopkeeper and service provider in the community was the poorer because of the loss of business that resulted.

The improvements during the war and the post-war period were immediately evident when Rowntree conducted his survey of York one more time in 1950, and found that only 2.8 per cent of the working class (not of the population as a whole) lived in poverty. How far off the mark was Rowntree's figure? Sidney Pollard claims that 'abject poverty' was 20 per cent of the population in 1953; by 1973, it was 2.5 per cent of the population. While he does not state what standard was used for measuring poverty, it was probably based on the government's own standard of who was eligible for National Assistance payments – the welfare payment for those who were deemed to be in poverty. A 1965 study found 3.8 per cent of the population living below this level, many because they were unwilling to apply for National Assistance on top of their existing benefits, but some because they were working for exceptionally low wages. Later studies of Great Britain (excluding Northern Ireland) from the early 1970s to the mid-1980s showed those below the official standard to be from about 3–5 per cent of the population, with the lower number reached in 1974 and the higher number in 1983. If one includes those *at* as well as below the level at which income support kicked in, however, the percentage jumped up to 14 per cent in 1979.[74]

By the early 1960s, however, the use of an absolute standard to measure poverty was being challenged, primarily by sociologists on the left who were not happy that people were treating poverty as a solved problem. More to the point, they did not accept that poverty could be eliminated simply by a general rise in the standard of living; real reduction required reducing the number of poor relative to the rest of the population.[75] Thus, the relative measure of poverty was invented. The difference could be substantial because, while incomes were rising in the 1950s and early 1960s, welfare payments like pensions and child benefit rose much less. Hence, the incomes of people who were dependent on these state payments fell further and further below the national average. Rising rents (before the introduction of housing allowance) could also drive people below the poverty line who earlier had been above it. Such factors help explain how one study found that poverty had actually gone up between 1953 and 1960, from 7.8 to 14.2 per cent. Another study in 1968–9 found 21.8 per cent of the population 'on the margins of poverty', with 6.1 per cent living in poverty.[76] This leaves us pretty much where we were in 1900, though, of course, with an entirely different and more inclusive measure of poverty. By the 1970s, a consensus had developed around a relative standard: all who were more than 50 per cent below the national mean household income. Using this definition, about 7–8 per cent of the population of Britain* were below the 50 per cent cut-off in 1979.[77]

Who were the poor of the 1960s and 1970s, when the official statistics showed absolute poverty to be low? Nationally they were mostly 'separated, divorced and widowed women; the sick and disabled; the unemployed; and the elderly'.[78] However, there were urban concentrations. The St Ann's district of Nottingham was an example of the 'classic slum' of the era. Sociologists Ken Coates and Richard Silburn found '91 per cent of the St Ann's sample had an outside lavatory, 85 per cent no bathroom and 54.5 per cent no hot water'. Half of those whom Coates and Silburn studied were working; their poverty was due to low wages. Finally and importantly, many of these people were not 'stuck' in poverty; they moved in and out depending on what was going on in their lives. For example, the poor often had young children. Family allowances had hardly increased since the 1940s; hence, given the steady increase in prices over the next two decades, children plus low wages meant poverty. Thus, poverty touched many more people than a single percentage at a single moment of time conveys.[79]

There is little question that poverty was higher in the 1980s and 1990s, though how much is again a subject for debate. Now it was the political right who were not inclined to admit what was happening, since they denied that Thatcherite economic policies increased poverty. The statistics seemed to support them, as the absolute standard showed little increase in the 1980s, rising only to around 8–9 per cent for the whole United Kingdom. The problem is that if eligibility requirements are tightened or if the cut-off point for eligibility does not rise as fast as inflation, then fewer people are defined as poor (because they are now ineligible for supplementary benefit), even though more people may be worse off. This is exactly what happened in the 1980s. Certainly, given the enormous increase in unemployment and in the number of aged, it is unpersuasive that poverty increased so little.

---

* Northern Ireland added about 1 per cent to the percentage in poverty in the 1970s and 2 per cent in the 1980s, when one uses relative poverty as the criterion.

Yet the relative standard had its own problems. It jumped up after 1985, peaking at 21 per cent in 1990–91, and then fell back to 17 per cent in 1995.[80] This enormous increase partly reflected the fact that the incomes of the rich went up much faster than those of the poor. The mean income went up, leaving a greater number of people more than 50 per cent below it. Thus relative poverty had increased, even though some of these people were not poorer. In an attempt to break free of the politics of all this, 117 governments in 1995 agreed on the minimum requirements necessary to maintain a minimally adequate standard of life – in effect, a reconfigured absolute standard. A 1999 survey of European countries, undertaken by scholars at Bristol University and the London School of Economics, asked people to assess their ability to meet these requirements and then measured poverty by how many people could not meet the standard. For Britain, the survey found that 9 per cent of the population had an income that was 'a lot below' what was needed to achieve the minimum standard of living, while another 8 per cent had an income that was 'a little below' what was necessary.[81] The first number is comparable to that yielded by the absolute standard, the two together to what the relative standard found.*

These new poor were no different from those of the years of prosperity; only the numbers had increased. The largest group was the elderly. Longer life was increasing the numbers of poor, for those over seventy-five were significantly more likely to have an income more than 50 per cent below the mean than were those aged sixty-five to seventy-four. Furthermore, the average income for both of these groups declined in the 1980s; the average for even the younger group was so close to the 50 per cent mark that large numbers must have fallen below it.[82] A second large pool was coming from the unemployed. The numbers ballooned in the early 1980s and, with some fluctuation, stayed

---

* Poverty in Britain was greater than in the rest of Western Europe and more like that in the United States, in part because inequality is more acceptable in Britain and the United States. See below on inequality.

high until well into the 1990s. Long-term unemployment (i.e. those unemployed for more than a year) was especially prevalent for men over fifty. By 1986–7, about 35–40 per cent of the unemployed were long-term.[83] The other large group of unemployed was school-leavers, including large numbers of non-whites. Beginning in 1982, however, many school-leavers went into job training programmes, which meant they were not eligible for supplementary benefit and so did not appear in the absolute measure of poverty. The final large group of new poor was single parents. While there was a big increase in births outside marriage in the 1980s, most single parents were women who were divorced or widowed, not teenage mothers. The percentage of single parents relying on public assistance rose from 38 to 70 per cent between 1979 and 1992. Their biggest problem was the cost of child care; if they could not afford it, they could not hold a full-time job. Thus, more mothers went into part-time work, while there was a trend in the 1990s towards more work being done in the home – such as making clothes or assembling electrical goods. In 1993, the Major government abolished the wages councils that had been created in 1909 to set minimum wages for home workers, who were primarily women. Thereafter, there was no floor on their wages until Labour introduced a national minimum. This reference back to 1909, however, should warn us that female poverty is not new. In 1908, 61 per cent of those on poor relief were female, while in 1983 60 per cent of those receiving supplementary benefit were women.[84]

Clearly, the debate over how to measure poverty is tied to attitudes about inequality. How important *is* inequality as a measurement of wellbeing in the society? Americans have focused more on equality of opportunity rather than equality as a policy goal. Since the war, however, Europeans have enacted more progressive tax structures and more elaborate welfare states than the US, reflecting a stronger interest in reducing inequality. Socialists, in particular, have seen greater equality as a fundamental measure of the fairness of a society. The British people may see it that way too. A 1988 study found that slightly over 70 per cent of the sample believed that the distribution of income and wealth was unfair, while 80 per cent thought there should be some redistribution of wealth to benefit those at the bottom.[85] Inequality, of course, has been the norm in Britain, as it has in all developed countries (and most less developed ones as well). The Industrial Revolution almost surely increased income inequality, as the rich got richer more quickly than benefits flowed to the bottom of society – although, based on the meagre data available, W. D. Rubinstein finds little evidence of an increase in inequality until the last third of the nineteenth century.[86] The twentieth century, however, saw a clear narrowing of the gap in earnings between those at the top and the bottom (as measured by their percentage of the national median) until the mid-1970s. The pattern is roughly the same if we look at estimates of net family income (i.e. adding in transfer payments from the state, subtracting out taxes paid and taking the household as the unit) after the advent of the welfare state: declining inequality from the Second World War to the mid-1970s.[87]

Estimates of the concentration of wealth also show some increase in equality after the First World War. Wealth inequality was far greater than income inequality in the nineteenth century because of the concentration of land ownership in relatively few hands. In the 1920s, the wealthiest 5 per cent of the population still owned over 80 per cent of the nation's wealth; by the late 1950s, that number had fallen to between 70 and 60 per cent; and by the mid-1970s it had fallen further to around 40 per cent, where it stayed for the rest of the century. This decline occurred because the possession of wealth spread further and further down the social hierarchy, as more people were able to save money, buy goods (like cars), own their own homes and even (thanks to Thatcher's privatisation policies) own some shares. If one adds in the wealth people owned in the form of pension rights, the share of the wealthiest 5 per cent falls to about 25 per cent since the mid-1970s, while the share of the bottom 50 per cent rises from 7 to 17 per cent of total wealth.[88]

While the distribution of wealth remained fairly static after the mid-1970s, income inequality got worse. According to a report by the Office of National Statistics, the incomes of the top 10 per cent of the population grew by 38 per cent in the 1980s, while those of the bottom 10 per cent grew by 5 per cent. The gap continued to widen in the early 1990s, though at a slower rate, but then it started to narrow again.[89] These statistics, however, do not take into account the effects of either taxation or welfare benefits (including non-cash benefits like education and health care). The Joseph Rowntree Foundation found that incorporating transfer payments would give the bottom 20 per cent of the population a 13 per cent increase in incomes from 1979 to 1993 instead of a 6 per cent increase. Nonetheless, given that the Thatcher and Major governments cut the taxes of the richest, increased taxes for the poorest and limited eligibility for and the rate of growth of transfer payments, the gap incorporating the 'social wage' also widened after 1979, at least until the mid-1990s.[90] Furthermore, this inequality was not spread evenly over the country. The gap that had existed from 1918 to 1939 between the South of England on the one hand and most of Wales, Scotland, Northern Ireland and the North of England on the other hand still existed in 2000. Prosperity was disproportionately concentrated in the South, while poverty was disproportionately concentrated in the regions of the Industrial Revolution.

Education

If people were going to be able to do more than merely move out of poverty – if they were going to be able to improve their place in society – the education system had to be directed towards that goal. As we saw in Chapter 5, education was one culprit blamed for Britain's economic performance between 1945 and 1979. Yet before 1945, few saw the education system as a vehicle to promote social mobility, except on a very limited basis. Britain did not have mandatory secondary education until the Education Act of

1944. Children, of course, had gone to secondary school before then, but in 1939 under half of those in England and Wales attended secondary schools. Furthermore, many of these were not getting a free education, as the grammar schools charged fees while providing some free places. In 1949, only 12 per cent of adults had a secondary education. By 1951, the numbers in state-supported secondary schools in England had almost quadrupled over the 1938 number, helped by the fact that the school-leaving age was increased to fifteen in 1947. Thereafter, the numbers kept growing until about 1980 – in part because of the baby boom, and in part because the school-leaving age was raised again, to sixteen in 1972. These numbers excluded those going to private schools, who usually comprised roughly 5–8 per cent of all pupils.[91] While the latter increased the number of free places they made available, they inevitably mostly served those from the upper and middle classes.

This increase in the student population could only be achieved by devoting more resources to education. In 1930, 2.4 per cent of the net national income of the UK was spent on education (capital as well as current expenditure). By 1975–6, 6.3 per cent of GDP went to education, the post-war peak. Thereafter, it fell with the school-age population to 4.8 per cent in 1990–91. So education clearly benefited from the expansive economy of 1950–75 and suffered from the cuts thereafter.[92] Britain's spending compared well with its principal economic competitors when the basis of comparison is percentage of GDP: it was significantly higher than in West Germany, France and Japan in 1965 and 1975, while roughly even with them in 1986–7. When the basis of comparison is expenditure per student, however, British spending on secondary education was well below the United States and its European competitors.[93]

The result was a steady improvement in the level of training of the British population. Table 8.1 (p. 300) showed the pattern of improvement for girls; Table 8.2 opposite gives the comparable numbers for boys. As with the girls, the numbers with no qualifications fell steadily throughout the post-war period; the

Table 8.2. Highest Level of Qualifications Achieved by
Adult Males, by Date of Birth
(Percentage with Qualification)

	1910–19	1930–39	1940–49	1950–59	1960–69	1970–79
None	61.0	45.2	35.9	24.5	13.4	7.8
O-level, CSE, etc.	21.4	25.3	27.0	29.1	42.5	41.6
A-level	2.4	5.9	9.5	14.9	19.9	33.8
University/ Professional	15.5	23.6	27.3	31.5	24.3	16.7

Source: George Smith, 'Schools', in Halsey and Webb, *Twentieth-Century Social Trends*, p. 209.

numbers with A-levels, university degrees or professional qualifications went up at a comparable rate. The same information can be approached from the other direction, by looking at the performance of school-leavers at O-level and A-level. In 1961, 14 per cent of those in England and Wales achieved at least five passing grades at O-level; in 1996–7, 45 per cent of English fifteen-year-olds had done that well at GCSE. The percentage who passed at least two A-levels was 8 in 1961 and 25.6 in 1991; Scottish numbers for the 1990s were similar.[94] It all added up to a much more educated and qualified population, though one that was still behind Germany and Japan, where the percentage of pupils passing the national equivalent of five O-levels was higher – and the gap in mathematics was greater still. By the end of the century, 75 per cent of those aged 12–18 were at school and 70 per cent of adults of working age (those 16–69) had a qualification, though it may not have been earned at school.[95]

The working class had to be major beneficiaries of this expansion of secondary education. Nonetheless, as the numbers with qualifications went up, the residual with none were probably coming almost entirely from that class. Those of middle-class origin or higher had a much better chance of getting an A-level qualification, as did those in private education. In the 1950s, most working-class children were being tracked into secondary modern schools at the age of 11, meaning an end of their education at 15 or 16. Furthermore, the education they received there contributed little to making them better workers or better able to improve themselves. During the decade, there was a growing reaction against the whole system. Many parents were not happy about having their children written off at eleven – or indeed, earlier, since there was streaming in elementary schools based on who was deemed most likely to do well in the exam. At the same time, educational sociologists were providing data showing that intelligence tests given at eleven favoured children of higher social classes. Furthermore, grammar schools were not equally available throughout the country; thus, in some areas able pupils were cut off from the fast track simply because there were not enough places. The overall conclusion was that the system was in many ways arbitrary and so not promoting equal opportunity.

In 1965, Labour decided to push local authorities to restructure the system by ending the 11-plus exam and converting to comprehensive schools. Comprehensives combined the grammar school and secondary modern into one school; the school-leaver and university-bound pupil would be educated together. In theory, a higher quality of education would be available to all, with the decision about university made later in the child's career. Throughout the 1960s and 1970s, comprehensives were at the centre of the debate between the parties over educational policy, as the Tories resisted the abolition of the grammar schools. Thatcher, as Education Secretary from 1970 to 1974, managed to save some, while others opted to go private. Yet many middle-class parents feared the 11-plus exam, so even Tory education authorities often chose to go comprehensive. As a result, Thatcher approved more schemes to convert to comprehensives than any other Education Secretary (primarily because no one else was kept in the position so long). By the mid-1980s around 85 per cent of English children in state schools were in comprehensives, while Wales and Scotland were virtually 100 per cent comprehensive.[96] There was still a class bias, however, since comprehensives in middle-class residential areas were likely to be of higher quality.[*] Nonetheless, comprehensives probably helped increase the numbers of working-class children leaving school with qualifications, including among racial minorities. For over the decades after 1970, West Indian and Indian children did just as well at securing qualifications as white children.[97] Yet progress was limited among both the black and white working class in the inner cities. Run-down facilities, a family culture that sometimes did not put a high value on education, home conditions that made learning difficult and resistance from the children themselves, who believed education was irrelevant to their lives, all combined to undermine the success of secondary education in these areas.

Conservatives saw the whole move to comprehensive education as a formula for reducing quality to a fairly low level, even though streaming according to ability remained common in the comprehensives. Furthermore, the new policy coincided with the adoption of new teaching methods which emphasised the development of the child and his or her thinking skills rather than learning information. The result, they believed, had been a decline in standards due to a retreat from the mastery of the basics of English and mathematics, which were fundamental for those not continuing to university. New approaches to teaching science and history, which emphasised the method of analysis rather than memorisation, were similarly attacked. It is not clear how much change actually occurred, but the perception of declining standards, by many parents as well as by politicians, shaped education policy in the 1980s and 1990s.

[*] The introduction of comprehensives also marked the final transition to full coeducation within the public sector, except for some of the few remaining grammar schools.

The Thatcher and Major governments introduced regular testing for several age groups, plus a national curriculum which set a minimum level of knowledge for each subject that students in each age group should be able to achieve. They also sought to revive the quality associated with the grammar schools by allowing schools to opt out of local authority control. In England, about 20 per cent of secondary school children in 1997 were in these 'grant-maintained' schools.[98] Government-funded assisted places at independent schools, introduced in 1980, and parental choice within the state system also promoted greater selectivity by helping the best pupils go to the best schools.

For those concerned about education and Britain's economy, the third track offered after the 1944 Education Act, technical education, was also important. Since the late nineteenth century, critics had denounced the failure of the education system to provide adequate training in the technical and vocational skills necessary for the economy, and especially for industry. Yet the British belief in the value of a liberal education always seemed to trump efforts to develop technical education at the secondary level.[99] In 1945, civil servants at the Ministry of Education envisaged the third track as providing much more than vocational education. They saw the technical colleges as training grounds from which some students would go on to higher education courses in engineering, while others would go directly into business – almost scientific counterparts to the grammar schools. The local authorities, however, had little interest in technical colleges, given the difficulties of telling at the age of eleven which students should go to them. Anyway, parents wanted their children to go to grammar schools. Thus, as education authorities coped with building more schools to accommodate the baby boom, they concentrated on the other two tracks. In the latter half of the 1950s, the Conservative government turned away from the third track altogether, concluding that appropriate technical and scientific education should be provided in the grammar and secondary modern schools. In the 1960s it was wound up with the move towards comprehensive education.[100]

The effect was to leave Britain short on both of the possible options for the technical colleges. On the one hand, the system did not provide enough pupils interested in engineering to fill the places that were available in the universities and polytechnics. On the other hand, Britain was left with a growing skills shortage among its industrial labour force. Throughout the early post-war decades, industrial workers were left to get their training from an apprenticeship system which Gertrude William claimed in 1957 was 'exactly the same as the method introduced more than 800 years ago for an entirely different economy'.[101] In most firms, it meant no formal classes or any system of certification; workers simply learned on the job and were treated as adequately trained when their apprenticeship was over. In the 1970s and 1980s, however, it became clear that the system was no longer serving the interests of either industry or workers very well in the rapidly changing economy. By then, from one-fifth to one-half of firms at some time were suffering from shortages of skilled labour, with the building trades especially badly hit.[102]

In the 1970s, governments started to focus on youth training programmes for the increasing numbers of unemployed school-leavers. These schemes were developed as the number of unemployed youth jumped from 10,000 in July 1974 to 240,000 in July 1977. With the rapid increase in unemployment in the early 1980s, the Conservatives introduced a new Youth Training Scheme for sixteen- and seventeen-year-olds. The objective of this programme was to combine work and training – initially for a year, but from 1986 for two years. By that time, over a quarter of sixteen-year-olds were involved in the scheme, while one-eighth were unemployed. The programme included *ad hoc* provision of job skills, but its main aim was to reduce unemployment, and it achieved some success: in 1986 nearly three-quarters were in a job for which they had received some training within three months of completing the programme.[103] Yet the Youth Training Scheme did not solve the larger problem of an undertrained workforce, as most of the jobs were low-skill and gave the employees little prospect for improvement. Most importantly, it did not offer a systematic vocational training, based on a combination of course work and apprenticeship, that would provide transferable as well as specialised skills. This was the norm in Western Europe and Japan (but not in the United States), and it resulted in their having a better trained and more adaptable workforce. Thus, in 1988 less than 30 per cent of Britain's workers had formal intermediate vocational qualifications (something beyond a GCSE from secondary school), while nearly two-thirds of Germany's had such qualifications. In 2000, the Labour government was talking about closing the gap by guaranteeing all youths between sixteen and eighteen a place in either a private- or public-sector apprenticeship programme if they chose not to stay at school.[104] Overall, while an ever larger percentage of Britons reached adulthood with school certification and some training, Britain still remained well behind competitor nations in the quality of what it provided.

Although it took longer, Britain eventually undertook an expansion of higher education that was similar to that for secondary education. In 1900, there were fewer than 25,000 students in universities, representing about 1 per cent of the college-age population. In 1962–3, there were still only 118,000 university students (about 4 per cent of the relevant age group), plus another 55,000 in teacher-training colleges. By the end of 1996, there were nearly 1.8 million students at universities and other institutions of higher education; nearly one-third of the college-age population was in higher education full-time. Another radical change occurred in continuing education. In 1910, there were some 26,000 full-time students in further education, 68,000 part-time students and 558,000 night-school students. By 1950 the total was some two million, and by the end of the century it was over four million. All told, by the end of the century there were about five million students in post-secondary education, of whom overseas students comprised about 9 per cent.[105]

The seminal moment in British higher education was the 1963 report of a committee headed by Lord Robbins; however, much had been done before then. There had been a steady increase in the number of university students since the war. A new university college was founded at Keele in 1949; between 1952 and 1962, it and five other university colleges became independent universities;* and from the mid-1950s the existing universities expanded the number of places. Furthermore, seven new universities founded in England in the 1960s had all been approved by 1961.† Yet the population getting higher education was still a very small and fairly elite group. Robbins therefore called for a further substantial expansion of numbers to assure that everyone who had the ability to benefit from a university education also had the opportunity. The most immediate response was to give university status to the ten colleges of advanced technology, which meant new building so that they could increase their student intake. At the same time, in the early 1960s the government introduced guaranteed grants for fees and maintenance for all students. The cumulative result was a rough doubling in the number of universities, university faculty, university students and percentage of the age group attending university between the late 1950s and 1971.

Yet the system was still criticised for not providing the kind of education that the economy required. Following their foundation in the nineteenth century, the 'red brick' universities and university colleges had had close ties to their communities – both in terms of their governance and their student bodies. As a result, they had served industry well. After 1918, however, the older ones began to adopt more narrow assumptions about whom they

---

* The five were Exeter, Hull, Leicester, Nottingham and Southampton. University colleges could not confer degrees. All of these has been associated with the University of London; that is, their students took London examinations and received London degrees.
† The seven new universities were East Anglia (in Norwich), Essex (in Colchester), Kent (in Canterbury), Lancaster, Sussex (in Brighton), Warwick (in Coventry) and York.

should educate and the kind of education they should provide, as they sought to replicate what was on offer at Oxford and Cambridge. After 1945 all universities (old and new) went in this direction. The polytechnics and area and regional colleges that were started in the late 1960s to teach new kinds of students and new kinds of subjects were now supposed to fill the gap. By 1970–71, there were thirty polytechnics (as against fifty-three universities), most of them upgraded local technical colleges. Each was supposed to serve its community, including the business community. Hence, they offered vocational, engineering and business courses as well as traditional courses, and they enrolled part-time as well as full-time and older as well as college-age students. Their research was also expected to be useful, which meant that they became centres for the social sciences, grappling with socially 'relevant' issues. Their primary business, however, was to teach undergraduate courses. The 1960s also saw the founding of the Open University by Wilson's government. Even more than the polytechnics, its purpose was to provide adult students with the opportunity to work part-time towards an under-graduate degree. Its courses were taken by a combination of corre-spondence, broadcasts and weekend tutorials, so they were especially accessible to women – a crucial service as increasing numbers of housewives sought to enter the job market. 'By the end of the century it was admitting 100,000 students a year . . . and it was ranked seventh in the UK for the quality of its teaching and research.'[106]

One of the functions of these new institutions of higher educa-tion was to offer the courses in engineering and business which had long been identified as necessary to improve Britain's economic performance. Yet it was difficult to change the nature of higher education if the broader national culture remained unal-tered. In 1971, for example, there were 1,968 places available in universities for engineering students; however, there were only 1,240 applicants. Even in pure science, there were not enough applicants – 2,700 for 3,571 places.[107] If the demand was not there for engineering and science degrees, the universities could hardly be blamed for not supplying enough. In part, the demand was not there because the job opportunities were lacking; the British economy was still not using their skills. Each year between 1956 and 1961, an average of 7–8 per cent of young scientists and engineers already on staff at British universities emigrated to the United States, while in the early 1960s something under 20 per cent of recent Ph.D.s were emigrating.[108] In 1977, Britain still had a much smaller portion of its workforce employed in science and engineering than did the United States, West Germany and Japan.[109] The low prestige of technology degrees meant that the best people were still not attracted to these courses. A 1989 assessment by the Universities Funding Council found that the eight technological universities had only one excellent department among them (based on the quality of faculty research), while fourteen were rated poor.[110]

There were signs of a change in the culture, however. The public schools had completely retooled in the 1950s and 1960s. With the help of money from industry, they made themselves into outstanding educators in mathematics and science, and in the boys' schools these had become preferred areas of specialisation. The ethic at most of them was now closer to one of training for a successful career than of training to be a gentleman. By 1977, engineering courses were the most popular destination for pupils leaving private secondary schools (not just the public schools), as pupils saw them as a vehicle to success in business.[111] That trend continued for the rest of the century. Thus, if there was a shortage of outstanding students in engineering, it was because those at public-sector schools were not following the lead of the elite.

British higher education was much slower to respond in the realm of business education than in engineering. As already mentioned, the first two business schools were started in London and Manchester in the 1960s. While other universities had added courses by the 1980s, much of undergraduate business education was being provided by polytechnics and colleges. The universities only had places for about a quarter of those who applied.

As a result, by the mid-1980s still only 2 per cent of managers were getting formal management training, while in large corporations only 12 per cent of managers and about half of higher management had any kind of degree. Over a fifth of managers had no qualifications at all, not even O-levels.[112]

The 1990s saw the next big breakthrough in higher education. By the late 1980s, still only about one-sixth of college-age students were being served, with the polytechnics, regional colleges and Open University educating two-thirds of them and the universities educating one-third.[113] The Major government sought to further break down the elitism of higher education by converting the polytechnics into universities. The effect was to make the kinds of practical courses that the Tories wanted to encourage – like business, accounting, computing and nursing – into university degree courses. At the same time, the intake into higher education at all levels started to expand again. As a result, by 1997–8 one-third of eighteen- and nineteen-year-olds were entering full-time higher education courses (not just those at the universities), with 45 per cent of those in Scotland and Northern Ireland doing so.[114] These numbers were comparable to those in the United States and well above what was happening on the Continent.

We can ask the same question about higher education that was asked about secondary education: how much did the working class benefit from this expansion? Given the scale of the increase, they had to benefit. Only 3 per cent of working-class children went on to university in the 1960s, and they accounted for about 7 per cent of entrants. By the 1980s, that percentage had increased, as they accounted for about one-fifth of matriculating students between 1986 and 1988, while their share of students in polytechnics and the Open University was significantly higher. In the 1980s and 1990s, ethnic minorities, in particular, took advantage of higher education opportunities at rates that were significantly greater than those of white people.[115] The 1990s, however, saw a move to greater fees and tuition as a means of reducing costs to government. In the mid-1960s, government grants had accounted for nearly 80 per cent of universities' income. The Tories had sought to reverse that dependency, and by 1993–4 it was down to 30 per cent.[116] The Blair government went further by insisting that universities charge tuition. While tuition was waived for the poorest, and loans were available for others, these extra costs hurt the ability of those in the working class to continue with university education. The policy was unpopular with students, universities and Labour's own supporters. It was repudiated for Scotland by the new Parliament. Yet with spending per pupil having fallen substantially because of spending cuts in the 1980s and the increase in numbers in the 1990s, Labour was in a bind. By the new century, income per pupil at Harvard was 4.5 times greater than at Oxford, while at Yale it was 3.2 times greater.[117] Something clearly had to be done to increase the resources of the universities, and marginal increases in government spending could not do the job. In looking for ways to make students (or graduates) take on more of the burden, Blair was inching towards the American approach.

There was one further way in which higher-education reform was Americanising the system: there was a greater diversity of intellectual ability among the students. It would be impossible to go from a student body comprising 8 per cent of the college-age population to one incorporating over one-third of the age-group without significant changes in quality. Yet this did not necessarily make for a worse system, just one that had a broader function than educating an elite. Intellectual ability does not always measure potential for success in society. Less intellectual students could still benefit from a higher education, and they would be more successful with a higher education than without one. The nation therefore gained by having them so educated. By the second half of the decade, Britain had progressed much further than either France or Germany in embracing this approach to higher education. Indeed, according to a 1998 OECD study, it had surpassed the United States in the percentage of its population that had completed a university education.[118] Thus, it seemed the groundwork for greater social mobility was being laid.

Class and Social Mobility

It is a universally accepted truism that British society has long been defined by its class system. As the sociologist A. H. Halsey writes, 'A sociologist may refine it into abstractions, but no one could grow up in England without acquiring a deep personal-cum-anthropological knowledge of class and status.'[119] Halsey and others clearly mean something beyond the simple fact that Britain has fairly distinct social classes. The United States has classes: even the myth of the American dream, based on assumptions of opportunity and mobility, implies that there are classes that people can move out of and in to. Furthermore, Americans themselves tend to be able to identify themselves as working or middle class.[120] So when analysts claim that Britain is a singularly class-bound society, they must mean more than this. The implication is that there is a unique consciousness of class in defining personal identity, with relatively little social mobility. The upper class is entrenched and benefits from a privileged position, while those below it, particularly the working class, are resentful and hostile. All of this is taken to be a problem for Britain. Most importantly, it is seen as a source of decline, as the economy was slow to adapt to the merito-cratic demands of the modern world, with excessive class conflict as one result. Furthermore, it is seen as a distinctly British problem; somehow class is different in Britain than in other developed countries, including other European countries with a similar social history.

Yet class is a remarkably elusive concept. Karl Marx's defini-tion provides a starting point: a class consists of people with a common relationship to the means of production and with a consciousness of a common identity and a common interest in opposition to other classes. The old landed aristocracy most clearly fit this definition. Marx's bourgeoisie, however, consisted only of the industrialists, financiers and merchants. In *The Communist Manifesto*, he said that the petite bourgeoisie of shop-keepers and clerical staff would disappear, while professionals were merely the hired labour of the bourgeoisie. In fact, the lower middle class proved to be one of the most expansive of all social groups, while professionals appropriated an enhanced status over the next century. All of these together could be seen as a middle class. Yet there are still problems. For that expanding lower middle class consists of clerical staff, salespeople, schoolteachers, etc, whose income through much of the nineteenth and twentieth centuries was not much different from that of a skilled industrial worker. At the end of the nineteenth century, the distinction between the two still seemed pretty clear – based on education, accent, where one lived, how one dressed, etc. Yet even then, there was quite a bit of inter-marriage and crossover between the two. Moreover, within the working class itself, the sense of common identity was limited, as skilled workers felt socially superior to the unskilled. Nonetheless, it is Marx's model that most people have in mind when talking about class in Britain – especially as, by the twentieth century, the workers had the political and economic power to assert their interest (and express their hostility) against those above them. Furthermore, while there may have been differences among skilled and unskilled workers, they were nothing compared to their sense of commonality *vis-à-vis* the rest. At least that is the theory. In fact, workers in the first half of the century imposed a very high level of differentiation within their own ranks, with many rungs on the working-class hierarchy, and a determination by those at the upper end to assert their respectability so as to distinguish themselves from the 'rough' end of the class.[121]

The advent of a numbers-driven sociology in the 1960s led to efforts to give greater precision to definitions of class so that sociologists could measure change over time. They turned to census classifications by occupation and income to define social groups; however, by themselves these groups were not the equivalent of classes. For example, Anthony Heath and Clive Payne defined six groups to analyse social mobility:

1. Higher salaried professionals and administrators
2. Lower salaried semi-professionals and administrators
3. Routine white-collar workers
4. A petite bourgeoisie of farmers, small employers and the self-employed
5. Skilled manual workers and supervisors
6. Semi-skilled and unskilled manual workers.[122]

The first thing to notice is that the landed aristocracy has disappeared as a separate group. That, in itself, represents a radical change in the structure of British society since the nineteenth century. While the very richest landowners in the nineteenth century derived their income from a wide range of sources, including stocks and bonds and urban rents, the bulk of them still depended on agricultural rents. This income was decimated by the agrarian depression that began in the 1870s and lasted until the Second World War. Eventually they had to retrench, cutting back on extravagance and selling land. Others sold land not because they had to, but in order to buy investments that would yield a decent income. Increases in inheritance taxes accelerated the trend. By 1945, much of the agricultural land was held by owner-farmers (often former tenants), and the sell-off continued in the 1950s and 1960s. In 1967, about nine hundred owners of large estates remained, some two hundred of which were peerage families.[123] The old aristocracy still existed in the post-war era, but theirs was a narrow world of hunting, hunt balls and debutantes, all of which were reported in the press that catered to those who liked to watch the rich and famous. The monarchy itself was at the head of this society, but the royal family was watched by a much broader popular press that sought to sniff out scandal. Some of the old titled families joined the entrepreneurial culture (as their ancestors had in the eighteenth and nineteenth centuries) by opening their houses to visitors and tourists and renting them out for parties, weddings, concerts and any group that would pay. While individual members of the aristocracy might still become important politicians and major corporate shareholders, as a group they operated on the margins of national life and of the decision-making elite who ran the country.

What, then, defined being upper class? First and foremost, it was wealth. In *The Sunday Times Book of the Rich*, Philip Beresford 'found twelve billionaires in Britain in 1990 headed by the Queen who has a fortune worth over £6,700 million. A total of seventy-eight individuals were listed as super-rich with fortunes of £100m+ ... Finally, Beresford also identified 118 very rich families with £50m+ and 192 rich families with £20m+ including landowners, industrialists, politicians and pop stars.'[124] While many of the upper class were not among the very rich, a great many by the 1990s had annual incomes well over £100,000. Apart from great wealth, education was by far the most important criterion, especially in the first three post-war decades: a secondary education at one of the elite public schools and/or a university education at Oxford or Cambridge. This education provided the entrée to the most prestigious and powerful jobs – in politics, in finance, in the civil and foreign service, in higher education, in the media, in the law, and more. Increasingly, however, the younger generation was choosing the private sector and money over the public sector and service.[125] These people networked on corporate boards and as members of exclusive clubs. What was so at the national level (with the rich and powerful centred around London) was also true on a lesser scale at the local level. For example, a study of Newcastle-upon-Tyne in the 1970s found that its ruling class was descended from the capitalist families who had made the city a centre of coal, industry, commerce and finance in the eighteenth and nineteenth centuries. They 'tended to sit on local authorities . . . on local planning bodies, on the boards of finance corporations and multinational companies (where they were also substantial shareholders), had usually been educated at Eton, Harrow, Winchester, or Rugby, held substantial family seats in rural Northumberland, belonged to the Northern Counties Club in Newcastle's Hood Street, and . . . [to] exclusive London clubs . . .'. By profession, these men were bankers, accountants or insurance managers.[126]

The Newcastle-upon-Tyne elite look suspiciously middle class. And indeed, Heath and Payne's first two groups roughly represent an upper and upper-middle class who are mainly distinguished from each other by the size of the enterprises they are engaged in and the amount of money they earn. Since their last two groups are clearly working class, does that mean the two middle groups are *the* middle class? It is difficult to completely separate them from the first two groups, with whom they share many values and even some of the same kinds of jobs. A. H. Halsey solves this problem by separating the lower-middle class (groups three and four) from the middle class (groups one and two), with no upper class at all.[127] Yet even this is not fully satisfactory, for purely in terms of income the skilled workers could have as much or more than some of those in this lower-middle class, while some farmers and small business-owners (group four) could have more income than some lesser professionals (group two). The clearest divide may still be between the first four groups and the last two: the former are not manual workers and the latter are. With the old landed aristocracy irrelevant, this division is at the heart of what remains of the claim that Britain is a class society, with limited opportunities for mobility.

Heath and Payne used their six-group classification as the basis for trying to measure social mobility and how much it had changed over time. Their data came from the election surveys that were conducted during every general election from 1964 to 1997, in which people answered questions about their own social group and that of their father. Heath and Payne looked at two measures of mobility: the percentage of people in each group that had come from another group, and the chances that people from any one group would have of moving up, staying where they are or moving down. The first measure showed a very high level of upward mobility. About 65 per cent of those in the first group and 70 per cent of those in the second group (the upper-middle class) came from a lower group; 40 per cent of the first and 50 per cent of the second came from the working class. Working-class recruitment into group four was comparable, while that into group three was even greater. The degree of downward mobility into the working class was relatively small: only about 20 per cent of those in each of the working-class groups came from outside the working class. In short, because the working class was so large, it was a major source of recruits for all social groups, while overwhelmingly the largest for the working class itself. Perhaps surprisingly, there was not a lot of change over time, with two exceptions: there may have been some expansion in recruitment into the upper-middle class from below between 1949 and 1964, and there was expansion of recruitment into the petite bourgeoisie (group four) from both above and below between 1964 and 1987.[128]

When looking at the chances of improvement, however, the picture is less optimistic. Upper-middle-class men and working-class men were most likely, by far, to stay where they were. The men with the best chance of upward mobility were those whose fathers were white-collar workers (group three). When looking at change over the course of the century, Heath and Payne found that those in the upper-middle class had actually improved their chances of staying where they were. The privileged had consolidated their position. Yet the opportunities for the working class to move up also improved significantly. The least stable group was the white-collar workers; by the time we get to those born in the 1930s (and so entering the job market in the 1950s and 1960s), virtually all of them came from some other group. Hence, the best opportunity for working-class sons was to move into this group. Overall, Heath and Payne found a significant net surplus of upward over downward mobility in the sample as a whole. The pattern for women was somewhat different.* Those from the upper-middle class were more likely to be downwardly mobile than the men; those from the working class were more likely to

---

* The class of a woman was defined by her own job. Housewives were excluded, as were women who never had a job. Women who were retired were (like retired men) classified by the last job they held. The analysis only included men and women aged thirty-five or over at the time of the survey.

be upwardly mobile than the men; and women as a whole were much more likely than men to end up in the white-collar group, whether from above or from below. There has been some improvement over time in the ability of women in the upper-middle class to stay there, while there has been much more significant improvement in the ability of women in the working class to move up – more improvement than for men.[129]

What does all this add up to? While those at the top were usually able to stay there, the working class provided a steady and increasing flow of people (especially women) to higher classes, and the chances of moving out of the working class improved somewhat during the post-war period. Other studies showed much the same thing. A. H. Halsey could write in 1995, 'Two out of every three middle-class men today were not born into a middle-class family.' By 1992, less than 50 per cent of those born into the working class had remained there. Furthermore, social mobility in Britain was not much less than in the United States, while it was significantly greater than in Germany or Japan.[130] The overall result indicates that class in Britain by 2000 was looking very much like class in other developed countries. Upper, middle and lower classes were defined by wealth and education. Leisure had ceased to be a defining characteristic of the upper class, while the lower class was something broader than just the working class. Finally, there was considerable upward mobility, even though those at the top and the bottom tended to be entrenched in that position over generations.

Education was the crucial vehicle for upward mobility, especially for those moving into the upper-middle class, just as it was crucial for preserving the position of those already in that class. In 1972, a selective secondary education accounted for over two-thirds of those moving into the highest group. Yet those most likely to get such an education were already at the top. They were also the ones most likely to leave school with A-levels, most likely to get into a prestigious university and so most likely to get the kinds of high-status jobs that such credentials opened up. A university education, however, still did not count for so much in

1972. Amazingly, about three-quarters of those in the upper-middle class did not have a university degree. Nonetheless, for those in the working class who were trying to move up, it was very important: a university degree or some further education accounted for about half of those who had moved into the middle class in 1972.[131] The expanded educational opportunities of the next three decades thus had to benefit the working class, though the access they gave was to less prestigious institutions and degree courses.

Analysts on the left have been more troubled by the fact that privilege remains entrenched than they are encouraged by the evidence of working-class upward mobility. Indeed, as with the decline in poverty between 1945 and 1970, they argue that the latter hasn't really happened – because change was not the result of government policies designed to create greater equality by breaking the privileged position of the upper and middle classes. Instead, whatever progress that occurred was the result of the long-term change in the structure of the economy. The opportunities to move up came because more jobs in the service sector were created, while manufacturing jobs were shrinking. The former process had been going on since the end of the nineteenth century; the latter began in the mid-1960s. Between 1966 and 1991, manufacturing employment fell by over 40 per cent, while service employment increased by over 30 per cent. Sixty per cent of the decline occurred in the 1980s alone, when Thatcherite policies devastated manufacturing. As a result, manual workers accounted for only 38 per cent of the workforce, while in 1993 industry only accounted for about a quarter – comparable to the United States, but well below Germany and Japan. White-collar workers in 1991 made up 56 per cent of the workforce, with clerical workers accounting for more than 15 per cent, managers and administrators another 15 per cent and professionals 19 per cent. The latter two numbers alone demonstrate why a better educated population was necessary, while all these white-collar jobs had to be filled at least partly from a working class that, in 1951, still made up about two-thirds of the population.[132]

This long-term trend poses a threat to the whole Marxist model: it is the working class that seems to be disappearing into the lower-middle class, rather than the other way around. Many left-wing social scientists are therefore redefining the proletariat to include clerical workers. On purely economic grounds, there was always a large overlap between these two groups. Yet clerical workers saw themselves as part of the middle class at the beginning of the century. Marxists argue, however, that the loss of the work's semi-skilled character and the unionisation of clerical workers since the war have led to proletarianisation. Like Marx's proletariat, they have no leverage against the employers; apart from their own solidarity, they are completely open to exploitation. Neither deskilling nor unionisation, however, has been universal, while for many, clerical jobs represent either a clear step up from where they started or the first stage in an upward career path – especially, in recent years, if they involve the acquisition of information technology skills. Finally, there is little evidence of working-class identity among clerical workers.[133] That identity always involved something more than just income or even skill. While union membership was one part of it, the spread of unionisation among professionals like teachers and nurses and among white-collar public employees has eroded its power as a marker of class. A secondary education also helped to identify the middle class at the beginning of the century. Education as a marker changed after 1945 – first to leaving school with qualifications, and then to a university education. But all these distinctions are also breaking down. What, then, is left to define the working – or middle – class? To answer this question, we need to look at what happened to British culture after 1945, since some of the most important constituents of class identity were cultural.

9

THE CULTURE OF ELITISM

Britain's cultural history, like that of all Europe, is based on hierarchy and inequality: a hereditary monarch and aristocracy provided the ruling class. Merchants and bankers were eventually able to carve out a place for themselves in the cities where they lived, but, overall, power and standing were defined by birth and the ownership of land. This was the system that had to adapt to the onset of large-scale capitalism and industrialisation between the seventeenth and nineteenth centuries. By and large, it adjusted very well. While new elites were incorporated at the top, equality came to Britain only slowly and hesitantly. Equality had not been the watchword of England's revolutions of the seventeenth century, except among the most radical. Indeed, the radicalism of some of the common people in the 1640s, along with the Terror in the French Revolution 150 years later, were sufficient warnings of the dangers of real equality. Thus hierarchy, with the expectation that those lower down the social scale would defer to their social betters, remained part of Britain's political culture, even as the social structure and political system underwent a radical transformation in the nineteenth century. Furthermore, that mentality survived to shape the character of democratic Britain in the twentieth century as well. Whether politicians or civil servants, conservatives or socialists, all seemed to have a residual belief that those who governed knew what was best for the people.

This elitism characterised cultural attitudes more broadly. The aristocracy assumed that it was civilised, while the masses were barbaric and had no culture. The education system trained the children of the elite; it would be dangerous to educate the masses, who might become dissatisfied with their station in life. In the nineteenth century, the elite education system incorporated the children of the expanding middle class, which in turn embraced the attitudes and culture of the aristocracy that were taught at the public schools and universities. These new urban elites built libraries and museums and founded orchestras in their cities as a means of promoting literature, art and music – thus validating their credentials as custodians of a culture which, in the twentieth century, came to be identified with them. All this survived during the half-century following the Second World War. Oxford and Cambridge continued to define what it meant to be an educated man (and now an educated woman) and trained the ruling class in their own image. The standing of other universities depended on their ability to deliver a comparable education to the two most prestigious institutions. Thus, the political and educational hierarchy continued to be nearly identical.

Yet this elitism was also questioned in ways that weakened traditional authority and cultural attitudes. These challenges to the domination of the traditional elite are the subjects of the next three chapters. This one focuses on the challenges that came from within the institutions of elitism – government, academia and the artistic world. We have already seen how, beginning in the 1960s, university education was expanded to incorporate a far broader population. At the same time, the very nature of knowledge and culture as they had been taught at universities began to be impugned. The unique status of 'elite culture' as something worthy of study, or as something to be valued above any other product of a society, was denied. These attacks reverberated back into the world of literature and the arts. The makers of art ceased to see themselves as part of a continuous Western tradition dating back to the Renaissance. Art and everyday life ceased to be separated; the artist ceased to be respected as someone with unique insight. The mass and the elite were merged, as art seemed to follow theory. The paradoxical effect of these changes was to render Britain, which historically had not been a leader in art and music (though it had been one in literature), closer to other nations as a centre of artistic culture.

These changes in the academic and artistic world reflected changes in the society at large. Chapter 8 showed how traditional hierarchies of class, race and gender were being challenged and rejected. Similarly, people were no longer as inclined to defer to authority, whatever the source of that authority might be. Thus, the authority of government itself began to be challenged. The result was growing pressure for constitutional reforms, such as changing the structure of the House of Lords, enacting a bill of rights or introducing proportional representation. Similarly, popular, youth and immigrant cultures and even violence (to be discussed in Chapter 10) were means of defying the primacy of traditional elite culture. Finally, a more assertive Celtic nationalism (to be discussed in Chapter 11) rejected deference to London and England. All these phenomena helped to make Britain a more open and diverse society than it had been before 1945. The changes in academic thought and artistic culture helped to articulate these broader changes that were going on – changes that were contentious and upsetting, but which on balance were very much for the better.

The Politics of Authority

As a broad generalisation, one could characterise American political culture as anarchic and British political culture as authoritarian. The chaotic nature of the American political system is evident in the Byzantine divisions of authority between federal, state and local governments on virtually every issue from education to health care, as well as in the potential of the constitution to limit what government can do on any issue from gun control to campaign financing. In Britain, by contrast, central government in theory can do anything it wants. This does not mean it does so: democracy, public opinion and interest groups all act as checks on government. For example, even as the authority of government came to be omnipotent, it remained reluctant to manage the economy by any sort of detailed planning that would involve telling capital and labour what they must do. Some scholars have even claimed that Britain's economic problems resulted from this failure, because industry required a radical shaking up from the top to force it to modernise management, production and industrial relations.[1] Yet while the authority was there, the belief in economic *laissez-faire* and the resistance to interference by business and labour trumped it.

How did the nation which prides itself on being the cradle of liberty, individual rights and representative government evolve a political system that is potentially so authoritarian? It was not always this way. Eighteenth-century Britain was a raucous society. Central government was weak, as most authority rested with local landowners and urban merchants, while there was a remarkable tolerance of violence. There were two reasons for this state of affairs. The landowners interpreted their own revolution against the monarchy in the seventeenth century as one against tyranny; therefore, they distrusted executive authority and saw a police force and an army as symbols of continental despotism. They therefore accepted disorder as long as it did not threaten their rule. Second, the revolution of 1688 had established the principle of parliamentary sovereignty. Parliament meant monarch, Lords and Commons, so in theory checks were built into the system to prevent tyranny. In practice, the only check that existed in the eighteenth century was the ability of the King and the Lords to influence the Commons through a use of patronage that we would now call corrupt. Indeed, it was called so then by those who were excluded from power, and their rhetoric of corruption and tyranny influenced the American colonists and helped spark their revolution against parliamentary sovereignty. In fact, there was no threat of tyranny. The eighteenth-century system worked remarkably well – in part because the rule of law was real, however much it was weighted in favour of property, and in part because violence (such as food riots), protest and even crime (such as smuggling and poaching) gave the masses the means to influence and resist the system.

All this ended with the French and Industrial Revolutions. The former showed that violence by the common people could be politicised and used to destroy the political system and threaten property. The latter meant that this danger now threatened Britain, with the emergence of a politically active working class. Parliament therefore cracked down on violence and crime. It tried to suppress mass radical politics after 1793 and authorised urban police forces, starting with London's in 1829. At the same time, corruption was gradually eliminated during the century after 1780, while the political process was partially democratised. Political reform, however, undermined the power of the monarch and the House of Lords as effective checks on the Commons, and so on the government of the day. By mid-century, the monarch was relegated to Walter Bagehot's 'dignified' role in the constitution,[2] while in 1911 the House of Lords, which had become the instrument of the Conservative Party, lost its absolute veto.

Local government could not serve as an alternative check on the Commons because its authority was derived from Parliament. Parliament abolished the old medieval corporations and created representative government in the cities and towns in 1835; it created elected government in the counties and metropolitan London in 1888. However, what Parliament gave, it could take away. For example, when public elementary education was enacted in 1870, Parliament created elected school boards for England and Wales; in 1902, it abolished those school boards and gave power over education to the county and city councils. Local governments had no choice in this matter. Nor did they have a choice about supporting Anglican and Catholic schools or about teaching religion in state schools, all of which was mandated. Education was managed and paid for locally, but the system of education was determined at the centre. Nonetheless, nineteenth-century government still remained local rather than centralised. In 1886, local spending was about twice that of the central government for civil purposes.[3] At the same time, local government remained a patchwork, as new units like city and county councils, school boards, boards of guardians (to manage poor relief) and boards of health existed side-by-side with medieval parishes and eighteenth-century creations like improvement commissioners.

The advent of the welfare state in the twentieth century completely reversed the balance, as both the direction and the money increasingly came from the centre and a more uniform system of government was created. For example, the 1834 Poor Law was abolished in 1929. Now the criteria for determining who was eligible for every imaginable form of social welfare, and what the amount of the benefit would be, were defined by Parliament. The introduction of the NHS meant that Parliament also determined the structure of the health care system, the conditions under which health care would be provided and the scale of remuneration for the providers. If certain parts of the country had a shortage of doctors, they could not offer more money except if authorised to do so by Parliament. Each of these reforms, like the Education Act of 1902, also abolished the local authorities that had provided the services involved.

After 1945, the responsibilities of local authorities were redefined. For example, policing was made a county function and hospitals came under the NHS, but new social services and planning authority were given to local government. The net effect was an augmentation of responsibilities at the local level, but with more intrusive central control, especially as an increasing share of the money was provided by the Treasury. The process of rationalisation also continued. In 1972, the Heath government passed a Local Government Act which not only reformed the structure of local government, but also redefined boundaries – abolishing counties (like Rutland), changing the boundaries of others, creating new counties (such as Avon around Bristol) and creating metropolitan counties around the six largest urban areas in England.* Historic boundaries dating back to the Middle Ages were jettisoned, as local government was reconstructed according to rational principles. Bentham would have been delighted, Burke appalled! The people affected sided with Burke. They had strong attachments to historic local identities and disliked changes that were foisted on them, without their having any say in the matter.4 Conservative politicos, however, focused on the fact that the reforms entrenched Labour power in the large urban areas. Thatcher therefore abolished the six metropolitan governments and the Greater London Council in 1985, while the rest of the reforms remained in place. The same political considerations induced Thatcher to reduce the powers of local education authorities, set caps on local property taxes and weaken local government as much as possible. Such centralised dictation was not limited to the Conservatives, however. Tony Blair retained rate capping, while in 1998 his government tried to force West Sussex County Council to plan to build 12,800 more houses than it wished to build over the next twenty years.5 Local authorities now had little leverage in dealing with the centre on such issues, since central government provided 80 per cent of local government funding.6

Why were Heath, Thatcher and Blair so indifferent to local opinion? Britain's ruling classes had long had an elitist attitude towards the masses. The old aristocracy had resisted democracy because it did not believe that ordinary people had the intelligence, specialised knowledge or understanding to make judgements about complex issues of policy. That residual sense that the governors knew best remained strong in the democratic age. At the same time, the politicians and civil servants who made policy had a self-interested stake in being free from effective oversight. Their instrument of protection was the Official Secrets Act of 1911, which was passed by a Liberal government. It codified a culture of secrecy by protecting policy-makers in the name

---

* The greater London area had been reorganised as a metropolitan county in 1963.

of the security of the state. Britain's rulers were no different from those of any other country in their desire to assure that no one had the information with which to criticise them; nor were they any different in their willingness to use national security to shield them from public scrutiny. Parliamentary sovereignty, however, made it especially difficult to challenge the authority of government, even from within the system. With the Commons under the control of the executive and the Lords a weakened and partisan institution, there was no counterbalancing force against ministerial authority. Wilson's introduction of standing select committees of the Commons in the mid-1960s was a start, but they did not do the job, for they did not have the powers that American Congressional committees could wield against the executive.

Indeed, the advent of Labour made little dent in the politics of elitism. The British brand of socialism was partly defined by the Fabian Society, whose founders could be as hierarchical in their outlook as any aristocrat. Labour also had a latent belief in socialist centralisation and the power of planning which, while muted in the party's approach to the economy, was more evident in its social policies. Finally, Labour's leaders benefited from the protection that official secrecy and the lack of checks gave them. So while Labour claimed to want to make government more democratic and accountable, in practice it did little in this direction. For example, following the Lords' veto of steel nationalisation, Attlee further limited their ability to delay legislation; after 1949, a bill became law if it was passed a second time by the Commons, whatever the Lords did. The Lords could still make life difficult for a prime minister by holding up a bill. Indeed, in the 1980s, they emerged as an unlikely critic of some of the Thatcher government's more egregious attacks on civil liberties. Despite such spasms of political neutrality, however, the Lords remained overwhelmingly a partisan Conservative institution. Labour therefore was committed to reforming the Lords when Blair became Prime Minister in 1997. He proceeded on the first stage of reform in 1999: expelling the hereditary peers, except for ninety-two who were elected by their fellow hereditary peers and who were to remain until a final reform was enacted. His views on that reform, however, looked remarkably undemocratic, with a heavy weighting towards nominated peers. For an elected second chamber would have some popular mandate and so a claim to a limited sovereignty that would check the Commons' authority. Blair did not want that, any more than any previous prime minister who had grappled with Lords reform did.

Clearly prime ministers liked their authority and they tried to enhance it. The whole thrust of post-war politics seemed to be towards 'Americanisation', which meant increasing control from the centre. One manifestation was in elections themselves, as the party organisations in London mapped out every aspect of a general election campaign in response to the dictates of television and the judgements of public relations firms. 'Americanisation' also described a prime minister who seemingly was becoming ever more 'presidential'. In part, this simply meant a greater focus on the Prime Minister as the embodiment of the government. More substantively, however, it involved making the British Cabinet more like that of the United States, where it is simply a set of advisers appointed by and answerable to the President. Anything that undercut the collective responsibility of the Cabinet, and the exclusive responsibility of individual Cabinet members for their ministries, enhanced the authority of the Prime Minister. There were a variety of ways in which prime ministers did this. One was to turn outside the Cabinet for advice, by making 10 Downing Street an alternative to ministries as a source of policy (not unlike the White House staff and the National Security Council in Washington). Even without turning to outsiders, however, prime ministers undercut collective responsibility by making decisions on key policy issues with one or two ministers who headed the relevant departments. These decisions were then presented to the Cabinet on a take-it-or-leave-it basis, when leaving it would inevitably provoke resignations and a government crisis. Thus, cabinets went along, even when individuals were not happy with the agreed policy, and the independence of the Cabinet was weakened.

Criticism of authoritarianism began to surface under Wilson, who consciously set out to increase his authority. Critics claimed that he allowed his personal secretary and 'kitchen Cabinet' too much influence in decision-making. At the same time, he tried to assure that he and an inner Cabinet had shaped the outcome by the time he took an issue to the Cabinet. Wilson's ongoing war with the press and the BBC after 1966 also contributed to the impression that he would brook no criticism. Thatcher took prime ministerial authority even further. Unlike Wilson, once she had established her dominance as Prime Minister, she was not prepared to tolerate people whom she did not trust in the Cabinet. At the same time, she tried to weaken the influence of top civil servants in making policy, for she believed they had a stake in maintaining the status quo. Finally, she distrusted lower levels of government, non-governmental organisations and pressure groups, all of which she thought propped up the welfare state. She therefore set out to undermine all such organisations – including local government itself. Thus, whereas historically the Conservatives had been suspicious of centralisation, which was associated with socialist planning, Thatcher promoted a centralised state far beyond anything that Labour had imagined.

Indeed, the whole impetus of Thatcherite reform was towards centralisation. Tory policy after 1985 increasingly aimed to promote accountability in government and value for money spent. Towards these ends, central government departments gathered data from, monitored spending by and assessed the performance of local units such as police, hospitals and schools. The effect was to vastly increase central oversight, as the centre judged the quality of service and determined how funds would be spent, while pushing local units in the direction that government policy wished them to go. At the same time, the state became less democratically accountable. For as Thatcher reduced the powers of elected bodies, she appointed extra-governmental organisations (called quangos) to take on some of their responsibilities. Members of quangos were outside the civil service, so they could be partisan and more subject to central influence. By 1993 over

5,500 quangos, with a membership and staff totalling over 70,000 people, oversaw one-third of all public spending.[7]

Thatcher's authoritarian instincts also led her to chip away at civil liberties. The revival of IRA violence in Northern Ireland in the 1970s had already led to the suspension of due process under the law there. The Conservatives went further by circumscribing liberties on the British mainland. The new focus on law and order led the government to expand the authority of the police – giving them more power to control marches and processions and to stop and search people without having a specific reason to do so. The 1988 Criminal Justice Act ended the right of the defence to challenge jurors without a reason. The Major government followed up by compromising the right of the accused to remain silent; juries were allowed to take the refusal to answer questions into account. Sometimes, the Tories went to extremes which seemed, at best, peculiar. For example, convinced that the IRA was benefiting from excessive media publicity, Thatcher made the broadcast of live interviews with anyone associated with a named terrorist organisation illegal. For a while, television viewers could watch Gerry Adams, the Sinn Fein leader, make comments while someone else read his words, as if this somehow made Britain safer. Thatcher in any case distrusted the BBC (which was by far the most influential media organ that was not Tory). Thus her efforts to impose the government's standard policies of cost-cutting and an internal market on the Corporation were seen by some as an attempt to undermine its independence.

Perhaps the most bizarre of Thatcher's assaults on freedom of expression was the effort to stop the publication of *Spycatcher*, the memoirs of Peter Wright, a former agent with MI5 (the agency responsible for counterintelligence within the UK). The whole trend in recent decades had been to relax the censorship inherited from the Victorians. Parliament had passed a new Obscene Publications Act in 1959, which loosened the old Victorian law on obscenity. Then a series of legal decisions, beginning in 1960, when Penguin Books was acquitted for publishing D. H. Lawrence's *Lady Chatterley's Lover*, undercut even that regulation.

The power of the state to censor plays was finally abolished in 1968. These changes in the law, along with the more liberal social attitudes of the 1960s, ended self-censorship by writers, who started to show greater willingness to challenge public norms and sensibilities in the name of art. National security, of course, was a different matter. Wright had long resided in Australia, where his book was to be published. The British government sent its top civil servant to persuade the Australian courts to suppress the book before publication, but they refused. Yet the government still blocked publication in Britain and stopped the press quoting from the book, even though everyone who cared now knew what was in it, and newspapers could use foreign press reports as the basis for articles (something which the government also tried to prevent). One of the book's most sensational revelations was that MI5, fearful of the Labour left, had tried to destabilise the Wilson government in 1974–5. Some of its more paranoid spies (including Wright) believed Wilson might be a Soviet agent, and they fed such rumours to the press. Yet Wilson, who had become suspicious of an MI5 plot against him towards the end of his term, supported Thatcher's effort to suppress the book.[8]

Naturally, Labour attacked Thatcher's authoritarianism and promised to open up government and redirect power away from the centre. While Blair did give some self-government to Scotland and Wales, he demonstrated authoritarian instincts of his own. For example, having created new governing institutions in Wales and London, he tried to dictate who would lead them. As of 2001, his government was trying to impose a partial privatisation of the London Underground that was opposed by the new mayor and most Londoners. He had his own Peter Wright case when another former agent, David Shayler, wrote a book claiming that there had been a plot to kill Libyan President Muammar Gaddafi in 1996. Once again, the government tried to block publication. This time, when it failed, it prosecuted Shayler. Blair's government also chipped away at civil liberties as the Conservatives had. It proposed to reduce the number of cases subject to trial by jury, while Blair himself floated the idea of giving the police the power to fine troublemakers or close down rowdy pubs on the spot. The government also urged modifying the double jeopardy rule in the aftermath of the Stephen Lawrence fiasco. Lawrence, an eighteen-year-old A-level student of West Indian descent, was stabbed to death by a group of white youths at a bus stop in 1993. Although the police identified five suspects, none could be brought to trial, in part because of the botched investigation. The government eventually proposed to allow a person acquitted of certain serious crimes to be retried if there is 'compelling' new evidence.

An obvious protection against the erosion of civil liberties would be a bill of rights, comparable to that in the American constitution. Over the past couple of decades, the European Convention on Human Rights has served as an approximation. By the late 1980s, the Convention had been used to success-fully challenge some eighty British laws or regulations in the European Court of Justice.[9] Blair went further, incorporating the European Convention into British law, meaning the govern-ment could now be challenged in British courts. He was more cautious, however, when it came to amending the Official Secrets Act. The 1997 election manifesto promised to guarantee a right of access to information and to define rights for whistle-blowers, and such legislation had enthusiastic support from the back benches. The Home Secretary, Jack Straw, however, showed every inclination to whittle down such rights and protect politicians and civil servants. Indeed, in some ways Straw's proposals would make it *more* difficult to get access to information from government, while increasing penalties for those who leaked information.

Its tentative approach to freedom of information and House of Lords reform showed just how conflicted Labour was about curbing the culture of secrecy and centralised authoritarianism. Labour backbenchers were mostly enthusiastic reformers, but Blair did not want to compromise the power of a government to do what it wanted. Thus, he also backed away from a referendum on proportional representation – which would be another way of checking the authority of government by one party. Yet he granted Scottish and Welsh devolution and floated the possibility of assemblies for the English regions. Similarly, he gave London an elected mayor, again with hints that other large cities may follow. There was at least the rhetoric of bringing government closer to the people at the expense of the centre. Furthermore, Labour may well have compromised Parliament's sovereignty permanently. For constitutional change in Britain comes by custom and usage as well as by legislation. Convention may quickly dictate that it is impossible for Parliament to take powers away from the Scottish and Welsh governments or to compromise human rights that are now guaranteed by British law, just as it dictates that the monarch cannot veto legislation and the Prime Minister cannot sit in the House of Lords.

Revolution in the Academy

In his revisionist history of the Reconstruction period following the American Civil War, Eric Foner describes how the traditional interpretation of the period came into being. That narrative was based on the views of Southern whites. It posited that Reconstruction was a blunder – an effort by ignorant and self-interested Yankees to let blacks help run the South while Northerners bilked it economically. These policies were misguided because African-Americans were an uneducated, uncivilised people, with no ability or desire to improve themselves. Thus, they were totally incapable of self-government. Northerners eventually accepted this account. Indeed, its most respectable and scholarly incarnation originated with a group of professors at Columbia University in New York around the turn of the century. By then, it had been validated by the 'objective' science of anthropology, which confirmed the inferiority of black people. Northerners, however, had been absorbing and incorporating the Southern version of the Civil War and Reconstruction for the previous forty years. Most of them did not believe in racial equality, while they had a powerful interest in achieving a successful reconciliation between North and South. So an entire mythology of a romanticised South and the Civil War was incorporated into American history. Slavery became a benign institution aimed at uplifting an inferior people, while the war was converted into a struggle over states' rights, with slavery entirely marginalised as a cause.[10]

This story, much of which is fiction, offers two lessons as we approach the changes in intellectual thought that were launched in the 1950s and 1960s. First, it is a myth that the new scholarship politicised disciplines that had previously been based on objectivity. The earlier scholarship could be every bit as politicised as the new research that challenged it. Nor could research which ignored a vast amount of evidence that would have undermined its conclusions – including the letters, diaries and memoirs of the supposedly illiterate former slaves – have much claim to be objective. The second lesson is the obverse of the first: however politicised some of the new research may have been, some of it was first-rate and provided a far more nuanced, comprehensive and accurate analysis than we had before. For this very reason, the new scholarship helped to revolutionise the way knowledge was produced in the universities – so much so that even a traditional historian like myself *must* make use of it in analysing Britain's social and cultural history after 1945. At the same time, the new scholarship represented a profound challenge to elitism. It asserted that all classes and groups in society were of equal importance, an equality that applied to culture as much as to every other aspect of human existence. Hence, the new theories undermined elitism in the production and evaluation of art, as the culture of the aristocracy and the middle classes of Europe lost its primacy of place. Furthermore, many of the artists themselves began to accept the view of art propounded in the new theories. Those theories were reflected in their works, while the boundary between popular and elite culture became increasingly blurred.

Literary criticism was the vanguard discipline in the development of the theories that contributed to an emerging Postmodernism,[*] and language was at the centre of the arguments of the theorists.[II] Language, they claimed, shapes and defines our thoughts – not just the 'mother tongue' but also the languages of everyday life and work. Within a single society there are multiple languages, of class and religion and race and gender and ethnic groups; of every conceivable form of work and every conceivable profession; of every site where we live our lives, such as the shop and the school and the hospital. All the conventions of usage and modes of expression that define a 'discourse' (in the jargon of the discipline) have the effect of cutting off communication as well as promoting it, as those outside cannot fully comprehend those within. The multiple nature of language, with its many meanings determined by all the variables that define each person's cultural relations with it, calls into question whether there can ever be a single meaning. Can the same statement mean the same thing to a man and a woman, a worker and a businessman, a black and a white, a Scotsman and an American? The new theory argues that it is impossible. So there can be no clear, objectively determined meaning in a literary text. Indeed, in the very process of writing something down, the author cannot convey exactly what he or she means; the conventions of language come between the author and the meaning, distorting the latter. Similarly, the reader will impose his or her own meaning on what is written. One role of literary criticism, then, is the determination of multiple meanings while sorting out all the different language systems in a text – especially unintended meanings, meanings that contradict the apparent meaning and meanings conveyed by what is not said

---

[*] This is, for most theorists, an unacceptable use of the term, as it involves imposing some coherence and homogeneity when the possibility of doing so is denied, while Postmodernism has its own fairly specific set of meanings. Nonetheless, it is useful to have a term to encompass all the change that has gone on since the 1960s, and Postmodernism serves that function well. What follows is an oversimplification of what is incredibly complex, with the fusing together of different movements and methodologies that are distinct and perhaps should not be fused.

(because, for example, it is understood or it is too painful to say) as well as by what is written.

The power and authority of the state introduce another dimension to this slippery and multiple character of language. Their understanding of a discourse, and of the practices and conventions that are attached to it, gives those with authority (e.g. doctors, teachers, bureaucrats) power over those whom they deal with. Language then becomes an instrument of domination, and another function of literary criticism is to identify the means by which texts affirm traditional power relationships – such as those of men over women or of Europeans over non-Europeans. Yet the very fact that communication and understanding are never fully possible also provides people with the means of resisting power. For they interpret language according to their own understanding and cultural conventions; they are as much involved in producing meaning as are those in charge. They may therefore act in ways quite different from what is intended and which subvert authority rather than validating it. Such resistance may be as simple as not doing what the teacher or the parent wants – or what whites or the middle class or the politicians define as appropriate.

What follows from this analysis that would influence other disciplines? First, if meaning can never be clearly conveyed or determined, then reason as a basis for analysis, understanding and effecting change is destroyed. The whole Englightenment tradition of human progress and human improvement is undermined. Any narrative can only speak for the author, and even then neither accurately nor clearly. Thus, there can be no objective truths, and there are no universal models of human existence and development that apply to all – like those of Marx or Freud or Adam Smith. Life is too chaotic and elusive, too much is not known and cannot be known, and the author/thinker is too narrowly located in the particularity of his or her being for universally applicable generalisation to be possible. Similarly, a single, coherent, knowable self or identity is also impossible. What is left is an individual with fragmented, multiple and contradictory identities, and so who is ultimately unknowable – whether he or she is a historical figure, an artist or a character in a novel or play. Finally, the view that certain authors or artists are people with special understanding or insight, with something uniquely important to say, is also denied. For the entire construction of a European tradition of culture involved a process of inclusion and exclusion which reflected the values of white European males of the upper and middle classes. Thus one function of scholars of literature, the arts and history became to seek out the voices and narratives of those who had been excluded – in particular women, the working class, minorities in Europe and the United States, and the non-European peoples of the world. These people have to be allowed to speak for themselves, for they cannot be fully understood by outsiders. Furthermore, their views, their lives and their cultures are as valuable as those of the people who have traditionally been the subject of humanistic study in a Western university.

While the French were the leaders in developing these theories, British intellectuals made a centrally important contribution: a means of reinterpreting Marx. The innovators came out of the New Left that organised among Marxist intellectuals under the umbrella of the *New Left Review*, which was founded in 1960. They were responding to a variety of crises in British and Communist history: Crosland revisionism and Suez, Khrushchev's revelations about Stalinism and Hungary, all of which occurred in 1956. Raymond Williams took the lead in formulating an alternative view of culture that had much in common with the new literary theories. He argued that the identification of *culture* with the culture of the elite was a convention that had been defined by the elite themselves. Anthopologists used the term quite differently, applying it to the totality of the way of life of a whole people – all of the materials and practices, signs and symbols of a society that give meaning to people's lives. Williams argued that research should try to understand how objects, rituals and customs convey meaning in contemporary society and the power relationships that are involved. Scholars began to focus on the culture of the common people – such as cinema, sport and popular music – which was now deemed to be as worthy of investigation as the culture of the elite. At the same time, they looked at the relationship between the media which communicate so many forms of culture and the people who are the audience. This approach to culture was the basis of the new discipline of cultural studies, which emerged at the University of Birmingham under Stuart Hall in the late 1960s and early 1970s. Cultural studies was explicitly political and left wing, as it sought to give ideological content to the actions of ordinary people – to discover how their cultural practices expressed values different from those of the dominant elite, offered means of dissent or resistance and gave dignity to their lives. At the same time, in breaking down the boundaries between elite and popular culture, cultural studies looked at the interaction between the two and how each could make use of the other – as when a Richard Hamilton picture incorporates a Chrysler or when an advertisement uses Mozart. Art could not be segregated from society; they were integral to each other.

This approach to culture provided the basis for a new social history which influenced Foner and his generation in America. E. P. Thompson and Eric Hobsbawm pioneered this history that was 'from the bottom up' instead of 'from the top down'. They wanted to recover the ways of life and the values of people who were not literate (or were only somewhat literate) and did not leave the kinds of written records that were the usual documents of historians. Thus, they looked to alternative documents – such as police records, trial records, medical records, wills, defunct newspapers, broadsheets, etc. – and to real objects as windows into the lives of these people.* As Marxists, they were particularly interested in labourers, class conflict and the development of a working-class consciousness and working-class political activism. Their

---

* They also found, as the story of the historiography of Reconstruction illustrates, that many of these people did leave written records. Historians just had not bothered to look for them or at them before.

methodology, however, could be applied to the study of any group whose lives and point of view had been excluded from historical narratives, such as women, slaves (or freed slaves), colonised peoples or peasants. Social historians now tried to reconstruct the lives of such people and the meanings of those lives. They sought to rehabilitate the common people from simply being the masses or the mob, ignorant and purposeless in their actions, reacting or adapting to what others did or imposed. Rather, they showed how these people constructed their lives for themselves.

Literary theory, cultural studies and the new social history revolutionised the methods of scholars far beyond the political left; many of their methods came to be mainstream in Europe and the United States. The effect of such an analysis on literature, art, music and philosophy was to undermine the traditional 'canon' of great works and great authors that had increasingly been the subject of study at universities since the First World War. In England, the constituents of a literary canon had been defined in London and the provincial universities in the second half of the nineteenth century as part of a larger movement to characterise English (as opposed to British) national identity. The study of English literature as a distinct course was thus only formalised at Oxford in 1894 and Cambridge in 1911.* After the 1960s, however, the subject, in the words of novelist and English professor David Lodge's don Bob Busby, 'expanded vastly'. 'Now we have linguistics, media studies, American Literature, Commonwealth Literature, literary theory, women's studies, not to mention about a hundred new British writers worth taking seriously.'[12] At other universities, some of these subjects would be separate courses, but all of them had to be covered. It was a far cry from the nineteenth-century Oxbridge curriculum that focused primarily on Classical studies and mathematics, and only slowly added political economy, theoretical science, modern history and modern languages.

---

* Before it became a separate discipline, English was part of the Medieval and Modern Languages course at Cambridge. At Oxford, English literature still stopped at 1830 in the 1950s.

The social sciences were less affected by these new methodologies than were the humanities. Sociology, however, a relatively new discipline in Britain* – and one which leaned to the political left there – was an exception. All the social sciences wanted to emulate economics, whose 'scientific' status was validated by a relatively coherent body of theory. Sociologists were able to assimilate aspects of literary and cultural theory into an expanding corpus for their own discipline, thus providing them with a 'neutral' basis for examining issues and policy questions. Political science did the same thing, incorporating game theory and theories of rational choice from other disciplines. The biggest revolution for social scientific methodology, however, was the statistical analysis made possible by the computer. On the one hand, modern societies generated more and more numbers that social scientists could use with growing sophistication. On the other hand, they created their own data, especially with the use of the poll and the survey. Quantitative analysis gave greater 'scientific' authority to the policy judgements of social scientists; so they were employed more frequently as experts in making public policy. As a result, the standing of the social sciences within the university increased, while they became ever more popular with students. Furthermore, the pragmatic thrust of social scientific research meant that it could flourish at newer universities and polytechnics; these disciplines therefore could be somewhat free of Oxbridge domination.

The sciences, unlike the other disciplines, did not undergo major revolutions of methodology and approach, although scientists, too, had new technologies (like the laser) at their disposal to use in their research. Still, there was a continuous revolution in scientific theory. Throughout the century, science had been advancing far beyond what the ordinary lay person

* Sociology was something of an American import, which arrived at British universities in the 1950s. There were still only forty sociologists in British universities in 1960; the US had about two thousand. The *Journal of the British Sociological Association* was not founded until 1967. W. A. C. Stewart, *Higher Education in Postwar Britain* (Basingstoke: Macmillan, 1989), p. 87.

could understand; so university science was only accessible to specialists. Indeed, the humanities and social sciences were becoming more like the sciences as they employed theories, methodologies and discourses open only to experts. At the same time, the sciences, like the other two areas, were ever more inter-disciplinary. Biological and medical research were indistinguishable; chemistry was crucial to biology and physics; and biochemistry and neuroscience emerged as independent disciplines, while subjects like scientific ethics (linking the sciences and the humanities) began to be subjects of scholarly study. The whole academic world seemed to be becoming increasingly inter-related.

The effect of both 'Postmodernist' theory and the new social science was to help make the universities into centres of political debate between the left and the right. For the right was by no means quiescent before the advance of the new literary theory, while it could mobilise its own social scientists and philosophers. Friedrich von Hayek (who will be discussed with Thatcherism), for example, won the Nobel Prize for Economics in 1974 for his pioneering work (dating back to the 1930s) in anti-Keynesian theory. The philosopher Michael Oakeshott attacked the whole Enlightenment belief in the improvement of society according to principles of reason. He was not only suspicious of any universal political truths; he was also sceptical of the ability of the state to satisfy specific needs, since the very process involved using reason, which he distrusted.* Isaiah Berlin similarly doubted that society could be reconstructed according to a coherent set of principles. In *Two Concepts of Liberty* (1958), he attacked 'positive liberty' as a basis for social improvement. The adherents of positive liberty (dating back to the 1870s in Britain) claimed that government policy could restructure society so that people were liberated to achieve some form of self-realisation. The danger of any such project, however, was authoritarianism. For who was to

---

* This scepticism about reason, the Enlightenment tradition and universal systems links Oakeshott with the new left theorists discussed above. As we will see, this is not all that links the right with the new left.

decide what principles would define the positive action by the state that would liberate the individual? While positive liberty had been used to justify the British welfare state, similar language was used by Fascists and Communists to rationalise far more radical social reconstructions. In the end, therefore, the only secure form of liberty was negative – the freedom from any interference by the state. Beyond towering figures such as Hayek, Oakeshott and Berlin, there were also innumerable historians and literary critics, many also very distinguished, who continued to pursue their work using traditional modes of analysis. The ensuing battle between the new and the traditional shook up higher education throughout the West and brought it closer to the ideal of the university as a centre of intellectual ferment and debate.

Yet to conservatives, it seemed increasingly clear that the left had the upper hand. They saw the universities as centres of left-wing politics and faddish methodologies that were irrelevant to real education.[13] They believed that faculty members were able to get away with this because life was soft. Government money had been readily available to fund research in the 1960s, and, while the increases were smaller in the 1970s, there was still no pressure for retrenchment. The Thatcher government was determined to end this privileged position. As it looked to cut spending and waste throughout government, the universities were going to contribute their share. In addition, the Thatcherites wanted to reform the universities. They despised the kind of elitism that the British university system cultivated – showing how close they could be to their left-wing enemies. The Conservatives accepted the cultural interpretation of Britain's economic decline: the culture of higher education, which had been shaped by Oxford and Cambridge,[14] had contributed by promoting a hostility to business and money-making. The seeming irrelevance of the new theoretical developments and methologies to any practical application in the real world merely confirmed such views. Thus, the aim of university reform was to push the whole system away from Oxbridge ideals and in the direction of educating entrepreneurs rather than gentlemen.

The result was what the universities perceived to be a systematic attack on higher education. Between 1980 and 1983 they had to reduce their budgets by about 15 per cent, and there was more belt-tightening on a smaller scale thereafter. At the same time, the Conservatives imposed a level of central control in the allocation of funds that was far beyond what had existed before. They tried to break the system whereby salaries were nearly uniform across universities and departments and were determined primarily by rank and seniority. Pay would in part be determined by merit, which was to be judged by the quality of research and teaching – both notoriously difficult to measure by quantitative means. Eventually, tenure was abolished, thus ending the security of life appointment that they believed protected failure. Government grants would also reflect student numbers and merit, with more money going to universities whose faculties showed a higher research output. Similarly, financial incentives from the centre encouraged a more market-driven approach to the curriculum, based on providing course programmes which had the highest student demand. To increase university resources, faculties were prodded into developing relations with business to get research funding, while university administrators got more involved in fundraising. Finally, as we saw in the last chapter, the numbers were vastly expanded, in another attack on the old elitism. Taken together, these reforms were a clear effort to push the British system towards the American model, but with British universities lacking both the financial resources and the elaborate infrastructure for raising money from private sources that the best American universities have.

Not surprisingly, the effect was a collapse of morale among university faculties. Some escaped to the United States, where there were jobs for the younger ones and substantially higher salaries for senior scholars. Underlying this demoralisation, however, was not just the budget cutting which shrunk departments and even obliterated courses at some universities. It was, in the words of one London arts professor, 'the present government's sustained disparagement of intellectual life, its denial that it is an inherent good, part of the life of a civilised society'.[15] In truth, the government was trying to reshape people's perception of what constituted a civilised society, as part of its effort to reverse economic decline. In doing so, it joined its left-wing critics in challenging the conception of civilisation that had been promoted at Oxford and Cambridge at least since the days of Matthew Arnold. The right contested the view that the purpose of education was to build character rather than train for a career; the left rejected the view that civilisation was the cultural tradition of Western European elites since Classical times. Besieged from within the academic community since the 1960s and from government since the 1980s, elitism was being challenged by two of its traditional allies. Yet that was not all: there was a third front. Traditional perceptions of culture were also coming under attack from within the world of elite culture itself, as practitioners played out the theories of Postmodernism in their art.

The Transformation of Elite Culture

THE PROVISION OF ART

The approach to culture throughout the Western world until the 1960s was paternalistic. Civilisation was defined by an understanding and appreciation of the culture of an educated aristocracy. As the masses were integrated into a liberal society – politically with the vote and socially with universal education – they had to be civilised. This attitude was epitomised by John Maynard Keynes, who at the end of the Second World War saw a 'leisure problem' in Britain. Technological progress would give the working class ever more free time, yet they would not know how to use it intelligently. They would waste it. Thus, they had to be taught by their betters to appreciate culture so that they could use their time in a civilised fashion.[16]

Many socialists, often themselves middle-class intellectuals who were surprisingly elitist, shared Keynes's outlook. Hence, the Labour government accepted and supported the Arts Council, which was created in early 1945 to facilitate the 'civilising' process. The provision of the arts in Britain historically had been private and local. Some national institutions had evolved out of private collections or bequests – like the British Museum and the National Gallery. In the provinces, however, the initiative for the creation and support of cultural institutions had come entirely from local elites. The wartime government created the Council for the Encouragement of Music and the Arts (CEMA), the first ever central government endeavour to deliver arts to a wider public – in this case as part of the effort to sustain morale. Keynes, who became chairman of CEMA in 1942, assured that this mission would focus on elite culture provided by professionals. The Arts Council was to continue CEMA's work. Financial constraints, however, limited what it aspired to, as did lingering notions that support of the arts was a matter for the market and civic philanthropy rather than the state. Thus, British government contributed much less in subsidies to the arts than government did in France or West Germany.* Furthermore, the Royal Opera House, the English National Opera, the National Theatre and the Royal Shakespeare Company got around half the money, as the Arts Council set out to create institutions that would rank Britain as a world centre of performance.[17] Neither the Royal Shakespeare Company nor the National Theatre existed in its present form until the 1960s. Arts Council subsidies helped make both into great national companies. The opera and ballet were similarly built up after the war. The Sadler's Wells Ballet, which became the Royal Ballet in 1956, had some reputation before the war, but the predecessor to the Royal Opera had little. After 1945, both companies moved to Covent Garden, where, underpinned by Arts Council money, they developed worldwide reputations that enabled them to attract performers of international stature. Yet

---

* In the early 1980s, the British taxpayer spent about £2 per person on the arts, compared to about £25 for the West German.

the blossoming of the 'big four' with central government help was the exception. Much of the work in the provision of art still had to be done by local governments, whose powers in this direction were expanded by Labour in 1948. The London County Council, for example, commissioned some seventy sculptures for public places from 1956 to 1965.[18]

Britain could not have grown into a major player in the provision of art if it had just depended on government, which was not prepared to make available the necessary resources. Private initiative was crucial, although public financing might supplement it. Theatre offers a good example of the possibilities and problems. Experimental repertory theatres sprang up all over London from the mid-1950s. They were modelled on the Royal Court, which had been promoting riskier modern plays since the turn of the century. The result was a 'fringe' which John Elsom has described as 'positively anarchic'. The fringe, however, which was entirely the product of private entrepreneurship, was dominated by London. The Arts Council therefore helped build thirty new regional theatres in the 1960s, in part to counter charges of a London bias in its giving.[19] When harsher economic times came in the 1970s, and an unsympathetic political climate followed in the 1980s, the Arts Council faced growing financial constraints on what it could do and had to retrench. As a result, many of the new regional theatres faced bankruptcy, while all arts institutions and museums were pushed to get serious about raising money from the private sector. The National Lottery was created in 1993 in part to help pick up the slack from reduced government funding, as capital projects in the arts were one of the designated areas for support.

Music performance, like theatre, blossomed as part of a cultural boom, especially after 1960, and mostly it was done without government help. In addition to the two opera companies and the ballet, London had four major orchestras, two of which were founded after 1945. Thomas Beecham, perhaps Britain's greatest musical entrepreneur, started the Royal Philharmonic in 1946, while the Philharmonia was launched as

EMI's in-house orchestra. There were also several regional orchestras, but none of any distinction. Indeed, the quality of orchestral performance in general was pretty low after the war. Over the next decades, however, personalities like Beecham, Otto Klemperer (at the Philharmonia), Colin Davis (at the London Symphony), John Barbarolli (at Manchester's Hallé) and Simon Rattle (at the City of Birmingham) built up orchestras of international reputation, while there were many other regional orchestras, and the BBC supported a number of orchestras as well. At the same time, there was an explosion of new chamber orchestras and ensembles. The best known was the Academy of St Martin-in-the-Fields under Neville Marriner, but there were many others, as Britain developed as a centre of first-class groups performing with period instruments.[*] All these orchestras and chamber groups were staffed primarily by home-grown musicians, as Britain became known as a seedbed of quality musical training. Finally, Britain became a home for music festivals: a 1996 BBC brochure listed no less than 172 summer festivals in the UK.[20]

Thus, by the end of the century, Britain and especially London were among the world's major centres of performance. Despite the economic problems of the 1970s and 1980s, there were still some 140 regional repertory theatres, while London was (with New York) the world's centre of English-speaking theatre.[21] Theatre was big business for Britain. Some thirty million people went to the theatre in 1998, keeping some sixty thousand people employed and making it much more important than football or

---

[*] The chamber orchestras include the English Chamber Orchestra, the Scottish Chamber Orchestra, the English Concert, the Academy of Ancient Music, the English Baroque Soloists, the London Classical Players. The music directors, all British, include Trevor Pinnock, Christopher Hogwood, John Eliot Gardiner, Roger Norrington and Jeffrey Tate. New orchestras that were founded after the war included the Scottish National Orchestra and the Bournemouth Symphony Orchestra. Finally, the BBC added three regional orchestras – in Scotland, Wales and the North of England – to the London-based BBC Symphony, which was actually London's first permanent orchestra, founded in 1930.

cinema to the British economy.[22] Similarly, while London was not exactly a backwater of classical music in 1900, the advance since 1945 was staggering. In 1998 it had over one hundred symphony and chamber orchestras, and the *Daily Telegraph* could plausibly call it 'the world's capital of music'.[23] Britain had become what it had never been before: a recognised centre of artistic performance throughout the world.

LITERATURE

It was in this context of ambivalent national support, backed by an environment of cultural expansiveness and individual entrepreneurship, that British writers, musicians and artists plied their trade. In Europe, Britain had not been known as a major centre of artistic creativity, with one exception: it had been a leader in the world of literature for centuries. It was the home of Shakespeare. British authors had virtually invented the novel in the eighteenth century. Britain was the centre of Romantic poetry in the early nineteenth century. Finally, from the time of Hobbes and Locke in the seventeenth century and Smith and Hume in the eighteenth, British writers were major contributors to the literature of political and economic thought and of philosophy more broadly conceived. It was an awesome record, and one that the British sustained throughout the nineteenth century. By the twentieth century, however, the initiative in literary innovation in English was being seized by outsiders – like the Irish, in the persons of W. B. Yeats and James Joyce; or the Americans, such as Henry James and T. S. Eliot; or the Pole Joseph Conrad. In short, the British were not in the vanguard of Modernism.

Modernism emerged in the latter part of the nineteenth century. It reflected a loss of confidence in the principles of objectivity and rationality that had guided thought and culture at least since the Enlightenment. For example, Friedrich Nietzsche and Sigmund Freud, among others, focused on the power of the irrational in determining human behaviour. Albert Einstein's theory of relativity and other developments in modern physics called into question the power of an objective, reason-based science to understand and explain every aspect of human existence. In literature and art, Modernism was in part a reaction against the Victorian view that art must be a narrative with a moral purpose. Was there even a single clear basis for judging right and wrong; and if not, how could art comment on values and social relations? People like Joyce and Eliot went further, breaking away from the traditional structures of the novel and the poem altogether. Yet Modernism was not solely destructive and negative. It was ambivalent. Modernists continued to believe in the power of reason and science. While the catastrophe of two world wars subverted notions of progress and the ongoing improvement of mankind, Modernists believed in the promise of reshaping society according to some universal ideal.

Mostly, British writers were not much interested in Modernism during the first half of the twentieth century. Excluding the Irishman Joyce, the most modern of British novelists was Virginia Woolf, whose novels wrestle with the inner workings of the human psyche, explore multiple identities and the functioning of the unconscious, and experiment with the traditional narrative form. Other 'canonical' figures, however, like D. H. Lawrence and E. M. Forster, were fairly traditional in their approach, with narratives that develop plot and character and deal with moral issues. British theatre was, if anything, even more conventional. The one 'giant', George Bernard Shaw, was another Irishman, and while he was a brilliant satirist and political polemicist, he broke no new ground in terms of style or subject. Terence Rattigan typified the best of English theatre coming out of the Second World War. Although his plays deal with potentially controversial subjects (like repressed sexuality and implied homosexuality), his style is genteel and so still embodies middle-class respectability. The main source of excitement and innovation was again foreign, in the persons of the Americans Tennessee Williams and Arthur Miller.

British poetry was similarly bound to a tradition – the Romanticism that was defined in the early nineteenth century.

In reacting against the rationalism of the Enlightenment, the Romantics idealised nature. It could be beautiful, awesome or terrifying, but it was always unspoiled by mankind and unpredictable. Similarly, feeling, emotion and imagination were truer expressions of our humanity than reason and were the real sources of creativity and genius. Hence excess could be justified as natural, while the Classical ideals of balance and harmony were artificial. The Romantic hero (or artist) acted impulsively, was unrestrained, and so sometimes violated social norms. In part, the opposition to reason grew out of the French Revolution. Percy Bysshe Shelley, however, gave British Romanticism a radical political strain, claiming that poetry should serve as a voice for liberty and social justice. He politicised Romanticism's belief in the moral power of art – a tradition that was continued in the 1930s by the poet W. H. Auden and in the 1960s by E. P. Thompson and Raymond Williams. The dominant poet of the inter-war period was the American expatriate T. S. Eliot. *The Waste Land* (1922), according to literary critic Andrew Sanders, is characterised by 'jarring juxtaposition, inconsistency of perception, multiplicity of narration, and fluidity of time and place' – a catalogue of some of the central qualities of Modernism and even of Postmodernism.[24] The Welshman Dylan Thomas, however, was more typical of British poetry coming out of the Second World War. Thomas was almost a self-conscious neo-Romantic: egotistical and self-indulgent, passionate and emotional, musical in his use of language. Most appropriate of all for the Romantic hero, he drank himself to death before he reached the age of forty.

Thus, Modernism had not progressed very far in British literature by the 1950s, and its most successful practitioners were nearly all foreigners. Yet even that influence was too much for the poets who were associated with 'the Movement'. While the Movement poets were partly reacting against the Romantic emotionalism of Thomas, they also hated the pretentiousness and elitism of Modernism. Their model was George Orwell, who 'encouraged a down-to-earth and plain-speaking intimacy with the Common Reader'.[25] Thus, they aspired to poetry that used clear language rather than metaphor and symbolism that might obscure its meaning. Philip Larkin is the best known of the Movement poets.[*] His preference is for plain, direct writing and traditional poetic forms and meters which could speak to an audience. There is no Romantic sentimentality. His poetry offers a cold, hard look at reality.

This emphasis on the plain rather than the elusive linked the Movement poets to the writers who came to be called the 'Angry Young Men'. Both groups were assertively English, rejecting 'foreign experimentalism' in their style and in what they had to say.[26] They shared a hostility to the cosmopolitanism and pretension associated with London, so their novels flaunted their provincial settings. What were the Angry Young Men angry about? Mostly, their target was the continued survival of the Victorian value system in a post-war world that was supposed to be meritocratic. Joe Lampton, the hero in John Braine's novel *Room at the Top* (1957), is a working-class boy who has moved up: he is a decently paid local-government civil servant. But Joe wants more, and he shows a complete disregard for Victorian morality in pursuing it. The implication is that he is doing no more than the middle class had done throughout the ages in getting to the top. So the target is the hypocrisy of Victorian values. John Osborne's play *Look Back in Anger* (1956) attacks a different characteristic of Victorian morality. His hero Jimmy Porter, another child of the working class, finds the conventional life of the middle class stifling and totally without feeling – especially as embodied in his ice-cold, passive, traditional wife Alison. He also hates the class snobbery of Alison's upper-middle-class parents, who do not accept him. Joe's rebellion is in the form of his amorality and immorality; Jimmy's is in the form of his vulgar behaviour and emotionalism. Kingsley Amis's *Lucky Jim* (1954) attacks middle-class pretentiousness and pomposity. His target

---

[*] Other Movement poets were D. J. Enright, Thom Gunn, Elizabeth Jennings, Robert Conquest and Donald Davie.

is the world of the provincial university, where the faculty tries to imitate the aristocracy in its way of life and general arrogance and Oxbridge in its professional culture. Both are equally superficial and phony.*

Yet Victorian hypocrisy and pomposity were also the targets of Shaw and Rattigan. There was thus nothing very radical in the work of the Angry Young Men. They were not offering any political alternatives, partly because, like the Movement poets, they were rebelling against the politicised Modernism of the 1930s. The success of these writers derived from the anger itself rather than a particular political message. They aimed to shake up British society, when Conservative rule seemed to indicate nothing much had changed and people were becoming complacent because they had 'never had it so good'. At the same time, their style, and especially their language, was much earthier than was the norm for the British novel. Hence, their working- and lower-middle-class heroes reflect the social milieu of the North in a way that had never been done before – even by the great nineteenth-century writers on urban society like Elizabeth Gaskell. Osborne was the most radical in this regard, employing the coarse bluntness of the music hall and thus breaking with the kind of tiptoeing around forbidden subjects that characterised Rattigan. He seemed almost to be shaking Britons out of their passivity and propriety, telling them that it was time to end the deferential society. After Osborne, it was open war between the sexes and classes, not some discreet sniping. At the same time, Osborne opened the theatre to the working-class accent; thereafter, it was mandatory that all actors cultivate one.

Osborne helped to launch a revolution in British theatre that generated the vitality and excitement associated with the fringe. Yet with all its energy and commercial success, mainstream British theatre remained fairly conventional. One explanation may be that the theatrical revolution was largely executed by the

* Other Angry Young Men were John Wain and Alan Sillitoe. Wain and Amis were also identified with the Movement as poets.

traditional elite. Most of Britain's dramatists and directors came out of a public school, Oxbridge or (more occasionally) other universities – one reason, perhaps, that British theatre remained preoccupied with language, as it had been since Shakespeare and Shaw.[27] The one genuine Modernist and innovator was an outsider, Harold Pinter, an East End Jew who is possibly England's greatest dramatist since the seventeenth century (for the greats in between were Irish). Plays like *The Birthday Party* (1958), *The Homecoming* (1965), *No Man's Land* (1975) and *Betrayal* (1978) explore the psychology of human, and especially family, relationships. Pinter's plays are open-ended about time, as characters bring into the drama much baggage, only some of which is explained. The plays have a strong element of the absurd, which is reflected in the dialogue, as characters talk past each other, contradict each other, repeat what they have just said, answer a different question from the one asked, but fail to communicate. Because honest communication is so frightening and threatening, they deceive, they simply say nothing, or they ignore what is said to them. Thus, what is not said is as important as what is said. The action, like the characters, does not always connect. Things happen that are not clearly understood and are never fully explained. The effect is to create a sense of menace that is all the more alarming for being implied.

In their use of language – with its uncertain meanings, the inability of people to communicate, the importance of the unspoken and the elusiveness of a clearly understood reality – Pinter's plays anticipate and reflect elements of modern literary theory, and thus show how much Modernism and Postmodernism share. Yet while the theatre of the 1960s and 1970s was more adventurous and less tied to respectability than it had been before Osborne, the norm was the traditional, naturalistic literary play, with a clearly structured plot and resolution at the end. The most 'Postmodern' of Britain's post-1960s playwrights is Tom Stoppard, a Czech immigrant and so another outsider. Stoppard likes to construct word games using a combination of the historical past, literary tradition and his own imagination and intellectuality. For Stoppard, it is impossible to know; so his central characters are usually trying to work out a reality that is beyond their understanding, or they are caught in the middle of events that at best they can only partially grasp. At the same time, the settings allow the characters to discuss 'big' ideas, often with a certainty that becomes absurd. *Travesties* (1974), for example, is constructed around Lenin, James Joyce and the Dadaist writer Tristan Tzara all being in Zurich during the First World War. Stoppard creates an imaginative intersection of these people, giving each of them an opportunity to expound on his view of reality, while shaping the play partly around Oscar Wilde's *The Importance of Being Earnest*, which also has a role in the play. *Arcadia* (1993) intermingles modern chaos theory, eighteenth-century country house garden design and the slippery nature of historical truth while juxtaposing 1809 and the present and commenting on gender stereotyping.

This same Postmodern awareness of the links between the present and the past, leading to a breakdown of distinctions of time, began to characterise poetry in the 1960s and after. The new generation of poets also challenged the use of Standard English diction as the single 'correct' form, as the voices of outsiders entered the British poetic domain and introduced the point of view of the formerly excluded. For example, Caribbean poets like James Berry, Grace Nichols and Fred D'Aguiar use the 'fractured' English of the immigrant communities to express both their anger and their ambivalent relationship to the dominant culture. The Northern working-class poet Tony Harrison, who is angry over attempts by his social betters to correct his pronunciation in school, takes his revenge by using the dialect of the working class, including much swearing, in his poetry. Similarly, the Northern Irish poet Seamus Heaney employs a County Derry vernacular to assert his rural Catholic background in opposition to mainstream English culture and the language that has colonised Ireland. Paul Muldoon, who is a generation later than Heaney, uses the full panoply of Postmodern devices as he tries 'to circumvent the iron oppositions, antitheses, polarities and dualities of Northern Ireland since 1968'.[28] He finds instead an Ireland whose identity is changeable and manifold. Muldoon uses the opposition of the Irish and English languages as one among many juxtapositions – including elements of Irish history and culture, American Indian culture, the European and American literary canon and modern popular culture – to establish that there is no fixed point of view from which to observe and understand Ireland.

This 'collage' or 'pastiche' character of Postmodernism also came to characterise the novel, as did moral relativity and the multiplicity of identities and points of view. William Golding, for example, breaks dramatically with traditional notions of a 'civilised' humanity. In *Lord of the Flies* (1954), man's animal nature takes over when boys are stranded on an island, while in *The Inheritors* (1955), 'homo sapiens [overrun] and [corrupt] the innocent world of Neanderthal man'.[29] The novels of Iris Murdoch employ elements of fantasy, magic, the supernatural and the spiritual to explore the nature of reality, truth and moral certainty – all of which are elusive and open to question. Thus, at times, she undermines the traditional narrative that is linear in time and plot and explores new possibilities for the novel as a form when there are no clear messages to convey. *The Black Prince* (1973), for example, contains 'various narrators and narrative deceptions, and six different and self-contradicting postscripts'.[30] The contingent nature of personal identity and understanding is at the centre of Doris Lessing's *The Golden Notebook* (1962). Lessing's heroine, Anna Wulf, is a politically active artist who keeps a separate notebook to record her thoughts on each aspect of her life, embodying the fragmentation of identity and the difficulty of integrating those fragments into a coherent whole.

Lessing is one example of the influences of feminism in literature. Martha Quest, the heroine of her five-novel series *The Children of Violence* (1952–69), wants to be a liberated woman, yet ultimately she is frustrated. Women cannot be sexually liberated when men remain conventional in their expectations and so unable to give women the kind of relationship they want. Margaret Drabble is similarly ambiguous about the possibilities of liberation. Novels like *The Millstone* (1965) and *The Ice Age* (1977) explore the problems faced by women who are raised with traditional views about gender and seek to break free, but without fully rejecting the old values. Inevitably, there is tension and ambivalence, as her heroines are partially liberated women, caught between a new confidence and the old deference and insecurity. V. S. Naipaul, who was born in Trinidad, explores similar sorts of tensions for immigrants. While the Trinidad of his early novels is claustrophobic – limited by its parochialism and by the expectations of Indian family life – England hardly offers a satisfactory escape. For Western freedom does not help the colonial immigrant cope with an alien culture while living in poverty. Naipaul eventually comes to doubt the adequacy of the novel as a vehicle for exploring racial issues, which are far too complex for the form. In some ways, it is simply another Western structure that does not quite work when employed by an outsider trying to navigate Western society.[31]

This typically Postmodern conclusion shows how much the new theories were penetrating literature by the 1970s and 1980s, as the traditional linear narrative form was abandoned by some. Muriel Spark's characters are conscious participants in creating the fictions they are part of. In the novels of Angela Carter, 'elements of dream, fantasy, fairytale and magic mingle with social and historical narrative'.[32] Writers like Carter, Martin Amis and Salman Rushdie mix styles and genres and literary traditions, past and present, realism and fantasy, authorly distance and active commentary about what is going on. At the same time, in the age of Britain's 'decline' and Thatcherism's rise, decadence, selfishness, amorality, violence and chaos play a prevalent part in the literature of the last twenty years of the century.

The effect of Postmodernism and the world that it reflected on Britain's literature was thus somewhat paradoxical. On the one hand, whereas British writers had generally been resistant to the influences of Modernism, and so somewhat retrograde as they stood by time-honoured styles and the Romantic and Victorian traditions, by the 1980s and 1990s they were much more integrated into a worldwide movement that reflected Postmodern thought. Thus British literature had moved from a laggard position that resisted experimentation and change to one that embraced both. Yet as literature became more democratic, and incorporated voices from all over the world and from all parts of British society, Britain also lost its perceived position of 'greatness' as a producer of literature. Thus, the literary critic Gilbert Phelps believes the British novel declined after 1945 from the great heights that it had achieved between 1800 and 1939.[33] However, these same phenomena – democratisation and Postmodernism – had the opposite effect on Britain's place as a producer of music and art. The narrow world of European culture had viewed British production in these realms with contempt. Yet in the fine arts, as in literature, the playing field was levelled a good bit after 1960, but now to Britain's benefit – as we have already seen was the case with music performance.

Music

Like the other arts, classical music was constructed around a canon of great composers and great works. That canon was defined in the nineteenth century, when the classical concert moved out of the palaces and drawing rooms of Europe and became a public event aimed at the middle class. British music did not fare well in the canon, which was defined and dominated by Germans. After 1890, however, there began a change, as Edward Elgar actually received the German seal of approval (through Richard Strauss). Elgar saw himself (and was seen by others) as a Modernist in the tradition of Wagner and Strauss: the warmth and lushness of his style evoked a nineteenth-century Romantic music that was defined by Germans.[34] By contrast, Ralph Vaughan Williams sought to construct an English tradition that was more backward-looking than contemporary. He was active in the folk music and Tudor music revivals, incorporated folk songs and Anglican hymns into his work and tried to evoke the English countryside. Vaughan Williams had another decade of composition before him in 1945; however, three composers who emerged in the 1930s would be the standard-bearers of British music in the immediate post-war era: Benjamin Britten, Michael Tippett and William Walton. Britten, even more than Elgar and Vaughan Williams, came to be identified internationally as a 'great' composer who was worthy of enshrinement in the classical music pantheon. Indeed, with Richard Strauss, he was probably the greatest opera composer of the century. *Peter Grimes*, in particular, which had its premier immediately after the war, hit the musical world like a bombshell – the first ever English opera that was immediately accepted as a masterpiece, perfectly integrating music and drama.

Britten's Modernism was one reason for his success. Even as British composers were achieving some notoriety between 1890 and 1939, the continentals were discarding the structures, tonalities and rhythms that had been associated with classical music since the seventeenth century. Thus, the music of the British renaissance of 1890–1939[*] was, in many ways, *passé* – Vaughan Williams thought atonal music was ugly. Britten, however, linked British music to the Modernist mainstream while retaining aspects of Britain's Romantic tradition, such as the use of English folk themes and the evocation of nature. For example, the sea infuses the score of *Peter Grimes*, which is set in a fishing village: 'the grinding of surf against shingle as the gulls cry overhead in the first interlude, the jangle of rigging against masts in the

---

[*] In addition to Elgar and Vaughan Williams, there was a second tier of composers – some composing in the Romantic pastoral tradition of the latter and some in the more Germanic tradition of the former – who collectively justified the perception of a musical renaissance in Britain between 1890 and 1939. Some of these included Arnold Bax, Frank Bridge, Peter Warlock, John Ireland, Arthur Bliss, Gerald Finzi and George Butterworth. Gustav Holst, a contemporary of Vaughan Williams, achieved higher status than these composers, as eventually did Frederick Delius, who was a contemporary of Elgar and was also well regarded by the Germans.

storm, the play of light in the morning sunshine as the church-bells sound, and the dense fog of the final interlude – all are evoked.'[35] Yet the sound achieved is not Romantic, but thoroughly Modern. Neither Tippett nor Walton achieved anything like Britten's reputation. Walton's post-war work is considered disappointing, too 'conventionally tonal', and too Romantic.[36] Tippett, however, was much more of a Modernist, especially after the war, when he broke decisively with tonality and with musical conventions more generally. As a result, Tippett became the model for the post-war Modernists, who rejected the more pastoral and nationalist approach of Vaughan Williams and even Britten.

The British Modernists fully embraced continental serialism, the approach to composition defined by Arnold Schoenberg and Anton Webern, whose music was meticulously structured while breaking completely with tonality. Thus, composers like Peter Maxwell Davies, Thea Musgrave and Richard Rodney Bennett approached music 'as an intellectual and technical problem'.[37] The staunchest and most unbending of the Modernists was Harrison Birtwistle. The musicologist Jim Samson wrote of him, 'There is a real sense in which Birtwistle composes the same piece again and again in many different manifestations.'[38] This is not stated as a criticism. Rather, it is a reflection of his intellectual approach to composing, which continuously struggles with the same difficulties; each piece is a way of working them out. By the 1960s and 1970s, new influences were being incorporated into classical music: new technologies such as the computer, electronic recording, acoustical amplification and the synthesiser; popular music such as jazz (especially improvisation) and ethnic music; and classical music of earlier eras. At the same time, Britain's musical institutions – orchestras, opera companies, music festivals and the BBC – started to commission more new works by British composers, and new specialist ensembles were founded to perform contemporary music. The next generation of composers therefore diversified their approach to composition, as they combined elements of Modernism with a Postmodern eclecticism that borrowed from everywhere, including the pre-Modern musical past. Michael Nyman, for example, is a practitioner of Minimalism (developed by the American John Cage), which emphasises simplicity based on repetitiveness and a 'non-directional' linear development, while Robin Holloway overtly borrows from earlier eras, as exemplified in orchestral pieces entitled 'Scenes from Schumann' (1969–70) and 'Wagner Nights' (1989). His compositions are not avant-garde, as they are 'still linked to traditional norms of rhythmic structure and tonal ambience (even if "tonality" as such is avoided or kept on a long leash) . . .'.[39] In other words, a result of Postmodernism is that tonality is acceptable again.

ART

Postmodernism had much the same effect on British art. A world that had resisted Modernism and so often was seen as behind the times suddenly became *au courant* as Modernism itself was rejected and variants on traditional approaches were as acceptable as any other. As in music, Britain had not fared well when it came to defining a canon in art. Until the nineteenth century, Britain's strength was in portrait painting.[*] Then the Romantic era produced a school of landscape painters, of whom John Constable and J. M. W. Turner were the most distinguished. Turner, in particular, was embraced by later art critics because the less representational nature of his paintings was seen as foreshadowing the Modern future. The Victorians defined a third British artistic tradition: narrative paintings that conveyed a strong moral message. Yet the British art establishment remained assertively conventional after 1870, while art on the Continent was being transformed. Thus, the National Gallery refused a

---

[*] The one exception, and the eighteenth century's most distinctive artist, was William Hogarth. While Hogarth's works are much loved by present-day scholars for their social commentary, and while he had an original style which broke free from the aristocratically dictated approach of the portraitists, he was not treated as a 'great' between his death and the 1960s.

painting by Edgar Degas that was offered to it in 1904. The artist C. R. W. Nevinson complained of this conservatism in the foreword to the catalogue of a 1918 exhibition of his work: 'owing chiefly to our Press, our loathsome tradition-loving Public Schools and our antiquity-stinking Universities, the average Englishman is . . . suspicious of the new in all intellectual and artistic experiment . . .'.[40]

Modernism in art, as in music, meant the rejection of the traditional forms that had shaped the aesthetic since the Renaissance. Artists no longer sought to portray reality. The view could be subjective, as was the case with the French Impressionists; it could express the inner response of the artist, as with the German Expressionists; or it could be from multiple perspectives, as with the Cubists. Underlying all these and subsequent Modernist schools was the belief that a work of art speaks for itself – in its use of colour, line, shape, texture and materials. In its most extreme form, the trend was towards abstraction, dispensing with all representation. Like non-tonal music, such art was intellectual and elitist. It was aimed at the few who were in the know, while seeking to shock middle-class propriety and taste. Hence, it is not surprising that Britain, the home of Victorian morality, would come to terms only slowly with such a radical change. Yet it did – although there was always a tension between those who believed in the centrality of form and material as the vehicles for expressing art and those who believed that art needed to connect to the real lives of the people. The artists who were most successful as Modernists integrated their work with the existing British traditions of landscape, portraiture and narrative.

While the Scottish Colourists had reflected the influence of Henri Matisse in the first decade of the century, the big breakthrough for Modernism in Britain came with two Post-Impressionist exhibitions in London in 1910 and 1912. Only in the 1930s, however, did a new generation of British artists emerge who were both Modern and successful. The best known is the sculptor Henry Moore, whose abstract shapes elicited the organicism and flow of natural and human forms. Thus, Richard Cork writes of Moore's 1929 *Reclining Figure*: 'Hills, valleys, caves and cliffs are evoked in the dip and swell of her massive body.'[41] Such a distortion of the human form was controversial in Britain; yet the avant-garde found Moore too conventional. Barbara Hepworth and Ben Nicholson were even more abstract. After the war, St Ives in Cornwall developed around Hepworth and Nicholson as a centre of British abstractionism. The post-war era, however, saw a continued struggle between artists who evoked Britain's landscape or narrative traditions, like the neo-Romantics of the 1940s and the Kitchen Sink School of the 1950s, and Modernists like the Independent Group, who were associated with the Institute of Contemporary Arts, which was founded in 1946 to promote and exhibit Modern art.[*]

Independent Group artists like Eduardo Paolozzi and Richard Hamilton were in the vanguard of Pop Art.[†] The Independent Group wanted to break from the domination over Modern art of an elitist European avant-garde. Paolozzi, for example, used the debris of industrial society to create his sculptures. Pop expressed these artists' fascination with American technology, mass production and popular culture. It offered the means to explore the links between art and everyday life. The emblematic work of 1950s Pop was Hamilton's *Just What Is It That Makes Today's Homes So Different, So Appealing?*. Hamilton's collage reflected Pop artists' fascination with advertising, fashion and design, the products of modern capitalism, and the explicit appeal to sexuality that was used to sell goods and media stars. Pop was art with humour. The style was to juxtapose the symbols of the fantasies of the new consumer society, while using collage to intermingle all forms of art and cultural symbols – painting, photography, television, cinema, music, journalism, comic books, posters and advertising.[42]

[*] The best known neo-Romantic painters were Paul Nash, Graham Sutherland and John Piper. The Kitchen Sink School artists included John Bratby, Derrick Greaves and Edward Middleditch.
[†] Other artists in the Independent Group included Nigel Henderson, William Turnbull, Peter Reyner Banham and the architects Alison and Peter Smithson.

By mixing elite art, mass culture and the products of everyday life, Pop anticipated many aspects of Postmodernism in art. Postmodernism denied a separate status both for the artist as someone with unique insight or talent and also for the art of the Western elite as worthy of canonisation. Similarly, no style should be privileged; indeed, styles could be combined in any way that moved the artist, just as elite and popular culture could be mixed. Art should be approachable, both intellectually (i.e. one should not need special knowledge to understand it) and physically. Accessibility was all the more important because Postmodernists believed that the audience gives meaning to the art every bit as much as the artist does.

From the 1960s, a new generation of artists was being taught the new theories in the art schools, and new galleries sprang up in London to exhibit their work. Almost anything was possible. New fields of art included 'Performance Art, Film, Photography, Video, Community Art in all its nuances, Street Theatre, Art with a Social Purpose and the Art of Organizing Art.'[43] Many of these were forms that actively involved the audience; others produced something ephemeral, that ceased to exist as soon as it was over, and so could not be packaged for showcasing. A couple of examples will give a sense of what Britain's artists were creating. Richard Long, whose work was called Conceptual Art, offered a Postmodern take on Britain's long tradition of idealising nature. Long's approach to the countryside was realistic; there was no Romantic interpretation. He took walks; what he did thereafter varied. He might map his walk; he might write a narrative on it; he might photograph it. All or any of these could form the art work that was displayed. Or sticks and stones that he had gathered might be brought back to the gallery and formed into a design that was part of the art work. For a while in the early 1970s, Bruce McLean made his body into a sculpture. Gilbert & George also started as 'living sculptures', but eventually they turned to photo-montages. Each work combined photos of themselves and photos that offered an increasingly astringent social commentary on life in London's East End – its people and social outcasts, its buildings and streets, its graffiti, its political tensions and racism.

It is hard to escape the suspicion that Postmodern artists were, in the words of Edward Lucie-Smith, seeking 'to explore the frontiers of the acceptable – in fact, to see just what the audience will swallow without protest'.44 For one aim of the Postmodernists was to have fun, to mock and play with the viewer. They certainly succeeded in outraging traditionalists, who wished to reassert the reality of a hierarchy of value based on talent and taste. Yet ironically, Postmodernism assisted this conservative counterattack. For in rejecting a canon, Postmodernism called into question the tendency in Modernism to validate certain trends – like abstractionism in art or serialism in music – while trashing all art that went elsewhere. Now there was a re-evaluation of British artists who had been painting for years. For example, Francis Bacon and Frank Auerbach were associated with a loose grouping of artists called the School of London who set out to reassert 'a return to figuration' in the late 1970s.* Their aim was to make art more accessible to ordinary people.45 They painted pictures that mixed elements of pre-war Modernist styles, like Surrealism and Expressionism, with traditional British art forms. Bacon's paintings of human figures were not exactly portraits; they also had some attributes of narrative painting without being narratives either. He sought to convey something inner and psychological about the people he painted. Auerbach, whose figures and landscapes were less representational than Bacon's works, was Expressionist in his use of textures to convey a reality that was rather coarse and harsh. A Neo-Expressionist revival in the 1980s that was centred in Germany more than in Britain suddenly gave his work a currency that it had not had before.

Like painting and sculpture, British architecture lent itself to a Postmodernist approach. The British did not embrace

---

* Others associated with the School of London were Lucien Freud, Leon Kossoff, Michael Andrews, Howard Hodgkin and R. B. Kitaj. Kitaj, an American Jew who came to England in the late 1950s, coined the phrase in 1976.

Modernism in architecture until post-war reconstruction. James Stirling, Richard Rogers and Norman Foster led a new generation of architects who had spent time in the United States and were influenced by the modern buildings there. Yet Modernism in architecture came under attack in the 1970s: buildings from new materials or prefabricated parts had serious structural flaws, council tower blocks were environmental disasters and other experiments were judged either ugly or non-functional. As a result, there was a new interest in renovating old buildings, as had been done in central Leeds, while Prince Charles emerged as a kind of Postmodern critic, condemning the 'ugliness' of modern designs and calling for a return to traditional architectural styles. Such a return to the past was perfectly acceptable in Postmodernism, which condemned all notions of a single 'correct' tradition in architecture, as in all arts. Any and all styles, whether historic or contemporary, had something to offer, and they could be mixed in any way that suited individual taste. Simplicity and austerity were rejected, while ornament, humour and architecture as a language of communication were embraced. Stirling, Foster and Rogers all migrated to a Postmodernist approach, as exemplified by Rogers' design for the Pompidou Centre in Paris (completed in 1976) and Stirling's Stuttgart Staatsgalerie (1984), which incorporates references to a range of different historical styles.[46]

By the end of the century, Britain was well established as a centre of modern art. There was a Scottish revival in the 1980s, associated on the one hand with Neo-Expressionism and on the other with social realism and socialist criticism. Glasgow, whose down-and-outs were the subject of some of this new art, was now a recognised centre of culture. English art continued to flourish, too. This was the era of Britpop and 'Young British Art'. The latter was described by Matthew Collings as 'a movement of everything mixed up and everyone chopping and changing between different mediums and styles'. It is the essence of Postmodernism in art that no one is a star, or at least not for long, though Damien Hirst and Tracey Emin were coming close. In a 2001 article, the

New York Times noted that the young British artists, who 'in seasons past fetched high prices for whatever was on offer', had not done so well in Christie's modern art auction that summer. Nonetheless, thirteen secured record prices.[47] The symbol of Britain's new standing in the art world was the 2000 opening of the new Tate Modern gallery, exclusively for Modern art, in an abandoned power station, an appropriately Postmodern space, to virtually universal critical acclaim. Barely regarded at the beginning of the twentieth century, Britain was now a major player in the production and exhibition of art, as it was in the production and performance of music and drama.

This astonishing rise of Britain, however, was simply one facet of a general levelling of the playing field in literature and the arts after 1945 – a levelling that Postmodern theories both anticipated and justified. It is often the case that theory, intended to be universal in its application, has its origins in the specific circumstances of a particular place and time. Jean Bodin, John Locke, Adam Smith, Karl Marx and John Maynard Keynes are just a few of the theorists whose works were in part a response to crises or dramatic changes that they were living through. The new theories that culminated in Postmodernism can be viewed in the same way. Radically democratic in their intent while radically elitist in their expression, they embodied some of the contradictions of a time when elitist society was being challenged from below – by decolonisation, by feminism, by immigration and integration and by a more thorough democratisation of the political and education systems. Postmodernist theories helped validate such changes while using them as a launching pad for attacks on the culture that European elites had been promoting for centuries – including not only the fine arts and literature, but also the kind of university education that had moulded Britain's elite since the Victorian era. Only government itself seemed to resist change; it seemed more secretive, authoritarian and elitist than ever. Yet even here, the bases for changes that could limit the power of central government were taking shape – in guaranteed civil rights, freedom of information, an effective second chamber and the devolution of power to regional and local authorities.

Conservatives were outraged by the values that Postmodernism promoted, just as they were disgusted by much of what passed for art from the 1970s on. Yet the conservative counterattack was hampered because Postmodernism was merely helping to make sense of what was going on anyway. Their challenge was also circumscribed because conservatives shared some of the radical left's suspicions of elitism. Modern conservatism is more rooted in capitalism and a belief in the market than in the values of the aristocracy. Conservatives thought that one reason for Britain's decline was the values promoted at the public schools and Oxbridge. They were determined to end that supposed hostility to everything experimental and innovative that Nevinson had complained about in 1918 with reference to art. So they joined the attack on elitism, even as they condemned it. They forced change on higher education and sought to broaden what a university education was. As we shall see when we turn to the Thatcher years, they challenged the entrenched position of other elites in the same way they did that of the dons – including doctors, lawyers, civil servants, the BBC and City financiers. They were also Postmodernist in their dislike of Modern art, architecture, music and literature that was divorced from what ordinary people could understand or like, even as they were critical of the kind of community art and street performance that Postmodernism sometimes promoted as an alternative. It is not clear, however, that the cultural future lay with any of these options – the elite culture of Modernism, the anti-elite culture of Postmodernism or the earlier forms of elite culture that conservatism wished to resurrect. There were other cultures out there competing, including one that the left and right were equally sceptical about – American-influenced mass culture.

10

ALTERNATIVE
CULTURES

For centuries, ordinary people in the four kingdoms had developed their own means of challenging and even resisting the cultural dictates of the English and British elite. In the 1960s, the new social historians set out to identify two such alternative cultures: the rural culture of the eighteenth-century common people that was destroyed by the Industrial Revolution, and the urban culture of the working class that was developed during the nineteenth century. The constituents of the latter in the first half of the twentieth century were first laid out by Richard Hoggart in his 1957 classic, *The Uses of Literacy*. The sociologist Geoff Pearson has summarised them this way: 'the closely-knit extended kinship group, the corner shop, the pub, the Saturday football match, the bowling green, the brass band, the cloth cap, the local dialect, the rattle of clogs on cobbled streets, neighbours sitting out on the door-step on summer evenings sharing local gossip.'[1] Like the pre-industrial rural past, this urban past was idealised by Marxists and New Left social observers as a golden age. And just as the first golden age was destroyed by the inexorable progress of capitalism, they now saw the culture of the workers being undermined by a capitalist-driven mass culture imported from the United States.

From the beginning of the twentieth century, the British elite had worried about 'the Americanization of the world' (the title of a book written in 1901). The problem, as the English writer Goldsworthy Lowes Dickinson wrote at the time, was that 'essentially America is a barbarous country . . . without leisure, manners, morals, beauty or religion . . .'.[2] The United States had no culture that the elite recognised as such, apart from what was derived from European culture. Instead, it had what cultural historians call mass culture. Americans have a talent for producing and marketing goods for the multitude. Their genius is in working out what people will buy, persuading them that they want to buy those things, and then getting those things to them at prices they can afford to pay. Their products, moreover, transcend class, sex and even nationality. In the 1920s, one word came to embody all that the elite feared: Hollywood. After 1945, it was joined by many others: McDonald's, Coca-Cola, Disney – the list is endless. For Britain's elite, such mass culture meant the triumph of materialism and a lack of standards and taste. For the left, it threatened the destruction of all that the working class had struggled so painfully to build in the face of the assault of industrialisation and urbanisation.

Yet the very concept of a homogeneous mass culture is questionable. Whatever genre of mass culture that one names – whether it be television, music or sport – the market was broken up by producers into audiences that were more narrowly defined by age, sex or class. Thus mass culture often could reaffirm or rework class culture, though in the case of the working class it was not the same class culture that was being idealised by scholars. This process of segmenting and reworking was evident in one of the most important cultural phenomena of the postwar period, the emergence of a distinct youth culture. When it first appeared in the 1950s, it too looked American, with its roots in rock and roll music, blue jeans and hippiedom. Like mass culture, it crossed both class and national boundaries. Yet in 1960s Britain, middle- and working-class youths each created their own culture, and in the 1970s black youths created theirs. These youth cultures offered a means of rebelling against parental authority and white middle-class values. They were the repudiation of a culture based on deference. For some in the working class, youth culture was more: an attempt to reconstruct a working-class culture by combining aspects of the old one with elements of the new mass culture. Especially for those who were on the economic margins (immigrants as well as whites) – those for whom a meagre prosperity in the good times turned into unemployment in the 1970s and 1980s – youth culture offered a way to challenge everything that middle-class society stood for: education, respectability, propriety and the law. These youths went out of their way to outrage by their looks and behaviour, even turning to violence.

It is important, however, not to exaggerate the extent of this rejection of the mainstream. The middle-class value system remained the prime determinant of morality and behaviour for most British people, and not just for those within the white middle class. Indeed, the working class was often more morally conventional than the middle class, as were first-generation immigrants. While religion was down and crime and violence were up, British society remained Victorian in many of its beliefs. Thus, the value system that was emerging in the 1980s was a combination of what might be called the traditional and the modern. This synthesis, however, was much more open to change and much less deferential to authority than the society of 1945 had been.

The Masses and the Classes

Throughout the twentieth century, the United States was the world's largest economically developed market. It was a very segmented market, however, for the US was a country of great regional, ethnic, racial, religious and class diversity – and divisions, for many of these groups did not like each other very much. American capitalism could take advantage of this enormous market only if it created products that cut across these fissures. It became very good at doing so and at marketing what it produced. Not surprisingly, the goods liked by this varied population also appealed to people in the countries of Europe which had supplied so many Americans. To the British elite, however, such products could not be conceived of as part of a culture. Culture reflected creativity. Even popular culture (such as folk music) had 'authenticity' because it emanated directly from the people, reflecting their lives, values and experiences. Mass culture, by contrast, was dehumanised; it contained nothing of the unique experience of a group, because it did not come from any group. On the contrary, it was created to appeal to all groups.

The search for a genuinely English culture to set against the growing pervasiveness of American non-culture helped drive several phenomena after 1900: a revived interest in the folk culture of rural England, an assertion of the centrality of English literature as embodying timeless national values, and the 'discovery' of working-class culture. All these movements centred England's culture in the past, and an idealised past at that. Two people, from opposite ends of the political spectrum, epitomised this reaction by developing an intellectual critique of mass culture. F. R. Leavis, a professor of English at Cambridge, burst on the scene as a radical reformer in the early 1930s. He asserted the primacy of 'high' culture as interpreted by a specially trained intellectual elite. English literature was pre-eminent because of its moral force, and it was that very moral sensibility that was being undermined by mass media and advertising. Richard Hoggart was a young tutor at Hull when he published *The Uses of Literacy* in 1957. He articulated left-wing fears that an authentic working-class culture, one that grew organically out of the community (the one of Hoggart's youth in Leeds), was being swamped by a mass culture that was driven by commercialism and so was artificial and promoted uniformity. As a result, wrote Raymond Williams in 1962, 'At certain levels, we are culturally an American colony.'3

Yet this conception of a homogeneous mass culture imposed on the British people by American capitalism is a vast over-simplification. How, indeed, are we to define mass culture when media like television, radio, cinema and popular music targeted audiences – by class, race and ethnic origin, gender and age? Arguably, a musical by Andrew Lloyd Webber had as much mass appeal as any television show or singing group. *Phantom of the Opera* (1986) earned nearly twice as much money as the movie *Titanic*, the largest grossing film ever (as of 2000).[4] Yet the audience for both was overwhelmingly middle class. In the 1950s, perhaps the form of mass culture that was most successful at transcending class was the woman's magazine, as 'five out of six women read one magazine a week, [and] many saw more than one'.[5] With the advent of the paperback book, some popular literary forms could also appeal to mass audiences. For example, Agatha Christie and later Dick Francis poured out bestselling detective stories for decades, while Ian Fleming's James Bond novels netted him sales of around eighty million on an international market.[6] The audience for such literature probably crossed class lines, as did that for romances like those of Barbara Cartland. The segmentation for Francis, Fleming and Cartland was more likely to be based on gender than class. The tabloid press also drew readers from both classes, although the working class was more likely to read first the *Daily Mirror* and later the *Sun*, while the middle class read the *Daily Mail*.

There were forms of popular culture with a mass appeal prior to the 1920s. The circus, for example, cut across every conceivable dividing line within European society. Even the British music hall, although primarily a working-class entertainment, attracted people from the middle class. They differed from the radio and cinema, however, in one crucial way: there was a direct contact between performers and audience. Thus, the new mass media of the inter-war era were truly unique. Cinema, in particular, seemed to embody American values of commercialism and mass entertainment. That was why Hollywood conjured such fear in the hearts of the arbiters of taste in Britain. Yet there was no stopping its popularity. Already in 1926, 95 per cent of the movies distributed in Britain were American, and the popularity of American movies just kept growing. People loved movies, which were relatively cheap. As a result, Glasgow alone supported

127 cinemas.[7] Radio was every bit as pervasive: there were roughly eight million wireless sets in Britain in 1939 for roughly twelve million households.[8] Radio, however, was under the censorious monopoly of the BBC and its first director-general, John Reith. Reith was elitist in his approach to culture. Entertainment, as entertainment, was suspect; therefore a paternalistic BBC had to educate, instruct and improve its audience. Yet as radio became a universal medium of entertainment, even Reith could not be totally indifferent to what his audience wanted. By the 1930s there was American-style jazz and swing music, while half the listening audience tuned in to football and cricket broadcasts.

The popularity of both radio and cinema peaked immediately after the war; then both went into decline. Radio's decline was less decisive. It continued to thrive in the 1950s, as television spread only slowly into British households. That decade was a golden age of radio comedy, with programmes like *The Goon Show* (which introduced Peter Sellers and influenced *Monty Python*), *Educating Archie* and *Hancock's Half Hour*. Even as television superseded radio as the principal form of home entertainment, however, the latter continued to have an important niche. It could be listened to in the car or even at work. Transistors made possible portable radios that could be carried to the park or the beach. Television simply did not have this versatility.

Furthermore, the expanding youth market embraced radio as the means to listen to the new rock and roll music – and in so doing it transformed British broadcasting. The BBC had already retreated somewhat from its Reithian mission after the war, as it gave 'light' music its own station. Light music, however, did not include rock and roll. Young people listened to the new music on Radio Luxembourg, a commercial station that had been broadcasting to Britain since the 1930s. In 1964, home-grown 'pirate radio' stations began broadcasting from off-shore ships. The pirates were shut down in 1967, when the BBC introduced a pop music station. Pop was not rock, however, so market pressures continued to push against its monopoly. Heath's government permitted local radio stations that were private, though still subject to some legal constraints. Even this was not enough. New unlicensed stations sprang up in the 1970s and 1980s that catered to Britain's increasingly diversified urban market by specialising in reggae, soul, hip-hop and rap on the one hand and dance music on the other. Finally, in the 1990s, with the advent of the private Classic FM, the BBC's classical music monopoly was broken. Thus music assured that radio continued to thrive, while its very diversity destroyed elitist control over the medium. The average weekly listening per person settled at roughly half the number of hours as the weekly average of television viewing.[9]

The decline of the cinema was much more dramatic. The number of cinemas fell from 4,900 in 1939 to 1,560 in 1979 and 495 in 1996. The number of admissions peaked in 1946 at 1,635 million, when one-third of the population and 40 per cent of the working class went to the pictures at least once a week. In 1950, the British were the most cinema-going people in the world, accounting for one-tenth of all cinema attendances world-wide. The core of this audience was working-class adolescents, which may have been one reason why the elite of all political stripes feared American influence. Thereafter, however, admissions fell to 510 million in 1960 and 96 million in 1980. They fell further in the 1980s, before slowly climbing back to 141 million in 2001, a thirty-year high.[10] Despite this decline, Britain remained an important source of film-making talent in the post-war era. Partly with the help of regulatory legislation, Hollywood's domination had been eroded somewhat by the 1940s, as about 30 per cent of the movies shown were produced in Britain.[11] The British, however, were unable to sustain that rate of production after the war.

The post-war years were something of a golden age for high-quality British films. The wartime and post-war experiences infused British movie-making for a generation, as the British people took pride and pleasure in reliving their 'finest hour'. Thus, films that captured the glories of the war were popular. Often based on bestselling books – like *The Dam Busters* (1954), *The Cruel Sea* (1955) and *The Wooden Horse* (1959) – they celebrated

British ingenuity, tenacity and humour in besting the Germans.[12] David Lean's *Brief Encounter* (1945) focused on the home front, as it showed the disruptive impact of the war on ordinary people. Yet Lean did not limit himself to replicating the wartime experience as he tried to convey what the war was about. His two remakes of Dickens classics, *Great Expectations* (1946) and *Oliver Twist* (1948) – which, like *Brief Encounter*, ended up on an end-of-century list of the century's top one hundred British films[13] – celebrated the English culture, rooted in Victorian values, that the British people had fought to save. Lawrence Olivier's Shakespearean classics – *Henry* V (1944) and Hamlet (1948) – did much the same thing. For nothing embodied Britain's greatness for the middle class more than its literature. The Ealing comedies of the late 1940s and early 1950s offered a different take on Britain coming out of the war. They 'drew on the democratic and egalitarian temper of the war years, but with a confidence that allowed them to subvert the bureaucratic solemnity and over-inflated idealism of "the age of austerity".'[14] The Cold War and the advent of the superpowers provided British movies with the opportunity to celebrate a solid, practical knowingness in the ways of the world that contrasted with the blundering naivety of the Americans. Carol Reed's classic *The Third Man* (1949), about occupation Vienna, was later voted the greatest British film of the century. However, the 1960s films (and the later television series) based on the novels of John le Carré and Len Deighton developed the same theme, as did the movies based on Ian Fleming's James Bond in a more humorous and self-mocking way.

By the 1960s, when the first Bond movies were made, British film was becoming integrated into the American movie industry. While pictures could be made by small British production companies, the financing and distribution had to come from the United States. The British simply could not afford the kind of big-screen productions that were now favoured by Hollywood and which were as popular with British as with American audiences. What Britain could contribute was an incredible array of talented actors, actresses, directors and specialists who worked on films in both countries. Lean's *The Bridge Over the River Kwai* (1957) and *Lawrence of Arabia* (1962) and Tony Richardson's *Tom Jones* (1963) were all blockbusters that were well suited for the American market. All developed the same themes that had proven themselves over the previous twenty years – the war and the classics of British literature. Thereafter, British history and literature continued to be the subjects of Britain's most successful glossy films with international appeal – like *Chariots of Fire* (1981), *Gandhi* (1982) and the films of Ismail Merchant and James Ivory.

Yet the British did not have to imitate Hollywood to succeed. Movies, like theatre and rock and roll, brought the working class into a broader culture that had to appeal to the middle class to succeed. The socially realistic working-class film was launched when the novels of the Angry Young Men were converted into films in the late 1950s and early 1960s. Movies like *Saturday Night and Sunday Morning* (1960) and *This Sporting Life* (1963) completely undermined the warm, comfortable and bumbling stereotype of British life that was projected in the comedies of the 1950s. *Alfie* (1966) showed that a working-class film could even be a commercial success. In later decades, Ken Loach and Mike Leigh emerged as important makers of small-budget, domestically produced working-class movies. Some of this type, like Leigh's *Secrets and Lies* (1995) and Danny Boyle's *Trainspotting* (1996), even succeeded in the American market.

The villain of the declining public appeal of cinema and radio was, of course, television. It inherited the BBC monopoly that had been established for radio. The television monopoly, however, was challenged by a new generation of Tories who suspected the BBC of left-wing bias and disliked state monopolies. Hence, despite the resistance of a portion of the cultural elite and the political left, who feared the debasing effects of Americanisation, the Independent Television network (ITV) was launched in 1955 to introduce an element of private-sector competition into this new medium. It was still subject to regulation, however; it was not going to be commercialism run rampant on the American model. Yet initially ITV had to rely on American programming, and the BBC soon followed it into the market for American television shows. Ultimately, competition led the two networks to refine their programming and create the high quality news, current affairs, drama and comedy that came to characterise British television. At the same time, they had no choice but to start producing shows that people wanted to watch – however much it might disturb those who saw television as the negation of culture. The embracing of the American soap opera realised the elite's worst fears in this direction. At the turn of the century, Britain's longest running show was *Coronation Street*, a soap opera of working-class life in the North that was launched in 1962, while its most popular was the more recent *EastEnders*, which was watched by about twenty million viewers weekly.

It quickly became evident in the 1960s that British television shows were exportable to the United States. *That Was the Week that Was* (known as *TW3*), which was first aired in the autumn of 1962, was the first export. It introduced a format that would be imitated many times on both sides of the Atlantic, using current events as a basis for sharp political commentary and humour. *TW3* was followed in the 1970s by the much more successful *Monty Python's Flying Circus*. Bringing together a group of comic geniuses, its humour was a combination of the sick, the absurd and the incomprehensible, as well as the more usual poking fun at the stuffy establishment and the politics of the day. The big commercial breakthrough, however, was the twenty-six-part series *The Forsyte Saga*, based on John Galsworthy's novels. Produced in 1967, it eventually had an audience of 160 million in 26 countries plus another 18 million in Britain.[15] Its success launched a new genre of high-quality, middle-brow costume dramas which, like Britain's most successful movie exports, were based on works of British literature or on British history – thus reaffirming stereotypes about Britain. A third genre that proved exportable was the historical documentary: the first was *The World at War* (1973), ITV's twenty-six-part story of the Second World War. Finally, there were detective serials – using classic heroes like Sherlock Holmes, Miss Marple and Hercule Poirot, and more recent ones such as Inspector Morse and DCI Jane Tennison. The advent of cable television in the 1980s and 1990s created a potential American market for almost any kind of British show – including travel, nature, cooking and gardening. The flow was by no means one way, however. The best American melodramas and police shows were as popular in Britain as in the United States. Increasingly, the English-speaking market was becoming a single one.

British television had a remit beyond the production of popular shows. It was supposed to produce plays that were written for the medium. In the 1960s, the BBC and ITV were broadcasting seven or eight plays each week, as they commissioned works from the likes of Osborne, Pinter and John Mortimer.[16] Dennis Potter started as a dramatist, but then stayed with television as a writer of screenplays. All told, he wrote some forty between 1965 and 1996, the best known being the series *Pennies from Heaven* (1978) and *The Singing Detective* (1986). As Britain's domestic movie industry shrunk, the BBC and Channel 4 (the second and more experimental independent station) also became important producers of movies, the best of which were then distributed to cinemas and even made it overseas.

Television therefore became a major export industry. Cinema and theatre also made important contributions to Britain's exports. Rather than Britain being swamped by Americanisation, there was a more complex cross-flow between the two countries in which Britain gave as well as got. British giving was even more evident in the most substantial mass cultural innovation of the post-war era, rock music. Rock and roll started as yet another American import that threatened to take over Britain. It was derived from rhythm and blues and so identified with African-Americans, one reason it seemed dangerous to adults. However, teenagers loved it! Britain's first rock and roll star, Cliff Richard, was really a pop singer, but he had the look of a teen idol, and teenagers were initially his audience, though he quickly broadened it. Singers needed teenagers because they bought records.

The new 45 rpms were so cheap that almost any boy or girl with some money could afford them. Sales leapt up from 4.6 million in 1955 to 51.8 million in 1960. The rate of growth was tailing off by 1963, however, when the Beatles came on the scene.[17]

The Beatles revolutionised the industry. Their sound was identifiably English rather than American, and it transcended both class and nationality. Their image was working class, but slightly toned down to make it acceptable to the middle class. Young people of all classes loved them. At first, the older generation responded with horror; however, eventually it decided that they actually were rather nice and clever. This acceptance was symbolised by their appearance at the Royal Variety Performance in November 1963 and their award of the MBE in 1965. At the same time, the Beatles made rock and roll into something that had to be taken seriously as a form of art. This change took time. John Lennon and Paul McCartney wrote their own songs, and once the Beatles had established themselves most of their records were their own creation. They took a major turn towards 'seriousness' in 1965 with *Rubber Soul*, their first album to be conceptualised as a coherent whole. Most of the songs were written for the album rather than released first as singles – including 'In My Life', which was voted the greatest song of all time by a panel of songwriters at the end of the twentieth century.[18] The album itself was an artistic statement, and its more experimental and drug-infused successor, *Revolver*, was even more so. Suddenly, mass culture was . . . culture!

The Beatles became a major export industry very quickly – from record sales, from their tours of the United States, from the sale of the goods of 'Beatlemania' and from their two movies, *A Hard Day's Night* (1964) and *Help!* (1965). At one time in 1964 the Beatles had the top five hits in America. The Beatles' sales from all sources to January 1968 were £225 million, while their gross receipts just from record sales between 1963 and 1968 were £70 million. Clearly big money was to be made by anyone who could achieve international stardom. In 1974, at least a hundred British rock stars made more than £100,000 per year, while the

Moody Blues were making £2 million. The record companies made a killing from this new product. In 1963-4, EMI's pre-tax profits from music rose 80 per cent, while in 1973 the company estimated that sales from two Beatles anthologies would account for nearly 30 per cent of pre-tax music profits. By 1977, the sale of singles had reached 80 million, while that of albums was at 122 million (compared to 9 million in 1955). In the late 1970s, top hit albums could sell 10 million, while Paul McCartney was reported to have been offered some £8 million for three albums and some Beatles back numbers.[19]

After 1963, new groups were discovered everywhere, though mostly in London, which already had a well-established rhythm and blues circuit. The most famous groups of the 1960s – like the Rolling Stones and the Who – cultivated a working-class image even more aggressively than the Beatles did, although many of the band members were middle class. The Rolling Stones, in particular, embodied in both their songs and their behaviour an arrogance and anger, an overt sexuality and a hostility to the affluent society, that frightened the middle class – enough to get Mick Jagger and Keith Richards sentenced to prison for a minor drug charge in 1967.* The young loved it, however, and the Beatles had to remake themselves in 1966 and 1967 to fit the new anti-Establishment mood. The image came out of the art schools, which many leading rock musicians had attended.† These schools promoted a nineteenth-century Romantic view of the artist as an individualist and rebel who sought to challenge the norms of society. The art school graduates helped to redefine the character of rock as provocative, anti-Establishment and anti-commercial. Artistically, it had to be 'authentic', which meant it continued to combine the sounds of

---

* The sentences, which even *The Times* considered outrageously harsh for a first offence, were overturned on appeal.
† A partial list of those who attended art schools includes John Lennon of the Beatles, Keith Richards of the Rolling Stones, Pete Townshend of the Who, Eric Burdon of the Animals, Jimmy Page of Led Zeppelin, Malcolm McLaren of the Sex Pistols (founder and manager), Eric Clapton, Cat Stevens and David Bowie.

black America with the 'attitude' of the British working class. Furthermore, words mattered. The lyrics were not the insipid sentiments of teen romance so common in American rock and roll. Instead, they expressed protest or some form of the Romantic ideal.[20] In short, rock aspired to be another form of Pop Art, and it began to be treated as such. Just as art was turning towards performance in the 1970s, performance was becoming art. And while new American influences like Bob Dylan and Jimi Hendrix continued to be felt, Britain (especially London) rather than the United States was now the centre of artistic creativity.

How did this movement towards music as an avant-garde artistic statement work itself out? Once again, the Beatles led the way with *Sgt. Pepper's Lonely Hearts Club Band* (1967), which became the subject of serious artistic criticism and commentary. It helped launch the progressive rock era. Drugs were now integral to the music and the culture. Performers were more political, experimented with new sounds and new forms of instrumentation, and incorporated new technologies and new musical influences. English folk, music hall and neo-Romantic classical; continental Modernist and American minimalist; Caribbean reggae and Indian sitar music were all cannibalised. Like all avant-garde artists, groups tried to shock. The Stones deliberately offended everyone they came in contact with, while the Who destroyed their instruments on stage. In the 1970s, David Bowie's onstage dress and behaviour flaunted his bisexuality, and the Sex Pistols shouted abuse and spat at their audience (who did the same back). The punk rock Sex Pistols were shaped by their manager, Malcolm McLaren, to be avant-garde artists who outraged middle-class values with their music, their behaviour and their look while also mocking the pretensions of rock.

Another vehicle for artistic expression was the rock festival. Some festivals sought to be countercultural and to challenge local communities and the police. For example, the Windsor festival in Windsor Great Park was closed down after a couple of years because of its confrontational ambiance. By far the most famous and long-lasting of these festivals was at Glastonbury. Inaugurated in 1970, it became the nation's best-known happening in the 1980s. A draw for ageing hippies and new age youth, it was tied not only to music, but to the pagan associations of nearby Stonehenge. Each summer solstice, there was a clash between the young and not-so-young who wanted to celebrate there and the police who were trying to keep people away from the endangered stones. Glastonbury was politicised in the early 1980s, when it started to support the revived Campaign for Nuclear Disarmament, while in the 1990s it gave profits to Greenpeace and Oxfam. The authorities came to view it as a magnet for illegal drug use as well as radical political causes, so they tried to limit its size and regulate it, with some success. By the beginning of the new century, it had become almost an establishment event – well organised, with tickets sold in advance.

These forms of rock as art divorced it from mass culture, for its appeal was increasingly to a segment of the middle class. Working-class guys liked the heavy metal music that was launched around 1970. It was aggressive and masculine and had none of the artistic pretensions of progressive rock. The broadest appeal, especially among the girls, lay with pop-rock performers like Van Morrison, Rod Stewart, Elton John and the Bee Gees. Some groups, like Led Zeppelin, which produced only albums, crossed over and succeeded with both audiences. During the second half of the 1970s, however, the real innovation in music was no longer coming from either the white working class or from the middle-class art school graduates, but from the West Indian immigrants who were importing new sounds from the Caribbean and the United States.

By the late 1960s, Caribbean music was already penetrating the British pop and rock markets. There was a reggae festival at Wembley in 1969, while many hits of 1969–72 were influenced by Jamaican music, as was the punk music of the mid-1970s. Reggae had roots in the same American rhythm and blues that influenced rock, as well as in indigenous Jamaican music, so the bases for a crossover appeal to white audiences were there. Its popularity was spread by the Jamaican star Bob Marley, who marketed it worldwide while developing it as a vehicle for asserting black pride and black identity with his overtly political lyrics. Marley's *Exodus* album was in the charts for fifty-six consecutive weeks in Britain during 1977–8.[21] The American influence became more important in the 1980s. Political changes in Jamaica muted the oppositional nature of its reggae music, while the advent of the Reagan era in the United States politicised African-American music. During the decade, British black groups began to develop their own style that was distinct from both its Caribbean and American sources, while the divisions between reggae and soul – reflected in distinct radio stations and clubs – began to break down.

The 1980s and 1990s also saw the advent of a new and more politically radical music, coming from New York: hip-hop. Hip-hop was almost a Postmodernist popular cultural form:

> Records are deprived of the authority and reverential treatment appropriate to a fixed and final artistic statement. They become little more than a basic tool in complex processes of creative improvisation . . . A patchwork or collage of melody, voice and rhythm is created when these sounds [from various records and sources of percussion] come together with rapped vocal commentary and chants which draw on Afro-America's older traditions of communication . . . The original records become a vehicle for the imagination of the DJ or scratcher who, together with rapper(s), interacts with the audience.[22]

The effect was to remake meaning with each performance, as new sounds (including recorded political speeches by the likes of Martin Luther King and Malcolm X) could be introduced. While Britain produced some hip-hop groups of its own, it did not have the market to produce its own industry, as it had with rock, and hip-hop remained on the fringes of the music scene. In the 1990s, however, it caught on with non-black audiences; in 1999 70 per cent of hip-hop sales in the United States were to white people.[23] In Britain, Asian artists began to reflect hip-hop influences in their own music. For example, the rap group Smiley Culture's 1984 song 'Cockney Translation' incorporated dialogue between Caribbean immigrants speaking their patois and white policemen speaking with Cockney accents; similarly, the lyrics of songs by the Asian rock group Apache Indian in the 1990s combined Punjabi, Jamaican patois and the street English of Birmingham youth. Like hip-hop, new Asian musical forms such as bhangra were a mix of styles – from Punjabi folk and Western disco music to 'Bollywood' film music and reggae. Britain's popular musical culture was increasingly becoming a mishmash of sounds borrowed and mixed from all the cultures of British society. Yet despite this cross-fertilisation, the market remained segmented and segregated: a survey in 2000 showed that only 2 per cent of blacks liked rock music. Their primary interest was in the music of the African diaspora: reggae, soul, gospel, hip-hop or African.[24]

Thus music, like television, radio and cinema, was not exactly a mass medium at all, as different products appealed to different classes, races and sexes. The effect could be to reaffirm aspects of traditional cultures rather than to create a uniform mass culture. Spectator sports similarly had aspects of both mass and class culture. Following sports was the preferred pastime for lots of working men, as the tabloid papers devoted about 15–20 per cent of their space to sports coverage and nearly half the space for a major event like football's World Cup.[25] Football had long been a constituent of class identity among working men. At the beginning of the twentieth century, Liverpool had more than 200 football clubs and 13 amateur leagues, while in 1930 the city provided more than 170 football pitches.[26] The professional spectator sport was built on this grass-roots popularity. Every city had a team (though initially professional football was centered in the North), the largest had two, and London and Glasgow had more. The team offered a source of local identity, as the stadiums were in working-class areas and provided some jobs for locals. The Saturday game was a means of getting out of the house with your mates. Every season, the FA Cup was the focus of English fan loyalty and inter-city rivalry; the Final regularly drew crowds of 100,000. For the Scots, who may have been even more fanatical about football than the English, the annual match against England was almost a national crusade. In 1937, it drew nearly 150,000 to Hampden Park in Glasgow, while up to 60,000 Scottish fans would travel to Wembley to see it when it was played in England.[27]

Average attendance at football matches in England and Wales peaked at 41 million in 1948–9, and then declined to about 18 million in 1984–5. Scotland suffered a similar decline. One of the principal reasons was television, as some 7–10 million people watched the match of the day from their living rooms in the 1980s.[28] Yet television is not the whole story. Affluence opened up competition from other forms of entertainment for the more prosperous workers, while there was pressure from wives to spend more time with the family. Some of these workers were becoming more middle class in their lifestyle, even as some of their children moved into white-collar jobs. The fan base of football had always been the industrial workers of England and Scotland; as the old industries declined, so did the number of fans. Slum clearance, urban development and the consequent movement of workers out of the old neighbourhoods and into the suburbs had the same effect: the territorial loyalty that had been passed down from father to son was broken. The new immigrant children (especially the Asians) did not have the same identification with the game or with the local team.

A more extensive professionalisation of the sport may also have contributed to declining attendance. There had been a maximum wage until a threatened players' strike in 1960–61 led the League to abandon it. Then in 1963, the system that prevented players from changing clubs was declared illegal by the courts. Over the next decades, players' salaries shot up, while the best of them could jump to other clubs in England or Europe. By the 1980s, the Scottish clubs could no longer field quality teams with just Scottish players and had to start recruiting in England and abroad. Rangers, the team of Glasgow's Protestants, even began to recruit Catholic players as it went after foreigners. All these changes may have diluted the link between the players and their working-class fans. Players whose wages had been roughly those of a skilled worker now lived like pop stars. No longer could they be seen as one of the lads. Nor did they any longer have an attachment to the local club; for the right money, they would move on.

In response to the decline in attendance, clubs began to improve stadiums to attract an audience beyond the local working-class fan base. The sport tried to reinvent itself as family entertainment for the middle class, which was drawn to football following England's World Cup triumph in 1966. This more aggressive campaign succeeded. Manchester United's gate receipts increased from £43.9 million in 1994 to £87.9 million in 1997, while receipts from television, sponsorships and merchandising increased from over £20 million to over £50 million in the same period. Thus the whole bond between football and working-class identity was weakened. It continued to be popular among working men: the high level of participation in 'park' football testified to that. However, with some public schools dropping rugby in favour of football and others offering both, it had ceased to be identified exclusively with the working class as a participatory sport too. Indeed, the largest concentrations of recreational football were in counties that had a large middle-class or small working-class population, like Lincolnshire, Essex, Surrey and Cornwall.[29]

The growth of sport as a major capitalist enterprise affected other sports besides football. Most notably, commercialisation destroyed amateurism and the class distinctions that it implied. Television, once again, was the culprit. For sports could not get a significant piece of television money unless they assured that the best athletes were competing, and the athletes would no longer accept distinctions that kept them from maximising their earnings when so much money was available. All this interest in money – on the part of clubs, players and sports organisations – signified the decline of a culture where upper-class gentility dictated that money did not matter, though amateurs were glad to take payments under the table, in the form of excess travel expenses or sinecure jobs with clubs. Thus, a system based on class and deference broke down after 1960, as sport became a business almost like any other, although not quite so.

Cricket, the national game of England, and rugby, the national game of Wales, were both affected by this change. Cricket was the sport of all classes in England. The Bolton area, for example, had over 170 clubs in the early 1930s, sponsored primarily by churches and workplaces. Many of the players were workers in the cotton factories.[30] Most communities of any size would also have one or more clubs that were socially exclusive. This exclusivity was identified at the top level with county cricket. It had started as an amateur sport concentrated in the South, while league cricket was more professional and was northern. By the inter-war years, however, both were a mix of professionals and amateurs; but while the professionals came to be dominant, the amateurs controlled the sport. Only amateurs could captain county teams or England's national team in test matches. Amateurs travelled first class and stayed in good hotels while professionals stayed in pubs. In short, amateurs were treated as gentlemen and professionals were not. Yet the amateurs were well compensated through the system of indirect payments – often better than the professionals. Not surprisingly, the professionals resented the whole system. After the war, the supply of amateurs (usually coming from the public schools) started to dry up. The distinction was finally abolished in 1963, as it became evident that cricket was suffering from the same drop in attendance as football. Over the next two decades, the sport tried to reinvent itself to broaden its appeal and accommodate television – introducing a new county league based on weekly one-day matches (instead of the traditional three-day matches) and an increased number of test matches. Nonetheless, cricket could not duplicate the popularity of football and so did not generate the same kind of money. In the 1980s, its stars only made about £10–12,000 per year plus expenses, so many had to hold other jobs during the off-season. With the decline of the aristocracy and the empire, the sport of gentlemen had become less central to English cultural life – even with the influx of devoted cricket fans from the West Indies and South Asia. No effort was made, however, to draw the immigrants and their children into the sport. Thus cricket was eventually replaced by football, which had a broader mass appeal, as the English national game.

Rugby, even more than cricket, had a mixed identity. It was the sport of the English public schools, but in the last third of the nineteenth century it was embraced by the coal-mining towns of the South Wales mountains as a source of community identity. While professionals and amateurs played cricket together, this was not the case with rugby. In the North of England, the Rugby League had a quasi-professional character (the players were part-timers with another paying job); however, those who controlled rugby in Wales, Scotland and the Southwest of England (the Rugby Union) kept it amateur and therefore gentlemanly. England and Scotland had recruited their amateurs from the public schools; however, as the sport declined after 1945, Rugby Union had to become less socially exclusive. Since Wales had always drawn its players from all classes, its teams were able to thrive after the war. Matches there could regularly draw from 20,000 to 30,000 fans, with big ones sometimes drawing many more. The identification of Welsh rugby with the coal mines, however, eventually meant decline there too, as the industry died out, and with it an important source of players. While rugby transcended class in Wales, it was the sport of an expanding middle class in England and Scotland. Interest grew in the 1980s and 1990s, focusing on international matches like the annual Five Nations competition (which included Ireland and France) and tours by other national sides – especially New Zealand, Australia and (after a hiatus) South Africa. In the late 1980s, the Rugby World Cup was launched. With more money coming into the game, it proved impossible to retain the distinction between professionals and amateurs, which was finally abolished in 1995. Once again, capitalism had broken down the old class divisions in a big-time sport. Capitalism and television had made it possible for sports – golf and tennis as well as football, cricket and rugby – to become mass cultural events, but at the expense of weakening local identities and, at least in the case of football, declining attendance. The role of sport in society had completely changed.

Working-Class Identity

The vast expansion of mass culture, with the erosion of old and the construction of new class divides that it entailed, exemplifies how class divisions in Britain were becoming more fluid. Some of the social changes discussed in Chapter 8 – prosperity, suburbanisation, expanding education – had the same effect. Was Britain moving, then, towards a classless society – an assertion made in the 1960s that has been trashed since that time? Those who made the claim meant that the working class was becoming more like the middle class, both in its values and its way of life. At the same time, middle-class society became more accepting of the working class on its own terms. Whether in plays, novels, movies, television shows or music, working-class origins and identity no longer needed to be cleaned up. On the contrary, they could be asserted. By the 1990s, a television show like *Taggart*, the story of a Glasgow police detective, highlighted the accents of characters, while the movie *My Name is Joe* provided subtitles – both emphasising the 'foreignness' of Ken Loach's working class for the rest of Britain and helping out those who could not decipher the Glasgow accents. Thus, the working class now contributed to the mainstream culture of the nation, if not on an equal basis, at least on a more equal basis. Did this mean that a distinct working-class culture was disappearing, and with it the bases of working-class identity?

There can be no question that the old Marxist working class survived throughout the period after 1945. The limited nature of both the upward mobility of the working class and the downward movement of others into that class assured that many remained who inherited the attitudes of their parents and grandparents.

The very existence of a movie like *My Name is Joe* was evidence of how much the workers in Glasgow were still a class apart, and one with a powerful consciousness of class distinctions. They saw the middle class as snobs who put on airs, acted as if they were better than everyone else, and were preoccupied with keeping up appearances. Working people had little patience with such behaviour and no desire to imitate it. Such people were identified with 'them' – those people who held positions of authority and so were an object of distrust. Thus, even as the disappearance of class was being floated in the 1960s, class was still the most common source of identity for most Britons. It was the single most important explanation of voting behaviour from 1945 to 1970 – although 29 per cent of workers voted for the Tories in the 1950 general election.[31]

What were the bases of identity for these working people? Work was crucial in defining the lives of the men. One described 'a friendship generated of common experience, common income and common worktasks. Out of this shared pattern of experience grows a common culture of the workplace . . . [including] the need to identify myself with the workgroup in opposition to all forms of authority from the chargehand up.'[32] There is disagreement concerning how they felt about the work itself. John Goldthorpe and David Lockwood, in their classic study of car workers in Luton, suggested it was purely instrumental: work was a means of making money to buy more goods and improve their standard of living. The sociologist Paul Willis, however, claimed that they took real pride in how hard the work was and their ability to master it. The work itself was part of what defined them as men. The difference, however, may relate to the kind of work they did, for there was less satisfaction with assembly line work than with other kinds of industry.[33] Many of these jobs were eliminated as Britain's industry shrank, and the numbers decreased dramatically after the mid-1960s. The decline of this industrial working class changed the nature of trade unionism, once an important source of working-class identity. By the 1980s, unions were as likely to consist of middle-class white-collar workers as factory workers, and the former were as likely to be militant. Thus, even strike activity, which peaked between 1966 and 1985, was an ambiguous sign of class identity and class conflict.

The changing nature of the economy threatened another source of pride for the working man – his ability to support his family. In the 1950s and 1960s, some skilled workers achieved a real if modest prosperity. They became homeowners, car owners and television owners. Yet increasingly, in order to pay for these goods and maintain the standard of living they wanted, the women had to work in order to supplement the family income. They could do so because, as 'men's' jobs in heavy industry were disappearing, 'women's' jobs in light industry and services were expanding. However, new attitudes about gender roles took hold very slowly in the working class. It was not easy for a man to accept that he could not support the family on his own. For those in the declining industries, it was even worse. By the 1980s and 1990s, they were beset by anxiety about losing their jobs and not being able to support the family at all. According to a 1990 study, 'They attached considerable importance to owning their own [home] . . . and to equipping it with an array of basic and luxury items. They also attached great significance to having money over and above household expenses for leisure activities for themselves and their children including holidays abroad.'34 In short, their aspirations had become very middle-class even as their attitudes about work and the family remained working-class. Both were threatened by industrial decline.

Although working men retained many traditional views of family life, they spent more leisure time with the family than their fathers had. While the companionate marriage was less accepted by workers, from the 1960s there were new pressures to stay home with the wife and children instead of going to the pub, club or union hall. Even between the wars, men who moved into council housing did not have the same need to escape the home that earlier generations had felt. They had a greater interest in undertaking home improvements or working in the garden or allotment. Their numbers increased radically after 1945. At the same time, smaller families and more household amenities meant their wives were beginning to have time to devote to other things besides sewing, knitting and housework (all while listening to the radio), with the occasional evening at the cinema. With longer summer holidays, the family could do more together. Thus, leisure was becoming less segregated by gender. The conversion of football from a sport for the working man into a sport for families of all classes was one sign of the change. Another was a similar transformation of the pub – perhaps the single most powerful symbol of working-class culture in the nineteenth century. In the decades after the Second World War, local pubs were bought up by the big breweries. The effect was to cut them off from local ownership, homogenise their ambiance and broaden their appeal to women, the young and the middle class. By the 1980s, even the old pub menu was being diversified and upgraded. Thus, what was once distinctively working class was now no longer so, as the pub became as important to some middle-class communities as a place to eat and socialise as it was to the working class. Working-men's clubs suffered the same sort of homogenisation, as they were taken over by big nightclub chains and modernised. Such changes encouraged working men to do more with their wives, whether it was going to the pub, the club or the races.

One reason the football match and the pub became less identified with the working class was the destruction of neighbourhoods which had been the centres of working-class life since the Industrial Revolution. Neighbourhoods created communities in which extended families lived and socialised, and where neighbours helped each other when the need arose. The women of the neighbourhood gossiped and shopped there while competing with each other for status.[35] Slum clearance, urban renewal, council tower blocks and German bombs all contributed to levelling some of these neighbourhoods and dispersing workers. Prosperity must also have contributed something. For while the British working class was not known for its mobility, children who were moving into the lower middle class or higher surely moved out of the old neighbourhoods too. The new environments were not always built around a neighbourhood with its local shops and pubs. For the more prosperous, shopping and leisure activities like cinemas became more centralised in towns or cities or in shopping centres. For the poorer, blocks of flats were less conducive to an outdoor street life. Yet when the opportunity arose, most working people preferred to move for the better housing, and they were not particularly sentimental about the neighbours and the community they left behind.36

So even as the size of the old industrial working class shrank, the constituent components of a working-class identity eroded. By the 1980s, their sense of what constituted class had changed considerably: the working class were 'the majority of people who had to work for a living. They were distinct from the rich and the poor . . .'.37 This much vaguer conception of class was paralleled by a decline in the significance of class as a determinant of how a person voted. The division now was between a prosperous South based on newer industries and a distressed North that housed the old declining industries; or between those who owned their homes and those who did not. These were divisions within the working class: the former in both cases were more likely to vote Conservative and the latter Labour. Even the hard times of the 1980s did not necessarily lead to greater class hostility. At a time when the numbers unemployed had reached the levels of the Great Depression, a survey found that the majority of workers were reasonably satisfied with their lives, as much so as those in the middle class.38 In part, that may have been a sign of how modest their expectations were; but it was also a sign of how much their world had changed since 1939.

Youth Culture

One of the most radical developments of the post-war era was the emergence of youth as a separate segment of society with a culture of its own that seemed to transcend both class and nationality.

Youth culture expressed itself in distinctive behaviour, dress, speech and leisure activities. Like many other attributes of popular culture, there was an aspect of Americanisation – in the attraction of jeans and T-shirts, rock music and fast food. In 1968, when youth throughout America and Europe took to the streets and occupied university buildings, it looked political and very radical. Yet in reality, this vision of youth culture exaggerates the rebelliousness and the homogeneity. Not surprisingly, most British youth were not rebels, nor even very alienated from their parents. In the 1970s, anyway, the biggest sources of tension between parents and sixteen-year-olds were dress and how late the children came in at night. A 1986 survey of northeastern working-class men and women aged sixteen to twenty-eight found 'non-political, pragmatic young adults who were still eager for employment even on modest wages, who were conservative on most social issues, and who had turned their frustration not against their elders but against themselves'.[39]

The perception that something more was going on resulted from the fact that adults often mistook youth 'subcultures' as representative of youth in general. These subcultures were segmented by class and often *were* rebellious. They were also more visible than mainstream youth, got much more media attention and so generated anxiety and even panic among adults. As a result, while parents saw little generational conflict with their own children, the younger generation as a whole looked very different from themselves and was rather troubling. Furthermore, adults often projected their own hopes and fears on these youths: the right saw in their behaviour the collapse of traditional values, respect for authority and elite culture, while the left saw an idealistic rebellion against capitalism, the class system and a stifling middle-class conformity. These stereotypes might apply to some subcultural behaviour, but only bits of them characterised mainstream youth.

Adults' anxieties about youth (especially working-class youth) went back to the beginning of the twentieth century, when they began worrying about what were to become well-worn themes:

juvenile delinquency, gang behaviour and hooliganism and dress. These fears were enhanced in the 1950s by concern over the disruptive effects of the war and the post-war shortages on the children of the 1940s. Then, in the late 1950s and early 1960s, Britain's baby-boomers began to reach their teens just when the economy emerged from austerity. While prosperity was not universal, working-class school-leavers were likely to have a job and some money with which to purchase goods. At the same time, larger numbers of middle-class youths were continuing their education; they had free time on their hands and money to spend. Thus, 'youth' became a distinct market in a way it had never been before. The market was segmented, as there were differences, by class and gender, as to how much money young people had, how independent they were, and, of course, tastes and interests. Yet for certain kinds of goods – like clothes and cosmetics, magazines and records, food and drinks, movies and television shows – it was a very substantial market, and capitalism, ever adaptable, could either transcend differences or appeal to submarkets as circumstances dictated. The dress, styles and music of even the most rebellious subculture could be exploited by business and diffused through a broader youth market which welcomed a distinctive means of self-expression. Young people were adaptable too, so they appropriated what suited them from different subcultures and ignored the rest. Since most subcultures were working-class, the diffusion of youth culture became yet another agent for incorporating aspects of working-class culture into the mainstream.

The theory of youth subcultures was developed by sociologists and cultural studies scholars in the 1970s. They saw a subculture as a vehicle for working-class boys to reassert and reconstruct their class identity when the traditional bases of that identity were being destroyed, weakened, compromised or appropriated by the broader culture. School offered them nothing; they found it boring, effeminate and a waste of time. So they tried to create a way of life outside school that had some colour and excitement, while thumbing their noses at the authority and values of school, middle-class society and their own parents. That way of life combined immediate gratification through consumption and a tough masculinity which they associated with the traditions of working-class manhood. It expressed itself in distinctive styles of dress, modes of communication and patterns of behaviour that often deliberately offended middle-class values. Part of the satisfaction was in upsetting the mainstream by their conduct and evoking outraged responses from the media and politicians. These actions could be read as resistance to or rebellion against domination by middle-class norms and the homogenising effects of modern society.[40] While working-class girls could engage in antisocial activity too, they were more subject to parental control than boys were. Their space for informal socialising was in the bedroom, where friends could talk, share magazines and listen to music. Male subcultures, by contrast, were an extension of the traditional street life of working-class adolescents that dated back to the previous century.

The first subculture to burst on the scene in the 1950s was the Teddy boys, who came mainly from the unskilled working class. The Teds' distinctive style of dress was a mix of the Edwardian dandy and the American river-boat gambler or gangster. Especially in the 1950s, America was a powerful influence on the working class, so part of their style was to try to be American. America could symbolise rebellion against any form of authority – the police, the schools, the elite and the culture they provided, as well as their parents. Not surprisingly, they embraced American rock and roll, and music remained integral to all youth subcultures thereafter. An important attraction was its sexuality – as expressed in the way the performers dressed, in how they moved their bodies, in how and what they sang and in the audience's response. That was one reason it frightened adults; therefore, rock and roll became a source of middle-class hysteria and panic. Confrontations could turn violent. When authorities tried to stop kids from dancing during early showings of the movie *Rock Around the Clock* in 1956, it led to riots and vandalism in the cinemas. Eventually they stopped showing the film. The Teds had been associated with violence (including fights in dance halls and cinemas) long before then. They were labelled thugs and hooligans almost as soon as they appeared in 1953–4 and were identified with the juvenile delinquency that was a preoccupation of the decade. By the end of the 1950s, almost any violence was blamed on the Teds, even though they had disappeared. The successors to the Teddy boys were the mods and the rockers of the mid-1960s. Following some fights and damage during the spring and summer of 1964, the press played them up as competing 'gangs' of 'thugs' terrorising British seaside resorts. The rockers, with their macho image of a 1950s motorcycle gang, were the old working class of unskilled manual labourers; the mods, with their image of Italian high fashion, were the new lower stratum of white-collar workers. Everything about the mods spoke of a preoccupation with style: how they dressed, looked and danced, even how they rode their scooters. Their obsession with consumption seemed to embody the newly affluent society.

The mods were the vanguard of the new youth culture of the Swinging Sixties, with London as the centre of fashion and the Beatles and Stones as worldwide phenomena who were redefining rock music. The music and the look helped to bring middle-class youth into a culture that had been primarily working-class. Swinging London was a lifestyle. It was a nightlife built around loud, amplified music with a heavy beat; it was girls wearing Mary Quant miniskirts, rather than dresses below the knees, and acting . . . liberated; it was Carnaby Street as a centre of men's fashions that were inspired by rock groups and gay culture rather than businessmen. The lines between male and female blurred, as girls wanted to be flat-chested with short hair and wore slacks, while boys let their hair grow long, wore beads and earrings and became fashion-conscious with loud, colourful clothes. Suddenly Chelsea was challenging Paris as a centre of fashion, while working-class (and lower-middle-class) youths were defining styles and a way of life for those above them. At the same time, middle-class musicians were starting to make rock music, and in doing so they did their best to look and act working class. They performed at nightclubs that were patronised by both. The whole language and ambiance became rebellious and seemed to break down class distinctions.

Yet even as the classes merged in a single youth culture, the middle class split off again. On the one hand, it turned rock into art, and so cut the music off from the working-class audience that had spawned it. On the other hand, it created its own subculture, imported from the United States: that of the hippie radical. The hippies were mostly students. They adopted the shabby look of the 1950s American 'beatniks'; they stood for sex and drugs, love and brotherhood, doing their own thing. Mysticism, astrology, science fiction, and J. R. R. Tolkien's *The Hobbit* and *The Lord of the Rings* all spoke to their Romantic aspiration after an idealised fantasy world, free of the impersonal bureaucratic state, where all was simple and clear. They were politically active. Middle-class youths had provided the energy, the numbers and even much of the idealism behind the Campaign for Nuclear Disarmament of 1958–62. Indeed, CND's annual Easter march between Aldermaston and London was a 'happening' – a joyful combination of political statement and reassertion of the importance of community and morality. Now they supported environmentalism and opposed the Vietnam War. Peace demonstrations at the American embassy in the autumn of 1967 and spring of 1968 turned violent. The first sit-ins at universities occurred in 1967, and there were more over the next few years, again sometimes with violence. Not only did the students protest about political issues; they also pressed for university reforms, like broadening the curriculum and incorporating students into university governance. All their actions were a protest against middle-class respectability – not only with their drugs and violence, but also their rejection of the work ethic, materialism and Victorian prudery. Mostly, however, they were not revolutionaries – apart from a small London underground, which even set off some bombs. The activities of the underground attracted the attention of the authorities, who slowly strangled extremism (and drove many of its alumni into Labour politics). None of it, however, approached the violence of the movements in France, West Germany, Italy or even the United States.

A teenager did not have to be a hippie or a revolutionary to be excited by all that was going on in the 1960s, to welcome the new freedom from inhibitions and so to pick and choose among the many options of self-expression. Young people could enjoy listening and dancing to rock music without intellectualising its significance. They could enjoy the less repressive attitudes towards sex without turning to free love. They could experiment with drugs without becoming regular users. The freer styles of dress allowed a young woman to express her sexuality by wearing a miniskirt without being pegged as a tart, or if she preferred, to wear trousers and a man's shirt without being deemed masculine. Opposition to the Vietnam War allowed political involvement without participating in violence and the destruction of property. All the energy of the 1960s created a more expressive, less deferential youth who were rebellious without being rebels. Indeed, the decade marked the end of deference, whether it was of youths to their elders, of the working class to its social betters, or of women to men. Authority was to be questioned and, if necessary, challenged, not deferred to. *That* was the real revolution.

Working-class youth were not much interested in the political rebellions of the middle class. Yet they, too, appropriated from more radical subcultures what they wanted in the way of styles and behaviour to create a distinctive identity. These could easily be integrated into their traditional social activities: associating with friends, girls worrying about how they looked and going dancing, boys hanging out on the streets and being threatening. Their taste in rock music was also integrated into the working-class lifestyle. The girls preferred pop-rock, which was better to dance to or listen to on the radio; the boys liked the more aggressive style of the Who or of heavy metal bands.

After 1969, as economic times got worse, unemployment crept up and trade union militancy increased, the subcultures became more menacing. The skinheads, like earlier subcultures, had their own look and way of dressing. They embodied aspects of the customary working-men's culture: defence of territory, toughness, misogyny. They were violent, attacking those associated with the liberal middle-class values that were undermining the old way of life: hippies, immigrants and homosexuals. They were succeeded in the mid-1970s by the punks. Some punk styles continued to be embraced by rebellious youth for the rest of the century: 'Hair was shaved close to the head, dyed outrageous colours, then later, spiked up into cockatoo plumes of startling design . . .'[41] Punks were scruffy and down-at-heel, employing symbols of bondage and even self-mutilation. Working-class girls were involved, challenging traditional notions of femininity. Indeed, everything about the punks was a rejection of middle-class propriety. The punk bands were supposed to be the embodiment of an angry, unemployed, working-class youth. Their lyrics were often explicitly political, expressing anger at a life with no future and rejecting consumerism. The Sex Pistols deliberately promoted a raunchy, vulgar, nihilistic image. This musical culture was constructed by middle-class musicians as an art form, but it also was taken up by working-class youths who might well have seen it as a vehicle for outraging an Establishment they did not like. The punks generated a media hysteria comparable to that produced by the Teddy boys: the Establishment saw in them evidence of Britain's decline and the breakdown of authority that haunted the 1970s. This was exactly the kind of response the punks wanted. At the same time, because their music was influenced by West Indian reggae, and because both the punks and the West Indian Rastafarians were involved in the 'Rock against Racism' movement of the late 1970s, they represented the first intersection between the cultures of working-class whites and Britain's immigrant populations.

Immigrant Cultures

By the mid-1970s, times were at least as hard for West Indian youths as for their white working-class counterparts. They suffered from the same burgeoning unemployment, while also facing increasing numbers of attacks from skinheads and harassment from an unsympathetic police force. The promise of equality and opportunity that liberal Britain had offered appeared to them to be a sham. Instead, they saw a society based on racism and discrimination, and their parents apparently passively accepted the status quo, trying to live by the values of white society. Even the traditional black religion looked 'white' – a variant of the Church of England. Young Caribbean men were no longer prepared to adopt the accommodating ways of their parents. This was the attraction of the Rastafarian movement: it was a rejection of both white Britain and the parental culture. At the same time, it was an assertion of black pride and dignity, when the white society told them they were inferior, and it identified black strength with their cultural roots in the West Indies and Africa. It offered young blacks a clear explanation for their present predicament, based on racism, and a promise of future deliverance. Like white working-class subcultures, however, Rastafarianism only appealed to a small minority of youths. And as with white subcultures, the press and the authorities gave it a disproportionate prominence because it appeared so threatening to middle-class society and its values.

Rastafarianism was part religion and part radical politics. It was developed in Jamaica in the 1930s, inspired by the 'back-to-Africa' movement of the black nationalist Marcus Garvey. The Rastafarians believed that Haile Selassie was God, and that he would ultimately act as saviour, destroying the white world that had enslaved and suppressed blacks for the last four hundred years and making possible their return to Africa. These beliefs were brought to England, and indeed to the whole African diaspora, by Bob Marley, a follower and prophet who used the lyrics of his reggae hits to spread the message worldwide. For English blacks, Marley defined the symbols of black pride which became their means of rejecting the standards and values of white society: allowing their hair to grow naturally and be twisted as dreadlocks, wearing the Ethiopian colours (red, black and green) and shabby clothes, speaking in a Jamaican patois. However, just as whites could appropriate elements of a subcultural look or behaviour to make a statement without being part of the subculture, blacks could assume aspects of Rastararianism without espousing the religion. The aim was to repudiate white expectations of propriety and respectability in speech, looks, beliefs and behaviour.

Like white working-class youths who turned to crime as an expression of alienation, Rastafarians challenged the norms and authority of white society by rejecting the law, whose legitimacy they did not recognise because it was an instrument of black oppression. For black and white alike, criminal behaviour asserted their masculinity. At the same time, both cultures saw thieving as acceptable if a person and his family were in need and if the victim could afford the loss – a modern variant of Robin Hoodism. In the case of the Rastas in London, the victim was often an Asian shopkeeper who had a little too successfully absorbed the capitalist culture of white society. But it was not only whites and Asians who found the Rastas' aggressive behaviour threatening; so did mainstream West Indians. At various times, white authority identified Rastafarianism as a religious cult, a racist black power movement, and an organised criminal gang who terrorised communities. In this last guise, the police attributed to the Rastafarians a level of organisation that they did not have. The result was a much closer policing of West Indian communities, as the police sought to reaffirm their authority and that of the law. Crime came to be seen as endemic to black culture, requiring radical means to stamp it out. Anyone who looked like a Rasta or whose behaviour was challenging was treated as a potential criminal. The new police strategy led directly to the riots in Bristol in 1980, in Brixton in 1981 and in Birmingham in 1985.

The rioting of the first half of the 1980s was in part an expression of frustration in the face of Thatcherite conservatism and the explosion of youth unemployment. In America, too, there was a conservative reaction against the liberalism of the 1960s, and there it produced a much more politically aggressive black music: rap. Rap literally spread the message of the rioters – 'Don't push me, 'cause I'm close to the edge' – in the lyrics of the New York group Grandmaster Flash and the Furious Five. Rap exported to Britain the beliefs of the American Civil Rights movement, the Black Power movement, black separatism and Pan-Africanism, since excerpts from the speeches of black leaders were incorporated into the lyrics. As a result, the United States began to replace Jamaica as the source of inspiration for politically or spiritually aware British blacks, with a variety of African-American musical styles – soul, gospel and hip-hop – contributing to the reshaping of the British Caribbean youth culture in a way that did not exclude the Rastafarian, but supplemented it.

At the same time, there was a new interest in engaging white culture. The riots seemed to show that the Rastafarians' rejection of white society as 'Babylon' ultimately led to a dead end. Furthermore, blacks liked *EastEnders* as much as whites did. There was something in the working-class culture that both shared. Yet the music still remained political and oppositional to the mainstream of Thatcherism. In particular, a critique of the capitalism that had produced slavery in the past and mass unemployment in the present was embedded in the lyrics of the songs of the 1980s, as it was in those of the 1970s. So was a denunciation of the political and legal systems and an assertion of the principles of equality and social justice.[42] The result over the next two decades was to create a culture that was critical of mainstream society yet sufficiently spontaneous and creative to appeal to that society. The culture of the youth of the British black diaspora was exportable to the youth of the rest of Britain, although, as was always the case with subcultures, the full political message of those at the extreme was not necessarily what was embraced by the majority either of young blacks or of British youth more generally.

Asians as well as whites were drawn to the musical forms and political messaging of hip-hop. The West Indians viewed the Asians with a certain amount of suspicion and admiration at the same time. To Caribbean youth, the Asians seemed to come too close to selling out to white society, as many of them continued to value traditional religion, turned to education as a means of self-improvement and embraced the possibilities that capitalism offered. There was no rebellion or rejection on the part of the younger generation; they seemed to be as passive in accepting British society, with its racism, as their elders were. Yet blacks also admired the closeness of the Asian communities, which separated and sheltered them from the indigenous English. There was something remarkably self-sufficient about the Asians, which provided some protection from whatever racism they faced, and Rastafarianism was in part an attempt by young blacks to create such a community for themselves.

The Muslim, Hindu and Sikh immigrants who made up the south Asian communities certainly did not see themselves as being like the English. On the contrary, they were proud of their distinct cultures, which they thought were better than a British culture that was becoming ever more permissive. Thus, they had no desire to adopt the latter, as the first-generation West Indians seemingly had done. And indeed, Asian immigrants were cut off from mainstream society in a way the West Indians were not – because of differences in language and religion. Among Muslims and Sikhs in particular, neighbourhoods were based on people of the same religion, often from the same part of the Indian subcontinent, who spoke Urdu or Punjabi. Pakistani ties to the home country were reinforced by further immigration of relatives, by marriages to cousins from home, by Pakistani imams at the mosques, by Pakistani newspapers that were available, and by Urdu language magazines and radio programmes in cities like Bradford and Pakistani television shows that later became accessible on cable. The first generation always claimed that they would return to Pakistan; in the 1990s, half the men belonged to funeral associations that would help pay the expenses to send the dead back to the ancestral village for burial.[43]

While Hindu and even Sikh communities were not quite as closed as those of Pakistani and Bangladeshi immigrants, Asian children in general felt no need to break from an environment based on strong family and community ties. Their desire was to accommodate their parents while succeeding at school, establishing successful careers and having greater freedom within British society. Thus, they accepted the traditional values but sought compromises that would allow them to be more 'British'. They were intensely loyal to family, believed they should obey parents and were conscious of the importance of maintaining the family's reputation in the community. Mostly, their closest friends were Asian, while they would not think of marrying outside their religion. Children accepted that their parents should have a say over whom they married; they saw nothing to admire in the Western 'love marriages' when one-third of them ended in divorce. However, they did not share their parents' concern about caste, and Muslims were not always inclined to marry a cousin from the home country who knew nothing of British ways. In most cases, both generations sought a means of modifying the traditional arranged marriage in a way that would respect the parents' role in arranging and give the children the right to have the final decision. By the new century, Asian marriage websites, chat rooms and personal ads had all been adapted to parental arrangement.44 Thus the incidences of forced marriage for women, while highly publicised in the media, were rare.

Women of the younger generation were like the men: they wanted an education and a job or career, valued the freedom that British society offered, but accepted traditional values. Furthermore, this was just as true of Muslims as of other South Asians – although, as in the white community, aspirations tended to be higher among those in the middle class than among working-class girls, who were more likely to see O levels as the end of their schooling and did not expect to work after marriage unless it was necessary to the family. Yet even among the middle class, some young women accepted traditional views of female modesty, appropriate dress, separation of the sexes and not going out with boys – sometimes so as not to create problems in the family, but also for more complex reasons. For example, a pharmacist explained why she wore a headscarf this way:

> I am not covering up because I am oppressed. But because I want to show people I am not ashamed of my family and my religion. But more than that, I hated the way when I became a teenager, I became a piece of sex for the boys in school . . . I want to be myself, not somebody's fantasy.[45]

For young Sikh men, too, preserving traditions was important to their identity. They therefore did not cut their hair, and Sikh communities fought (mostly successfully) for the right of boys to wear turbans in school, just as Muslims secured the right of girls to wear more modest dress that deviated from the school uniform.

Clearly religion and the values that it taught were important to many young Asians, although there was some falling away among the generation born in Britain.[46] Religion provided both sexes with a basis of identity and a source of stability and even clarity as they negotiated between their Asian and British worlds. Yet the younger generation of women saw an obvious distinction between the behavioural dictates of religion, for example concerning abstinence from alcohol and sex, and the dictates of cultural tradition. Indeed, their education enabled them to understand the religion, and they used it to argue against traditions that had no basis in the faith: for example, showing that Islam encouraged female education and did not endorse forced marriage. Nor did they want a marriage where they had to submit to their husband and could not have a career.

Religion took on greater importance for young Sikhs and Muslims because of specific crises of the 1980s which brought them into conflict with mainstream British society. For Sikhs, it was the storming of the Golden Temple at Amritsar in 1984 by the Indian government, and the subsequent assassination of Prime Minister Indira Gandhi by her Sikh bodyguards, which many British Sikhs welcomed because Mrs Gandhi had failed in

her duty to maintain order and protect the holy site. More notorious within the white community, however, was the response of
British Muslims to the publication of Salman Rushdie's *The
Satanic Verses* in 1988. For Muslims, there was one fundamental
issue: Rushdie had apparently deliberately insulted the Prophet
by impugning his moral integrity. He gave his fictional Prophet
the name Mahound, which means false prophet, while he gave
the prostitutes in a brothel the names of Muhammad's wives. As
Bhikhu Parekh, deputy chair of the Commission for Racial
Equality, a professor of political theory and a non-Muslim,
explained: 'Like any great religious text, the Koran is full of rules
and injunctions about forms of worship . . . [and] moral purity
. . . *The Satanic Verses* mockingly reduces it to a book "spouting"
rules about how to "fart", "fuck" and "clean one's behind".'[47]
Muslims felt as if they had been personally insulted, their honour
impugned. Huge demonstrations were organised in Birmingham
and Bradford in the autumn of 1988, and Muslim youth, who
had not participated in the riots of the early 1980s, joined in. Yet
the white community either denied that Muslims had a legitimate grievance, patronised them with explanations about free
speech or ignored them. Some Muslims therefore turned to more
extreme actions to attract attention: burning Rushdie's book or
endorsing (or refusing to condemn) the 1989 fatwa by the
Ayatollah Khomeini against Rushdie – although the vast majority
of Muslims probably did not support the fatwa.* Ten years later,
the sociologist Jessica Jacobson found there was still enormous
resentment over the Rushdie affair among the Waltham Forest
Muslims whom she interviewed.[48]

It is probably no coincidence that a more rebellious Asian
youth culture appeared at this time. Music became a vehicle for
asserting Asian identity among Asian youth, as well as expressing
some identification with the culture of the African diaspora –

---

* There was no survey of Muslims at the time, but a poll in January 1991 (i.e.
two years later) by Bradford City Radio found that 90 per cent of Muslims
opposed the fatwa. Lewis, *Islamic Britain*, p. 170.

both Afro-Caribbean and African-American. At the core of this Asian musical culture were traditional Asian music and newer sounds, such as remixed soundtracks from Bollywood Indian movies. During the 1990s, however, this music became increasingly eclectic and political, as traditional bhangra dance music incorporated the 'sounds, instrumentation, expressive styles, and production techniques of disco, pop, hip-hop, house, rave, and reggae'.49 For the most part, this music was an expression of an Asian youth culture that was broadly based. It was promoted on Yorkshire Television's *Bhangra Beat* and the national Asian station Sunrise Radio. The weekly newspapers *Eastern Eye* and *The Asian Times* were aimed at the same Asian youth market, as were some films and television shows. The music, however, could take on a more extreme and political purpose. For example, the Asian hip-hop group Fun-da-mental used excerpts of speeches by Louis Farrakhan, Malcolm X and Enoch Powell, as well as extracts from the Koran and expressions of support for the fatwa against Salman Rushdie, in its lyrics. The implication was that blacks and Asians shared a common cause in the fight against racism.

The evolution of this more politicised music coincided with the emergence of an assertive Muslim radicalism among a minority of Asian youth. Like the culture of the northern white working class among whom many of them lived, this Asian youth culture was aggressively masculine and misogynistic. Unlike the white culture, it used religion to justify a worldview where women were the key battleground in the fight against Western values. Like the Rastafarian movement, it was a rejection of the more passive and accepting approach to white society of the older generation. It grew out of the resentment following the Rushdie crisis, which made an overt identification with Islam a badge of pride and a means of showing young Muslims' indifference to the views of a white society which they viewed as hostile and racist. As these men sought to learn about their religion, they turned to local imams who had mostly come from South Asia, were cut off from English culture and had a narrow and parochial understanding of the teachings of the faith. These men became the recruits for radical, anti-Western Muslim groups like Hizb-ut-Tahrir. They were never more than a small minority of Muslims, but they were one manifestation of a broader anger among Muslim youth which exploded in the first large-scale Asian riots in 1995 and 2001.

The Culture of Violence

Historically, Britain had not been a violent society in the modern era. Yet after 1945, there was a staggering increase in crime. Suddenly criminal behaviour and violence were becoming a part of British culture in ways which made it seem depressingly similar to the United States. In 1900, there were just 300 recorded crimes per 100,000 of the population in England and Wales, most of them petty thefts. This was the lowest level since statistics were first published in 1857. The crime rate went up after the First World War and doubled between 1927 and 1937, when there were about 10,500 people in prison, but only 850 with sentences of longer than three years. By 1997, however, the crime rate was 8,576 per 100,000, while there were 61,000 prisoners, 24,000 of whom had sentences of three years or more.[50] Unfortunately, these statistics cannot be taken at face value. The number of crimes depends on what is actually reported to the police, as well as on what is considered a crime and what society encourages people to report. The most obvious examples in the last thirty years are rape and domestic violence against women and children. In both instances, the culture before 1970 encouraged keeping quiet about such violence; since then, the culture has placed increasing emphasis on reporting and punishing it. Authorities who used to discount such charges, and so did not record them, are now more likely to take them seriously. As another example, poor people or immigrants often do not report crimes because they distrust the police and have little confidence that they will take the crimes seriously.

Nonetheless, while the statistics may not be literally correct, they reflect the general trend. Crime roughly doubled between

1937 and 1945, but the rate slowed down significantly from 1945 to 1955. Then it took off, doubling again from 1957 to 1967 and yet again from 1967 to 1977. Thereafter, the rate of increase slowed down – to 50 per cent from 1977 to 1987 and only 20 per cent from 1987 to 1997. The rate actually dropped each year from 1992. By 2001, following a 12 per cent drop from the previous year, crime in England and Wales had reached the lowest level in twenty years. What kinds of crimes were people committing? There was some increase in violent crime, but not a great deal. After falling from 2.4 per cent of recorded crimes in 1900 to about 1 per cent in 1937 and 1947, crimes of violence went up to 3.8 per cent in 1987 and 5.6 per cent in 1997. The murder rate at the end of the century, however, was about the same as at the beginning, and that was one of the lowest in the world. Most of the increase in crime after 1957, therefore, was directed against property. Indeed, in the early 1990s Britain surpassed even the United States in this category of crimes. The number of burglaries increased from 105,000 in 1957 to over one million in 1997, while the number of thefts went from 400,000 to 2.3 million.[51] The most important factor accounting for these numbers was the increase in the amount of valuable property that was portable and so easily stolen – from televisions and video recorders to cars, which accounted for nearly half of all thefts in 1987 and 1997. The influx of drugs during the last two decades of the century provided a new impetus for people to steal, in order to get money to support the habit. In addition to these major sources of crime, there was a large number of other offences (most commonly criminal damage), as well as non-indictable offences. By far, the most common of the latter were driving offences, followed by drunkenness.

As the number of crimes and convictions went up, so did the prison population. Like crime statistics, numbers in prison vary with changing social attitudes to imprisonment and sentencing. Between the wars the culture was hostile to imprisonment and optimistic about the possibilities of reforming criminals. After the Second World War, cautioning was the norm for juveniles and even youths arrested for indictable offences, which meant fewer imprisonments. Parole was introduced in 1967, which made possible the shortening of prison sentences and the reduction of the prison population. Thus, the general attitude was to avoid imprisonment when possible, and the long-term effect was a dramatic decline in imprisonment as a sentence between 1900 and 1977: from 90 per cent of those sentenced in the crown court in 1900 to under 50 per cent in 1977; and from about 50 per cent of sentences in the magistrates' court in 1907 to 6 per cent in 1977.* The Conservatives reversed this trend after 1979. They made crime a major political issue, and punishment replaced treatment as the goal of the criminal justice system. Spending on law and order increased nearly 60 per cent in real terms between 1978 and 1979 and 1987 and 1988, an additional ten thousand police officers were employed, the conditions for parole were toughened and government pressed for longer sentences. As a result, the numbers imprisoned went up – to over 60 per cent of sentences in the crown court and over 10 per cent in the magistrates' court in 1997. Because of these longer sentences, the number of prisoners increased by 50 per cent between 1987 and 1997. The effect was to accelerate the long-term trend towards more prisoners serving sentences of three years or more, which went from under 10 per cent of male prisoners in 1937 to half in 1997.[52]

Many of these culprits were young men. Thus, one reason for the rise in crime from the mid-1950s to the late 1970s was the increase in the size of that population because of the baby boom. This fact also helps account for the fixation on juvenile delinquency that began in the mid-1950s. From 1955 to 1961, the number of males in age groups 14–17 and 18–21 convicted of crimes more than doubled, while the numbers convicted of violent crimes in both age groups tripled. Yet there was also a rise in female crime beginning in the late 1960s, and violence

---

* The crown court heard indictable offences, including all felony trials; magistrates' courts heard some indictable offences and all non-indictable offences.

by females also increased. The number of girls imprisoned for violent crimes jumped by over 40 per cent between 1991 and 1996, while projections for the future indicated that the numbers might exceed those of boys between 14 and 17 within a decade.[53] Just as natural assumptions about the sex of criminals have to be somewhat modified, so do those about their class. Thus, the community in southeast London with the highest rate of crimes against the individual in 1987 was the borough of Bexley, a middle- and lower-middle-class white suburb. According to the police, the perpetrators tended to have jobs and cars and liked to get drunk.[54] Murder, at any rate, still occurred mostly in boroughs with large concentrations of poor people, like Westminster, Lewisham, Brent, Lambeth and Hackney.* Between 25 and 50 per cent of murders were 'domestic', while many of the rest were related to drugs and organised crime, often in black neighbour-hoods. In addition to drugs, drink was closely associated with violent crime. In 2000, 40 per cent of such crimes were alcohol related, and one third occurred near a pub or other licensed facility.[55]

How are we to account for this boom in crime? Caution is required when answering this question, for the subject is politi-cised, while the explanations of both the left and the right are plausible. The left attributed the rise in crime to poverty and unemployment. Even before unemployment became a serious problem in the 1980s, life offered little joy, excitement or hope for working-class boys, especially those from the poorest segment of that class. Their main aspiration was to earn some money: work was what men did. Yet the jobs they got were boring and dead-end. So they lived for the moment because the future offered little. One outlet was youth culture or subcultures. Some, how-ever, went further: crime was a more radical means of challenging the system. The 1980s made matters worse. Since young men were disproportionately represented among the unemployed,

---

* In 1997–9, the five London boroughs mentioned each had between twenty-five and twenty-nine murders, while Bexley had only two.

even the hope of a job after school was now gone for some. Most reacted with fatalism and apathy. Others turned to crime.

The right is not inclined to accept such sociological explanations of crime. Rather, it is an individual choice and so a sign of moral failing. Yet it is plausible that youth responded to the market forces so beloved by conservatives, and it was a relatively simple cost-benefit analysis for young men to judge whether crime against property paid. Furthermore, the urban poor came from a culture that had long tolerated theft in hard times, especially if it was directed against outsiders who could clearly afford the loss. However, the statistics do not correlate well with an association of rising crime with poverty and unemployment. Crime started to get worse from 1957 to 1977, when both were relatively low. While it continued to get worse in the 1980s, when both rose rapidly, the crime rate went down in the 1990s, while poverty and unemployment remained relatively high. So something more must have been involved.

In fact, the right had its own socio-cultural interpretation of rising crime: it was due to the breakdown of the family and the erosion of traditional Victorian values. There is much to be said for this view. The Victorian social system had been based on both a fairly rigid social hierarchy of class and gender and a fairly repressive morality. The intention was to impose order when the threat of disorder seemed very real, and it succeeded – not only in keeping the lower classes in their place, but in getting them to accept that place. All this was breaking down even before the First World War, and it accelerated afterwards. The 1920s, in particular, saw a retreat from rationality, social responsibility and self-discipline as people sought greater self-gratification.[56] Such a change in values could help explain the rise in crime that occurred between the wars. The Second World War dealt a much more serious blow to the Victorian heritage. Over the decades that followed, consumerism and personal fulfilment became positive virtues in a society that was changing radically. Neighbourhoods were destroyed, and with them the communities that had imposed discipline on working-class boys for generations.

At the same time, the class system became less rigid and the rhetoric changed. The lower classes were no longer expected to accept their place in society; the new ethic claimed that there should be opportunity for all who had the ability to move up. Here was one challenge to the culture of authority, hierarchy and deference that had been passed down from the Victorian era. Feminism was another. It may not have progressed very far in the working class, but mothers were working, the relations between husbands and wives were changing and divorce was on the increase. Parent–child relations were changing too: youth culture also challenged the old order. Finally, society *was* getting more permissive, or tolerant (choose your word), while the indiscriminate use of force by authority was no longer acceptable. There had been very few checks on what policemen, teachers and parents could do in 1900; there were many more in 1980. Superimposed on all this change was immigration, which replenished the bottom of the working class with people who did not come from the old Victorian culture. The immigrants brought their own culture, which was also reconstituted within the fluid state of post-war British society. They had no reason to accept a place at the bottom of that society, especially when attacks by white people subverted the liberal values which the society claimed. Yet for white people, they simply represented one more change destroying the world of their parents and grandparents.

It is inconceivable that all these changes, as they influenced adolescent males, had no effect on the amount of crime in the society. It is important to remember that we are talking about a minority – not only of youth, but of working-class youth.* These boys were from the poorest and least educated segment of that class, those who got only limited benefits from prosperity and who suffered first and most lengthily from the harsher economic times that began in the 1970s. Both drinking and violence had

---

* Most of the changes discussed affected middle-class adolescents as well, and so could contribute to an increase in crime in communities like Bexley. The largest number of criminals, however, still came from the working class.

long been part of their culture; they were associated with manliness, with toughness and with a kind of rite-of-passage through adolescence to adulthood. Nor had this class ever had much use either for authority or for the middle-class value system that authority represented. Hence, there was a long history of resorting to violence or petty crime. Relations between the police and the working poor had been tense from the beginning, as the latter saw the police as instruments of a government authority which they distrusted. As a result, in the mid-nineteenth century 'in the cramped city slums of London and Liverpool, Birmingham and Glasgow, officers normally had to patrol in pairs and there were districts that were to all intents and purposes "no-go" areas'.[57] While the danger had disappeared by 1900, there is no reason to believe that the hostility ever did.

It expressed itself not only in formal crime, but in all sorts of violent and anti-social behaviour – such as that of the Teddy boys, the mods and the rockers and the Rastafarians. Part of the attraction of such subcultures was the possibility of some action, whether it was directed at other boys or at the police. The football hooliganism that emerged in the late 1960s had some of the same quality. Football had always had some sporadic violence, but it usually was individual and spontaneous. The one exception was in Glasgow, where gangs of Catholic Celtic and Protestant Rangers supporters squared off against each other regularly between the wars. Now, however, something more prevalent and threatening was occurring – though most games still had no violence at all. Groups of rival fans (usually drinking) chanted, taunted, abused and shouted obscenities at each other on the way to the games or from opposite sections of the terraces. It was the street culture of two gangs who were involved in a turf war brought to the football stadium. Yet there could also be much more extreme behaviour. Hooligans hurled racist abuse at the growing number of black players (even on their own team), vandalised British Rail special trains, smashed the windows of shops near the grounds or trashed city centres. A 'firm' of hooligans might prowl the streets outside their local pub before or after a match, looking for a fight if opposing fans encroached. The situation deteriorated in the 1980s, especially for international matches on the Continent, as British fans fought foreign fans and police. The result could be catastrophic.* During the 1985 European Cup Final in Brussels, Liverpool fans invaded the terraces of the Juventus fans. When the Italians tried to escape, a wall collapsed and forty-one people were crushed or trampled to death and another four hundred injured.[58] Hooliganism was contained in the 1990s by more intensive policing, the use of video cameras, the renovation of stadiums to replace terraces with all-seater stands and higher prices to appeal to the middle class. At international matches, however, it remained a serious problem.

Hooligans were mostly 'white, urban, unskilled school-leavers in their teens'.[59] Interviews indicated that these youths romanticised the world of their fathers, when men were men and fighting was part of the culture. Beginning in the late 1960s, adult men started to stay home to watch games on television or opted for seats, leaving a younger crowd standing in the terraces unsupervised. At the same time, prosperity meant that more youthful fans travelled to away games, which previously had been rare. It was therefore more likely that two opposing groups of young men faced each other without any older adults to moderate behaviour. Since the football club had territorial associations with the working-class community, there was something of the character of gangs from two neighbourhoods squaring off. This territorial identification took on a chauvinist dimension when England played a foreign team in an international competition. The vulgarity and violence, both ritualised and real, may also have provided a means of reasserting the working-class identity of football – by offending middle-class sensibilities at a time when the appeal of the sport was expanding – since workers did not

---

* The biggest tragedy of all did not result from violence. Ninety-six Liverpool fans were crushed to death at the outset of a 1989 FA Cup semi-final at Hillsborough when the crowd panicked in an overcrowded terrace.

view middle-class supporters as 'true' fans. The intensive media coverage of and outrage over acts of violence may have offered a further attraction to such behaviour. All this could be exploited by troublemakers and criminals who were seeking ways to provoke violence.[60]

One source of such troublemakers was the neo-fascist political movements that appeared at about the same time. The National Front started as an anti-Semitic party; however, there was little political capital in anti-Semitism, so it turned its hostility on immigration to mobilise support. New members flowed in following the arrival of the Ugandan Asians in the early 1970s. As a result, the party achieved some success in local elections in areas with relatively large immigrant populations – like some London boroughs, parts of greater Birmingham and smaller cities such as Leicester, Blackburn and Bradford. In parliamentary elections, however, National Front candidates only occasionally achieved more than 5 per cent of the vote. The pre-1972 membership was more interested in violence anyway. They marched through immigrant neighbourhoods, seeking to intimidate and to provoke attacks from immigrant youths and the radical left. The mobilisation of a more broadly based anti-Nazi campaign in the later 1970s, plus efforts in the schools to blunt the National Front message, helped stop its growth. But the violent and racist core remained.

Many of the National Front were skinheads. The skinheads attracted men who hated everything that had happened since the 1960s – equal opportunity, women's lib, gay rights and the loss of job security. At the same time, they had seen their neighbourhoods deteriorate and immigrants move in. They blamed the immigrants for stealing jobs which mostly they did not want anyway; for getting 'privileged' access to council housing because of laws against discrimination; and for sticking to their own culture rather than trying to assimilate and become 'British'. So they attacked: first Asians in the North of England, most of whom were Muslims – thus the term 'Paki-bashing' – but increasingly, towards the late 1970s, Asians and West Indians in London as well.* Violence meant assaults and murder, but more common was the constant harassment, abuse and petty crime directed in particular at Asians, who lived in constant fear. One young member of the National Front conveyed the underlying attitude: 'I don't want to be with black people. I don't want a multi-racial country . . . If I ran over a black in my car, I wouldn't just leave him lying in the road; I'd kick him into the gutter.'[61] Such hatred was validated by tabloids like the *Sun*, which constantly denigrated foreigners and immigrants. As the National Front's political influence declined in the late 1970s, it became dependent on these youths for support. So the number of violent incidents accelerated.†

The police weren't much help; in fact, immigrants saw them as part of the problem. They thought the police had no interest in protecting their communities, did little to find the perpetrators of racial violence (even when murder was the result) and treated the victims as more guilty than their attackers. Indeed, policemen seemed to treat all non-whites as prospective criminals, as crime came to be seen as a 'black problem'. By the late 1970s, they were adopting 'saturation' policing in West Indian neighbourhoods, which meant stop-and-search operations directed at the residents, especially young men who had adopted the Rasta look. Too often, the typical police view seemed to be that of the deputy chairman of the Police Federation (the policemen's union), who explained the problem of crime this way in 1982: 'There is in our inner cities a very large minority of people who are not fit for salvage . . . the only way in which the police can protect society is quite simply by harassing these people and frightening them so they are afraid to commit crimes.'[62] There was only limited improvement over the next two decades.

---

* Hippies and homosexuals (or those who looked as if they might be homosexual) were also the objects of skinhead attacks.
† The number of attacks on minorities increased from roughly 2,700 in 1975 to more than 7,000 in 1981. These figures are only for violent crimes that were reported to the police. Weight, *Patriots*, p. 538 and note 43.

A 1994 survey found that 75 per cent of West Indians believed that the police could not be relied on to protect them from racial harassment; the number was 85 per cent for those aged sixteen to thirty-four. In 1997, only 2.9 per cent of the Metropolitan Police were from minority populations, while the 1999 Macpherson Report, on the Met's handling of the murder of the black youth Stephen Lawrence, claimed that the department was permeated by systematic racism which affected its ability to treat blacks fairly and take their complaints and fears seriously.[63]

This police attitude contributed to the urban riots of the 1980s and after. Black youths were frustrated with the lack of improvement in their lives. They saw little benefit from the kind of respectfulness and respectability represented by their first-generation parents, who were often reasonably satisfied with their work (even in dead-end jobs) and lives.[64] The children, by contrast, had much less interest in adapting themselves to white society, either in behaviour or speech. At the same time, they were breaking away from the traditional deferential family structure at home. The first major anti-police riot was by West Indians in Bristol in 1980. Riots in London's Brixton and Liverpool's Toxteth communities in 1981 were also primarily West Indian. Both of these were areas of very high unemployment (black youth unemployment in Brixton was over 50 per cent), but the riots were primarily the result of a decade or more of tense relations with the police. Since poor white youths also hated the police and the values of respectability, they joined in, and some of the rioting occurred in all-white neighbourhoods. Yet like E. P. Thompson's food rioters in eighteenth-century England, the rioters of the 1980s were not necessarily a purposeless mob. Their human targets were mostly policemen and representatives of the media, while in an attack on a shopping area during the 1985 riots in the London district of Tottenham, 'the supermarket and off-licence was looted and burned, but not the launderette, the fruit and veg shop or the hairdressers (all run by community co-ops); nor the welfare rights centre nor the neighbourhood office'.[65] Clearly, the rioters thought they knew who their friends were, as well as their enemies.

There were also riots in Handsworth Park, Birmingham, in 1985, and more in Bradford in 1995, where it was Asian youth who were at the centre of the violence. Most recently, Asians in the depressed Lancashire textile towns of Oldham and Burnley rioted in the summer of 2001, and there were also more riots in Bradford. In Burnley, senior figures – both Asian and white – claimed that race relations had historically been pretty good. Yet the neo-fascist British National Party (BNP)* had gained 11 per cent of the vote at the general election that year, so clearly there was white resentment. In Bradford North, however, the BNP candidate had received only 4 per cent of the vote, while a National Front rally on the day the riot started drew only twenty people. In Burnley and Oldham, both Asian and white youths rioted, often fighting each other in what seemed a form of turf war. In Bradford, however, the rioters were mostly Pakistani youths, with relatively little white participation or provocation, and their main aim was to make their neighbourhood a no-go area for the police. A report commissioned prior to the riot but published after it criticised the politicians, the community leaders and the police, none of whom had confronted 'the gang culture, the illegal drugs trade, and the growing racial intolerance, harassment and abuse that exists'.[66]

The Survival of Traditional Values

The sixties looked like a transforming decade to those who lived through them, and thirty years later they still do. Seemingly all of the traditional values of society were challenged. Youth culture, feminism and crime all took off. Divorce was facilitated, abortion was legalised, contraception was made easily available, homosexuality was decriminalised, censorship was relaxed and the death penalty was ended. There was a general easing of sexual constraints, a rejection of deference and a flouting of authority.

---

* The BNP broke from the National Front in 1982 and then replaced it as the predominant party of the extreme right.

In the latter part of the sixties, trade unionism became more militant, while political and popular action became more violent. University places were expanded while traditional notions of culture came under attack. Most of this continued in the decades that followed. While the trade unions were tamed in the 1980s and crime started to go down in the 1990s, the culture of violence remained entrenched, and all the consequences of the liberating movements that began in the 1960s were still working themselves out.

To traditionalists, much of this looked like a catastrophe – the triumph of moral relativism, amorality and immorality. One villain they identified was the secularisation of society. Yet the decline of religion, which had been going on over the whole century, can easily be exaggerated. The numbers who saw themselves as atheists or with no religious identity at all increased only moderately. It has been estimated that about 85 per cent of the population in 1900 had some religious affiliation, while 72 per cent did in 1995. The nature of the religious community changed significantly during that time. Nearly all of it was Christian in 1900, while in 1995 Christians were 65 per cent of the population and non-Christians 7 per cent. Anglicans comprised about 70 per cent of the Christians throughout the century. However, the Catholics grew from 7.5 per cent of the Christians in 1900 to 15 per cent in 1995, while others declined from 22 per cent in 1900 to 16.5 per cent in 1995.[67] The latter decline was primarily among the old Nonconformist sects like the Baptists, Presbyterians, Congregationalists, Unitarians and Methodists.

Church membership offers a much narrower test of religiosity than simple identification. For example, while 23.1 million in 1900 are estimated to have been part of the Anglican community, only 3.2 million were members of the Church. The gap is so large because so many English people felt a vague association with the Anglican Church without having formal ties to it. The gap was not so great for the other Christian churches, but it was still significant – 7.2 million Nonconformists affiliated and

3.6 million members; 2.5 million Catholics affiliated and 1.6 million members. This gap shows how easy it is to exaggerate how religious Britain was in 1900: church members were only about one-third of the population (excluding what is now the Republic of Ireland). By 1997, that percentage had been halved, to 17 per cent. While membership in the Anglican and Nonconformist churches had fallen, the number of Catholics had increased somewhat. Because of immigration, however, the biggest increase was in the number of non-Christians, who had gone from a few hundred thousand in 1900 to 22 per cent of those who formally identified with a faith in 1995. By comparison, Anglicans were 22 per cent of church members, Catholics were 23 per cent and other Christians were 33 per cent.[68]

Attendance at religious services is an even narrower measure of those who were reasonably serious about their religious practice. However, church attendance has only been measured intermittently, and attendance at a place of worship by non-Christian communities has hardly been measured at all. The only census of attendance at the beginning of the century was for London, which showed 19 per cent of the population attended a service on census Sunday. It is probable that attendance rates were higher elsewhere – because Wales and Scotland were more religious than England, and because London was a centre of British secularism, especially among the working class. A survey of 1948–9 showed 15 per cent of the population attending church. An English survey in 1979 showed 11 per cent of adults attending – a number which hardly changed in a 1989 census. The numbers for Wales and Scotland were higher: 13 per cent of adults in Wales in 1982 and 17 per cent of adults in Scotland in 1984. The attendance rate in Northern Ireland was surely higher still, since it had a much higher membership rate than other parts of the UK.[69] Assuming that the 1902–3 London numbers were a little low for England as a whole, the rate of attendance in England roughly halved over the course of the century, and approximately half of that decline had taken place by the end of the Second World War. Estimates between 1980 and 2000 showed that the big gainers among Christians were new churches such as Seventh-Day Adventists, Mormons, Pentecostals and Jehovah's Witnesses, while the Catholic Church was the big loser. Immigrants were especially important to the continued vitality of religion in Britain. By 2001, Muslims and Hindus comprised 9 per cent of regular worshippers, even though they were only 3 per cent of the population. Among the black community, one-third said in a 2000 survey that they attended religious services weekly.[70]

Overall, then, the level of religiosity in Britain roughly halved between 1900 and 1995, whether measured by membership of a faith or attendance at a service. This decline is not as great as the image of a collapse into secularism implies – partly because, using these two criteria, Britain was not that religious in 1900, and partly because, using a broader sense of religious identification, Britain in 1995 was more religious than myth would have it. Furthermore, the decline was less in the rest of the UK than in England. In England, however, the decline of Christian church attendance was greater than the aggregate percentages show, for England benefited most from the inflow of non-Christians from Asia in particular.

In the 1960s, the consciousness of this decline led to self-appraisal by all the traditional Christian churches, which took their lead from the Second Vatican Council. Over the next decades, the Anglican Church offered a new translation of the Bible (as an alternative to the King James Version) and a modernised Book of Common Prayer. There was a new interest in ecumenicalism and new projects to reach the poor. Seeking to recapture for the Church a national role as the conscience of the nation, Robert Runcie, Archbishop of Canterbury from 1980 to 1991, spoke out on behalf of the urban poor and criticised excessive materialism. This brought him into direct conflict with the Thatcher government and brought to the surface the debate within the Church over how much it should resist or adapt to changing social mores. The battle between modernisers and traditionalists was encapsulated in the fight over the ordination of women. The Anglicans were the last Protestant denomination in Britain to ordain women, with the first ordinations occurring in 1994. Even then, some bishops refused to do it, while some Church members became Catholics. By the 1990s, however, the Catholics were declining too. The aura of persecution by a Protestant society was gone (except in Northern Ireland), and the Church was more integrated into the national community. This change was symbolised by the visit of Pope John Paul II to Britain in 1982, the first by a pope since the Reformation. The big gainers after 1970 were the alternative Christian churches. With both Anglicanism and Nonconformity modernising, but still apparently lacking something, they offered the spiritual zeal that some people were looking for.

Who was religious? Throughout Western Europe and the United States, women were the core group to whom religion appealed. Every possible measure of religiosity showed this:

> Women attend church more often than men and in greater numbers. Women are more likely than men to claim for themselves denominational membership, to pray, to read their bibles, to report religious and mystical experiences, to watch religious television programmes and to express belief in God. They are also more likely to hold traditional religious beliefs, to report feeling close to God . . . and to report deriving comfort from religion.[71]

Religion was also likely to appeal to those over fifty-five more than to those in their twenties, and to those in the middle class more than to those in the working class. Yet there is paradox: while people in the middle class were more likely to attend church, those in the working class actually had a more positive attitude towards Christianity.[72] Middle-class church-going may partly have been a legacy from the era when it was a sign of class status and respectability; some of the belief was gone. Among the older generation, too, there was contradiction. Despite their greater religiosity, a survey in the mid-1980s found that only

40 per cent of Christians over fifty-five believed strongly in the value of religion, while most saw little value in an institutionalised church.

Yet three-quarters of the total sample in the same survey believed in God, nearly half drew some comfort from religion and felt the need for prayer, nearly 70 per cent believed in sin and nearly 60 per cent believed in heaven and the soul.[73] What did all this mean? It is not clear. Another survey, this one in Islington in the late 1960s, asked: 'Do you believe in a God who can change the course of events on earth?' One answer was, 'No, just the ordinary one.' The authors of the survey concluded that such a belief in God was not much different from superstition. And indeed, later surveys showed that about as many people believed in the paranormal and astrology as believed in God; many believed in both.[74] For most people, church membership was a step further than this kind of generalised religious belief. Historically, for Christians it had meant relying on the church for key rites: baptism, marriage and burial. In 1945, about two-thirds of all British births still resulted in a baptism; however, by 1990, that number had fallen to about one-third – still a substantial number, but also a substantial decline.[75] A religious burial or cremation service is probably more common now than a baptism, though there are no hard numbers.

Religion continued to have a hold on many Britons because it was still integrated into their lives. Anglican, Catholic and Jewish schools had been part of the national school system since 1902; the Labour government approved incorporating the first Muslim school in 1998 and the first Sikh school in 1999. In rural areas, the parish (Anglican) school was still likely to be the only one available. Denominational schools were popular even with some people outside the faith, who liked the discipline, traditional education and integration of faith and values into the teaching that they offered. Religion was also taught in the state schools according to a common syllabus. In 1945, it taught only about Christianity, but increasingly it became instruction in the major religions of the world. For much the same reason that religion remained part of the education system, many people (including working-class parents) still sent their children to Sunday school – to provide a basic grounding in values of decency, humanity and concern for others. In other ways, too, religion is given a role in national life. The monarch is the head of both the Church of England and the Church of Scotland. The bishops of the Church of England still sit in the House of Lords, which gives them a political forum for expressing their views. The symbols of religion are integrated into the ceremonies of state: the coronation or marriage or burial of the monarch, the marriage or burial of other members of the royal family, Remembrance Sunday honouring the fallen in wars, services of thanksgiving for key national occasions (like the victories of the Second World War and the Falklands War) are all religious services. All this seems to imply that the British people want to continue to be perceived as a faith-based community, even though one faith has a privileged status in the symbolism of the nation.

Since the Middle Ages, one of the central functions of churches in national life was to provide charity. The welfare state was supposed to have destroyed the ethic of charitable giving and voluntarism in Britain, but, in fact, they are alive and well. There was no culture more vibrant with voluntary organisations and activity than the one that grew up in Britain in the eighteenth and nineteenth centuries. Charities, hospitals, asylums, schools, museums, art galleries, all were the product of voluntary initiatives or a combination of private and public action. It is true that many of these institutions and activities were taken over by government in the twentieth century, as it came to dominate the funding of health care, welfare provision, education and the arts. Yet after the Second World War, private charities were at the forefront in developing programmes to help neglected or abused children, the disabled, the homeless and the elderly, when such care was not fully integrated into the welfare state. Then, as government accepted responsibility for such services, it paid the charities to continue to provide them. At the same time, new charities sprang up to deal with subjects that were hardly on the radar screen in 1945, like international aid, medical research, conserving the environment, animal rights and historic preservation. Charities were required to register after 1960, and the numbers since then give a sense of their growth: 57,000 in 1965, more than 135,000 in 1980 and nearly 190,000 in 1998. Most of them were very small. In January 1998, 70.5 per cent of the charities accounted for only 1.5 per cent of charities' income, while 248 charities took in 40 per cent of all the income. Thatcherism and the rise in poverty that came with it gave an enormous boost to charitable activity. In 1987, the four hundred largest charitable foundations made grants of £204 million; in 1996, that sum had increased to £1,157 million. Even after allowing for inflation, this was nearly a fourfold increase. By far, the largest beneficiaries of giving were medical and welfare charities, which accounted for over half the voluntary income of the top five hundred charities in 1993–4. International aid charities accounted for another 17 per cent. The three top fundraisers were Oxfam, the National Trust and the Imperial Cancer Research Fund.[76]

With their increase in size and money, the biggest charities became professionalised, with large paid staff and highly polished marketing and fundraising programmes.* By 1990, registered charities accounted for 2 per cent of employment (including part-time workers) in Britain. While paid staff filled supervisory positions, all charities relied on a large corps of volunteers to get key tasks done. Yet voluntarism went well beyond work for charities. Depending on how broadly it is defined, it can include work for arts and educational institutions, trade unions and political parties, professional organisations and even coaching the children's football team. The distinctions are important, for voluntarism is much more a middle-class than a working-class activity, and much more a female than a male activity, unless one includes

---

* The largest charities received government grants, which were often a major source of funds. Following the introduction of the National Lottery in 1994, some of its money also went to charities.

political and union work and coaching. Using a broad definition, about half the adult population participated in voluntary activities; using a narrow one, about one-fifth did. A 1984 survey of values found that over half the adult population were members of voluntary organisations, while one-fifth undertook voluntary work. Furthermore, religiosity was, with class and gender, the most important factor in determining who would be an active charitable volunteer.[77] The religious middle-class female activist of the Victorian era was still thriving in postmodern Britain. This bias is not surprising, for voluntarism had long been central to the social lives of middle-class women, and its importance in that respect continued in the post-war era – especially if they were not full-time workers.

If religion and voluntarism were more vibrant than myth would lead one to expect, perhaps larger generalisations about a revolution in values are also exaggerated. The 1984 values survey referred to above found that the people sampled were ambivalent, uncertain and inconsistent in their attitudes. There was only occasionally a difference among classes and virtually none between the sexes. The one group that was different was the young (those aged eighteen to thirty-four), among whom very few had traditional values – although more were ambivalent than anti-traditional.[78] Yet despite this expressed uncertainty, people remained very conventional in their attitudes. The family was at the centre of life for most. They were married or expected to marry, expected faithfulness in marriage (though, in practice, perhaps half had had or would have an extra-marital affair), and (in somewhat smaller numbers) expected marriage to last a lifetime. Two-thirds thought that children needed a home with two parents, while half 'disapproved' of single parents – though disapproval was half as likely among the young as among those aged fifty-five and over. Almost exactly half thought divorce was unjustified. There was a similar ambivalence about whether it was a child's duty to respect his or her parents – 56 per cent overall thought it was, though with a substantially larger percentage among unskilled workers and those over fifty-five.

Clear majorities of 60–65 per cent thought homosexuality and abortion were immoral – again, with the level of disapproval significantly stronger among the older generation (though with over half of the younger generation still opposed), while it was less among the middle class.[79]

Thus, religiously based values held up very well among the British people. There were a few obvious ways in which a large proportion of the population began to discard those values in the 1960s and after: the acceptance of sex outside marriage and the rejection of the subordination of women (which all traditional religions affirmed) are the most obvious. But in most respects, people still remained good neo-Victorians. In addition to their traditional views about the family, they believed in individual responsibility for personal actions and rejected moral relativism. Those of the ten commandments that apply to moral rather than religious behaviour still held good, whatever a person's religion, or lack of religion. They respected traditional authority, condemned violence and crime, and took pride in their country. Nearly 80 per cent of those in the sample who were employed took pride in their work, though the percentage fell to around 70 among the young and among unskilled workers. The British actually scored higher in terms of pride in their work and job satisfaction than other Europeans in a comparable survey. Nearly 60 per cent thought it was bad that work had become less important in people's lives, with very little difference by age or class.[80]

Hence, once more there was a paradox: some genuinely radical change, the appearance of much more, and the reality of a people who either remained profoundly traditional or else were confused and ambivalent. There was only a hint in 1984 of more permissive attitudes among the young (those aged eighteen to thirty-four), a hint that was confirmed by later surveys of social attitudes, with conservatism somewhat more strongly entrenched among the working class than the middle class.[81] Furthermore, this adherence to traditional values had been reinforced by the immigrant population that had come to Britain over the previous decades. Yet the perception was of a much more comprehensive rejection of conventional morality – a perception that conservatives began to emphasise as they blamed the sixties for Britain's moral decline. After the mid-1970s, a reaction set in against the permissive society. The Catholic Church set out to change the law on abortion, while the police cracked down on pornography and prostitution after a period of leniency. Mary Whitehouse sought to revive a Christian-based morality, as she organised campaigns against sex education in schools and smut in the media. Barbara Cartland minted money by writing romance fiction for women who wanted to believe in the old ideals of romantic love, glamour and sexiness without sex. Traditionalism may have been stronger among women – for unlike in the United States, the political gender gap in Britain saw women favouring the Conservatives. This latent traditionalism and disillusionment with the sixties – reinforced by a decade of economic crisis and social turmoil – provided the foundation for the triumph of a Conservative party led by Margaret Thatcher selling a return to Victorian values as part of its creed.

11

NATIONAL IDENTITIES

Since the late 1960s, there has been a surge of separatist nationalism among the Celtic peoples of Scotland, Wales and Northern Ireland. In part, its emergence as a serious political phenomenon reflected the same kind of resistance to elitist centralised authority that spurred other cultural phenomena around the same time. For the Celtic peoples the centralised authority was located in London, and for the nationalists the elitism it represented was English. Celtic nationalists had a lurking suspicion that British national identity had long been simply another way of describing an English hegemony which was insensitive or indifferent to their national concerns and which implied a belief in English superiority. Their suspicions seemed to be corroborated over the next twenty years and more by new scholarly approaches to colonialism that developed the concept of internal imperialism, which enabled a particular national group to dominate others within the nation-state, not just in Britain but elsewhere. At the same time, in the 1980s and 1990s the new theorists began to tackle more directly the subject of national identity and the cultural traditions which shape it. They showed how often traditions that were supposed to go back to time immemorial were in fact of fairly recent vintage and were the result of conscious nation-building by ruling classes. In some instances, they questioned the reality of national identity at all – in the sense that it was something that was objectively felt by all citizens of the nation, rather than something that was the product of a particular time and circumstances, and was even the expression of the interests and identity of a particular class rather than the whole people.

All this research validated the questioning of whether there was such a thing as a British identity or a British nation, and so whether there was any reason for the different parts of the United Kingdom to stay together at all, if self-interest did not demand it. At the same time, it raises the question of what is the identity of each of the Celtic states and of England, and how much do identity and interest provide a centrifugal force impelling the parts of the United Kingdom towards separation. Certainly, each of the Celtic nations has a long history that includes resistance to English domination. Furthermore, as each came to be more fully incorporated into a modern British state that was centred in London, the attributes of an identity began to be constructed and articulated in ways that would assure that the people continued to think of themselves as distinct from the English, and even as separate from a common British identity. The Celtic nationalists of the post-war period could draw on these identities, as well as on indigenous political nationalist movements whose roots were in the nineteenth century, as they demanded greater autonomy from London or, in the more extreme cases, separation.

Does this nationalist challenge mean, then, that Britain as we know it is doomed? Are there neither interests nor identity to hold the constituent parts together? And what does all this talk of separation mean for the English, whose own identity was so much focused on being at the centre of a great nation which in turn was at the centre of a great empire? One view is that Celtic separatism, in conjunction with the end of empire, is simply one more very powerful manifestation of Britain's decline since the Second World War. If, however, Britain transforms itself into some sort of federal state, which accommodates the distinct identities of the Celtic peoples and so retains their loyalty, then this period will have marked the beginning of a revolution that changed the very nature of the United Kingdom while preserving it. The historian is not in the business of predicting the future. The American, however, who has seen federalism succeed, can be optimistic that Britain can 'reinvent itself' (to use a term favoured by the new theorists) as some sort of federal state which, because the peoples who comprise it have a shared history and even a shared culture, can not only survive but continue to thrive.

The Re-emergence of Celtic Nationalism

Celtic nationalism was no new phenomenon. It was most firmly established in Ireland. Indeed, the seeds of dissolution between Ireland and Britain were planted virtually from the moment they were joined in 1801. The Irish leaders who confirmed that union were Protestant; the Catholic majority was not a party. When Daniel O'Connell, the father of modern Irish nationalism, eventually mobilised that majority, his programme in the 1830s and 1840s was to repeal the Act of Union and restore an independent Irish Parliament under the Crown. A more radical form of Irish separatism, based on a fully independent Irish republic, emerged with Fenianism in the 1860s. Republicanism, however, remained marginalised in the nineteenth century. Instead, in the 1880s Charles Stewart Parnell forced the Liberal Party in Britain to accept Irish Home Rule, with an Irish parliament responsible for Irish affairs. For the first time, a British party recognised the legitimacy of Irish nationalism and sought to accommodate it in a way that would preserve the United Kingdom. However, the resistance of the Tory-dominated House of Lords, the Conservative Party more generally and the Protestants of Ireland, who were centred primarily in the northeast province of Ulster, blocked Home Rule. This delay allowed the more radical strain of Irish separatism to reassert itself. Thus, when Irish nationalism exploded after the First World War, it was in support of the Fenian goal of a republic. Ireland's war of independence finally forced the British to give way in 1921. While Ireland remained technically subject to the Crown as a dominion, by the mid-1920s the British had conceded that dominions were fully sovereign independent states. The South of Ireland was free. The North, however, was hived off under the 1921 treaty, in conformity with the wishes of the Protestant majority.* Irish independence therefore did not end the movement for Irish separatism. In 1990, only 10 per cent of Catholics in Northern Ireland identified themselves as British; the rest saw themselves as Irish or Northern Irish. By contrast, 93 per cent of the Protestants saw themselves as British or Ulstermen, while a mere 4 per cent identified themselves as Irish.[1] Thus, while the union of Northern Ireland with the rest of the United Kingdom was secure as long as the Protestants were in the majority, there would be unending pressure from Irish Catholics for change.

While Wales and Scotland also had strong nationalist traditions, they were not separatist. Welsh nationalism was primarily cultural. Wales, unlike Ireland or Scotland, had been politically and administratively integrated into England – in the 1530s by the Tudors, who were Welsh in origin. As a result, Wales was left with no distinct institutions. It did, however, have two important badges of cultural separateness. The most important was the Welsh language. Far more than in Scotland or Ireland, the indigenous Celtic language survived in Wales into the twentieth century. The second symbol of Welsh difference was religion. Although Wales, like England and Scotland, had an aggressively Protestant identity, that Protestantism was Baptist and Methodist. Since the Anglican Church was the established church of Wales, it was an important source of Welsh resentment. When a small Welsh nationalist party, including the young David Lloyd George, appeared in the House of Commons in the 1890s, the disestablishment of the Anglican Church in Wales was one of its principal goals.

---

* Only six of the nine counties of historic Ulster remained as part of Northern Ireland; the other three went with the South. So it is incorrect to call Northern Ireland Ulster.

Scotland, unlike Wales and Ireland, had not been conquered by the English. The union between England (and Wales) and Scotland was a voluntary act on the part of the Scots. Thus, although they gave up their parliament, the Scots were able to preserve key institutional expressions of their separate identity: the Presbyterian Church as the established church of the nation, the continued application of the Scottish system of law and the preservation of their own distinct systems of education and local government. The rise of Scottish nationalism in the last third of the nineteenth century had more to do with discontent over London domination than any specific grievances. Nonetheless, because of the power of Scotland within the Liberal Party, Gladstone created a Scottish Office in 1885 to pay some attention to Scottish affairs.

The emergence of Scottish and Welsh nationalism at the same time as the movement for Irish Home Rule gave rise to the possibility of accommodating the nationalism of all three countries. A proposal for 'home rule all around', or devolution, meant that Scotland and Wales as well as Ireland would get some sort of council with responsibility for administering specified local services. Since devolution was offered as a substitute for Home Rule, it was unacceptable to the Irish and so was never a serious possibility. In fact, it had a very limited appeal even among the Welsh and the Scots, since the numbers looking for political separation from England at the time were small. Indeed, in one of the great ironies of history, the only people to get devolved government before 1999 were the Northern Irish Protestants, who had threatened rebellion before the First World War in order to thwart Home Rule. Yet in 1920, Britain gave Northern Ireland a parliament with responsibility for a wide range of internal affairs. The effect was to hand political control of the province over to the Protestants, who used it as an instrument to dominate the Catholic minority. Thus, the Northern Irish experience was not a happy model for devolution as a means of accommodating national differences within the United Kingdom.

Because Scotland, Wales and Northern Ireland had nationalist traditions, those traditions were available for mobilising popular discontent, should it arise. After 1945, the economy increasingly became a source of frustration in all three countries. All of them had benefited from the Industrial Revolution. Indeed, it is possible that the prosperity that came with industrialisation was an important cement that helped bind the Celtic fringe to the English centre. When the old industries began to decline after 1918, however, so did the regions in which they were concentrated. Furthermore, new industry tended to locate in the English Midlands and South, and since Britons of all nationalities were far less mobile than Americans, the poverty associated with economic decline persisted over generations, apart from a brief respite during and after the Second World War. Labour governments tried to help; except in Northern Ireland, these regions of decline were the Labour heartland. Government policies therefore sought to encourage industry to locate in those areas that had been suffering from prolonged unemployment. While they succeeded in providing new sources of employment, the long-term haemorrhage in manufacturing jobs continued. Thus, while England was booming in the 1950s and 1960s, the Celtic states did not fully participate in that boom; and as the economy turned worse from the late 1960s on, the Celtic peoples felt that they were suffering disproportionately from the economic pain. This discontent was an important reason for the strengthening of political nationalism in all three nations.

In fact, it is not true that they suffered more than their English counterparts. Table 11.1 overleaf compares unemployment rates and average gross income per family in the North of England with the Celtic regions during the period from the crisis of 1973 to the peak of the late 1980s recovery. While Northern Ireland was clearly the worst off, Scotland and Wales compared very favourably with the equally troubled North. None of them, however, could compare with the obvious prosperity of London and the South of England that developed in the 1980s under Thatcher. It was this comparison with England as a whole, rather than with the deprived regions of England, that left the Celtic

Table 11.1. Unemployment Rate and Average Gross Household Income, 1973–88, North of England, Scotland, Wales and Northern Ireland

	Unemployment 1973 (%)	Unemployment 1979 (%)	Unemployment 1986 (%)	Household Income 1988 (£)
Northwest England	2.9	5.9	14.1	246
Northern England	3.9	7.3	15.3	220
Scotland	3.8	6.8	14.0	234
Wales	3.0	6.3	13.9	227
Northern Ireland	4.9	9.7	18.6	214

Source: S. N. Broadberry, 'Unemployment', in Crafts and Woodward, *The British Economy since 1945*, p. 217 (unemployment); Boyle and Hadden, *Northern Ireland: The Choice*, p. 52 (average gross household income).

peoples feeling that they were the victims of discrimination, and that feeling helped feed the resentment that fostered a more aggressive nationalism.

The Celtic peoples blamed Westminster for their chronic economic troubles in part because the continuing encroachment of central government seemed to leave those at the centre responsible for everything. We have seen how absolute the power of Parliament to dictate to the country was. Wales had no protection at all against that power, as it was fully incorporated into England for administrative purposes. In theory, Scotland and Northern Ireland did have protection because of their separate administrative structures. Edward Heath, for example, passed a separate Local Government Act for Scotland in 1974, after consultation with the Scots through a Royal Commission. There was no constitutional obligation to consult, however, and Thatcher showed no interest in the wishes of the mainly Labour Celtic peoples when implementing her policy reforms. The most controversial was the introduction of the 'poll tax', a reform of the system of local government finance. It was applied first in Scotland, and the Scots rebelled – mobilising a resistance which was eventually exported to England and helped to bring Thatcher down. Thatcherite economic policies were also unpopular with the Scots and Welsh. They had enthusiastically supported the nationalisations of 1945–50, so they did not like the Conservative privatisation policies. The closing of coal mines and the halving of employment in the steel industry destroyed *their* jobs.

No policy, however, irked Labour supporters more than the privatisation of the utilities – electricity, gas and water. Utilities had been brought under municipal control, or even initiated by local governments, in the second half of the nineteenth century because they were natural monopolies and public necessities. They had been nationalised after 1945 in order to create an integrated system of supply. Now, they were to be turned over to the private sector, and the communities which had originally created them or taken them over were to have no say in the matter. The Conservatives were utterly indifferent to these local feelings. When Strathclyde (the Glasgow region with a population of over two million) held an unofficial referendum by postal ballot on the privatisation of water, over 95 per cent of those who voted were against it.[2] The government of John Major, however, ploughed on. To the Scots and Welsh, this was dogmatism gone wild – totally ignoring the wishes of the people in the name of ideology, and oblivious to the possibility that a different policy might be appropriate for Scotland or Wales. It is little wonder that Scottish nationalism in particular thrived in the 1990s, and that the Conservatives were wiped out in both Scotland and Wales in the general election of 1997. As had so often been the case with Ireland, the Tory Party, while committed to preserving the Union at all costs, pursued policies that did much to undermine it.

The situation in Northern Ireland was different from that in Scotland and Wales, but here, too, British centralisation provoked an anti-British response. In 1972, to counter the escalating violence there, the Heath government suspended the Northern Irish parliament and imposed direct rule. Direct rule alienated everyone. As part of the war against the Irish Republican Army (IRA), the normal procedures of law that protected the accused were suspended, thus alienating the Catholic population. The Protestants, however, did not like British policies to promote equality of opportunity in employment, to assure fair policing and to limit marches through Catholic neighbourhoods. Most important of all, Protestants thought British insistence on some sort of power-sharing arrangement that included Catholics was a rejection of the principles of democratic government, and it caused a few of them to call into question the British connection. The policies of the Thatcher and Major governments, which broke new ground by involving the Irish Republic in the affairs of the North, merely reinforced the doubts of such Protestants, who saw any participation by the Republic as a first step towards Irish union. For these few, the alternative to British rule was an independent Northern Ireland. In this limited sense, then, Westminster centralisation provoked a Northern Irish separatism that paralleled that in Scotland and Wales. Furthermore, since Northern Irish Protestants had a distinct identity, their separatism might even be called nationalist.

This evolving Celtic separatism was reinforced by events outside the United Kingdom. Parochial nationalism and tribal separatism were on the march all over the world – from Canada to Nigeria to India. In Europe, separatist nationalist movements sprang to life following the collapse of authoritarian regimes that had suppressed them. In Spain, for example, the end of the dictatorship following Francisco Franco's death allowed long-suppressed Basque and Catalan nationalist movements to re-emerge. The most dramatic example, of course, was the disintegration of the great Russian empire, some three hundred years old, following the fall of communism in the 1990s. The splintering of Yugoslavia, after the death of its long-time ruler Marshal Tito, was another manifestation of the same phenomenon, as was the splitting up of Czechoslovakia after the end of Soviet domination. All these cases, however, involved the removal of the threat of force that had kept the centrifugal effects of nationalism in check. This was hardly the case in Britain – though Northern Irish Catholics might argue otherwise. But the forces of fragmentation were also evident in other democratic states of Western Europe. The Flemings of Belgium were pressing for separation from the French Walloons, while the Northern League was organised around separating northern Italy from the south. These movements, like those in the Celtic states, were fuelled by some sense of economic grievance – though in Belgium and Italy it was the economically strong rather than the economically weak who were threatening secession. The European Community gave cover for all such campaigns in Western Europe. Separatists assumed that all new states would remain part of the EC and so economically viable, while independence would give the people greater control over their own economic resources. As a result, nationalist parties in Scotland and Wales, which initially had opposed the EC because it appeared to be another institution that would suppress national identity, eventually threw their support behind it in the 1980s. Thus, broader geopolitical trends, as well as developments within the United Kingdom, helped make Celtic separatism seem both a desirable and a credible alternative.

The Scots and Political Nationalism

In many ways, the Scots seemed to have the best of both worlds. On the one hand, they were a people very secure in their identity as a nation. With their own established Church and systems of law, education and local government, they were well barricaded against English institutional or cultural absorption. True, the Celtic language had pretty much died out by the end of the nineteenth century, except in parts of the Highlands and Western

Isles;[*] however, Scottish identity was daily reinforced by an English-language press that was overwhelmingly Scottish in ownership and content. Scottish ownership has ebbed in recent decades, while television and radio have provided London-based sources of information and culture. Even the new multinational owners, however, preserved the Scottish focus of the Glasgow and Edinburgh press, and there remained a large number of regional and local papers that were exclusively Scottish. Furthermore, while television offered only limited Scottish programming, BBC radio had substantial Scottish content, and there were numerous independent Scottish radio stations. Hence, the opportunities for English cultural domination through the language and the media were limited. Scotland's cultural self-assurance was further reinforced by an intellectual output that made Scots leaders in the English-speaking world. Its great universities had enabled Scotland, rather than England, to be the centre of an eighteenth-century Enlightenment that included Adam Smith and David Hume, as well as numerous less famous but still distinguished thinkers. Nineteenth-century Scots like Thomas Carlyle and William Thomson (Lord Kelvin) also matched, or nearly did, the best that England produced.

Carlyle and Kelvin, along with the likes of James and John Stuart Mill, reflected the other side of the Scottish story – the ability of Scots to take advantage of their union with England. Scots of talent were able to migrate to England or overseas and succeed. The Scots saw themselves as one of the linchpins of the British Empire, providing both military and administrative resources for British expansion and governance abroad. Indeed, the empire was one of their principal sources of British, as opposed to Scottish, identity. The economic ties to England and the empire enabled the Glasgow region to become one of the centres of the Industrial Revolution, producing textiles, iron and steel, engines and machinery, and ships, as well as being a major

---

[*] It was estimated that less than 5 per cent of the population spoke Gaelic at the end of the nineteenth century.

port for overseas trade. Scotland's political integration was equally successful, once political reform broke the control of the eighteenth-century oligarchy. After the 1884 Reform Act, no fewer than eight British Prime Ministers were Scots or had Scottish roots.* This integration of Scots into the nation's political elite continues to the present: John Smith was leader of the Labour Party from 1992 until his death in 1994, while Tony Blair's Cabinet in 1997 included Gordon Brown as Chancellor of the Exchequer, Robin Cook as Foreign Secretary and George Robertson as Defence Secretary. Scottish nationalism certainly could not complain about political discrimination within the British system.

Integration had its disadvantages, however. Scotland's ties to England and the empire meant that there was a steady outflow of population. Between 1861 and 1911, emigration averaged nearly 150,000 per decade, and that number doubled in the two decades from 1911 to 1931.[3] Those who departed were not Scotland's poorest citizens, but entrepreneurial artisans, semi-skilled workers, farmers and even professionals looking for greater opportunity elsewhere. Though emigration declined dramatically during the Depression, it picked up again when prosperity returned in the 1950s and even more in the 1960s. At the same time, Scotland's integration into the British economy meant that it took a terrible beating once Britain's staple industries began to decline. Paradoxically, even though industries like coal, steel and shipbuilding began to suffer between the wars, the Second World War made Scotland even more dependent on them, as industries that were not essential to the war effort were closed down. Post-war reconstruction again focused on these industries to promote British exports. They did well in the 1950s, but there was a general indolence about modernising in the good years. In shipbuilding, for example,

---

* They were Gladstone, Lord Rosebery, Balfour, Sir Henry Campbell-Bannerman, Andrew Bonar Law, MacDonald, Macmillan and Home. Five of these were born in Scotland, while the other three (Gladstone, Bonar Law and Macmillan) had recent Scottish ancestry.

the failure to invest in new technology or production methods – a judgement jointly supported by management and unions – led to a collapse by 1968 and the pressure to nationalise the industry, which finally occurred in 1976.

In order to counter the decline of the staple industries, governments (especially Labour governments) embraced regional planning as a means of directing new investment and new industries into the 'sick' regions of Northern England and the Celtic fringe. This meant providing tax incentives, loans and government subsidies to firms (including foreign companies) to locate plants in these regions. Scotland, as a result, received levels of public investment significantly above the British average: between 1964 and 1973, with 9.3 per cent of the British labour force, Scotland got 15 per cent of government spending on industry and agriculture. There were some significant successes – for example, the electronics industry, which employed 7,500 in 1959 and 30,000 in 1969. By 1973, American firms employed over 87,000 people in Scotland.[4] Yet problems got worse following the devaluation crisis of 1967. Planning was frequently put on hold because of the financial constraints imposed by the need to protect the pound and fight inflation. Once the immediate incentives to locate in Scotland dried up, often there were no long-term cost benefits for the new plants and industries. At the same time, foreign-owned firms inevitably made business decisions based on imperatives determined outside Scotland. As a result of all these factors, from 1968 unemployment began to grow, and at a faster rate than in England.

Political nationalism in Scotland had originally been identified with economic deprivation. It had emerged in the Highlands in the late nineteenth century, inspired by Parnell's success in mobilising Catholic Ireland behind Home Rule. As in Ireland, the Scottish movement was linked to grievances over land, as crofters were being evicted as a result of collapsing rents. The nationalist demand was for land reform and Home Rule. The Liberals conceded the former and formally committed to the latter. Thereafter, however, despite the enthusiastic support of

Scottish Liberal MPs, Home Rule took a back seat because of the far greater pressure for Irish and Welsh demands. When Labour replaced the Liberals as the party of the left, it appropriated Home Rule, but with little conviction (except among some Scottish Labour MPs). The politics of working-class solidarity and the dictates of socialist planning both implied treating the United Kingdom as a unit. Furthermore, Labour would be weakened at Westminster if Scottish representation were reduced. This Labour indifference to devolution, along with the economic hard times between the wars, provided the context for the formation of the Scottish National Party (SNP) in the 1930s. The leaders were an amalgam of intellectuals and dissident members of the left-wing Independent Labour Party,* but the SNP did not have much of an intellectual dimension. While there was an important literary revival in Scotland during this period – one with political over-tones in its hostility to urbanisation and the effects of modern capitalism – it did little to feed the new nationalist movement. Unlike its Welsh counterpart, the SNP's aims were solely polit-ical, not cultural. Although it managed to elect an MP in 1945, the SNP hardly made a blip on the British political radar screen until the 1960s; its appeal was too narrow.

The period after the Second World War saw an erosion of some of Scotland's traditional sources of national identity. The Presbyterian Church, which had been damaged earlier by internal divisions, was now further weakened by increasing secularisa-tion and the waning of Victorian values with the sixties revolu-tion. As a result, Church membership fell after the mid-1950s. Hence, religion became less of a mark of Scottish identity. Scotland's education system, too, had lost some of its distinc-tiveness. The preeminence of the Scottish universities disap-peared in the nineteenth century, as Oxford and Cambridge

---

* The Labour Party had been founded as an alliance of trade unions and socialist organisations that chose to affiliate. The Independent Labour Party, founded by the Scotsman Keir Hardie in 1893, was one of the socialist parties that affili-ated at its founding in 1900. It is distinct, therefore, from the Labour Party.

reinvented themselves as major research institutions. The Scottish landed and capitalist elite followed their English counterparts by sending their children to English public schools and Oxbridge so that they could be part of the British ruling class. At the same time, the prestige of the Scottish universities declined as they lost their reputation as research centres. After 1945, they improved again, but it was according to the English model with more English students and faculty. A similar process was evident in secondary education. In the eighteenth and nineteenth centuries, Scotland had been way ahead of England in providing elementary education to a large segment of the population, and after 1872 it did significantly better in secondary education as well. Scotland's best schools, however, became more like England's in the nineteenth century in order to staunch the flow of students south. The gap in state-provided education also eroded once England went into the business seriously. By the 1960s, the two systems were becoming increasingly alike.

To counter this trend of assimilation, however, there was a growth of new administrative institutions exclusively for Scotland. In the nineteenth century, the tradition was to leave Scottish business to be settled by Scottish law officers and MPs. A more formal recognition of Scottish distinctiveness came in 1885, when Gladstone created the Scottish Office, headed by a Scottish Secretary, to satisfy the demands of Scottish Liberal MPs. The Scottish Office took on more responsibilities after the First World War and was moved to Edinburgh in 1937. It came into its own, however, during the Second World War, when Churchill – eager to maximise support behind the war and to free Parliament from having to worry about Scottish legislation – gave unprecedented new powers to the Scottish Secretary Tom Johnston, a Labour MP and Home Ruler. After the war, there was increasing pressure on the central government to recognise Scotland as a separate area for economic development and planning. At the same time, more and more Whitehall functions for Scotland were transferred to Edinburgh. The effect was to give Scotland its own executive bureaucracy, with the number of civil servants expanding from 2,400 in 1937 to 8,300 in 1970 and 10,700 in 1992.[5]

Thus, the decades after the Second World War saw a reconstruction of Scottish identity. On the one hand, the elements of the old triumvirate of religion, education and law were either less important or less differentiated from their English counterparts. On the other hand, the British government was increasingly treating Scotland as a separate unit with its own problems which needed to be administered by Scots. At the same time, the historic bases of Scottish identity with *Britain* were diminished by the loss of empire and economic decline. The effect was to reduce the traditional routes of initiative and self-advancement for Scots through the British connection, while increasing the opportunities through a Scottish civil service. Finally, most Scots, whatever their background, had appropriated the clan, the clan tartan and kilt – which were invented as symbols of the once despised Highlanders in the eighteenth and early nineteenth centuries – as unique signifiers of their Scottishness. A romantic mythology had grown up around the Highlands and the clans in the nineteenth century, fuelled by the successes of the Highland regiments in the wars against France, the novels of Sir Walter Scott and Queen Victoria's summer holidays there. In part to counter this trend, the poets of the Scottish renaissance between the wars, like Hugh MacDiarmid and Edwin Muir, had sought to define a more assertive Scottish identity that rejected the sentimentalised version promoted by Highland nostalgia. Yet people do not give up their myths easily, as the annual Military Tattoo at Edinburgh Castle to kick off the Edinburgh Festival showed. With its regiments dressed in kilts and bands playing the bagpipes, it appealed to Scots as much as to tourists. The Festival was launched in 1947 as a mixture of elite and popular culture. It grew into a centre for experimental theatre and music, as well as a showcase for Scotland's cultural organisations, like the Scottish National Orchestra. As it became a major international event, it helped to confirm culture as a source of national pride. So did Glasgow's designation as the Cultural Capital of Europe for 1990 and the emergence of hard-hitting

Scottish cinema during the decade. Thus, another aspect of the new Scottish identity was defined, one that harked back to the days of the Scottish Enlightenment. Scotland was once more a centre of European culture.

The combination of a new kind of national consciousness among ordinary Scots, discontent over Scotland's economic problems and some hard work organising at the local level, enabled the SNP to start to make an impact on the Scottish political scene in the mid-1960s.* It achieved a breakthrough victory in a parliamentary by-election for Hamilton in 1967, where Winifred Ewing erased a previous Labour majority of sixteen thousand. It followed with a smashing success in the 1968 municipal elections. Yet most Scots remained satisfied that their interests were adequately protected by Parliament and the Scottish Office. Two factors transformed the situation: the Heath government's attack on the trade unions, which alienated many Scots, and the discovery of North Sea oil in 1970. Oil was potentially the miracle product that would solve Britain's chronic balance-of-payments problems by converting a major import into a major export. The jump in its price in the seventies suddenly made its extraction from the North Sea economically feasible. The desperation of government to get the oil flowing as quickly as possible alarmed ordinary Scots and gave some conviction to the SNP claim that it was Scotland's oil, but Scotland would get few of the benefits. If Britain's economic necessity meant an assault on the Highland environment, or the reliance on imported equipment rather than retooling Glasgow's engineering facilities, that was what would be done, whatever Scotland's interests might be. As a counterweight to the perception that Britain was somehow taking Scotland's oil, there was the British claim that Scotland benefited from the net flow of taxes from Scotland to the Treasury and payments going in the other direction. While the SNP contested the statistics, it seems pretty clear that Scotland was a net gainer. In 1997, official figures

---

* There were twenty local branches of the SNP in 1960 and 470 in 1969. Devine, *The Scottish Nation*, p. 577.

showed the net benefit to Scotland would be about £3.2 billion in the coming year, and it had been as high as £6 billion during the decade.[6]

Oil was the decisive influence on Scottish voters in 1974, as the SNP won 22 per cent of the vote in February and 30 per cent in October, compared with 11.4 per cent in 1970.[7] While most of the gains were at the expense of the Tories, the SNP vote sent a message to both parties that people disliked oil policies that were conceived in haste and without adequate concern for Scottish wishes. The oil reinforced a perception, particularly among the younger generation, that Scotland always played second fiddle to England when government dealt with the nation's economic problems, and that Scotland did not have enough leverage to secure its own interests in negotiations with foreign corporations. These voters, however, did not want all of the oil to go to Scotland; nor did they want the SNP policy of independence. Devolution fitted perfectly what seemed to be needed – greater Scottish control over Scottish affairs, but within the United Kingdom. Labour's belated commitment to devolution therefore satisfied many of these people. The bill that emerged from 1977 to 1979 had many problems: powers and responsibilities granted to the elected assembly were repeatedly hedged by exceptions; the assembly had no taxing powers; the Scottish Secretary had substantial veto powers. Nonetheless, a new principle was affirmed, and the bill was endorsed in the unsuccessful (because of insufficient turnout) devolution referendum of 1979 by 32.85 per cent of the electorate, while 30.8 per cent voted against it.[8] On the other hand, the closeness of the vote reflected the ambivalence generated by the proposals, especially among Labour supporters.

By 1979, the SNP was a declining force. It had always been beset by a tension: how political should it be apart from its commitment to independence? The natural leaning of many of its members was left-wing; however, its emerging base in the northeast Highlands was rooted in an anti-Labour rural populism which competed with the Liberals. Purists resisted any policies that watered down the centrality of independence. Yet if it was going to expand, it would have to attack Labour in its heartland along the Clyde, and that seemed to the leftists to require a socialist programme. Devolution became integrated into this dispute. Should a party of independence collaborate with more limited proposals for self-government? Moderates assumed that Labour voters supported the bill and so argued that devolution should be accepted as good in itself. This position, however, was resisted by party purists. These divisions were constantly on display between 1975 and 1979, with the opponents of devolution ultimately gaining the upper hand. The party paid the price for its divisions with an erosion of its popularity, as its share of the vote in the 1979 general election fell to 17.3 per cent. It then proceeded to alienate this remaining base by three more years of internecine warfare, climaxed by the expulsion of the socialist group in 1982.

Salvation came in the form of Thatcherism. Its neo-liberal economic policies, which allowed industries to go to the wall and kept the pound high as a hedge against inflation, devastated what remained of Scottish manufacturing, including the new industries launched since the 1960s. Scotland's manufacturing capacity fell over 30 per cent between 1976 and 1987, while unemployment soared to a peak of 15.6 per cent in 1985. Between 1985 and 1994 manufacturing employment fell by another 23 per cent.[9] Industries that had been the mainstay of Scotland since the nineteenth century, but had been in decline since 1921, were wiped out. Many major firms that remained began to be absorbed by larger corporations based in England or overseas. In 1985–6 alone, takeovers by British firms halved Scottish manufacturing capital from £4.7 billion to £2.3 billion.[10] Scottish capitalism hardly seemed to exist any more. Much of this may have been inevitable. The Scottish economy ultimately was strengthened by its diversification, especially with the advent of more high-tech and financial firms. Edinburgh (helped by home rule) was one of Britain's fastest growing and most prosperous cities by 2000, while Scottish unemployment by then had fallen to the national average for the first time in thirty years.

Scots, however, were not inclined to accept such a precipitous and radical change that maimed their community simply because it had to come. At least the abruptness and brutality for the victims might have been muted. Yet there was little evidence of any concern in London for men whose way of life was destroyed, who wanted to work, who had supported their families all their adult lives, but who were now left stranded. On the contrary, the Tories seemed to revel in the 'rationalisation' of British industry and the transition to a service-based (and more English-based) economy as the way of the future. Furthermore, the revenues from North Sea oil, along with the money from the privatisation of industries that were especially well represented in Scotland, were being used to finance tax cuts that benefited the privileged, who were disproportionately English. The symbol of the Thatcherite constituency – Essex man – located its concerns very firmly in the southeast, in the London suburbs and with the financial interests of the City of London.

At the same time, Thatcherism involved a new level of central dictation. The predominant theme of Scottish political development since 1940 had been an increasing effort by Westminster to recognise Scottish distinctiveness, and the consequent creation of institutions to mediate and negotiate policy in a way that paid some deference to that distinctiveness. Under the dictates of Thatcherite ideology, however, there seemed to be no room for any form of singularity that implied exception; it applied equally to all parts of England, the United Kingdom and the world. The climax of this central dictation came in the latter part of the 1980s. Privatisation began to be extended to public services, and the Scots bitterly resented having their services sold off without any gesture of consultation. An ideology shaped for England was being imposed on Scotland against its will. The poll tax, and the Scottish revolt against it, further reflected both Tory indifference to Scottish sensibilities and Scottish resentment. The Major government continued the privatisation of public services. In addition, it imposed a reform of Scottish local government that was clearly political in its intent to destroy Labour power bases.

Once more, there was no consultation, in contrast to the extensive consultation involved in the parallel reform that was pushed in England. In 1997, the Tories paid the price for these policies when they did not win a single Scottish seat.

Labour should have been well positioned to benefit from Scotland's disillusionment with the new conservatism. However, in its strongholds around Glasgow, government had been dominated by Labour for so long that it had come to be controlled by an entrenched oligarchy that was intolerant of dissent, monopolised patronage in its own interests and too often was corrupt. Local disillusionment, combined with the weakness of the national Labour Party, opened the way for the SNP to attack Labour seats with the argument that working-class interests could be better protected in an independent Scotland. So the socialists won the argument in the end, as the SNP became more explicitly social democratic in its policy orientation. At the same time, it recast its goal for Scotland as independence within the European Community – a break with its anti-EC past. The implication to voters was that Scottish independence would not be such a radical change, since the EC defined so much of the economic and even social framework within which they operated. The payoff came for the SNP in a 1988 by-election when Jim Sillars (himself a former Labour MP) won the previously safe Labour seat of Glasgow Govan. The poll tax was a further godsend to the SNP, comparable to North Sea oil in the 1970s. The Labour leader, Neil Kinnock, had seen his party burned too often because its radical left flouted the law; so he could not support non-payment of the tax. The SNP was therefore able to take the lead in Scotland in promoting a tax boycott.

As had been the case in the 1970s, Labour was again placed in the position of having to catch up with nationalist sentiment before Scotland got away from it. The anger of Labour's Scottish MPs over the imposition of Thatcherite policies drove the party to embrace the nationalist concept of the Scottish mandate. The claim was that the people of Scotland were the ultimate determinants of what was good for Scotland; therefore, the

Conservatives had no mandate to govern Scotland because of their puny Scottish representation, which was reduced to 10 out of 72 MPs after the 1987 general election. Once Labour accepted this argument, the case for devolution, as the means both to determine what the Scottish people wanted and to limit the claims of a sovereign Westminster government, was unassailable. Labour also moved closer to the SNP view of the powers of a Scottish Assembly, including the powers to tax on a limited basis and to shape an economic policy for Scotland. By the early 1990s, therefore, there was not much to choose between the SNP, Liberal Democrats and Labour ideologically, as all supported leftist domestic policies and Scottish autonomy. At the same time, the Thatcher era had moved the centre of gravity in a radical direction by 1992 – away from a large consensus in favour of devolution, towards a more even division between devolution and independence, at about 35–40 per cent in support of each.[11]

The Labour government elected in 1997 held a referendum prior to introducing any legislation, asking whether voters wanted a separate Scottish parliament (nearly 75 per cent of those voting did) and whether it should have limited taxing powers (63.5 per cent voted yes). People voted 'yes' because they thought that a Scottish parliament would be more responsive to them – in particular, that it would improve social services, which had been run down under the Tories. The bill that resulted offered a legislature with far more substantial powers than the devolution bill that failed in 1979. After 1998, the Scottish Parliament sat in Edinburgh under a Labour–Liberal coalition government. The SNP was the official opposition with just under 30 per cent of the vote. Voters now trusted it more than Labour to serve Scotland's interests.[12] In its first two years, Parliament succeeded in eroding the domination of the centre by approaching issues like education and health care with distinctly Scottish policies that broke from the line dictated in the south by the Labour government. Thus, the Parliament at Edinburgh rather than the one at Westminster was becoming the focus of Scottish politics.

The Welsh and Cultural Nationalism

While Scotland's identity was firmly rooted in its separateness from England, Wales's relationship with its more powerful neighbour was more ambiguous, in part because there was considerable interpenetration between the two. The result has been a greater Welsh willingness to embrace a British identity, as was described by John Osmond:

> Indeed, it is possible to argue that the particular Britishness of the people of Wales is the thing that most distinguishes them from the rest of the peoples of the United Kingdom. At more than one historical moment the very idea of Britain was forged in Wales: from the times of Arthurian myth, through the roles of key leaders like Henry VII and Lloyd George, to the more modern experiences of the industrial revolution and the creation of the Labour movement.[13]

The Welsh identity, therefore, has been infused by an exchange with England. Nonconformist religion (that is, non-Anglican Protestantism) and trade unionism were two especially important English imports which were embraced by the Welsh, given a distinctively Welsh character and incorporated into a Welsh cultural identity. Religion, in particular, became central to Welshness in the nineteenth century. The perceived oppression of Nonconformists by an established English Church representing a minority of the Welsh people helped define an emergent nationalism after 1880, while the first triumph for Welsh distinctiveness was the disestablishment of that church in 1920. As in Scotland and England, however, Welsh Protestantism declined in the twentieth century as a result of urbanisation, secularisation and migration, a decline that accelerated after 1945. Thus religion ceased to provide a strong basis for national identity.

That left the language as the key badge of Welshness. Nineteenth-century Wales was divided between the north and west, which were predominantly Welsh-speaking and agricultural, and the south and east, which were closer to the English border. More importantly, after 1870 the south was a centre of in-migration from England as a result of the region's coal mines and the industrialisation they brought. This population influx made Wales unique among the Celtic nations: as late as 1901–11, the rate of immigration into Wales was surprisingly close to that of the United States at a time when the flow to America was at its peak.[14] English hegemony in the nineteenth century assured an attack on the Welsh language, which a commission report in 1846 branded as 'evil'. It was not used in the elementary schools until the end of the century, and even then it was only used to teach English. In fact, the inclination of Welsh local education authorities was to facilitate Welsh integration into an English-speaking mainstream – where all administrative and legal business was conducted in English, all official documents were in English and the most likely routes to economic improvement required a knowledge of English.[15] More important than institutional discrimination, however, it was industrialisation and the immigration it brought that reduced the proportion of Welsh speakers. Still, in 1911 43.5 per cent of the population over the age of three spoke Welsh, and the absolute number of Welsh speakers, which had roughly doubled during the century, broke one million. Enough of those were in the industrial south to assure that it remained a genuinely national language – one that was fed by a Welsh-language press and literature.[16]

The twentieth century brought fresh forces that eroded the number of Welsh speakers. While the depression reversed the flow of migration between the wars, the old pattern reasserted itself after the Second World War. Post-war prosperity along the south coast drew immigrants from England, as did the expansion of greater Liverpool in the northeast. The coastal areas of the northwest drew English retirees, while more recently a booming tourist industry based on the rugged mountain and coastal scenery brought English entrepreneurs and those who saw Wales as a beautiful place to have a summer home. Mass media and entertainment also played their part. Films, of course, were always in English. Prior to the advent of separate Welsh-language stations in 1980, radio and television were London-based, and broadcasts were in English with some Welsh programming. While Scotland had a vibrant indigenous press, Wales did not. Some local newspapers were in Welsh, but there were few national newspapers at all, as most of the population read the British papers. Thus, the decline in the percentage of Welsh speakers continued – from about 37 per cent in 1931 to 28 per cent in 1951 and about 20 per cent from 1971 to 1991.[17]

The Welsh language helped to shape Welsh cultural identity in a variety of ways, beyond the mere fact that large numbers of people spoke it. All nations have cultural symbols that almost become stereotypes, as outsiders somehow take them as the sum total of the national culture. For Wales, there are two such: rugby and singing. The Welsh musical tradition was invented in the eighteenth century, but it spread through the population more broadly between 1780 and 1850 with the hymn singing of the Nonconformist chapels. After 1945, Welsh music-making became internationalised with the founding of several classical music organisations that began to travel – the BBC National Orchestra of Wales and the Welsh National Opera being the best known – and the production of a string of world-famous opera singers.[*] Poetry, which might be viewed as a different manifestation of musicality, was as important to the cultural revival of the eighteenth century as music was. The national eisteddfod – a gathering of Welsh poetic and musical culture, as well as of literature, oratory and pageantry – emerged in its modern form between 1790 and the mid-nineteenth century. More recently, it was expanded to include the artistic, intellectual and popular. The introduction of a Welsh-only rule in 1950 more clearly identified that culture with the language.

There was a vibrant Welsh-language literature that flourished

---

[*] Among the best-known singers were Gwyneth Jones, Stuart Burrows, Margaret Price, Geraint Evans and Bryn Terfel.

between the wars and after the Second World War. Yet Wales's most famous poet of the twentieth century – Dylan Thomas – wrote in English. Herein lay the problem of tying Welsh identity solely to the language. It might seem puzzling that anyone could say that Thomas and the other writers whose works were in English were somehow less Welsh. Yet cultural nationalists did say so. Furthermore, many writers in English, like the post-war poet R. S. Thomas, accepted their inferior place in the Welsh cultural hierarchy because they believed the language to be central to defining the nation. Nevertheless the English-language literature very much reflected Welsh sensibilities and issues. Between the wars, writers in English broke new ground, as novelists like Jack Jones and Gwyn Thomas rejected a romanticised rural (and Welsh-speaking) Wales and took the industrial (and Anglo) Wales of the south as their subject. The Welsh-language novels of Kate Roberts offered the same kind of unvarnished view of the slate-mining communities of North Wales.

As the works of Thomas and Jones show, there was another Wales that was self-consciously Welsh in a way that was divorced from the language. This was the Wales of the mining and manufacturing districts of the south – a Wales created by the coal and iron of the Industrial Revolution and populated by immigrants, whether from the Welsh-speaking north or from England. Its Welsh identity was tied to trade unionism and the Labour Party, just as the identity of the north had been tied to Nonconformity and the Liberal Party. Aneurin Bevan was the representative political hero of the former, David Lloyd George of the latter. At the turn of the century, nearly half the population of Wales was either directly or indirectly dependent on the coal industry. Thus industrial Wales, like industrial Scotland, suffered mightily from the inter-war depression. Unemployment in 1932 was 38 per cent for all of Wales, and over 50 per cent in some of the mining areas.[18] After the war, decline continued – despite full employment and a programme of modernisation, including the sinking of new mines. Facing the conversion of the economy to other fuels, the National Coal Board closed more and more old and inefficient mines. As a result, the 130,000 miners in Wales in the 1950s fell to 50,000 in the early 1970s and 20,000 in the early 1980s. By 1992, only four collieries were left in South Wales employing 1,300 men. Steel did well in the 1950s and 1960s, with expanding demand and new investment. By the 1970s, however, it, too, was becoming a sick industry. British Steel employed 63,000 in Wales in 1979; following Thatcherite rationalisation, the number had fallen to 19,000 by 1983.[19]

Because of the decline of the staple industries, Wales, like Scotland, was the target of government development policies. Direct government investment in nationalised industries sought to slow their decline, while incentives encouraged private sector investment in new industries so as to diversify the economy and soak up some of the unemployment that resulted from that decline. South Wales was the major beneficiary of this policy. During the war the government had begun to bring new industries (like chemicals and vehicles) into the region. Now that process expanded. Between 1945 and 1949, Attlee's government sponsored 112 of the 179 new factories or extensions of factories built there, while reducing unemployment to 2.8 per cent.[20] Over the next decades, new industries sprung up around Cardiff and Newport – mostly light industries, like consumer goods, but also a sprinkling of heavy industries like chemicals, oil refining, cars and engineering. At the same time, South Wales benefited from the rapid growth of the service sector, not least due to the location of government offices and non-governmental organisations in Cardiff. The net effect by the 1980s was a far more diverse economy and a higher level of prosperity for most of the population, including the working class, but also a much higher level of unemployment than had existed in the 1950s and 1960s. The main loser in this restructuring, apart from the coal-mining areas, was rural Wales. Rural areas benefited only sporadically from new industry and the growth of tourism. Although agriculture was modernised and subsidised by the state, some rural areas were as poor as any region in the EC. Indeed, despite all the improvements, Wales was the poorest region of the UK in the

1990s, or second to Northern Ireland, depending on the measure.[21]

The effect of economic decline in the mining valleys of the south was to reinforce Welsh radicalism. Since the advent of meaningful democracy in 1867 and 1884, political radicalism was far more central to the Welsh identity than to Scotland's. The party of the left therefore dominated Welsh politics after 1885. The Liberals' appeal was based on Nonconformist grievances and a populist anti-landlordism directed at rural Wales. The effort to disestablish the Anglican Church in Wales was the first great nationalist crusade there. Success in 1920, however, brought a collapse of nationalism during the depressed inter-war years, while Labour replaced the Liberals as the party of the left. Labour's appeal was based on working-class issues of importance to the south – nationalisation of industry, full employment and trade union rights. Its dominance verged on the overwhelming after the Second World War, as the party won from 27 to 32 of Wales's 36 seats between 1950 and 1970. Nonetheless, its programme did not have much to offer the rural north; so it left an opening for a nationalist movement based on language.

Plaid Cymru was founded in 1925 to pursue the goal of dominion status for Wales; however, its real aim was to defend Welsh culture, and most particularly the Welsh language. The driving force in articulating its vision was J. Saunders Lewis, a major Welsh-language writer from the 1920s to the 1970s. Lewis detested industrialisation, urbanisation and centralisation. Yet he loathed socialism because it was just as materialistic, centralising and as impersonal as capitalism itself. A romantic, he believed that Welsh-speaking rural communities would serve as a much more effective barrier than socialism against a soulless international capitalism. Lewis's goal therefore was not merely preservation of the language, but its primacy in Wales as the language of government and of speech. Such views appealed only to a narrow group of academics and intellectuals and assured that the party remained on the fringe of politics until the 1960s.

The factors that contributed to the rise of Welsh nationalism and an interest in devolution after the war were much the same as in Scotland. The apparent failure of state centralism to reverse the decline of key industries led to an erosion of the solid support for Labour after 1966. At the same time, pressure on the central government after 1945 to recognise Wales as a separate area for economic development and planning, and to devolve ever more responsibilities to separate Welsh organisations, culminated in the creation of the Welsh Office in 1964. While Wales was far behind Scotland, it began to take on a separate administrative identity, which in turn made the argument for democratic oversight of this burgeoning bureaucracy more compelling. The decline of Britain as an economic and imperial power simultaneously made separation seem less drastic in its consequences. Finally, people were increasingly annoyed that Tory governments could dictate policy for a Wales that consistently returned large anti-Tory majorities. The issue that crystallised this discontent was water – which had some of the same galvanising effect in Wales that oil had in Scotland. In the late 1950s, Macmillan's government approved the flooding of the Tryweryn valley, with the destruction of a Welsh-speaking village, to provide a water supply for Liverpool. No Welsh body at any level had a legal right to influence this decision, even though it drew universal condemnation in Wales. There could be no clearer evidence of how English concerns overrode Welsh wishes and interests. Water became a significant issue again in the 1970s and 1980s, as the reorganisation of water supply for Britain made manifest that, while 'Wales's water' was supplying England, the Welsh were actually paying higher water rates.

The Tryweryn affair helped turn Labour decisively in favour of the creation of a Welsh Office headed by a Secretary of State, paralleling the long-existing Scottish Office. Historically, Welsh Labour MPs, however nationalist they may have been, were more committed to the party's socialist agenda than to national claims for Wales. Bevan had embodied this priority and opposed Welsh devolution after the Second World War. However, Jim Griffiths, a trade unionist who was second only to Bevan in the Welsh

Labour pantheon, was much more of a nationalist. He persuaded Attlee to create a Council for Wales to vet Welsh issues and offer advice to governments. When its inadequacies became evident in the 1950s, Griffiths, backed by some of the younger Welsh Labour MPs, led the movement to create the Welsh Office, and he became the first Welsh Secretary when that campaign triumphed in 1964. Its initial functions were limited to housing, roads and local government; however, its responsibilities and the size of its staff continued to expand through the 1960s and 1970s, adding health, education and economic development.

Yet even as Labour showed greater sensitivity to Welsh distinctiveness, a new and more radical nationalism emerged, built around the preservation and revival of the language. It was led by a new generation of idealists who were the product of the University of Wales (whose constituent colleges were founded in the late nineteenth century), but many of them were English speakers. They focused on issues like Welsh-language schools, equal status for Welsh in government and law, Welsh road signs and Welsh-language radio and television stations. In the 1960s, they began to adopt the tactics of protest, civil disobedience and, at the extreme, attacks on property. Thereafter, violence (including arson and bombs) was an intermittent tactic of a fringe of militant nationalists. While the violence created some embarrassment for the political establishment, these extra-political movements achieved results. The Welsh language was given equal status in government and law in 1967; dual-language road signs became the norm in the 1970s; and the number of Welsh-language schools expanded throughout the 1960s and 1970s – first in the English-speaking areas of the south, where middle-class Welsh-speaking parents demanded them, and then in the Welsh-speaking areas of the north. By the mid-1990s, knowledge of Welsh had become an asset in getting a job. As a result, virtually all schools taught it. Yet this privileging of Welsh as *the* badge of national identity annoyed many English speakers, who resented the fact that they were viewed as 'less Welsh', even though they conceded the central importance of the language to Welshness.

Thus, the new language militancy created a problem for Plaid Cymru if it was going to be a successful political party. Its leader from 1945 to 1981 was Gwynfor Evans. Evans saw the need for the party to broaden its appeal beyond a narrow group of Welsh-speaking intellectuals, students and rural communities, and to embrace issues of concern to trade unionists and the growing suburban middle class. Evans shared Lewis's dislike of proletarianisation and a centralising socialism, but he rejected any backward-looking aspirations to an idealised rural past. His Nonconformist background and pacifism enabled him to appeal to the old moral tradition of Nonconformist liberalism. He fully supported the issues raised by the language activists, but he also recognised that both the issues and the militancy alienated English-speaking voters who might be attracted to a policy of devolution and ultimately independence. The potential for the party became manifest when Evans won the Carmarthen by-election in 1966. Even more important was the 1967 by-election in the Labour stronghold of Rhondda West in the coal-mining region, when a Labour majority of 17,000 in 1966 was cut to just 2,300. Suddenly, as the full effects of economic retrenchment began to be felt, Plaid Cymru had a political credibility for disgruntled working-class voters that it had never had before. It also benefited as voters were turned off by the corruption of Labour-dominated local governments that had monopolised power for too long. To capitalise on its new opportunities, the party began to articulate a more carefully formulated economic policy for Wales based on planned development. By February 1974, with the economy more of a mess than ever, Plaid Cymru was strong enough to win two seats, and in October it won three. At the same time, it began to expand its base in local government. By the mid-1970s, it had secured a position as the alternative to Labour in the rural Welsh-speaking northwest.

As Plaid Cymru was getting stronger, the character of the Welsh Labour Party changed. Historically, it had been dominated by the miners, but with the decline of coal a new generation of university men was being elected whose roots were rural. Thus, the old Bevanite priority of socialism before nationalism began to be challenged. The emergence of Plaid Cymru as a viable political force reinforced the pressure for Labour to develop a more ambitious policy for Wales. So did Labour's performance in the February 1974 general election, when for the first time since the war it got less than 50 per cent of the Welsh vote and won 'only' twenty-four seats.[22] Thus, the Labour government had to do something to satisfy Welsh nationalist aspirations. Yet Wales always remained a secondary concern compared to Scotland, and Labour's devolution bill reflected this lower priority, as it gave the proposed Welsh Assembly only attenuated administrative powers. Nationalists welcomed it nonetheless, on the assumption that those powers would be expanded later. While Plaid Cymru campaigned for the bill in the referendum, however, Labour MPs from the old industrial areas of the south took the lead in opposing it. Its overwhelming defeat, with only 20 per cent of the vote by only 10 per cent of the electorate, was seen as a blow for the nationalists. The evidence of opinion polls, however, indicated that there was substantially more support for devolution than for the government's proposals. People who voted 'no' felt that the additional cost of a new layer of government outweighed any gains from the few responsibilities devolved and the greater democratic accountability. The defeat also reflected the continuing power of the linguistic divide in Wales: people of each community (Welsh- and English-speaking) feared that an assembly would promote the interests of and become a vehicle of patronage for the other at their own expense.

Thatcherism had much the same effect in Wales as in Scotland, though perhaps not to the same degree. South Wales had adapted better to economic change than had the area around Glasgow, while Peter Walker, Thatcher's Welsh Secretary from 1987 to 1990, promoted economic and infrastructure development which further benefited the region. Both South Wales and those parts of North Wales near greater Liverpool profited from new foreign investment in the 1980s. Still, with 43 per cent of the workforce state employed in 1979 and 19 per cent of the male workforce employed in the mining or metals industries, there remained much room for further attrition in the face of the government's assault on the public sector.[23] The national response to the miners' strike of 1984–5 reflected the people's sense that something distinctively Welsh was under attack. People from all parts of the country came together as part of miners' support organisations in defence of the mining *communities*, rather than in support of the strike *per se*.

Plaid Cymru responded to Thatcherism by focusing less on parliamentary politics and more on revising its policies so it could expand its support. In 1981, it committed itself to a decentralised, community-based socialism that was quite different from the centralised socialism of Labour, while later in the decade it reversed years of hostility to the EC. After Labour's 1983 debacle, it set out to challenge Labour as the party of the left in Wales. In this it had only modest success. With the Welshman Neil Kinnock as Labour's leader after 1983, and with his efforts to pull the party back from left-wing extremism, the party was able to slowly rebuild its strength in Wales – from a low of 20 MPs in 1983 to a more normal 27 in 1992. The departure of Kinnock after the defeat that year, combined with the effects of more than ten years of Tory policies, opened the way for Labour to make a more decisive commitment in favour of devolution. At the same time, the efforts of John Redwood, Major's Welsh Secretary from 1992 to 1995, to impose full-blooded Thatcherite reforms on the Welsh bureaucracy, further accelerated the swing away from the Tories. Major's reform of local government, with the appointment of ever more non-representative 'quangos' to manage Welsh affairs, had the same effect. As in Scotland, reform was pushed through despite the angry opposition of the people, who were hardly consulted. Nonetheless, the popular support for the self-government that Labour offered, with limited legislative power and no power of taxation, remained shallow. The referendum held by the Blair government in 1997 passed by only 50.3 per cent to 49.7 per cent on a 50 per cent turnout, although this outcome was still a significant turnaround from the dismal result of 1979.[24] Support for reform came from Welsh speakers and those who saw themselves as Welsh, primarily because they hoped that self-government would lead to improvements in the NHS and the economy in Wales.[25] This base of support was reflected in the first election to the Assembly, which came into existence in Cardiff in 1999: Labour's margin over Plaid Cymru was only 37.6 per cent to 28.4 per cent of the vote. Plaid Cymru, which never before had been a significant electoral presence in Wales, was now clearly established as the most viable alternative to Labour when defining internal Welsh politics.

The Northern Irish and Religious Identities

The crisis in Northern Ireland began innocuously enough in the mid-1960s when Catholics, inspired by the American Civil Rights movement, launched a series of peaceful protests. The specific focus initially was the unfair allocation of council houses; however, the underlying agenda was a much broader assertion of the principle of equality as it is understood in every Western democracy: equality of rights, equality under the law and equality of opportunity. The 1920 Government of Ireland Act that gave Home Rule to Northern Ireland had built-in protections for the Catholic minority; however, the Protestant government had subverted or ignored them, and by 1930 it was clear that Westminster would not interfere. Political boundaries were therefore gerrymandered to assure Protestant domination at every level of government, while there was not full adult suffrage in local elections. Thus, there was no political equality. The overwhelmingly Protestant police force, the Royal Ulster Constabulary (RUC) and its paramilitary auxiliary the B Specials, reinforced Protestant domination by harassing and intimidating Catholics in times of crisis. The judiciary, like the police, was mostly Protestants and biased against the Catholic population, which many of them viewed with contempt. Thus, there could be no equality under the law. The arbitrariness of the law was symbolised by the Special Powers Act of 1922, which gave the government virtually unlimited power to issue any regulation it wished relating to law and order – powers that were used to reinforce Catholic subordination.

Nor was there equality of opportunity. On the contrary, job discrimination helped consolidate Protestant rule, for it assured a steady flow of Catholic emigrants to Britain and America. Emigration received a further impetus because Northern Ireland's economy was dependent on two failing industries, shipbuilding and linen manufacture. They employed roughly 60 per cent of the workforce between the wars, when they began their long-term decline. As a result, the province's rate of unemployment averaged 27 per cent in the 1930s.[26] These problems continued, with only brief hiccups, after 1945, while the most expansive sector – the civil service – overwhelmingly favoured Protestants in its employment practices. This combination of discrimination and a contracting industrial base limited job opportunities for Catholics; so many left. Their steady emigration assured that the Protestant majority of the population remained at two-to-one, even though the Catholic birth rate was higher. Hence there was nothing innocent about the Catholic demand for civil rights. It went to the heart of Protestant control of Northern Ireland, which was based on institutionalised discrimination just as much as white domination of the South in the United States was under the 'Jim Crow' era from the 1890s through the 1950s.

Northern Irish Unionists (those who supported the Union with Britain) were not inclined to make concessions to the Catholics. They had a siege mentality which saw conspiracies against Protestantism and the separate existence of their state everywhere. They never trusted the British government, and every time the British even hinted at the possibility of some sort of compromise with (or even negotiation with) the Irish Republic, they saw a sellout. At the same time, the very existence of the IRA, the para-military organisation committed to the union of all Ireland under the Republic, was sufficient evidence of the reality of the threat they faced. Ulster Protestants feared Catholicism, which they associated with papal domination and priestly rule. They claimed that both suppressed independent thought and sought to keep the people ignorant, obedient and submissive. Theirs was the rhetoric of the seventeenth century, when many of the Protestants had first settled in Ireland. At that time, both Protestants and Catholics had good reason to fear the other. Often enough during more than a century of warfare throughout Europe, each had sought to exterminate the other, or at least impose forced conversion on the other. The policies of seventeenth-century Europe, however, were not those of the twentieth century. While Catholicism was the established religion of the Republic, and it defined the values of the state, this ascendancy did not involve discrimination against or persecution of Protestants. Following the liberalisation of laws in Britain in the 1960s, however, it did mean that life would not be identical under British and Irish rule. Thereafter, divorce and abortion were relatively easy in the north and illegal in the south, until a referendum approved limited divorce reform in 1995. Northern Irish Protestants, however, were not social liberals. Indeed, opposition to pre-marital sex, pornography and homosexuality linked the Protestant and Catholic communities there.[27] In the end, it is difficult to escape the conclusion that, while religion was central to the identity of both communities in Northern Ireland, the fears generated by Catholic equality were political rather than religious. The Protestants were not prepared to compromise their power to dominate the minority.

Northern Ireland's Catholic community had simply withdrawn from politics in the 1920s. However, the Catholic middle class began to increase in size after the war, as a result of the introduction of free secondary education in 1947 and the expansion of university education in the 1960s. This generation showed a greater willingness to engage politically, and the civil rights movement grew out of this new political activism. The other impetus came from the government of Terrence O'Neill, who became Prime Minister in 1963. O'Neill wanted to promote the same kind of economic diversification that was going on in Scotland and Wales. An expansion of council housing was part of O'Neill's modernisation programme – thus defining the initial focus of the civil rights movement. O'Neill, who had some of the paternalism of his landowning ancestors, was willing to contemplate an agreement with moderate Catholics. The extent (or limit) of O'Neillite reform was defined in 1968: the equitable distribution of public housing, the end to gerrymandering in local government and the repeal of the Special Powers Act. The Protestant extremists, however, would accept no compromise. They responded to the civil rights movement as they had to every demand for Catholic equality since the 1790s, with counter-demonstrations, intimidation and violence. Given the overwhelming (and justified) Catholic distrust of the RUC, whose own biases became overt in these showdowns, the British government finally had to send troops to Northern Ireland in 1969 to protect the Catholic community. Since the Home Secretary James Callaghan was fully behind civil rights reforms, direct British intervention was welcomed by the Catholics.

Unfortunately, the British army's traditions were on the side of the Protestants, not the Catholics. Army officers had been sympathetic to the Ulster Protestants who had threatened rebellion in 1914, and, following the Easter Rising of 1916, the army had imposed martial law and treated all Catholics as potential traitors, even though only a tiny number had supported the rising. Army hostility to the Catholics erupted during the 1919–21 guerrilla war waged by the IRA for Irish independence – a war which begot atrocities on both sides. The attitudes of hatred and resentment generated by this history of conflict did not easily die out within the British army, any more than they did within the IRA. Thus, when a reconstituted Provisional IRA took advantage of the appearance of British troops to relaunch the war of independence, the soldiers responded as they had during previous conflicts – with the assumption that all Catholics were potential IRA sympathisers.* The army therefore increasingly focused its

---

* The IRA had split in 1969, between the 'official' IRA, which sought to pursue a Marxist agenda rather than the war against the British, and the Provisional IRA, which stood by the traditional aims and tactics. The Provisional IRA took the lead in the war against the British army. All those engaged in that war will be referred to here as the IRA.

policing functions on the Catholic population, not on the Protestants who had brought them there in the first place. By 1970 and 1971, the old war between the British army and the IRA was fully reactivated, and the army's treatment of the Catholic population helped the IRA to win the popular support that the army thought was there all along. The climax came on 'Bloody Sunday' in January 1972, when British troops fired on Catholic demonstrators in Londonderry (Derry), killing thirteen of them. (One of the wounded died later, his death attributed to injuries sustained that day.) With order in Northern Ireland breaking down, the Heath government took over direct rule of the province – one of the goals of the IRA, which saw it as the first step towards driving the British out altogether.

Why, then, didn't the British just leave? It is not an easy question to answer, though easy answers are offered. The Republican answer was imperialism. The British, they claimed, had long had an irrepressible drive to dominate the Irish; so British rule would end only when they were driven out. It may be true, but this explanation runs counter to recent British history. For whatever Britain's drive for empire once was, after 1945 British governments had let go if the colonial people were able to impose a cost to holding on. The IRA imposed such a cost, so why should Northern Ireland be different? In the past, Britain had a security interest in Ireland. British governments feared that a Catholic Ireland would link up with their continental enemies, who often were Catholic too. Every time the British tightened their grip on Ireland, it was in response to such a security threat during a war: against the Spanish in the 1590s, when Queen Elizabeth I launched the final successful conquest of Ireland; against the French in the 1690s, when William III reluctantly turned the government of Ireland over to the ascendant Protestants; and against the French in 1799–1800, when William Pitt the Younger bought the acquiescence of the Irish Parliament to the Act of Union. Even the misjudged British response to the Easter Rising of 1916 was provoked by a war and the threat that the Republicans would ally with the Germans. But Britain's security arrangements

495

had been transformed after the Second World War. On the one hand, Ireland was hardly likely to ally with the enemies of NATO; on the other hand, the Soviet Union did not need bases in Ireland to destroy Britain with nuclear weapons. Hence, Ireland had become irrelevant to Britain's security.

Another reason often offered for the British presence in Northern Ireland was economic. This is another version of the imperialism argument, but it is an imperialism based on economic self-interest rather than 'racial' domination. In the nineteenth century, Ulster was the most economically advanced and prosperous province in Ireland. This prosperity died, however, with the decline of linen and shipbuilding. Since the Second World War, Northern Ireland consistently had the highest unemployment rate in the United Kingdom (see Table 11.1)[28] – thus reducing its economic output and requiring more benefit payments from the British Treasury. The 'troubles' since 1969 merely made matters worse, as the violence discouraged new investment there. As a result, it became a terrible drain on British resources. In 1973–4, the net British subvention for Northern Ireland (i.e. the excess of British payments into Northern Ireland over tax revenues from Northern Ireland) was £313 million, or 37 per cent of total public sector expenditure there; by 1992–3, it was estimated at £3,500 million (including £300 million for the army), now 47 per cent of public expenditure there.[29] The primary expense for Britain clearly was not the military, but the pensions and insurance payments by the British welfare state. These figures, however, did not represent the whole of the cost, for they omitted the British soldiers killed in Northern Ireland (444 between 1971 and 1993),[30] the British civilians killed by IRA terrorist acts in Great Britain and the damage to British property as a result of IRA bombs. Surely, whatever pleasure the British got from dominating Irish Catholics could not begin to compensate for all this.

And yet the British would not walk away, although they did so in India and Palestine, and though most of the British people probably would have been glad to be rid of the whole Irish mess.

In part, perhaps, the persistence was due to cussedness – a determination not to be driven out and so appear to give way to IRA terrorism. In part, perhaps, there was a genuine sense of responsibility – recognising that this was a problem created by the British (far more than in India or Palestine), and so they had some obligation to try to resolve it. Finally, there was almost surely a genuine fear of civil war. For, contrary to Republican mythology, the Protestants in Northern Ireland were not the tools of British imperialism – although the Conservatives between 1886 and 1921 were glad to use them to political advantage. The Protestants were every bit as determined as the IRA, with their own paramilitary organisations dating back to the 1912–14 resistance to Home Rule, and they had shown just as much willingness as the IRA to fight for what they wanted. And what they wanted was to remain part of the United Kingdom – or rather, not to be part of the Irish Republic. So Protestant resistance was not likely to dissipate if the British pulled out, and a united Ireland could have a guerrilla war on its hands that is every bit as vicious as that which the British faced for nearly thirty years. The political leaders of the Republic did not want unification on these terms. Indeed, by the 1960s unification had ceased to be a preoccupation of the people of the South. As a result, from 1973 on, the Irish government consistently affirmed the principle that the status of Northern Ireland could not be changed except with the approval of the majority of its people. Thus, the British stayed, and with at least the implicit approval of the Irish government.

This acquiescence, however, did not mean that Irish politicians were happy with British rule in Northern Ireland. On the contrary, the period from 1972 to 1982 in particular was a disaster for Anglo-Irish relations. Between 1972 and 1975, the Heath and Wilson governments pursued a two-pronged strategy, based on trying to suppress the IRA while developing a system of government in which Catholics and Protestants shared power. The latter came close to success with the Sunningdale Agreement of December 1973. Brian Faulkner, the leader of the Ulster Unionist Party – the largest of the Protestant parties – was willing to risk working with moderate Catholics. In 1970, John Hume and Gerry Fitt had launched the Social Democratic and Labour Party (SDLP) as a constitutional nationalist party that was willing to accept British rule, in the short run, in return for justice for Catholics. Following the election of a new assembly for the province, the moderate Irish parties worked out a power-sharing agreement among themselves. At Sunningdale, Heath's Secretary of State for Northern Ireland, William Whitelaw, brokered a deal that brought the Irish government on board, creating a Council for Ireland with significant powers. In return, the Irish affirmed that Northern Ireland's status should be determined by the majority of its people, not of the Irish people as a whole. Thus, for the first time in the history of Northern Ireland, Catholics participated in the government.

This was too much for the Unionist rank and file, who repudiated the agreement. Militant Protestants, led by the Reverend Ian Paisley, opposed any accommodation of the Catholics and involvement of the Republic as the first step down the slippery slope towards Irish unification. Paisley came out of an Ulster evangelical Protestant tradition which viewed the Pope as anti-Christ. He had even condemned O'Neill's expression of sympathy to the Vatican upon the death of Pope John XXIII in 1963. During the resistance to the civil rights movement, Paisley had shown his ability to mobilise Protestant workers – who resented a paternalist political establishment that ignored them – behind the cause of sectarianism. Now the workers, supported by Protestant paramilitaries and Paisley, organised a strike in May 1974 that brought down the power-sharing government. Wilson then tried a new initiative with the election of a constitutional convention to negotiate a political arrangement agreeable to all the parties. It was an exercise in futility, however, since there was no common ground that linked them. Thereafter, much to the annoyance of the Republic's leaders, Labour defaulted on seeking a political solution.

The other prong of British policy undermined whatever Catholic goodwill might have come out of Sunningdale. The

Special Powers Act had always been there for the government of Northern Ireland to use to preserve the law. As the British army came to view the IRA as its principal enemy, the British government appropriated these powers with Prevention of Terrorism Acts. The most controversial, which was launched in 1971 before direct rule, was the power to intern without trial anyone suspected of subversive activities – which meant anyone thought to have an IRA connection. It was the aftermath of the 1916 Easter Rising all over again, as every Irish Catholic became a suspect. Since the RUC's intelligence was out of date, many of the people arrested had no IRA connection at all, while those who did often escaped over the border to the Republic. In addition to the arrests, many more Catholics were harassed by stop-and-search procedures. The IRA responded by stepping up the war against the army, and in 1974 it carried the campaign to the British mainland with bombs that took civilian lives. So the ordinary procedures of law were short-circuited at home, too, when dealing with terrorist suspects. People arrested for murders resulting from IRA bombs too often were convicted unjustly, based on insufficient or even fabricated evidence – convictions that many years later were overturned. Thus, the whole system of justice came unstuck – for understandable reasons, when British lives were lost, but resulting in perversions of justice nonetheless. A war waged with such ferocity on both sides led to a horrifying loss of life. Two hundred and sixty British soldiers and 1,234 Irish civilians were killed in Northern Ireland from 1971 to 1976 – in both cases nearly 60 per cent of the total number of violent deaths between 1971 and 1993. Half of all violent deaths in 1971–6 were the result of Republican violence; 12 per cent were inflicted by the security forces; the rest were perpetrated by Protestant Loyalists, whom the British army mostly ignored as it conducted its war with the IRA.[31]

The aim of the civil rights policy was to reconcile the Catholic community to British rule. Yet the effect of internment was merely to enhance the influence of the IRA, even though many Catholics were appalled by the violence. So in 1976 internment was ended, and the British tried to return policing functions to the RUC and the legal system. However, the system of justice still compromised fundamental rights that were guaranteed in a liberal society. Most importantly, suspects in terrorist offences were not given jury trials, as the British did not trust Catholic jurors and feared IRA intimidation. Furthermore, confessions were taken at face value, as was the evidence of infiltrators into the IRA, even when there was no independent corroboration. Inevitably the police sometimes resorted to unacceptable methods to secure confessions, while inside agents (supergrasses) sometimes gave the RUC the evidence they knew it wanted. Judges tended to accept both sources without asking too many awkward questions. As a result, while there was some easing of tension between the army and the Catholic population after 1976, the latter still had little confidence that the system of justice was fair. Their scepticism was reinforced whenever heavy-handed action by the army led to civilian deaths. The army and RUC seemed too inclined to resort to force when dealing with Catholics, especially when engaged in undercover operations against IRA suspects, while British soldiers were very rarely held accountable for the accidental murder of unarmed Catholic civilians.

The British, however, seemed satisfied with the status quo that emerged after the end of internment. A political solution based on agreement between Protestants and Catholics seemed hopeless, so the government stopped looking for one. Loss of life in Northern Ireland was reduced to 'acceptable' levels, especially among British soldiers. Even civilian deaths from the violence dropped significantly.* While Britain lost some respect in the international community because of human rights violations, the government and people were sympathetic to their troops. They felt that the soldiers were engaged in a thankless task, trying to root out terrorism among a hostile population while preserving

---

* Civilian deaths from violence had averaged 206 per year from 1971 to 1976; from 1977 to 1981 they averaged 55 per year. Boyle and Hadden, *Northern Ireland: The Choice*, pp. 70–71.

the peace between Catholics and Protestants. Any mistakes, they believed, were made in good faith – that is, accidental civilian deaths occurred when a soldier either genuinely believed he was under threat or that the civilian was a member of the IRA and was trying to escape. The British public had little use for an international community that criticised them but not the human rights abuses of the IRA, which deliberately murdered innocent people (as did the Protestant paramilitaries). The IRA occasionally was able to bring the cost directly to the British people, with terrorist acts in Britain itself. Nonetheless, the British were inclined to believe they were doing their best, discount Catholic grievances against them and accept the military stand-off.

The government of Ireland was very unhappy with this passive attitude. It was primarily Catholics who were being killed, and it was Britain's responsibility to try to find some way to end the violence. The IRA was also dissatisfied with the new status quo. For despite their grievances, Northern Irish Catholics were accepting life with the reduced level of violence. Hence, their support for the IRA waned. Some of the most high-profile murders came during this period – most notably the 1979 murders of Airey Neave,* Thatcher's likely Northern Ireland Secretary, and Earl Mountbatten, the Queen's cousin and the hero of Indian independence. At the same time, the IRA started to focus public attention on the status of its prisoners convicted of terrorist acts. It insisted they were political prisoners, for they had acted out of political motives, and so should not be treated like common criminals – wearing the same dress, being subject to the same discipline and having the same visiting rights. In their campaign for special status, IRA prisoners within the Maze (the highest security prison in Belfast) resorted to hunger strikes in 1980 and 1981. The IRA hunger strikes, however, gave Thatcher just the kind of opportunity she craved to demonstrate that she would not give way to coercion. In May and June of 1981

---

* Neave was murdered not by the IRA, but by the more militant Irish National Liberation Army.

the hunger strikers began to die – first Bobby Sands, their leader, and then nine more before the strikes were called off. The hunger strikes had just the political effect the IRA wanted, generating revived support for their cause among Catholics in Northern Ireland, the Republic and the United States, while increasing tensions between Britain and Ireland. Despite her victory, therefore, Thatcher saw that there had to be progress on the political front. The political costs of continued inaction were too high. Even after the IRA tried to kill Thatcher herself with a bomb at the Grand Hotel in Brighton during the Conservative Party conference in 1984, the impetus remained for her to negotiate – including pressure from Washington.

The result was the 1985 Anglo-Irish Agreement between Thatcher and the Irish Taoiseach Garret FitzGerald. FitzGerald's Fine Gael Party was more hostile to the IRA than Fianna Fáil; however, Irish politicians of all stripes had an interest in accommodation with Britain on acceptable terms. They did not want an increase in the influence of the IRA and Sinn Fein (the political wing of the IRA), while Ireland would benefit from cross-border cooperation between the North and South. The Anglo-Irish Agreement was a dramatic step in that direction, although for the most part it resurrected principles established at Sunningdale. Once again, the Republic affirmed that the status of Northern Ireland could not be changed except by the consent of a majority of its people. In return, the British affirmed for the first time that, should a majority vote in favour of joining the Republic, Britain's government would facilitate such a reunion. More importantly, the British agreed to a standing Anglo-Irish conference, with a permanent secretariat, to discuss ways to promote better relations between the communities in Northern Ireland. This meant a dimension of Irish involvement that was well beyond that provided by Sunningdale. Finally, the Republic promised to improve cooperation with the RUC and the British army in the fight against terrorism – surely a key provision for Thatcher, although one that disappointed in its results.

The Anglo-Irish Agreement precipitated an explosion in

Northern Ireland's Protestant community. They rightly saw it as a watershed. For the first time, the British conceded that Northern Irish issues were no longer exclusively their internal affair. While the Republic did not participate in making policy for Northern Ireland, and certainly it had no veto over policy, it now had a recognised right to be interested in Britain's policy and to say what it thought. To the Protestants, this fatally compromised British sovereignty over Northern Ireland and so was the first step towards Irish unification. And shockingly, it had been taken by a Tory government. The party whose very identity since the Home Rule Bill of 1886 had been with preserving the Union, and which had long been the benevolent protector of even the most violent and anti-constitutional actions by Northern Ireland's Protestants, had sold them out. Most amazing of all, it had been done by the hard-line Thatcher, who had faced down the IRA hunger-strikers, and whom the Protestants trusted to stand firm against the pretensions of the South. Yet, as she would show repeatedly during her eleven years as Prime Minister, Thatcher was no traditional Tory politician. On the contrary, she repeatedly challenged the accepted wisdom that had been handed down in the party by its established elite, as she challenged the domination of the elite themselves, and Northern Ireland turned out to be no exception.

This sense of betrayal by their best friends made the Unionists furious over the Anglo-Irish Agreement. Once again, the real nature of Protestant 'loyalism' was revealed – as it had been when it organised to resist Home Rule by force in 1914, and again when it helped bring down the power-sharing government in 1974. Its loyalty to the British constitution always was conditional; nothing could be done in Northern Ireland to which the Protestants objected. As they had with Sunningdale, the militants led by Paisley organised to destroy the agreement. The British had to be shown that they could not change the political status quo in Northern Ireland without even consulting the Protestant majority. Thatcher, however, was no more inclined to be intimidated by Protestant extremists than she had been by their Catholic counterparts. She stood firm in the face of massive Protestant demonstrations, efforts to paralyse the province's economy, an acceleration of Protestant paramilitary violence – which by the 1990s was accounting for more deaths than the IRA – and the boycotting of political institutions. Although the Protestants failed to destroy the Anglo-Irish Agreement, however, they assured that it contributed little towards a settlement in Northern Ireland and an end to the violence. Without the Protestants, there would be no Northern Irish government and no peace. By 1990, both Hume and the Irish government had accepted that any way forward must incorporate the Unionists.

Thus, the British and Irish governments continued the search for some way to break the deadlock. There was little doubt that the overwhelming majority of Northern Ireland's Catholics wanted some sort of settlement, even though it meant remaining inside the United Kingdom. Despite all the problems with the army and the RUC, many Catholics' lives had improved under direct rule as the British imposed the goals of the civil rights movement. The principal beneficiaries were the growing Catholic middle class that had benefited from free university education in the UK. These professionals and government employees were now a significant force in the Catholic community. The British required fair employment practices by all the larger private employers in the province; and while many small establishments remained segregated, Catholics had their own segregated firms. Yet Catholics still had a significantly higher unemployment rate, which meant that Catholic workers were not profiting as much from civil rights reforms. In part, this was because the Northern Irish economy remained a mess as a result of the 'troubles'. Government policy tried to attract the same kind of foreign investment that was coming to Wales and Scotland, but it generally failed. Nonetheless, much of the higher Catholic unemployment rate could be accounted for by the RUC, which remained overwhelmingly Protestant. If, somehow, a way could be found to replace the RUC with a police force that was 40 per cent Catholic (like the population as a whole), the unemployment rate of

Catholics and Protestants would be nearly the same.[32] If there could be peace, then, there was every reason to believe that the Catholic community would thrive – though prosperity would be limited by the larger economic problems that the province shared with other parts of the United Kingdom.

There was a second incentive for an agreement. It was now more than fifteen years since Britain and Ireland had joined the European Community. Membership had allowed Ireland to break free of its economic dependence on Britain. In the 1990s, the Irish economy flourished; the effect was slowly to eliminate the prosperity gap between the two countries. The benefits of economic cooperation between the North and the South could only grow in such an environment. Most obviously, the interests of Northern farmers (most of whom were Protestants) were much closer to those of farmers in the Republic than to those of Britain's farmers; so the Republic could more effectively represent them in EC agricultural negotiations. Ireland's tourist industry was also booming; but tourists were discouraged from heading north as long as the violence persisted. North–South cooperation could mean a joint tourism programme, while Northern Ireland was marginal to British tourist promotion.

How was an agreement to be reached, however, when extremists on both sides opposed all compromise? John Hume, the leader of the SDLP, believed that the key to breaking the impasse was to bring Sinn Fein into the peace process. The prospects for such a move hardly seemed promising. Sinn Fein and the IRA opposed any solution that kept Northern Ireland part of the United Kingdom. Furthermore, the British government refused to negotiate with terrorists, which meant Sinn Fein as the voice of the IRA. Finally, no Protestant politician in the North could have discussions with Sinn Fein without risking political obliteration. On the other hand, Sinn Fein was moderating its long-held opposition to any form of collaboration with the partitionist regime. Throughout the 1980s, its leader, Gerry Adams, had been educating militant Republicans to try a policy that involved active participation in the political systems in both the South and the

North – perhaps even contemplating an interim political solution short of immediate Irish unification. Hence Hume persevered – despite his own opposition to political violence and the IRA. If Sinn Fein and the IRA could be brought to accept a compromise and so to end Catholic paramilitary violence, they could take advantage of Unionist divisions by appealing to the moderate Protestants and isolating Paisley and the extremists. Talks between Hume and Adams had begun in 1988 and were resumed in 1993, while since 1992 Hume had also been talking to the Irish Taoiseach, Albert Reynolds of Fianna Fáil. In the autumn of 1993, Hume and Adams announced that they had agreed on a set of proposals. While they were never made public, Sinn Fein earlier had accepted two important principles which assured these proposals could become the basis for discussions with the British. Adams recognised that the British no longer had any interest in remaining in Northern Ireland, and he accepted that a solution must respect the distinct identity and interests of the Protestants. Both principles involved the repudiation of long-cherished Republican beliefs and so signalled Sinn Fein's readiness to take a more pragmatic approach to Northern Ireland.

Reynolds communicated the Irish proposals to John Major, the British Prime Minister, in launching his own initiative to get the British to agree to a joint declaration. After months of tense on-and-off bargaining, the two Prime Ministers signed the Downing Street Declaration on 15 December 1993. Major made explicit what had long been true: Britain had no interests in Northern Ireland, Britain wanted a peaceful settlement there, the people of Ireland should determine the ultimate status of Northern Ireland and the British government would facilitate the transition to a united Ireland if that was what the Irish people wanted. Much of this was aimed at removing the debris of Republican mythology about Britain and so eliminating any possible pretext for an IRA refusal to end the violence and enter negotiations. Nonetheless, Major resisted one Republican demand: Britain would not become an advocate for unification.

Rather, Britain saw itself as a neutral umpire between the two communities in the North, willing to help achieve peace and implement any settlement they agreed upon. For his part, Reynolds reiterated what Irish leaders had said in every formal document since Sunningdale: the consent of the Irish people meant a majority of the people of Northern Ireland. More importantly, in a concession to Protestant sensibilities, he indicated that Ireland would repeal the articles of its constitution that laid claim to the North, but only as part of an overall settlement. Major's government had kept the Unionist leader James Molyneaux informed throughout the negotiations, which assured that there was no perception of a stab in the back, as had been the case with the Anglo-Irish Agreement of 1985.

The payoff from the Downing Street Declaration came in August 1994, when the IRA declared a cease-fire. The unlikely hero was Bill Clinton, the American President. Clinton had infuriated the British when he had ordered the State Department to grant Adams a visa to visit the United States, despite America's promise since the Reagan–Thatcher era to treat the IRA like any other terrorist organisation. Clinton had acted for the most self-interested of reasons – to appeal to the Irish-American vote, while seeking a foreign policy success with little cost if he failed. Adams's tour of America helped persuade IRA leaders that his policy of negotiation could work, and the cease-fire was the result.* Now the pressure was on Major. The Tories, like the Unionists, did not really like bringing Sinn Fein into the bargaining process; it was giving in to terrorist violence. However, Conservatives could hardly be adamant on these grounds. The

---

* There is disagreement over whether the visa for Adams helped the peace process. Clinton was annoyed by Adams's grandstanding during the visit; so the effect may have been indirect, by making it risky to leave a potentially sympathetic President angry. The fact that the US denied Adams a later visa request prior to the cease-fire may be an indication of this danger. Or, as some of the British claim, the visit may have postponed the cease-fire by taking the pressure off the IRA. See Anthony Seldon, *Major: A Political Life* (London: Weidenfeld & Nicolson, 1997), pp. 443–5.

British had a long history of negotiating with terrorists if they were successful enough, including the 1921 negotiations with the IRA and Sinn Fein that led to the creation of the Irish state. Even during the current 'troubles', British governments had found it useful to communicate with the IRA, and Major's own government had done so indirectly throughout 1993. The British therefore advocated disarmament by the paramilitaries as a test of their commitment to the peace process. Some start on decommissioning weapons became a prerequisite if any paramilitary organisation (Protestant or Catholic) was to participate in discussions about a settlement. The IRA, however, like the British government, was not about to give up its weapons in case the war was resumed. Adams, like Major, was in a bind. Many in the IRA had no interest in a peace process that would postpone Irish unity, and the weapons issue defined the line he could not cross.

After a seventeen-month impasse, the IRA renewed the war in January 1996 with a bomb in central London. A second bomb in the middle of Manchester in June confirmed that British property would be a central target of the revived campaign. Now a resumption of the IRA cease-fire became a precondition for Sinn Fein's participation in talks. Major could not go any further in promoting peace, as he was dependent on the votes of Unionist MPs for his majority in the Commons. Therefore, the election of Tony Blair in May 1997 was necessary for a new political initiative by the British. With Clinton now a well-established medium for bringing pressure on Sinn Fein, the weapons issue was shelved and a new cease-fire was called. Clinton appointed former Senate Majority Leader George Mitchell to mediate negotiations, and for the first time Sinn Fein was part of the process, along with the SDLP and the moderate Unionist parties. By 1998 Blair saw that the negotiations could drag on indefinitely, so he set a 1 May deadline. If there was no agreement by then, Britain would propose its own settlement and put it to the people in a referendum. With Mitchell acting as a very effective mediator, the parties finally came to terms on Good Friday, 10 April. The terms of the Good Friday Agreement were those that had been on the table since Sunningdale: an elected assembly for Northern Ireland based on proportional representation, a power-sharing government that included the leaders of both Protestant and Catholic parties (and those that were neither), a council linking the North and the South to deal with matters of common concern, the acceptance that Northern Ireland would remain part of the United Kingdom until the majority determined otherwise. There were, however, some important additions which helped make these terms more palatable to the Ulster Unionist leader, David Trimble. The Agreement had to be approved by separate referenda in the North and the South, and the referendum in the South would include the proposal to repeal the articles of the Irish constitution laying claim to the North. Also, a separate council of the two islands was to be created that would include representatives from the Scottish and Welsh Assemblies, as well as from the British and Irish Parliaments and the Northern Irish Assembly. Thus, the Republicans got a council of Ireland symbolising that the island was a whole, and the Protestants got a council of the two islands symbolising that Irish affairs were linked to Britain. At the same time, this council gave further status to Blair's new assemblies for Scotland and Wales, and so greater credibility to his whole devolution strategy.

The future remains as unclear as ever in Ireland. The Good Friday Agreement was approved by an overwhelming vote in the Republic, and by nearly a three-quarters majority in the North. Still, roughly half the Protestants opposed it, and the process of getting Ulster Unionists and Republicans to work together was an arduous one. The weapons issue remained explosive. In February 2000, Trimble withdrew his party from the power-sharing government because there had been no start on IRA disarmament. Once again, the peace process seemed to be on the verge of collapse. The deadlock was broken later that year when the IRA for the first time agreed to the inspection of its weapons stashes by outside commissioners, and then their sealing to put them beyond use. As usual, Protestants had great difficulty accepting this seismic change by the IRA as meaningful, and Trimble barely got approval to return to the power-sharing government by 53 per cent of his party's governing council. The ritual was repeated in 2001. Trimble withdrew because no weapons had been destroyed, the IRA actually destroyed some weapons and once more Trimble returned, but with his party nearly split down the middle. So Trimble's influence among Ulster Unionists had become shaky. Adams, however, had his own problems. Immediately after the Good Friday Agreement, a group of dissidents calling themselves the Real IRA planted a bomb at Omagh that killed twenty-nine people, the largest single catastrophe in the entire 'troubles'. As Sinn Fein and the IRA move further along the road to compromise, the Real IRA's power could increase. There will surely be many more hitches along the road to stability – the one most immediately evident, apart from decommissioning, being a battle over the reform of the RUC.

On the other hand, Northern Ireland had benefited from the years of peace dating back to the initial cease-fire of 1994. Helped by British economic recovery and an American interest in peace in Ireland, there was an influx of foreign investment in high-tech industries. By the end of 2000, unemployment had plummeted to the relatively low 6.1 per cent from its 1986 high of 18.6 per cent.[33] Clearly, the population had an ever larger stake in the peace process holding firm. Yet should the day approach when the Catholics will be a majority in Northern Ireland, and the prospect of Irish reunion becomes imminent, it is impossible to predict how the Protestants (and especially the Protestant extremists) will respond. Perhaps the Good Friday Agreement will work as is hoped, and it will be a non-issue; but to effect such a constitutional change peacefully would be a first in modern Irish history – in itself, a revolution.

What Does It Mean to Be English?

With the Scots, the Welsh and the Irish all increasingly assertive in expressing identities that were distinct from the British, the question arises, what about the English? Did they, too, have an identity separate from their British one that was more strongly expressed after the 1960s? This is a question that scholars and pundits have been wrestling with since 1980 – making use of new theoretical work on the multiple, changing and 'invented' nature of identity, and of national identity in particular. Bernard Crick expressed the dilemma of an English citizen of the United Kingdom this way: 'I am a citizen of a country with no agreed colloquial name. Its official name is the most rarely used . . . The sense of identity of the English is almost as difficult to specify as the name of the state.'[34] By contrast, in the eighteenth century, Englishmen of all classes agreed on the components of a national identity: Protestantism, trade, liberty, prosperity. They believed that because they were a Protestant and commercial nation, blessed with a unique constitution that guaranteed the rights of free-born Englishmen, they were the most prosperous people on earth. All they had to do was to look at Catholic France to confirm their good fortune.[35] John Bull, Jack Tar, and 'Rule Britannia' were all eighteenth-century creations. John Bull, in particular, reflected English prosperity. His bluff, overfed face was a pictorial contrast to the poor benighted French 'in rags and tatters, barefoot or dragging the wooden clogs of servitude, for ever eating snails and raw onions'.[36] Jack Tar represented another aspect of the English identity: the island nation, the seafaring people who were cut off from Europe and happy in their 'splendid isolation'.

Ultimately many of these supposedly English characteristics were merged into a broader British identity (always excluding the Irish Catholics). The empire, too – that product of the commercial spirit of a seafaring people – was seen as explicitly British rather than English. Furthermore, imperial expansion in the eighteenth and nineteenth centuries enabled the English to export components of their identity to people all over the globe. The benefits of commercial and industrial capitalism, Protestant religion, liberty and parliamentary government became a heritage that was available to all peoples. This was the era when being English came to be identified with a smug sense of superiority. The English were civilising the world!

The English language was one of the most important of these exports. In Europe, language and literature have been seen as definers of a national culture and a national identity since the French Revolution. The English, already with a sense of identity, were behind the curve. Once superiority was challenged after 1880, however, English cultural nationalists sought to reassert the role of the language in defining the nation. English language and literature replaced Classics as the foundation for a liberal education, thus serving as a means of consolidating English identity in the education system. The public schools began to cultivate an appropriate accent that became the standard for correct pronunciation – first for the upper classes, and then, once it went out over the BBC after the war, for everyone. Scholarly works like the *Oxford English Dictionary* (or *OED*, 1884–1928) and the *Cambridge History of English Literature* (1907–16) were intended to be authoritative sources about the language and literature. Finally, F. R. Leavis and others provided the intellectual underpinnings for all this by defining English literature as the expression of an unchanging national character over the centuries and so as the foundation of the national culture.

Ultimately, however, the language did not work well as the basis of a national identity. The English of the *OED* and the BBC was the language of the upper and middle classes of the South of England. It excluded most English people. As we have seen, the languages of the working class and of the regions made a comeback in literature and popular culture after 1960, thus staking their claim to be part of the common heritage. At the same time, just because English was the language of other parts of the world, it became increasingly difficult for the English people to claim it as theirs. In particular, the English language, like everything else, was in danger of corruption from the United States, as Britons were exposed to American movies, popular fiction, magazines, television and an increasing onslaught of live Americans. Like everything else American, the slang and usage to some degree cut across class divides, or at least escaped class associations (one reason that working-class youth in the 1950s liked it), and so some of it came into general usage in Britain as well. Now the authors of the *OED* appropriate usage from every part of the English-speaking world (not just the United States) as they seek to create a genuinely inclusive and democratic reference book of the spoken language.

The latter part of the nineteenth century also saw a revived interest in historic English architecture. Like the language, the styles of the village church, the country house and the peasant's cottage from the late Middle Ages to the Georgian era of the eighteenth century were seen to embody the character of the people and the nation. The National Trust was founded in 1895 as a preservationist organisation; however, its real growth came after 1945. In that year, it had 800 members, while by 1997 it had 2.5 million and was one of Britain's top fundraising charities.[37] Some scholars have associated this incredible post-war growth, most of which was after 1960, with national decline. For the National Trust represented a nostalgia for England's historical and rural past, which was now idealised and mythologised. This yearning for the countryside as the embodiment of the true England has characterised the national culture since the Romantic era. For example, Leavis and Denys Thompson wrote in 1932, 'Folk-songs, folk-dances, Cotswold cottages and handicraft products are signs and expressions of . . . an art of life, a way of living, ordered and patterned . . . growing out of immemorial experience, [tied] to the *natural environment* and the rhythm of the year.' By implication, urban England, which incorporated over 90 per cent of the population, was artificial and 'unnatural'. Similarly, Ken Worpole found that in popular literature during the Second World War, 'the England which was evoked as the country being fought for and defended against fascism was one of oak-beamed pubs, punting on the Cam, and the image of cool summer evenings in country lanes or on velvet-smooth lawns'.[38] With the growing prosperity after the war, more and more people tried to claim a piece of this Arcadia. Those who had the money moved ever further away from the city (especially London) and commuted, or they bought weekend homes in the countryside. Those who could afford neither took a summer holiday in rural England. The latter, in particular, was promoted by the National Trust, which took control of significant swaths of the English coast, while the National Parks set aside more mountainous areas for tourists, walkers and climbers. All this led to conflict with the rural population. Property values were driven beyond what the locals could afford, while the city transients and immigrants fought to maintain historic rights of way and resisted any form of modernisation that threatened the look of the fields and villages that embodied their rural ideal.

Was this aspiration after an idealised rural past yet another symptom of the decline of an England which was no longer at the centre of a great empire – of a people who lived in the past rather than the future? The argument is a little difficult to buy – not least because its origins were in the nineteenth century, when England was at the height of its power. Furthermore, the English were not alone in seeing the soul of the nation in the countryside. The cult of the Highlands in Scotland and Plaid Cymru's early insistence that only Welsh-speaking rural communities were authentically Welsh reflected exactly the same phenomenon. Similarly, the French fixation on protecting their farmers supposedly reflects the tie that every French person feels to the countryside. In the United States, too, the myth has long existed that the small farmer represents the heart of the country. As W. D. Rubinstein points out, 'Classical American writers from Thoreau to Mark Twain, Robert Frost, and William Faulkner have . . . glorified the rural life, condemning urban America, machinery, and technology as inherently corrupting . . .'[39] The only decline that all of this reflects is that of the rural economy and of rural society itself. For the farming population in both France and the United States has been relentlessly shrinking for the last hundred years and more.

What, then, can be said of the other part of the National Trust's mission, the preservation of the buildings of the past – a past associated with England's and Britain's greatness? Initially, that past was associated with the elite – the owners of the country houses which the National Trust increasingly took over and showed to the public. During the decades after the war, however, heritage did not focus solely on the rich and famous. The York Castle Museum and the Newarke Houses Museum in Leicester followed the lead of the new social historians in trying the recreate the lives of ordinary people from the past. More recently, Britain's industrial past also began to be promoted as a source of interest and pride. Thus old factory buildings became part of the architectural past to be preserved as historic, while the Rhondda Heritage Park was developed to introduce people to the coal industry, and particularly to the miners themselves, placing both at the centre of the creation of modern Wales and so of Welsh national identity. The Rhondda example shows that the 'heritage industry' was not limited to England. All the nations of the British Isles became engaged in the same project, as did other European countries and the United States. Whether it is touring Southern plantations and the mansions of robber barons, or re-enacting Revolutionary War and Civil War battles, Americans have shown themselves just as intent on recapturing an idealised past as any Europeans. Hence, it is difficult to see how the new interest in heritage is a symbol of British decline.

The most visible representative of Britain's past is the monarchy. Why on earth do the British people still care about the monarchy? This is a question that many have struggled with over recent years, applying sociological, psychological, cultural and political analyses rooted in a variety of ideologies. The left, in particular, is troubled by the survival of this 'fossil' (Tom Nairn's term) from a past when aristocracy ruled. They see it as a perpetual reaffirmation of the centrality of class and of the privileged elitism which dominates the social structure. The royal performance is simply another means of pacifying the people and keeping them in their place (if the working class cares about the monarchy at all, which some on the left doubt). The right, on the other hand, asserts its value as a symbol of the nation and as a unifying force transcending class. They even embrace its entertainment value when they tie the appeal of the royal family to the supposed British love of ritual and ceremony. Furthermore, decline enhanced the value of the monarchy 'as something which was uniquely ours and which no country could match'.[40]

The royal family is not English in its origins. If we follow royalty itself in tracing lineage through the male line, Prince Philip is Greek, while Prince Albert, who married Queen Victoria, and the Georgian kings who preceded her were all German. Going further back still, the Stuarts were Scottish and the Tudors Welsh. Indeed, it sometimes seems as if the one bloodline that is missing is the English. Yet somehow observers see the monarchy, like Parliament, as part of the British heritage that came from England. It has not always been particularly popular. The first two Georges were foreign and were well hated. While George III (1760–1820) in his later (and mad) years did much to create a popular monarchy, his son George IV (1820–30) was probably as despised as any king who ever sat on the throne. Even Victoria (1837–1901) had her ups and downs – loved as an attractive young queen breeding a huge family, disliked as the reclusive widow who would not appear in public after Albert died, and loved again as the matron of the empire and the grandmother of Europe in her old age. Another low came at the time of the abdication crisis of Edward VIII in 1936. So the vacillations in royal popularity since the 1950s do not necessarily imply that the demise of the monarchy is imminent. It has done much damage to itself over the centuries, yet still it has survived and even thrived.

The functions and rituals of the modern monarchy were developed in the reign of George III, during the wars against France, and perfected in the latter part of the reign of Victoria.[41] George III and his wife Queen Charlotte were the first to promote domesticity as part of a British identity. It was one means of contrasting themselves with George's hated German predecessors. Later, the sanctity and security of the family was offered as part of what the British people were fighting for in the wars against revolutionary and Napoleonic France. Yet George in his prime still took an active, if increasingly limited, role in running the state. Similarly, while his successors could no longer make policy or create governments, they still could influence both and were often overtly partisan. Thus, it was only under George V (1910–36) and George VI (1936–52), when partisanship became clearly forbidden, that the royal family much more consciously cultivated its domesticity as the ideal of the nation. By then, the rituals of the modern monarchy had evolved under Victoria and Edward VII (1901–10) between 1880 and 1910. The present elaborate ceremonies at the coronation and death of the monarch were perfected, and the celebration of the monarch's jubilees was instituted. Under George V and George VI, the pageantry was expanded to include royal weddings for the children and state funerals for the mother of the monarch. At the same time, the newsreels and the popular press now publicised the royal family's activities far more widely than had been the case before, while the radio allowed the King direct communication with the people.

The monarchy was never more popular than during and after the Second World War. It had perfected the formula of embodying the ideal family, performing in key public ceremonials, touching the lives of ordinary people through choreographed photo opportunities and representing the character and the unity of the nation. Thus when Elizabeth II became Queen, there was enormous optimism and hope for a new Elizabethan era. Yet the class character of the monarchy remained firmly entrenched – as was the class character of the nation. Monarchy still inspired awe, and the royal family remained distant from the people, even when meeting them. Yet paradoxically, the royal family were celebrities without much style. While the coaches and the palaces were glamorous, the Queen and her family looked decidedly dowdy and seemed boring. In a notorious comment in 1957, John Grigg said that Elizabeth had the image 'of a priggish schoolgirl, captain of the hockey team, a perfect and a recent candidate for confirmation'.[42]

How would this mix of ordinariness and aristocracy hold up in the age of mass media and the social revolution that was launched in the 1960s? First television assured that every royal occasion was now watched by millions of people, thus consolidating popular interest. At the same time, the popular press became increasing intrusive, as newspapers scrambled to increase circulation. The effect was to undermine royalty's ability to dictate the terms of its communion with the people. Finally, the royal family proved to be susceptible to the changing temper of the times, as they married commoners and then divorced them. Slowly, the royal family found themselves at the centre of a soap opera. The marriages of Princes Charles and Andrew to Lady Diana Spencer and Sarah Ferguson respectively in the 1980s gave the show the sexiness and glamour it had lacked. As with any 'participatory soap', because

> the public has shared the ups and downs, the joys and sorrows of this family, has taken sides and passed judgment as they would on characters in *EastEnders* or *The Archers*, they feel they know them personally . . . Diana was the undoubted star of this 'super-soap'. Her eating disorders, suicide attempts, the broken marriage, the unhappy love affairs were all followed with the same eagerness and fascination that earlier generations of 'soap' fans had followed the fictional careers of Elsie Tanner and Meg Richardson.[43]

Clearly the old awe and deference were gone, replaced by a familiarity that characterised the new, more Americanised Britain.

The Queen and her entourage were not happy with the royal soap opera. This was certainly not their notion of the way the monarchy should serve as the symbol of the nation and its values. The emergence of Diana as the star of the show represented all that was wrong from their standpoint. Yet the rest of the court had great difficulty competing with Diana, who reflected the changing Britain in so many ways. She was brought up to be a traditional woman within the aristocracy, the least modernised section of British society. As Princess of Wales she was expected to produce an heir while deferring to the male-dominated culture of her husband's and mother-in-law's households. If her husband cheated, she was supposed to shut up – as all her predecessors had done in the same circumstances. Diana rebelled against all this, seeking to break free from the traditional constraints of womanhood and even of class. In doing so, she carried with her lots of women who shared her lack of self-esteem and had their own difficulties trying to become autonomous in the age of liberation. At the same time, she showed a thoroughly modern expertise at manipulating the media and using her star power and sex appeal to win a broader public support. Increasingly she represented both what the monarchy was not and what it might be by her human behaviour and ability to relate to ordinary people. For instead of being dull, stuffy and distant, Diana was emotional, warm, caring and exciting.

The royal family did not come off well in its fight with Diana. While many traditionalists were on Charles's side, and the Queen and Queen Mother never lost their popularity, the image of their entourages trying to destroy one not so helpless woman (and a good mother at that) could only harm the image of the monarchy, especially with the younger generations who mostly were indifferent to the pageantry of royalty. It seemed a clear case of tradition fighting modernity – perhaps a metaphor for England itself as it sought to carve out a new identity. Following the royal family's botched response to Diana's death, Tony Blair set out to modernise the monarchy, with only limited success. Whether modern or archaic, however, it is difficult to pin down what the monarchy has to contribute to national identity. It is useful (as every nation with parliamentary government has found it useful to have a politically neutral head of state), it is entertaining, it is tied to the history of the nation, but most of all it is uniquely theirs. Yet while the English *may* care more about it, the monarchy is and must be British.

Given the difficulty of defining exactly what it means to be English as opposed to British, many observers fall back on a bundle of characteristics and symbols of the nation. For some, those characteristics are associated specifically with the aristocracy, as embodied in the cult of the gentleman. Qualities such as moderation and restraint, anti-intellectualism and amateurism, respect for manners and style, smug superiority and eccentricity, snobbery and arrogance, a sense of honour and a sense of fair play all might be derived from those who ran the nation between 1688 and 1914.[44] Jeremy Paxman offers a more updated list that incorporates some of the above characteristics while also harking back to the eighteenth century:

> If I had to list those qualities of the English which most impress me – a quizzical detachment, tolerance, common sense, bloody-mindedness, willingness to compromise, their deeply political sense of themselves – I think I should praise most this sense of 'I know my rights'. The attachment to certain hard-earned freedoms lies deep.[45]

Most ordinary English men and women, however, would probably be more inclined to identify with the list put together by my friend Tracy: 'Maybe it's fish and chips, cricket, beer, and a tendency to call a single sunny day "summer" if that's all we get in a season.' Richard Weight, who uses more than seven hundred pages struggling with the changing identity of all parts of the United Kingdom since 1940, ends up in a similar place to Tracy: football and the re-emergence of St George.[46]

Yet that is not the end of it for Weight. He sees the English as slowly adjusting to and embracing a multi-cultural society. England, far more than the other parts of the United Kingdom, has been the recipient of immigration. Hence, Englishness is no longer identified either with white Anglo-Saxons or with the middle-class and working-class cultures and values that were inherited from the nineteenth century and which defined it from the Victorian era until about 1980. As Will Self wrote, 'While the old idea of a monocultural landscape is impossible to sustain, England as the centre of that great rolling, post-colonial ocean of cultural ferment is alive and kicking.'[47] And this view, oddly enough, brings us back to Princess Diana. Many analysts of the Diana phenomenon agree on the incredible breadth of her appeal over a wide spectrum of English society. It was not just that her most recent boyfriend was an Arab and a Muslim. She had included Muslims among her friends and associates before Dodi Al Fayed, as she had included blacks and gays. All her charitable activities in the years before her death symbolised an attempt to incorporate the excluded – war victims, the mutilated and disabled, the homeless and the sufferers from Aids. Furthermore, she was able to communicate with ordinary people in terms that they could identify with. Thus Diana sought to adapt the symbolic role of the monarchy since the wars against France – as the embodiment of national unity – to the new diverse and more egalitarian England.[48] Queen Elizabeth and her mother did it for white people of all classes, who had defined the nation in the first half of the century, but only within the framework of hierarchy. Diana went further, and her success was evident in the diversity of the crowds that lined the streets to mourn her upon her death. England, like the United States, had to learn that national identity did not mean uniformity and homogeneity. Rather, it had to acknowledge and embrace diversity – whether of class, region, race or ethnicity – and to recognise that all contribute to making the nation and its identity. And a system of devolution, which recognised the reality of distinct Celtic identities by accepting an autonomous political existence for the Celtic states within the United Kingdom, was a logical corollary to such an English identity. Progress had been made in both these directions by the time of Diana's death.

PART IV: 1979–2001
REVIVAL

12

THE NEW LIBERALISM

Has there been a Thatcher revolution? That is, did Margaret Thatcher and those working with her in the 1980s change the fundamental paradigm by which the British people analysed political issues – away from a focus on government and towards a focus on the individual as the solver of problems, and away from a view that the social and economic framework was the source of problems and towards a view that government was the problem? Certainly that was Thatcher's aim. Given her interpretation of the reasons for Britain's economic and moral decline, her ambitions could be little short of revolutionary if she was going to reverse that decline.

Commentators have offered three arguments to show that Thatcher did not make *that* much difference. First, many of the key elements of the Thatcherite economic agenda – giving primacy to limiting inflation, controlling the growth of the money supply, cutting government spending – were introduced by Callaghan's Labour government between 1976 and 1979, in the aftermath of the IMF bail-out. Thus, there was no Thatcherite revolution. Rather, there was a broader change in economic policy resulting from the need to adapt to the economic crisis of the 1970s. Furthermore, that change was not limited to Britain, nor, as the experience of the socialist government in France showed, to conservatives. A second argument is that there was no clearly articulated economic philosophy that the Conservatives embraced in opposition and then implemented after they came to power in 1979. On the contrary, Thatcher was the classic pragmatic politician who adapted and U-turned with the best of them as political necessity dictated. Most importantly, when monetarism – the one ideologically based economic policy that she started with – failed to reduce the budget deficit and control inflation, it was jettisoned. At the same time, privatisation of nationalised industries – the policy that Thatcher is most centrally identified with – was only a peripheral part of the Tory election manifesto of 1979. Rather, it became a defining policy in the mid-1980s when the government had to find sources of income to help finance tax cuts. Thus there was no ideological coherence to Thatcherism at all, and so there could be no ideological revolution associated with it. A third argument looks at the performance of the British economy under Thatcher. In particular, the decline in inflation after 1980 was an international phenomenon that was the product of global factors – most importantly, the collapse of the price of oil and other commodities. Thus, no credit is due to Thatcherite economic policies. At the same time, the performance of the British economy in the 1980s was not much different from its performance in the 1960s – hardly evidence of a revolutionary change.

Such arguments are reminiscent of those who claim that the New Deal of Franklin Roosevelt made little difference in pulling America out of the Great Depression. It may be true that Roosevelt's policies had only a marginal effect on the massive unemployment of the period, much less on the moribund American economy. Yes, ultimately it took the Second World War to end the Depression. But these arguments miss the point. The reality of what happened was much less important than people's perceptions of what happened, and to the generation of Americans who lived through the Depression, Roosevelt transformed their experience of it. Most of all, he gave them hope – a belief that they could have some control over their future, and a framework for thinking about government as a means to exercise that control. This is exactly what Thatcher did! There was a mood of hopelessness at the end of the 1970s – a mood that was not limited to Britain. Thatcher set out to reverse that mood, and she succeeded – by generating energy and new ideas, and so creating a conviction that people are not the prisoners of circumstances, but can make things better if they will. As was the case with Roosevelt and the New Deal, the change wrought by Thatcher was associated with a specific set of policies and attitudes which themselves came to be associated with the new confidence and improved circumstances of the era. So Thatcher gets the credit, and rightly so, for this psychological change would not have occurred without her, and the psychological change was centrally important.

Certainly this outside observer, who first lived in Britain during the crisis of 1974–5 and has visited the country regularly since then, perceives a noticeable change, and in directions that Thatcher sought to promote. There appears to be more economic energy and optimism, more interest in business and making money, and more attention to service and accommodating the customer. Furthermore, more professional observers than the author, especially within the business community, have commented on this changed environment. Yet it is important, too, to recognise the limits of that change. Britons remain strongly attached to their welfare state – especially to the National Health Service, but also more broadly to the underlying principles of welfare articulated by Beveridge sixty years ago. Nor has there been any rolling back of the revolution of values that was launched in the 'permissive sixties'. Indeed, there hardly has been any effort to do so, apart from a couple of votes on restoring the death penalty. The transformation in views about the roles of women and the nature of femininity, and the more tolerant attitude towards sex and homosexuality, appear to be integrated into the national culture. Divorce laws have been further relaxed since 1979, while abortion has rarely been a significant political issue. So it is to Thatcherism's economic policies that we must look for its most significant impact on British society.

Where's the 'ism'?

Sympathisers and critics alike agree that Thatcherism was not an ideology. Peter Riddell, a critical sympathiser, puts it like this: 'Thatcherism is essentially an instinct, a series of moral values and an approach to leadership rather than an ideology.' Shirley Robin Letwin, a much less critical acolyte, agrees that Thatcherism was not an ideology or a theory. Its goal, she says, was to promote 'the vigorous virtues', which she defines thus: 'upright, self-sufficient, energetic, adventurous, independent-minded'. These are contrasted with the '"softer" virtues such as kindness, humility, gentleness, sympathy'.[1] As is so often the case in British political debate, observers claim a lack of ideology because they fail to find a consistency and coherence that are rarely present in the real world of politics. Certainly, if the Labour Party is an example of socialism in practice, then socialism fails the test of ideology miserably. Since the underlying views that inspired Thatcher and her followers are deemed worthy of an 'ism', there must have been some level of coherence, and, as the Riddell and Letwin quotes indicate, that coherence was defined in moral terms. By placing morality at the centre of their political project, the Thatcherites followed a British political tradition pioneered by nineteenth-century liberalism and continued by twentieth-century socialism – the former, the ideology they most admired, and the latter the one they most despised.

The link to liberalism is evident in Letwin's vigorous virtues. Thatcherism aimed to liberate the individual from the trammels of government interference and control. In so doing, it hoped to release the inherent initiative and energies of the British people and so reverse Britain's economic decline. That decline was associated with Letwin's softer virtues, which were encouraged by twentieth-century liberalism and socialism. By training individuals to look to the state to supply all their wants, and by promoting a greater equality of income and wealth as a policy objective, these ideologies of the left had undermined entrepreneurship. In particular, they had discouraged making money, that pursuit of enlightened self-interest which Adam Smith had taught would operate to the optimum benefit of society as a whole. So Thatcherism involved a whole-hearted embracing of cultural explanations for Britain's decline. Furthermore, because the villains were all those who disparaged profit maximisation and business as worthy pursuits, the enemy was the gentlemanly ruling class produced by Oxbridge and the public schools as much as it was liberals and socialists.

The embodiment of the harmful effect of government interference was Keynesian economics and the culture of corporatism that had emerged in Britain. Economic policy had discouraged the entrepreneur from doing his job and making a fair profit: by micro-managing (and so mismanaging) the economy; by expanding the public sector at the expense of the private sector, and so driving up interest rates through the state's competition for scarce funds; by running budget deficits, and so fostering inflation; by maintaining a punitive level of taxation, which retarded saving and investment. The welfare state, of course, further harmed the economy by discouraging work. If the largest possible number of people were not putting in maximum effort, then inevitably worker productivity and economic output suffered. The other inhibitors of work and profit-making were the trade unions. Their rules made it impossible to dismiss the incompetent or inefficient, while their insistence on a uniform national wage scale divorced compensation from productivity and effort. The keys, then, to Britain's economic revival were several: get government out of the economy and cut the size of the public sector; end all consultation with industry and labour, which had no more right to participate in policy-making than any other interest groups; encourage entrepreneurship by reducing taxes, ending government competition for scarce funds and breaking the power of trade unions to keep wages artificially high; and promote a work ethic and individual self-reliance by cutting back the welfare state and, again, weakening the trade unions. The central first step was to end inflation, for rising prices destroyed the value of money, diminished savings and so, again, were a disincentive for work and entrepreneurship.

Given the close kinship of both its economic and moral analysis to nineteenth-century liberalism, it is not surprising that Thatcherism was identified with a return to Victorian values – especially since it also involved a reassertion of the patriarchal family roles and sexual propriety that are associated with the Victorian era. However, there were more recent sources of intellectual inspiration for Thatcherite economics. The first was Friedrich von Hayek, the Austrian-born economist who won the Nobel Prize for Economics in 1974. In part, Hayek was a traditional Burkean conservative. He saw society as the product of a complex evolution based on trial and error and experience which humans fiddled with at their peril. Like Burke, he attacked an Enlightenment-based social science which believed that institutions could be reconstructed according to principles of reason. Yet Hayek was also a nineteenth-century liberal. For the market itself was the product of this process of evolution, so it too should not be interfered with by social scientific theorists or governments. As a young professor at the London School of Economics in the early 1930s, he had been a critic of Keynes's economics, but his views were swamped in the Keynesian tide of the 1940s. His best-known book, *The Road to Serfdom* (1944), was an attack on socialist planning with an eye to the command economies of the Soviet Union and Nazi Germany. However, his larger critique of government planning, where insufficient information replaced the market as the allocator of resources, could also apply to Keynesian management and the income redistribution policies that became the norm after the Second World War. It was Hayek's attack on socialism and government planning, and his assertion of the infallibility of the market, that appealed to the Thatcherites. They were less interested in the broader Burkean framework in which he embedded his analysis, as they were themselves set on a radical reconstruction of society.

Another Nobel Prize-winning economist, Milton Friedman, was the other great intellectual mentor of the new liberals.

Friedman has been the guru of monetarism since the Second World War. Monetarists claim that all discretionary actions by government at best have no significant influence on the performance of the economy. More likely, government policies (monetary as well as fiscal) will aggravate fluctuations in the trade cycle and so make things worse because, acting on imperfect information and primitive models of a complex economy, they inevitably get it wrong. Government policy therefore should be limited to assuring a modest annual increase in the money supply, thereby providing a stable and predictable framework in which economic actors can go about their business. Friedman and his colleagues at the University of Chicago were not only critics of Keynesian management of the economy; they opposed all forms of government regulation or subsidy that interfered with the working of the free market. Trade unions, which interfered with the market in setting wages and the conditions of work, were equally condemned. Like his nemesis Keynes, Friedman was a brilliant publicist for his ideas – writing weekly columns in the American press and even hosting a television series on (ironically) public television in the United States. Thus, even during the heyday of Keynesianism, Friedman was able to keep his ideas before the public, and with the reaction against Keynes in the 1970s, they became the economic orthodoxy.

While Friedman was the most visible American intellectual influence on Thatcherism, he was not the only one. American supply-side economists were also important, with their emphasis on the impact of taxes and the welfare state on business and consumer behaviour. American thought had such a large impact on Thatcherites because America seemed to provide the model for the kind of society they aspired to. First and foremost, money counted in the United States, carrying both status and power. When people say that the United States is not a class society, what they really mean is that class in the United States is determined not by birth, but by how much money a person has. So access to the middle or upper class is open to anyone who can make sufficient money, and enough people are able to move up to give 'the American dream' some basis in reality. This was the kind of society Thatcherites aspired to. Furthermore, business was respected as a profession and was seen as the optimal vehicle for making money and so achieving status. As a result, American culture seemed to encourage entrepreneurship. The evidence was the large number of small businesses and the enormous turnover in businesses, as some folded while new ones started up. Such economic dynamism was what Thatcherites wanted to create in Britain. They thought that America was more entrepreneurial in part because the levels of taxation and government spending there were significantly lower than in Europe. In particular, the United States had a smaller welfare state. Services that were near-public sector monopolies in Britain – like health, education and social insurance – were a public–private mix in the United States, usually (except for education) with the weight very much on the side of the private sector. As a result, there was choice for the middle class (the rich, in Britain, could always go private), and there was no levelling down of quality to a lowest common denominator defined by bureaucrats. For all these reasons, the United States was a source of admiration and even inspiration for Thatcherism. That link was reinforced in 1981, when Ronald Reagan became President, embracing much the same ideological framework as Thatcher's in order to reverse America's perceived decline. Thereafter, throughout the 1980s the British and Americans looked to each other for ideas, inspiration and confirmation that they were on the right track in the policies they were implementing.

Inflation and Unemployment

It is hardly surprising that monetarism came into fashion in the 1970s. The British government had not paid much attention to the money supply in making policy until the late 1960s, while the inflation of the 1970s was associated with unprecedented budget deficits and a surge in the money supply, especially in the early part of the decade. One reason was the end of fixed exchange rates. Under the Bretton Woods system, the imperative to maintain the value of the pound had disciplined governments, forcing them to act quickly to combat inflation. After 1972, if rising inflation led to a balance-of-payments deficit, a government could simply let the value of the pound fall, which accelerated the inflation. To raise money to meet the higher costs that ensued, it might then sell government notes to banks, which would increase the money supply. To some degree, this was what happened between 1972 and 1979. Yet ultimately, it is impossible for a non-specialist to judge whether an expanding money supply led to more inflation, because economists themselves are not agreed on it.[2] It is sufficient to say that the new Conservative government accepted the monetarist analysis.

Thatcher and her Chancellor of the Exchequer, Sir Geoffrey Howe, were first and foremost committed to reducing inflation, and they looked to limiting the growth of the money supply as the means of achieving this end. Each year between 1979 and 1986, Howe and his successor Nigel Lawson set targets for the annual rate of growth of the money supply as the centrepiece of what they called their medium-term financial strategy (first launched in 1980). The money supply turned out to be difficult to manage, however, because it was not easy to define what money was. Historically, it had been treated as cash (including bank reserves) plus the amount of money in current accounts. However, building societies began giving their customers the same current account services as commercial banks. There was also the problem of inflows from overseas. High interest rates (which were one means of controlling the money supply) attracted foreign money, and the government was not about to regulate such flows. Indeed, it ended the remaining controls on the banking system. Nor was it going to limit the ability of British firms to borrow overseas if the terms at home were less attractive. Howe and Lawson tried several different strategies to limit the growth of the money supply, but they kept overshooting their targets.

Finally, in 1987 Lawson gave up setting targets altogether.[*]

Yet the government's anti-inflation policy was a success. Why was this so? In part, it was due to factors beyond its control. The fall of commodities prices which began in 1980, especially the collapse of the price of oil, helped a lot – just as the increase in these prices had helped trigger the inflation in the first place. Furthermore, Britain was now an oil-exporting nation, thanks to North Sea oil, which made the pound very attractive for the other oil-producing nations with surplus money to invest. The resulting influx of money kept the value of the pound higher than Britain's economic strength justified. An overvalued pound meant a fall in the price of imports, thus dampening inflation. Finally, the government never put all its eggs in the monetarist basket. The medium-term financial strategy involved using interest rates and targets for reducing public sector borrowing (which meant reducing government spending) to reinforce the message that everything necessary would be done to bring inflation down.[†]

Initially, everything went from bad to worse. Again, the main

---

[*] True believers among monetarists, beginning with Milton Friedman, claim that the government never properly implemented monetarist policies, in part because it used the wrong definition of money, in part because of other policies it employed simultaneously. So they deny that the Thatcher era was a monetarist experiment at all. Opponents of monetarism, by contrast, contend that the whole performance of the economy from 1979 to 1992 proved the failure of relying solely on monetary policy instruments to manage the economy.

[†] The British use the Public Sector Borrowing Requirement (PSBR) – which is the budget deficit plus the borrowing of local government and nationalised industries – rather than the budget deficit as the economic indicator to judge the inflationary or deflationary effects of government policy. Because the PSBR includes capital as well as current expenditure, it is, in the words of Alec Cairncross, 'a much more exacting target than a balanced Budget'. In fact, it was nearly always in deficit in the post-war years prior to its emergence as the fixation of policy-makers in the mid-1970s. Alec Cairncross, *The British Economy since 1945: Economic Policy and Performance, 1945–1995*, 2nd edition (Oxford: Blackwell, 1995), p. 206. As we shall see, it proved very difficult even after that time to drag it into surplus, while the effect of focusing on it rather than the budget deficit made for systematic underinvestment in infrastructure and the nationalised industries.

reason was outside the control of the government – an enormous increase in the price of oil following the Iranian revolution and the American hostage crisis. The jump in all oil-based costs not only triggered an inflation, but with it a worldwide recession as demand for exports shrank. Yet government policy also contributed a lot to Britain's problems. Its insistence on reducing the budget deficit while cutting income tax forced it to increase the value added tax (VAT) from 8 to 15 per cent – providing a second large and sudden jolt up for prices. Finally, it accepted the recommendation of an independent commission appointed by the Labour government for a large salary increase for civil servants. All these factors contributed to a dramatic rise in inflation, from 8.3 per cent in 1978 to 17.9 per cent in 1980, reaching a maximum of 21.9 per cent in August.[3] The government responded by increasing interest rates to a record high of 17 per cent, which not only choked off the demand for credit but reinforced the upward pressure on the pound, with its deflationary effects on import prices. The effect was to make more acute the recession that was already under way. In particular, by pushing up the value of the pound, government policy made exports more expensive. British industry was savaged: manufacturing production plunged 14 per cent between 1979 and 1981, as manufacturing capacity decreased nearly 25 per cent.[4] Yet with inflation still unacceptably high in the spring of 1981, and desiring to lower interest rates to relieve the overvalued pound, Howe further tightened the vice of fiscal policy. This was the moment of Thatcher's famous claim, 'The Lady's not for turning.' There would be no Heath-like U-turn in her government's commitment to slay inflation once and for all, whatever the costs. This was the message sent to the international financial markets and the trade unions alike. But with unemployment soaring, the unions had little leverage anyway, so the rate of wage increases fell substantially. This muting of wage hikes, in conjunction with the fall in commodity prices and the government's tight economic policies, finally produced the desired result, as inflation fell to a low of 3.7 per cent in May and June of 1983. Thereafter it stabilised at between about 4 and 7 per cent until the late 1980s.[5]

A heavy price was paid for this success. Britain's manufacturing sector was decimated. Industrial output did not surpass its 1979 level until 1987, while manufacturing's share of total economic output fell from about one-third to less than a quarter.[6] The collapse of industry meant a corresponding increase in unemployment: it more than doubled from 1.3 million in May 1979, when the Conservatives came in, to 2.7 million at the end of 1981. A year later it broke through the psychologically powerful three million barrier, where it stayed (with fluctuations) until early 1987.[7] These were levels unseen since the Great Depression, and although the number of workers was larger now, three million was still roughly 12.7 per cent of the workforce. Furthermore, the numbers recovered more quickly in the 1930s; the 1986 unemployment rate of 11.3 per cent was higher than the 10.1 per cent of 1937.[8] Nor do even these drastic numbers fully capture how unemployment in the 1980s compared with earlier years. For the government changed the way in which the statistics were calculated twenty-eight times![9] Most importantly, instead of counting those registering as unemployed, the statistics now counted those claiming unemployment benefit, which eliminated many married women; and they excluded most men over sixty and youths in job-training schemes. Many of the men, in particular, simply dropped out of the labour market, as they gave up looking for jobs and either took early retirement or lived on invalidity or sickness benefits. These changes meant that some 600,000–750,000 people who would have preferred to work were not counted in the late 1980s, and most of them would have been counted in the late 1970s.[10]

Many of those affected were men who became long-term unemployed. Nationalised and private-sector industries alike shed the least productive workers and closed down inefficient plants and mines. The effect was traumatic on individuals and communities alike. Those who lost their jobs tended to be middle-aged men who had worked their whole adult lives. They were not the lazy and shiftless, who preferred to live off welfare, of neo-liberal myth. On the contrary, they were men who desperately wanted to work, and they were of a generation and a class whose sense of manhood was tied up with their ability to support their family. It was a personal failure when they could not and had to watch the family fall into poverty.* The result for many was mounting debt, deteriorating health, depression and increased tension in the family.[11] Many of these jobs were probably doomed in any case. Industries like steel and textiles were in long-term decline, as they could not compete against newly industrialising countries with cheaper labour. Coal was up against cheaper and cleaner fuels like oil and gas. As a result, the number of coal miners fell from 712,000 in 1949 to 517,000 in 1964, 287,000 in 1970–71, and roughly 150,000 in 1985.[12] Comparable collapses occurred in other heavy industries. These men were like the handloom weavers of the first half of the nineteenth century – the victims of technological change and an evolving world economy that had effectively rendered them irrelevant. The justification, from the government's standpoint, was a phenomenal improvement in worker productivity, especially in the industries that shed the most workers. For example, steel had seen total productivity *decline* by an average of 1.4 per cent per year from 1968 to 1978; now, after more than halving the number of workers, the industry's productivity increased by an average of 4.6 per cent per year from 1979 to 1983 and 9.0 per cent from 1983 to 1987.[13]

By the beginning of 1988, the Conservatives looked as if they could legitimately claim to have solved Britain's chronic economic problems of the last couple of decades. The average annual growth rate was about 2.3 per cent from 1979 to 1988 and 3.9 per cent

---

* Far more often than might be thought, wives did not work to make up for lost wages, and some even stopped working. Since women's wages were lower, the benefit system often penalised their work (especially part-time employment), while many wives of semi-skilled men had no skills of their own for the job market in a region that was already depressed. But it was also true that they were protective of their men and devoted their time to helping and caring for them.

from the bottom of the recession in 1981 to 1988, while the average annual growth of labour productivity was 2.1 per cent from 1979 to 1987. The improvement in productivity in manufacturing was even more striking.[14] While monetarism had apparently failed, Lawson had come up with an alternative policy which was containing inflation. To limit public sector borrowing, he used interest rates to fix the sterling exchange rate with the German mark. The theory was simple. Everyone had confidence that the Bundesbank would manage the German economy to assure low inflation. So if the pound 'shadowed' the mark, the markets could be sure that Britain's inflation would be under control. The problem was that Thatcher disliked shadowing the mark, which looked suspiciously like preparing the pound to join the European exchange rate mechanism (ERM), whereby participating countries maintained fixed exchange rates among their currencies. Thatcher was adamantly opposed to any such abdication of Britain's authority over its own economy. So Lawson had to do it surreptitiously.

Unfortunately for Lawson, just as this source of tension emerged with the Prime Minister, everything started to go wrong with the economy. The stock market crash in October 1987 led all the leading central banks to cut interest rates in order to prevent a concurrent economic collapse. He then had to keep interest rates down so that the pound would not appreciate relative to the mark. Yet with the economy (and the money supply) growing rapidly, Lawson chose to cut income taxes in 1988 to deliver another instalment on the Tories' long-run tax-cutting policy. The accelerating expansion fuelled a demand for imports, so the balance-of-payments deficit grew. A housing boom in the South, fuelled by low interest rates and credit expansion, helped to stimulate inflation. By 1989, Britain was in a classic 'stop-go' situation. Increasing inflation and a large balance-of-payments deficit seemed to indicate that falling unemployment had come at exactly the same cost as similar booms in the 1960s and 1970s (see Table 12.1 opposite). So the government had to slam on the brakes by raising interest rates to as high as 15 per cent, again

Table 12.1. The Crisis of 1989–92

	Inflation (%)	Unemployment (maximum for year)
1987	4.2	3,297,000
1988	5.0	2,722,000
1989	7.7	2,074,000
1990	9.5	1,850,000
1991	5.9	2,552,000
1992	4.1	2,983,000
1993	1.6	3,062,000

Source: Butler and Butler, *British Political Facts 1900–2000*, pp. 401 (unemployment), 411–12 (inflation).

with exactly the same cost as in previous 'stop' phases of the cycle – a jump in unemployment.

The onset of the recession completed the discrediting of Lawson with Thatcher. She was finally able to force his resignation in October 1989. But his successor, John Major, turned out to be equally enthusiastic for Britain to join the ERM, and he finally wore Thatcher down in October 1990. Britain joined, however, with the pound overvalued; therefore, interest rates had to stay up because the cost of German unification was forcing the Bundesbank to keep Germany's high. Hence, as in 1979–81, Britain suffered worse during the slowdown of 1989–92 than other Western countries, and, as in 1979–81, it did so because of government policies – which had first allowed inflation to get out of control and then maintained high interest rates to protect the pound. By 1992, unemployment had again reached the levels of the Great Depression, with the middle class and the South suffering much more than before. It was impossible to maintain the present exchange rate indefinitely. Finally, in September 1992 a massive speculation against the pound forced the Prime Minister John Major and the Chancellor Norman Lamont to bail out of ERM and allow the pound to float once again. 'Black Wednesday' left Tory economic policy in a shambles. In particular, Lawson's policy of using the exchange rate to limit inflation was finished. Lamont and his successor, Kenneth Clarke, turned to fiscal policy (raising taxes and cutting spending), which had been discredited in the Thatcher years, although controlling inflation remained the priority.

Taxing and Spending

Balancing the budget became an important component of the government's anti-inflation strategy, which in turn required cutting government spending. Such retrenchment was all the more necessary because the Tories believed that a radical tax cut was essential to reverse Britain's economic decline. They believed that exorbitant levels of direct taxation (i.e. income and corporate taxes and death duties) deterred entrepreneurship, since people with money had to be the savers and investors in a capitalist economy. Yet, having proved that they had what it takes to succeed in a competitive environment, the wealthy were being penalised for having exactly the qualities that the nation should be encouraging. This argument would not seem to hold for inheritors of wealth; however, Tories claimed that the ability to pass money on to one's heirs was an important incentive for economic achievement. So even high death duties were an object of criticism.

Taxes could not be cut significantly, however, without a substantial reduction in government spending. Thatcher always claimed that she did not want to dismantle the welfare state. Rather, it should be pared down to provide a safety net for those genuinely in need, rather than a way of life for those who could work. It is hard to believe, however, that she and her followers wouldn't have preferred to end the whole thing, for their ideological outlook posited a uniformly harmful effect of government activism. On the one hand, its spending diverted resources from the private sector; on the other, by definition, government could not provide any service as efficiently as private enterprise could. So any reallocation of resources to the public sector simply meant an inferior and more costly product. Welfare services had a secondary harmful effect: they destroyed the incentive to work and save, undermining individual initiative among those who benefited from them. In areas like insurance and health care, the new liberals preferred private provision, which would assure higher quality and also force people to save in order to purchase the service. Help from family and private charity would fill any gap that remained, as they had before the welfare state. Government, therefore, should limit itself to the triad of defence, law and order and foreign policy. Everything else should be left to the market.

Whatever her secret wishes may have been, however, Thatcher understood that there could be no elimination of the welfare state. Indeed, she had to spend much of her eleven years in power denying that was her intention. For the public's perception of Thatcher was much the same as mine. By 1987, they thought the welfare state was unsafe in her hands; they thought things had got worse, even though the government had increased welfare spending; and they claimed (in polls) that they would accept higher taxes to get improved services, even as the government was cutting taxes. So the Tories had a serious public relations problem when it came to the welfare state, one which they had created with their own rhetoric. Pensions and the NHS, in particular, were far too popular to be slashed, and the 1979 election manifesto had promised to protect them. Spending on both, in any case, was bound to go up in the 1980s. The increasing proportion of the population that was living to old age and the revolutionary improvements in medical care led to accelerating costs in all developed countries. Thatcherite policies then gave a further impetus to welfare spending because of the enormous increase in unemployment, while layoffs in nationalised industries were bought by giving employees redundancy payments.

Given the limitations, the government worked hard to control the financial burden on the state. One significant change was to phase out the government's contribution to the insurance fund; by 1988, all contributions were coming from the insured and their employers. Beyond that reform, the government changed lots of rules to chip away at costs – including cutting back on eligibility for some benefits, trying to introduce means tests for others, redefining how some benefits were calculated and even eliminating some. The rate of increase of the basic pension was cut significantly. While spending on the NHS went up, it did not go up as fast as it had under previous governments, nor enough to enable NHS services to keep up with the accelerating cost of health care. Popular suspicions thus reflected real constraints imposed on the provision of medical care. Nonetheless, real spending on both health and social security increased by about one-third between 1978–9 and 1988–9. Other welfare-related areas did take a significant hit: housing and employment spending fell by about three-quarters each over the ten years, transportation by 15 per cent.[15] Education increased by less than 10 per cent. These cuts were counterbalanced by increases in areas of Conservative priority: defence and law and order. Overall, while the medium-term financial strategy had budgeted for a cut of 5 per cent over the four years from 1980 to 1984, real spending actually increased by about 8 per cent. By the second half of the decade, however, with the economy growing again and unemployment going down, the record improved, as spending remained fairly steady. More importantly, while government spending had increased from 43.2 per cent of GDP in 1978–9 to 46.8 per cent in 1982–3, by 1988–9 it had fallen to 39.5 per cent, the lowest ratio since 1967.[16] Once the recession started, however, the ratio went back up to 1970s levels, especially after Major replaced Thatcher. Indeed, spending on social welfare (including education and the NHS) as a percentage of GDP from 1992–3 to 1995–6 was the same as or more that it had been from 1974 to 1979.[17]

The government's problems reducing spending made it more

difficult to bring the budget deficit under control. Cutting public-sector borrowing was an important adjunct to the larger policy of reducing inflation and encouraging entrepreneurship. For borrowing by the state supposedly forced up interest rates, thus discouraging private investment, while deficits fuelled the growth of the money supply. Chancellors tried to impose discipline on government departments by strictly enforcing their annual allocations. Initially, the recession again undermined the government's goals, as the deficit did not shrink nearly as much as projected in the medium-term financial plan. Unemployment benefits and shrinking tax receipts assured this. The recovery after 1984, however, meant that the discipline imposed by the Chancellors' cash limits finally had an effect, and by 1987–8 the budget was in balance. However, this success too was undone by the subsequent inflation and recession, and by 1992 the deficit had returned to 1970s levels, while the Major years as a whole saw the national debt double from 1990 to 1997.[18] As a result, Major's Chancellors focused their policies after 1992 on reducing the deficit – not just squeezing public spending, but doing the unthinkable by raising taxes (the largest peacetime increase since the war) and imposing a public-sector wage freeze.

One difficulty in imposing fiscal restraint was local government spending, especially by Labour-controlled city councils. The government's first response was to set a ceiling on the spending by each local authority, with the loss of some portion of the central grant if an authority overspent. Labour councils, however, responded by increasing the rates on property owners. The government then introduced rate-capping, whereby the responsible minister set a maximum rate for local authorities which persistently overspent. The ultimate sanction if an authority ignored its cap was a central government takeover of the powers of the council. Yet the whole situation was profoundly unsatisfactory, not least because Tory-dominated councils bitterly resented the loss of autonomy that came with dictation from the centre about their budgets. Furthermore, hostile councils simply borrowed money to finance their services, thus replacing the central government as a competitor for funds and so undermining the Tories' whole fiscal strategy.

In 1988 Thatcher decided to reform the whole rating system by introducing the community charge, or poll tax. Rating reform had a long pedigree, going back to Liberal anti-landlord agitations between 1880 and 1914. The Tories began toying with the problem in the early 1960s, as rising rates created resentment among their voters, and they spent the first half of the 1980s deciding which way to go with reform. For Thatcher, the problem with the rate was that it fell on property. So like the income tax, it penalised the 'doers' in society, and in the hands of irresponsible socialists it became a vehicle for milking the rich to provide services for the poor. If everyone had to finance those services, however, local governments would have to answer to the whole community if they raised taxes. The poll tax sought to create this situation by placing the tax on all adults in the household. The poll tax was deeply unpopular, however, and the Major government finally replaced it with a council tax that was a combination of the community charge on individuals and a modified rate that increased in stages (bands) with the value of the property.[19] Nonetheless, Major kept the pressure on local spending by making rate-capping universal rather than selective. At the same time, increased centralisation of finances meant that local tax paid for only 15 per cent of spending in England by the mid-1990s. The counterpart to this trend was the creation of centrally appointed extra-governmental organisations (quangos) with multifarious oversight functions but not subject to local control. By the mid-1990s, quangos managed some 35 per cent of public expenditure.[20] Elected local government was effectively being neutered by the Tories.

The poll tax reflected exactly the same taxing philosophy as the government's approach to national taxation. People of property should be relieved of an excessive tax burden, so they would have incentives to invest their surplus income. Since government services had to be paid for somehow, part of the burden was transferred to the poor through VAT. Since the poor were not investors, taxing them would be less harmful to the economy. Income tax cuts were at the centre of the Tories' election campaign in 1979. Howe's budget that year reduced both the top marginal rate and the standard rate of income tax, while nearly doubling VAT. Once the recession was over, income tax rates came down further, so that a standard rate that had been 33 per cent in 1978 had been reduced to 25 per cent by 1988, while the top rate had been reduced from 83 per cent to 40 per cent. The corporation tax rate was cut from 52 to 35 per cent. Overall, while the total tax burden had increased from 33.1 per cent of GDP in 1978–9 to 37.6 per cent in 1988–9, the share of income tax in government revenue had fallen from 30 to 24 per cent.[21] This enormous increase in tax revenue came not only from VAT, but also from increased yield of income and corporate taxes because of the economic expansion of 1982–8.

Taming the Unions

If inflation was to be lowered and government spending contained, there had to be smaller wage settlements. Thus, the unions had to be brought into line. The one mandate the government surely had when it was elected was to limit union power. The lesson of the failure of Heath's measure of 1971 was to proceed piecemeal. Thatcher's governments therefore passed a series of acts in 1980, 1982, 1984, 1988 and 1990, each of which added more constraints on union freedom of action. Cumulatively, the effect of these measures was wide-ranging. All key union officials now had to be elected by a secret ballot every five years, and the government provided money for these ballots. All strikes also had to be authorised by a secret ballot; failure to do so made a strike illegal, which meant the union could be sued for damages. Unions also could now be sued for illegal acts committed by their members during a strike if union responsibility could be proved. Strikes could only be aimed at employers involved in a direct dispute with workers over wages and conditions of work; secondary (sympathy) strikes were also now illegal.

The reforms also narrowed the definition of legal picketing and effectively made closed shops illegal, while protecting workers who did not wish to join unions or to join strikes.

The most draconian of these measures only came in the last two acts, but even the early ones probably had an effect – though it is impossible to disentangle how much worker restraint resulted from trade union legislation and how much from massive unemployment. The level of strike activity dropped precipitously from the crisis levels of the 1970s (see Tables 6.4 on p. 223 and 12.2 opposite). At the same time, trade union legislation facilitated other changes that helped improve productivity – greater flexibility in job descriptions and manning levels, the end of practices and customs which hampered output, the relaxation of demarcation definitions (i.e. the defining of which union claimed responsibility for which job). Indeed, it is likely that management concentrated on these kinds of issues rather than wages in its bargaining, for real earnings continued to grow at a rapid rate in the 1980s. These were the issues that could most easily be dealt with in negotiations that continued the longer-term trend towards bargaining at the plant level through shop stewards.

Table 12.2 shows that labour was not completely passive in the face of the government's onslaught on industrial jobs and trade union privileges. For a while, the unions were convinced that Thatcher's economic policies were failing, and she would have to reverse them and bring the TUC back into the consultation process. Hence, there was early defiance, such as a thirteen-week strike in the steel industry in 1980 and a railway and tube strike in 1982. After the 1983 election, the TUC was more interested in talking; however, ministers were firm that the days of unions influencing policy were over. All the while, periodic high-profile strikes kept the trade unions in the headlines and helped the government remind the public why it had been elected. One of the most notorious was the 1986 battle of the printers against Rupert Murdoch's News International, the publishers of the *Sun* (Britain's largest-circulation daily) and *The Times*. The printers' unions were notorious for featherbedding and resisting new

Table 12.2. Strike Activity 1979–88

	Number of Stoppages	Days Lost to Stoppages (000)
1979	2,125	29,474
1980	1,348	11,964
1981	1,344	4,266
1982	1,538	5,313
1983	1,364	3,754
1984	1,221	27,135
1985	903	6,402
1986	1,074	1,920
1987	1,016	3,546
1988	725	3,752

Source: Riddell, *The Thatcher Era*, p. 50.

technology. They embodied the image of unjustified privilege, the desire not to work, the insistence on outmoded work rules and job definitions, and the resulting high costs and inefficiency imposed on business that was the stereotype of all that was wrong with unionism. When Murdoch moved production to a new, fully modernised plant at Wapping in London's docklands, he fired all his unionised production workers and employed replacements associated with another union. The result was a bitter year-long industrial action, attended by well-publicised violence, which broke the printers' unions' stranglehold on the newspaper industry. Murdoch was himself the embodiment of an aggrandising international capitalism, with no national home, that was the stereotype demonised by the left. That was part of what made the confrontation so fascinating; it looked like evil against evil.

But the liberal *Washington Post* fought an equally bitter strike in the United States at about the same time, while Alastair Hetherington, the former editor of Britain's most liberal newspaper, the *Guardian*, considered both Thatcher and Murdoch the saviours of the industry.[22] So it was not easy for the left to defend trade unionism in the newspaper wars.

It was at a similar disadvantage in the most spectacular of all the confrontations of the Thatcher era – the miners' strike of 1984–5. Arthur Scargill, the president of the National Union of Mineworkers (NUM), was to the right what Murdoch was to the left, the embodiment of all they hated – in Scargill's case, irresponsible union leadership. He was worse. He was a Communist – not just in name, but a true believer! Industrial relations, for Scargill, were an extension of the class struggle. He had made his reputation during the 1972 miners' strike as a successful mobiliser of flying pickets – the practice of concentrating large numbers at a location where the strike could be broken. The intimidating effect of numbers, backed up by the threat and even reality of violence, assured, for example, that no coal got through to power stations. The fact that the flying pickets were not necessarily even picketing their workplace merely reinforced, for conservatives, all that was wrong with the current system of industrial relations. Scargill, on the other hand, had proved his success at fighting their corner for his men. That success, not his politics, got him elected president of the NUM at the end of 1981 with a record 70 per cent of the vote. It was a major victory for the left in its struggle to gain the ascendancy in the union movement, and for Scargill it was a mandate for action. He saw a strike as a political instrument to bring down the government, harking back to the glory days of 1974 when the miners had driven Heath from office. The legitimacy of trying to intimidate a government was always problematic. It was more untenable in 1984, since the Conservatives had just received a fresh mandate in a landslide victory the previous year. Scargill seemed to be claiming for the miners (and the unions more generally) a sovereignty beyond the electorate to make and unmake governments.

Most of the TUC wanted no part of Scargill's political agenda; therefore, the miners were never able to mobilise broad support among the trade union movement, much less a general strike as they had in 1926. Neil Kinnock, the new leader of the Labour Party, was disgusted by Scargill's tactics. He was careful always to support the miners publicly, not wishing to give Scargill the escape of blaming the party if the strike failed. When it was over, however, his indictment of the NUM leadership became part of a more comprehensive campaign to expel Marxists from the party.

There is some debate over whether Thatcher and her advisers took advantage of Scargill's eagerness for confrontation to provoke a strike. In fact, there was so much mutual distrust by 1984 that each side was convinced the other was looking for an excuse for a showdown. Certainly the government was not going out of its way to avoid one. It had already been forced to back down in 1981, when the National Coal Board had wanted to shut down some loss-making mines. If the opportunity arose again, it was determined to break the NUM. Otherwise, the trade unions would never be put in their place and governments and businesses would never be free to do their jobs. The Cabinet therefore prepared well in advance for the coming struggle. It pressed power stations to accumulate large stockpiles of coal so that neither industry nor consumers could be held hostage by power rationing or powercuts. Also at government urging, some power stations installed equipment to enable them to convert to oil if necessary. It explored arrangements to transport coal by road rather than rail so as to sidestep possible sympathetic action by the rail unions. Finally, the police planned more systematically to move large numbers of their forces to regions where disorder threatened. By the autumn of 1983, the Cabinet was ready. The appointment of Ian MacGregor, a Scottish-born American who had just presided over the halving of the workforce at British Steel, as the new chairman of the Coal Board seemed the signal for a showdown.

Scargill played right into the government's hands. The NUM was one of the few unions prior to the reforms of the 1980s that required a ballot before a strike. Furthermore, at least 55 per cent had to vote for the strike; a bare majority was not sufficient. Three times after he became president of the NUM, Scargill sought authorisation for a strike, and three times he failed. This time he called a strike without a ballot – thus confirming all existing views about politically motivated union leaders who did not truly represent their members. Scargill's action made the strike illegal, so the union became liable for damages under the common law. The new trade union legislation did not have to be employed at all, thus denying the NUM a lever for mobilising broader union support. While some union leaders sympathised with the strike, many workers were turned off by the miners' violence and showed little inclination to risk their jobs at a time of high unemployment. The illegal strike also split the NUM, as miners in the more efficient (and so profitable) mines of the Midlands voted against joining it and eventually formed their own union. With about a quarter of the miners still working, with significant supplies of coal already accumulated and more being imported during the strike, and with a mild winter mitigating demand, the strike was never able to cause significant inconvenience to industry or the public.

Thus the strike was doomed as soon as it began. Nonetheless, Scargill persisted. The Yorkshire miners organised massive flying pickets in an attempt to shut down the Nottinghamshire mines, and less often to shut down power stations. At their peak in May and June 1984, they numbered between 11,000 and 18,000 per week, with as many as 8,000 at a single site.[23] There was sabotage of the mines; there was destruction of property, including attacks on the homes of working miners; there was intimidation and violence against individuals. The police mobilised too – some working as long as sixteen-hour days – trying to prevent strikers from travelling to the targeted areas and to protect working miners. Violence inevitably occurred on both sides. Despite the police violence, however, it was the miners who took a beating with public opinion, as television showed barrages of missiles hurled at police, miners and members of the media. Yet the strike was not a complete public relations disaster, for there was real sympathy for the strikers. The central issue of the strike was mine closures. The miners were fighting to preserve their jobs, their way of life, their communities (where virtually all jobs in a village depended on the mines) and the public could identify with these goals. Even more, people sympathised with suffering families trying to get by on a minimal welfare payment, and with the collective efforts of mining communities to help all survive. Shops and even utilities were understanding about bills that could not be paid. Money came from all over the country to help – much from fellow trade unionists, but much also from ordinary people who were not necessarily socialists. But the miners were never able to convert such sympathy into support – because of the violence, and because Scargill was indifferent to public relations.

The government got little popularity from its victory over the miners, but it got all that it wanted. Not only was the myth of irresistible NUM power broken. The miners' defeat, which was almost universally blamed on Scargill, enabled the moderates within the trade union movement to reassert themselves. The number of strikes fell off dramatically (see Table 12.2). Just as important, unions were more open to multi-year wage settlements, deals that linked wage increases to productivity, more flexible work arrangements and even no-strike agreements. This new realism was also reflected in a greater sensitivity to the importance of winning the public over to the workers' cause, which meant better public relations, making certain that union demands seemed reasonable, and not inconveniencing the public too much. The unions were not broken, but they now had to be much more careful, moderate and responsible. A successful railway dispute in the summer of 1989 showed what could be achieved by a more savvy leadership.

Moderation was all the more important because the long-term trend of increasing union membership was dramatically reversed in the 1980s. Between 1948 and 1969, members had slowly increased from roughly 9 to 11 million. Rapid growth in the 1970s had brought the total to over 13 million by 1979; however, after

1980 an even more rapid decline set in – to 10 million in 1990 and under 7 million by 1997.[24] Part of this collapse was due to the decline in British industry and the concurrent expansion of a service sector with large numbers of part-time and female employees; however, such a precipitous retreat also reflected the fact that union membership had become less attractive after 1980. Even as unions were being weakened, however, the European Union emerged as the new protector of workers' rights. Increasingly in the 1990s, Britain came into conflict with European Commission regulations, and as often as not it was forced to back down on issues ranging from maternity leave to workplace safety. As the Thatcherites fear, the EU may yet be the Trojan horse that undoes their success in liberalising the British labour market.

Public versus Private

Even with the substantial increase in tax revenues that the economy produced in the 1980s, the government would have found it difficult to achieve both a balanced budget and income tax cuts without two other sources of revenue. In the first half of the decade, it got substantial royalties from North Sea oil at a time when the price of oil was high. Later, when oil prices collapsed, it got an annual injection of money from the sale of nationalised industries. Thus, the government's privatisation policy was an important adjunct to its fiscal policy. Furthermore, nationalised industries ran at a tremendous financial loss. Ending that loss would eliminate an important drain on government resources and so make it easier to balance the budget. The record of the nationalised industries merely confirmed the basic premise that underlay Conservative thinking under Thatcher: the government could not possibly provide a service as efficiently as the private sector could.

Yet the premise was a doubtful one. The nationalised industries accounted for little of the manufacturing sector, which was the focus of criticism over the years. Steel, which went back and forth between public and private ownership, was the main exception. So the problems of British industry were located in the private sector. For example, here is how the economic historians J. Dunkerley and P. Hare describe the situation at British Leyland when it was created in 1968 from the merger of two other motor car companies:

> The new company had too many product lines; most of the cars being produced were old models, and some of them no longer profitable; some of the plants were not integrated production units and production took place at too many sites . . . There were deficiencies in the design of BMH's [British Motor Holdings] models and the company had a record of poor productivity and mediocre marketing.[25]

This experience was not exceptional. Dunkerley and Hare provide an equally damning description of the shipbuilding industry in the 1960s, while the bankruptcy of Rolls-Royce was another example of mismanagement. This is not to argue that the public sector is preferable to the private; there are plenty of counter-examples to refute such a claim. For example, one study in 1982, which compared public and private corporations in three different industries, found greater productivity and profitability in the private corporations in each case. Two of the three industries studied were in the service sector – airlines and sea ferries; the third was gas and electrical appliances.[26]

While there were certainly gross inefficiencies in the nationalised industries by the 1970s, this record resulted from government's failure to demand anything else. In its effort to balance the budget, Thatcher's administration showed how efficiently nationalised industries could be managed if the dictate was there. Management had to close down loss-making plants, shipyards and mines; to end overmanning; and to adopt market-based pricing policies. Cash limits assured that there would be no back-up money coming from the Treasury if managers were not able to operate within more stringent budgets. Once the government looked towards privatisation, the private sector had no interest in buying loss-making ventures. So the nationalised industries had to be making a profit, or at least show the prospect of doing so, in order to facilitate a share flotation. The outcome of Conservative policy, therefore, was to prove that government *could* manage industry efficiently, if the politicians insisted on it being done and left management free to make decisions according to business criteria. Indeed, once nationalised industries were sold off, their performance in the 1980s was no better than that of the industries that remained in public ownership.[27]

The real key to efficiency was not public or private ownership, but a competitive market. For example, the government opened long-distance bus routes to competition without privatising the industry. The result was a vastly improved service at reduced costs, with lower prices for consumers. The greater efficiency applied as much to the publicly owned National Bus Company as to its private competitors. It could be difficult, however, to create a competitive market when industries were natural monopolies. Yet the 1980s led to a rethink even of public utilities. The break-up of American Telephone and Telegraph in the United States showed that the government could mandate access to that part of the system which had been the source of the monopoly (in this case, the telephone lines) and so foster competition. Economists saw the same possibility with electricity. Yet the Thatcher government did little to use privatisation to promote competition. British Telecom was not broken up at all, while electricity generation was divided into only two companies. For the most part, therefore, effective monopolies were preserved in the privatised industries. Separate regulatory authorities were set up to oversee each one as it was privatised: telephone, electricity, gas and later water and railways. The regulators have had mixed success, depending primarily on the individual in charge, in getting benefits for consumers in the forms of reduced prices, better service and more extensive investment in the industry.[28]

Why didn't the government do more to promote competition, something that it firmly believed in as a matter of principle? The explanation lies in the reasons for privatisation. Its initial plans in 1979 were limited to undoing some of Labour's most recent nationalisations – like British Aerospace and Cable and Wireless. The proposals seemed to presage the kind of battle between Conservatives and Labour over the margins of what should be public and private that had engulfed steel in the two decades after the war. A real privatisation programme only took off after the government's landslide victory in 1983. By that time, its anti-inflation policy was focused much more on reducing public borrowing, and privatisation offered a means of bringing in revenue to supplement taxation while shedding assets that drained the state coffers. The first target was British Telecom, which was already a money-making venture. The economic purpose of the sell-off was to free up telecommunications to borrow on the private market in order to modernise – since borrowing as a public corporation would increase the burden on the budget through interest payments. The assumption, however, was also that privatisation would encourage entrepreneurship, making possible market-driven innovations. The government was warned by its advisers in the City, however, that breaking up British Telecom would require a more lengthy preparation for privatisation, when ministers wanted relief to the budget immediately. Anyway, unsurprisingly, it was a much more attractive investment as a monopoly. So the Conservative government did exactly what it had criticised earlier governments for doing in their oversight of nationalised industries: it allowed political considerations to override economic ones, and decided to sell many of the nationalised industries as single units.

The British Telecom offering in 1984 was an extraordinary success, as the shares were oversubscribed. Service improved, too. The company's monopoly on providing equipment was ended, and within a very short time Britain's telephone system was transformed into Europe's most modern and efficient. Prices, however, remained high. Overall, the British Telecom experience showed ministers the enormous possibilities of a comprehensive privatisation policy, both in terms of providing revenues for the Treasury and deepening the support for the government. So Jaguar, British Gas, British Airways, Rolls-Royce and British Steel, as well as the government's remaining shares in North Sea oil, British Petroleum and Cable and Wireless, followed between 1984 and 1988. The docks and the airports were privatised as well. Each share flotation was a smashing success with the public. The Tories' larger goal was to broaden the base of capital ownership in the country and so increase the number of people who felt they had a personal stake in the system. Between 1979 and 1989, the number of individual shareholders increased from 3 to 9 million (from 7 to 20 per cent of the adult population). About half the owners of shares in privatised companies in 1989 were new shareholders. Most of these new shareholders, however, had a small stake in a single company, while about 40 per cent of purchasers sold fairly quickly to make a profit.[29] As a result, the balance of the value of shares held by institutions, rich individuals and small shareholders did not change despite the enormous increase in the number of shareholders.

The main beneficiaries, indeed, seemed to be the rich, and that was one of the criticisms of the whole privatisation process. First, the costs were high, with the gains accruing to the Tories' friends in the City. Second, the offerings tended to be underpriced, meaning that the public did not get good value for its assets, while purchasers of shares got windfall profits as prices were bid up. The justification for undervaluing the shares, especially after the British Telecom experience eliminated fears that the offering would not be fully subscribed, was to encourage their purchase as far down the social scale as possible. As we have seen, this certainly happened. The biggest winners, however, were managers and executives, who always got a portion of the offering, and often stock options as part of compensation packages; and those in the know in the City, who did not sell quickly, like the small shareholders, but held on to reap the long-term gains of appreciating shares. In the end, the National Audit Office estimated that the government's privatisation policies cost taxpayers some £2.4 billion in expenses and lost revenues due to undervaluation.[30]

Privatisation was not the government's only policy to encourage an increase in the number of property owners in society. Indeed, its first such policy, launched in 1980, was the sale of council houses (i.e. those owned by local government) to their tenants. The right to buy had been a Conservative policy since the 1960s, and a significant number of sales had occurred during the Heath years. Now, the Thatcher government forced councils to sell at a discounted price if the tenants wanted to buy, and subsequent legislation improved the terms for the buyers. The policy was incredibly popular and seemed an unambiguous success, as over one million tenants bought their houses between 1979 and 1988, and another three-quarters of a million had done so by 1995.[31] The inflation and then recession of 1989–92, however, showed the dangers of popular capitalism. Interest rates leapt up even as the housing market collapsed. As a result, many of the new homeowners were stuck with high mortgage payments which they could not meet out of their relatively meagre incomes, while their houses were now worth less than those mortgages. Others lost their jobs (including many in the middle class) and so their sources of income. As a result, mortgage payments were defaulted and the period saw a record number of homes repossessed, while 350,000 mortgage holders in 1992 were at least six months in arrears.[32]

Government policy to promote privatisation of pensions also had adverse consequences. In 1975, Labour had introduced a state earnings-related pension scheme (SERPS) to supplement the basic pension. People could opt for comparable private schemes, and many better-off people did so because their employers provided pension schemes. Most working people, however, relied on the state scheme as a way to top up the basic retirement pension. The Tories now weakened SERPS and introduced financial incentives to push people to move to a private pension plan. Some five million people had opted out by 1993. The government, however, paid no attention to the schemes that were promoted. Some people were misled over the benefits and ended up in a plan that offered less than SERPS had. Eventually, the Major government introduced legislation to bring the value of the personal pension funds of all those who lost money up to the level they would have been at under the state scheme. The Blair government was still grappling with the problem as of the end of 2003, with the estimated total cost to the Treasury being some £19 billion.[33]

Such abuses occurred because neo-liberal ideology insisted that the private sector was always better than the public and could do no wrong – the result of a real contempt for the public sector. That contempt meant that, on the one hand, Conservative governments aimed to make public services more economically efficient, while on the other, they were eager to degrade the status and sense of privilege of those who worked for the state. Public institutions from local government to the NHS were eventually required to introduce competitive bidding for the provision of some services, as a way of introducing competition into the public sector and so enforcing efficiency. The public provider could bid, but it had to come in lowest or lose the right to provide the service. Examples of services that were contracted out included janitorial and cleaning services for buildings, rubbish collection for local authorities and catering for the NHS. The provision of personal social services offers another example of how Thatcherism tried to circumscribe local authorities. Spending on these services for the elderly, children, the handicapped and the mentally ill was one of the fastest growing areas of welfare provision, more than doubling between 1978–9 and 1995–6. Most of this was spending by local government. Conservative policy, as much as possible, sought to limit its roles to the assessment of needs and purchase of services from specialist organisations, whether private sector companies or charities.

In this way, Thatcher's reforms aimed at undermining the authority and independence of local government, which she saw as inefficient, wedded to traditional ways of doing things and often the prisoner of its unions. The service which Conservatives thought best epitomised these problems was state education, and a series of measures, climaxing in the Education Acts of 1988 and 1993, stripped away the power of local education authorities. The Tory reforms aimed to impose standards through national testing and a national curriculum; give parents choice within the state system, so promoting competition among schools; give head teachers freedom to manage their budgets, so they could set priorities, benefit from savings and innovate; and, most radically, allow schools to withdraw from local control altogether, if the parents voted to do so. Schools that contracted out (called grant-maintained schools) had complete control over their policies and budgets and were answerable to the Ministry of Education rather than the local authority. The effect of these reforms was virtually to divorce the local education authorities from setting policy. Not surprisingly, teachers bitterly resisted the reforms, not least because the extra testing put enormous additional burdens on them, while their compensation remained stagnant. Parents liked the choice and heads liked the flexibility, but there was little interest in opting out of the system. Indeed, the Major government had to offer bonuses to induce schools to take advantage of that option. At the same time, the Major government instituted a more rigorous evaluation system, aimed at 'naming and shaming' failing schools, with the ultimate sanction of a central government takeover if they were not able to improve their performance.

In many ways, the government's 1990 changes in the NHS mirrored its education reforms. In both cases, it sought to replicate the market by creating competition within the state system. In both cases, it sought to give the principal providers of the service control over their own budgets in order to encourage efficiency and innovation. In both cases, it sought to weaken the power of trade unions and local authorities. The new internal market allowed groups of general practitioners who had enough patients to have control over their own budgets. These groups (called fundholders) could buy services wherever they chose (i.e. they were not locked into a specific hospital, or even a specific health authority); their efficiency was rewarded by their being able to retain money they saved and to use it to improve the practice. District health authorities could also buy services from wherever they wanted (e.g. a hospital outside the district or even a private provider). The intention of these reforms was to force hospitals to compete for patients and so to improve services. To give hospitals greater freedom, they could choose to become independent trusts (still within the NHS), with control over their budgets, the right to purchase and sell services wherever they wanted (including the private sector) and greater flexibility over employment contracts. Most hospitals did eventually choose trust status. GPs were required to meet minimum standards of service and were monitored concerning their prescriptions and their referrals to hospitals – again an attempt to impose a test of efficiency. In the 1990s, league tables seeking to measure hospital performance by a range of criteria were introduced. So too was the 'Patient's Charter', which defined consumer rights. It offered yet one more basis for accountability within the system and so for measuring its effectiveness. While many GPs feared that the reforms were the first step towards dismantling the NHS, and the British Medical Association (BMA) maintained an unrelenting opposition, many were attracted by controlling their budgets and opted in. Overall, however, the reforms never generated great popular support, and patients did not see noticeable improvements. Indeed, things seemed to get worse in the 1990s, with hospitals closing, waiting lists for elective surgery getting longer, and patients waiting for hours to see their GP. At the same time, critics claimed that too much money was being spent on management and that a two-tier system had been created, where hospital trusts favoured private patients and those of GPs fundholders.

The education and health reforms generated just the anguished howls of opposition from teachers and doctors that the government would have expected – and, indeed, probably welcomed. The opposition demonstrated that the reforms were hurting exactly where it was intended that they should. For

Thatcher loved to attack what she saw as entrenched privilege. Indeed, nothing about Thatcherism so identified it with Victorian liberalism as this hatred of privilege. In both instances, the attack came from a middle class that was outside the charmed circle and resented the elite. The Thatcherites' favoured target, apart from the trade unions, was a professional elite associated especially with Oxford, Cambridge and the oldest of the public schools. Since 1962, Anthony Sampson had been showing in a series of editions of his *Anatomy of Britain* that this public school- and Oxbridge-educated ruling class controlled most of the levers of power and influence in the country. These people were supposedly the propagators of a version of the values of the Victorian aristocracy – including the anti-competitive, anti-money mentality – that Thatcherites believed explained Britain's economic decline.[34] Doctors were certainly part of that elite. Universities, the civil service, the law, the BBC, the City and the Church of England all were identified with it, and all were targets of the Thatcher revolution.

The reforms took one of two forms. One was to try to impose business methods inside the public sector on people who were not used to operating according to such criteria. The reason was simple: the government was looking for ways to save money. So civil service reforms looked to reduce costs, while taking an Oxbridge-bred elite down a peg. Thatcherites distrusted the civil service, which they thought had been coopted by socialism, interest groups and their own interest in seeing greater power and authority given to the bureaucracy. The Prime Minister wanted to get Permanent Secretaries out of the business of policy-making and into the business of managing their departments. This meant that the ethic of business had to be inculcated so as to cut red tape, reduce costs and eliminate jobs. In 1988, the government launched a complete reorganisation of the bureaucracy aimed at hiving off the delivery of services into separate agencies from the policy-making departments, although still subject to their authority. The new agencies were then subjected to market-based criteria to reduce costs and improve services, while agency heads had more autonomy but were also held accountable for meeting targets. Under Major, these heads increasingly came from outside the civil service, as the positions were advertised. At the same time, Major's Citizen's Charter initiative made customer satisfaction a defining test of success. Agencies were now expected to provide annual targets for improved performance, and citizens were offered effective vehicles for complaint and even redress. Major also began subjecting tasks in the central bureaucracy to competitive bidding (called market testing), with the possibility of contracting them out to the private sector. Research and information technology were examples of services that were contracted out, while in some cases whole agencies were privatised. The effects of these reforms were mixed. By 1990, the civil service had been reduced by 22.5 per cent, but most of this drop was accounted for by privatisation; the size of the white collar civil service was static between 1984 and 1994. Thereafter, however, the government's retrenchment campaign brought substantial cuts in bureaucracy. Furthermore, by 1997 over 80 per cent of those who remained were working for the new agencies.[35] However, the constant attacks by ministers increased demoralisation within the service, while the loss of privileged status made it a less attractive career.

The second way in which the government attacked privilege was to end guild-like rules within some professions that limited entry, reduced competition and increased costs to the consumer. For example, the so-called Big Bang of 1986 deregulated the London Stock Exchange by changing the way it charged commissions, eliminating job demarcations and opening its firms up to outside ownership. The goal was to enable it to diversify its services and improve its competitiveness in an industry that was being revolutionised by technology and becoming increasingly international. Only reform could secure its place as the pre-eminent exchange in Europe and one of the 'big three' with New York and Tokyo. It took a while for the brokers to embrace change, but once they saw that their survival depended on it, Big Bang was implemented with a good deal of enthusiasm among an elite that was as pro-Thatcher as any in the country. The proposed reform of the law profession, however, generated much more heat. Lord Mackay ended the monopoly of solicitors on conveyancing, thus opening it up to financial institutions and estate agents. More controversially, he tried to allow solicitors to plead cases in higher courts, thus ending the barristers' monopoly as litigators. Graham Zellick described the Thatcherite approach to law reform in this way: 'to pile on the pressure, undermine the foundations, facilitate a free-for-all, and withdraw to watch the resulting consternation'.[36] This description encapsulated the effect of all the Prime Minister's challenges to entrenched privilege in revered institutions and professions. It is hard to escape the feeling that she enjoyed the show.

The Legacy in the 1990s

The economic crisis of 1989–92 seemingly undid the economic successes of Thatcherism. The whole combination of government policies from 1987 to 1992 gave Britain high inflation, balance-of-payments and budget deficits and unemployment, all at levels similar to those of the Callaghan (though not the Wilson) years of the 1970s. The decision in September 1992 to allow the pound to float, however, eventually turned the economy around, enabling the government to lower interest rates and making exports cheaper. Helped by an unprecedented economic expansion in the United States, Britain's economy began a period of prolonged growth. By the time Labour took over in May 1997, the new Chancellor Gordon Brown, in the words of the socialist historian Ben Pimlott, 'inherited a sounder base than any chancellor since before the first world war'.[37] It was an impressive, though perhaps unintended, tribute by a political opponent to the success of the policies of Major and the Chancellor, Kenneth Clarke, from 1993 to 1997. The economy continued to do well under Labour. Inflation fell to around 2 per cent in 2000, and in 2001 unemployment fell below one million for the first time since 1975 (though employing the new definition, rather than the one used before 1979).* Times looked good again. The moment seems a propitious one for trying to evaluate the impact of Thatcherite policies on economic and social welfare policy-making.

Labour's first action upon returning to power in 1997 was to give the Bank of England complete independence in setting monetary policy, thus removing the politicians from the equation. The Bank's position was now comparable to that of the Federal Reserve in the United States. Brown was trying to do what Labour governments have had to do since Ramsay MacDonald became the first Labour Prime Minister in 1924 – assure the financial markets that the economy was safe under Labour. The experience of 1974–9 had undermined any earlier successes of Labour governments in that direction; so Brown and the Prime Minister, Tony Blair, determined that dramatic action was necessary to convey the message that 'New Labour' was different. Just as important was the charge that Brown gave the Bank concerning how it should determine policy. Controlling inflation was to be its top priority, with a target of a 2.5 per cent annual rate – although he allowed for some fluctuation around that number. Thus, the economic framework for policy-making that had been defined by the Thatcher government was institutionalised. As had been the case under Thatcher, Labour's policy meant that industry took a back seat. British manufacturing took a beating, as an overvalued pound increased export prices to countries in the euro-zone. All was made worse by the collapse of the euro following its launch in 1999. As plants had to close because they could not compete and jobs were lost, the trade unions pressed Brown to give the Bank greater flexibility to take unemployment as well as inflation into account in setting interest rates. The message from manufacturers was the same: industry in Britain would be wiped out if the value of the pound wasn't

---

* Using something closer to the older definition, based on people looking for work but not claiming benefit, unemployment in 2001 fell to 5 per cent at around 1.5 million. Charlotte Denny, 'Warning as pay rises reach record level', *Guardian* (on-line edition), 14 June 2001.

pushed down, preferably as a prelude to Britain joining the euro. But the Chancellor stood firm. The economy was doing well; the overall labour market was expanding, despite the loss of manufacturing jobs; and any devaluation would risk inflation. So there would be no change of policy. As had been the case throughout the century, the interests of the City took precedence. The days of government rescuing firms to save jobs were also gone, although short-term subsidies were still permissible under EU rules. Hence, while the Trade Secretary Stephen Byers scrambled to help facilitate a purchase of Rover when the German car giant BMW decided to offload it, a buyer had to come from the private sector. Similarly, the government refused to provide the subsidies necessary to fit power stations with 'clean coal' technology to help save the now-privatised coal industry. Blair would countenance nothing that conjured up the image of past irresponsible Labour intervention in the economy.

Within limits, Labour was also committed to the Thatcherite approach to taxing and spending – though the Tory legacy on both was not what they would have wanted. Total tax receipts were actually larger as a percentage of GDP in 1997 than they had been from 1951 to 1964, while corporate tax receipts as a percentage of GDP were higher in 1997 than they had been in either 1973 or 1979. Similarly, spending as a percentage of GDP in the 1990s was comparable to the proportion in the 1970s and above that of the 1960s.[38] Still, Labour was not about to let the Tories paint them as a 'tax-and-spend' party. Fiscal policy would promote low inflation by seeking to balance the budget and so eliminate public-sector borrowing. There was to be no return to Keynesian management of the economy. To guarantee probity, Brown promised before the 1997 election to adhere to the Conservatives' spending plans during Labour's first two years of government, while the only new tax would be on the excess profits of the unpopular privatised utilities. Despite pressure from party supporters, Brown stuck by his policy, even when economic prosperity started to produce a budget surplus. As a result, government spending as a percentage of GDP went down in Labour's first three years, and in 2001 it stood exactly where it had been in 1987.[39]

Labour also worked hard to project an image of Thatcherite toughness on welfare, by targeting more benefits to the poorest and emphasising welfare-to-work policies involving further training and education. The old Labour belief in universal and uniform benefits was jettisoned. At the same time, Blair bent over backwards to be sympathetic towards business by watering down several worker-friendly proposals. Yet Labour also identified areas where it could differentiate itself from Thatcherism by trying to strengthen the welfare state. Its most important policy was the introduction of a national minimum wage. The support for a minimum wage was given new impetus when the Major government abolished Wages Councils in 1993. They had been created by Churchill in 1909 to protect workers in sweated industries, but their scope had been expanded over the years to many workers who could not unionise. Now, without a minimum wage, these workers had no protection. Blair, however, kept the minimum low enough not to upset business too much; even the amount of increase proposed in 2001 secured the support of the Confederation of British Industry. In another effort to appeal to traditional Labour values, Blair looked for ways to reduce poverty without busting the budget. So just as Thatcher made lots of cuts in welfare on the margins, Blair started making additions – such as a winter-fuel supplement and the waiving of the television licence fee for pensioners, and a tax credit for working families. After an uproar over niggardly pension increases, Brown offered something far more substantial in the two years leading up to the 2001 general election – increases that could really make a dent in pensioner poverty. At the same time, Labour made another effort to rework the whole pensions system, with a balance of public and private provision, so as to assure an adequate pension for the lowest paid workers forty years hence. Overall, in its first term the Labour government succeeded in changing the balance of its budgets in favour of those at the bottom of the income distribution, a reversal of Thatcherite priorities.[40]

The Chancellor was able to be more generous to pensioners because of the budget surplus that came with prosperity. For the same reason, by 2000–2001 the government could develop programmes to pump substantial sums of money into health and education, the two areas of most importance to voters. The NHS, in particular, gave Blair as much difficulty as it did Thatcher. It had been run on a shoestring for too long – indeed, virtually for its entire existence. In 2000, Britain spent 6.9 per cent of its GNP on health care (which included the small but growing private sector), compared with 9.8 per cent in France, 10.4 per cent in Germany and 14.2 per cent in the United States. As a result of chronic underfunding, by 2000 Britain was suffering from an acute shortage of nurses and doctors: its doctor–patient ratio of 1.7 per 1,000 in the population compared miserably with the EU average of 3.1.[41] Given this constant squeeze on resources, Britain got amazing value for its money – surely better than the US, which, however high the quality of care on offer, left over forty million people uncovered by insurance and not eligible for the Medicaid programme serving the poor. It was a classic case of British muddling through. But the effect of decades of inadequate funding was evident in ever longer waiting lists for non-essential operations and too many instances of shoddy service and incompetence. Britain had the worst record in the developed world for cancer survival and one of the worst in Europe for treating heart disease. As troubling were the growing number of cases of negligent screening and incompetent specialists. The final crisis came with a flu epidemic in the winter of 1999–2000, when the press headlined overwhelmed hospitals which did not have enough beds. Blair had come into office promising to improve the NHS; but it only seemed to get worse during the government's first two years. While the Thatcher reforms had improved the quality of NHS management, fundholding had not delivered the benefits hoped for. Blair retained the hospital trusts, ended the GP fundholding system and tried to reform the internal market so that it would work more effectively.

Still, he was left with an NHS that was too bureaucratic,

centralised and insensitive to its users. To win public support, the government introduced reforms to make health care more accessible. A twenty-four-hour telephone hotline, staffed by nurses, was set up to answer patient questions and give advice. Walk-in clinics, staffed by doctors and requiring no prior appointment, would help bypass the long waits to see GPs. The budget surplus, however, allowed something much more ambitious. In 2000, Brown proposed a 6.1 per cent increase in spending over four years, double the average annual increase from 1979 to 1999. The goal was to raise spending on health care as a percentage of GDP to the European average by 2006.[42] The government could then promise more doctors and nurses, shorter waiting times for operations and to see GPs, and more hospitals and more hospital renovations with some credibility. More radical was Blair's proposal to prohibit private practice for new consultants during the first seven years of their contract with the NHS. The aim was to counter the accelerating trend of NHS doctors devoting ever more time to private patients. At the same time, however, the Prime Minister encouraged partnerships with the private sector when they would improve NHS service. In response to the seemingly steady stream of reports of incompetent doctors practising for years without anyone paying attention, the medical profession was also put on notice that it had to do better in dealing with complaints and disciplining the incompetent, or self-regulation would end. In true Thatcherite fashion, doctors' pay rises and hospitals' budgets would be tied to annual performance reviews. All affected interest groups had kind words for the Labour plan, except for the proposals for private practice by consultants, which provoked the expected howl of protest from the BMA.

While the Blair government struck out on its own in trying to improve health provision, it stood by the Thatcherite education reforms of 1988 and 1993 – giving control over school budgets to the heads, keeping the grant-maintained schools and retaining parent choice of schools within the state system. It also stuck with the national curriculum, testing and league tables of test results to rank schools' performance, and subjecting schools to periodic rigorous evaluation. Those that did not measure up were given a timetable for improvement, with the ultimate sanction of central government takeover and the appointment of outside management if a school continued to fail. More money was pumped into teachers' salaries and given to the schools, but pay rises were to be tied to merit evaluations. This last proposal led to an ongoing war with the teachers' unions.

Overall, however, the trade unions were remarkably quiet during Blair's first term, with most of their pressure focused on pushing the government to be more generous in its welfare policies. Rarely was there a word about repealing the Thatcherite trade union reforms. Indeed, Blair enthusiastically embraced the Thatcherite belief that a flexible labour market was essential to a competitive economy. For this reason, his government put the emphasis on job training rather than job protection. It gave the unions one significant benefit, allowing unionisation of a workplace if 40 per cent of eligible workers voted in favour. This was a far cry from 1974–9, however.

The most ambiguous of the Thatcherite legacies was privatisation. The Major government continued the unloading of the nationalised industries with coal and the railways. The latter, however, along with the sale of the water industry, turned out to be very unpopular. The British Rail sell-off was hurried, as the government wanted to complete it before the general election so that Labour would be faced with a *fait accompli*. It was broken up into 100 units, including 25 companies to operate the passenger services, 5 freight companies, 19 maintenance suppliers, 3 rolling-stock leasing companies, and Railtrack, which took over the track, signals and stations. The only justification for such a complex privatisation was to improve British Rail's increasingly bad service record – the result of decades of under-investment – and to begin the process of modernisation that had been so long postponed. Neither happened. Instead, people saw rising fares of incredible complexity, poorer service, more overcrowding and little in the way of new investment to improve the quality of the network. Yet the new companies made substantial profits, some of which came from continuing government subsidies that were to be phased out.[43] And all the while, management was raking in enormous salaries and bonuses. Public alienation was reinforced by a series of high-profile accidents which could plausibly be attributed to cost-cutting. Such accidents had occurred periodically under British Rail too, but they were supposed to be eliminated by private management and private investment. In the autumn and winter of 2000–2001, the whole system seemed to be falling apart, with miles of track under emergency repair requiring slowdowns along extensive stretches of track. The result was trains cancelled, timetables in chaos and public patience worn out and wishing for renationalisation. By 2001, Blair's government was gradually asserting a stronger control over the management of the privatised franchises.

The public verdict on the 1989 water privatisation has been much the same. After ten years, average water bills had gone up 97.4 per cent, roughly 40 per cent in real terms. The money was to be used to modernise a system that had hardly been touched since the Victorian era. For many years, however, all people saw were annual hosepipe bans in some regions during the summer, the loss of large quantities of water due to pipe leakage and soaring dividends for shareholders and salaries for executives. The companies finally had to respond to the constant public-relations hammering they were getting and in 1997 began a serious effort to repair leaky underground pipes. Yet it was not enough. In 1999, the water regulator finally cracked down – cutting prices and insisting on £15 billion in new investment over the next five years.[44]

Stricter regulation would seem to offer one means of meeting public dissatisfaction with the privatisation of industries that were monopolies, or nearly so. The Labour government made some noises in that direction, as it did about limiting executive compensation in these industries, but not much happened. For the government had no quarrel with privatisation. There was no talk of renationalisation, apart from an occasional plea from the Labour left to take back the railways.[45] Indeed, in the face of intense resistance from many Labour MPs, the government was determined to privatise the air-traffic control system and impose a public–private partnership on the London Underground. Some of the controversy over the utilities may be resolved by the real hero of the Adam Smith model – competition. For what was unimaginable in the nineteenth century or even in 1945 is now possible. Companies can compete in the delivery of water, gas, electricity and telephone service; it is beginning to happen; and it is likely to become European-wide under the EU. So eventually, consumers could see benefits in lower prices and better service, though the chaos in California in 2001 following electricity deregulation shows how speculative such benefits remain.

A Radical Transformation?

The justification for Thatcherism was that it would begin to cure the 'British disease' and reverse Britain's economic decline. What provisional assessment can be offered? In the 1980s, Britain's annual growth rate averaged 1.8 per cent; over the whole period from 1979 to 1997 GDP grew by an average of 2.1 per cent, while from 1992 to 2000 the average was about 2.7 per cent. All but the last is significantly below the 2.8 per cent of 1951–73, but above the 1.3 per cent of 1973–9 (see Table 5.1). Overall, the Thatcherite record was comparable to that of the much-maligned 1960s, and may even have been worse.[46] Similarly, the improvement in labour productivity hardly brought it back to earlier levels (see Table 5.6). The annual average rate of growth from 1979 to 1988 was 2.3 per cent, while in the 1990s it was 2.1 per cent – comparable to, but below, the 2.3 per cent for 1951–64 and 2.6 per cent for 1964–73.[47] The inflation story is, surprisingly, the same. The average annual increase in the retail price index for 1979–97 was 5.8 per cent – well below the inflation rates of the 1970s, but higher than the 4.6 per cent of 1964–70 and 3.4 per cent of 1951–64.[48] All of the post-1979 statistics would be better if we could carry them up to 2000, but the Thatcher legacy would still not look better than the 1960s. On the other hand, if one believes that Britain's undeniably weak performance in the 1970s was simply the first stage in a much more precipitous economic decline that would have continued if Thatcherism had not changed the whole framework for thinking about the economy and economic problems, then comparisons with the 1960s are not really relevant. The real basis for comparison would be what the 1980s and beyond would have been without Thatcherism – something which is, of course, unknowable, and a subject on which views are inevitably politically determined.

The one area of obvious decline which Thatcherism could not touch was the manufacturing sector, and especially the export of manufactured goods. The Thatcherite reforms did improve manufacturing productivity, achieving an annual average growth rate well above that of the 1960s – 3.8 per cent in 1964–73 and 4.5 per cent in 1979–88. Privatised British Steel reflected the character of the changes that took place at their most successful. By the late 1980s, it was more efficient than the steel industries of the US, Germany and Japan. During the next decade, it was the world's fifth largest producer, but as a much-shrunken corporation, with a workforce less than half the 1980 level.[49] Yet manufacturing now accounted for a much smaller share of the economy and the workforce than it did in 1979, with a significantly smaller percentage than in Germany and Japan – but no smaller than in other industrialised countries. While Britain's share of world manufacturing exports had already collapsed from 1950 to 1970 (see Table 5.4), it shrunk a bit more between 1979 and 1992.[50] Furthermore, with the pound overvalued for some of the 1990s, British manufacturers had trouble competing in Europe, the market that was most important to them. The primacy of finance over manufacturing continued to be the rule in British economic policy-making, with the result that financial services accounted for 7 per cent of Britain's national income by 2001 – well ahead of its share for other developed economies.[51]

How, then, does Britain's overall economic performance

compare now with the rest of the developed world? The 1990s was not a good decade for Japan and Western Europe. As a result, Britain's average annual growth rate based on real GDP per capita over the whole period from 1973 to 1997 was virtually the same as that of the United States, France and Germany. Only Japan remained higher, and given Japan's continued problems since 1997, that gap must be shrinking too.[52] Britain has also closed the gap in productivity growth rates with its main competitors, although its overall growth rate of worker productivity still remains well below that of Japan and Germany, while being ahead of the United States.[53] The success of the British economy since 1992 has allowed it to pass France as the world's fourth largest. Even more strikingly, Nobel Prize-winning economist Robert Mundell claimed in January 2000 that Britain could compete successfully within the euro-zone at the sterling–Deutschmark exchange rate that was unsustainable in 1992.[54] Overall, the record is ambiguous – not surprisingly, since the record of decline was far more ambiguous than myth would have it. Indeed, it seems that the real aberration was the extraordinary performance of the war-torn economies of Western Europe and Japan until the early 1970s, and now all have fallen back to a more normal level, comparable to Britain's. In the earlier period, they were catching up on Britain and especially the United States; more recently, it is Britain that has done some catching up.

Thatcherism was as much about changing British attitudes as about reviving the nation's economic performance. Indeed, Thatcher and her supporters saw the two as centrally linked. So *has* Britain become more entrepreneurial? One of the Thatcher government's most significant efforts in this direction was to encourage small business. A combination of tax incentives, loan guarantees and advice initiatives helped to promote a leap in the self-employed by over one million (nearly 60 per cent) between 1979 and 1988 – more than six times greater than the numerical increase of the previous *thirty* years! Similar data are on offer for the creation, expansion and failure of new businesses and the emergence of a venture-capital industry from virtually nothing.[55]

There is also some evidence that more university graduates were attracted to business than once were; its status as a profession improved. However, all this enterprise and talent went into the service sector (finance, leisure, etc.), not into manufacturing. By 1997, services accounted for 70 per cent of GDP, with business services and finance; hotels, catering and entertainment; and education and health as the most important service industries.[56] The decline of manufacturing had been going on since the 1960s. Yet the fact remains: manufacturing, whose failures everyone had been fretting about for over thirty years, continued to decline despite the Thatcher revolution. The structure of that manufacturing sector was changing, however. The old industries that had been a source of problems for much of the century were now of little importance compared to new industries like information technology, electronics, pharmaceuticals, chemicals and aerospace. Between 1995 and 2000, for example, output in technology industries increased 37 per cent, compared to a 1 per cent decline for the rest of manufacturing. At the same time, the transformation from manufacturing to services was not neutral in its effect on Britain's long-term economic performance, for services cannot be as easily exported, while they have less potential for generating employment.[57]

Entrepreneurship should mean more investment; however, the record on investment was mixed. Between 1987 and 1998, Britain's business investment as a percentage of GDP matched that of France and Germany.[58] Yet the British invested just over £1 billion of private capital in new businesses, compared with America's £28 billion. Not surprisingly, given Thatcherite attitudes, British government invested significantly less than its European competitors: an average of 2 per cent of GDP from 1987 to 1998 compared to Germany's 2.3 per cent and France's 3.2 per cent. The private sector did not fully succeed in making up the difference, in part because of a long-standing weakness in spending on research and development (R & D). As of 2000, Britain's R & D spending had been static since the mid-1980s, with the slowest rate of growth of any country in the OECD (which includes the most developed nations of the world). California businesses alone spent four times as much as Britain on R & D, while Britain spent half as much per capita as Sweden.[59] Furthermore, a disproportionate amount of British investment in R & D remained tied to the armed forces. Thus, insufficient investment (including investment in research) continued to be a major problem for the British economy.

So did weaknesses in education. Most economists agree that Britain's worker productivity problems are tied to the education system, and especially to insufficient levels of technical and vocational education. There were substantial improvements in the last two decades of the century, but these did not affect previous generations of workers. Clearly many British school-leavers were not getting sufficient qualifications, and it is too soon to tell whether recent improvements will do the job. While British universities remained among the best in the English-speaking world, they, too, were not contributing enough, especially as spenders on research and development. In 2000, Britain still stood well down the OECD rankings in the growth of university R & D spending, as spending per capita was half that of American universities.[60] Although there was a fair amount of recent investment in business education, Britain was still behind its competitors in training managers. So while the culture does seem to have become more entrepreneurial, more needs to be done in the areas of education, research and development and government investment in infrastructure.

Furthermore, the gains of the last two decades were achieved at a significant cost. One of the great achievements of the 1950s and 1960s was full employment, and with it a reduction of poverty to lows unheard of in Britain's history. Despite the economic woes of the 1970s, the level of poverty remained fairly steady. The poor were not the principal sufferers from Britain's inflation; indeed, one reason for the explosion in government spending in the 1970s was to try to assure that benefits kept up with prices. Thatcherism changed all that. While there is much politicised debate about where poverty actually stood in the 1980s and 1990s, an OECD report claimed that between 1991 and 1996, 'poverty affected 20% of the population, and during the same period 38% spent at least one year below the poverty line'.[61] At the same time, with unemployment higher, welfare benefits trimmed, taxes reallocated from direct to indirect taxation and more people in poverty, there was a significant increase in income inequality. The Conservatives would not have seen a problem with these trends. They denied that income redistribution was a function of government. The purpose of welfare and tax policies was to provide sufficient protection for those at the bottom, not to narrow the gap between the top and the bottom. Indeed, they had deliberately reversed attempts to discourage income and wealth accumulation at the top – believing that past disincentives were one reason for Britain's economic decline.

The Blair government accepted Tory views on inequality. A further cut in income tax occurred in 1999, although the 2001 budget targeted tax cuts at lower-income people. More generally, Labour sought to portray itself as friendly to business and entrepreneurship. Labour was less inclined, however, to accept the Thatcherite view of poverty. Neo-liberals claimed that poverty was an absolute, not a relative, state. It should be based on the spending power of the poor, not on their income in relation to the income of the rest of the population. Thus, when Peter Lilley, the Social Security Secretary under Major, commissioned a study of the spending of the lowest 10 per cent of earners, he found that it had increased by 30 per cent since 1979. Furthermore, 84 per cent owned a refrigerator, 75 per cent owned a video recorder and 57 per cent owned a car.[62] For Lilley, as for most Tories, such data undermined any notion of growing poverty. Labour, however, found it more difficult to ignore the evidence of increased poverty since the 1970s. Indeed, the demand that the government should act to reduce poverty, which did not change much after Blair became Prime Minister, came from a much broader cross-section of the party than just the left. Thus, the reduction of poverty was an area where both government rhetoric and policies sought to reverse some of the Thatcher legacy, as Blair looked for ways to appeal to Labour's core constituency.

Yet overall, Blair and 'New Labour' accepted enough of the Thatcherite interpretation of the economy to justify the view that a real shift had occurred away from the consensus of the Keynesian era. The British economy was doing well during Blair's first term, and there was some inclination to attribute that performance at least in part to the changes that had been implemented under Conservative rule. It is much less clear, however, that the economy actually did any better in the 1980s and 1990s than it did in the 1950s and 1960s, while unemployment was much higher for most of those years, and poverty almost surely had increased significantly.

13

AMERICA OR EUROPE?

While Thatcherite economics had much in common with nineteenth-century liberalism, the two deviated when it came to foreign policy, empire and defence. The radicals of the Victorian era saw defence as the principal area in which to slash government budgets, as there was little else that central government spent money on. They opposed a forward foreign policy and an expansionist imperial policy because both led to confrontations with other powers, and thus to more defence spending. The new liberals, by contrast, concentrated their retrenchment scalpels entirely on a welfare state that did not exist in the nineteenth century. Their belief in a strong national defence and a foreign policy that put Britain at the centre of world affairs provided one of their strongest links to traditional conservatism.

Thatcher herself had only one foreign policy agenda when she was elected in 1979: reversing Britain's declining influence (as she saw it) in international affairs. She was not very clear, however, about how to go about her task. She wanted to rebuild Britain's military strength; yet her commitment to limiting government spending meant that piles of money could not be thrown at defence.* She was not particularly hostile to Europe; but her

---

* In this, she was very different from her friend Ronald Reagan, who poured money into defence while cutting taxes, and thus accepted a chronic and large budget deficit throughout his presidency.

efforts to get a handle on domestic finances meant that she would fight like a dog to get Britain's contribution to the European budget scaled back to a more modest level. She was by instinct an imperialist; but the empire was long gone, and what was left was not worth either the international or financial cost of hanging on to if that proved difficult. It is not even clear that she had any particular interest in the special relationship with the United States until Ronald Reagan was elected President in November 1980. As a result, *The Times* and others could predict during the 1979 general election that Thatcher would be more European and less Atlanticist than Callaghan was.[1]

After her election, Thatcher was content to let her Foreign Secretary, Lord Carrington, take the lead in defining foreign policy. Carrington was an odd choice, for his curriculum vitae incorporated much that she distrusted. Educated at Eton and Sandhurst, he had held a series of defence and imperial political appointments since the mid-1950s. Such a background meant that he was far more inclined to embrace the Foreign Office outlook than Thatcher would have liked. The Foreign Office was the epitome of the bureaucratic establishment, rooted in elite education, that Thatcherism attacked in the 1980s. The Foreign Office had another black mark against it: it was too flabby in defending Britain's interests. She thought it was far too inclined to see the other side of any question and so to seek compromise in order to avoid a breakdown in relations. It was just such spinelessness that she thought had contributed to Britain's decline. To appoint Carrington as Foreign Secretary was to put a product of the system she hated in charge. Yet his long experience of foreign affairs, as well as his standing in the party, meant there really was no other choice. Her interest was in domestic change, Carrington was not an active opponent of her domestic policies and so their relationship was a good one.

All was transformed by the Falklands War. The political fallout forced Carrington to resign at the outset, and, following Britain's victory, a newly confident and engaged Thatcher took charge. In 1983 she appointed Sir Geoffrey Howe as Foreign Secretary.

Howe's standing in the party was her own creation; hence he was likely to defer to her will. Yet for all her assertiveness, foreign and defence policies proved to be much less susceptible to distinctive Thatcherite initiatives than domestic policy was. Financial constraints assured that she could never build up Britain's defences in the way she wished. Indeed, like everyone before her, she had to look for places to cut in order to assure that a modernised nuclear deterrent remained the centrepiece of Britain's defence. Both her enthusiasm for the Atlantic alliance and her ambiguity about Europe had characterised her predecessors, with the exception of Heath. Given her problems with American policies, it is not even clear that the 'special relationship' was much closer than it had been in the past, despite her efforts to trumpet it. While her style of dealing with the EC was undoubtedly more confrontational, it was only towards the end of her tenure that her views changed decisively towards a hostility that assured Europe would be the dominant foreign-policy concern of the 1990s.

The Reluctant Anti-Imperialist

Given that Conservatives had identified the empire with British patriotism for a hundred years, that the present fixation on decline had coincided with the end of empire, and that Thatcher was determined to end decline and restore Britain to prominence on the world stage, she should have been a strong imperialist. In fact, there was little she could do. She could not take back what was lost, and there was little to be gained politically by standing tough on remaining issues like Rhodesia and Hong Kong. The one thing she could do she did: she stood up to the leaders of the liberated colonies in Africa and Asia, refused to apologise for Britain's behaviour as a colonial power or to accept any obligation of guilt as a result of its colonial role, and even criticised them for their failures to build successful, liberal societies. The lion would no longer walk with its tail between its legs at Commonwealth conferences; it would accept no moral lectures from others. The mentality that Margaret Drabble had identified in the 1970s was to be exorcised, especially as there was political capital to be gained at home from standing up to the 'coloured' peoples.

Thatcher would have liked to have done more. Her instincts were with the imperialist wing of her party. Yet the Rhodesia crisis showed how little she could do, and thus why she was willing to let herself be guided by Carrington towards a settlement that reflected the Foreign Office view of Africa. Rhodesia had been a constant headache for Wilson and his successors. On the one hand, African countries organised pressure within the Commonwealth for Britain to do *something* about the white minority government's declaration of independence. At the same time, the right wing of the Conservative Party opposed the bi-partisan British policy on Rhodesia and pressed for an end to sanctions. By the late 1970s, the situation was coming to a crisis, as both the sanctions and a guerrilla war against the government of Ian Smith had taken a toll.

In 1978, Smith launched his own compromise, based on a limited acceptance of majority rule, with reserved powers for the whites. As a result, a new government came into being, headed by the black Anglican Bishop Abel Muzorewa. Thatcher's instincts were to support Muzorewa, who had been chosen in an election that was relatively fair and open. Yet there were two crucial problems: the guerrilla leaders were excluded from election and the constitution that legitimised it was devised by the white government to secure white power. Thatcher had no sympathy for guerrillas, especially when the leader of one of the factions, Robert Mugabe, was a self-proclaimed Marxist. But she understood the need for international support if a settlement was to be final, and she liked the idea of Britain taking the initiative to try to reach one. She therefore came around to Carrington's view that Britain should repudiate the new constitution and convene a conference that included the guerrilla leaders – Mugabe and Joshua Nkomo. Thatcher liked this policy because it excluded the Commonwealth from negotiating and implementing a settlement.

Britain would take charge of and resolve Britain's problem, without outsiders telling it what to do. However, she was not altogether happy with the new constitution that resulted, for, contrary to Foreign Office assurances, Mugabe swept to power in the elections, and Mugabe, she knew, would simply be another African leader lecturing Britain on what it should do. Thus, the outcome confirmed her distrust of the Foreign Office, if it needed such confirmation.

Thatcher's approach to the Falkland Islands was not very different from that to Rhodesia: they were a nuisance to be resolved so that they would cease to be a sore point in Britain's relations with the rest of the region. This was the Foreign Office view, and it was the Thatcher government's as well. For the Falklands had no strategic value and no resources to offer, while the Argentine claim meant that they represented something of a security burden. British governments had been negotiating with Argentina since the 1960s to try to come up with a solution that was acceptable to both the Argentinians and the islanders. There was no such solution, however, for the islanders would not accept any compromise of British sovereignty or British rule, the Argentinians would not accept anything less than total sovereignty and the power that came with it and the British would not act against the wishes of the islanders. A Conservative government certainly could not easily do so because its imperialist wing acted as the islanders' *de facto* representatives in the Commons. Since Thatcher had already braved her right wing in bargaining away the white government of Rhodesia, there was no political capital to be gained from risking their wrath over something as unimportant as the Falklands. Nonetheless, negotiations had continued under her premiership, and a possible leaseback solution had even been floated and rejected.*

By 1982, however, the military government in Argentina was

---

* Leaseback meant a transfer of sovereignty to Argentina, which would then lease the islands back to Britain for some stated number of years – like the lease Britain had on the territories adjacent to Hong Kong.

no longer prepared to tolerate an endless stalemate. It needed to revive its waning popular support, and the Malvinas (the Falklands) seemed to offer a perfect opportunity. The signals from Britain were of indifference. The government, as part of its cost-cutting, had decided to reduce the navy's ability to project power outside the NATO region. As a result, it withdrew the only symbol it had in the South Atlantic of a commitment to defend the Falklands – the survey ship *Endurance*. It was inconceivable to the Argentinians that the British would then fight to reclaim a cluster of islands they so obviously didn't want anyway. Though the Argentines began stepping up the rhetoric at the beginning of March, the British were not troubled. They expected that any crisis would involve a gradual build-up of pressure over many months. Thus, the Argentine invasion on 2 April took the Foreign Office completely by surprise – the main reason that Carrington felt he had to resign. Yet the Argentine junta had completely misjudged the situation in Britain. For Thatcher believed that if Britain did not recapture the islands, it would never again be taken seriously as a power and her premiership would be over. The shadow of Suez hovered over everyone in the government; not only must they act, but they must succeed. At the same time, Thatcher saw a clear moral issue involved. An unprovoked invasion of British territory could not be tolerated. There could be no giving way to aggression, no appeasement of dictators.

All these factors assured that the British sent a substantial task force to recover the islands. Yet virtually from the moment it sailed, the pressure began for a negotiated settlement. Most importantly, a divided Reagan administration did not want to have to choose between Britain and Latin America. While Secretary of State Alexander Haig and Defense Secretary Caspar Weinberger were firm Atlanticists, the Latin Americanists, led by UN Ambassador Jeane Kirkpatrick, pressed for neutrality. Haig therefore tried to broker a compromise. The British were not happy; it looked as if it could be Suez all over again. Yet to under-mine negotiations would make it look as if Britain wanted war. That in itself would undercut the moral high ground that

Thatcher was claiming, confirmed by a UN Security Council resolution calling on Argentina to withdraw. The UN resolution, however, enabled Britain to insist that Argentina vacate the islands as a prerequisite to any understanding, without fear of being accused of obstructionism. Even if only for a moment, the status quo ante had to be restored before a new agreement was implemented. The Argentine junta, however, could not possibly accept this public recantation of the justification for the invasion. Such humiliation would mean the end of its power. Thus, Haig eventually had to give up. Although others then took up the task, they also failed because neither side wanted to compromise.

Thatcher certainly didn't. Throughout the long period of negotiations while the task force slowly sailed the eight thousand miles to the South Atlantic, she supported the armed forces' view of the crisis. There could be no dallying; the task force had to be used or brought home. There had to be meaningful deadlines to negotiations, and if they weren't yielding anything substantive, then the option for war had to be taken. When there was pressure for delay – after the recapture of South Georgia had demonstrated Britain's willingness to use force, and again after the successful landing on East Falkland, to prevent the complete humiliation of the Argentinians – she supported the military commanders in pushing for decisions. Once military action was under way, it could not be halted. Her military advisers loved her because she was decisive and did not back away from the consequences of her decisions. By contrast Francis Pym, the new Foreign Secretary, was the voice of moderation. In their public pronouncements, Thatcher tended to emphasise the government's determination not to compromise its bottom-line terms and its willingness to use force, while Pym tended to emphasise Britain's desire for a peaceful resolution.

Thatcher showed her toughness when she took the flak generated by the sinking of the Argentine cruiser *General Belgrano*, even though it was outside the two hundred-mile exclusion zone that the British had declared around the islands. One of the two most powerful ships in the Argentine navy, the military commanders believed that, by definition, it posed a potential threat to British forces. There was evidence of a possible Argentine naval offensive against the task force. If Britain was to establish superiority at sea, the ship had to be removed from the equation. The sinking of the *Belgrano* cost the British the strong moral position they had occupied up to that time. Thatcher, however, never wavered in insisting that it was right, whatever evidence was produced to show that the ship was not a threat. Some even claimed that the British sank the *Belgrano* in a deliberate attempt to sabotage negotiations, but this was probably not true. In fact, the British were sufficiently shaken by the erosion of EC support in the aftermath of the *Belgrano*, plus the subsequent sinking of the *Sheffield* by the Argentines, to give a positive response to peace proposals by the President of Peru, even though the government did not really like them. The sinking of the *Belgrano*, however, had made it even more difficult for the junta to compromise, and it rejected the Peruvian plan.

The war itself, against a demoralised and inadequately supplied army and a navy and air force whose commanders in Buenos Aires were hesitant to risk their prize hardware (especially after the sinking of the *Belgrano*), was easier than the British had expected. Once victory was secured, however, the government was not inclined to compromise on the larger issue of sovereignty. It had not sacrificed 255 British lives in order, for example, to turn the islands over to a United Nations trusteeship. The veto of the inhabitants was therefore much more firmly established than ever before. Consequently, a very costly war was followed by a costly commitment to defend and supply the Falklands (since they could no longer trade with Argentina).[2] And all this was for some forlorn islands that the British still didn't want!

Given all the effort that Britain had expended to hold on to the worthless Falklands, one would expect Thatcher to have fought to keep the incredibly prosperous colony of Hong Kong – whose people no more wanted to be turned over to China than the Falkland Islanders wanted to join Argentina. Yet Thatcher understood that Britain held none of the cards in negotiating with China on Hong Kong. The British lease over the territories on the mainland adjacent to the island would expire in 1997. Thereafter, Hong Kong could not be a viable entity except with Chinese collaboration, since it depended on the mainland for water and electricity. China insisted on the cession of Hong Kong. Thus, there could be no talk about the wishes of the people; Thatcher simply negotiated the best deal she could in 1984. It wasn't a bad one, as the Chinese promised to respect Hong Kong's capitalist system and traditions for fifty years after the transfer in 1997.

In truth, Thatcher had little interest in the empire – especially in the Commonwealth, which to her mind was just a talking shop that wasted time. Following Britain's entry into the EC, the already declining economic importance of the Commonwealth accelerated.[3] It remained only as a faded symbol of Britain's imperial past, and of the futile hope of the 1950s that somehow the power embodied in the empire could be preserved. Only Queen Elizabeth seemed to care about that symbol any more. Thatcher certainly didn't, and the Queen was none too happy about her barely concealed contempt when it showed, most notably in her bitter battles over economic sanctions against the apartheid regime in South Africa. Britain was the country most affected by sanctions against South Africa, though Germany was closing in; their citizens were the major investors and traders there. Thatcher did not believe in sanctions, full stop. She argued, as did all opponents of sanctions, that they would hurt the poor South Africans, not the government they were aimed at; that they would not work; and that they would only lead the South African government to dig in all the more stubbornly (as she undoubtedly would have done if Britain had been the target of sanctions). While there was some truth to all these arguments, they ignored the fact that the resistance movements in South Africa supported sanctions. Furthermore, sanctions did adversely affect the willingness of Western corporations to invest and do business there, and so had the potential to do some long-term damage (both real and psychological) to the regime. Thatcher's opponents retorted that her policy of 'constructive engagement' in South Africa merely enhanced the standing of the government with its white constituents by breaking its international isolation.

While Thatcher genuinely opposed apartheid and was critical of the actions of the South African government, she could never quite shake off a belief that resistance movements in Africa, like the IRA closer to home, were simply terrorist organisations, and so were to be opposed rather than supported. It did not help that South Africa's resistance organisation, the African National Congress, was openly allied to the Communist Party there. She also hated the sanctimonious moralising by her fellow Commonwealth leaders (white as well as black), who were happy to impose sanctions that would cost them little or nothing but would cost Britain much. She thought the leaders of India and Africa, in particular, were hypocrites who ignored the corruption (and in most African countries the oppressiveness) of their own regimes, but were glad to blame Britain, the Europeans and the Americans for all their problems and to demand more from them. As a result, the more they preached, the harder she resisted. Following the 1985 Commonwealth conference at Nassau, Thatcher made every effort in public to discount the very limited sanctions that had been agreed upon and to emphasise how much she disagreed with the majority. At the June 1986 EC summit, after fighting against sanctions for two days, she finally agreed to some limited sanctions. Yet the whole battle over sanctions merely served to confirm for her how much she had in common with her friends in the United States, and how little she shared with her fellow Europeans.

Repairing the Special Relationship

The 'special relationship' with the United States had always represented an effort by Britain to give itself an influence in international affairs beyond that of its European partners. While no one but the French had seen America and Europe as mutually exclusive alternatives, to some degree they were. Each represented a way for Britain to pool power and so count for more on the international stage than the country's objective power would warrant. It might be possible to 'pool' with both; however, after 1970 British leaders usually tended to look to one or the other. Thus, Thatcher's resurrection of the 'special relationship' in the 1980s was a logical corollary of the growing tensions with her European partners. Thatcher viewed 'the US as the primary upholder of an international order which was good, from which Britain benefited greatly and which, hence, it had an obligation to help maintain'.[4] Most importantly, she believed the American presence had been crucial to preserving peace in Europe, and she was very nervous about any EC initiative that might weaken America's interest in staying there.

At the time of Thatcher's election, the 'special relationship' seemed to be on the way out. Although Callaghan was an ardent Atlanticist, Britain had become a less attractive partner to the Americans once it had eliminated its commitments east of Suez, a process that was completed by the mid-1970s. Indeed, there was a real contempt for Britain by many American policy-makers, who saw it as a weak, effete power that could not even manage its own trade unions. However, the United States was not very appealing as a special partner either. Never was American standing lower than in the wake of Richard Nixon's resignation over Watergate and the country's defeat in Vietnam. Jimmy Carter's apparent weakness further contributed to a perception of American decline. The main focus of US foreign policy in the aftermath of Vietnam was nuclear arms reduction talks with the Soviets. The British did not like being excluded from these negotiations, which affected European security. At the same time, they feared that an agreement could compromise their access to American nuclear weapons systems, while arms reduction might presage a reduced American commitment to the defence of Europe. Since France, like Britain, was not about to have the Americans negotiate away its nuclear deterrent, and since others in NATO were fearful of a weakened American presence in Europe, the negotiations drove Britain closer to its continental allies in the late 1970s.

Yet at the same time, there were ways in which the links between Britain and the United States were so strong, whatever the attitudes of the politicians, that the relationship was inevitably special. There was constant dialogue between the military establishments, which led to common ways of thinking about problems as well as the sharing of technology. If anything, the intelligence operations of the two countries were even closer. There was, of course, the nuclear tie, while the United States made use of more than one hundred military bases and other facilities in Britain, not to mention British overseas bases in places like Bermuda and Diego Garcia.[5] Add to this the growing economic ties, with the enormous presence of American corporations in Britain and British corporations in the United States, and the cultural ties that were made possible by a common language (far greater than those that had existed in 1945), and the concept of special relationship had a meaning beyond the particular focus of either British or American foreign policy. Whatever the tensions, both sides agreed that they had more in common with each other than either had with any other ally.

The centrepiece of the special military relationship remained nuclear weapons. The Thatcher government decided to replace the increasingly obsolete Polaris missile system with America's latest, the Trident. The new missiles would carry many more warheads which could be independently targeted, they were more accurate, and they had a greater range, so they were more likely to penetrate Soviet defences and thus serve as an effective deterrent. The system, however, was very expensive, and Britain was trying to cut public spending. To Thatcher, Britain's nuclear weapons were an essential symbol of its position as a power that counted in world affairs, as well as a key component of Britain's own defences. There was no point in having a deterrent if it was not powerful enough to threaten. Therefore, an upgrade was necessary.

The decision to purchase Trident was part of a broader debate about nuclear weapons that was going on at the same time. In the 1970s, Europeans began to fear that the defence of the United States was being uncoupled from the defence of Europe because the Soviets were deploying intermediate-range nuclear missiles which could hit any target in Western Europe, but not the United States. European leaders worried whether American public opinion would support launching a missile attack from the US in response to an attack on Europe, thus inviting a Soviet attack on the American mainland. NATO therefore agreed in 1979 that American Cruise and intermediate-range ballistic missiles would be sited in allied countries. Then a nuclear attack on those countries would be an attack on Americans and so would trigger an American response. At the same time, NATO would try to get the Soviets to negotiate the reduction or removal of all intermediate-range nuclear weapons. For the first time, West Germany agreed to accept nuclear weapons, as did Italy, Belgium and the Netherlands. Britain, too, was targeted to receive these weapons, in the form of Cruise missiles.

The NATO agreement, in conjunction with the Trident decision a year later, was a red flag waved in front of the left all over Europe. In Britain, it triggered the revival of CND and led the Labour Party to embrace a policy of unilateral nuclear disarmament. Comparable movements against deploying the American weapons were organised on the Continent. The European left's distrust of the United States merely increased with the election of Reagan as President in 1980. Reagan used a kind of Cold War rhetoric not heard since the 1950s, while his government seemed more interested in deploying nuclear weapons than in negotiating them away. It would not even submit Carter's SALT II agreement to the Senate for ratification. The result was very powerful European peace movements, which looked as if they had a real chance of winning public opinion because they spoke to anxieties that were shared by a broad segment of the population. They represented a substantial challenge to Thatcher and West German Chancellor Helmut

Schmidt, whose Social Democratic Party did not support him on the issue. Siting the missiles in Britain and on the Continent became a test both of NATO's willingness and ability to follow through on the policy. In order to neutralise the opposition, Thatcher tied Britain's Cruise missiles to the alliance, which remained popular. There could be no caving in to Soviet pressure, threats or blackmail, which were aimed at dividing and weakening NATO. For four years, Thatcher fought the opposition until the missiles arrived at British bases in 1983.

The decision to deploy intermediate-range missiles was part of a larger policy of upgrading NATO's defences in response to the perception that it had lost ground to the Soviets in the 1970s. After 1977, Britain was subject to a NATO agreement to increase defence spending in real terms by 3 per cent annually. Years of cutting had left the British armed forces needing to modernise weapons and equipment, as well as to increase the pay for the armed forces in order to stop the haemorrhage in skilled personnel. Thatcher embraced the NATO policy with enthusiasm. Britain's spending as a percentage of GDP had been declining: from 6 to 7 per cent in the 1960s to 4.7 per cent in 1978–9. By 1983–4 spending was back up to 5.4 per cent of GDP.[6] Yet the imperatives of reducing public spending and getting the budget deficit under control soon forced the government to backtrack. In 1980–81, Thatcher launched a comprehensive review of defence priorities. Given the absolute primacy of the army and air force in West Germany (Britain's NATO commitment), of the air force in Britain's home defence and of the nuclear deterrent, there was only one place left to cut. The result was a proposal to reduce the size and importance of the Royal Navy – which would have been a mini-revolution in British defence policy. The Falklands War junked that plan, however, by demonstrating how the cuts would have crippled Britain's ability to carry out operations independent of NATO and outside the NATO area. For the time being, therefore, defence budget paring concentrated on Thatcherite standbys like increased bureaucratic efficiency, competitive bidding for contracts, contracting out in-house functions and privatisation.

Thatcher's toughness on NATO issues helped to consolidate a burgeoning love affair with President Reagan after he took office in 1981. The 'special relationship' was always most meaningful when there was a real personal relationship underpinning it, and that was certainly the case with Thatcher and Reagan. First and foremost, they saw themselves as fellow cold warriors engaged in the struggle against a hegemonic communism that aimed at world conquest. The West, they claimed, had been weakened by a period of wimpish leadership on both sides of the Atlantic which had pursued détente and so allowed the Soviets to secure strategic advantages. Their job was to restore Western superiority. Secondly, they were both engaged in a project of reversing national decline by pursuing similar domestic agendas. For despite significant differences, the Reagan administration followed the trail of economic liberalisation that Thatcher had been blazing since 1979. Finally, both were moral absolutists who saw foreign and domestic issues in clear terms of right and wrong, without shades and nuances; and they were both fervent proselytisers for their beliefs. Their close relationship, however, was based on two inequalities. One was the obvious superior power of the United States that made Britain a junior partner. The other was Thatcher's clear superiority to Reagan as an intellectual and a workaholic. One suspects that a consciousness of that superiority was part of what made the relationship attractive to her, especially as her premiership lengthened, and with it her experience and her confidence.

Nonetheless, the 'special relationship' was not nearly as harmonious and trouble-free as Thatcher's rhetoric implied. A series of crises in the 1980s created trouble between the two countries. The first came when the United States sought to impose sanctions against the Soviet Union following the imposition of martial law in Poland in 1981. The sanctions would have terminated the building of a gas pipeline from Siberia to Western Europe because of the American technology involved, which in turn would have bankrupted several European companies participating in the deal. The incident smacked of the United States dictating foreign policy to the European allies, while the exclusion of US grain exports to the Soviet Union made the Americans appear hypocritical. In effect, the American sanctions would punish Europe but not the Soviets; they would have a major effect on the European economy, but virtually none on the American. Thatcher was no more supportive of sanctions against the Soviet Union than against South Africa. She became Europe's envoy to America, persuading the Reagan administration that it had to find a way out that would preserve the pipeline deal. Eventually the US backed down, though it took a year.

The Falklands crisis also created some problems between Britain and the United States. The British had little patience with the initial American position of even-handedness, which implied that Britain was somehow an ally of equal importance to Argentina or Latin America. Yet conscious of the Suez precedent, the Washington embassy launched a mammoth (and successful) public relations campaign to win the support of Congress and the American public, as well as the Reagan administration. Once the administration came off the fence, American support for the British in the war was solid. Even during the period of uncertainty, Britain's friends in the defence and intelligence establishments were providing assistance; now it increased substantially. Yet the enormous goodwill that resulted from the Falklands War was completely undermined a year later when the United States invaded the Caribbean island of Grenada in October 1983. The pretext was a coup, and the threat to American medical students on the island if there was a breakdown in order. However, the Reagan administration welcomed the opportunity to overthrow a Marxist government long considered excessively sympathetic to Cuba and the Sandinistas in Nicaragua. Although Grenada was a member of the Commonwealth, Reagan had not informed Thatcher of American plans because of the need for secrecy. Indeed, the United States deceived the British government of its intentions right up to the moment of invasion. Thatcher was furious, not least because the British had already decided that an invasion would be unjustified under international law. The

Americans could not understand her attitude; they had assumed that, with her well-known anti-communism, she would endorse the enterprise. As always, the disagreement was patched up, but not before Thatcher had made her displeasure known in some not very oblique public statements.

Winning the Cold War

Following her victory in the 1983 general election, a more confident Thatcher began to assert herself as a Western stateswoman. She toned down her anti-Communist rhetoric and started to promote the recently discredited policy of détente. It was in this context that Mikhail Gorbachev, a rising star in the Politburo, was invited to London in December 1984. He made a deep impression on all who met him, including Thatcher, who famously said, 'we can do business together'. She found him intellectually engaging, interested in what he saw in Britain and supportive of disarmament. Gorbachev was interested in Thatcher as someone who could influence the Reagan administration, which seemed hopelessly immersed in a Cold War mentality. The Soviets were not alone in being troubled by American rhetoric and behaviour. British and European public opinion was becoming more fearful of the Americans than of the Soviets in world affairs. Indeed, the United States had never been less popular with the British people. A cowboy mentality now seemed to infuse American policy-making, as evidenced by the support of guerrilla wars against Marxist governments in Nicaragua, Angola and Afghanistan. The same disregard for international law seemed evident in an April 1986 air strike, launched from British bases (with the Cabinet's reluctant permission), against Colonel Muammar Gaddafi of Libya, who was thought to be behind a series of terrorist attacks in Europe. With a restless public on her hands, Thatcher needed to play the role, much aspired to by British Prime Ministers, of interpreter between the Soviet Union and Europe on one side and the United States on the other. That role now meant not only explaining and defending

American positions and policies, but also trying to influence the Americans to tone down the bombast and be seen to be genuinely seeking peace.

At the time of the Gorbachev visit, the Soviets' immediate concern was Reagan's proposed Strategic Defense Initiative (SDI). Intended to shoot down missiles in space (hence the sobriquet 'star wars'), SDI threatened to destroy the system of deterrence, based on mutual assured destruction, which had been the basis of nuclear peace between the superpowers since the 1950s. The British shared a general scepticism over whether a space-based system could work. More importantly, they were troubled about its implications for the Anti-Ballistic Missile Treaty and so for Britain's own deterrent. For if the Soviets took it as a repudiation of that treaty and constructed their own missile defence system, Britain's nuclear weapons could be neutered. At the same time, SDI called into question America's commitment to defend Europe. For if the United States was protected from a nuclear attack, could it be trusted to go to war in the event of a Soviet attack against a Europe that was no longer the first line of defence for the US? Thatcher was able to persuade the Americans to accept a statement that SDI-related systems would be subject to negotiation, thus limiting the ability of the United States to act unilaterally, and that SDI was a complement to deterrence rather than a replacement for it. Publicly, she supported research and development of SDI systems, thus staying on side with the Americans. As far as she was concerned, however, all the principles of nuclear balance that had tied the United States to Europe and preserved the peace for forty years were being undermined by Reagan's chimerical vision of a world free from the fear of nuclear weapons.

This was the vision behind Reagan's near agreement with Gorbachev, at Reykjavik in October 1986, for the eventual elimination of all strategic nuclear weapons. Gorbachev was still trying to kill SDI and get American medium-range missiles out of Europe. Reagan, however, would not agree to any limitation on SDI; so the agreement collapsed. Thatcher was appalled. Again, as with SDI, Reagan appeared willing to weaken the European defence system to get security for the United States. For intermediate and short-range nuclear weapons were built into NATO's defence strategy, since the Soviets had overwhelming superiority in conventional forces. Reykjavik also implied the bargaining away of British and French nuclear weapons, something the President clearly had no power to do. The whole performance seemed to be another example of the Americans failing to consult the Europeans when making decisions that impacted the alliance as well as the United States. Reagan had not intended this. The near agreement on 'zero option' happened almost by accident, not as the result of a carefully planned American initiative. Indeed, Reagan's own advisers apparently were as horrified as the Europeans were. Thatcher immediately rushed to Washington and secured three promises from Reagan: NATO's strategy remained unchanged, disarmament negotiations would include conventional as well as nuclear weapons and the United States would follow through on its promise to sell Trident missiles to Britain.

The effect of Reykjavik was to make radical arms reductions viable. The following year, Reagan and Gorbachev agreed to eliminate all medium-range nuclear weapons within ten years. Thatcher was not happy. For even though their elimination had been the justification for the NATO deployment, she had never been a supporter of the 'zero option'. She saw the deployment as a necessary part of a broader project to modernise NATO's nuclear deterrent. The negotiation track was a tactic to carry along the countries that would be deploying nuclear weapons for the first time, helping them with the inevitable domestic opposition they would face. It helped Thatcher, too, to portray these weapons simply as a response to a Soviet escalation of the nuclear arms race. She never actually believed the Soviets would agree to the 'zero option'. The advent of Gorbachev, however, had upset all her calculations. Now there was a real possibility that the enthusiasm of the two leaders for nuclear disarmament would be extended to other nuclear weapons.

Thatcher focused on blocking negotiations about short-range nuclear weapons, which were central to NATO's strategy of repulsing a Soviet ground offensive. By 1968, the Soviet Union had the missile capability to level the United States and Europe together. With the likelihood of anyone using intercontinental nuclear weapons hopefully nil, NATO was left without a strategy for deterring a conventional Soviet attack. NATO therefore adopted the policy of 'flexible response': if driven by the threat of defeat following a Soviet incursion, NATO might use battle-field or short-range nuclear weapons. The premise was this: if the Soviets were convinced that a limited war could escalate to a nuclear war, that risk would be a more effective deterrent than building up NATO's conventional arms. At the same time, flex-ible response tied the US more effectively to Europe's defence, since such an escalation would bring American intercontinental missiles back into play. However, this strategy also implied that NATO could be the first to use nuclear weapons and that it would do so on German soil – which understandably made the West Germans unhappy. Now, with the Cold War winding down, the Germans saw an opportunity to get what they really wanted: the end of Germany's position as a potential nuclear battlefield.

Thatcher therefore had difficulty achieving her goals. She wanted NATO to modernise its theatre weapons. She also insisted that all further steps towards nuclear weapons reduction be tied to progress on reducing conventional arms in Europe – a logical position since the two were linked through flexible response. Once again, however, Gorbachev's flexibility undercut her position, as he announced radical unilateral cuts in Soviet conventional forces in Europe. The Germans therefore lost interest in modernising nuclear forces and were ready for NATO to negotiate a short-range missile reduction while modifying the doctrine of flexible response.* On all these issues, US President

---

* The Soviets had a substantial quantitative and qualitative superiority in short-range nuclear weapons, as they did in conventional forces, so the advantage of reductions lay with the West.

George Bush deferred to Germany's preferences rather than Britain's. Even to the United States, Thatcher was looking more and more like a Cold War dinosaur in her approach to European security. Western Europe was getting everything that it had ever dreamed of, and she was only able to throw up roadblocks.

The end of the Cold War meant the end of one of Britain's favourite roles: the interpreter of each of the superpowers to the other, trying to encourage dialogue and prevent a breakdown in relations. After 1990, there was no threat of superpower conflict, and, indeed, Russia for the moment ceased to be a superpower. Thatcher similarly had sought to assume the role of interpreter of the United States and the EC to each other. This one, too, was predicated on Britain's 'special relationship' with the United States. As Thatcher increasingly marginalised herself in Europe, however, she ceased to be of much use to the Americans as a reliable interpreter of European views. So the 'special relationship' went into hibernation again until 1997, when the personal chemistry between Bill Clinton and Tony Blair, as fellow baby-boom generation proponents of moderate left-wing politics, sought to revive it.

The European Wars

Thatcher's initial confrontations with her partners in the European Community were over the same issues that had preoccupied her Labour predecessors: Britain's disproportionate contribution to the EC budget and the cost of the Common Agricultural Policy (CAP). In negotiating the treaty with the EC, Heath had secured a period of transition before the full weight of Britain's budget and CAP obligations came into effect. That period was now drawing to a close. Britain and West Germany were left as the only net contributors to the EC budget, even though Britain's economy ranked seventh (as measured by GDP per head) among the nine members. A rebate formula had been introduced as a result of Wilson's renegotiation, but it was insufficient. With Thatcher trying to reduce public spending in

Britain, the contribution to the EC budget was an obvious target. A reform of CAP to limit its cost would have been her preferred way to secure her goal, since CAP accounted for such a large proportion of total expenditure. The other members were unwilling to touch CAP, however, so a rebate was the only means available to reduce Britain's contribution.

Britain had been a difficult member since it joined the EC, and the others were getting tired of the constant griping of its leaders. Why did they always take a narrow, self-interested approach to Community issues like the budget, rather than a broad European outlook?* The dictates of domestic politics always seemed to be pushing the British to resist proposals for European cooperation. For example, Wilson and Callaghan had fought a common energy policy, fearing that it would be a vehicle for the other members to get hold of North Sea oil. Similarly, they had resisted joining the exchange rate mechanism of the 1970s, which created fixed exchange rates among participating currencies, for fear that the weakened British economy could not handle the deflationary pressures that would result. Britain therefore had a history of friction with the other EC states even before Thatcher became Prime Minister. She took this tension to a new level, however. Her style was alien to the other European leaders, who were much more used to *politesse*, the language of diplomacy and compromise in negotiating issues. All of this embodied the Foreign Office mentality that Thatcher hated. She was much more direct, strident and stubborn. She was even willing to threaten to immobilise European business or to withhold Britain's budget contribution altogether to get her way. The Europeans were not

---

* There is a lot of myth in this continental stereotype of the British. De Gaulle and the French had shown the way in using the EC for self-interested purposes, and all the other countries fought hard to protect their interests when necessary. However, the British were not willing to pay lip service to the European idea in their rhetoric. Thatcher, of course, hated the European idea, but to most of the British leaders there was a lot of humbug in it. This was the real source of division between Britain and the original six members. Other new members, however, learned quickly how to soften their self-interested actions with the words of European idealism; the British never would do so.

used to the public and blunt airing of differences, accompanied by threats, that Thatcher adopted.

Thatcher was convinced that moral right was on Britain's side, so she was not inclined to compromise. She seemed to revel in the impasses in meetings of the European Council (the heads of government). Yet her style made it all the more difficult for others to make concessions, which would look like caving in to British dictation. Britain had two means of putting pressure on them: spending was pressing up against revenues, and any revision of the budget formula to increase resources required British consent; and the farm price supports each year required unanimous approval. But the other members could retaliate by withholding Britain's budget rebate. The negotiations dragged on for four years, with interim compromises that gave Britain less than it wanted while it accepted some increase in price supports. When negotiations opened again in June 1983, Thatcher insisted that there would be no increase in the EC budget until the British problem was settled. Twice the exasperated French President François Mitterand spoke of relaunching the EC without Britain. Once it became clear, however, that Thatcher was not going to withhold Britain's budget contribution, Mitterand was able to push for a final resolution, which was achieved at Fontainebleau in June 1984. The British did not get the full amount of their original demand in 1979, but the rebate formula treated them generously. The rest of the EC got an increase in the size of the budget, while they managed to shelve CAP reform. There has been enormous debate between pro- and anti-Thatcherites over whether Britain gained from her belligerent behaviour; however, Britain probably would not have done as well with someone else using more traditional methods of diplomacy. The Thatcher style was distasteful, but it forced concessions that the French, in particular, were not inclined to make. CAP, however, was what concerned the French the most, and they were very effective at blocking change. A formula to control agricultural spending was finally agreed on in 1988, but significant cuts only came in 1992 as part of a larger GATT agreement to reduce agricultural tariffs.

Yet even with the 1992 reform, CAP imposed an enormous cost on British and EU consumers: the increase in agricultural prices that it caused ranged from 25 to as much as 40 per cent in any given year.[8]

Following the settlement of the British budget issue, the EC leaders could focus on how to equip the Community to compete more effectively with the United States and Japan (the economic superpower of the 1980s). The British wanted a single market and got it with the Single European Act of 1986. The purpose of the Act was to remove non-tariff barriers and assure the free movement not only of goods, but of services, capital and labour in the Community by 1992. For Thatcher, it not only reflected her belief in a free economy; it would open up the Community (West Germany, in particular) to British financial services, the nation's great economic strength. Thatcher, however, had to pay a price to secure the Single European Act. She had to concede the end of the national veto with the introduction of qualified majority voting (i.e. majority voting weighted to give more votes to larger countries) on specified issues. There were also two vaguer commitments in the act that would come back to haunt her – those to monetary union and to European union.

Just as importantly, the Single European Act itself turned out to be a Trojan horse for interventionism, since many matters could be related to fair competition within the EC. For example, the European Commission in Brussels believed that the equali-sation of trade union rights, pension costs and taxation was insep-arable from creating a genuine single market in which all competed fairly. If, for example, British firms could undercut their French counterparts because they paid lower taxes or made smaller contributions to pension funds, that would give them an unfair advantage competitively. The Commission wanted to avoid the kind of competition engaged in by American states, which offer tax breaks and other incentives to induce corporations to locate there. Thus, a whole range of social, financial and indus-trial policies were justified by the Commission as necessary to consolidate the single market. The kinds of regulations that the

Commission wanted to impose, however, were just those that Thatcher had worked so hard to dismantle at home. Lower taxes and weaker trade unions had been at the centre of her policies to make British industry more competitive; now the Europeans wanted to undermine that competitiveness again.

In truth, the creation of a single market meant a level of European interdependence which inevitably compromised the sovereignty of individual states – something that Thatcher refused to admit. This reality was central to the alternative vision of the EC: to make it more like a federal state, a 'United States of Europe'. The single market was simply one aspect of the radical institutional reform that was necessary to achieve this end. Britons (especially the anti-European press) came to identify this vision of the future with Jacques Delors, the President of the European Commission from 1985 to 1994. Delors was a friend and former colleague of France's socialist President, François Mitterand. Delors's proposals for a European Union included monetary union, guaranteed social rights, tax harmonisation, common foreign and defence policies, a more democratically responsible European Parliament and more majority voting within the European Council. Thatcher supported the single market and cooperation on foreign policy and defence, but none of the rest. Indeed, she despised Delors's interventionism, with its strong tinge of socialism and its close regulation of the economy. Her speech at Bruges in October 1988 was her declaration of war against this vision. There she made her famous statement, 'We have not successfully rolled back the frontiers of the state in Britain only to see them reimposed at a European level, with a European super-state exercising a new dominance from Brussels.'[9] She emphasised not merely the futility, but the danger, of trying to suppress national identities that had a long historical tradition and had been the source of European vitality. In later speeches, she focused her attacks on Delors as a socialist pursuing a socialist agenda and on the irresponsible Brussels bureaucracy, answerable to no electorate, which sought to make policy by regulation. She defined as a principle for Community policy-making what came to be known as subsidiarity: policy should be made at the lowest appropriate institutional level. The Community should only act when the state clearly could not – that is, when action was impossible without incorporating all states in a single policy.

The next step on the agenda towards greater European union was a single currency. Monetary union had been a Community goal since the 1970s, and Heath had agreed to it in his first EC summit after Britain joined. Since 1979, many EC states had been participating in an exchange rate mechanism (ERM), whereby their exchange rates fluctuated within a narrow range around a defined parity relative to the German mark. Central banks were required to intervene to preserve the parity rate, though the possibility existed for a revaluation or devaluation if members judged that the parity was no longer appropriate. The ERM was not the same as monetary union; it was more like a Bretton Woods arrangement for participating EC members. The pound was not tied to the ERM, but by 1988 and 1989 the Chancellors (first Nigel Lawson and then John Major) and Foreign Secretaries (first Geoffrey Howe and then Douglas Hurd) all wanted sterling to join. Thatcher resisted, believing that membership in the ERM was the first stage towards monetary union (a view confirmed by Delors). Her colleagues did not want a single currency. Rather, they saw the ERM as a pragmatic form of European cooperation whose link to monetary union could be broken once Britain was inside. Britain should join in order to gain extra leverage in its battle against inflation, with the German Bundesbank operating as the enforcer. Thatcher, however, saw the line in the sand drawn when the EC committed itself to a single currency managed by a European central bank. If a country did not control its own money, it had lost one of the fundamental attributes of sovereignty; therefore, monetary union had to be resisted as the first step towards a European superstate. While Thatcher ultimately agreed to the pound entering the ERM, she did so protesting all the way, and she was never happy about it.

The ideological struggle over Europe's future made Thatcher

increasingly offensive in her dealings with her European partners. She went out of her way to insult the French in 1989, during
the commemoration of the two hundredth anniversary of the fall
of the Bastille and the outbreak of the French Revolution – an
event of such consequence that historians have long treated it as
marking the advent of the modern world in Europe, if not in
Britain. Yet Thatcher said that it was not all that important, for
its principles of liberty had been invented by the English one
hundred years earlier without any of the French violence.* She
was trying to upstage Mitterand during one of the great moments
of his presidency. Such behaviour came back to haunt her when
she needed French cooperation in resisting German unification
following the fall of the Berlin Wall. Brought up on the lessons
of the first half of the century, Thatcher saw a strong Germany
at the centre of Europe as inherently destabilising. She also shared
the Germanophobia of so many Britons of her generation, which
was so carelessly expressed by her colleague Nicholas Ridley in
1990, when commenting on the EC: '[It's] all a German racket
designed to take over the whole of Europe . . . You might as well
give it to Adolf Hitler, frankly . . .'[10] Thus, she fought German
unification, arguing instead that there should be no border
changes for ten years, giving everyone (including the Germans)
plenty of time to consider what they wanted.

The Bush administration, however, had lost patience with a
Britain that was persistently obstructionist in Europe. The
Americans cared only that any change should reflect the will of
the people and that a united Germany be part of NATO. Thatcher
expected Gorbachev to be her ally; the Soviet leader, however,
thought he could use unification to secure a neutral Germany,
and Thatcher, of course, could not even consider such an option.
Gorbachev conceded unification in principle and then backed

---

* Her comments were not only insulting; they were false, ignoring Britain's revolution in the 1640s which involved a violent civil war, the execution of the King
and the abolition of the nobility and the monarchy. Thatcher's remarks reflected
her tendency to see events exactly as she wished – thus disproving her own
insistence that history is a matter of fact, not of interpretation.

away from his insistence on neutrality. Finally, there was France – Germany's other historic enemy. Mitterand, however, believed the EC provided a sufficient check on German nationalism; the more integrated the Community was, the more effectively it would perform that role. He therefore gave his approval to unification on the condition that German Chancellor Helmut Kohl support the next steps towards European union. Thus Thatcher lost the nation that should have been her strongest ally in resisting the Germans, and in the name of the cause she hated.[11]

By 1990, Thatcher's European policy was a shambles. She believed that a strong European state would be the vehicle for projecting revived German power while pursuing long-standing French policy goals. It would be protectionist and anti-American, and would thus encourage the United States to withdraw from Europe. Yet in trying to block German unification, she had been unable to influence any of her allies (or Gorbachev) and had failed in her aim. At the same time, she had provided some impetus towards a closer European union, including monetary union. Neither Kohl nor Mitterand had any use for her. She was isolated as the other EC members agreed to press forward on all fronts, political and economic, towards closer integration. Her frustration that she was losing the argument in the councils of Europe probably helps account for the stridency of her language and her obstreperous hostility during and after the Rome summit in 1990 – which contributed to her fall from power. Yet Thatcher was not as isolated as she seemed when she attacked the Brussels bureaucracy that was interfering in the affairs of member states. On the contrary, the evidence of the next few years would show that many ordinary Europeans shared her anxieties concerning the loss of national sovereignty. They were ignored by elitist political leaders who thought such issues were beyond the understanding of the democracy – leaving their people to be wooed by the anti-European neo-fascist right. The only responsible leader who articulated their concerns was Thatcher. Yet the famous Thatcher style had left her weakened in the discussions about Europe's future and British foreign relations in a mess.

The Thatcher Legacy: The 'Special Relationship'

Her successors had to pick up the pieces. Even relations with the United States were in need of repair, as the Bush administration had little use for a Britain that was isolated in Europe. John Major, who was not all that interested in foreign policy, was happy to leave its management to his Foreign Secretary, Douglas Hurd, who was by training and temperament a diplomat. Like Major, he was a moderate, so they worked well together. Major did not share Thatcher's emotional attachment to the 'special relationship'. But then, neither did Bush, who resented Thatcher's domineering style and seeming control of Reagan. Major and Bush got along well and respected each other. Their laid-back personalities and unpretentious styles were quite similar, as were their politics. The fact that they had to fight a war together provided an added incentive for them to learn quickly to work together.

Following Saddam Hussein's invasion of Kuwait, the Bush administration (encouraged by Thatcher) began a process of building up forces in the Persian Gulf and marshalling support in the United Nations aimed at forcing the Iraqis to withdraw. The resulting Gulf War was not really Major's war. The key decisions had been made before he became Prime Minister, and thereafter Washington was always in control. The British, however, felt the need to make a major military contribution to prove their reliability as an ally. Major's job when he succeeded Thatcher was to get British public opinion, which was not as divided as in the United States, behind the war. In doing so, Major kept the leaders of the opposition informed of what was planned – something Thatcher had never dreamed of doing during the Falklands War. When the vote came in the Commons, only the Labour left voted against British participation. Major's real contribution came after the war was over. Despite discouragement from the Bush administration, he took the initiative in organising European support for the creation of a safe haven for Iraqi Kurds, who were being massacred by Saddam Hussein.

The Gulf War saw the United States and its European allies

working together in relative harmony. By contrast, the escalating crisis in the Balkans following the break-up of Yugoslavia put a greater strain on the alliance than any issue since the days of Communist and Nationalist China. The British were very reluctant to get involved in what they saw as a civil war in a region that was hopelessly prone to violence. Furthermore, if intervention were called for, they wanted to see those allies most affected by the influx of refugees – Germany and Italy – take the lead, especially since they had not contributed to the Gulf War. A residual sympathy for Serbia and distrust of Croatia also contributed to British inaction. British mythology had long portrayed Serbia as the victim during the First World War, when Britain had supposedly gone to war to protect small nations from aggression. Post-war Yugoslavia, however, had institutionalised Serb domination; therefore, the Croats had collaborated with the Nazis during the Second World War, while the Serbs had been part of the resistance.* Hence, once more the British saw the Serbs as the good guys. With so much history linking the British and the Serbs, the former were slow to admit just how vicious Slobodan Milosevic and his cronies were as they sought to incorporate the Serb regions of Croatia and Bosnia into a greater Serbia. Thus, the British did not want to get involved in 1991–2 when, following Croatia's declaration of independence, the Serb areas (supported by the Yugoslav army) launched a brutal war to break away from Croatia and join Yugoslavia. It was a war in

---

* It is impossible to talk about the Balkans without dealing in multiple mythologies. While Serbia *had* been invaded by Austria-Hungary to launch the First World War, the Allied myth ignores the level of provocation that the Serbs had offered Austria-Hungary over many years, as they sought to encourage a rebellion by the Slavs within that empire. Not many major powers would have tolerated such sustained efforts to destroy the state. The Yugoslav regime of the inter-war years oppressed its non-Serb nationals. So Croat nationalists saw the German invasion as an opportunity to get out from under the Serb yoke and to get even. Yet the Croat puppet regime that worked with the Nazis was far more brutal than the pre-war Yugoslav government had been. Not all Croats were Nazis, however; many fought in the resistance, which in fact included people from all the south Slav nationalities.

which initially the preponderance of power, and so of atrocities, was on the side of the Serbs. Yet the British tended to give equal weight to Croatian and Serb crimes, and thus to see little to choose between the two sides. As far as the Foreign Office was concerned, all Slavs were pretty much alike: barbaric.

By 1992, a new struggle was developing in Bosnia, a multi-national Yugoslav state that included Serbs, Croats and Muslims. Following Bosnia's declaration of independence, Serbia and Croatia each tried to hive off territory that included its nationals, and the partisans of each massacred Muslims in doing so. Major, already faced with a divided party on Europe, was told by the whips that backbenchers would not support a large British military involvement in Bosnia. In an effort at even-handedness reminiscent of the non-intervention agreement during the Spanish Civil War of 1936–9, the British insisted that an arms embargo be applied to all sides, which favoured the Serbs and Croats, who were being supplied by Yugoslavia and Croatia. As the brutal ethnic and religious war played out on the television screen, however, pressure for a more activist policy grew – from some Tory backbenchers, from the Liberal Democrats and their leader Paddy Ashdown, and from Thatcher. All these critics believed that intervention had become a moral imperative, as more and more evidence came out of the savage Serb (and Croatian) policies.

Ultimately, a British military commitment was dictated as the international community got involved. The United Nations needed effective military help to get humanitarian aid to Bosnia. The election of Bill Clinton in the United States meant that the Americans were now interested in a more activist, anti-Serbian policy. Yet for domestic political reasons, Clinton did not want to take the lead by committing troops. Indeed, there was a good deal of friction between the US and its allies over the Americans' willingness to risk the lives of everyone's soldiers but their own in pursuing American policies. Initially, however, the Europeans welcomed the opportunity to show that they could act without the US. The Germans, who had been at the forefront in pushing for EC recognition of the breakaway states, felt precluded from acting militarily by the legacy of the wartime occupation. Britain and France, who had resisted Germany throughout on the independence issue, were thus left to pick up the pieces and provide NATO troops for the humanitarian effort. When the Serbs continued their aggression and atrocities, the allies then fought over whether to lift the arms embargo as it applied to the Bosnian government (i.e. the Bosnian Muslims). They also fought over whether to use air attacks to deter Milosevic. The British, acutely aware that *their* soldiers' lives would be put at risk if the Serbs retaliated against European troops, resisted all moves to escalate the war, bringing them into direct conflict with the Americans. It was only following Serb massacres in UN safe areas, with the danger of more if Sarajevo fell to the Serbs, that Britain acceded to air attacks and the Clinton administration got serious about investing political capital to end the fighting. The whole sorry scenario was replayed a second time in the late 1990s, when Milosevic escalated a campaign of 'ethnic cleansing' against the majority Albanian population in the Serb province of Kosovo. NATO finally responded with a massive bombing campaign, which itself generated even more massacres of Albanians. As Yugoslavia held out, the allies had a new fight about committing ground troops to the war – with Tony Blair taking the lead in insisting on using them if necessary and the Americans, ever leery of casualties, resisting. Milosevic finally gave way following the loss of Russian support, and NATO ground troops occupied Kosovo to preserve the peace. American and European cooperation had improved slightly, but the problems of the Balkans seemed no closer to resolution.

The crisis in the Balkans showed the Europeans how difficult it was for them to act effectively without the Americans. This was especially the case when military action was involved, as the Europeans simply did not have the range of high-technology weapons possessed by the United States. The result was to give new life to proposals for a European rapid-deployment force that would be self-contained, modernised, integrated and capable of acting without the US or within NATO as appropriate. Britain historically had been cautious about such proposals, fearing they were simply part of a French ploy to weaken NATO. Britain's own declining military capabilities, however, were pushing its governments towards a rethink. While Thatcher had tried to build up Britain's defences, in the late 1980s she was forced to retreat before revived inflation. As a result, in 1989 defence spending as a percentage of GDP was at the lowest level of the post-war era, sinking to 4 per cent.[12] The end of the Cold War, combined with the need to cut expenditure in order to reduce inflation following 'Black Wednesday' in September 1992, merely provided a further impetus for slashing defence spending and so eroding defence capabilities.[13] Even nuclear weapons were subject to retrenchment. Yet the Gulf War and the Balkans crisis showed that Britain's foreign policy ambitions required a battle-ready military capability. Hence, Blair showed more sympathy to proposals for a European defence force than his Conservative predecessors had, and at the December 2000 Nice summit it was agreed to in principle.

The Thatcher Legacy: The Crisis over Europe

Blair's agreement on European defence was a rare example of active British collaboration in a major European initiative. For while both Major and Blair came to the premiership promising a more positive and constructive relationship with the EC, Thatcher had so fundamentally altered the terms of the domestic debate over Europe that both were very cautious in what they were willing to risk. Yet all started promisingly in Major's first two years as Prime Minister. Major was a pragmatic moderate on Europe, and the Foreign Secretary Douglas Hurd was a pro-European. Major believed his job was to reduce the temperature of Britain's negotiations in the councils of Europe while pursuing the Thatcherite aim of preventing moves towards a European federal state. At the same time, he was eager to secure the reduction of agricultural tariffs in the GATT negotiations then going on – a long-standing British aim – which meant persuading his reluctant EC partners (most notably France) to make concessions. He was successful on all these fronts.*

Major's tactics in approaching the negotiations over further European integration were to try to limit innovation. The Community, however, was already committed to a transition to a European monetary system, with a single currency and a European central bank. Furthermore, the collapse of the Soviet Union and the crisis in the Balkans put closer cooperation on foreign and defence policy on the agenda, especially when the United States used the 'peace dividend' to reduce its military presence in Europe. Finally, the collapse of the Eastern bloc also opened up the possibility of expansion of the EC, as neutralist Sweden, Austria and Finland all wanted to join. Expansion would make existing EC institutions even more cumbersome and so would increase the pressure for institutional reform. Britain was not necessarily opposed to all these developments. It had long supported cooperation on foreign policy. Furthermore, it was an enthusiastic proponent of expansion, hoping that it would water down the Euro-enthusiasm of the founding six. For it seemed implausible that a Community consisting of most of the states of Europe could agree on much of anything beyond what already existed. So a larger Community would help block movements for integration or federalism.

Major's only chance of success was to get Germany on his side. Thus, he worked hard to cultivate Kohl – whose recent relationship with Thatcher had been, to say the least, frosty – trying to convince him that Britain's goals in Europe were constructive rather than destructive. At the same time, his whole tone towards the EC was much more accommodating than Thatcher's had been. Both strategies paid off, as Major secured

---

* A new GATT agreement was signed in December 1993, with lower tariffs on agricultural goods. It also created the World Trade Organization to enforce world tariff agreements, something that originally had been floated in the 1940s, but then had been abandoned as something that could not be sold politically in the United States.

many concessions in the Maastricht Treaty of 1991. The most important were the right for Britain to opt out of the single currency and the Social Chapter. The latter, which defined basic minimum rights for EC citizens, including workers' rights, was hived off from the rest of the treaty and became the subject of a separate agreement among the other eleven states. There were other successes too: the removal of a federal goal from the Preamble; the failure to give the European Parliament the right to initiate legislation or to have a role in foreign and defence policies; the inclusion of the principle of subsidiarity in the Treaty. On the other hand, Major made concessions – on the level of European cooperation on defence and foreign policies, as well as on intelligence and police, and on more powers for the European Parliament. The British had also to agree to another inter-governmental conference on institutional reform in 1996, after expansion. More broadly, Major had no more success than his predecessors in limiting the growth of the Community budget. It was three times larger in 1992 than in 1971, due to the increase in the size of the Community and the resources now being directed towards development; yet CAP still accounted for two-thirds of it.[14]

The defeat of the Maastricht Treaty in the first Danish referendum of June 1992, and its near defeat in a French referendum in September (called unnecessarily by Mitterand to prove what good Europeans the French were), convinced the British that the tide had turned against the overly centralised European state. British leaders thought democratic pressure in the member states would now force all of them to embrace subsidiarity. At the 1992 Lisbon summit, the EC leaders even agreed to a review of existing legislation to see if it needed to be altered to conform to that principle. The break-up of the ERM in July 1993 looked like another stake in the heart of the rush towards a federal state. At the same time, Europe's economic problems in the 1990s, which included high unemployment and slow growth, generated new pressures towards deregulation, privatisation and cutting the costs of business in member states. All these forces appeared to indicate that the British way was replacing the Delors way of defining EC policy.

Yet there were also factors working in the other direction. Major's ability to influence the direction of the Community was weakened, first by the very opt-outs he had negotiated, and second because his good relationship with Kohl was destroyed when the British tried to blame 'Black Wednesday' on the Bundesbank's refusal to lower interest rates. Nor did enlargement work out as the British had expected. New members wanted to prove their European credentials, and they were not interested in offending Germany and France as their first act of membership. This had been true of Greece, Spain and Portugal when they joined in the 1980s, and it was true again of Sweden, Austria and Finland in 1995. Hence, they did not serve as very effective brakes on the movement to 'deepen' the Community. Most important of all, however, was the impact of Major's domestic difficulties after September 1992. As Europe became a contentious issue within the Conservative Party, he abandoned his earlier efforts at constructive engagement. He now felt that he had to prove his toughness in European negotiations, so he became much more obstinate. This new persona was on display in the summer of 1994, when the time came to name a successor to Delors as President of the Commission. Major vetoed the Belgian Prime Minister, Jean-Luc Dehaene, whom the Tory right had declared was too much of a federalist. The fact that his candidacy was promoted by Germany also made a veto attractive, since Euro-scepticism in Britain had a very strong anti-German tinge. The Germans finally had to abandon Dehaene, and the former Luxembourg premier Jacques Santer was selected instead. Yet Santer turned out to be every bit the integrationist that Dehaene was supposed to be. Major seemed to have adopted Thatcher's strident obstructionism without achieving the successes that she was able to secure.

The dominant issue of the decade for the European Union (renamed in 1993) was the single currency. After the virtual disintegration of the ERM, the questions were whether EU leaders would be able to pull it off by the target date of 1999, and whether the Community would survive if they did not. The very fact that the latter question was being asked provided an enormous impetus to assure that they *did* pull it off. Three convergence criteria had to be met for a country to join, relating to its rate of inflation, the size of its budget deficit and the amount of its national debt. Major did not want to make a definitive statement concerning whether Britain would join the single currency if it met the criteria – thus alienating the anti-Europeans at home, but enabling him to participate in EU decision-making about the new currency (the euro). Ironically, as the date for deciding approached, Britain satisfied the three criteria far more easily than did some countries that were committed to the euro; however, the very success of its economic performance since 'Black Wednesday' provided a strong impetus to stay out. It was Germany and France, now, that had stagnant economies with high unemployment and structural inefficiencies that undermined their competitiveness on world markets. The lesson since 1992 seemed to be that Britain was weakened economically by being tied financially to its European partners.

This position was not changed significantly by the triumph of Labour in 1997. Labour had promised a referendum before taking Britain into the single currency, and once in power, the Chancellor Gordon Brown defined five economic criteria that would have to be met before such a decision was taken. Brown's priorities were, first, to prove Labour's financial probity and, second, to preserve the relatively successful economy that he had inherited. He was not inclined to risk the latter by joining the euro when it was finally launched on schedule in January 1999. Tony Blair's caution was more political than economic. With a second electoral victory taken as virtually certain from the moment he was elected in 1997, he did not want to do anything that threatened that certainty. A referendum campaign to persuade Britons to accept the euro would have done just that – especially with the post-Major Tories firmly planted in the anti-euro camp. So it quickly became clear that Labour would make no decision on the euro until after the next general election, which meant that Britain would not join at launch.

In other respects, however, Blair tried to be a good European, even as his close friendship with Clinton gave a revived personal dimension to the 'special relationship' with the United States. Labour accepted the Social Chapter and enacted the European Convention on Human Rights into British law. He signed on to a European defence force with the French, accepting that it provided Europe with a means of acting when the United States did not want to. At last, a long-standing French goal could be achieved, with the integration of the West European Union into the EU as its military arm. On the other hand, Blair, like the Tories, resisted tax harmonisation, more powers for the European Parliament and the erosion of Britain's veto on matters it cared about. Gordon Brown fought doggedly and successfully against a uniform tax on financial transactions, which he thought would hurt the City. Furthermore, Blair's policy for tackling unemployment and improving the EU's economic performance was a heavy dose of Thatcherite deregulation and 'labour flexibility' – which was not what other members had in mind. His position on other issues, like reducing and reforming CAP, subsidiarity and further expansion of the Community, were also exactly those of his Tory predecessors. Thus, apart from the single currency, an issue on which Blair only began to commit himself in 2001, the differences of substance between him and the Conservatives were not obvious.

Indeed, with a couple of important exceptions, Britain's policies towards the EC/EU have been quite consistent since the 1970s. The British never were European enthusiasts who embraced the vision of a single Europe that inspired the founding fathers of the 1950s. From the start, they were profoundly ambivalent. Their history as a nation was based on trade and interests that were worldwide rather than European-centred, and their governments' policies towards the Community reflected that fact. Furthermore, the basic premise of opponents of the Community is incontestable: it *has* eroded sovereignty. That erosion has proceeded apace since 1980, with increased economic regulation by the Commission, more European court challenges to the laws of individual states and, finally, monetary union. Indeed, there is no department in Whitehall that does not have to deal with the EU to some degree. The counterargument is that countries no longer have full control over their economic affairs anyway. They are constrained by the global economy, the mobility of capital, the emergence of giant multi-national corporations and international agreements they have signed – most notably, the Bretton Woods Agreement, various GATT agreements and, in the case of Europe, the Treaty of Rome and its successors. All these limit their freedom of action on economic matters. NATO has had the same effect on Britain's ability to define its national defence policies.

The larger issue, however, is psychological. A full-fledged commitment to Europe *would* involve a significant transformation in Britain's identity – especially if Europe evolves towards a federal or 'super' state. Parliamentary sovereignty is integral to the British self-identity, going back to the seventeenth and eighteenth centuries. Britain as a worldwide trading nation is similarly part of that identity. Britain as part of a European state would be tied to the Continent as it has not been since the Middle Ages; identity would be transformed. It would inevitably mean a jettisoning of aspects of the 'special relationship' with the United States in its political dimension – though the ties of language, history and culture would remain. In fact, the British are not alone in being troubled by what is happening. Many other EU peoples are just as unhappy about seeing national sovereignty so fully compromised by the EU. The Danes have already shown themselves to be sceptics, as have the citizens of some of the newer member states, like Austria and Sweden. The Germans and French have never allowed their people to debate the national identity and sovereignty issues; however, the indications are that many would no more welcome a more fully integrated EU than the British or the Danes. British ambivalence stands out among EU members just because there has been a constant debate in

Britain since the late 1980s. Although leaders often tried to obscure the larger issue of sovereignty, Britain is way ahead of the other states in engaging its people in a discussion. This, too, was Thatcher's legacy to foreign policy in the post-Thatcher era.

14

A NEW CONSENSUS?

One only has to read the opening chapter of Corelli Barnett's *The Audit of War* to see why it appealed so to Thatcherites. Barnett looks at the wartime decision to commit Britain to a full-blown welfare state and asks how such an obligation could have been undertaken when Britain's economy was in no condition to underwrite it. The people involved were a mixture of civil servants, politicians and other public figures; they were Christian moralists, post-Victorian romantics, socialist and liberal intellectuals and Tory paternalists. Not one, Barnett tells us,

> was an engineer, an industrialist or a trade unionist; not one of them had ever had experience of running any kind of operation in the real world in which Britain competed commercially . . . [They] were no better equipped to design a working New Jerusalem for this real world than Adolf Hitler, another kind of romantic fantasist, was equipped to run a real war.[1]

Each time Barnett brings a new player into the drama, he cites the man's educational pedigree – almost invariably a public school and an Oxford or Cambridge college. These were the people whom Barnett calls the '"enlightened" Establishment', and they were the people he and Thatcher held responsible for Britain's post-war decline.* Thatcher's political goals were to destroy the power and influence of all of their type and to shatter the post-war consensus which their successors presided over.

Thatcher's own background was not so very different. Like them, she was middle class; like them, she went to Oxford. Unlike them, however, Thatcher was an outsider. As a female politician in the Tory Party, how could she have been otherwise? The daughter of a Lincolnshire grocer, Thatcher came from middle England and the lower-middle class, not from the South and the more privileged background of most of the elite. Her people had provided the political base for the Conservative Party since the passage of the third Reform Act in 1884. More importantly, their numbers had been increasing steadily throughout the twentieth century, making them ever more important in the political nation. By the Thatcher era, they had a voting power comparable to that of the shrinking working class. Despite her Oxford education, Thatcher had never foresworn the values of this class. Those values were rooted in the Victorian middle class that had fought the aristocracy, not the Victorian professional class that had ultimately merged with the aristocracy through the elite education system. For decades, this middle class felt as if somehow they had been losing out relative to the working class, by being taxed more and getting less out of the welfare state. These were the people whom Thatcher was conscious of representing. She believed they embodied all that was best in British conservatism, and she shared their resentment at being patronised and talked down to by an elite that always thought it knew what was best for everyone.

Thatcher believed that the established elite had more to answer for than just Britain's economic decline – and, with it, Britain's decline as a great power. Britain by the 1970s seemed an ungovernable nation. This perception was not just Tory hysteria; a wide range of observers, both British and foreign,

---

* Since Barnett thinks that, after the war, the Labour government should have forced the modernisation of British industry, it is also puzzling why he appealed so much to the Thatcherites.

commented on it. The term 'ungovernable' carried with it several meanings. One was the impossibility of promoting a level of economic growth that would support the nation's welfare system. In other words, government could no longer come up with a workable policy that would sustain the structure of society that had evolved since the Second World War. The result was a fraying of the political consensus that had governed the country since 1945, a fragmentation of the party system and the emergence of political extremism which threatened to paralyse government. Another meaning of ungovernable, however, carried the connotation of a breakdown of order. It referred to strikes that brought the country to a halt, IRA violence, the rise of football hooliganism and an increase in crime. Tory ideology claimed that the solution was strong rule from the top. Only then could the primary objects of government be achieved: social stability, the security of property and the upholding of the rule of law. All these seemed to be under attack in the 1970s, and the rot could be stopped only if strong government replaced the indecisive leadership that had characterised the decade. Thatcher believed that the elite were responsible for this collapse into ungovernability. Theirs were the values of moral relativism and misplaced sympathy which excused weakness, failure and disorder. Her mission, then, in addition to destroying the power and authority of the traditional elite, was to discredit their value system, to restore respect for government and to restore order in society. What Britain needed was strength at the top, and Thatcher was determined to provide it.

The Dries versus The Wets

Chapters 9 and 12 showed how Thatcher attacked the privileges and power of a variety of institutions dominated by the traditional elite – most notably the civil service, the professions and the universities. 'One-nation' Tories were part of the same elite establishment. The Thatcher years therefore launched a struggle for the soul of the Conservative Party. The term that came into use for the old Tories was 'wets', with its connotations of flabbiness and weakness. Wets were too prone to Shirley Robin Letwin's 'softer virtues' like sympathy and kindness. Tories of this stripe were committed to the consensus policies that Thatcher hoped to smash. Thatcher claimed that consensus was 'the process of abandoning all beliefs, principles, values and policies'.[2] For her, there was no principle in seeking out a middle way, in advocating compromise, in wanting to conciliate opposition and reconcile differences in order to get things done. All such tendencies were evidence of personal weakness, and so wet.

The opposite of wet was 'dry'. The term implied solidity and uprightness. The dry was free from the damage that liquid could do: from the flimsiness that it could impart to an object and from the blending that it could facilitate when mixed with other substances. Foreign matter did not adhere to the dry; dryness was pure. This was the Thatcher image – free from contaminating influences, a pure conservative, a person driven by an absolute morality. It was an image of strength and rigidity, underpinned by a willingness to work harder, master the details of issues better and argue her position more forcefully than anyone else. With this image, she projected an unbending adherence to principle, a rejection of sympathy and sentimentality in making judgements and a killer instinct when confronting the enemy. The enemy was socialism, and the willingness of 'one-nation' Tories to fraternise with this enemy, and to imply some commonality between welfare socialism and conservatism, made them dangerous. Hence, they had to be neutralised politically.

All the evidence of the polls throughout Thatcher's premiership indicated that people (apart from the Conservative faithful) did not much like her. She did not seem to care. Her aim was not popularity; it was to restore Britain to its greatness, to reverse its decline, to defeat its enemies – internal as well as external. She could not be nice to achieve all this, for unpopular decisions had to be made and sometimes people had to be hurt. Respect and admiration were what Thatcher aspired to, for they would vindicate her. The whole of this image – the image of dryness –

was what people came to associate with Thatcherism. For the 'ism' was as much about style as about ideology. Restoring the confidence and self-respect of a people in decline was a matter of psychology as well as policy. Thatcher understood this, so her style and image were meant to transform the psychological outlook of Britons (or at least the English).

In challenging the consensus that governed Britain between 1945 and 1979, Thatcher could draw on a conservative tradition that had evolved since the end of the nineteenth century. As liberalism had become more interventionist and socialism had emerged as a viable political creed in Britain, the middle class had moved over to the Conservative Party and brought its liberal individualism with it. The Russian Revolution of 1917 and the triumph of communism there, as well as the replacement of the Liberal Party in Britain by Labour as the party of the left, had helped to consolidate the role of the Conservatives as the opponents of socialism and the supporters of market capitalism. This individualist conservatism lived side-by-side with 'one-nation' Toryism. Among Tory parliamentarians, however, it held a distinctly subordinate position, as the party elite did not have that strong a commitment to competition as a matter of principle.3 Hence, the anti-ideological strain of conservatism dominated, even between the wars, and decisively after the Second World War. This conservatism sought to wed the party's commitment to individualism and not telling industry what to do with promoting social harmony through selective state intervention. Nonetheless, throughout the post-war period, and especially from the late 1950s on, there was constant pressure from Tory loyalists in the constituencies and a minority of MPs to repudiate such flirtations with socialism and assert a more full-blooded conservatism that was anti-government, anti-trade union, anti-immigration, anti-Europe and anti-majority rule in Africa.4

The first powerful spokesman for these dissenters was Enoch Powell, who had resigned from the government in 1958 because he thought its spending policies were promoting inflation. He was an advocate of the supremacy of the market, a critic of government spending as the source of inflation and a promoter of cuts in direct taxation. Thus, throughout the 1960s Powell attacked incomes policies, Keynesian management of the budget, efforts to prop up the pound and all state subsidies. He was hostile to the trade unions and critical of universal benefits. A British chauvinist, Powell hated Britain's subservience to the United States, opposed the nuclear deterrent and disdained the Commonwealth and the romantic imperialism that underlay it. He had little use for Britain's great power pretensions and even denied that Britain was in decline, either because of the loss of empire (which he saw as irrelevant) or because of the loss of industrial preeminence (which he saw as inevitable). Clearly Powell was a very unusual breed of Conservative. In 1968 he made headlines with his inflammatory speeches against 'coloured' immigration. While anti-immigration legislation was already on the books and more was on the way, such explicit appeals to racism were not politically acceptable, however popular. In excluding Powell from government, however, Heath freed him to be a bitter critic of the economic policies of 1970–74. He also opposed British entry into the EC because it impinged on British sovereignty; therefore, in the February 1974 general election, he implied that people should vote Labour. Having thus abandoned the Conservatives, Powell retreated to Ireland, where the Ulster Unionists provided him with a safe seat. Not surprisingly, Powell generated strong passions. To the *Daily Telegraph*, he was 'one of the greatest Conservative thinkers of modern times . . . as the inspiration behind Thatcherism'. Fergus Pyle of the *Irish Times*, however, called him 'probably the most repulsive politician on the scene, first in British politics, when he accurately predicted the rise of racial tension but in terms that made the nastiest and most boneheaded racist feel intellectually justified; later in the North [of Ireland], where he performed the same service for the Unionists'.[5]

Powell's successor as the voice of the intellectual among Tory politicians was Sir Keith Joseph, the man behind the Thatcher run for the party leadership in 1975 and the person who influenced her thinking most directly. Joseph was a man divided. He had a strong social conscience and a desire to help the poor; yet he had toyed with *laissez-faire* economic ideas throughout the 1960s. Powell tended to see issues clearly and speak with certainty. Joseph, by contrast, engaged in internal intellectual struggles over issues and ideas and so waffled. He sat on the fence as a member of Heath's government, but came off it following defeat in 1974. The Heath failure, he concluded, was a product of the whole socialist political culture that had shaped British government since 1945. More specifically, he identified as villains the same policies that Powell had attacked: Keynesianism, government spending, incomes policies and indifference to the money supply. The government was trying to do too much when it tried to manage the economy in order to promote growth. Instead, it should stand aside, limit its spending so as not to promote inflation, not worry about unemployment, and allow growth to take care of itself. Because of the close relationship that developed between Thatcher and Joseph, he was the main intellectual source behind Thatcherism as a set of economic principles.

Only a watered down version of these principles, however, was the basis of the party's campaign in 1979. Indeed, the programme in the election manifesto looked strikingly similar to Heath's in 1970: tax cuts, control of public spending and the money supply and freeing up individual enterprise and the private sector. The rhetoric on trade unions was mild, and that on privatisation was barely visible. Furthermore, there was much to convey consultation and consensus in the pursuit of change. Nonetheless, in the campaign the Conservatives portrayed their programme as a radical break with the past, aimed at defending the liberty of ordinary Britons against the stifling effects of socialism. This contrast between moderation and radicalism reflected the reality in the party. Inevitably, most of its leaders were the kind of moderate, 'one-nation' Tories who had run the party since the war. Thatcher had to rely on these men in opposition, and the party programme reflected their view that change should be achieved incrementally, while carrying the bulk of the people along with them.

These 'one-nation' Tories were well-represented in Thatcher's first government – William Whitelaw, Lord Carrington, Sir Ian Gilmour, Peter Walker, James Prior, Francis Pym. While she kept them away from economic policy, they held key positions because of their standing in the party. Whitelaw, the most important, was loyal to Thatcher, whatever his doubts about her policies. Unlike the other wets, he believed that the party could not turn back from the reforms she launched; for the foreseeable future, conservatism was Thatcherism. He became her Deputy Prime Minister and acted as an essential mediator and brake on wet rebellion. Carrington was the least ideological of the wets; the others were more dangerous. They had opposed Thatcher in her run for the leadership and still had little respect for her. If she could be arrogant towards them in her assertiveness, they could be equally arrogant towards her in their condescension. Her problem, they thought, was that she simply did not understand the realities of politics, which required compromise and consensus. Once she faced those realities, she would either have to adapt or see her premiership collapse. The most distinguished of all the wets, Edward Heath, did his best to assure such a failure. Still bitter over being dumped in 1975, he remained on the outside, constantly lashing out at his nemesis and her policies – the voice of a consensus that he had been unable to promote, and had hardly conveyed that he valued, when he was Prime Minister.

The wets feared an economic and social collapse as a result of the government's economic policies. When the Prime Minister insisted on standing by those policies in 1980 – in the face of high inflation, soaring unemployment and a major recession, not to mention a prolonged steel strike – they thought she was crazy, literally. To Thatcher, their fears were simply evidence of the timidity that helped define them as wet. Her self-image was captured in the statement she is reputed to have made, 'I am the rebel head of an establishment government.'[6] Hence, she fought them – indeed, she relished fighting them. There might be short-term gains for the wets, as when Prior was able to pursue a go-slow approach to trade union reform – though the lessons of 1971–4 pointed in that direction anyway. But in the medium term, they were doomed, for they stood for policies that were discredited with the Conservative rank and file. They did not even try to organise a rebellion. All they did was privately snipe at and express contempt for the Prime Minister and the Chancellor, Sir Geoffrey Howe, with an occasional public voicing of dissent (especially by Gilmour). The struggle over economic policy, therefore, was really no struggle at all. As long as Thatcher remained firm, there would be no change of course, and once she had made up her mind, Thatcher relished remaining firm when others pressed her to change. The budget of 1981, which further squeezed the economy when deep in recession, signalled once and for all that there would be no retreat. There was not a single resignation in protest. That same year, the riots in Brixton and Toxteth seemed to confirm the kind of social breakdown the wets had been predicting. Yet mostly they merely groused at the Prime Minister behind her back and hoped for her fall.

While the wets sat immobilised, Thatcher gradually picked them off as she grew more confident. Each Cabinet reshuffle involved the sacrifice of wets while bringing in new people who were at least potential Thatcherites. The first significant change came in September 1981, when Gilmour was fired and Prior was banished to Northern Ireland. Nigel Lawson moved into the Cabinet for the first time as Energy Secretary, while Norman Tebbit – perhaps the driest of all the Thatcherites – replaced Prior as Employment Secretary with responsibility for trade union legislation. The Falklands War forced the resignation of Carrington in 1982. Thatcher did not really want Carrington to go. The Tory backbenchers, however, had been schooled by Thatcher to hate the Foreign Office and took advantage of the humiliation to go on the warpath. More importantly, the government needed a fall guy. For the Falklands invasion was a policy failure, and the British system usually assumes that someone will take responsibility for failure. If it was not to be the whole government (requiring the resignation of the Prime Minister), then it had to be the minister responsible for conducting the negotiations. Thatcher derived no advantage from Carrington's departure, for she felt compelled to replace him with Pym, a far more militant wet whom she hated. However, he had experience in foreign affairs, he was a skilled parliamentarian and there was no obvious alternative. When, after the election landslide of 1983, she was free to shape a Cabinet more suited to her taste, Thatcher dumped Pym and replaced him with Howe, while Lawson took Howe's post as Chancellor. This team was to dominate the firmament at her side for the next six years – the cautious, slightly plodding Howe and the brilliant, sharp Lawson. At the same time, Whitelaw moved to the Lords and was replaced by Leon Brittan as Home Secretary. Apart from Whitelaw (a unique case), Walker was the only dry who proved sufficiently adaptable and useful to last through Thatcher's second term.

Her war with the wets helped Thatcher cultivate her image as 'the Iron Lady'. Political scientists like to emphasise that Thatcher was as flexible and willing to retreat from a defined position as any other politician. Simon Jenkins goes further, claiming that she was often a quite timid reformer and reluctant Thatcherite.[7] Yet ultimately her image was based on confrontation, and that larger picture transcended any behind-the-scenes hesitations or compromises she made on specific issues. Hers were conviction politics. Stubbornness was merely firmness in defence of principle and the national interest. Her overbearing manner and assertiveness were a refusal to allow her government or Britain to be bullied. Thatcher was a master at identifying an enemy who embodied some sort of evil that had to be resisted. She then used confrontation with that enemy to impress the British public with her toughness and so win its support. The wets hardly counted in this taxonomy; they were dangerous, but certainly not evil. Yet her fights with them helped her to define and sharpen the image.

Her battle with the anti-nuclear movement had a similar effect. The revival of the long-moribund CND was the product of three factors: the NATO decision to site Cruise missiles in Britain, the Thatcher government's decision to purchase Trident from the United States and the Cold War rhetoric of the Reagan administration. The latter was especially frightening, as the Americans actually seemed to contemplate the use of nuclear weapons, with Europe as the principal battlefield and the American mainland free and clear. Since these missiles also posed a qualitative increase in the threat to the Soviet Union, nuclear war looked like a possibility for the first time since the Cuban missile crisis in 1962. The anti-nuclear movement demanded the removal of all nuclear weapons and American nuclear bases from British soil. It mobilised the anti-Americanism of the British left, which saw the Cold War as an expression of American imperialism more than as an ideological conflict. Some were attracted to the old 1940s vision of Europe as a 'third force', removed from the whole nuclear mess and independent of both superpowers.

As in the 1950s, the anti-nuclear movement spoke to the fears of many ordinary men and women. Polls showed public opposition to both the Cruise missiles and Trident. CND could thus mobilise impressive numbers: in October 1982 some 250,000 people turned out for a London demonstration against Cruise missiles, while some 70,000 protested at Greenham Common air base (where they were to be sited) in January 1983.[8] Tens of thousands of women joined a semi-permanent peace camp at Greenham. A confrontation with CND was the kind of test of wills that Thatcher relished. She faced down all the demonstrations and deployed the missiles in the autumn of 1983. Behind her, she had public support for NATO and Britain's independent nuclear deterrent. So she stood firm – for the nation's security against the romantic chimera of unilateral nuclear disarmament and, as the protests turned violent and attacked property, for enforcing the law and refusing to allow the country to descend again into the anarchy of the 1970s.

There were other such battles in the early 1980s – such as those against the IRA hunger-strikers over political status and against the rest of the EC over Britain's budget contribution. It was the Falklands War, however, that proved to be the decisive test for Thatcher, for it provided a crisis in which her character was an unambiguous asset. Had the British failed to recover the islands, her premiership would have been over; instead, her public standing was transformed. It was an ideal situation because Thatcher could adopt the moral high ground while resisting the forces of evil. No Argentine grievance could justify the unprovoked invasion of a nation with which they had peaceful relations. The image of Nazi aggression in the 1930s was reinforced by the fact that the Argentine junta was a brutal dictatorship with an appalling record of terrorising its own people. How could citizens of democratic Britain be abandoned to such a regime? Britain's honour and its standing as a nation were involved. So Thatcher stood firm, unwilling to countenance a compromise. There would be none of the hesitations and ambivalence of Suez this time, and most of the British people welcomed both her stubbornness and her decisiveness. Thatcher's strength contrasted well against Pym, the wet Foreign Secretary, who seemed prepared to appease the Argentinians through a negotiated settlement, and Michael Foot, the leader of the Labour Party, who supported sending the task force but then yearned for a peaceful denouement. Thus, when Britain won the war, everyone remembered Thatcher's strength and willingness to stand by what was right, no matter what the consequences were. It was *her* victory.

The Falklands War had a riveting effect on the British people. As the task force sailed, many had doubts whether the Falklands were worth British lives. Once the fighting began, however, they were as chauvinistic as all people are during a war. Nightly, the television broadcast two-week-old film of the battle, and the nation watched, gripped by what it saw, even though it already knew the outcome. There was enormous pride in an operation that logistically was incredibly complex, involving mobilising and supplying on short notice a considerable force to fight a war eight thousand miles away in horrendous weather. Furthermore, it seemed to have been carried out remarkably efficiently and at relatively low human cost (255 British dead), although at a considerably greater financial cost.[9] While a victory over Argentina could not suddenly transform Britain into an international heavyweight, Argentina had a substantial military force that caused British commanders some anxiety, and it had fought just well enough for there to be no doubt that the British had been in a real fight.[10] So victory represented a clear statement that Britain was not going to be pushed around any more. The ghost of Suez was purged! It was an important psychological step for the nation, just as economic recovery was also getting under way. Instead of everything becoming worse, as had seemed to be the case from 1972 to 1981, things were beginning to get better. A corner was turned, and the nation was starting on its way back up again. Given this effect, the war inevitably led people to reconsider their views about the Prime Minister. Her popularity soared from unplumbed depths to unaccustomed heights, and while it would fluctuate often enough in the years ahead, there was a new respect and admiration for her. But the war also reinforced her self-confidence and conviction that she was right. More than ever, after 1982 Thatcher would not be a person to compromise with those who opposed her.

Like the Argentine generals, Arthur Scargill suited Thatcher perfectly as a foil. He was as rigidly ideological as she was, and since that ideology was Marxist and seemed aimed at bringing down a constitutionally elected government, she could again represent morality and democracy. At the same time, in the aftermath of the last purge of the wets in 1983, a war against the miners could unite the party. For there was hardly a Conservative anywhere who did not yearn for revenge for the humiliations of 1972 and 1974. As Energy Secretary, the wet Walker was the government's point-man with the press, a job he performed superbly. Thatcher herself took on the role of ratcheting up the temperature during the summer of 1984, presenting the issue in stark terms as a fight to the death against a unionism that would tyrannise the nation if it were to triumph. The violence of the miners also enabled her to portray the struggle as one between the forces of law and order and the forces of anarchy. As if to punctuate the reality of the threat of tyranny and anarchy,

Thatcher herself was the target of an IRA bomb during the party conference in Brighton that October. It came close enough to getting her, while it killed five people, seriously injured Tebbit (and left his wife paralysed), and reduced parts of the Grand Hotel to rubble. Thatcher did not hesitate to draw the link between the miners' leadership and the IRA. Each, in its own way, sought to destroy the British system of government. It was just the kind of role that most appealed to her: strong, unbending, impervious to danger, taking on the forces of evil and ultimately triumphing. Thus, as the defeated miners trickled back to work during the winter of 1984-5, Britain's slayer of dragons could rack up another trophy for her wall. Further acts of violence in the summer of 1985 – the football disaster at Brussels, the Birmingham race riots – enabled Thatcher to reinforce the message that she was engaged in a final battle against the anarchic elements that had made the seventies 'ungovernable', and that she would defeat them.

The Disintegration of the Left

Thatcher had plenty of time to consolidate her hold on the Conservative Party and bounce back from the economic disaster of 1979-81 because the Labour Party was a mess. The election result in 1979 represented the most decisive defeat for Labour since 1931.[11] Inevitably, a search was launched for scapegoats: the right blamed the trade unions and the strikes of the 'winter of discontent', while the left blamed the government's incomes policy and the innocuousness of its programme. More generally, the left was tired of the party leadership pursuing policies, on every issue from wage controls to the Vietnam War to membership in the EC, that ignored the expressed wishes of the majority of the party. Hence there followed a struggle for control of the party, in which the left had the advantage.

The left had been consolidating its position in the party for years. Since the late 1960s, young men and women had been joining constituency Labour parties that were often thinly populated and so were under oligarchic control. Many of these new members were from the middle class, often university-educated and local government employees, but there were also working-class trade union activists. They brought with them an enthusiasm and commitment that any party sorely needs to be successful, and so at the local level their influence could be revitalising. Some of them had been part of the militant political movements that had taken off in the late 1960s, especially in the form of community activism. Their numbers were not necessarily enormous, especially outside London; however, their experience in political activism enabled them to take control of local party organisations and use them to pursue their goals.[12] They used these constituency organisations as a base from which to try to seize control of the national party.

Under Wilson's leadership, they believed the Labour Party had jettisoned the bedrock moralism which should be at the heart of socialism. In the early 1970s, they joined with the growing number of left-wing trade union leaders to capture the National Executive Committee (NEC). The NEC was, in theory, the supreme policy-making organisation of the party. It oversaw the resolutions at the annual conference as well as the drafting of the election manifesto. In practice, however, the parliamentary leaders used their influence to get election manifestoes watered down into a more acceptable form, while they simply ignored party resolutions and policies that they deemed too extreme. It was just this waffling on socialist ideology that the left believed accounted for the party's weakness in 1974–9, and they were determined to end it. Thus, while using the NEC to secure the approval of a series of radical policies by the party conference, they also launched a campaign to make the parliamentary party more accountable to the rank and file. Their effort to democratise the party involved three reforms: all MPs must resubmit themselves to their constituency parties once during a parliament for reselection; the party would elect the leader and shadow Cabinet; and the NEC would have final authority over the election manifesto. Reselection of MPs was approved by the party conference in 1979; the other two proposals, however, divided the party, as direct election of the leader was barely approved in 1980, while NEC authority over the manifesto was rejected by an equally narrow margin.

Seeing the direction in which the party was going, Callaghan resigned as leader after the 1980 party conference, so that his replacement could still be elected by the parliamentary party. A 1979 Gallup poll had shown that Labour voters and trade unionists preferred the right-wing Denis Healey as a successor to Callaghan; while Labour defectors preferred the even more moderate Shirley Williams, with Healey second.[13] Yet the winner was the leftist Michael Foot. Foot was a compromise candidate between the more extreme Peter Shore and Healey, whose leadership MPs feared would never be accepted by the left, thus leaving the party perpetually at war. Thus, Labour ended up with a leader who was far weaker than the more controversial Healey and who also commanded little support among the party's own constituencies – much less the electorate at large. Foot chose Healey as his deputy leader in an effort to pull the party together, but once the new 'electoral college' for choosing the leadership had been approved, Tony Benn insisted on challenging him. Foot and trade union leaders opposed a contest that would further divide the party. Benn, however, took a 'hard left' view: he had no interest in preserving party unity if it meant accommodating a non-socialist (or even anti-socialist) right wing. So he went his own way. Under the electoral college, the trade unions had 40 per cent of the vote, while the local parties and parliamentary party each had 30 per cent. Benn wooed the first two, in the case of union members trying to appeal over the heads of their leaders. Despite an overwhelming victory in the constituency parties, Benn barely lost (by 50.4 per cent to 49.6 per cent) because the trade union rank and file supported Healey, who also won the parliamentary party. The whole process of reforming the Labour Party and selecting its leadership between 1979 and 1981 revealed it to be divided right down the middle, with an increasingly aggressive and militant left wing pursuing its agenda whatever the electoral costs.

The success of the left finally drove a group of right-wing Labour MPs to break with the party in March 1981 and form a new Social Democratic Party (SDP). The leaders were Shirley Williams, David Owen and William Rodgers. All had been in Callaghan's Cabinet (Owen as Foreign Secretary), and all feared that the dominance of the left not only meant that Labour was unelectable, but that it had become dangerous. They were joined by Roy Jenkins, who returned to Britain following a term as President of the European Commission to make the SDP leadership into a 'Gang of Four'. Initially the SDP had 13 Labour MPs and 1 Conservative, but within a year the number reached 29, as it served as a convenient retreat for Labour moderates who might not be reselected by their local parties. Almost immediately, there was discussion of an alliance with the Liberals. David Steel, the Liberal leader, had made it his top priority to convince the nation that the Liberals were a party of government. That was why he had agreed to the Lib-Lab pact with Callaghan in 1977. The agreement with Labour, however, had alienated many of his own activists, while the Thorpe scandal had hurt the party with the country. The SDP split was a godsend for him. An alliance that included four former ministers made his party look like a viable alternative to the established parties. Suddenly, Britain had a real three-party system (with smaller parties in the Celtic regions) in a way that had not been the case since the inter-war period.

In its first year, the alliance of the SDP and Liberals seemed unstoppable, as they won one high-profile by-election after another – including the return to the Commons of Williams, who had been defeated in 1979, and Jenkins. They did equally well in local government by-elections, winning nearly half the seats contested in the second half of 1981. Their standing in polls soared to as high as 50 per cent, a fair indicator of how unpopular the major parties were by the end of the year. Yet the bloom of youth began to fade in the first half of 1982, despite Jenkins's by-election victory at Glasgow, Hillhead, in March. While the stronger partner looked to be the SDP, with its high-profile leaders, it was actually the Liberals, who had the local organisations. For the Labour Party in the constituencies held firm behind the leadership, as the SDP did not appeal to Labour's core working-class base. Many of the SDP defectors were therefore vulnerable to Labour challenges, as the May local government elections demonstrated. Thus, the party had little to offer local Liberals who had long cultivated these constituencies. The two leaders, Steel and Jenkins, had a good working relationship, and each was able to push his rank and file towards agreement over which party would contest each seat. The public bickering, however, brought the Alliance's standing in the polls down to more plausible levels, even before the Falklands War transformed the political landscape. By July, the Conservatives had opened a gap of 20 per cent over Labour and the Alliance, and this was pretty much how the parties remained up to the general election in 1983.

As an unknown quantity, however, the Alliance continued to worry the Conservatives – probably more than Labour did. First, Foot was a hopelessly weak leader. His job was made miserable by Benn, who seemed to go out of his way at times to embarrass Foot by his actions. More broadly, Foot was unable to prevent the divisions in the party from boiling to the surface, while he was ineffectual in the Commons when facing Thatcher. The Tory press pointed out his every difficulty and subjected him to constant ridicule so the voters would not take him seriously. Second, the left saddled the party with an election manifesto which Gerald Kaufman, a member of the shadow Cabinet, called 'the longest suicide note in history'.[14] Among its proposals were massive spending to bring down unemployment and improve infrastructure, foreign exchange and import controls, a new version of the social contract with the unions, more aggressive government planning in managing the economy, worker participation in corporate decision-making, unilateral nuclear disarmament (with the closure of American nuclear bases in Britain) and withdrawal from the EC. There was also a likelihood of more nationalisation and higher taxes to finance all this. The programme was actually a watered-down version of what the left had achieved through various party conferences, but it was still far more radical than anything that had been proposed before. It was too extreme for voters outside Labour's heartland in the North of England, Scotland and Wales.

The divided left, Foot's lack of credibility and the economic recovery all helped to shape Thatcher's election campaign. In contrast to Foot, she was a strong leader who had been staunch and unbending in adversity, both domestic and foreign. Now the British people were seeing the economic payoff, if they just stuck with her. The Tory manifesto promised more privatisation and trade union legislation, tight budgeting and tax cuts – in other words, another dose of Thatcherism. To vote Labour, on the other hand, was to retreat to the failed policies of the past. The Alliance, however, was no alternative. All three of the opposition parties, she claimed, were socialist, and it was socialism that had ruined the country. Given the divisions on the left, it probably did not matter much how the Tories ran their campaign; they could not lose. Their share of the vote actually fell slightly, but that was irrelevant; their majority over all other parties was 144. The Alliance did spectacularly well with 25 per cent of the vote, compared to 28 per cent for Labour. Its votes, however, were spread fairly evenly over the country, while Labour's were concentrated in its heartland, which it won handily. Hence, the Alliance won a mere 23 seats compared with Labour's 209, and the weakness of the SDP was further exposed.[15] Its appeal was too much to a professional, white-collar electorate. With such a narrow base, only six of its MPs were able to hold their seats, as both Williams and Rodgers went down to defeat.

The catastrophe of 1983 finished Foot as a leader. He was replaced by Neil Kinnock, a young, personable, energetic Welshman whom everyone hoped would be able to compete effectively on television with the Tory public relations juggernaut. Kinnock was from the party's left, but, unlike Benn, he was fully committed to holding the party together. In fact, he had abstained in the 1981 deputy leadership contest because of his resentment at Benn's divisive actions. Kinnock understood that if the party was going to win elections, it had to retreat from left-wing extremism, for it was losing a portion of its core voters. Both the 1979 and 1983 general elections had seen a significant swing against Labour by workers (especially skilled workers) and trade unionists. Most of this swing was in the South and Midlands, which were least affected by industrial decline and were to benefit from the economic revival of the 1980s. Skilled workers and the young, in particular, were no longer interested in such touchstone Labour issues as nationalisation, social welfare spending and trade union rights. They supported Tory policies of home-ownership and getting tough on crime. Indeed, their values were not so very different from those of a middle class that was increasing in size with the expanding service sector. Given this long-term restructuring of the economy, it was folly for Labour to think it could win elections based on a shrinking blue-collar constituency. Kinnock saw that it not only had to win back the prosperous workers, but some among the growing middle and professional classes as well. In his efforts to achieve this goal, he was supported by the trade union leadership – even many of those on the left. The unions' priority since 1945 had always been to elect a Labour government. Many had been alienated by what they perceived to be the unnecessarily divisive tactics of Benn and his allies, while after the collapse of the miners' strike in 1985, direct industrial action was a proven failure.

First and foremost, Kinnock needed to divorce the party from left-wing extremism. There were two facets to the campaign that followed: purging the party of its so-called 'loony left' and revamping its policies so that they would appeal to a broader electorate. As part of its effort to capture the party, the left had begun to get involved in local government in the 1970s. This was a natural outgrowth of their efforts to re-energise participatory democracy at the community level. Local government offered a means to test socialist ideas and, after 1979, to resist Thatcherism. Leftist policies included subsidising public transport in order to keep fares down; involving workers and the poor (such as council house tenants and welfare recipients) in decisions about spending for the services aimed at them; assuring that local government spending promoted jobs within the community; and even local economic planning. Some of this was no more controversial than any other radical policy experiment, and some leftist leaders, like David Blunkett in Sheffield, were successful.

Other Labour-led governments, however, were deliberately provocative. The reigning genius at getting under the skin of the Tories (and not just the Tories) was Ken Livingstone, the leader of the Greater London Council (GLC) from 1981 until it was abolished by Thatcher in 1986 – as a means of getting rid of Livingstone. With Scargill, Livingstone was the right's principal exhibit of the extremism that characterised Labour. Here, for example, is how Shirley Robin Letwin describes the policies that were funded by the GLC under Livingstone:

> There were the usual good causes such as blacks, gays, one-parent families and peace campaigners, as well as a Police Committee which used its budget of 2.9 million [pounds] in 1985–6 to fund forty-nine anti-police organizations . . . And there were also more exotic causes – the United Filipino Association, the Armenian Democratic Front, the Marx Memorial Library, and Babies Against the Bomb.[16]

The most irresponsible of the left-wing city councils was Liverpool's, whose borrowing and spending nearly bankrupted the city. Liverpool's council was controlled by Militant Tendency under Derek Hatton, the foremost of the Trotskyist organisations that had penetrated the party in the 1970s.* Like Scargill and Livingstone, Militant became a code-word for all that was wrong with Labour. Although the numbers in the party were small, the press associated them in the public mind with the party's radical

---

* The term Trotskyist is a general one for Marxists who pursue alternative models to the Stalinist model developed in the Soviet Union or the Maoist model developed in China. Their views had very little to do with those of Leon Trotsky, the leader of the Russian Revolution who, because he was purged and then assassinated by Stalin, became a symbol for principled opposition to Stalin.

left. Hence, the purging of Militant was a prerequisite for any revamping of Labour's image. The process had begun under Foot, who expelled five editors of the newspaper *Militant* from the party for violating the prohibition in Labour's constitution against any autonomous organisation with its own principles and programme.

Kinnock could not move much further, however, until he established his supremacy. His weakness was evident when he failed to push through a compromise on reselection of candidates at the 1984 party conference. That conference also voted to support the miners and condemn the police during the strike and endorsed defiance of rate-capping by Labour councils – both votes taken against Kinnock's advice. Kinnock understood that such support for law-breakers alienated ordinary voters (including many in the working class). The 'hard' left, however, stood firm for socialist solidarity and saw Kinnock as yet another leader vainly trying to win the centre. Ultimately, however, non-parliamentary resistance to Thatcherism was futile. The denouement of the miners' strike and the actions of the Liverpool councillors helped Kinnock consolidate an alliance between the 'soft' left and the right wing of the party. Armed with a damning report on the political activities of the Liverpool party, including evidence of intimidation, Kinnock secured expulsion from the party of the Liverpool Militant leaders by the 1986 party conference. Since many local parties, taking their cues from the centre, had expelled their own Militant members over the past two years, the strength of the movement was broken.

Changing the party's platform was more difficult – not least because Kinnock, a child of the left, sympathised with policies like unilateral nuclear disarmament and public investment in infrastructure. Furthermore, there were limits to how much of a retreat the trade unions and young MPs on the 'soft' left would accede to. Thus, while the new leadership accepted EC membership, unilateralism remained in place, as did the principle of public ownership that was embodied in Clause IV of the Labour constitution. It proved especially difficult to construct a credible economic policy, as the leaders sought to reconcile some recognition of the importance of markets and private enterprise, their own residual Keynesianism, and remnants of the leftist commitments of 1983. As a result, they did not accept key elements of the Thatcher revolution. The revised programme supported renationalisation of privatised utilities, bailing out sick industries, and reversing Tory trade union legislation. Since Labour's own research showed that people thought its solutions were out of date and its policies would lead to higher taxes and inflation, it is hardly surprising that this mishmash of the old and the new did not play well at the general election.

The Alliance, like Labour, remained a divided force. In 1983 David Owen replaced Jenkins as leader of the SDP. Owen was vehemently opposed to unilateral nuclear disarmament and was none too keen on the EC. The Liberals, however, had a left wing that supported unilateralism, and the party had long been enthusiastic Europeanists. Furthermore, Owen wanted the SDP to accept the Thatcherite emphasis on the primacy of the market, while the Liberals emphasised the role of the state in promoting social justice. Overall, Owen seemed to be leaning towards the Conservatives; by contrast, the whole drift of the Liberals since 1970 had been towards the left. This division became apparent in 1986–7, as the two parties constructed a joint policy statement that tried to reconcile their views, and then as the two leaders attempted to maintain a balance between the two major parties during the general election campaign.

Given the continued divisions on the left, both as a whole and within the two political blocs, the 1987 general election did not pose much more of a problem for the Tories than had that of 1983 – although there was a good deal more anxiety because Labour ran such a strong campaign. They made effective use of Labour's 'loony left', associating it not only with radical socialism and trade unionism, but also with extremist special interests that were promoted by the likes of the GLC. They also focused on nuclear disarmament, which they claimed would leave Britain unprotected in the event of a nuclear threat. Finally, the Tory campaign emphasised Labour's irresponsibility in managing the economy as the party of taxing and spending. All three of these issues resonated with the electorate, including the skilled, home-owning working class of the South. Labour responded by portraying itself as the party that cared about people and would protect the public services that they wanted and valued. While sympathetic, voters were more influenced by the fact that they were doing well in the economic recovery. Hence, the Tories lost only 19 seats, leaving them with a majority of 102 over all other parties. Labour's share of the vote hardly increased, to 30.8 per cent from 27.6 in 1983, while the Alliance's fell to 22.5 per cent from 25.4.[17] As long as both sides on the left seemed equally viable (or unviable), the Tories were safe.

Political Earthquake

Margaret Thatcher had never been a particularly popular Prime Minister. From the start, her hard-edged style unsettled people. She could overcome any electoral handicap that might arise because she got results and because people respected and admired her strength. In the last years of her premiership, however, the image of 'the Iron Lady' did not play so well. Suitable enemies were harder to come by. Teachers, doctors and poll tax resisters did not look like threats to democracy and the national interest in their struggles against Thatcherite reforms; indeed, they evoked a good deal of popular support. Moreover, increasingly her conflicts were not with Tory 'wets', whose power in the party had been neutralised, but with men who had helped to make the Thatcher revolution and who commanded popular respect in their own right. Their only fault was that they disagreed with a leader who would brook no dissent.

The first such clash occurred in the winter of 1985–6, over the sale of Britain's only helicopter manufacturer, Westland, which was on the verge of bankruptcy. Thatcher's opponent was Michael Heseltine, the Secretary for Defence. Heseltine was certainly no wet. He was a believer in efficiency and the private sector and so had supported making nationalised industries competitive, privatisation, contracting out public sector services and making the civil service more accountable. Thatcher had moved him to Defence in 1983 for just this purpose – to make it more efficient. At Defence, he had been a high-profile opponent of CND at the climax of the Cruise missile crisis and had aggressively defended the government on the sinking of the *Belgrano*. Thus, his record of loyalty was a good one. Crucially, however, Heseltine was a Europeanist. He wanted Westland to be purchased by a European consortium, which he helped to assemble, so that it would remain under European control. Unfortunately, the better offer came from the American company Sikorsky. That was the offer Westland's management and shareholders wanted to take, and they were supported by the Secretary for Trade and Industry, Leon Brittan.

Thatcher supported Brittan. But Heseltine was determined. He mobilised the Europeans and lobbied the leaders of British businesses that would be affected by the sale. Under American ownership, he argued, Westland would be excluded from participating in European defence contracts. Thatcher finally asked the Solicitor-General, Sir Patrick Mayhew, for a legal opinion about Heseltine's contention. Mayhew wrote Heseltine a letter, with copies to Thatcher and Brittan, indicating that he thought the Defence Secretary was claiming more than was justified. This letter was leaked to the press. Mayhew was furious; his confidential advice had been made public, and in a way that distorted what he had said to make it much less even-handed and more decisive. The leak, it turned out, had come from Brittan's Department. Furthermore, Brittan had given an ambiguously conditional consent, subject to Downing Street approval, which also apparently had been secured. Brittan was eventually forced to resign as the fall guy for the breach of confidence. Heseltine resigned first, however, making the Prime Minister's dictatorial style in Cabinet an issue. In her statement to the Commons, Thatcher insisted that she knew nothing of Mayhew's letter or the authorisation to leak it. Given Thatcher's reputation for being on top of everything, and given her closeness to the people in her office who had at least implicitly approved the leak, her denials were hard to swallow. For a moment, Thatcher seemed vulnerable for having misled the Commons; but one more statement, that was reasonably candid, got her off the hook. Yet Westland ended Thatcher's aura of invulnerability while marking the first blood-letting of the Thatcherites.

Far more significant was her conflict two years later with Nigel Lawson, who arguably was the architect of the Thatcherite economic policy, first as the developer of the medium-term financial strategy and then as Chancellor of the Exchequer. Their falling out came in 1988 over Lawson's policy of shadowing the Deutschmark – that is, keeping the value of the pound fixed relative to the currencies in the EC's exchange rate mechanism (ERM). Although Thatcher forced him to stop, Lawson kept pressing for sterling to enter the ERM. Thatcher, however, now saw the EC's erosion of national sovereignty as the dominant issue of international politics. To her, the ERM was a Trojan horse that would fatally undermine British sovereignty by ending government control over monetary policy. Was the management of the economy now to be turned over to the Germans, and was Britain thereby to be brought under a German hegemony that it had resisted, at great cost, in two world wars? Although Thatcher's suspicion of European integration probably reflected the attitude of most Britons, her fight with Lawson was not presented in these terms. The public saw a disagreement over whether Britain could fight inflation more effectively in the ERM rather than outside, and some very cautious Thatcherites, in the persons of Lawson and Howe, were saying that sterling should be in. Furthermore, with inflation beginning to take off again in 1988 and 1989, the evidence seemed to support the implication that Britain needed outside help. Thus, it is not clear that Thatcher had popular support on the narrower issue; rather, she seemed to be stubbornly insisting that she was right and everyone else was wrong.

In July 1989 Thatcher struck, not against Lawson but against Howe, who had imbued too much of the Foreign Office mentality for her taste. She shunted him off to lead the Commons. At the same time, to strengthen herself in the battle with the Treasury, Thatcher brought back to Downing Street her old economic adviser, Alan Walters, an open critic of ERM. Lawson finally resigned in October rather than allow himself to be superseded by Walters in shaping economic policy. John Major succeeded to the Treasury, while Douglas Hurd became Foreign Secretary. But Hurd, an old Heathite and Foreign Office man, was no improvement on Howe, while Major agreed with the Treasury view that Britain should be in the ERM. Thatcher was no better off for the changes, while she looked increasingly capricious and imperious. That autumn, an obscure backbencher named Sir Anthony Meyer challenged Thatcher for the party leadership, making her style the centrepiece of his challenge. Sixty MPs either voted for Meyer or did not bother to vote at all. This was not a number to make the Prime Minister's position untenable, but it was enough to provide a base for a more formidable challenger should the opportunity arise. And there were far more than sixty unhappy Tory MPs, who feared they could lose their seats in a close election.

A Labour victory no longer looked out of the question, primarily because of the poll tax. While the issues that triggered Thatcher's collapse were linked to Europe, the underlying cause was her stubborn insistence on following through with this unpopular reform, which generated a full-scale tax revolt in Scotland. There were other reasons as well for Tory MPs to be nervous. All polls indicated (and had for some time) that the welfare state remained popular, and even that people were prepared to accept higher taxes for improved public services. Despite three election victories, Thatcherism had not captured public support. The Tories could keep winning despite this fact because Labour was divided and people saw the Conservatives as the party of strong government, best fit to manage the economy. Now, however, the economy was beginning to collapse into recession, while the behaviour of the Prime Minister – the embodiment of strong government – was making her into a liability rather than an asset. Nor was the Tory rank and file particularly

Thatcherite, either.[18] Hence the base of support for Thatcher was far thinner than one would expect for someone who had been such a successful Prime Minister for ten years.

A year later, all was worse. The economy was a mess, especially in the South, the Tory heartland. The poll tax rebellion had spread to England. At the same time Labour, under Kinnock's reforming whip, was beginning to look like a viable competitor again. So when Howe resigned on 1 November, following a deliberately provocative anti-European statement to the Commons by the Prime Minister, and in his own statement offered a damning commentary on her shrill and bullheaded approach to Europe, the dam burst open. Heseltine challenged Thatcher as leader of the party, and, while he did not win, his 152 votes (to Thatcher's 204) denied her the 15 per cent margin of victory that party rules required. Then an astonishing thing happened: most of Thatcher's colleagues advised her to resign, in the interest of party unity and to block a possible (though by no means certain) Heseltine victory. Evidently, despite all the purges, the Cabinet was hardly more Thatcherite in 1990 than it had been in 1979. For if people like Lawson and Howe, who bore central responsibility for the policies of the last eleven years, were not dry enough, who could be? And given the Prime Minister's disloyalty to those who had served her so well, why should those who remained count on anything better?* Thus all they saw was the potential disaster of fighting the next election under Thatcher's leadership. They felt not obligation to her personally and were indifferent to the constitutional implications of throwing out a sitting Prime Minister, chosen in a national election, by a vote of Tory MPs. In the end, Thatcher withdrew, and the Tories chose John Major, a man with uniquely little parliamentary and Cabinet experience, to be Prime Minister.

---

* Others whom Thatcher was perceived to have abandoned included Brittan; Norman Tebbitt who was too openly ambitious to succeed the Prime Minister; and, most recently, Nicholas Ridley, who had made his strong anti-German views too public for his own good.

The Labour Party looked well positioned to take advantage of the Tory collapse. The 'hard' left completely discredited itself following the 1987 election, when Benn challenged Kinnock as party leader. Most of the remainder of the left now became fully integrated into the Kinnockite party – well represented in the shadow Cabinet and with positions of authority throughout the party structure. Furthermore, given the party's meagre improvement on its 1983 performance, no one, apart from the Bennites, could deny the need for fundamental changes in its policies. Kinnock therefore launched a major Policy Review between 1988 and 1991 that incorporated both MPs and trade unionists. The result was an acceptance of much of the Thatcher revolution. It explicitly asserted the positive role of the market in distributing resources efficiently and meeting consumer demands. It backed away from Keynesianism and accepted the Thatcherite regimen of low inflation, low interest rates, a stable exchange rate and low income taxes. It repudiated the renationalisation of privatised industries and even accepted the Tories' trade union reforms. The only roles Labour now saw for government were investment in infrastructure, encouragement of research and development and the organisation of workforce training programmes. Perhaps the most traumatic sacrifice for the 'soft' left was unilateral nuclear disarmament; there was certainly much resistance to jettisoning the policy. Ultimately, it was made easier by the end of the Cold War, the collapse of the Warsaw Pact and the arms reductions that the Americans and Soviets were actually negotiating. Finally, and most ironically, Labour became the party of Europe, embracing the ERM and the European Commission's interest in the kind of protection for workers that Thatcherism had done so much to undermine.

The end result of the Policy Review, then, was the abandonment of long-standing Labour policies, some dating back to 1945 and earlier: full employment, redistributive taxation, trade union rights, nationalisation, withdrawal from the EC and unilateral nuclear disarmament. State planning and incomes policies were also jettisoned. Labour's rhetoric now sounded a lot like the 'new liberalism' of 1890–1914. It was committed to a society based on individual liberty, with the government staying out of the economy. However, true freedom for the individual to realise all his or her talents required education and health. Society did not benefit, and values of work and self-help were not encouraged, if people were brought down by circumstances beyond their control and beyond their means to provide against. Thus government intervention to assure basic welfare services to all was justified to secure genuine equal opportunity within a competitive society. This meant national provision of health care; sufficient insurance against unemployment, old age and poverty; and education and training adequate to a modern industrialised economy, while assuring that those who were able could improve themselves.

As the Policy Review was winding its way forward, Kinnock also tightened his grip on the party. Most important, symbolically, was the conference vote mandating reselection of MPs. Kinnock did not try formally to reverse that vote; instead, he sought to undermine its effects. His preferred means was to require that reselection be by the vote of the full local party membership rather than by the general committee. The latter might be captured by the left, but the party rank and file was more likely to be moderate. The trade unions resisted this reform, however, because they saw it as a first step towards replacing their block vote in party conference by a similar system based on one member, one vote. For the moment, therefore, Kinnock had to be satisfied with a new rule requiring the local party to choose from a list of approved candidates. Several times the NEC rejected a candidate preferred by or already selected by a left-wing constituency organisation, and then imposed its own candidate after the locals refused to nominate anyone from its list. Kinnock did, however, secure one member, one vote as the basis for electing the constituency representatives to the NEC, and the effect by 1993 was to help give the right its largest number of constituency representatives since the 1940s. Similarly, constituency delegates to the party conference were now to be elected by the whole membership rather than by the general committee. The whole thrust, then, of Kinnock's organisational reforms was to parry left-wing control of local party organisations with votes by all local party members. Democracy would counter a Leninist organisational coup.

As Kinnock's revamped Labour Party was looking stronger, the alternative on the left was having difficulty. After the defeat of 1987, David Steel forced merger negotiations between the Liberals and Social Democrats, with the SDP rank and file over-riding the opposition of David Owen. Nor would Owen accept the decision of the party to approve the merger once the terms were agreed. Instead, playing a kind of left-wing Heath, he relaunched the SDP and continued to pursue his spoiler role until the party finally folded in 1990. Unfortunately, Owen was by far the best known of the remaining leaders of the Alliance, so his every move was followed in the press. The effect was to exaggerate the divisions resulting from the merger and to weaken the new Liberal Democrats as they worked to establish their cred-ibility under a new leader, Paddy Ashdown. The Liberal Democrats' heritage from Owen was the acceptance of most of the Thatcherite economic policies. Ashdown attempted to posi-tion them as the party of individual freedom, emphasising the authoritarian, anti-individualist aspects of Thatcherism's attack on local government. He promoted decentralisation as the liberal alternative to Thatcherite centralisation. At the same time, Steel had left the party a legacy of policies that seemed especially rele-vant in the 1990s: protection of the environment, freedom of information and Scottish and Welsh devolution. Ashdown added the defence of consumer interests through effective regulation of privatised utilities or the breaking up of privatised monopo-lies to secure competition. In many ways, it was a more distinc-tive programme than Labour's, and by 1992 Ashdown had established himself as the most respected of the three major party leaders. But the Alliance's strength in the 1980s had been pred-icated on Labour's weakness. How well could the Lib Dems do now that Labour was a real alternative government again?

They would not be able to count on Conservative weakness to bale them out. Under Major, the party retooled its image in preparation for the imminent general election. Major's leadership victory mandated only two changes from mainstream Thatcherism: the ditching of the poll tax and the projection of greater empathy with ordinary voters (the British equivalent of George Bush senior's 'kinder and gentler' conservatism). A man of humble background and limited education, Major wanted to be liked. Kind, generous and sensitive, he felt insecure around those, like many of the Thatcherites, who were dogmatically assertive and intellectually self-confident (if not arrogant). Major was a conciliator and a consensus-builder, just the kind of person whom Thatcher hated. His style in the Cabinet was collegial; he wanted his government to be a harmonious team. The effect of the Major approach up to the general election was to create a period of rest and consolidation for the party and the nation, after a decade of high-decibel and high-tension politics, when everything seemed to be about radical change.

The result was just what the parliamentary party had hoped for when it dumped Thatcher. The Tories leapt ahead of Labour in the polls, and while they fell back after the initial rush brought on by Major's appointment, they held their own thereafter. Most importantly, voters were not inclined to blame Major for the nation's deep recession; instead, they blamed the worldwide recession or the Thatcher government. As a result, enough people still believed that the Conservatives were better qualified than Labour to manage the economy, or that they would be worse off under a Labour government, to enable Major to win. This perception was reinforced during the election by Tory attacks on Labour's 'shadow budget', with its proposed tax increases.[19] At the same time, years of abuse by the tabloid press had undermined Kinnock's credibility as a prospective Prime Minister. Too many voters saw him as a political lightweight. Even the Policy Review was an ambiguous asset because it had required so many U-turns. The Tories constantly asked, what did he stand for? The implication was that he was purely an opportunist. In the end, according to Hugo Young of the *Guardian*, Major 'and not Neil Kinnock was seen as the man to trust . . . doggedness and quiet decency, the anti-Thatcher side of Major . . . saw him through'.[20] As a result, contrary to most expectations and polls, Major led the Conservatives to a stunning victory in the 1992 general election, winning 336 seats to 271 for Labour and 20 for the Liberal Democrats.[21] Major would never look as strong as he did that April, after the returns came in.

The Dissolution of the Tories

There is a myth that Conservatives are loyal to their leader, in contrast to Labour, whose leader constantly has been undermined by internal party struggles.[22] It is a myth with little basis in reality. Indeed, only a decade after the Conservative Party was formally born in 1834, it overthrew Sir Robert Peel when he repealed the Corn Laws in 1846. In the twentieth century alone, Joseph Chamberlain launched his Tariff Reform campaign in 1903, crippling the party for eight years and finally leading to the overthrow of Balfour as leader in 1911; Churchill continually attacked Baldwin and Neville Chamberlain in the 1930s over Indian self-government and appeasement; Macmillan showed a tenuous loyalty to Eden as the party dumped him after Suez in 1957; Thatcher led the revolt against Heath in 1975; and, of course, Thatcher in turn was jettisoned as an election liability in 1990. Since 1945, however, Tory rebellion involved the quick axing of a leader perceived as a loser – not the ceaseless carping which undermined Labour governments in power. In this sense, John Major faced something that had not been seen among Tories since the days of Chamberlain and Churchill – a constant challenge to his leadership from those who disagreed with him on a fundamental issue, Europe.

The rebellion was slow to develop. The obvious success of Major's low-key style with the public seemed to confirm the party's wisdom in getting rid of Thatcher and electing him leader. The unexpected victory in the general election gave him an enhanced authority in the party and the country. That authority was destroyed, however, by 'Black Wednesday' – that day in September when Britain was forced to withdraw from the ERM. Major was personally identified with the ERM – both as the Chancellor who had taken Britain in and as the Prime Minister who insisted throughout the summer of 1992 that it was essential to economic stability and recovery from the recession. The Prime Minister's credibility was shattered following the humiliating U-turn of September. Instantly, he lost the leverage he needed to contain the party's divisions over Europe. Once the party began to fracture on him, Major's lack of experience as a leader who had worked his way up through the ranks over many years began to tell. He simply did not have the standing that came with all that time spent among the party's leadership, engaged in political warfare both with the opposition and within the party. Nor did he have the political savvy of Harold Wilson in negotiating the shoals of party divisions over a contentious issue. Given that even Wilson's efforts ultimately failed to prevent Labour's divisions from ripping the party apart, it is hardly surprising that Major failed even more spectacularly – especially since the fallen leader was always looming in the shadows as a reminder to the faithful of what might have been.

Major had been the Thatcherites' candidate in the leadership election, primarily because he was not Heseltine, but probably also because he was so obviously a creation of Thatcher that they expected him to be beholden to them. They should have been satisfied with their choice. His strong belief in equal opportunity, public services that were responsive to the people they served and small government led him to extend Thatcher's policies on privatisation, health, education and the civil service. In dealing with the recession, he made control of inflation the top priority, and he succeeded. Even on Europe, he bent over backwards to accommodate a Thatcherite right which continually sniped at him from the moment he took over. He embraced Thatcher's key European principles – arguing for a community of sovereign nations rather than a single European state and promoting subsidiarity, i.e. the principle that policy decisions should be made at the national level unless it was clearly unsuitable. He attacked the Euro-bureaucracy in Brussels and back-door socialism. His great achievement, the Maastricht Treaty, was initially welcomed by Conservatives for limiting the supposed march towards a European superstate. At the same time, he had preserved Britain's freedom of action by negotiating opt-outs on the Treaty's commitment to a single currency and the Social Chapter.

Yet still he turned out not to be the kind of right-winger that Thatcherites wanted. Major was not a person who thought in ideological terms, so he could never be an effective voice for Thatcherism. At the same time, his style was too accommodating and consensual. He seemed a weak reed in comparison to the deposed leader – though he was strong enough to dispense with many of the Thatcherites whom he had inherited, often for reasons having little to do with ideology.[*] Most of all, the right resented him because he was not Thatcher. And all the while, sometimes in the background and sometimes quite openly, Thatcher was egging them on, showing her contempt for her successor, attacking his policies, and generally doing to him what Heath had spent fifteen years doing to her by making his life miserable. Europe served her and her acolytes alike as a means for attacking him.

Since the 1870s, the Conservative Party had been the party of nationalism. Conservative foreign, defence and imperial policies were all concerned with enhancing the power and prestige of the nation. Thus European integration always represented a

---

[*] In the end, only three true 'dries' were left in his Cabinet. They were Michael Portillo, ultimately the 'great white hope' who was expected to restore Thatcherism to its rightful place of glory in the Conservative Party; John Redwood, the most intellectual of the three, who ultimately challenged Major for the leadership; and Peter Lilley, the most senior of the three, having achieved Cabinet rank in Thatcher's last year. The three were the 'bastards' whom Major was referring to during a notorious BBC interview, when he was talking informally after he thought the microphone had been turned off. All wanted to see the Maastricht Treaty fail. However, Michael Howard, too, was very right wing and Euro-sceptic.

fundamental challenge to traditional Conservative ideology. Conservative pragmatism, however, had dictated compromise and accommodation since Macmillan first applied for entry to the Common Market in the 1960s. Furthermore, Europe potentially offered a way for Britain to project a strong foreign policy in conjunction with its EC partners – in current parlance, a means for Britain to punch above its weight in world affairs. Thus, the EC could allow Conservatives to pursue their traditional policy of asserting British power and interests aggressively. However, as the EC began to encroach on sovereignty through European Commission directives and European Court decisions, the potential was always there for the nationalist strain of conservatism to rebel against this undermining of the nation. This was what happened in the last years of Thatcher's premiership. Her Bruges speech in September 1988 set her seal of approval on resistance to further European integration. The pro-European elements in the party seemingly triumphed by forcing Thatcher's resignation; however, Thatcherites saw her vindication in the clear harm done to the economy by the ERM. Following 'Black Wednesday', they declared open war on the Prime Minister over Europe. They would not be placated; no compromise was acceptable. Indeed, as Major became ever more Euro-sceptic in his pronouncements and actions, they kept upping the ante, hoping ultimately to force a break with his Europhile Chancellor Kenneth Clarke.

The Thatcherites could keep the issue alive because they were not alone in their unease over European developments. A 1994 poll of backbench Conservatives on a series of statements relating to Europe indicated that roughly 50–60 per cent of them were Euro-sceptic and roughly 30–40 per cent were pro-European, depending on the issue.[23] There was overwhelming opposition to extending qualified majority voting (meaning the end of the national veto) to issues of foreign and defence policy, clear symbols of sovereignty, and to any further supranational powers for EU institutions. The number of rebels was much smaller than this, but this broader base of anti-European sentiment, which was reinforced by the intake of new Tory MPs from the 1992 general election, made it difficult for Major to quash the issue. As a result, from the autumn of 1992 until the general election in May 1997, the Tory Party and its leader were torn apart over Europe.

The rejection of the Maastricht Treaty by the Danes in June 1992 and 'Black Wednesday' the following September unleashed the dammed-up opposition. The Tory right wanted Major either to abandon the treaty or to submit it to a referendum. Major, however, resented their behaviour and stubbornly stood by his greatest foreign policy triumph. By the autumn, the bill to implement the treaty brought open rebellion in the Commons – a rebellion that Thatcher encouraged both behind the scenes and with her public statements. A bruising battle between the government and the rebels followed. Twenty-two Tories had voted against the second reading prior to the Danish referendum, while another four had abstained. Now in committee the government suffered one defeat, while Liberal Democratic support was necessary to avoid another. Some amendments were conceded rather than risk a vote. By the third reading, there were 46 rebels, 41 of whom voted against the government.[24] Nor did the sniping stop once the Maastricht legislation was passed. The government lost a vote in July 1993 confirming its Social Chapter opt-out, forcing it to call for a vote of confidence. Major finally withdrew the party whip from eight persistent rebels in November 1994 when they abstained on another EU vote that had been made a vote of confidence. It was a futile gesture, however, as the whipless eight immediately helped to defeat the government on a tax proposal. The whip finally had to be restored the following April. Major's decision to resign the party leadership and submit himself for re-election in the summer of 1995 was another desperate attempt to end the divisions over Europe and re-establish his authority over the party. Major beat back a challenge from John Redwood by 218 votes to 89 with 20 abstentions, but the exercise did not achieve his goal. The European issue could not die, with the introduction of the single currency due in 1999. Major refused to rule out

Britain's joining, even though he had no intention of doing so.

One reason that Major could not end Tory divisions was the collapse of the party's support in the country. Two factors had assured Conservative victories in 1987 and 1992: the perception that they were the most competent party to manage the economy and the fact that the opposition was divided and lacked credibility. Those assets were reversed by 'Black Wednesday' and the civil war over Europe. Conservative economic policies had proved a failure, while it was the Tories who were divided and losing credibility. The effect was immediately evident in public opinion polls: Labour's lead shot up from an average of 2.5 per cent from July to September to nearly 18 per cent in the last three months of 1992. The local government elections of May 1993 drove the point home. The Conservatives' share of the vote plummeted to 31 per cent, the lowest ever, while they lost strongholds that had been under Tory rule since the introduction of elected county councils in 1888 – Dorset, Kent and Norfolk. On the same day, the Tory vote in the Newbury by-election collapsed from 56 per cent at the general election to 27 per cent, as the Liberal Democrats captured the seat. Later in the summer the Liberal Democrats won another 'safe' Tory seat at Christchurch. That summer of 1993 saw the Lib Dems move ahead of the Tories in the Gallup polls.[25] The performance in subsequent local government elections was, if anything, worse. Following the May 1996 elections, the Conservatives controlled only three local authorities, compared to 212 for Labour and 55 for the Liberal Democrats.[26] Each new by-election or local election catastrophe brought the knives out again, with new talk of a leadership crisis and the need to dump Major. By the spring of 1996, the right had written off the next general election and was conspiring to assure that one of its own succeeded Major, either before or after the inevitable defeat.

Other factors contributed to this disintegration, as the Conservatives showed all the signs of a party that had been in power too long. A series of scandals involving sex, corruption or questionable actions by Tory MPs or members of the government (shorthanded as 'sleaze' in the press) were made worse because Major had briefly tried to make the nation's moral decline central to the party's message. Major could never work out how to handle the steady flow of revelations, and his constant U-turns made him seem hesitant and bumbling. That impression was reinforced in 1996 by the government's slow and uncertain response to the panic created when it was determined that 'mad cow disease' might be passed to humans. Finally, the party's traditional supporters in the press turned against Major. *The Times* and the *Sun* of Rupert Murdoch and the *Daily Telegraph* of Conrad Black relentlessly hammered his European policy and his ineffectual leadership. Black (a Canadian) was an Atlanticist; Murdoch (an Australian turned American) promoted an anti-French, anti-German chauvinism. Both were unhappy that Major wasn't Thatcher, and their papers punished him for it.[27] Their unending attacks were supported by Norman Lamont, who waged a personal vendetta against Major following his dismissal as Chancellor in May 1993. Reinforced by the constant bickering within the party, this ceaseless abuse shaped the image of Major as weak and indecisive. Major's inability to put his own stamp on his government's domestic policies also contributed to that image. He seemed to be a leader without an agenda, except what had been Thatcher's. His most distinctive programmes, like the Citizen's Charter and the 'back-to basics' campaign, both bombed as defining statements for the government and became targets of derision – the former unjustly, as it became a considerable success. All these factors helped to undermine his credibility as Prime Minister. As a result, long before May 1997, Major had become a liability to his party, just as the party had become a liability to its leader.

The Rise of New Labour

'Black Wednesday' was fundamental to the revival of Labour as a party of government. For analysis of voter attitudes following the 1992 election showed that Kinnock's efforts to reshape

Labour's image had not accomplished very much. According to Eric Shaw, a historian of the party:

> It was still seen as backward-looking, out-of-touch, economically incompetent, unreliable, vulnerable to an extremist take-over and, above all, not meriting trust. It was associated with the unions, old-style industrial workers, 'minorities', the poor and the losers in life rather than with 'ordinary' people. It was seen as antipathetic to the upwardly mobile, the diligent and the able and there was little faith in its ability to govern, to protect individual well-being or promote popular aspirations.[28]

At the same time, the 1992 defeat confirmed that Kinnock was damaged goods. He could never escape the press image of him as weak and ineffectual, despite his success in breaking the power of the left and moving Labour's policies towards the centre. He recognised the reality and resigned to give someone else a chance, his last service to the party.

His successor, John Smith, was a man of the right. He was a strong supporter of EC membership and had backed right-wing candidates in the leadership contests of 1980 and 1983. As leader, he was inclined to loosen the reins of central control that Kinnock had established in order to impose discipline on his notoriously unruly party. Smith, like Major, was a conciliator with a more collective and consensual leadership style. Thus, he saw no need either to keep fighting the left, as Kinnock had done, or to move the party any further to the right. All the polls indicated that the welfare state was never more popular. The pendulum would eventually swing against the Tories, and Kinnock's reforms assured that Labour would benefit when this happened.

'Black Wednesday', the tax increases that followed and the Tory divisions over Europe opened up just the kind of opportunity that Smith was waiting for. Yet Smith's judgement was at odds with the view of Labour that Shaw described. If the party was to take advantage, something more needed to be done to convince voters (especially middle-class voters) that this was a 'new' Labour party – one that had broken decisively with the image that had evolved in the public mind between 1969 and 1987. This was the view of Tony Blair, Gordon Brown and a group of 'modernisers' on the right wing of the party. And in one fundamental way, it was Smith's view too. He saw that the party had to look less beholden to the trade unions. This required ending the unions' use of the block vote at party conference, in electing the party leader and in the selection of parliamentary candidates. Smith had had mixed success in securing this aim[*] when he died suddenly in May 1994. His successor, Tony Blair, had none of Smith's sensibilities about conciliating the unions. The brief interlude of laid-back leadership was over, as the modernisers were given full authority to finish the job that Kinnock had begun. Blair ended union sponsorship of candidates, kept the unions at arm's length in policy discussions and turned to business for money so as to make the unions' political levy less important to party finances.[†]

---

[*] Smith was able to reduce the trade unions' share of the electoral college in leadership elections to one-third. He also got a form of one member, one vote in the reselection of MPs. Just as reselection of MPs had symbolised the triumph of the left in the early 1980s, reselection by local party members (rather than the party organisation) became a touchstone for showing that the power of the left was fully broken. However, in order to secure union acquiescence to the reform, the resolution explicitly reaffirmed that there was no desire to weaken the trade union connection with the party. Since the outside world saw the whole process as a way to distance the party from the unions, Smith's concession negated that effect.

[†] Much of the change was for public relations purposes. Unions almost never tried to tell sponsored MPs how to vote. Union leaders mostly took their cues from the party leadership on policy matters (especially when Labour was in power), although since 1970 with formal consultation processes. And of course, there were disagreements both between unions and within unions on policy issues. The main way in which they influenced party debates was through the election of union representatives on the NEC, through union votes at party conferences, and (since 1981) through the electoral college to select the leader and deputy leader. In the 1970s, however, it had looked as if the unions were calling the shots, and that perception remained. See Lewis Minkin, *The Contentious Alliance: Trade Unions and the Labour Party* (Edinburgh: Edinburgh University Press, 1991), *passim*, but especially chaps 9, 10, 13 and 14.

He also sought to weaken the party conference as a forum for debate by creating a series of policy-making committees which would filter and control the content of what was finally discussed at the conference. It was one more way to take the initiative away from the constituency organisations and trade unions. With a nice populist touch, he submitted the election manifesto to a referendum of party members, thus further neutralising the policy-making influence of the conference.

Finally, Blair decided to prove how decisively *new* Labour had become by repealing Clause IV of the party's constitution, which committed it to nationalisation. The revised text was virtually the opposite of the one to be discarded, favouring an economy 'in which the enterprise of the market and the rigour of competition are joined with . . . high quality public services'.[29] Blair spent a year first working out the wording and then campaigning for the new clause among party members in order to neutralise union opposition. Membership ballots showed there was overwhelming support for the change, even among trade unionists. Combined with the earlier changes, the approval of the new Clause IV by a special party conference helped persuade people that Labour extremism was a thing of the past. Now it was the Tories who seemed to be in danger of being captured by their fanatics, not Labour. As the final seal of approval, following a Blair trip to Australia to cultivate Murdoch's News International group, Blair secured the support of the *Sun*.

Blair was, in fact, following in the path already blazed by Bill Clinton in the United States. New Labour, like the New Democrats, was offered to the voters as a slightly left-leaning centrist party which had repudiated its interventionist past and was now the natural home for those who were uncomfortable with the radical conservatism which appeared to be taking over the party of the right. The message had enough force behind it for a Labour victory to look inevitable by the time the general election came in the spring of 1997. Blair's focus groups had told him that people were most concerned about health and education, so these became the centrepiece of Labour's election campaign. At the same time, to pre-empt any Tory attempt to impose the tax-and-spend tag on them, Brown and Blair committed the party to the Conservative budget figures for their first two years in office and forswore a return to Keynesianism. The only new tax would be on the windfall profits of the unpopular privatised utilities. Otherwise, when talking about the economy, they sounded very Thatcherite. The whole of the leadership team was expected to toe the party line on all policies; there would be no public dissent for the opposition to exploit, and those who deviated were called to task. The contrast with the civil war being fought out among the Conservatives could not have been starker. The reward for this new discipline was a landslide on a scale not seen since 1906 – the last time a discredited and divided Conservative government faced the united forces of the left. Labour won 419 seats to 165 for the Conservatives, with the Liberal Democrats winning 46 – the party's best result since 1929.[30] Labour did well among those voters whom it had been losing since the 1970s – the middle class and skilled workers, including those in the South of England. While New Labour claimed the credit, the electorate also showed again that it was unforgiving of a divided party, especially one that had hung on too long.

In some ways, the most impressive result of the election was the performance of the Liberal Democrats. They had benefited from tactical voting: that is, Labour voters supported the Lib Dem candidate in some Tory constituencies because the Lib Dem had the best chance of defeating the Conservative.[31] Since there had also been tactical voting by Liberal Democrats, there seemed to have been an unspoken alliance between the two parties in the election. There was even talk (mostly on the left) of a new, natural centre-left majority in the country that would relegate the Tories to a permanent minority – an amazing turnaround, since after the defeat in 1992 some respectable observers speculated that Labour could never win another election. Blair and Ashdown tried to consolidate this centre-left majority by cooperating after the election. They created Lib-Lab consultative committees to look at constitutional reform and proportional representation, though Blair pointedly did not promise to support a change in the voting system. The Labour government also pressed ahead with other constitutional reforms supported by the Liberal Democrats – Scottish and Welsh devolution and the first steps towards reform of the House of Lords. Because elections to the Scottish Parliament and the Welsh Assembly were based on a form of proportional representation, in both cases they resulted in no party winning a majority of seats. Labour and the Liberal Democrats immediately agreed to form a coalition government in Scotland; after a period of minority Labour government in Wales, in 2000 they agreed on a coalition there too.

Yet the permanent triumph of the left began to look shaky, as New Labour and Blair were decidedly less popular by 1999. The most prevalent criticism of Blair was his preoccupation with 'spin'. Spin meant assuring that the media reported what the government wanted it to report, and that both the media and the public at large put the interpretation on events that the government wanted. This fixation on the media resulted partly from the belief that they were crucial to Thatcher's success in the 1980s and partly from the reality that the print media had historically been overwhelmingly anti-Labour. The effect, however, was to create an impression that New Labour did not stand for anything, that it was all presentation without any underlying substance. By 2000, leaks of confidential documents confirmed this preoccupation with spin and left the public very impatient with it. At the same time, Blair came to be perceived as excessively arrogant and controlling. In fact, the style was not so different from Thatcher's, and she had shown that it could be either an asset or a liability, depending on the circumstances. Blair had yet to make it an image of strength, while the insistence of the leadership team on controlling *everything* clearly hurt him. He was especially maladroit in imposing Alun Michael as leader of the new Welsh Assembly over Rhodri Morgan, when the Welsh party preferred the latter. Despite the uproar, Blair continued in the same vein when he used a patently unfair electoral college system to block Ken Livingstone from being the party's candidate for the newly created position of London mayor. In both cases, the opposed candidates were too 'Old Labour' for Blair's taste.

The left took advantage of growing public unease with Blair's fixation on spin and image, and its sense that he was too arrogant and controlling, to launch a counterattack. Union leaders and party activists had accepted all Blair's backtracking and reforms between 1994 and 1997 because, after eighteen years of Thatcherite government, they accepted the primacy of winning the election. As Prime Minister, however, Blair continued to equivocate on or abandon policies dear to old Labour in his desire to please business and 'middle England'. It was not just the left who were upset. Roy Hattersley, the deputy leader under Kinnock and a stalwart of the old Labour right, had been attacking Blair's abandonment of fundamental socialist principles since 1995. The result, critics argued, was the alienation of Labour's core supporters. The whole of London showed what they thought of Blair's approach to politics when Livingstone decided to run for mayor as an independent. He won an overwhelming victory over the candidates of the established parties, leaving Labour's Frank Dobson struggling in third place.[32] With a general election looming in 2001, Blair started to work much harder to generate enthusiasm in the Labour heartland. He sought to persuade voters that the government's accomplishments reflected the kinds of policies that they wanted, while modifying some welfare policies in a more generous direction.

Towards a New Consensus

Old Labour had reason to be worried. New Labour looked an awful lot like Thatcherism – perhaps toned down a bit, and with more emphasis on social justice, but Thatcherism just the same. Thatcher may not have liked consensus politics, but a new consensus seemed to have emerged which was based on her agenda and policies. Its economics accepted the beneficent supremacy of the market. Government therefore should pursue policies that were friendly to business and finance, which meant the primacy of controlling inflation. At the same time, government should reduce its role in the economy and society, which meant reduced social welfare spending and taxation and no Keynesian micro-management. The consensus accepted the importance to a society of work, self-improvement and individual initiative; thus, the welfare state and tax system should be structured to promote these values. Because competition secured efficiency, the ethos of the private sector should be introduced into the public sector – including market conditions when possible, criteria of efficiency in the delivery of services, and recognition that the public should get the same benefits of value for money that any private-sector consumer sought. The consensus accepted that there should be no role for trade unions in influencing policy and that the power of the unions to use the strike weapon should be circumscribed. Finally, it accepted the need to improve standards in education and incorporated tough rhetoric on law and order.

Was there nothing, then, that Labour stood for in the way of domestic policy that distinguished it from the Conservatives? In rejecting old Labour's commitment to equality through a combination of redistributive taxation, public provision of services and government management of the economy, did Blair have no alternative vision to offer? In part, New Labour contended that it did not reject the public sector as a matter of principle, and so was more dedicated than the Tories to the provision of high-quality services. Furthermore, in promoting Clinton-like welfare-to-work programmes, Labour claimed a stronger commitment to education and job training that would assure every person could realise his or her potential to the full. Yet after four years of Labour government, the NHS and the nation's transport system appeared to be worse than in 1997. While Labour swept to victory in the 2001 general election, the message was that it had better improve these services and education or risk a major backlash.

Yet New Labour claimed more. It offered a vision based on the importance of community, social cohesion and the bonds that tie people together, in opposition to Thatcher's assertion that there is no such thing as society. For New Labour, this meant reasserting the communitarian strand of socialism while rejecting both socialism's emphasis on class conflict and the Thatcherite focus on self. In some ways, it was yet another manifestation of a post-war political and cultural romanticism in Britain (especially but not exclusively on the left) that was constantly searching for alternatives to the impersonal and alienating life of modern industrial and urban society.[33] Towards this end, Blair developed a rhetoric that was a combination of nineteenth-century Christian socialism (rooted in his own religious faith) and early twentieth-century 'new liberalism'. While standing by the fundamental tenets of individualism, he insisted that it must be tied to social justice and genuine equal opportunity. People must be helped to help themselves, not simply left to struggle alone against the vagaries of the market. They must also be given some decent protection against poverty, rooted in simple humanitarian concern for one's fellow citizens, and Labour, he said, could claim some significant steps in this direction in its first four years of government.

It is still too early to tell whether such rhetoric will translate into policies that are distinct from what the Tories would offer. Major resigned as leader after the general election in 1997. His successor, William Hague, was chosen primarily because he was young and he was not Kenneth Clarke, the pro-European political heavyweight among the contenders. The Thatcherites had used the same kind of negative reasoning to elect Major, and they lived to regret it. Hague did much better in living up to right-wing expectations, as he embraced an increasingly hard line on Europe and promised massive tax cuts. Nonetheless, his election looked like a mistake, as Labour was able to paint him as an extremist, while he suffered the same kind of press ridicule that had made Kinnock unelectable. Consequently, he commanded little popular respect or credibility as a strong leader. In the run-up to the general election in 2001, Hague backed away somewhat from his radical tax policies and focused the campaign on saving the pound, which polls showed rated very low among public concerns. At the same time, the Conservatives hardly looked credible as critics of Labour's record on helping public services. After all, they were the ones who had sold off the railways and denigrated the public sector during their eighteen years in office. Most seriously of all, however, the Tories were still a party divided, especially over Europe, but more generally over what vision of British society they wanted to project to the country. As usual, the British electorate punished party division unforgivingly. Blair swept to a second term with an overall majority of 167, only slightly smaller than that of 1997, while the Liberal Democrats, whose new leader Charles Kennedy was the hit of the election, were able to push their representation up to 52.

Although there is at least the possibility of a consensus on domestic policy, there can be no foreign policy consensus while there is disagreement about Europe. Kinnock and Blair cultivated a positive attitude towards Europe to replace the old hostility that had characterised much of the Labour Party. But Conservative divisions showed just how volatile the European issue continued to be. Blair was determined not to let it divide Labour. During the 1997 general election, the touchstone issue was the single currency; so Labour promised a referendum prior to any decision to take Britain in. Since there was plenty of evidence that there was little popular support for a strong pro-European policy, the referendum was postponed, while Hague staked out opposition to Europe as the Tories' defining issue during the 2001 general election. The present Tory leader, Michael Howard, leads a party that is still overwhelmingly hostile.

Where does New Labour stand? Blair and the Chancellor Gordon Brown treated joining the euro as an economic rather than a political issue, thus trying to sidestep the explosive sovereignty question. Early in the government's term, Brown defined five economic criteria that would be the basis of judging whether Britain was ready to join, and these remain in place. Blair waffled on giving the people and the party a decisive lead on Europe, even though he clearly wanted Britain to be one of the 'big three' of the EU. Occasionally he revealed himself with a strong pro-European speech, as in November 2001. His general reticence, however, gave Tory Euro-sceptics the run of the debate throughout his first term, and public opinion remained anti-European as a result. A referendum would put Blair's prestige and even his government on the line. Hence, he would have to give a strong lead to try to stem the flow against Europe. With the Tories still weak, Blair remained disinclined to take the risk.

Even with a pro-euro result, however, there may be no consensus on Europe. The most extreme anti-Europeans in the Conservative Party now want to pull out of the EU altogether. There has even been talk of Britain joining the North American Free Trade Association, a bizarre reinvention of Atlanticism and the special relationship with the United States. Thatcher also weighs in periodically against any compromise on Europe. For the foreseeable future, therefore, the Tories will continue to be the anti-euro party. If a referendum yields an anti-euro result, that could possibly provide the basis for a consensus on Europe. The real problem comes if the referendum endorses joining the euro. For it is not clear that Thatcher and the Tory anti-Europeans would accept such a vote, making it impossible to construct a basis for a compromise. Then Europe will continue to divide the Conservatives and the parties. Without some broad agreement on Europe – one of the most fundamental issues defining Britain's future – there can be no talk of a political consensus of the kind that emerged after 1945.

CONCLUSION:
THE AUDIT OF PEACE

Economic Decline: It's All Relative

In recent years, the *New York Times* has devoted much attention to the economic problems of Japan. As Howard French, the Tokyo correspondent, wrote in February 2001, 'just 12 years ago, this country was seen by the United States and much of the world as a juggernaut . . .'. Everyone was predicting 'that Japan would dominate virtually every industry worth being in, and that a United States in decline would be left to play a supporting role'.[1] With Japan entering its fourth recession in a decade, people were now trying to figure out what was wrong. The problem was all the more confusing because the apparent strengths of the Japanese system from 1950 to 1990 suddenly looked like weaknesses in 2000. For example, one of the centrepieces of the Japanese economic miracle was the close collaboration between banking, industry and government, as all joined to promote investment in Japan's export industries. Currently, the banking sector is one source of Japan's economic woes. Many banks are technically insolvent with mountains of bad debt, and most are inefficient and ill-equipped to compete if financial services were to be opened up to outside competition. The civil service, too, which used to be praised for its role in overseeing Japan's economic growth, is now a barrier to the kinds of reforms that might get the economy going again. The emphasis on exports is

667

also being reassessed. For the effect over the years has been to cheat the Japanese people of some of the benefits of their own economic success. Prices are higher in Japan, houses and apartments are smaller, cities are more crowded and fewer people can afford the goods that have defined the consumer revolution in the West. According to the Japanese economist Haruo Shimada, 'The Japanese focus has never been on making Japanese richer, their lives happier or more convenient and predictable . . . Our future growth will come from an untapped market: investing in satisfying the family, making life happier for people.'[2]

This, of course, is exactly what British governments did after 1945: they concentrated on channelling resources to the people and making their lives happier, and for the past twenty-five years and more they have been damned for it and blamed for Britain's economic decline. Britain had other strengths compared to Japan that Britain's homegrown critics ignored. Japan was way behind Britain in the quality of its financial services and the efficiency of its retail distribution, as Japanese policy-makers protected small farmers and shopkeepers. As a result, while Japan's rate of inflation may have been below Britain's, its prices were the highest in the developed world.[3] There may be social benefits in protecting specific social groups, but there also are economic costs. Which is more important? The Japanese have long been admired for their work ethic and the quality of their education system, both of which have yielded a high-calibre workforce. Yet one result of both has been a suicide rate that was twice as high as Britain's in 1980.[4] One of French's articles looks at the 'scientific gap' and Japan's weakness in theoretical science – a British strength. Indeed, readers will remember that Britain has long been criticised for its weakness in applied science. A third article looks at the failure of women's liberation to make much impact in Japan, which affects the contribution women can make to the labour force and economic output. Such Japanese 'failures' are attributable to cultural differences. Even the scientific gap is explained by an aversion to competition, which is a theme running through all analyses of Japan's ordeal. Yet one consequence of this preference not to compete is a far more equal income distribution in Japan than in Britain, the United States or even continental Europe.[5]

Clearly, governments and peoples make decisions about policies and even ways of life that partly are culturally determined. Judgements about whether the decisions were the right ones depend very much on who is looking, what they are looking for and when they are looking. From the perspective of 1970–90, the decisions made by the British after the war seemed somewhat questionable, while Japanese decisions looked brilliant; from the perspective of 2001, the British do not look so bad and the Japanese don't look so good. Japan's is not the only economy that is not doing as well as it was twenty years ago. Another article in the *New York Times* from April 2001 is headlined, 'Germany Looks Like Europe's Weak Economic Link' – and Germany's performance over the following two years merely confirmed this perception. Part of Germany's problem is the high cost and inefficiencies of unification. Part of the problem, however, is very rigid labour markets and '[industry-wide] collective bargaining agreements [which] give companies little ability to negotiate better terms with labor unions'.[6] And there was Britain in the 1960s, lamenting the breakdown of national agreements as companies negotiated separate deals at the factory level! Right now, a flexible labour market is all the rage. The article in the *Times* asserts that the relative success of France and the Netherlands compared to Germany is the result of government policies that enable companies to employ part-time or temporary workers. In Britain, the move towards part-time work is bemoaned by the left and cheered by the right. As usual, it seems impossible to make unambiguous judgements about what is best that are free from political bias.

Yet we must try. The first is that the British economy did very well between 1950 and 1973. By any measure, even including the rate of inflation, this was a period of exceptional performance that was not matched in the 1980s and 1990s. The latter decades produced a somewhat lower growth rate, a somewhat higher rate of inflation and much higher levels of unemployment and poverty.7 To some degree, both the success of the two early decades and the problems later were beyond the control of any government. Britain's strong economic performance conformed to the trend in all industrialised countries, as an expansive world economy was fuelled by low prices, much pent-up demand and a stable system of exchange rates. The problems since then have also, in part, been beyond anyone's control – especially the oil-price increases of the 1970s, but also the disappearance of the unique conditions coming out of the war.

Nonetheless, there were many things that government *could* control. The British governments of the late 1940s and early 1950s made several decisions that were fundamental in their effect on the British economy. The first was that there should be full employment. By the 1950s, the definition of what that meant came to be an unemployment rate of between 1 and 2 per cent. Second, it was decided that sterling's role as a reserve currency, and thus the exchange rate of the pound, would be defended at all costs. Third, it was decided that Britain's role as a power greater than all others but the United States and the Soviet Union would be maintained. A conservative would add a fourth – the decision to maintain an expansive welfare state. The third and fourth could both be seen as a matter of politics: the left saw Britain's defence role as untenable, while the right saw the welfare state as untenable. Yet by the standards of other Western European states (but not of Japan and the United States, whose cultures are entirely different), Britain's welfare state was not excessively generous. If anything, it was a bit stingy. The others, however, did not have Britain's overseas commitments and atomic weapons; so they could more easily afford the welfare state. Could Britain have got away with a smaller welfare state, and if so, would it then have been able to afford the defence commitments it had taken on? We can never know. My own guess, however, is that it was polit-ically impossible for Britain to reduce the welfare state to a level that would have enabled it to afford all the defence commitments

it embraced. Even in the last two decades, Conservative governments that wanted to cut welfare while enhancing defence found
that there were severe limits as to how far they could pare back
the welfare state. So they were forced to retrench the much more
attenuated defence policy that they had inherited. Thus, the third
decision mentioned above really does seem much more critical
than the fourth.

These three decisions meant that British governments faced
perpetual, if relatively minor, economic crises throughout the two
decades of prosperity. Furthermore, their efforts to cope with those
crises may well have had an adverse effect on economic growth
and helped to account for Britain's slight underperformance
compared to other industrialised nations. That underperformance
should not be exaggerated. The data show it to be more ambiguous
than myth would have it. Furthermore, the countries devastated by
the war were bound to catch up with Britain, which meant that
they were going to have higher growth rates during these decades.
Nonetheless, there are a couple of economic indicators that show
unambiguous British decline: the fall in Britain's share of world
manufacturing exports and the decline of Britain's standing in the
rankings of nations according to GDP per head. Both are accounted
for by the problems of British industry, which ultimately led to a
massive contraction of the manufacturing sector from the 1960s
onwards. How are we to explain these problems? Economists come
down on almost every possible side in this debate. As best as a
non-economist can judge, cultural explanations have made a
distinct comeback in the last decade or two. In particular, British
management really did fail in giving consumers what they wanted.
They could not offer an attractive array of product lines, they could
not deliver goods on time and they could not provide the support
services that were required. Firms were slow to reorganise in the
most efficient way and so costs were higher. They invested less in
research and development than those in other countries. The blame
for some of these problems, however, must be shared with labour.
Trade unions did not want reorganisation either, their work rules
and battles over demarcation did drive up costs and they contributed

to the failure to meet deadlines on delivery. Finally, Britain's system of education and vocational training was inferior to competitor nations. As a result, Britain had a less skilled and less adaptable workforce in addition to less well trained managers.

The reforms of Thatcherism tried to correct some of these weaknesses, as well as addressing other explanations for economic 'failure' that probably had little to do with it. The Thatcherites certainly attempted to change the culture to make it more competitive, more entrepreneurial and more concerned with serving consumers, and they probably had some success. There was a vast expansion in education at the university level with the upgrading of the polytechnics, and there was an effort to give more status to the kind of education that the latter offered – including business and applied science and engineering. Less was done, however, in improving vocational training and upgrading the skills of ordinary workers. The trade unions were tamed. British industry, however, continued its unrelenting decline, which actually accelerated in these years. At the same time, British wages remained low in comparison to other developed nations, while the level of anxiety was higher as workers had to work longer hours with less job security. Did Thatcherism make a difference for the better? At this point, it gets more difficult to be non-political. Even some of Thatcher's critics almost concede that some change was necessary – e.g. cutting back on the role of the state, imposing ceilings on how high welfare spending could go, insisting that inflation must be controlled. That is the implication of seeing Thatcherism as part of a longer-term trend in these directions among all developed countries. The power of the trade unions also needed to be limited. It is more doubtful, however, that so much had to be done at the expense of the poorest section of society, or that the big payoffs to the rich did anything to help Britain's economic performance. That performance was helped by Thatcherite reforms, but those reforms also left a legacy of poverty and pathetic public services that are going to take some time to reverse.

Decline in Power: What Role?

In one of the most quoted of all statements about Britain's foreign policy dilemma, Harry Truman's Secretary of State, Dean Acheson, said in 1962, 'Great Britain has lost an Empire and has not yet found a role.'[8] How true is Acheson's statement? The answer depends on one's views on the role of the empire in making Britain great. By the twentieth century, it is questionable how much the empire contributed to British power. The dominions, which had contributed the most, were virtually independent by 1914 and so not subject to British control. Other parts of the empire – like Gibraltar, Malta and Singapore – contributed important bases from which the navy could project power. The most important part of the empire that remained was India, which had an army that British governments could use at their own discretion. The rest of the empire was irrelevant to British power, while all the empire had become impossible to defend. Indeed, the empire distorted both Britain's foreign policy and its economy in ways that may well have worked against rather than in support of British power and interests. What, then, was lost between 1945 and 1965? With the advent of NATO and American hegemony, the dominion military forces, like those of Britain itself, were integrated into the American defence umbrella. The naval bases and the Indian army had existed primarily to defend the empire; thus, if the empire was not worth defending, then they were not much of a loss. And the empire was *not* worth defending. Its demise freed Britain from the untenable financial burden imposed by its defence, and so made possible a foreign policy that genuinely pursued the national interest.

Yet there is another way to read Acheson's statement: that the perception of Britain as a power was derived from its possession of its enormous empire. Read this way, the statement surely is true. By the twentieth century, the other world powers took Britain's empire as the symbol of what made it a great power, as did the British people themselves. Thus, the loss of the empire not only meant that others might not take the British as seriously in world affairs. More importantly, it meant that the British did not take themselves as seriously. No wonder they were at a loss to define a new role in the world. Part of the problem was that Britain's leaders completely misread the situation in 1945. Schooled in the belief that Britain's empire defined its power, and seeing most of Britain's competitors weakened (like France) or devastated (like Germany and Japan) by the war, they really thought that Britain was in a position to compete on a nearly equal basis with the other powers that were left standing – the United States and the Soviet Union. Yet Britain's economy had long ago begun to constrain what it could do to project power when military hardware was becoming ever more costly. That fundamental limitation only got worse after 1945. For the economy was a mess coming out of the war, and while the British did a reasonable job of straightening it out by the 1950s, it still could not underwrite the level of defence spending demanded of it. Ranging from nearly 10 per cent of GDP at the beginning of the decade to around 6–7 per cent by the early 1960s, military spending was way beyond what the economy had been asked to sustain in peacetime when spending began to accelerate after 1890 or between the wars. Hence, British governments from 1945 to 1964 were trying to do far more than ever before – including supporting an army in Europe and building a nuclear deterrent – at far greater cost than ever before, in order to place Britain with the superpowers, or just below them.

This was not trying to prevent Britain's decline. It was aspiring to achieve something very new. For Britain had not been the world's, or even Europe's, greatest power in 1900. It was simply one of many. Now, because of the accidental circumstances of war, British governments dreamed of a power status far above any that Britain had attained earlier. It was an impossible goal, and by the time Acheson made his statement in the early 1960s, governments were reluctantly recognising its impossibility. This reality was made clear not only by the loss of empire, but also by the loss of independence for the nuclear deterrent, by the humiliation of succumbing to American dictates at Suez and by the realisation that the economy was not performing as well as the economies of competitors. The search for a role had to take all of these facts into account. Other realities were also becoming evident by 1962. The Commonwealth was not going to provide the basis for Britain to project a power and influence in world affairs beyond its size. The whole of the illusion that the empire meant power had to be jettisoned; it could not be preserved, even in this attenuated form. Finally, while it was not yet admitted, by 1962 it was also becoming impossible to maintain the international role of sterling – like the empire, another symbol of prestige rather than a source of real power. Thus, Acheson's statement was very timely, even though it was greatly resented. The time had come for the British people and their leaders to rethink their nation's role in world affairs.

The one weakness British governments had always understood was that Britain had little means to exercise power and influence in Europe itself, except in conjunction with other states. Furthermore, two world wars had taught that the United States had to be one of the other states. No other combination was sufficient to assure that British (and French) interests were adequately protected. Yet Britain's leaders quickly decided they wanted more from America than a mere alliance. They wanted to build on their shared past and shared language to fashion a special relationship that would make Britain the most important of America's allies, with unique access to and a unique influence over the President and his advisers. In many ways they got what they wanted. By all accounts, the relationships between the military and intelligence establishments of the two countries really are uniquely close. Recent wars in the Falklands, the Persian Gulf and Afghanistan speak of the way each can count on the other in a pinch. The question remains, however, whether this was the way for Britain to make its weight felt in the affairs of the world. The relationship had to be unequal, for the United States was far more powerful. Therefore, not surprisingly, American administrations often showed a willingness to pursue US interests with indifference to the impact on Britain or the views of its leaders. The Americans also showed at times that they did not want to give greater importance to Britain than to America's friends (and even its rivals) on the Continent and in other parts of the world. Britain's relationship with the United States *perhaps* enabled it to act as a vehicle of communication between the US and Europe, but it could only be so if it was fully part of Europe and trusted as such by its European friends.

Thus, most true of all is the rest of Acheson's statement, which is almost never quoted: 'The attempt to play a separate role – that is apart from Europe, a role based on a "special relationship" with the United States, a role based on being head of a "Commonwealth" which has no political structure or unity or strength . . . – this role is about played out.'9 Acheson understood that Europe was the only way forward if Britain was to assume its full influence in world affairs – the more so as the members of the Community started to work to adopt a common posture on key foreign policy issues. The British were very slow to come around to this position. Indeed, it is arguable that they still have not. At first, they resisted (despite American pressure in the other direction) because they did not think economic integration could work. There was too much history of antagonism between France and Germany. At the same time, they still hoped that the Commonwealth could provide the basis for British economic strength. By the 1960s, both of these judgements were proved wrong. Even then, however, Britain's view of the European Community was primarily economic. The vision of a United States of Europe held little attraction for most Britons. British leaders were therefore reluctant to pool sovereignty, even though joining the EC involved just that, and they resisted every step thereafter that involved some further compromise of sovereignty. Yet the erosion of sovereignty continued anyway, most obviously through the regulations of the European Commission and the decisions of the European Court of Justice.

In the late 1980s, Margaret Thatcher launched a campaign to try to call a halt. She identified real problems. The Commission had too much power with too little democratic accountability. The other European leaders were pushing integration forward without consulting their own people. The whole European project looked like another example of quasi-authoritarian paternalism on the part of the European elite. There was a genuine case to be made here. Thatcher, however, with her shrill, confrontational style and her own record of indifference to what the democracy at home thought, was not the person to make it. With Tony Blair as Prime Minister, Britain seemed to have a leader with a stronger commitment to Europe. Yet even Blair remains cautious about taking the lead on the one issue that matters at the moment – joining the European currency, the euro. For the ambivalence of the British people to Europe remains unabated.

Cultural Decline: The Traumas of Americanisation

On 31 August 1997, Diana, Princess of Wales, was killed in a car crash in Paris. The outpouring of emotion and grief in Britain took everyone by surprise, not least the British themselves. Over the following week, some 10,000 to 15,000 tons of flowers piled up at various royal sites, until they became a health hazard. It took days to cart them away from the gates of the Princess's Kensington Palace residence after the funeral. Lit candles, pictures of the dead princess and messages to her sprang up everywhere. The funeral itself was an international extravaganza, comparable to Diana's marriage to Prince Charles, with crowds many rows deep lining the streets along the route of the funeral cortege and throwing flowers as her coffin passed. The Princess's funeral service in Westminster Abbey was broadcast on giant television screens around London and was seen by some 2.5 billion people around the world.[10] For the occasion, Elton John performed a reworking of one of the songs he had written to honour Marilyn Monroe, while professional royal watchers acted as television commentators. What on earth was going on? With the Hollywood-style spectacle and the wanton displays of emotion, the usually staid and stiff-upper-lipped British suddenly seemed to be behaving like . . . Americans! And that was exactly what some observers said: it was another example of the

Americanisation of Britain. On the first anniversary of the Princess's death, commentators for the *Guardian* were thoroughly embarrassed by what seemed a maudlin, excessive exercise in self-indulgence. The paper's writers used their articles of penance to launch a campaign for the abolition of the monarchy, a cultural relic of Britain's hierarchical, imperialist past that was no more attractive to the left-wing *Guardian* as a representation of what it meant to be British than Americanisation was.

In a world that has shrunk radically since 1945 – and this is especially so of the highly developed economies of the North Atlantic – Americanisation seems pervasive. It certainly appears to permeate every aspect of Britain's history during this period. Economic recovery, the defence of the pound, Thatcherism, the 'special relationship' and national security, the nuclear deterrent, women's liberation, race, youth culture, mass culture, crime and violence, the conduct of elections, the approach to education – wherever one looks, one sees the influence of the United States. Some of it was self-inflicted, some of it was inescapable, some of it was illusory, but always it seemed to be there. It is easy, however, to exaggerate that influence. For how is one to disentangle the directions of influence between the United States and Western Europe when their cultures became so inter-related and the exchanges between them so many? There is, for example, a much greater tendency to see American influences on British cinema, television and music than to see the British influences on the American versions of all three. In addition to the flow of British shows, films, songs and performers westward, American public television and public radio surely serve as a tribute to the BBC model. Again, while American fast food arrived in Europe, quality continental cuisine permeated American (and British) restaurants in the 1980s and 1990s to a degree it never had in the 1950s. Styles of dress also flowed in both directions across the Atlantic. At the same time, many phenomena attributed to the United States only partially reflected its impact. While women's liberation, youth culture and mass marketing all incorporated American influences, all occurred in Europe independently of those influences. Indeed, there was a tendency by Europeans (especially intellectuals) to attribute all varieties of phenomena that would have happened anyway to American influences, and to blame America for all the changes in their own societies that they did not like.[11]

Judgements about Americanisation, and more broadly about the cultural changes that have occurred in Britain since 1945, must reflect political biases to some degree; it is inescapable. My own biases are those of an American who was a youth (aged thirteen to twenty-two) in the 1960s, and whose father rose from a poor Jewish immigrant background to a position in government during the Second World War and economic success afterwards. A person with such a history believes in the power of the American version of egalitarianism and sees much more good than bad in the 1960s. Looking at Britain from this perspective, the changes that have occurred since 1945 seem unambiguously for the better. And Princess Diana's funeral is as good a place as any to start in search of the evidence of it – not in the outpouring of emotion that it evoked, but in the people who were most evident in this display: women, gays and ethnic minorities.[12] The public participation in the funeral was the new Britain in action!

The sociologist A. H. Halsey says of his country, 'Nowhere else in the Western world does the elite retain the confidence both to indulge its own cultural tastes and also to believe that these should be offered to or imposed didactically upon the mass of the population.'[13] It was this elitism, and the hierarchical society that underpinned it, that was challenged – and in many ways successfully challenged – during these years, and Britain is all the better for it. American influences contributed their share to the challenges and to the undermining of the power of this elitism. One does not want a society based on mass culture, pop culture and mass marketing; however, most people do not want a society without these either. All of them have given more to ordinary people (including the poor) than the culture of the elite has. As Britain became a society more sensitive to the wants of its people, and less inclined to tell them what they should want, it became a more genuinely democratic society. The goods that a modern economy produces may not be sufficient in themselves to create 'the good life' (a philosopher's concept). The poor and the working class may be left dissatisfied, as they compare what they have with what others have. Yet the first generation to benefit were very satisfied, as they got housing with basic amenities and some of the advantages of the consumer society. They had experienced the poverty that existed in Britain before 1939, and the changes that occurred after that were almost miraculous for them. At the same time, movies, radio and television all enriched their lives, if these people are accepted as judges by their patterns of consumption. The effect may have been to erode traditional working-class culture, but this phenomenon seems to have troubled socialist intellectuals much more than it did members of the working class themselves.

It could be argued, however, that the next generations were much less satisfied – that, whether expressed through youth culture or crime and violence, working-class youths and immigrant youths since the 1960s showed their discontent and their resistance. The fact that they did and that they could, however, reflects a second major change in British society since the war: it was much less deferential. All the traditional hierarchical rigidities that characterised British society in 1945 – whether of class, gender, race or generation – were weakened. None of them disappeared; the privileges associated with being prosperous, white and male remained. Nonetheless, the opportunities for improvement and the choices available to those who were female and from lower classes were greater than before. In part, this improvement was the result of the changing structure of the economy. Yet the fact remains that many people whose parents and grandparents were working class were able to climb into lower-middle-class jobs or higher. This change was made possible by the transformation of the education system from one that was fairly narrow and elitist before 1945 into one that was much more open and democratic by the 1990s – even at the level of higher education. Racial minorities did not benefit from these changes as much as white people did, but many of them did benefit. At the same time, the introduction of immigration into Britain had its own effect in challenging the accepted norms of a society that was fairly homogeneous as well as hierarchical. The result was to weaken a culture based on deference and simply accepting things because that was the way those in authority said they should be. In rejecting such a mentality, the more aggressive forms of youth culture, feminism and immigrant activism were simply the most extreme manifestations of the broader change.

There is a third change that has occurred since 1945. Following a lead coming from the Netherlands and Scandinavia as much as the United States, British society became much less repressive. The reforms of the 1960s relating to censorship, homosexuality and divorce contributed to a freer, more open and more tolerant society. Changing attitudes towards sex and marriage had the same effect. All these changes helped to undermine inherited Victorian notions of respectability every bit as much as did the challenges to social hierarchy coming from workers, women, people of colour and youth. Together with the improved standards of living and increased social mobility, they made Britain, not a classless society, but a society in which the nature of class was changing and its centrality to identity was decreasing. Someone from my background has to find the judgement of these changes by Krishan Kumar very appealing:

> Social groups in British society no longer confront each other as different social species. Many changes in material conditions, dress, speech, food, have contributed to this relative class convergence – more accurately put, to the erosion of differences of social status . . . Cultural institutions and cultural changes since the war have not produced a common culture but they have enormously reduced the cultural distances between social groups.[14]

Furthermore, it is difficult not to see progress in all this – and progress of a very far-reaching and radical kind, which far outweighs in importance whatever economic and political decline may have occurred over these years.

There is disagreement, however, over both the extent and the value of these changes. Many on the left deny their reality, or the value of whatever changes did occur. The probability that someone would move up from the labouring classes did not improve that much in the decades following the war. Similarly, the probability that someone from those classes would get a university education did not go up a lot. People from the next generation moved up and got more education because the structure of the economy changed, not because society did anything to make opportunity more equal and so to improve their chances. The power of privilege was as entrenched as ever. Indeed, as the private secondary schools and Oxbridge restructured their education for a meritocratic society, they more than ever served a fairly narrow elite who operated all the levers of power and influence in the nation. It was just a different elite from that of 1945.[15] Furthermore, for those remaining in the labouring classes, class remained a powerful shaper of their attitudes, values and way of life. In other respects, too, the left saw little change. Poverty still dominated the lives of many, many Britons, even in the prosperous 1950s and 1960s. And it just got worse thereafter. While there was some progress in reducing inequality, it was reversed in the 1980s and 1990s. Finally, the left did not like the values of American culture, which seemed to destroy what was distinctive of the British working class in the name of market-based capitalism and which emphasised consumerism at the expense of the individual. If intellectuals on the left wanted to abolish the monarchy and all in British society that it represented, they certainly did not want to replace it with the values of Princess Diana's funeral. To them, 'Socialism is not to be measured in living standards alone, but in new social relations, new values and opportunities, a new, more generous, more just, and less selfish way of life.'[16] Americanisation seemed to be the antithesis of these values. So the intellectual left's whole framework for viewing Britain's social and cultural history since the war has been virtually the opposite of the one presented here.

Yet the right seems no happier. Many of them did not like Americanisation any better than those on the left. It stood for a debasement of culture as most of them understood that term. The values associated with the 1960s, however, were even more fundamental for conservatives in ushering in decline – as reflected in the collapse of traditional morality, the loss of respect for authority (a different way of viewing the end of deference), and the watering down of standards of education and of culture more broadly conceived. Almost surely, conservatives exaggerate how far such change has progressed. There is much evidence of the tenacious hold of traditional values and morality on the British people, even as they accepted selected changes. At the same time, the very relationship of the right with social change is profoundly ambivalent – especially if we are talking about the followers of Margaret Thatcher. For while they hate moral relativism and the claim that popular culture is as good as elite culture, they seem to hate the values of the elite just as much. Hence, they did much to undermine elitism in Britain. With every attack on the universities, the civil service, the professions, the BBC, the Church of England and the paternalism of the post-war consensus and of 'one-nation' Toryism, they deliberately sought to weaken the authority of Britain's traditional rulers and the values that those rulers propagated. In holding up as their alternative the values of American entrepreneurial culture and the education system that supported it, they did much the same thing. Thus, it is one of the paradoxes of Britain's history since the war that, while socialism did much to transform British society and to open it up and make it fairer, so did the Conservatives who were socialism's greatest enemy. Together, they made a real social and cultural revolution which, on balance, created a substantial improvement on what existed in the first half of the twentieth century.

NOTES

Preface

1. The books were Geoffrey Barraclough, *An Introduction to Contemporary History* (London: Penguin, 1967), and A. W. DePorte, *Europe between the Super-Powers: The Enduring Balance*, 2nd edition (New Haven, London: Yale University Press, 1986).
2. Walter Laqueur, *Europe since Hitler: The Rebirth of Europe*, revised edition (London: Penguin, 1982), pp. 509–69.
3. Kenneth O. Morgan, *The People's Peace: British History 1945–1989* (Oxford, etc.: Oxford University Press, 1990). Peter Clarke, *Hope and Glory: Britain 1900–1990* (Harmondsworth: Penguin, 1996), provides a better sense of the broader picture, but covers a much longer period.

Chapter 1. The Character of Decline

1. While there is an enormous bibliography on this subject, the following books offer a useful start: Roderick Floud and Donald McCloskey, *The Economic History of Britain since 1700*, Vol. 2: *1860 to the 1970s* (Cambridge: Cambridge University Press, 1981), chaps 1, 3–5; Sidney Pollard, *Britain's Prime and Britain's Decline: The British Economy 1870 –1914* (London: Edward Arnold, 1989); Martin J. Wiener, *English Culture and the Decline of the Industrial Spirit 1850–1980* (Cambridge: Cambridge University Press, 1981); Corelli Barnett, *The Audit of War: The Illusion and Reality of Britain as a Great Nation* (London: Macmillan, 1986); W. D. Rubinstein, *Capitalism, Culture, and Decline in Britain 1750–1990* (London, New York: Routledge, 1994); Michael Dintenfass, *The Decline of Industrial Britain 1870–1980* (London, New York: Routledge, 1992); Jean-Pierre Dormois and Michael Dintenfass, eds, *British Industrial*

Decline (London, New York: Routledge, 1999). See also N. F. R. Crafts' assessment in N. F. R. Crafts, 'Economic Growth', in N. F. R. Crafts and N. W. C. Woodward, eds, *The British Economy since 1945* (Oxford: Clarendon Press, 1991), pp. 280–81.

2. Sidney Pollard, *The Development of the British Economy, 1914–1990* (London: Edward Arnold, 1992), pp. 37–9. N. F. R. Crafts and N. W. C. Woodward, 'The British Economy since 1945: Introduction and Overview', in Crafts and Woodward, *The British Economy since 1945*, p. 7.

3. See David Reynolds, *Britannia Overruled: British Policy and World Power in the Twentieth Century* (London, New York: Longman, 1991), chap. 1 and *passim*. I wrote this chapter four years before reading Reynolds, but our views on Britain's weakness in the nineteenth century are very similar. On the other hand, he is far more willing than I am to believe that it was reasonable in the period 1945–60 to view Britain as a potential 'superpower'.

4. Lance E. Davis and Robert A. Huttenback, *Mammon and the Pursuit of Empire: The Economics of British Imperialism*, abridged edition (Cambridge, etc: Cambridge University Press, 1988), pp. 30–44. The United States was also a major target for overseas investment.

5. Geoffrey Ingham, *Capitalism Divided? The City and Industry in British Social Development* (Basingstoke: Macmillan, 1984), pp. 123–5. India's role as a trading partner declined even more precipitously between the wars. By the 1930s, Britain had a trade deficit with India, though India remained very important to the stability of the financial system centred in London. P. J. Cain and A. G. Hopkins, *British Imperialism: Crisis and Deconstruction 1914–1990* (London, New York: Longman, 1993), pp. 176–7.

6. E. J. Hobsbawm, *Industry and Empire: From 1750 to the Present Day* (Harmondsworth: Penguin, 1969). As a Marxist, Hobsbawm enjoys proposing the irony that the empire actually hurt rather than helped Britain.

7. Davis and Huttenback, *Mammon and the Pursuit of Empire*, p. 133. Patrick K. O'Brien, 'The costs and benefits of British imperialism 1846–1914', *Past and Present*, 120 (1988), pp. 186–8, 193–4.

8. In the First World War, some three million men were mobilised from the empire; during the Second World War, the number was 4.5 million. India supplied nearly half of the total in the First World War, with some one million of them sent overseas; it supplied 2.5 million in the Second World War. But Britain had to pay the cost of the Indian troops in the Second World War. Reynolds, *Britannia Overruled*, pp. 23, 25, 29. Nonetheless, the British themselves provided nearly 90 per cent of the money for and took nearly 80 per cent of the casualties in the First

World War, when measuring the total contribution of Britain and its empire. O'Brien, 'The costs and benefits of British imperialism 1846–1914', p. 198.

9. Bernard Porter, *The Lion's Share: A Short History of British Imperialism 1850–1995* (London, New York: Longman, 1996), pp. 290–92, 346–7. See, also, Richard Weight, *Patriots: National Identity in Britain 1940–2000* (London: Macmillan, 2002), pp. 64–5, for the public's indifference to a propaganda campaign for the empire in 1940, and pp. 286–93 on the post-war era.

10. Margaret Drabble, *The Ice Age* (London: Penguin, 1977), p. 92.

11. Matthew Arnold, *Culture and Anarchy* (Cambridge: Cambridge University Press, 1960), pp. 50, 70, 74.

12. George Gissing, *New Grub Street* (London: Penguin, 1968), p. 496.

13. I use the term myth here as I described it in my article 'Liberals, the Irish Famine and the Role of the State', *Irish Historical Studies*, XXIX, 116 (November 1995), p. 513: 'The term *myth* as used here does not necessarily imply that the account is untrue. Rather, the myth comprises a combination of fact, fiction and the unknowable in a narrative of such power that, for the people who accept it, the myth provides a guide to future understanding and action.' This conception of myth was inspired by Georges Sorel's 1911 work on syndicalism, *Reflections on Violence*.

14. The identification of Thatcherism with this view of moral decline is very evident in Shirley Robin Letwin, *The Anatomy of Thatcherism* (London: Fontana, 1992), chaps 7, 9.

15. Drabble, *The Ice Age*, p. 92.

16. This is one of the arguments in Alan Sked, *Britain's Decline: Problems and Perspectives* (Oxford: Basil Blackwell, 1987), chap. 2.

17. See Arthur Herman, *The Idea of Decline in Western History* (New York, etc: The Free Press, 1997), for a full discussion of this tendency, and many others besides.

Chapter 2. The Hard Road to Prosperity

1. See the table in B. R. Mitchell, *British Historical Statistics* (Cambridge, etc: Cambridge University Press, 1988), pp. 869–70.

2. At the end of the war, sterling balances were about £3.5 billion (equivalent to about 40 per cent of GNP), while Britain's gold and dollar reserves were only around £600 million. Alec Cairncross, *The British Economy since 1945: Economic Policy and Performance, 1945–1995*, 2nd edition (Oxford: Blackwell, 1995), p. 47. B. W. E. Alford, *British Economic Performance 1945–1975* (Cambridge: Cambridge University Press, 1995), p. 12.

3. John Darwin, *Britain and Decolonisation: The Retreat from Empire in the Post-War World* (New York: St Martin's Press, 1988), pp. 135–6.

4. Peter Clarke, 'Keynes, New Jerusalem, and British Decline', in Peter Clarke and Clive Trebilcock, eds, *Understanding Decline: Perceptions and Realities of British Economic Performance* (Cambridge: Cambridge University Press, 1997), pp. 154–7. Clarke rescues Keynes from the caricature of his views by the enemies of Keynesianism.

5. Alford, *British Economic Performance 1945–1975*, is directed in part at showing how little economists still understood in the late 1980s about economic relationships.

6. Family allowances were introduced by the Churchill coalition before it broke up in 1945.

7. Brian Simon implies that much of the initiative for maintaining the tripartite system, discouraging the introduction of comprehensive schools, and making it difficult for pupils at secondary moderns to sit for exams came from the permanent officials at the Ministry of Education. There was little interest, however, on the part of the two Ministers under Labour or of the Cabinet as a whole to pursue a more radical policy, though there was much support for it from the party's rank and file. Brian Simon, *Education and the Social Order 1940–1990* (London: Lawrence & Wishart, 1991), pp. 102–15.

8. This analysis of the beneficial effects of subsidies to the poor on domestic demand for goods and services goes back to the liberal economist J. A. Hobson, who incorporated it into his 1902 critique of imperialism; see *Imperialism, A Study* (Ann Arbor: University of Michigan Press, 1965). It was taken up by Keynes.

9. Keynes also believed that, by taking money out of people's pockets, the insurance system would restrain post-war demand and reduce the risks of inflation, and he converted many others to this view during the war. Jose Harris, 'Social Policy, Saving, and Sound Money', in Clarke and Trebilcock, *Understanding Decline*, 3rd edition, pp. 170–77.

10. Samuel H. Beer, *British Politics in the Collectivist Age* (New York: Vintage Books, 1969), p. 133. The phrase 'distribution and exchange' was added to production by the party conference in 1929; *ibid.*, n. 8.

11. Randolph S. Churchill, *Winston S. Churchill*, Vol. II: *Young Statesman, 1901–1914* (Boston: Houghton Mifflin, 1967), p. 269. Gladstone had actually provided for the possibility of the state taking over the railways in an 1844 regulation act, when he was President of the Board of Trade in a Conservative government.

12. The Americans argued that the loan was a substitution for the transition period. Alan P. Dobson, *The Politics of the Anglo-American Economic Special Relationship 1940–1987* (Brighton: Wheatsheaf; New York: St Martin's Press, 1988), pp. 85–6.

13. Cairncross, *British Economy since 1945*, p. 68.
14. Macmillan actually made the statement in 1957, as a warning on the dangers of inflation. Kenneth O. Morgan, *The People's Peace*, p. 176.
15. S. N. Broadberry, 'Unemployment', in Crafts and Woodward, *The British Economy since 1945*, p. 225. Nicholas Woodward, 'Labour's Economic Performance, 1964–70', in R. Coopey, S. Fielding and N. Tiratsoo, eds, *The Wilson Governments 1964–1970* (London, New York: Pinter, 1993), pp. 73–4.
16. Malcolm Chalmers, *Paying for Defence: Military Spending and British Decline* (London, Sydney: Pluto Press, 1985), p. 55.
17. Pollard, *British Economy 1914–1990*, pp. 306–12. Reynolds, *Britannia Overruled*, p. 197.
18. One of the main criticisms of the Labour government now is its failure to take advantage of industry's dependence on government during this period to force industries to restructure and improve their efficiency. Alford, *British Economic Performance 1945–1975*, p. 37. Helen Mercer shows the level of resistance it faced for its fairly modest proposals: Mercer, 'The Labour Governments of 1945–51 and Private Industry', in Nick Tiratsoo, ed., *The Attlee Years* (London, New York: Pinter, 1991), chap. 5.
19. Alford, *British Economic Performance 1945–1975*, p. 62.
20. Cairncross, *British Economy since 1945*, p. 71.
21. See Robert Shepherd, *Enoch Powell* (London: Hutchinson, 1996), pp. 169–70, on the two views of inflation and Thorneycroft's view that they might have to allow unemployment to go up.
22. Roger Middleton, *The British Economy since 1945: Engaging with the Debate* (Basingstoke: Macmillan; New York, St Martin's Press, 2000), p. 88.
23. *Ibid.*, p. 103.
24. Richard Lamb, *The Macmillan Years 1957–1963* (London: John Murray, 1995), pp. 95–100.

Chapter 3. The Strains of Great Power Status

1. Winston S. Churchill, *The Second World War*, Vol. 1: *The Gathering Storm* (Boston: Houghton Mifflin, 1948), pp. 440–41; Vol. 2: *Their Finest Hour* (Boston: Houghton Mifflin, 1949), p. 23. According to Churchill, he sent Roosevelt some 950 pieces of correspondence, and Roosevelt sent him about 800.
2. Apart from the insistence on sterling's convertibility, the conditions

for the loan (including the cancellation of $20 billion in Lend-Lease debt) have been judged generous – despite almost universal condemnation in Britain at the time. See Bradford Perkins, 'Unequal Partners: The Truman Administration and Great Britain', in Wm Roger Louis and Hedley Bull, eds, *The 'Special Relationship': Anglo-American Relations since 1945* (Oxford: Clarendon Press, 1986), p. 52. Robin Edmonds, *Setting the Mould: The United States and Britain, 1945–1950* (Oxford: Clarendon Press, 1986), p. 101. However, just because of the conditions attached, others have judged the whole package draconian: Dobson, *The Politics of the Anglo-American Economic Special Relationship*, pp. 86–7. Part of the problem was that the British had expected to get a 'free gift' as a compensation for bankrupting themselves for the war effort. There was a lot of resentment when they found that the Americans did not see things in this way.

3. A. J. P. Taylor, *The Origins of the Second World War* (New York: Touchstone, 1996), chaps II and III, was the first to make the points that Germany was given the responsibility of enforcing the Treaty of Versailles on itself, and that, in fact, there was no other way of enforcing it.

4. See C. J. Bartlett, '*The Special Relationship': A Political History of Anglo-American Relations since 1945* (London, New York: Longman, 1992), pp. 12–15, 22–6, for this interpretation of the British position.

5. Ritchie Ovendale, *Anglo-American Relations in the Twentieth Century* (New York: St Martin's Press, 1998), p. 60.

6. Nick Tiratsoo and Jim Tomlinson, *The Conservatives and Industrial Efficiency, 1951–64: Thirteen Wasted Years?* (London, New York: Routledge, 1998), chaps 1, 7.

7. This is the view of American policy offered in John Charmley, *Churchill's Grand Alliance: The Anglo-American Special Relationship 1940–57* (New York, San Diego, London: Harcourt Brace, 1995), Parts II and III, with double-dealing thrown in as well. It is also the view reflected in Harold Macmillan's famous statement that the British were the Greeks to the American Romans.

8. Based on tables in Mitchell, *British Historical Statistics*, pp. 588–95, 837–41. Any numbers based on Mitchell's figures must be rough estimates, as the data that go into GDP were not collected at that time. See also, Reynolds, *Britannia Overruled*, p. 31.

9. Michael Dockrill, *British Defence since 1945* (Oxford: Basil Blackwell, 1988), p. 57.

10. Britain also had occupation forces in Italy and Austria for as long as those countries were occupied by the victorious Allies; however, only the army in Germany turned out to be a long-term commitment.

11. Wyn Rees, 'Britain's Contribution to Global Order', in Stuart Croft *et al., Britain and Defence 1945–2000: A Policy Re-evaluation* (Harlow: Longman, 2001), p. 31.

12. William Wallace, 'World Status without Tears', in Vernon Bogdanor and Robert Skidelsky, eds, *The Age of Affluence 1951–1964* (London, Basingstoke: Macmillan, 1970), p. 216.

13. Dockrill, *British Defence since 1945,* p. 29.

14. Anthony Adamthwaite, 'Suez Revisited', in Michael Dockrill and John W. Young, eds, *British Foreign Policy, 1945–56* (New York: St Martin's Press, 1989), p. 228.

15. The notes of the British ambassador on Macmillan's meeting with Eisenhower indicate that Macmillan hardly raised the Suez issue at all. Yet Macmillan's reports home were of the President's support. Clearly Macmillan was seeing what he wished to see. Alistair Horne, *Macmillan 1894–1956* (London: Macmillan, 1988), pp. 420–22. The one thing that even Dulles made clear when he was implying that military action was acceptable was that it should not take place until after the American election. See Richard Lamb, *The Failure of the Eden Government* (London: Sidgwick & Jackson, 1987), chaps 9–11, for the details of all the correspondence.

16. The United States had much less influence over France, especially after the advent of General de Gaulle as President in 1958, because there was no nuclear connection and the franc had no international role to be defended. The French had more independence of action because there was no pretext of a special relationship. De Gaulle even showed in the late 1960s that the French could threaten the dollar by demanding gold for their dollars, as any nation had the right to do under the Bretton Woods Agreement. However, French efforts to count militarily have been nearly as costly as Britain's, and certainly after the 1962 Polaris agreement the American relationship reduced Britain's military costs – if it is taken as given that Britain was going to have a nuclear deterrent, whatever the cost.

17. See John W. Young, *Britain and European Unity, 1945–1999* (Basingstoke: Macmillan; New York: St Martin's Press, 2000), pp. 26–32, for this interpretation. Young claims that the Attlee government was not automatically hostile to Schuman's proposal. Yet given such fundamental differences in outlook, it almost boils down to the same thing.

18. Weight, *Patriots,* pp. 101, 111–12.

19. Some scholars argue that there was a significantly greater British influence. See John Dumbrell, *A Special Relationship: Anglo-American Relations in the Cold War and After* (Basingstoke: Macmillan; New York: St Martin's Press, 2001), pp. 54–8, for an excellent summary of the arguments on each side.

20. Ingham, *Capitalism Divided?* pp. 123–5.

21. The argument that Britain could maintain its empire because it was cheap, and that the loss of empire corresponded with the increase in the cost of maintaining it to an unacceptable level, is developed in Porter, *The Lion's Share*, now in its third edition.

22. Nicholas Owen, '"Responsibility without Power". The Attlee Governments and the End of British Rule in India', in Tiratsoo, *The Attlee Years*, chap. 10, debunks the myths about British withdrawal from India. He shows how out of touch with realities in India ministers were, how completely they were unable to influence events there and how consciously they developed the myths that were used to characterise withdrawal thereafter.

23. Macmillan's diary, late 1961, quoted in Lamb, *The Macmillan Years*, p. 230.

Chapter 4. The Age of Consensus

1. David Butler and Gareth Butler, *Twentieth-Century British Political Facts 1900–2000*, 8th edition (Basingstoke: Macmillan; New York: St Martin's Press, 2000), p. 236. Morgan, *The People's Peace*, p. 27, puts the results at Labour 394, Conservatives 210. The difference presumably reflects how some Tory-leaning independents are counted.

2. This view of consensus politics is subject to some controversy. The arguments are laid out in David Dutton, *British Politics since 1945: The Rise and Fall of Consensus* (Oxford: Basil Blackwell, 1991), chap. 1.

3. The results gave Labour a margin of five MPs over all other parties in 1950 and the Conservatives a margin of seventeen MPs over all other parties in 1951. Butler and Butler, *British Political Facts 1900–2000*, p. 236.

4. See N. W. C. Woodward, 'Inflation', in Crafts and Woodward, *The British Economy since 1945*, p. 196; and Broadberry, 'Unemployment', in *ibid.*, pp. 225–6.

5. Lennox-Boyd to Eden, n.d., quoted in Lewis Johnman, 'Defending the Pound: The Economics of the Suez Crisis, 1956', in Anthony Gorst, Lewis Johnman and W. Scott Lucas, *Post-War Britain, 1945–64: Themes and Perspectives* (London, New York: Pinter Publishers, 1989), p. 168. Sir Evelyn Shuckburgh, Under-Secretary for Middle East Affairs, quoted in Adamthwaite, 'Suez Revisited', in Dockrill and Young, *British Foreign Policy, 1945–56*, p. 229.

6. The Conservatives in the constituencies were equally strong in their support of the government following the invasion. John Ramsden, *The*

Age of Churchill and Eden, 1940–1957 (London, New York: Longman, 1995), pp. 312–13.

7. David Dutton goes even further and raises the question whether Macmillan exaggerated the problems of sterling at the key moment when the Cabinet was deciding whether to agree to a cease-fire, since 'there is no documentary evidence of warnings on 5 or 6 November from his Treasury officials in the extreme terms of his advice to the cabinet'. Dutton, *Anthony Eden: A Life and Reputation* (London, New York, etc.: Arnold, 1997), p. 442. As the crisis continued, however, Dutton agrees that the threat to the pound was genuine. Throughout his extensive discussion of Suez, Dutton is sceptical of Macmillan's actions and motives.

8. Quoted in Ramsden, *The Age of Churchill and Eden, 1940–1957*, p. 316.

9. If this fact had been known, Eden would have had no choice but to resign immediately. In effect, Eden was left with a time bomb that could explode at any time if he remained.

10. This account is based on that in John Turner, *Macmillan* (London, New York: Longman, 1994), pp. 234–8. Powell, by 1958, was a convinced monetarist in the way described, which was different from the meaning in the 1970s and 1980s. Shepherd, *Enoch Powell*, pp. 163–8.

11. Philip Murphy, *Party Politics and Decolonization: The Conservative Party and British Colonial Policy in Tropical Africa, 1951–1964* (Oxford: Clarendon Press, 1995), pp. 107–11.

12. Alistair Horne, *Macmillan, 1957–1986: Volume II of the Official Biography* (London: Macmillan, 1989), p. 183. Wm Roger Louis, 'The Dissolution of the British Empire', in Judith M. Brown and Wm Roger Louis, eds, *The Oxford History of the British Empire*, Vol. IV: *The Twentieth Century* (Oxford, New York: Oxford University Press, 1999), p. 353.

13. T. A. Jenkins, *The Liberal Ascendancy, 1830–1886* (New York: St Martin's Press, 1994), argues for 1846; John Vincent, *The Formation of the British Liberal Party* (New York: Charles Scribner's Sons, 1966), suggests 1859 or 1865. D. A. Hamer, *Liberal Politics in the Age of Gladstone and Rosebery* (Oxford: Oxford University Press, 1972), argues that it was not really a party at all.

14. Morgan, *The People's Peace*, p. 63. The group had grown to forty-seven MPs by 1953, when it was disbanded in response to an effort from the centre to suppress 'parties within the party'. Mervyn Jones, *Michael Foot* (London, 1994), p. 192.

15. Kenneth Harris, *Attlee* (London: Weidenfeld & Nicolson, 1982), pp. 301–3, 307. James Hinton, *Protests and Visions: Peace Politics in Twentieth-Century Britain* (London: Hutchinson Radius, 1989), p. 150. For the evolving attitudes towards the Soviet Union and the United States, see Jonathan Schneer, *Labour's Conscience: The Labour Left*

1945–51 (Boston, London: Unwin Hyman, 1988), chap. 2.

16. Eric Shaw, *Discipline and Discord in the Labour Party: The Politics of Managerial Control in the Labour Party, 1951–87* (Manchester, New York: Manchester University Press, 1988), pp. 40–44.

17. Jose Harris, 'Labour's Political and Social Thought', in Duncan Tanner, Pat Thane and Nick Tiratsoo, *Labour's First Century* (Cambridge: Cambridge University Press, 2000), p. 35.

18. Butler and Butler, *British Political Facts 1900–2000*, p. 236.

19. This is the argument of Nick Tiratsoo, 'Popular Politics, Affluence and the Labour Party in the 1950s', in Anthony Gorst, Lewis Johnman and W. Scott Lucas, *Contemporary British History 1931–1961: Politics and the Limits of Policy* (London, New York: Pinter Publishers, 1991), pp. 53–8.

20. Quoted in Alan Sked and Chris Cook, *Post-War Britain: A Political History*, 2nd edition (Harmondsworth: Penguin, 1984), p. 183.

21. See Morgan, *The People's Peace*, p. 224, for the interpretation that it was a sign of panic.

22. There remains some disagreement over whether Butler was a viable candidate and how actively Macmillan organised his defeat. This account is based on Kevin Jeffreys, *Retreat from New Jerusalem: British Politics, 1951–64* (New York: St Martin's Press, 1997), pp. 177–84; and John Ramsden, *The Winds of Change: Macmillan to Heath, 1957–1975* (London, New York: Longman, 1996), pp. 150, 194–208.

Chapter 5. Understanding Economic Decline

1. K. Theodore Hoppen, *The Mid-Victorian Generation 1846–1886* (Oxford: Oxford University Press, 1998), p. 278. Real GDP adjusts for changes in the level of prices. These estimates have the same 2.2 per cent average for 1856–73.

2. The table in Hoppen puts the average annual growth rate for real GDP from 1899 to 1913 at 1.4 per cent. *Ibid.*

3. S. N. Broadberry, 'Unemployment', in Crafts and Woodward, *The British Economy since 1945*, p. 212. Nicholas Woodward, 'The Retreat from Full Employment', in Richard Coopey and Nicholas Woodward, *Britain in the 1970s: The Troubled Decade* (New York: St Martin's Press, 1996), p. 137.

4. R. M. Page, 'Social Welfare since the War', in Crafts and Woodward, *The British Economy since 1945*, pp. 482–3, offers an official measurement of 6.1 per cent in 1968–9, compared with a relative measurement (defined as less than 50 per cent of mean household income) of 9.2 per cent in that year. Sked, *Britain's Decline*, p. 73, claims it was 6.3 per cent in 1975, using the same relative measurement. Poverty will be

discussed in greater detail in Chapter 8, where we will see that there was plenty of evidence that the rate was under 5 per cent in the 1960s and 1970s.

5. Crafts and Woodward, 'The British Economy since 1945: Introduction and Overview', in Crafts and Woodward, *The British Economy since 1945*, p. 9. By 1987, Finland, Japan and Norway had also surpassed Britain, while Italy was on the verge of catching it.

6. Middleton, *British Economy since 1945*, pp. 5, 24.

7. Britain suffered a similar decline in the export of services as the economies of other nations caught up with Britain's in the decades after the war. Thus, Britain accounted for 18 per cent of service exports in 1952 and 8 per cent in 1989. By the latter year, France accounted for 9 per cent of exports and West Germany 7 per cent. Ranald C. Michie, *The City of London: Continuity and Change, 1850–1990* (Basingstoke: Macmillan, 1992), p. 25.

8. Charles Feinstein shows slightly higher growth rates for British productivity in the post-war expansion: 2.5 per cent from 1951 to 1964 and 3.0 per cent from 1964 to 1973. Feinstein, 'Success and Failure: British Economic Growth since 1948', in Roderick Floud and Donald McCloskey, eds, *The Economic History of Britain since 1700*, 2nd edition; Vol. 3: *1939–1992* (Cambridge: Cambridge University Press, 1994), p. 98.

9. See the table based on index numbers in Cairncross, *British Economy since 1945*, p. 16. The index numbers for 1973 (with Britain equal to 100) are 108 for France and 106 for West Germany. They had increased the gap even more by 1984, with France at 121 and West Germany at 112. Robert Millward shows that Japan was well ahead of Britain in manufacturing productivity by 1973; it was Japan's very low productivity in other sectors of the economy that pulled overall productivity down. Millward, 'Industrial and Commercial Performance since 1950', in Floud and McCloskey, *Economic History of Britain since 1700*, 2nd edition; Vol. 3: *1939–1992*, p. 136. Feinstein, in the same volume, shows Japan's overall labour productivity only about 20 per cent below Britain's in 1973 and slightly ahead of Britain's in 1988. Feinstein, 'British Economic Growth since 1948,' *ibid.*, p. 117. I cannot account for the difference between Feinstein's figures and the others.

10. Robert Millward, 'Industrial Performance, the Infrastructure and Government Policy: An International Comparison of British Performance and Policy 1800–1987', in Dormois and Dintenfass, *British Industrial Decline*, chap. 3. Feinstein shows that manufacturing productivity was the same as overall productivity for the economy from 1951–1964, significantly higher from 1964 to 1973, and lower from 1973 to 1979. Feinstein, 'British Economic Growth since 1948', in Floud and

McCloskey, *Economic History of Britain since 1700*, 2nd edition; Vol. 3: *1939–1992*, p. 98.

11. Cairncross, *British Economy since 1945*, p. 84.

12. See Alford, *British Economic Performance 1945–1975*, pp. 55–9, and chap. 8. Alford gives primacy to cultural explanations and has some fairly unkind words to say about economic analysis along the way.

13. The classic statement of the cultural interpretation of economic decline (including the discussion of education below) is Wiener, *English Culture and the Decline of the Industrial Spirit*, chaps 2, 7.

14. The triumph of what he calls the 'professional ideal' is the underlying thesis of Harold Perkin, *The Rise of Professional Society: England since 1880* (London, New York: Routledge, 1989). It is this ideal, at least as represented by the public sector professional, that Thatcherism was to challenge.

15. Tiratsoo and Tomlinson, *The Conservatives and Industrial Efficiency, 1951–64*, chap. 5. Derek H. Aldcroft, *Education, Training and Economic Performance, 1944–1990* (Manchester, New York: Manchester University Press, 1992), pp. 101–6.

16. David Edgerton, *Science, Technology and the British Industrial 'Decline' 1870–1970* (Cambridge: Cambridge University Press, 1996), p. 24 (on Oxford), and more generally, argues that business and technology were not discriminated against by the elite. So does Rubinstein, *Capitalism, Culture, and Decline in Britain*, chap. 3. Anthony Sampson, *Anatomy of Britain* (New York: Harper & Row, 1962), provides the argument that the public schools and Oxbridge were providing all the elite. Sampson followed with several revised editions which, until the most recent, argued much the same thing.

17. Alford, *British Economic Performance 1945–1975*, pp. 96–7 and *passim*. David Coates is more sceptical, while willing to give them a share of the blame: *The Question of UK Decline: The Economy, State and Society* (Hemel Hempstead: Harvester Wheatsheaf, 1994), pp. 188–9. S. A. Walkland defends their cautiousness and willingness to subordinate their views to those of politicians who can claim a mandate. A. M. Gamble and S. A. Walkland, *The British Party System and Economic Policy 1945–1983: Studies in Adversary Politics* (Oxford: Clarendon Press, 1984), pp. 154–6.

18. Middleton, *British Economy since 1945*, p. 128. N. F. R. Crafts, 'Economic Growth', in Crafts and Woodward, *The British Economy since 1945*, pp. 273–7. Aldcroft, *Education, Training and Economic Performance*, chaps 3, 4, and pp. 124–30, 141–6. It is not clear whether this failure in technical education goes back before 1945. See Michael Sanderson, *Education and Economic Decline in Britain, 1870 to the 1990s* (Cambridge, New York: Cambridge University Press, 1999), chaps 2, 3, and pp. 65–8,

for a sympathetic assessment of the period before 1914 and a more sceptical one of the inter-war years.

19. On Cambridge, see Edgerton, *Science, Technology and the British Industrial 'Decline'*, pp. 21–2. For the general statement of sufficiency, see Peter L. Payne, 'Entrepreneurship and British Economic Decline', in Bruce Collins and Keith Robbins, eds, *British Culture and Economic Decline* (London: Weidenfeld & Nicolson, 1990), p. 43, for the period before 1914. See chap. 8, pp. 51–2, for the period around 1970.

20. On Germany, see Harold James, 'The German Experience and the Myth of British Cultural Exceptionalism', in Collins and Robbins, *British Culture and Economic Decline*, pp. 110–15. James shows how the status of engineering and applied science in Germany declined after 1900, only to revive again after 1945, in part as a reaction to a collapse under the Nazis.

21. For example, British research and development funds were disproportionately directed towards science and away from engineering. Crafts, 'Economic Growth', in Crafts and Woodward, *The British Economy since 1945*, pp. 275–6.

22. Aldcroft, *Education, Training and Economic Performance*, p. 76. See chap. 7 for an extensive discussion of the impact of insufficient use of engineers on research and development and on the organisation of production. David Edgerton, however, claims that there is no proven link between investment in science and technology and economic growth and efficiency, and he also argues that Aldcroft and others underestimate the number of science and engineering graduates in industry. Edgerton, *Science, Technology and the British Industrial 'Decline'*, pp. 8, 25–6. Finally, Harold James argues that Britain was no different from Germany as to how it recruited managers right up into the 1960s. Most were recruited from business families in both countries. James, 'The German Experience', in Collins and Robbins, *British Culture and Economic Decline*, pp. 116–22.

23. Cairncross, *British Economy since 1945*, p. 19. Nicholas Woodward, 'Labour's Economic Performance 1964–70', in Coopey, Fielding and Tiratsoo, *The Wilson Governments 1964–70*, p. 89. Richard Coopey and Nicholas Woodward, 'The British Economy in the 1970s: An Overview', in Coopey and Woodward, *Britain in the 1970s*, p. 4. If we look at *manufacturing* investment (as opposed to all investment) as a percentage of output, Britain's ratio was comparable to West Germany's, but British capital productivity was half that of West Germany's because of British overmanning. Middleton, *British Economy since 1945*, p. 122. The strongest statement that insufficient investment was a crucial source of the problem is Sidney Pollard, *The Wasting of the British Economy: British Economic Policy 1945 to the Present* (London, Canberra: Croom Helm, 1982).

24. Tiratsoo and Tomlinson, *The Conservatives and Industrial Efficiency, 1951–64*, pp. 151–2. The principal advocate of 'stop-go' as a crucial explanation for insufficient investment is Pollard, *The Wasting of the British Economy, passim.* Pollard stood by his belief that 'stop-go' was a primary culprit in a 1997 interview (the year before his death) in Richard English and Michael Kenny, eds, *Rethinking British Decline* (London: Macmillan; New York: St Martin's Press, 2000), p. 81.

25. Peter Oppenheimer, 'Muddling Through: The Economy, 1951–1964', in Bogdanor and Skidelsky, *The Age of Affluence 1951–1964*, pp. 122–3. Geoffrey Ingham points out that the Bank of England and the Treasury had their own interests: the Treasury's in continuing to dominate the British budgeting process and the Bank's in managing world finances through the gold standard. They could use the interests of London's financial institutions as a means of forwarding those interests. Ingham, *Capitalism Divided?*, pp. 37, 131–3, 179–81, 215–16, 223, 230–32.

26. Ingham, *Capitalism Divided?*, pp. 52–3. Jerry Coakley and Laurence Harris, *The City of Capital: London's Role as a Financial Centre* (Oxford: Blackwell, 1983), p. 129.

27. Ingham, *Capitalism Divided?*, p. 46. Ingham points out that this sum was larger than the GDP of New Zealand.

28. The emergence of nationalism and so protectionism in the provision of financial services hurt London more, which is one reason Britain has been at the forefront of those countries who want to liberalise trade in services.

29. W. A. P. Manser, *Britain in Balance* (London: Longman, 1971), p. 28.

30. The surplus was small because income from the export of capital was still limited in the 1960s and 1970s by the continued use of exchange controls. Yet even after the Thatcher government ended exchange controls and British overseas investment jumped up, the surplus remained small compared to what it had been before the First World War. Michie, *The City of London*, pp. 113–14.

31. Pollard, *British Economy 1914–1990*, pp. 306–12. Sked, *Britain's Decline*, pp. 28–34. Foreign aid given to underdeveloped countries was also a source of government spending overseas. While governments had no great enthusiasm for this aid, they found it politically inexpedient to stop it.

32. The years included in the table were chosen for the following reasons: 1961 is the beginning of the series; 1964 is the advent of the Labour government and the final crisis before devaluation; 1967 is the devaluation of the pound; 1971 is the end of fixed exchange rates; 1974 is the first year after the 1973 oil price increase, which radically increased the cost of imports; 1978 is the last year before the Thatcher government

and the second oil price increase, and before North Sea oil fully removed a major source of payments deficit.

33. Sked, *Britain's Decline*, p. 30. Sked throughout is citing Manser, *Britain in Balance*, pp. 29–36, and especially pp. 35–6.

34. David C. Mowery, 'Industrial Research, 1900–1950', in Bernard Elbaum and William Lazonick, *The Decline of the British Economy* (Oxford: Clarendon Press, 1986).

35. Chalmers, *Paying for Defence*, pp. 120–23. Chalmers argues that, on the contrary, the dictates of military priorities drove the British to try to develop industries – aircraft production, nuclear power generators – that they would have done well to stay out of.

36. Dintenfass, *Decline of Industrial Britain*, p. 48. Edgerton, *Science, Technology and the British Industrial 'Decline'*, p. 36. Edgerton is much more sceptical that spending on R & D made much difference to growth; see pp. 43–4, 56–7, 62–3, 68.

37. Nicholas Crafts, *Britain's Relative Economic Decline: 1870–1995: A Quantitative Perspective* (London: The Social Market Foundation, 1997), p. 62. Between 1950 and 1962, direct investment in Britain by US firms increased by more than four times. Tiratsoo and Tomlinson, *The Conservatives and Industrial Efficiency, 1951–64*, p. 43.

38. Nor, even when there is no obvious political agenda, does there seem to be much agreement. For example, in the same volume, R. Richardson claimed in 1990 that quantitative analyses had yielded very little evidence to support claims that unions contributed to either Britain's low productivity or to its poor inflation record, while N. F. R. Crafts claimed that industrial relations did contribute significantly to Britain's lower productivity. R. Richardson, 'Trade Unions and Industrial Relations', in Crafts and Woodward, *The British Economy since 1945*, chap. 13, and more specifically pp. 417, 436–40; and N. F. R. Crafts, 'Economic Growth', in *ibid.*, pp. 273–7.

39. Dintenfass, *Decline of Industrial Britain*, p. 30. Dintenfass has little use for explanations based on workers and trade unions after 1950 as well.

40. One sociologist who worked for a year in the early 1980s at a Ford plant in Liverpool was 'completely exhausted' during her first weeks on the assembly line. See Michael Ball, Fred Gray and Linda McDowell, *The Transformation of Britain: Contemporary Social and Economic Change* (London: Fontana, 1989), p. 153.

41. Pollard, *British Economy 1914–1990*, p. 282.

42. Those deals became a problem for the German economy in the 1990s. Agreements that gave high benefits and long holidays, while making it extremely difficult to lay workers off, were now contributing to an economy suffering from chronically low growth and high unemployment. Thus,

as is also the case for Japan, the successful formula for one generation became a source of economic difficulty for a later one.

43. Coopey and Woodward, 'The British Economy in the 1970s', in Coopey and Woodward, *Britain in the 1970s*, p. 19.

44. Keith Middlemas, *Power, Competition and the State*, Vol. 1: *Britain in Search of Balance, 1940–61* (Basingstoke: Macmillan, 1986), p. 239.

45. Tiratsoo and Tomlinson, *The Conservatives and Industrial Efficiency, 1951–64*, chap. 4 and pp. 87–8, 92, 97.

46. *Ibid.*, p. 95.

47. Woodward, 'Labour's Economic Performance, 1964–70', in Coopey, Fielding and Tiratsoo, *The Wilson Governments 1964–70*, p. 74. Woodward, 'The Retreat from Full Employment', in Coopey and Woodward, *Britain in the 1970s*, p. 136. Yet as low as British unemployment was in the 1950s and 1960s, unemployment in West Germany and Japan was even lower in the 1960s and 1970s. Stephen Broadberry, 'Employment and Unemployment', in Floud and McCloskey, *Economic History of Britain since 1700*, 2nd edition; Vol. 3: *1939–1992*, p. 201.

48. As an example of the problem, at the beginning of 1961 government judgements were based on the belief that national output had grown 1.5 per cent between the end of 1959 and the end of 1960. In 1977, the estimate was that the growth rate had been 3.5 per cent. F. T. Blackaby, 'Narrative, 1960–74', in F. T. Blackaby, ed., *British Economic Policy 1960–74* (Cambridge: Cambridge University Press, 1978), p. 12. Blackaby gives several examples in this chapter of government making policy decisions on information that proved to be incorrect. In a couple of cases, the situation was actually better than the government thought, which meant that government policy was more drastic than was necessary.

49. Peter Clarke, 'Keynes, New Jerusalem, and British Decline', in Clarke and Trebilcock, *Understanding Decline*, p. 164.

50. Paul Johnson, 'The Welfare State', in Floud and McCloskey, *Economic History of Britain since 1700*, 2nd edition; Vol. 3: *1939–1992*, p. 300.

Chapter 6. Economic Upheaval

1. Mitchell, *British Historical Statistics*, pp. 740–41. My calculations are based on the government's official retail price index as reproduced in Mitchell's Table 10; 1962 is the break year because it is used to provide a new base year to measure price increases thereafter until 1974, whereas the base year for 1956–62 was 1956. A slightly different calculation, using 1963 as the base year for the whole index, shows that the annual average price increase in the years after the Korean War (1953–8)

was 4 per cent, roughly comparable to the 4.2 per cent average for the five years 1963–8, while there was a significant dip to an annual average of 2.2 per cent from 1958 to 1963. The average for 1968–73 calculated with this index is 8.5 per cent. See Butler and Butler, *British Political Facts 1900–2000*, p. 411. A table provided by N. W. C. Woodward, 'Inflation', in Crafts and Woodward, *The British Economy since 1945*, p. 189, gives the average annual rate for 1950–67 as 4.3 per cent, while that for 1968–73 is 7.5 per cent.

2. The commitment east of Suez actually dragged on further into the 1970s. From 1959 to 1960 and 1962 to 1963, defence spending as a percentage of GDP had remained fairly constant at 6–6.1 per cent. Between 1963 and 1964 and 1967 and 1968 it had fluctuated between 5.7 and 5.4 per cent. Now defence cuts dropped it to 5 per cent in 1968–9 and 4.6 per cent in 1969–70, where it settled for the rest of the 1970s. Chalmers, *Paying for Defence*, pp. 68, 88, 94, 100.

3. See the statistics in Butler and Butler, *British Political Facts 1900–2000*, pp. 400–401. The number given in the statistics at this time was based on the number of insured workers. Unemployment did break one million before the figures started to go down again.

4. Mitchell, *British Historical Statistics*, p. 593. The numbers were: £12,822,000,000 in 1970, and £19,965,000,000 in 1974. It is perhaps unfair to take 1974 as the end year, as the Conservative government fell in February, while the big oil price increase of late 1973 was driving prices up to new levels. The figure for 1973 was £17,689,000,000, yielding an annual average increase of 12.65 per cent.

5. Clarke, *Hope and Glory*, p. 336.

6. Jonathan Schneer points to the numerical strength of Communists in the trade union movement immediately after the war, when the unions were anything but militant. Schneer, *Labour's Conscience*, p. 134.

7. Clarke, *Hope and Glory*, p. 333.

8. Morgan, *The People's Peace*, p. 328.

9. N. H. Dimsdale, 'British Monetary Policy since 1945', in Crafts and Woodward, *The British Economy since 1945*, p. 125; Woodward, 'Inflation', in *ibid.*, p. 202.

10. Sir Alexander Cairncross, 'Economic Policy and Performance, 1964–1990', in Floud and McCloskey, *Economic History of Britain since 1700*, 2nd edition; Vol. 3: *1939–1992*, p. 70. Mitchell, *British Historical Statistics*, pp. 740–41. Inflation reached a maximum of 27 per cent in the summer of 1975.

11. Inflation would have gone down anyway in 1976, since the 1973 oil price increase was now fully incorporated into the price system and so would not push prices up any more, while commodity prices were

falling. Monetarists deny that wage controls had any effect on inflation. They claim that the fall was due to a dramatic collapse in the rate of growth of the money supply between 1973 and 1975. Martin Holmes, *The Labour Government, 1974–79: Political Aims and Economic Reality* (New York: St Martin's Press, 1985), pp. 32–3.

12. Mitchell, *British Historical Statistics*, p. 741 (inflation); Butler and Butler, *British Political Facts 1900–2000*, p. 418 (exchange rate). Holmes, *The Labour Government, 1974–79*, pp. 86, 93 (May and October 1976 exchange rates).

13. Morgan, *The People's Peace*, p. 402.

14. Ivor Crewe, 'Why the Conservatives Won', in Howard R. Penniman, ed., *Britain at the Polls, 1979: A Study of the General Election* (Washington, London: American Enterprise Institute, 1981), pp. 284–7.

Chapter 7. Political Failure

1. Hamer, *Liberal Politics in the Age of Gladstone and Rosebery*.

2. It could be argued that the American parties are more ideologically pure now than they were when the old Democratic coalition of New Deal liberals and Southern conservatives existed. The gradual movement of Southern conservatism to the Republican party has given both parties a somewhat more coherent ideological tint than they had thirty years ago. Still, both of them incorporate a fairly broad ideological spectrum.

3. Manser, *Britain in Balance*, p. 28.

4. Philip M. Williams, *Hugh Gaitskell: A Political Biography* (London: Jonathan Cape, 1979), p. 704.

5. John Campbell, *Edward Heath: A Biography* (London: Jonathan Cape, 1993), pp. 189, 200.

6. Thatcher, of course, was limited by the conventions of Cabinet solidarity, for she was Minister of Education. However, if she had been as much the creature of principle rather than expediency as she liked to portray herself, she would have resigned. As it was, she expressed some reservations privately, but stayed put. Ramsden, *Winds of Change*, pp. 358–9.

7. All these numbers come from Clarke, *Hope and Glory*, p. 410. In February, two of the seats representing 0.8 per cent of the vote went to independent Labour candidates. These are included in the calculation in the text.

8. Ramsden, *Winds of Change*, pp. 399–402.

9. Butler and Butler, *British Political Facts 1900–2000*, p. 238.

10. Isaac Kramnick, 'Introduction: The Making of a Crisis', in Isaac Kramnick, ed., *Is Britain Dying? Perspectives on the Current Crisis* (Ithaca, London: Cornell University Press, 1979), p. 12.

11. Keith Middlemas argues that, while wage indexes kept ahead of price indexes (real wages), once tax increases and losses due to cuts in benefits like food and rent subsidies are factored in, there was a substantial decline in 'real earnings' from 1973 to 1977. So those in work were hit much harder than the usual statistics on real wages would indicate. Keith Middlemas, *Power, Competition and the State*, Vol. 3: *The End of the Postwar Era: Britain since 1974* (Basingstoke: Macmillan, 1991), p. 157.

Chapter 8. Social Revolution

1. David Coleman, 'Population and Family', in A. H. Halsey and Josephine Webb, eds, *Twentieth-Century British Social Trends* (Basingstoke: Macmillan; New York: St Martin's Press, 2000), p. 72. These figures include the population only of Northern Ireland in 1901. Britain's baby boom slowed down during the war, briefly surged after the war and then took off again in the early 1950s.

2. Until very recently, it had been assumed that falling birth rates occurred first among the upper and middle classes and then spread to the lower classes in the twentieth century. That model is now questioned. Hoppen, *The Mid-Victorian Generation*, pp. 86–7.

3. Coleman, 'Population and Family', in Halsey and Webb, *Twentieth-Century Social Trends*, pp. 34–5. In Scotland, the slowdown came more gradually. If a woman married before she was twenty-seven before the First World War, she was likely to have six children (statistically, slightly under six). One-fifth of these women had ten or more children. T. M. Devine, *The Scottish Nation 1700–2000* (London: Penguin, 2000), p. 524.

4. Coleman, 'Population and Family', in Halsey and Webb, *Twentieth-Century Social Trends*, pp. 55, 58. The figure below for 1995 is also on p. 58.

5. *Ibid.*, p. 44.

6. Ray Fitzpatrick and Tarani Chandola, 'Health', in Halsey and Webb, *Twentieth-Century Social Trends*, pp. 95–100. The life expectancy figures are for England and Wales. Those for Scotland are lower by about two years at both the beginning and the end of the century; those for Northern Ireland are one year lower at the end of the century. There is considerable scholarly debate over how much difference improvement in and greater availability of health care have made to longer life expectancy. It is difficult to see how the development of vaccines and antibiotics could not have made a significant contribution to defeating childhood and infectious diseases. Nonetheless, nutrition seems to be more important. See *ibid.*, pp. 123–4.

7. Coleman, 'Population and Family', in Halsey and Webb, *Twentieth-Century Social Trends*, pp. 75–6.
8. Bruce Wood and Jackie Carter, 'Towns, Urban Change and Local Government', in Halsey and Webb, *Twentieth-Century Social Trends*, pp. 416, 425.
9. *Ibid.*, pp. 417–19.
10. James Meikle and Matthew Engel, 'Blair takes his message to the regions'; Polly Toynbee, 'Down on the farm'; *Guardian Weekly*, 10–16 February 2000, p. 9. Nationally, agriculture employed 2 per cent of the workforce in England.
11. Wood and Carter, 'Towns, Urban Change and Local Government', in Halsey and Webb, *Twentieth-Century Social Trends*, pp. 420–21. Alison Ravetz, *The Government of Space: Town Planning in Modern Society* (London, Boston: Faber and Faber, 1986), p. 71. The numbers on the new towns come from Ravetz.
12. Amanda Root, 'Transport and Communications', in Halsey and Webb, *Twentieth-Century Social Trends*, pp. 439–47, 451–2. Sarah Hall, 'Britain tops list for traffic jams', *Guardian Weekly*, 29 November–5 December 2001, p. 8.
13. Ceri Peach, Alisdair Rogers, Judith Chance and Patricia Daley, 'Immigration and Ethnicity', in Halsey and Webb, *Twentieth-Century Social Trends*, p. 132.
14. Joanna Bourke, *Working Class Cultures in Britain 1890–1960: Gender, Class, and Ethnicity* (London, New York: Routledge, 1994), p. 192.
15. Colin Holmes, *John Bull's Island: Immigration and British Society, 1871–1971* (Basingstoke: Macmillan, 1988), p. 119.
16. Peach *et al.*, 'Immigration and Ethnicity', in Halsey and Webb, *Twentieth-Century Social Trends*, pp. 138–41. Adam Woolf, 'Race equality: the issue explained', *Guardian* (on-line edition), 16 March 2001, claims that the total minority ethnic population shown in the 1991 census was 'about 3.5' million, or 7 per cent of the population. For the 2001 census, see Ian Burrell, 'Census reveals the changing face of Britain', *Independent* (on-line edition), 14 February 2003.
17. Many Poles were in Britain after the war, having been soldiers or otherwise part of the war effort; more migrated there in the years immediately after its end. The number of Polish-born residents therefore increased from about 45,000 in 1931 to over 160,000 in 1951. The Italian-born population increased from under 40,000 in 1951 (most of whom had come in the first half of the century) to nearly 110,000 in 1971. Holmes, *John Bull's Island*, pp. 212, 214.
18. Weight, *Patriots*, p. 715.
19. For the education of minorities in the 1990s, see Tariq Modood, 'Qualifications and English Language', in Tariq Modood, Richard

Berthoud, *et al.*, *Ethnic Minorities in Britain: Diversity and Disadvantage* (London: Policy Studies Institute, 1997), pp. 65–6, 69–75. For the incomes of West Indian women, see Modood, 'Conclusion: Ethnic Diversity and Disadvantage', in *ibid.*, p. 344. Indians were not really a single group. Sikhs tended to be the least successful and more like Muslim South Asians in their income, jobs and education, while Indians from Africa tended to be the most successful.

20. Harry Gouldbourne, *Race Relations in Britain since 1945* (Basingstoke: Macmillan; New York: St Martin's Press, 1998), p. 84.

21. Ball, Gray and McDowell, *Transformation of Britain*, pp. 201–2. The numbers for 1996 were fairly comparable: 27 per cent for Pakistanis and Bangladeshis, 12 per cent for Indians and 8 per cent for whites. Andrew Adonis and Stephen Pollard, *A Class Act: The Myth of Britain's Classless Society* (London: Hamish Hamilton, 1997), p. 256.

22. Middleton, *British Economy since 1945*, p. 57. Seumas Milne, 'Britain's foreign legions', *Guardian Weekly*, 7–13 September 2000, p. 16. Jonathan Steele, 'Europe confronts the unthinkable', *Guardian Weekly*, 2–8 November 2000, p. 14. Many of the nurses were in Britain on short-term contracts.

23. Ian R. G. Spencer, *British Immigration Policy since 1939: The Making of Multi-Racial Britain* (London, New York: Routledge, 1997), p. 32 and, more generally, chap. 2.

24. E. Ellis Cashmore, *United Kingdom?: Class, Race, and Gender since the War* (London, etc.: Unwin Hyman, 1989), p. 90.

25. Randall Hansen, *Citizenship and Immigration in Post-war Britain: The Institutional Origins of a Multicultural Nation* (Oxford: Oxford University Press, 2000), p. 132. The slogan is quoted everywhere else as, 'If you want a nigger neighbour, vote Labour.'

26. Spencer, *British Immigration Policy since 1939*, p. 133. In 1972, the number exceeded 60,000, while in 1984 it fell below 30,000. There had been a jump in immigration between 1960 and 1962 in anticipation of the 1962 Act. Immigration from Ireland was explicitly excluded from all of these acts.

27. Powell's exact words, after a long denunciation of the government's proposed Race Relations Bill, were: 'As I look ahead, I am filled with foreboding. Like the Roman, I seem to see "the River Tiber foaming with much blood".' Zig Layton-Henry, *The Politics of Race in Britain* (London, Boston: Allen & Unwin, 1984), p. 71. He was quoting Virgil.

28. See Shepherd, *Enoch Powell*, pp. 352–4, 401–3, for Powell's popularity after the 'River Tiber' speech and for his probable influence on the 1970 general election results. For a more detailed analysis of Powell's likely effect on the general election, see Douglas E. Schoen, *Enoch Powell and*

the Powellites (New York: St Martin's Press, 1977), pp. 55–66. Existing immigrants continued to have the right to bring in certain family members.

29. The average natural population growth for the UK in the 1990s was 107,000; average annual immigration was 104,000. In England and Wales, immigration surpassed natural population growth in 1994–5; by 1998–9, it was 194,000 compared to a natural increase of 72,000. John Carvel, 'Immigration rise was main social trend of 1990s', *Guardian Weekly*, 1–7 February 2001, p. 9.

30. Jeremy Paxman, *The English: A Portrait of a People* (Woodstock, NY: The Overlook Press, 2000), p. 73. Martin Wainwright, 'Image of Asian ghettoes dispelled by survey', *Guardian Weekly*, 26 December 2002–1 January 2003, p. 8. Sociologists use an index of dissimilarity, which measures what percentage of a population would have to move for the race distribution of an area in a city to be the same as for the population of the city as a whole. For West Indians, this index in 1991 was 49 for London and 54 for Birmingham. For Indians, it was 51 in London and 60 in Birmingham. For Pakistanis, the numbers were 54 and 74, for Bangladeshis 65 and 80. Birmingham was significantly more segregated than Manchester, slightly more so than Leeds and roughly comparable to Bradford. The average number for US cities with large African-American neighbourhoods was 80. Peach *et al.*, 'Immigration and Ethnicity', in Halsey and Webb, *Twentieth-Century Social Trends*, pp. 149–51.

31. Adonis and Pollard, *A Class Act*, p. 249. Woolf, 'Race equality', *Guardian* (on-line edition), 16 March 2001. All ethnic groups suffered from this disadvantage at the top, even Chinese. Modood, Berthoud *et al.*, *Ethnic Minorities in Britain*, pp. 142–3.

32. Race seems to trump class, however. At least in 1979, Labour did better among Asian and Afro-Caribbean middle-class voters than it did among white working-class voters. Zig Layton-Henry, *The Politics of Immigration: Immigration, 'Race' and 'Race' Relations in Post-war Britain* (Oxford, Cambridge, MA: Blackwell, 1992), p. 110.

33. Philip Lewis, *Islamic Britain: Religion, Politics and Identity among British Muslims*, new edition (London, New York: I. B Tauris, 2002), p. 216. Danièle Joly, *Britannia's Crescent: Making a Place for Muslims in British Society* (Aldershot, Brookfield, VT: Avebury, 1995), p. 97.

34. *Ibid.*, pp. 120–21. Layton-Henry, *Politics of Race*, pp. 173–5. Goulbourne, *Race Relations since 1945*, pp. 63–4. There were five Conservative minority councillors elected in 1982. Two of the Liberal Democratic candidates in 1997 were Chinese and one was Arab.

35. Warren Hoge, 'British City Defines Diversity and Tolerance', *New York Times*, 8 February 2001, pp. A1, A10.

36. Amit Roy, 'Thank you Britain for a new life', *Daily Telegraph* (on-line edition), 18 September 1997. James Meikle, 'Confidence on rise in the black community', *Guardian*, 28 August 2000, p. 6. Hoge, 'Britain's Nonwhites Feel Un-British', *New York Times*, 4 April 2002, p. A6. Modood, Berthoud *et al.*, *Ethnic Minorities in Britain*, especially chaps 3–5, 10. In his analysis of the 1994 survey, Modood found that most people from immigrant communities tended to identify themselves as *both* British and Asian/African/West Indian. However, a significant minority, ranging from 20 to 30 per cent depending on the ethnic group, did not view themselves as British. Tariq Modood, 'Culture and Identity', in *ibid.*, 328–30. The results of interviews reported in Tariq Modood, Sharon Beishon and Satnam Virdee, *Changing Ethnic Identities* (London: Policy Studies Institute, 1994), chap. 6, were similar. They found that most West Indians defined themselves in terms of colour as well as a general West Indian or Caribbean identity, while South Asians identified themselves first according to their country of origin, with very little sense of common Asian identity.

37. Bourke, *Working Class Cultures in Britain 1890–1960*, pp. 63–71.

38. Weight, *Patriots*, p. 78.

39. A. H. Halsey, *Change in British Society, from 1900 to the Present Day*, 4th edition (Oxford, New York: Oxford University Press, 1995), p. 124. Duncan Gallie, 'The Labour Force', in Halsey and Webb, *Twentieth-Century Social Trends*, pp. 291–3, 296–7. Many married working-class women had worked informally at the beginning of the century – e.g. by doing laundry, minding children or taking in a lodger. Such employment would not show up in the statistics. While single women of the middle and upper classes were new entrants into the workforce, their entry was countered by two factors that kept the overall percentage relatively constant: larger numbers of single working-class women were continuing their education after 1970, and so were not entering the workforce, and larger numbers of single working-class women were unable to get jobs after 1980. Thus, the participation rate among single women from school-leaving age to twenty-four years old actually went up from 73 per cent in 1911 to 85 per cent in 1951, before declining to 66 per cent in 1991. This increase in female participation was paralleled by a decline in male participation. In 1911, 93.5 per cent of males worked; in 1961 the participation rate was still 86 per cent; by 1998 it had fallen to 71.3 per cent. In part, this decline was the result of much higher male participation in education beyond the school-leaving age; in part, the big decline after 1961 was the result of increasing long-term male unemployment from the mid-1970s because of both redundancies among mature workers and school-leavers who could not get jobs.

40. Gallie, 'The Labour Force', in Halsey and Webb, *Twentieth-Century Social Trends*, pp. 293–5. Fiona Devine, *Social Class in America and Britain* (Edinburgh: Edinburgh University Press, 1997), pp. 148, 151. Sheila Rowbotham, *A Century of Women: The History of Women in Britain and the United States in the Twentieth Century* (Harmondsworth: Penguin, 1997), p. 495. Adonis and Pollard, *A Class Act*, p. 27. Kenneth D. Brown, *Britain and Japan: A Comparative Economic and Social History since 1900* (Manchester, New York: Manchester University Press, 1998), pp. 216–17. Jack O'Sullivan, article on female surgeons, *Independent* (on-line edition), 6 June 1998. O'Sullivan says 'for 15 years nearly half of medical graduates have been female'. Women were never more than 20 per cent of the elite specialities (consultancies).

41. Jane Lewis, *Women in Britain since 1945: Women, Family, Work and the State in the Post-War Years* (Oxford, Cambridge, MA: Blackwell, 1992), p. 80. A. B. Atkinson, 'Distribution of Income and Wealth', in Halsey and Webb, *Twentieth-Century Social Trends*, pp. 354–5. 'UK News, In Brief', *Guardian Weekly*, 1–7 March 2001, p. 8.

42. George Smith, 'Schools', in Halsey and Webb, *Twentieth-Century Social Trends*, pp. 210–11. By 1995–7, 10 per cent more girls than boys were getting pass grades in at least five A-levels in England and Wales or three of the Scottish equivalents. That trend continued over the next years, and in 2000, girls for the first time achieved more A grades. Emma Brockes, 'In no man's land', *Guardian Weekly*, 31 August–6 September 2000, p. 21.

43. A. H. Halsey, 'Further and Higher Education', in Halsey and Webb, *Twentieth-Century Social Trends*, pp. 228–9, 242.

44. In 1989, less than 15 per cent of teaching faculties (i.e. excluding full-time researchers) at universities were women, while at the polytechnics it was slightly over 20 per cent. A. H. Halsey, *Decline of Donnish Dominion: The British Academic Professions in the Twentieth Century* (Oxford: Clarendon Press, 1992), p. 222.

45. Coleman, 'Population and Family', in Halsey and Webb, *Twentieth-Century Social Trends*, p. 58. Ruth Lister, 'The Family and Women', in Dennis Kavanagh and Anthony Seldon, eds, *The Major Effect* (London: Macmillan, 1994), p. 352.

46. Coleman, 'Population and Family', in Halsey and Webb, *Twentieth-Century Social Trends*, p. 63. Devine, *The Scottish Nation*, 523. Eric Hopkins, *The Rise and Decline of the English Working Classes, 1918–1990: A Social History* (New York: St Martin's Press, 1991), p. 253. Lewis, *Women in Britain since 1945*, p. 43. Richard Berthoud and Sharon Beishon, 'People, Families and Households', in Modood, Berthoud *et al.*, *Ethnic Minorities in Britain*, p. 24. Among immigrant communities, the one exception was people from the Caribbean, who were more likely to be divorced than whites.

NOTES

47. Arthur Marwick, *British Society since 1945* (Harmondsworth: Penguin, 1982), pp. 173–5. Coleman, 'Population and Family', in Halsey and Webb, *Twentieth-Century Social Trends*, p. 53. Paxman, *The English*, p. 231. Change came more slowly in Scotland, as only 17 per cent of girls aged sixteen to nineteen had had sexual experience, according to a 1976 survey. The double standard is made evident by the 1969 survey: only 26 per cent of men were virgins at the time of marriage, while 20 per cent had married the woman with whom they had their first sexual experience.

48. Elizabeth Wilson, *Only Halfway to Paradise: Women in Postwar Britain 1945–1968* (London, New York: Tavistock Publications, 1980), p. 97.

49. Coleman, 'Population and Family', in Halsey and Webb, *Twentieth-Century Social Trends*, pp. 59–60. For a comparison, in 1979–82 the number of first marriages preceded by cohabitation was 25 per cent and the number of remarriages was 65 per cent. We have no earlier statistics because the question had never been asked before. For ethnic minorities, see Berthoud and Beishon, 'People, Families and Households', in Modood, Berthoud *et al.*, *Ethnic Minorities in Britain*, p. 24.

50. Coleman, 'Population and Family', in Halsey and Webb, *Twentieth-Century Social Trends*, p. 51. Lewis, *Women in Britain since 1945*, p. 45. Halsey, *Change in British Society*, p. 126. Berthoud and Beishon, 'People, Families and Households', in Modood, Berthoud *et al.*, *Ethnic Minorities in Britain*, pp. 39, 24, 56–7. Berthoud and Beishon do not provide numbers for those of Chinese origin, but they are likely to be at least as small as among South Asians.

51. As an indication of how the higher estimate is arrived at, Ross McKibbon offers the following analysis of abortion in the 1930s: 'The Inter-Departmental Committee on Abortion (1939) suggested that there were probably 40–66,000 abortions each year, but if to that figure the number of self-induced miscarriages is added, the total might have been between 110,000 and 150,000 a year.' McKibbon, *Classes and Cultures: England 1918–1951* (Oxford, New York: Oxford University Press, 1998), p. 307.

52. Lewis, *Women in Britain since 1945*, p. 57. Coleman, 'Population and Family', in Halsey and Webb, *Twentieth-Century Social Trends*, p. 50. The new law did not provide for abortion on demand. Two doctors had to certify that the woman needed the abortion for either medical or psychological reasons.

53. Melanie Henwood, Lesley Rimmer and Malcolm Wicks, *Inside the Family: Changing Roles of Men and Women* (London: Family Policy Studies Centre, 1987), pp. 11–13, 25.

54. Hopkins, *Rise and Decline of the Working Class*, p. 72.

55. Devine, *The Scottish Nation*, pp. 550–51, 562.
56. Hopkins, *Rise and Decline of the Working Class*, pp. 128, 229–30.
57. Cairncross, *British Economy since 1945*, p. 297.
58. Alan Holmans, 'Housing', in Halsey and Webb, *Twentieth-Century Social Trends*, p. 487. There is a tendency to exaggerate how much building resulted in the appalling tower blocks of the 1960s. Even after the Thatcher sell-off of council housing was well along in the mid-1980s, 'almost two-thirds of council dwellings were houses, around a quarter low-rise flats and a mere 6 per cent high-rise flats'. Ball, Gray and McDowell, *The Transformation of Britain*, p. 228. However, it was the houses in the suburbs that were most popular for purchase, so the public authorities were left by the 1990s with a larger percentage of flats, including all the blocks.
59. Holmans, 'Housing', in Halsey and Webb, *Twentieth-Century Social Trends*, pp. 482–5. Devine, *The Scottish Nation*, p. 311. John Burnett, *A Social History of Housing 1815–1985*, 2nd edition (London, New York: Methuen, 1986), p. 243. There are two ways of measuring overcrowding. The most common is to treat anything less than one room per person as overcrowding. Holmans, however, looks at how many households (including grown children living with parents and aged parents living with children) were sharing housing. That number as a percentage of all households yields the percentage of overcrowding. The two measurements, however, show comparable progress. Jane Lakey uses yet another measurement in looking at rates of overcrowding among immigrants; however, she still finds considerable reductions in overcrowding between surveys in 1982 and 1994, even among the most disadvantaged groups. Lakey, 'Neighbourhoods and Housing', in Modood, Berthoud *et al.*, *Ethnic Minorities in Britain*, pp. 210–12, 219–20.
60. Holmans, 'Housing', in Halsey and Webb, *Twentieth-Century Social Trends*, pp. 474, 479–80. The 1971 percentages without all three amenities were comparable: less than 10 per cent were without a bath or shower, a bit over 10 per cent were without an indoor toilet and 13 per cent were without hot water. The 1991 percentages were about half a per cent. The estimates for percentages in 1947 are calculated by subtracting the numbers of houses built from 1948 to 1951 in Butler and Butler, *Twentieth Century British Political Facts*, pp. 356–7, from the total dwellings in 1951 stated in Holmans, p. 474, to secure an estimate of the 1947 housing stock. The Butler and Butler number is for the whole of the UK, however, rather than just England and Wales. So the effect is to underestimate the housing stock for England and Wales and slightly to overestimate the 1947 percentages. In Scotland, in 1951, 43 per cent of households 'did not have access to a fixed bath', while one-third shared a WC. Devine, *The Scottish Nation*, p. 530.

61. Hopkins, *Rise and Decline of the Working Class*, p. 240.
62. Howard Glennerster, John Hills, eds, *The State of Welfare: The Economics of Social Spending*, 2nd edition (Oxford, New York: Oxford University Press, 1998), p. 158. The Welsh figure is for 1993. The standard of fitness was raised significantly in 1986. Using the older standard, the percentage in England was 4.1 per cent.
63. Holmans, 'Housing', in Halsey and Webb, *Twentieth-Century Social Trends*, pp. 487–90. Steven Fielding, Peter Thompson and Nick Tiratsoo, *'England Arise!' The Labour Party and Popular Politics in 1940s Britain* (Manchester, New York: Manchester University Press, 1995), pp. 121–2. Hopkins, *Rise and Decline of the Working Class*, p. 237. Ball, Gray and McDowell, *Transformation of Britain*, p. 234.
64. Root, 'Transport and Communications', in Halsey and Webb, *Twentieth-Century Social Trends*, p. 449. Jonathan Gershuny and Kimberly Fisher, 'Leisure', in *ibid.*, p. 629. Hopkins, *Rise and Decline of the Working Class*, pp. 179, 240, 261.
65. This is the interpretation of Samuel Hays. See Meredith Veldman, *Fantasy, the Bomb, and the Greening of Britain: Romantic Protest, 1945–1980* (Cambridge, New York, Melbourne: Cambridge University Press, 1994), pp. 243–4.
66. British carbon emissions per capita were 2.4 metric tons, compared with 5.5 in the United States, 2.8 in Germany, 2.5 in Japan, and 1.6 in France. Edmund L. Andrews, 'Frustrated Europeans Set to Battle U.S. on Climate', *New York Times*, 16 July 2001, p. A3. On the rivers, see Paul Brown, 'Rivers are cleanest since the industrial revolution', *Guardian Weekly*, 8–14 November 2001, p. 8.
67. These are the numbers employed in the two census categories hotels, catering and restaurants and entertainment, sport and recreation. Gershuny and Fisher, 'Leisure', in Halsey and Webb, *Twentieth-Century Social Trends*, p. 636.
68. Tony Mason, 'Football', in Tony Mason, ed., *Sport in Britain: A Social History* (Cambridge, New York: Faber and Faber, 1989), pp. 149–50.
69. Marwick, *British Society since 1945*, p. 252. Halsey, *Change in British Society*, p. 42.
70. John Tagliabue, 'Buona Notte, Guten Tag: Europe's New Workdays', *New York Times*, 12 November 1997, p. C1. John Vidal, 'Give us a break', *Guardian*, 28 August 2000, p. 13. Polly Toynbee, 'Caught in the whirl of work', *Guardian Weekly*, 20–26 January 2000, p. 13. Polly Toynbee, 'Stand up to the bullying bosses', *ibid.*, 29 March–4 April 2001, p. 11.
71. Barnett, *Audit of War*, p. 193.
72. Quoted in Devine, *The Scottish Nation*, p. 531.
73. Hopkins, *Rise and Decline of the Working Class*, pp. 30, 39–40, 110.
74. *Ibid.*, p. 110. Pollard, *British Economy, 1914–1990*, p. 271. Atkinson,

'Income and Wealth Distribution', in Halsey and Webb, *Twentieth-Century Social Trends*, pp. 372–4. Devine, *Class in America and Britain*, p. 234. Devine gives a number of 6 per cent below the poverty line in 1979, compared to 4 per cent on Atkinson's chart. So her figures (which include the 14 per cent at or below) tend to be a bit above Atkinson's, perhaps because they include Northern Ireland.

75. See Chas Critcher, 'Sociology, Cultural Studies and the Post-War Working Class', in J. Clarke, C. Critcher and R. Johnson, eds, *Working-Class Culture: Studies in History and Theory* (New York: St Martin's Press, 1980), p. 24, who is quite blunt in making this argument.

76. Hopkins, *Rise and Decline of the Working Class*, pp. 148–9. It is claimed that relative poverty went up continuously from mid-century; Richard Wilkinson, 'Health, Redistribution and Growth', in Andrew Glyn and David Miliband, *Paying for Inequality: The Economic Cost of Social Injustice* (London: Rivers Oram Press, 1994), pp. 38–9.

77. Atkinson, 'Income and Wealth Distribution', in Halsey and Webb, *Twentieth-Century Social Trends*, pp. 373–4. Atkinson's text says 8 per cent were below, but the graph on p. 373 looks like 7 per cent.

78. Rodney Lowe, *The Welfare State in Britain since 1945*, 2nd edition (Basingstoke: Macmillan; New York: St Martin's Press, 1999), p. 156.

79. Critcher, 'Sociology, Cultural Studies and the Post-War Working Class', in Clarke, Critcher and Johnson, *Working-Class Culture*, p. 26, summarises Coates and Silburn.

80. Atkinson, 'Income and Wealth Distribution', in Halsey and Webb, *Twentieth-Century Social Trends*, pp. 373–4.

81. John Carvel, '5m Britons "living on the breadline"', *Guardian* (on-line edition), 8 March 2001.

82. Ball, Gray and McDowell, *Transformation of Britain*, pp. 191–2.

83. *Ibid.*, pp. 167, 186, 201. Hopkins, *Rise and Decline of the Working Class*, p. 216.

84. Lister, 'The Family and Women', in Kavanagh and Seldon, *The Major Effect*, p. 353. Lewis, *Women in Britain since 1945*, p. 99.

85. Devine, *Class in America and Britain*, pp. 91–2.

86. W. D. Rubinstein, *Wealth and Inequality in Britain* (London, Boston: Faber and Faber, 1986), pp. 68–72. Rubinstein still believes there was probably some growing inequality between 1760 and 1870; see pp. 87–8.

87. Atkinson, 'Income and Wealth Distribution', in Halsey and Webb, *Twentieth-Century Social Trends*, pp. 353–6, 365. As a second measure of the narrowing income gap, Atkinson offers the ratio of higher professional average earnings relative to those of unskilled workers, which more than halved between 1913–14 and 1978.

88. *Ibid.*, pp. 358–60.

89. Alan Travis, 'Rich and poor: the gap widens', *Guardian Weekly*, 18–24

May 2000, p. 8. 'In Brief', *ibid.*, 5 April 1998, p. 19. The judgement that the incomes of the top and bottom 10 per cent began to narrow again in the last years of Major's administration was made by the Joseph Rowntree Foundation, whose liberal credentials are impeccable.

90. Cairncross, *British Economy since 1945*, p. 300. Philip Johnston, 'New report dismisses claim that poor are getting poorer', *Electronic Telegraph*, 23 May 1997. Paul Johnson, 'Taxes and Benefits, Equality and Efficiency', in Glyn and Miliband, *Paying for Inequality*, pp. 162–3. While transfer payments have much more impact on income distribution than taxation does, the income tax cuts by the Conservatives were the single most important contributor to growing inequality after 1979. *Ibid.*, pp. 161–3; and Atkinson, 'Income and Wealth Distribution', in Halsey and Webb, *Twentieth-Century Social Trends*, pp. 368–70.

91. George Smith, 'Schools', in Halsey and Webb, *Twentieth-Century Social Trends*, pp. 185, 187. The increase in Scotland between 1938 and 1950–51 was from 150,000 to 230,000, which shows how much more common secondary education had been there, dating back to the nineteenth century. *Ibid.*, pp. 183–5.

92. *Ibid.*, pp. 201–3.

93. Aldcroft, *Education, Training and Economic Performance*, p. 23. Aldcroft compares public expenditure on education as a percentage of GNP rather than GDP. Britain spent slightly less than the United States in 1965 and 1975. Will Woodward, 'Britain tops US in the degree league', *Guardian Weekly*, 25–31 May 2000, p. 23, gives the spending per pupil for 1997. In that year, both spending per pupil and public spending as a percentage of GDP in Britain were below the OECD average.

94. Smith, 'Schools', in Halsey and Webb, *Twentieth-Century Social Trends*, pp. 210, 212–15. See note 42 above for a description of the qualifications. As with the girls, the number with advanced qualifications goes down for the younger groups because many have not yet finished their education. Over the next two decades, that number for those born from 1960 to 1979 should climb, while the number with A-levels as their highest qualification should go down as some with A-levels get more advanced qualifications.

95. *Ibid.*, p. 180. Aldcroft estimates about 60 per cent of German school-leavers in the early 1980s secured the equivalent of 5 O-level passes, when the figure was 27 per cent for England and Wales. He estimates that twice as many pupils in Germany, France and Japan as in Britain were securing the equivalent of an O-level pass in mathematics. Aldcroft, *Education, Training and Economic Performance*, p. 41. By contrast, English school children tested well in science compared to those of other countries. Howard Glennerster, 'Education: Reaping the Harvest?', in Glennerster and Hills, pp. 50–51.

96. Smith, 'Schools', in Halsey and Webb, *Twentieth-Century Social Trends*, p. 199.

97. Glennerster, 'Education: Reaping the Harvest?', in Glennerster and Hills, *The State of Welfare*, pp. 57–9, 65–6. Modood, 'Qualifications and English Language', in Modood, Berthoud *et al.*, *Ethnic Minorities in Britain*, pp. 69–75. Pakistanis and Bangladeshis, however, were doing significantly worse than whites. Adonis and Pollard argue that there was more opportunity for the working class under the old system of grammar schools in the state sector and state-supported free places in the private sector. Adonis and Pollard, *A Class Act*, pp. 39–40, 54–5.

98. Smith, 'Schools', in Halsey and Webb, *Twentieth-Century Social Trends*, p. 199. Hardly any schools in Wales and Scotland opted out.

99. On the other hand, by 1914 the British had developed an extensive system of continuing education based at local colleges that focused on technical education, and these schools offered degrees. Sanderson, *Education and Economic Decline in Britain*, pp. 27–9, 34–5.

100. The narrative is based on Michael Sanderson, *The Missing Stratum: Technical School Education in England 1900–1990s* (London, Atlantic Highlands, NJ: Athlone Press, 1994), chap. 7.

101. Quoted in Aldcroft, *Education, Training and Economic Performance*, p. 55.

102. Sanderson, *The Missing Stratum*, pp. 154–61.

103. Roy Lowe, *Schooling and Social Change, 1964–1990* (London, New York: Routledge, 1997), p. 37. Ball, Gray and McDowell, *Transformation of Britain*, pp. 181–2, 204.

104. At that time, some 250,000 were on apprenticeship schemes, 80,000 of them on a government programme. Will Woodward, 'Labour offer of apprentice place for all youngsters', *Guardian*, 28 August 2000, p. 7. For the British and German comparisons, see S. J. Prais, *Productivity, Education and Training: An International Perspective* (Cambridge, New York, Melbourne: Cambridge University Press, 1995), p. 17. See p. 41 for France (which was between Britain and Germany) and the Netherlands and Switzerland (which were closer to Germany).

105. A. H. Halsey, 'Further and Higher Education', in Halsey and Webb, *Twentieth-Century Social Trends*, pp. 222–6, 250–51. The percentage of overseas students was higher among full-time students and highest among full-time post-graduates.

106. Weight, *Patriots*, p. 389.

107. Lowe, *Schooling and Social Change*, p. 40. As a basis of comparison, there were some 2,000 places in arts subjects, and there had been over 10,000 applicants, while there had been 6,000 for 900 social science places. There were still university places in science and engineering going begging in 1993. Sanderson, *The Missing Stratum*, p. 174.

108. J. G. Crowther, *Science in Modern Society* (New York: Schocken, 1968), pp. 68, 160. A 1962 Royal Society Report indicated a minimum of 12 per cent of recent Ph.D.s were emigrating, while estimating the number at close to 19 per cent. It should be pointed out that West Germany lost a slightly higher percentage of scientists and engineers to the US between 1956 and 1961.

109. Aldcroft, *Education, Training and Economic Performance*, pp. 89–95. The numbers in 1977 were roughly 57 per 10,000 employed as scientists or engineers in the United States, 50 in Japan, 40 in West Germany, and 30 in Britain. Around 1980, fewer than half of those with science or engineering degrees were employed in the field.

110. Lowe, *Schooling and Social Change*, p. 42.

111. Sanderson, *Education and Economic Decline in Britain*, pp. 102–4.

112. Aldcroft, *Education, Training and Economic Performance*, pp. 116, 111–13.

113. Halsey, *Decline of Donnish Dominion*, pp. 4, 91.

114. Halsey, 'Further and Higher Education', in Halsey and Webb, *Twentieth-Century Social Trends*, p. 227.

115. Hopkins, *Rise and Decline of the Working Class*, pp. 157, 250–51. W. A. C. Stewart, *Higher Education in Postwar Britain* (Basingstoke: Macmillan, 1989), p. 280. Halsey, 'Further and Higher Education', in Halsey and Webb, *Twentieth-Century Social Trends*, pp. 243–5. Modood, 'Qualifications and English Language', in Modood, Berthoud *et al.*, *Ethnic Minorities in Britain*, pp. 76–7.

116. Halsey, 'Further and Higher Education', in Halsey and Webb, *Twentieth-Century Social Trends*, pp. 246–7.

117. 'The ruin of Britain's universities', *The Economist*, 16 November 2002, p. 51. Between 1990 and 2002, funding per pupil fell 37 per cent in real terms. The number of students increased 90 per cent.

118. Cecilie Rohwedder and David Wessel, 'Despite Proud Past, German Universities Fail by Many Measures', *Wall Street Journal*, 26 February 2001, pp. 1, 8. According to the OECD study, the percentages were 35 for Britain, 33 for the United States, 23 for France and 16 for Germany.

119. Halsey, *Change in British Society*, pp. 12–13.

120. Devine, *Class in America and Britain*, chaps 3 and 4.

121. The two classic memoirs which reflect these attitudes are Robert Roberts, *The Classic Slum: Salford Life in the First Quarter of the Century* (Harmondsworth: Penguin, 1973), for the period before 1914, and Richard Hoggart, *The Uses of Literacy* (London, New Brunswick, NJ, 1998: Transaction Publishers; reprint of 1957 edition), Part One, for the period between the wars. The argument is developed, in the context of the breakdown of post-war solidarity and community, by Fielding, Thompson and Tiratsoo, '*England Arise!*', pp. 121–4.

122. Anthony Heath and Clive Payne, 'Social Mobility', in Halsey and Webb, *Twentieth-Century Social Trends*, pp. 258–9.

123. John Scott, *The Upper Classes: Property and Privilege in Britain* (London, Basingstoke: Macmillan, 1982), pp. 133–4. In 1873, 5,000 people had owned estates of 1,000 acres or more in Britain (excluding Ireland), while 7,000 people had owned 80 per cent of the land. *Ibid.*, p. 86. In the nineteenth and early twentieth centuries, people held on to land, even though it was a poor investment, because of the political influence it yielded. However, with the limiting of the veto of the House of Lords in 1911 and the onset of full democracy, political power was eroded, while the incentive for public service was reduced.

124. Quoted in Devine, *Class in America and Britain*, p. 121.

125. See Adonis and Pollard, *A Class Act*, p. 93, for a comparison of the careers chosen by the Oxford classes of 1971 and 1994.

126. Marwick, *British Society since 1945*, p. 209.

127. Halsey, *Change in British Society*, p. 35.

128. Heath and Payne, 'Social Mobility', in Halsey and Webb, *Twentieth-Century Social Trends*, pp. 267–70.

129. *Ibid.*, pp. 259–67. Heath and Payne's analysis may underrepresent the amount of upward mobility, since they treat movements from the skilled working class into either the white-collar or petit bourgeois groups as lateral (i.e. they treat groups three, four, and five as the same class). This is an assumption that may make sense based on income, but does not make sense if there were cultural class distinctions that separated skilled blue-collar workers from white-collar workers. This, of course, would be equally true of movement down from groups three or four to group five. However, given the general trend of working-class upward mobility, the likelihood seems to be towards a net undercounting. For an alternative view that argues that women were somewhat less mobile than men, see Devine, *Class in America and Britain*, pp. 63–6. She argues that gender segregation in the labour market limited mobility opportunities for women. Some of the difference, however, may be due to how one views low-paying jobs in the service sector, which were heavily populated by women.

130. Halsey, *Change in British Society*, pp. 66 (quote), 151. Devine, *Class in America and Britain*, chap. 3. Devine analyses a wide range of sociological studies of mobility and comes to much the same conclusions as Heath and Payne.

131. Halsey, *Change in British Society*, pp. 153–4, 160. Smith, 'Schools', in Halsey and Webb, *Twentieth-Century Social Trends*, pp. 217–18.

132. Gallie, 'The Labour Force', in Halsey and Webb, *Twentieth-Century Social Trends*, pp. 282–9. Devine, *Class in America and Britain*, pp. 20–25. Charles Pattie and Ron Johnston, 'The Conservative Party and the

Electorate', in Steve Ludlam and Martin Smith, eds, *Contemporary British Conservatism* (New York: St Martin's Press, 1996), p. 46. N. F. R. Crafts, 'Industry', in Kavanagh and Seldon, *The Major Effect*, p. 218.

133. Richard Hoggart, a young socialist who was looking at these changes when they first became evident in the late 1950s, was still inclined to put clerical workers and shop employees in the lower-middle class; *The Uses of Literacy*, p. 7. Fielding, Thompson and Tiratsoo claim that skilled workers and clerical workers hated each other in the early 1950s, as the latter still saw themselves as middle class. *'England Arise!'*, p. 123. Gordon Marshall, *Repositioning Class: Social Inequality in Industrial Societies* (London, Thousand Oaks, CA, New Delhi: Sage Publications, 1997), pp. 73–7, chap. 6, makes the argument about career paths. He also claims that statistical analysis points against the proletarianisation thesis, and that clerical workers tended to identify more with the middle than with the working class.

Chapter 9. The Culture of Elitism

1. This is the implicit argument of Corelli Barnett's *The Audit of War*, and also of David Marquand, *The Unprincipled Society: New Demands and Old Politics* (London: Jonathan Cape, 1988).

2. Walter Bagehot, *The English Constitution* (Ithaca, NY: Cornell University Press, 1966), pp. 61–5.

3. As another example, in 1840, local expenditure was roughly 20 per cent of all national expenditure, while in 1910 it was half the national total. Hoppen, *The Mid-Victorian Generation*, pp. 106–8, 123.

4. A 1994 survey found that people still remained attached to the abolished counties and wanted them restored, while the new administrative units continued to be unpopular. Simon Jenkins, *Accountable to None: The Tory Nationalization of Britain* (Harmondsworth: Penguin, 1996), pp. 256–7.

5. Mark Rowe, 'Dismay over rural housing ruling', *Independent on Sunday* (on-line edition), 2 August 1998.

6. This figure is for 1997. Stephen Driver and Luke Martell, *New Labour: Politics after Thatcherism* (Cambridge: Polity Press, 1998), p. 144.

7. Quango stands for quasi-autonomous non-governmental organisation. Martin J. Smith, 'Reforming the State', in Ludlam and Smith, *Contemporary British Conservatism*, p. 150. See Jenkins, *Accountable to None, passim*, for the argument that centralisation became inherent in Thatcherite policies of cost-cutting and improved provision of services.

8. There are a number of other examples of the Thatcher government trying to stop either the publication of an article or the broadcast of a

show prior to publication or release. The government always succeeded initially in stopping publication or broadcast, though sometimes it eventually relented. See Peter Thornton, *Decade of Decline: Civil Liberties in the Thatcher Years* (London: National Council for Civil Liberties, 1989), chap. 2.

9. Thornton, *Decade of Decline*, p. 92.

10. Eric Foner, *Reconstruction: America's Unfinished Revolution, 1863–1877* (New York: Harper & Row, 1988). Part of this account is also based on a review of David W. Blight, *Race and Reunion: The Civil War in American Memory* (Cambridge, MA: Harvard University Press, 2000), by Jonathan Yardley of the *Washington Post*, in *Guardian Weekly*, 15–21 March 2001, p. 38.

11. A good brief summary of the meanings of and distinctions among the literary theories of semiotics, structuralism, deconstruction (poststructuralism), postmodernism and some of the attempts by Marxists in particular to make use of them is in Silvio Gaggi, *Modern/Postmodern: A Study in Twentieth-Century Arts and Ideas* (Philadelphia: University of Pennsylvania Press, 1989), chap. 6. A good introductory discussion of all the different meanings of Postmodernism (and all the battles over what it means) in all the different academic disciplines is Tim Woods, *Beginning Postmodernism* (Manchester, New York: Manchester University Press, 1999).

12. David Lodge, *Nice Work* (Harmondsworth: Penguin, 1988), p. 253.

13. University and polytechnic faculties *did* have a left-wing bias by the 1970s, and it became even greater with the reforms of the 1980s. The bias was somewhat less at Oxford and Cambridge than elsewhere. Of course, even Conservatives might come disproportionately from the left wing of the party. Halsey, *Decline of Donnish Dominion*, pp. 236–8.

14. A. H. Halsey refers to 'the general homogeneity of intellectual and cultural values that pervaded all ranks, all faculties, and all institutions, including the polytechnics as well as the universities' in the 1980s. *Ibid.*, p. 126.

15. Said in 1989; quoted in *ibid.*, p. 2.

16. Keynes's 'Economic Possibilities for our Grandchildren', cited in Gershuny and Fisher, 'Leisure', in Halsey and Webb, *Twentieth-Century Social Trends*, p. 622.

17. Despite pressure to direct more money to the provinces, the 'big four' still got nearly 40 per cent of the grants in 1980, while only 20 per cent went to the regions. Krishan Kumar, 'The Social and Cultural Setting', in Boris Ford, ed., *The New Pelican Guide to English Literature*, Vol. 8: *The Present* (Harmondsworth: Penguin, 1983), pp. 27–8.

18. Margaret Garlake, *New Art New World: British Art in Postwar Society* (New Haven, London: Yale University Press, 1998), p. 228.

19. John Elsom, *Post-War British Theatre* (London, Boston: Routledge & Kegan Paul, 1976), pp. 7, 147, 132.

20. Andrew Blake, *The Land without Music: Music, Culture and Society in Twentieth-Century Britain* (Manchester, New York: Manchester University Press, 1997), p. 196.

21. In 1998, there were sixty-nine regional repertory theatres that produced plays and about the same number which staged other theatres' productions. David Lister, 'Debt-hit theatres battle to survive cash crisis', *Independent* (on-line edition), 13 July 1998.

22. Fiachra Gibbons, 'Britain's great unsung success story', *Guardian Weekly*, 6–12 January 2000. Of those 60,000 employed, 40,000 were in London.

23. Brian Hunt, 'Why does London still have no concert hall worthy of its great orchestras', *Daily Telegraph* (on-line edition), 10 January 1998. Hughes and Stradling judge that British composition had not progressed far over the course of the twentieth century in terms of foreigners' (especially Europeans') recognition of it. Meirion Hughes and Robert Stradling, *The English Musical Renaissance 1840–1940: Constructing a National Music*, 2nd edition (Manchester, New York: Manchester University Press, 2001), pp. 287–8.

24. Andrew Sanders, *The Short Oxford History of English Literature*, revised edition (Oxford: Clarendon Press, 1996), p. 533.

25. Blake Morrison, *The Movement: English Poetry and Fiction of the 1950s* (Oxford, New York, etc: Oxford University Press, 1980), p. 130.

26. The phrase is Phelps's in 'The Post-War English Novel', in Ford, *The Present*, p. 432.

27. C. W. E. Bigsby, 'The Language of Crisis in British Theatre: The Drama of Cultural Pathology', in C. W. E. Bigsby, ed., *Contemporary English Drama* (London: Edward Arnold, 1981), pp. 13–14.

28. Neil Corcoran, *English Poetry since 1940* (London, New York: Longman, 1993), p. 209.

29. Phelps, 'The Post-War English Novel', in Ford, *The Present*, pp. 435–6.

30. Malcolm Bradbury, *The Modern British Novel* (London: Secker & Warburg, 1993), p. 371.

31. Much of this paragraph is indebted to Gāmini Salgādo, 'V. S. Naipaul and the Politics of Fiction', in Ford, *The Present*, pp. 314–27.

32. Bradbury, *The Modern British Novel*, p. 387.

33. Gilbert Phelps, 'The Post-War English Novel', in Ford, *The Present*, p. 417.

34. Jeremy Crump, 'The Identity of English Music: The Reception of Elgar 1898–1935', in Robert Colls and Philip Dodd, eds, *Englishness: Politics and Culture 1880–1920* (London, Sydney, etc: Croom Helm, 1986), pp. 167–9, discusses Elgar's Englishness.

35. John Caldwell, *The Oxford History of English Music*, Vol. II: *From c. 1715 to the Present Day* (Oxford, New York: Oxford University Press, 1999), p. 409.

36. *Ibid.*, pp. 422–3.

37. *Ibid.*, Vol. II, p. 469.

38. Jim Samson, 'Instrumental Music II', in Stephen Banfield, ed., *Music in Britain*: Vol. 6, *The Twentieth Century* (Oxford, Cambridge, MA: Blackwell, 1995), p. 327.

39. Caldwell, *Oxford History of English Music*, Vol. II, p. 483.

40. Modris Eksteins, *Rites of Spring: The Great War and the Birth of the Modern Age* (New York, London: Doubleday, 1989), p. 217.

41. Richard Cork, 'The Emancipation of Modern British Sculpture', in Susan Compton, ed., *British Art in the 20th Century: The Modern Movement* (Munich: Prestel-Verlag, 1986), p. 38. Compton's book has a spectacular collection of plates of the art work of all of the artists discussed here. The essays, too, were extremely helpful.

42. This discussion of the Independent Group relies heavily on Anne Massey, *The Independent Group: Modernism and Mass Culture in Britain, 1945–59* (Manchester, New York: Manchester University Press, 1995). One of Massey's aims is to prove that there was no direct link between the Independent Group and the Pop Art that emerged in Britain in the 1960s, contrary to the standard art historical narratives. Nonetheless, there seems to have been enough overlap of interests and concerns to justify treating some of the works of Hamilton and Paolozzi as forms of Pop Art and treating the Group's thinking about art as anticipatory of what was to come.

43. Caroline Tisdall, 'Art Controversies of the Seventies', in Compton, *British Art in the 20th Century*, p. 83.

44. Edward Lucie-Smith, *Art in the Seventies* (Ithaca, NY: Cornell University Press, 1980), p. 80.

45. Frances Spalding, *British Art since 1900* (London: Thames and Hudson, 1986), p. 229.

46. Paul Thompson, 'The Late Twentieth Century: Collectivism and Competition', in Peter Kidson, Peter Murray and Paul Thompson, *A History of English Architecture*, revised edition (Harmondsworth: Penguin, 1979), p. 363. Woods, *Beginning Postmodernism*, pp. 114–16.

47. Matthew Collings, *Blimey! From Bohemia to Britpop: The London Artworld from Francis Bacon to Damien Hirst* (London: 21 Publishing Ltd, 1998), p. 59. Carol Vogel, 'Monet's Haystacks Ignites Bidding at Sotheby's in London', *New York Times*, 2 July 2001, p. B6.

Chapter 10. Alternative Cultures

1. Geoff Pearson, '"Paki-Bashing" in a North East Lancashire Town: A Case Study and Its History', in Geoff Mungham and Geoff Pearson, *Working Class Youth Culture* (London, Boston: Routledge & Kegan Paul, 1976), p. 61.

2. Dickinson, who was in the United States in 1901, was writing home to C. R. Ashbee; quoted in Wiener, *English Culture and the Decline of the Industrial Spirit*, p. 89. This view of America was confirmed for Europeans by America's own intellectual elite, especially those from the Northeast. European commentaries on American culture were no more contemptuous than those of Americans themselves. See Henry Fairlie, *The Spoiled Child of the Western World: The Miscarriage of the American Idea in Our Time* (New York: Doubleday, 1976), p. 51.

3. Quoted in Robert Hewison, *Too Much: Art and Society in the Sixties 1960–75* (New York: Oxford University Press, 1987), p. 12.

4. Gibbons, 'Britain's great unsung success story,' *Guardian Weekly*, 6–12 January 2000.

5. Rowbotham, *A Century of Women*, p. 296 (quote). Wilson, *Only Halfway to Paradise*, p. 38.

6. Peter Lewis, *The Fifties* (New York: J. B. Lippincott, 1978), p. 59.

7. D. L. LeMahieu, *A Culture for Democracy: Mass Communication and the Cultivated Mind in Britain Between the Wars* (Oxford: Clarendon Press, 1988), p. 90. Devine, *The Scottish Nation*, pp. 316–17.

8. The estimate of the number of households is in Holmans, 'Housing', in Halsey and Webb, *Twentieth-Century Social Trends*, p. 470. The estimate of the number of wireless sets is in Richard Holt and Tony Mason, *Sport in Britain 1945–2000* (Oxford, Malden, MA: Blackwell, 2000), p. 94. Some households, of course, had more than one wireless. Devine estimates that over 40 per cent of Scottish homes had a wireless in 1939. Devine, *The Scottish Nation*, p. 317; however, England was surely more prosperous than Scotland, so the percentage there would have been higher.

9. Arthur Marwick claims that in the late 1970s the average for television was 16 hours per week in the summer and 20 in the winter, while the average for radio was about 9 hours per week. Marwick, *British Society since 1945*, p. 250.

10. Gershuny and Fisher, 'Leisure', in Halsey and Webb, *Twentieth-Century Social Trends*, p. 638. For the 1946 peak figure, see Garlake, *New Art New World*, p. 71; for the percentages see Arthur Marwick, *Culture in Britain since 1945* (Oxford, Cambridge, MA: Blackwell, 1991), p. 57. For the most recent figure, see 'In Brief', *Guardian Weekly*, 14–20 March 2002, p. 9. The claim of the world's top cinema-going people is based

on a per capita measurement of attendances. McKibbon, *Classes and Cultures*, p. 419.

11. Fielding, Thompson and Tiratsoo, *'England Arise!'*, p. 145.

12. See Weight, *Patriots*, pp. 342–8 on popular Germanophobia.

13. For the list of the top one hundred, see Fiachra Gibbons, 'Third Man voted best of British', *Guardian* (on-line edition), 23 September 1999.

14. Kumar, 'Social and Cultural Setting', in Ford, *The Present*, p. 41.

15. Louise Jury, 'Heroine of "Forsyte Saga" Dies Aged 65', *Independent*, 12 April 2001, p. 7.

16. Robert Hewison, *In Anger: British Culture in the Cold War 1945–60* (New York: Oxford University Press, 1981), p. 149.

17. John Davis, *Youth and the Condition of Britain: Images of Adolescent Conflict* (London, Atlantic Highlands, NJ: Athlone Press, 1990), p. 166. The sales for 1963, with the Beatles already having released their early hits, only were up to 61.3 million.

18. Colin Blackstock, 'Beatles head list of greatest songs', *Guardian* (on-line edition), 13 July 2000. 'Satisfaction' by the Rolling Stones was number two on the list of the one hundred greatest songs.

19. Hopkins, *Rise and Decline of the Working Class*, p. 174. Simon Frith, *Sound Effects: Youth, Leisure, and the Politics of Rock 'n' Roll* (New York: Pantheon Books, 1981), pp. 83, 135. Richard Middleton, 'The Rock Revolution', in Banfield, *The Twentieth Century*, p. 84.

20. See Simon Frith and Howard Horne, *Art into Pop* (London, New York: Methuen Books, 1987), which is the basis for much of this discussion of the art school connection and its influence.

21. Paul Gilroy, *'There Ain't No Black in the Union Jack': The Cultural Politics of Race and Nation* (Chicago: University of Chicago Press, 1991), pp. 168, 170. All the discussion of black music in Britain that follows is based on Gilroy, pp. 165–217.

22. *Ibid.*, p. 211.

23. Christopher John Farley, 'Hip-hop nation', *Guardian* (on-line edition), 19 March 1999. See also, Michael Odell, 'Brit-hop . . . why it didn't happen', *ibid.*, (on-line edition) 19 March 1999; and Michael Odell, 'Cockney rebel', *ibid.*, 17 March 2000 (on-line edition).

24. The percentages saying they liked different kinds of music were as follows: reggae, 39 per cent; soul, 34 per cent; African, 32 per cent; gospel, 29 per cent; hip-hop, 24 per cent; and rock, 2 per cent. James Meikle, 'Confidence on rise in the black community', *Guardian*, 28 August 2000, p. 6.

25. Holt and Mason, *Sport in Britain 1945–2000*, pp. 115, 118.

26. Richard Holt, *Sport and the British: A Modern History* (Oxford: Clarendon Press, 1989), pp. 151–2.

27. Devine, *The Scottish Nation*, pp. 361–2.

28. Mason, 'Football', in Mason, *Sport in Britain: A Social History*, pp. 163, 165.

29. Grant Clark, 'Will business bankrupt the beautiful game?,' *Independent on Sunday* (on-line edition), 12 July 1998. Tony Mason, *Sport in Britain* (London, Boston: Faber and Faber, 1988), p. 85.

30. Jack Williams, 'Cricket', in Mason, *Sport in Britain: A Social History*, p. 126.

31. Fielding, Thompson and Tiratsoo, '*England Arise!*', p. 195.

32. Marwick, *British Society since 1945*, p. 119.

33. Goldthorpe and Lockwood's study, *The Affluent Worker in the Class Structure* (1968–9), is summarised in Critcher, 'Sociology, Cultural Studies and the Post-War Working Class', in Clarke, Critcher and Johnson, *Working Class Culture*, pp. 27–30. Paul Willis adopts the second argument in 'Shop Floor Culture, Masculinity and the Wage Form', in *ibid.*, pp. 189–91, 196–7. Luton was a new manufacturing centre in the South, while Willis was referring to northern workers whose ancestors had been doing similar work in the same place for generations.

34. Devine, *Class in America and Britain*, p. 209.

35. The sense of community among the working class may not have been all that mythologists of the left would make it. See Bourke, *Working-Class Cultures in Britain 1890–1960*, pp. 142–4 and, more generally, chap. 5. In particular, she draws a distinction between a neighbourhood and a community and between a neighbour and a friend. In both cases, she argues, it is wrong to assume that the former implied the latter; mostly, it did not.

36. *Ibid.*, pp. 156–9.

37. *Ibid.* This view of class is confirmed by the recent survey which showed that 68 per cent of the people regarded themselves as working class, including 55 per cent of people who would normally be considered middle class. Steve Boggan, 'Forget the classless society – two-thirds of us now say we're working class and proud', *Independent* (on-line edition), 21 August 2002.

38. Mark Abrams, 'Demographic Correlates of Values', in Mark Abrams, David Gerard and Noel Timms, eds, *Values and Social Change in Britain* (Basingstoke: Macmillan, 1985), pp. 47–8.

39. Frank Coffield, Carol Borrill and Sarah Marshall, *Growing up at the Margins*, quoted in Davis, *Youth and the Condition of Britain*, pp. 5–6, and also p. 7.

40. Two useful, though highly politicised, discussions of youth subcultures are Michael Brake, *Comparative Youth Culture: The Sociology of Youth Cultures and Youth Subcultures in America, Britain, and Canada* (London, Boston, etc.: Routledge & Kegan Paul, 1985), and Mungham and Pearson, *Working Class Youth Culture*, especially the first chapter,

Graham Murdock and Robin McCron, 'Youth and Class: The Career of a Confusion'. Stanley Cohen's 'Symbols of Trouble: Introduction to the New Edition', in *Folk Devils and Moral Panics: The Creation of the Mods and Rockers* (New York: St Martin's Press, 1980), is an especially good warning of the dangers of overtheorising youth behaviour, particularly juvenile delinquency.

41. Brake, *Comparative Youth Culture*, p. 77.
42. This analysis is based on Gilroy, '*There Ain't No Black in the Union Jack*', pp. 193–209.
43. Joly, *Britannia's Crescent*, p. 53.
44. Lizette Alvarez, 'Arranged Marriages Get a Little Rearranging', *New York Times* (on-line archive), 22 June 2003.
45. Yasmin Alibhai-Brown, *Imagining the New Britain* (New York: Routledge, 2001), p. 246.
46. In a 1997 survey, 'two-thirds of the survey's Pakistani respondents aged 16–34 stated that religion is "very important" to the way they live their lives, compared to just over 80 per cent of those from older age groups . . .' As a comparison, 18 per cent of Caribbeans and 35 per cent of Indians between sixteen and thirty-four said religion was 'very important' to their lives. Jessica Jacobson, *Islam in Transition: Religion and Identity among British Pakistani Youth* (London, New York: Routledge, 1998), pp. 32–3.
47. Lewis, *Islamic Britain*, p. 155.
48. Jacobson, *Islam in Transition*, p. 78.
49. Kathleen D. Hall, *Lives in Translation: Sikh Youth as British Citizens* (Philadelphia: University of Pennsylvania Press, 2002), p. 141.
50. Roger Hood and Andrew Roddam, 'Crime, Sentencing and Punishment', in Halsey and Webb, *Twentieth-Century Social Trends*, pp. 675–6, 680.
51. *Ibid.*, pp. 680–85. The statistics on 2001 come from 'In Brief', *Guardian Weekly*, 1–7 November 2001, p. 10. All these statistics are for England and Wales. The big jump in violent crimes after 1987, when the overall rate of increase was tailing off, was almost surely due to increased reporting.
52. Hood and Roddam, 'Crime, Sentencing and Punishment', in Halsey and Webb, *Twentieth-Century Social Trends*, pp. 690–700. Ball, Gray and McDowell, *Transformation of Britain*, p. 367. The increased severity of sentences was due to the increase in the rate of violent crime after 1945 and the increase in drug-related crime after 1980, as well as the changed environment.
53. Davis, *Youth and the Condition of Britain*, p. 151. The number of girls aged ten to seventeen committing crimes actually increased faster between 1937 and 1967 than the number of boys; thereafter, the ratio

of males to females in that age group remained relatively constant. Hood and Roddam, 'Crime, Sentencing and Punishment', in Halsey and Webb, *Twentieth-Century Social Trends*, pp. 688–9. Glenda Cooper, 'Girl violence on the increase', *Independent* (on-line edition), 22 July 1998.

54. Ball, Gray and McDowell, *Transformation of Britain*, p. 367.

55. Nick Hopkins, 'Hotspots fuel capital's soaring murder rate', *Guardian*, 10 August 2000, p. 6. On drink, see Patrick Wintour, 'Ministers plan crackdown on yob culture', *Guardian* (on-line edition), 1 December 2000.

56. Eksteins, *Rites of Spring*, p. 293 and chap. IX.

57. Terence Morris, *Crime and Criminal Justice since 1945* (Oxford, New York: Basil Blackwell, 1989), p. 55.

58. The numbers ninety-six and forty-one come from Holt and Mason, *Sport in Britain 1945–2000*, pp. 158–9. Elsewhere, the numbers have been given as ninety-four and thirty-nine.

59. Holt, *Sport and the British*, p. 329.

60. *Ibid.*, pp. 335–6. Holt's whole discussion of football violence is superb.

61. Marwick, *British Society since 1945*, p. 223.

62. Layton-Henry, *Politics of Race*, pp. 164–5. He was speaking at a fringe meeting, sponsored by an anti-immigration group, at the 1982 Conservative Party conference.

63. South Asians had much more confidence in the police, but still over 40 per cent (50 per cent of those sixteen to thirty-four) did not think the police would protect them from racial harassment. Satnam Virdee, 'Racial Harassment', in Modood, Berthoud *et al.*, *Ethnic Minorities in Britain*, p. 280. Adonis and Pollard, *A Class Act*, p. 249.

64. Ron Ramdin, *The Making of the Black Working Class in Britain* (Aldershot: Gower, 1987), pp. 266–8, citing survey evidence published in 1977. Given where they had started upon arrival in Britain, parental expectations were probably quite low.

65. S. Platt, 'The Innocents of Broadwater Farm', *New Society*, 11 October 1985, quoted in Gilroy, '*There Ain't No Black in the Union Jack*', p. 239.

66. Vikram Dodd, 'Pre-riot report admits Bradford plagued by race divisions', *Guardian* (on-line edition), 10 July 2001. See also, Jeevan Vasagar and Vikram Dodd, 'Poverty and racism create an explosive mix', *Guardian* (on-line edition), 9 July 2001; and Sarah Lyall, 'Shadowy Party Heats Up British Racial Tensions', *New York Times*, 4 July 2001, p. A3.

67. Peter Brierley, 'Religion', in Halsey and Webb, *Twentieth-Century Social Trends*, pp. 652–3.

68. *Ibid.*, pp. 654–5. The rough numbers for the Asian religious communities in 1990 were 1.1 million Muslims, 400,000 Hindus and over 400,000 Sikhs. The estimated number of Jews was 330,000, a decline

since 1950. Grace Davie, *Religion in Britain since 1945: Believing without Belonging* (Oxford, Cambridge, MA: Blackwell, 1994), pp. 64–6. These numbers compare with the following for Christian church membership in 1995, as given by Brierley: 1.8 million Anglicans, 1.9 million Catholics and 2.7 million other Christians. Since the percentage of Anglicans and non-Christians was the same, the numbers above may be for affiliates. There would be only a tiny gap between affiliates and members in the non-Christian faiths compared with the Christian churches.

69. Brierley, 'Religion', in Halsey and Webb, *Twentieth-Century Social Trends*, pp. 657–62. The numbers of children attending church were higher than the number of adults – by a couple of percentage points in England and Scotland, but by 8 per cent in Wales. Anglican attendance was fairly steady between 1980 and 2000, as was the numbers of Hindus and Jews. For Northern Ireland, see Davie, *Religion in Britain since 1945*, pp. 14, 47.

70. Stephen Bates, 'Decline in churchgoing hits CoE hardest', *Guardian* (on-line edition), 14 April 2001. James Meikle, 'Confidence on rise in the black community', *Guardian*, 28 August 2000, p. 6.

71. William K. Kay and Leslie J. Francis, *Drift from the Churches: Attitude toward Christianity during Childhood and Adolescence* (Cardiff: University of Wales Press, 1996), p. 10.

72. *Ibid.*, p. 6.

73. Abrams, 'Demographic Correlates of Values', in Abrams, Gerard and Timms, *Values and Social Change in Britain*, pp. 30–33. David Gerard, 'Religious Attitudes and Values', in *ibid.*, pp. 58–60.

74. Davie, *Religion in Britain since 1945*, p. 79. The statement on the paranormal is based on Polly Toynbee, 'The Pope versus the aliens', from the *Guardian Weekly*. I do not have the date of the article, but it is probably from 1998, prior to September, when the *Guardian*'s on-line database begins.

75. Davie, *Religion in Britain since 1945*, p. 81. There were 365,000 baptisms in the Church of England in 1940 and 150,000 in 1995. Alan Travis, 'Labour commits itself to promoting family life', *Guardian Weekly*, 2 August 1998, UK News.

76. Brian Harrison and Josephine Webb, 'Volunteers and Voluntarism', in Halsey and Webb, *Twentieth-Century Social Trends*, pp. 589–90, 600, 602.

77. *Ibid.*, pp. 595–6. David Gerard, 'Values and Voluntary Work', in Abrams, Gerard and Timms, *Values in Britain*, pp. 202–3, 207–9.

78. Abrams, 'Demographic Correlates of Values', in Abrams, Gerard and Timms, *Values in Britain*, pp. 29–31.

79. *Ibid.*, pp. 33–7. Jennifer Brown, Miriam Comber, Karen Gibson and

Susan Howard, 'Marriage and the Family', in *ibid.*, pp. 110–19. Martin P. M. Richards and B. Jane Elliott, 'Sex and Marriage in the 1960s and 1970s', in David Clark, ed., *Marriage, Domestic Life and Social Change: Writings for Jacqueline Burgoyne (1944–88)*, (London, New York: Routledge, 1991), pp. 48–52.

80. Abrams, 'Demographic Correlates of Values', in Abrams, Gerard and Timms, *Values in Britain*, p. 40. Michael Fogarty, 'British Attitudes to Work', in *ibid.*, p. 186. There was no significant difference between the unemployed and the sample as a whole in their attitudes towards work. For the continued strong belief in the fourth to the tenth commandments, see Gerard, 'Religious Attitudes and Values', in *ibid.*, p. 78.

81. By 2002, the annual survey of British social attitudes found far greater tolerance towards drug use and homosexuality than had existed in 1985, when the survey began. John Carvel, 'Rising education standards creating a nation of liberals', *Guardian Weekly*, 12–18 December 2002, p. 10.

Chapter 11. National Identities

1. Kevin Boyle and Tom Hadden, *Northern Ireland: The Choice* (Harmondsworth: Penguin, 1994), pp. 59–60.

2. Christopher Harvie, *No Gods and Precious Few Heroes: Twentieth-Century Scotland*, 3rd edition (Edinburgh: Edinburgh University Press, 1998), p. 177.

3. *Ibid.*, p. 47. If one includes emigration to England, Scotland surpassed even Ireland as the European country with the largest rate of emigration for much of the period from 1815 to 1914. If one excludes emigration to England (a form of internal UK migration), then Scotland's rate was surpassed only by Ireland's and, in some decades, Norway's. Devine, *The Scottish Nation*, p. 468.

4. Harvie, *Twentieth-Century Scotland*, pp. 144–5, 150.

5. Christopher Harvie, *Scotland and Nationalism: Scottish Society and Politics 1707–1994*, 2nd edition (London, New York: Routledge, 1994), pp. 118–19.

6. Anne Segall, 'Scotland could pay dearly for devolution', *Daily Telegraph* (on-line edition), 9 September 1997.

7. Harvie, *Scotland and Nationalism*, pp. 182–3, 188–9.

8. Harvie, *Twentieth-Century Scotland*, p. 164.

9. *Ibid.*, pp. 166, 169. Devine, *The Scottish Nation*, p. 592.

10. Harvie, *Twentieth-Century Scotland*, p. 169.

11. Harvie, *Scotland and Nationalism*, p. 211.

12. Powers include 'health, education and training, local government, housing, social work, economic development, transport, the law and

home affairs, the environment . . . agriculture, fisheries and forestry, and sport and the arts'. Peter John, 'New Labour and the Decentralization of Power', in Gerald R. Taylor, ed., *The Impact of New Labour* (Basingstoke, London: Macmillan; New York: St Martin's Press, 1999), p. 125. Paula Surridge and David McCrone, 'The 1997 Scottish Referendum Vote', in Bridget Taylor and Katarina Thomson, eds, *Scotland and Wales: Nations Again?* (Cardiff: University of Wales Press, 1999), pp. 47–8, 52, 61. A 1997 survey at the time of the referendum showed that just over 60 per cent of voters trusted both Labour and the SNP to serve Scotland's interests well, but many more trusted the SNP to serve Scottish interests 'just about always'.

13. John Osmond, 'Introduction: Coping with a Dual Identity', in John Osmond, ed., *The National Question Again: Welsh Political Identity in the 1980s* (Llandysul: Gomer Press, 1985), p. xx.

14. *Ibid.*, p. xxix. The comparative immigration rates were 4.5 immigrants per 1,000 of population in Wales as against 6.3 per 1,000 in the United States.

15. Sir Reginald Coupland, *Welsh and Scottish Nationalism: A Study* (London: Collins, 1954), p. 360. Tim Williams, 'The Anglicisation of South Wales', in Raphael Samuel, ed., *Patriotism: The Making and Unmaking of British National Identity*, Vol. II: *Minorities and Outsiders* (London, New York: Routledge, 1989), pp. 197–201.

16. Kenneth O. Morgan, *Rebirth of a Nation: Wales 1880–1980* (Oxford, New York: Oxford University Press, University of Wales Press, 1981), p. 242. John Davies, *A History of Wales* (London: Allen Lane, The Penguin Press, 1993), p. 498. Hoppen, *The Mid-Victorian Generation*, pp. 537–8. By 1911, most of these Welsh speakers were bilingual.

17. Morgan, *Rebirth of a Nation*, pp. 243, 359. Denis Balsom, 'The Three-Wales Model', in Osmond, *Welsh Political Identity in the 1980s*, pp. 3, 6. D. Gareth Evans, *A History of Wales 1906–2000* (Cardiff: University of Wales Press, 2000), p. 193. Balsom claims that polls in the 1970s showed that the percentage of Welsh speakers was closer to 30 per cent, indicating that census figures throughout may not have been altogether accurate. The census showed something over five hundred thousand Welsh speakers in 1971 and 1981. Davies, *History of Wales*, p. 644.

18. Osmond, 'Introduction: Coping with a Dual Identity', in Osmond, *Welsh Political Identity in the 1980s*, p. xxx. Davies, *History of Wales*, pp. 272–3. Davies says that unemployment peaked at 42.8 per cent of insured males in August 1932. It was still 28.1 per cent of insured males at the end of 1936. *Ibid.*, pp. 549, 585.

19. Osmond, 'Introduction', in Osmond, *Welsh Political Identity in the 1980s*, p. xxvi. Evans, *History of Wales 1906–2000*, pp. 162–3.

20. Marwick, *British Society since 1945*, p. 33.

21. See Evans, *History of Wales 1906–2000*, pp. 175–6, for an evaluation of the state of the Welsh economy by 2000.

22. Morgan, *Rebirth of a Nation*, p. 396.

23. Balsom, 'The Three-Wales Model,' in Osmond, *Welsh Political Identity in the 1980s*, pp. 10–11. Charlotte Aull Davies, *Welsh Nationalism in the Twentieth Century: The Ethnic Option and the Modern State* (New York, Westport, London: Praeger, 1989), p. 64.

24. Butler and Butler, *British Political Facts 1900–2000*, p. 460. Kenneth O. Morgan, 'Welsh Devolution: The Past and the Future. The British Academy Lecture, 18 September 1998', in Taylor and Thomson, *Scotland and Wales*, p. 200.

25. Richard Wyn Jones and Dafydd Trystan, 'The 1997 Welsh Referendum Vote', in Taylor and Thomson, *Scotland and Wales*, pp. 81–2.

26. Alvin Jackson, *Ireland 1798–1998: Politics and War* (Oxford: Blackwell, 1999), pp. 350–51.

27. Boyle and Hadden, *Northern Ireland: The Choice*, p. 62. This is based on a 1990 survey. Abortion was the one social issue that divided Northern Irish Catholics and Protestants.

28. Broadberry, 'Unemployment', in Crafts and Woodward, *The British Economy since 1945*, p. 217, gives figures for years preceding those in Table 11.1.

29. Boyle and Hadden, *Northern Ireland: The Choice*, p. 140.

30. *Ibid.*, pp. 70–71.

31. *Ibid.*

32. *Ibid.*, pp. 46–9. The RUC did not necessarily have to be replaced; however, it has proved nearly impossible to persuade Catholics to join it.

33. 'As Violence Ebbs, Northern Ireland Renews Itself', *New York Times*, 12 December 2000, p. C10, and Table 11.1 above. Unemployment in Northern Ireland is still higher than in other parts of the United Kingdom. The article in the *New York Times* says that unemployment was 16.8 per cent in 1986; Broadberry's table in Crafts and Woodward says 18.6 per cent.

34. Bernard Crick, 'The English and the British', in Bernard Crick, ed., *National Identities: The Constitution of the United Kingdom* (Oxford, Cambridge, MA: Blackwell, 1991), pp. 90–91.

35. Linda Colley, *Britons: Forging the Nation 1707–1837* (New Haven, London: Yale University Press, 1992), chaps 1–2.

36. Jeannine Surel, 'John Bull', translated by Kathy Hodgkin, in Samuel, *Patriotism*, Vol. III: *National Fictions*, p. 8.

37. Paxman, *The English*, p. 155. See Wiener, *English Culture and the Decline of the Industrial Spirit*, pp. 64–72, on the revived interest in old architecture.

38. Both quotes are from Ken Worpole, 'Village school or blackboard jungle?', in Samuel, *Patriotism*, Vol. III: *National Fictions*, p. 138. Richard Weight, however, claims that the Second World War was a period when rural and urban Britain came to understand each other better than ever before, while no one had any doubts that victory would be determined by industrial Britain. Weight, *Patriots*, pp. 72–5. For the general phenomenon of rural idealisation since the Industrial Revolution, see Wiener, *English Culture and the Decline of the Industrial Spirit*, chap. 4.

39. Rubinstein, *Capitalism, Culture, and Decline in Britain*, p. 61.

40. Philip Ziegler quoted in David Cannadine, 'The British Monarchy, c. 1820–1977', in Eric Hobsbawm and Terence Ranger, eds, *The Invention of Tradition* (Cambridge, New York: Cambridge University Press, 1983), p. 157.

41. The creation of a new monarchy around George III is explained in Colley, *Britons*, chap. 5, while the period after George III is laid out in Cannadine, 'The British Monarchy, c. 1820–1977', in Hobsbawm and Ranger, *The Invention of Tradition*, chap. 2.

42. Quoted in Tom Nairn, *The Enchanted Glass: Britain and its Monarchy* (London: Radius, 1988), p. 63.

43. Jeffrey Richards, 'The Hollywoodisation of Diana', in Jeffrey Richards, Scott Wilson and Linda Woodhead, eds, *Diana, The Making of a Media Saint* (London, New York: I. B. Tauris, 1999), p. 61.

44. This list is based on Crick, 'The English and the British', in Crick, *National Identities*, pp. 94–5; and the qualities identified by the German visitor Odett Kuen in 1934, cited in Paxman, *The English*, p. 132. But the person who most uncompromisingly asserts that there is nothing to English identity apart from what the aristocracy has tried to make it is Stephen Haseler, *The English Tribe: Identity, Nation and Europe* (Basingstoke: Macmillan; New York: St Martin's Press, 1996), *passim*.

45. Paxman, *The English*, p. 133.

46. Weight, *Patriots*, pp. 708–12.

47. Quoted in *ibid.*, p. 713.

48. Mica Nava, 'Diana and Race: Romance and the Reconfiguration of the Nation', p. 111; Jatinder Verma, 'Mourning Diana, Asian Style', p. 121; and Richard Johnson, 'Exemplary Differences: Mourning (and not Mourning) a Princess', pp. 33, 36, all in Adrian Kear, and Deborah Lynn Steinberg, eds, *Mourning Diana: Nation, Culture and the Performance of Grief* (London, New York: Routledge, 1999). Linda Woodhead, 'Diana and the Religion of the Heart', in Richards, Wilson and Woodhead, *Diana, The Making of a Media Saint*, p. 130.

Chapter 12. The New Liberalism

1. Peter Riddell, *The Thatcher Era – And its Legacy*, 2nd edition (Oxford, Cambridge, MA: Blackwell, 1991), pp. 2–3. Letwin, *Anatomy of Thatcherism*, pp. 33, 39–40.

2. See Max-Stephan Schulze and Nicholas Woodward, 'The Emergence of Rapid Inflation', in Coopey and Woodward, *Britain in the 1970s*, pp. 116–22; and Christopher Johnson, *The Economy Under Mrs. Thatcher 1979–1990* (Harmondsworth: Penguin, 1991), chap. 2. There is also no agreement that the public-sector borrowing requirement has any relationship to the growth of the money supply. See Christopher Allsopp, 'Macroeconomic Policy: Design and Performance', in Michael Artis and David Cobham, eds, *Labour's Economic Policies 1974–1979* (Manchester, New York: Manchester University Press, 1991), pp. 30–31, and David Cobham, 'Monetary Policy', in *ibid.*, pp. 43–6, 52–3.

3. The statistics are derived from Butler and Butler, *British Political Facts 1900–2000*, p. 411. The maximum is in Riddell, *The Thatcher Era*, p. 27. The wage increases of the 'winter of discontent', as well as the hike in VAT, contributed to the rise that began in 1979.

4. Eric J. Evans, *Thatcher and Thatcherism* (London, New York: Routledge, 1997), p. 20.

5. Riddell, *The Thatcher Era*, p. 27.

6. *Ibid.*, p. 26. Employment in manufacturing had been declining since the late 1960s, but the rate of decline was gradual until the 1980s.

7. Butler and Butler, *British Political Facts 1900–2000*, p. 401.

8. S. N. Broadberry, 'Unemployment', in Crafts and Woodward, *The British Economy since 1945*, p. 217. Dennis Kavanagh, *Thatcherism and British Politics: The End of Consensus?*, 2nd edition (Oxford, New York, etc.: Oxford University Press, 1990), p. 231. The years for comparison are chosen by Broadberry; both are when the economy was well into a recovery from the trough of the trade cycle.

9. Riddell, *The Thatcher Era*, p. 28. Evans says thirty-one changes; *Thatcher and Thatcherism*, p. 30.

10. Kavanagh estimates 600,000. Riddell guesses 400,000 unemployed not counted, plus another 350,000 on training schemes who were not counted. Kavanagh, *Thatcherism and British Politics*, p. 231; Riddell, *The Thatcher Era*, p. 29.

11. For a statistical study that shows the high psychological toll of unemployment in the 1980s, see Fogarty, 'British Attitudes to Work', in Abrams, Gerard and Timms, *Values in Britain*, pp. 186–8. See also, Eithne McLaughlin, 'Employment, Unemployment and Social Security', in Glyn and Miliband, *Paying for Inequality*, pp. 158–9.

12. Morgan, *The People's Peace*, pp. 190, 475. Martin Adeney and John Lloyd,

The Miners' Strike 1984–5: Loss Without Limit (London: Routledge, 1986), p. 14 (for 1970–71).

13. Crafts, 'Economic Growth', in Crafts and Woodward, *The British Economy since 1945*, p. 284. Total productivity measures the changes in productivity of capital as well as labour. However, Crafts says later that the improvement was not associated with increasing investment (i.e. improved capital productivity). See p. 285.

14. Riddell, *The Thatcher Era*, pp. 26, 40. Samuel Brittan, 'The Government's Economic Policy', in Dennis Kavanagh and Anthony Seldon, eds, *The Thatcher Effect* (Oxford, etc.: Clarendon Press, 1989), pp. 11–12. Brittan's overall productivity figure is 1.9 per cent over the period 1979–88.

15. Spending on housing did not fall as much as official figures implied. The government ended direct payments to local authorities to subsidise rents and buildings programmes: thus the fall in the housing budget. However, it introduced housing benefit, which came from the social security budget, to help the poor pay market rents, and some of that money went to local authorities who could use it for building. Lowe, *The Welfare State in Britain since 1945*, pp. 337–9.

16. Riddell, *The Thatcher Era*, pp. 32–5; Kavanagh, *Thatcherism and British Politics*, pp. 212–17, 227–9. The numbers in these two sources are not identical, but they are close enough. For example, Riddell's numbers for public spending between 1980 and 1984 are a projected 4 per cent cut and an actual 6.3 per cent increase. However, it is not clear that they are talking about exactly the same thing. The one significant exception is that Kavanagh's table on p. 213 indicates an *increase* of 73 per cent in spending on employment over the decade, which is surely a misprint; it should be a decrease.

17. Howard Glennerster, 'Welfare with the Lid On', in Glennerster and Hills, *The State of Welfare*, p. 309. The highest percentage under Labour was 25.9 per cent of GDP in 1975–6; the lowest was 23.7 per cent in 1978–9. After 1979–80, the Thatcher government did not go below that figure until 1987–8; its low was 21.6 per cent in 1989–90. Under Major, the percentage went back up to 26.6 per cent in 1993–4, before starting to go down again.

18. Diane Coyle, 'Is Brown mad or bad, or is it just that there really is no war chest?', *Independent* (on-line edition), 4 June 1998.

19. The poll tax was also a fiscal catastrophe that had the perverse effect of increasing public spending. It cost about £1.5 billion merely to set it up and then abolish it again. Beyond that, in order to make it politically palatable, the government added a complex system of rebates, exemptions and funds to subsidise the transition. These cost the Treasury approximately £20 billion by 1993. Jenkins, *Accountable to None*, p. 59.

20. John Kingdom, 'Centralisation and Fragmentation: John Major and the Reform of Local Government', in Peter Dorey, ed., *The Major Premiership: Politics and Policies under John Major, 1990–97* (London and Basingstoke: Macmillan; New York: St Martin's Press, 1999), pp. 49, 61–2. The local rate had covered over 50 per cent of spending in 1989–90.

21. Kavanagh, *Thatcherism and British Politics*, p. 230. Riddell, *The Thatcher Era*, p. 72.

22. Alastair Hetherington, 'The Mass Media', in Kavanagh and Seldon, *The Thatcher Effect*, pp. 290–93.

23. Adeney and Lloyd, *The Miners' Strike 1984–5*, p. 93.

24. Butler and Butler, *British Political Facts 1900–2000*, pp. 400–401.

25. J. Dunkerley and P. Hare, 'Nationalized Industries', in Crafts and Woodward, *The British Economy since 1945*, p. 394. See p. 393 for their description of the shipbuilding industry. For excellent brief histories of both industries, showing how they got that way, see Edward Lorenz and Frank Wilkinson, 'The Shipbuilding Industry, 1880–1965', and Wayne Lewchuk, 'The Motor Vehicle Industry', in Elbaum and Lazonick, *The Decline of the British Economy*. Barnett's *Audit of War* is as damning of British management between 1870 and 1945 as it is of the trade unions and the wartime government, and the implication (sometimes stated explicitly) throughout the later chapters is that nothing changed in the post-war years. See especially chapters 4–9 and 13.

26. Dunkerley and Hare, 'Nationalized Industries', in Crafts and Woodward, *The British Economy since 1945*, p. 409.

27. *Ibid.*, p. 408. Riddell, *The Thatcher Era*, p. 93.

28. Simon Jenkins argues that privatisation with regulation had one important advantage over the nationalised industries. All the pressures and lobbying and bargaining over policies and rates, which had always gone on behind closed doors, was now brought out into the open and became more public. As a result, people could see the bases on which decisions were made. Jenkins, *Accountable to None*, p. 38, and chap. 2 more generally.

29. Riddell, *The Thatcher Era*, pp. 118–19. It may well be that more than half of the new shareholders were not purchasers of shares in privatised corporations. Beginning in the 1980s, some of the building societies converted from mutual societies to public corporations. When the largest, the Abbey National, went public, some four million savers became shareholders, many for the first time. Johnson, *The Economy Under Mrs Thatcher*, pp. 169–70.

30. Jenkins, *Accountable to None*, p. 32.

31. Hills, 'Housing', in Glennerster and Hills, *The State of Welfare*, pp. 153,

185. Not all council houses were bought by sitting tenants. The total sold between 1979 and 1995 was 2.2 million, of which 1.7 million were bought by the tenant.

32. There were 345,000 repossessions from 1990 to 1996. In 1992, almost 1.8 million mortgage holders had houses that were worth less than their mortgages. *Ibid.*, p. 176.

33. Nicholas Timmins, *The Five Giants: A Biography of the Welfare State*, new edition (London: HarperCollins, 2001), pp. 400–401. 'In Brief' (Finance), *Guardian Weekly*, 7–13 December 2000, p. 17.

34. This is the interpretation presented in Wiener, *English Culture and the Decline of the Industrial Spirit 1850–1980, passim*, which is discussed in chapters 1 and 5 above. For the rise of this professional ethic and class, see Perkin, *The Rise of Professional Society*. For a more systematic and quantitative discussion of the educational background of Britain's post-war elite than Sampson offers, see Scott, *The Upper Classes*, pp. 158–75.

35. Evans, *Thatcher and Thatcherism*, p. 55. The numbers fell from 732,000 to 567,000 by 1990, and then to 476,000 by Major's fall in 1997. Dennis Kavanagh, *The Reordering of British Politics: Politics after Thatcher* (Oxford, New York, etc.: Oxford University Press, 1997), p. 123. Kevin Theakston, 'A Permanent Revolution in Whitehall: the Major Governments and the Civil Service', in Dorey, *The Major Premiership*, pp. 28, 38–9. John Willman, 'The Civil Service', in Dennis Kavanagh and Anthony Seldon, *The Major Effect* (London: Macmillan, 1994), pp. 79–80.

36. Graham Zellick, 'The Law', in Kavanagh and Seldon, *The Thatcher Effect*, p. 288.

37. 'Blair's End-of-Term Report: Can Do Better' (review of *Did Things Get Better? An Audit of Labour's Successes and Failures*, by Polly Toynbee and David Walker), *Guardian Weekly*, 29 March–4 April 2001, p. 15.

38. Middleton, *British Economy since 1945*, pp. 36, 38, 77. According to Middleton, Britain's spending as a percentage of GDP in the 1990s was 5–10 per cent below that of its principal EU partners. *Ibid.*, pp. 82, 110.

39. Niall Ferguson, 'Britain's Bloodless Race for C.E.O.', *New York Times*, 30 May 2001, p. A23.

40. Timmins, *The Five Giants*, p. 613.

41. Jon Henley, 'France serves up first-class treatment – but at a price', *Guardian*, 21 June 2000. Lucy Ward, 'Blair gets tough with doctors', *ibid.*, 5 June 2000.

42. 'In Brief', *Guardian Weekly*, 20–26 January 2000, p. 9. Will Hutton, 'War-chest of pirate treasure', *Observer* (on-line edition), 26 March 2000.

43. Larry Elliott and Rebecca Smithers, 'Successful sell-off or cynical sell-out?,' *Guardian* (on-line edition), 7 October 1999. According to *The Economist*, the 1998–9 profits of the rail companies represented roughly a 20 per cent rate of return.

44. *Independent* (on-line edition), 23 July 1998 (article on government plans to regulate the salaries of managers and directors of privatised utilities). Nicholas Bannister, 'Regulator orders £38 cut in water bills', *Guardian* (on-line edition), 28 July 1999. David Walker, 'Don't tell Sid', *ibid.*, 16 June 2000.

45. At the time of writing, Railtrack has been taken over by the government, but it is not clear what long-term solution it is going to offer.

46. The 1.8 per cent is from Dennis Kavanagh, *The Reordering of British Politics*, p. 121. The 2.1 per cent is from Middleton, *British Economy since 1945*, p. 86. The figure for 1992–2000 is an average of 2.6 per cent for 1992–7 and 2.8 per cent for 1997–2000 in Larry Elliott, 'Britain must tackle its growing deficit', *Guardian Weekly*, 10–16 May 2001, p. 14. Measuring from 1992 to 2000 exaggerates growth, since it is from near the trough of a recession to near the peak of an expansion. Middleton's is the most recent book, and his table on p. 86 actually shows an annual average growth rate of GDP for 1951–64 of 2.9 per cent, while that for 1964–70 is 2.5 per cent and those for the 1970s are 2.8 per cent for 1970–74 and 2.1 per cent for 1974–9. These rates are difficult to reconcile with Woodward and Crafts's 1.3 per cent for 1973–9. But it seems very clear that the Conservative record was no better than that of the 1960s, may well have been worse and may not even have been significantly better than the 1970s.

47. Riddell, *The Thatcher Era*, p. 39. Larry Elliott, 'El Dorado or bust for Gordon Brown', *Guardian Weekly*, 11–17 November 1999, p. 16.

48. Middleton, *British Economy since 1945*, p. 86.

49. Riddell, *The Thatcher Era*, p. 39. Leslie Hannah, 'The Economic Consequences of the State Ownership of Industry, 1945–1990', in Floud and McCloskey, *Economic History of Britain since 1700*, 2nd edition; Vol. 3: *1939–1992*, p. 183. Article commenting on British Steel in the Business section, *Independent* (on-line edition), 16 June 1998.

50. Middleton, *British Economy since 1945*, p. 36. For the comparison with other industrialised countries, based on the percentage of the labour force employed in industry in 1989, see Barry Supple, 'Fear of Failing: Economic History and the Decline of Britain', in Clarke and Trebilcock, *Understanding Decline*, p. 24.

51. Ed Crooks, 'Britain hopes for economic immunity', *Financial Times*, 4 April 2001, p. 15.

52. Supple, 'Fear of Failing', in Clarke and Trebilcock, *Understanding Decline*, pp. 4–5. The percentages are as follows: Britain 1.7 per cent, the United States 1.5 per cent, France 1.6 per cent, Germany 1.8 per cent and Japan 2.6 per cent. It is worth remembering that even in the period before 1973, the United States was comparable to Britain; see Table 5.3.

53. *Ibid.*, pp. 31, 33.

54. 'In Brief', *Guardian Weekly*, 16–22 March 2000, p. 12. Charlotte Denny, 'UK "could join euro at DM3"' *Guardian* (on-line edition), 10 January 2000. In 1998, Britain moved 'from seventh to fourth place in world competitiveness'. David Brierley, 'Our miracle economy is fading before our eyes', *Independent on Sunday* (on-line edition), 7 June 1998.

55. Riddell, *The Thatcher Era*, pp. 53, 75–6.

56. Middleton, *British Economy since 1945*, pp. 56–7.

57. This is the judgement of Middleton, *ibid.*, p. 47. He also claims that it is not at all clear that Britain gets greater comparative productivity in services (i.e. Britain's productivity problems may be the same in the service sector as in the industrial sector). Tweedale points out that there is disagreement over whether services are 'less desirable' than manufacturing, but seems to come down on the side that they are. See 'Industry and De-industrialisation in the 1970s', in Coopey and Woodward, *Britain in the 1970s*, pp. 269–70. The figures on output since 1995 come from Crooks, 'Britain hopes for economic immunity', *Financial Times*, 4 April 2001, p. 15.

58. Elliott, 'El Dorado or bust for Gordon Brown', *Guardian Weekly*, 11–17 November 1999, p. 16.

59. Andreas Whittam Smith, article on British entrepreneurship, *Independent* (on-line edition), 9 June 1998. Lee Elliot Major, 'Hey, big spenders', *Guardian* (on-line edition), 24 May 2000. A lot of the investment in California has now gone down the drain with the collapse of the technology boom. The same boom also inflated figures for the United States as a whole in the 1990s.

60. Major, 'Hey, big spenders', *Guardian* (on-line edition), 24 May 2000.

61. Riddell, *The Thatcher Era*, pp. 155–6. James Lewis, 'New report reveals Tories' poor record', *Guardian Weekly*, 20–26 January 2000, p. 8 ('The Week in Britain').

62. Philip Johnston, 'New report dismisses claim that poor are getting poorer', *Electronic Telegraph*, 23 May 1997.

Chapter 13. America or Europe?

1. Paul Sharp, *Thatcher's Diplomacy: The Revival of British Foreign Policy* (Basingstoke: Macmillan; New York: St Martin's Press, 1997), pp. 27–8.

2. The estimated cost of the war (including the lost ships and planes) was £1.6 billion; the estimated cost, including the cost of holding the islands for the next four years after the war, ran to £2 billion. Max Hastings and Simon Jenkins, *The Battle for the Falklands* (New York, London: W. W. Norton, 1983), p. 319.

3. For example, in 1960 Australia alone had accounted for 7 per cent of British exports and 4 per cent of imports; by 1981, those numbers had

fallen to 1.7 and 0.8 per cent respectively. Gerald Segal, 'Asia and the Pacific', in Peter Byrd, ed., *British Foreign Policy under Thatcher* (Oxford: Philip Allan; New York: St Martin's Press, 1988), p. 129.

4. Sharp, *Thatcher's Diplomacy*, p. 78.

5. Dan Keohane, *Labour Party Defence Policy since 1945* (Leicester: Leicester University Press, 1993), p. 20.

6. By comparison, France was spending about 4 per cent of GDP on defence, and West Germany 3.3 per cent. Peter Byrd, 'Defence Policy', in Byrd, *British Foreign Policy under Thatcher*, p. 171.

7. Hugo Young, *One of Us: A Biography of Margaret Thatcher* (London: Macmillan, 1989), p. 393. No one at the time could have predicted that Gorbachev would succeed to the leadership in the Soviet Union.

8. Martin Wolf, 'Farmer should go to market', in the *Financial Times*, 4 April 2001, p. 15. According to the OECD, prices were increased by 40 per cent from 1986 to 1988, 25 per cent in 1997 and 36 per cent in 1999.

9. Stephen George and Matthew Sowemimo, 'Conservative Foreign Policy towards the European Union', in Ludlam and Smith, *Contemporary British Conservatism*, p. 252.

10. Weight, *Patriots*, p. 633. Ridley was forced to resign as Minister for the Environment as a result of his remarks.

11. Gorbachev secured other concessions in lieu of German neutrality: NATO troops would not be stationed in the former East Germany, while Soviet troops could remain another three years, and the size of the German army was to be limited.

12. Jim Buller, 'Foreign and Defence Policy under Thatcher and Major', in Ludlam and Smith, *Contemporary British Conservatism*, p. 236. Paul Laurent, 'The Costs of Defence', in Croft, p. 91. As a reminder, the previous scale of spending was as high as 9 per cent of GDP in the early 1950s, 6–7 per cent in the 1960s, 4.7 per cent in 1978–9, and 5.4 per cent in 1983–4.

13. The projected 1996 defence spending was around 3 per cent of GDP, which is in the range of where it was before the First World War and between the wars. Lawrence Freedman, 'Defence Policy', in Kavanagh and Seldon, *The Major Effect*, pp. 272–3.

14. Young, *Britain and European Unity*, p. 196.

Chapter 14. A New Consensus?

1. Barnett, *The Audit of War*, p. 18.

2. Quoted in Kavanagh, *The Reordering of British Politics*, p. 10. For the 'softer virtues', see chap. 12 and Letwin, *Anatomy of Thatcherism*, p. 33.

3. Tiratsoo and Tomlinson, *The Conservatives and Industrial Efficiency, 1951–64*, chaps 1, 7.

4. Ramsden, *Winds of Change, passim.*

5. Obituary of Powell, *Daily Telegraph* (on-line edition), 9 February 1998. Fergus Pyle, Review of Robert Shepherd, *Enoch Powell: A Biography*, in the *Irish Times* (on-line edition), 7 November 1996, in 'Features'. Despite Thatcher's 'Powellite' economic policies, Powell attacked her too, because of her support for the special relationship with the United States, her support for the nuclear deterrent and her support of the Single European Act.

6. Young, *One of Us*, p. 242.

7. Jenkins, *Accountable to None*, p. 12. For specific instances, see pp. 36–7, 67, 74–5.

8. Mark Hoffman, 'From Conformity to Confrontation: Security and Arms Control in the Thatcher Years', in Stuart Croft, ed., *British Security Policy: The Thatcher Years and the End of the Cold War* (London: HarperCollins, 1991), p. 74.

9. The British dead were one-third of the numbers killed in the Korean War and one hundred fewer than those killed in Northern Ireland between 1969 and 1983. The immediate cost, including the lost planes and ships, was about £1.6 billion; but that does not include the cost of defending and supplying the Falklands for years after the war. Hastings and Jenkins, *The Battle for the Falklands*, pp. 318–19.

10. The British benefited from the unwillingness of Argentine commanders in any of the three services to risk serious losses, especially after the sinking of the *Belgrano*; the reliance of the occupying force on untrained conscripts; and the failure of the Argentines to provide adequate supplies of food and warm clothes for the soldiers on the islands, resulting in disastrously low morale.

11. This judgement is based on the percentage swing from Labour to the Conservatives and Labour's share of the total vote, not on the number of MPs elected. Crewe, 'Why the Conservatives Won', in Penniman, *Britain at the Polls, 1979*, pp. 296–7.

12. Duncan Tanner argues that their numbers have been exaggerated, not least by a Tory press that had an interest in doing so, but also by Labour historians. Duncan Tanner, 'Labour and Its Membership', in Tanner, Thane and Tiratsoo, *Labour's First Century*, pp. 263–6.

13. Among Labour voters, Healey got 36 per cent, Williams 14, Tony Benn 15 and Michael Foot 14 per cent. Among Labour defectors it was Healey 20 per cent, Williams 27, Benn 8 and Foot 5; and among trade unionists it was Healey 26, Williams 17, Benn 12 and Foot 9. Crewe, 'Why the Conservatives Won', in Penniman, *Britain at the Polls, 1979*, p. 302.

14. John Stevenson, *Third Party Politics since 1945: Liberals, Alliance and Liberal Democrats* (Oxford: Basil Blackwell, 1993), p. 82.

15. Butler and Butler, *British Political Facts 1900–2000*, p. 238.

16. Letwin, *Anatomy of Thatcherism*, p. 184.

17. Butler and Butler, *British Political Facts 1900–2000*, pp. 238–9.

18. See Patrick Seyd and Paul Whitely, 'Conservative Grassroots: An Overview', in Ludlam and Smith, *Contemporary British Conservatism*, p. 81.

19. Ivor Crewe, 'Electoral Behaviour', in Kavanagh and Seldon, *The Major Effect*, pp. 103, 105. David Sanders, 'Why the Conservative Party Won – Again', in Anthony King, Ivor Crewe, *et al.*, eds, *Britain at the Polls 1992* (Chatham, NJ: Chatham House Publishers, 1992), pp. 197–210.

20. Hugo Young, 'The Prime Minister', in Kavanagh and Seldon, *The Major Effect*, p. 21.

21. Butler and Butler, *British Political Facts 1900–2000*, p. 239.

22. See, for example, Kavanagh, *The Reordering of British Politics*, p. 116.

23. Steve Ludlam, 'The Spectre Haunting Conservatism: Europe and Backbench Rebellion', in Ludlam and Smith, *Contemporary British Conservatism*, p. 120.

24. *Ibid.*, pp. 104–5.

25. Crewe, 'Electoral Behaviour', in Kavanagh and Seldon, *The Major Effect*, pp. 109–13. Charles Pattie and Ron Johnston, 'The Conservative Party and the Electorate', in Ludlam and Smith, *Contemporary British Conservatism*, p. 61.

26. Kingdom, 'Centralisation and Fragmentation', in Dorey, *The Major Premiership*, p. 64. No party had a majority in the remaining 195 local authorities.

27. Editorial policy was set by the editors; but mostly the editors (including those of the *Sunday Times* and *Sunday Telegraph*) held views similar to those of the proprietor. Eventually, both of the *Telegraph* papers and the *Sunday Times* endorsed Major in 1997, while *The Times* endorsed Eurosceptic candidates (which would mostly favour the Tories). Of the papers mentioned, only the *Sun* supported Labour. See Anthony Seldon, *Major: A Political Life* (London: Weidenfeld & Nicolson, 1977), pp. 707–11.

28. Eric Shaw, *The Labour Party since 1979: Crisis and Transformation* (London, New York: Routledge, 1994), p. 174.

29. Eric Shaw, *The Labour Party since 1945: Old Labour, New Labour* (Oxford, Cambridge, MA: Blackwell, 1996), p. 199.

30. Butler and Butler, *British Political Facts 1900–2000*, p. 239.

31. The Liberal Democrats' share of the vote actually fell slightly, from 17.8 per cent in 1992 to 16.8 per cent in 1997.

32. The London mayoral election was conducted on a preferential ballot system, called the single transferable vote, in which people indicated

their second choice if their first choice was already eliminated. Thus, the ballots of all but the top two vote-getters were redistributed to the second choice. The results of the first choice ballots were: Ken Livingstone (Independent), 40.3 per cent; Stephen Norris (Conservative), 25.7 per cent; Frank Dobson (Labour), 13.8 per cent; and Susan Kramer (Liberal Democrat), 11.2 per cent. There were several other candidates.

33. See Veldman, *Fantasy, the Bomb, and the Greening of Britain*, p. 3 and *passim*.

Conclusion. The Audit of Peace

1. Howard W. French, 'In Stagnant Japan, Economic And Social Ills Match', *New York Times*, 6 February 2001, p. A1.
2. *Ibid.*, p. A8.
3. Indeed, one benefit of the prolonged malaise of the Japanese economy has been falling prices, which are approaching the level of the more expensive Western cities like London and New York.
4. Brown, *Britain and Japan*, p. 206.
5. Howard W. French, 'Hypothesis: A Scientific Gap; Conclusion: Japanese Custom', *New York Times*, 7 August 2001, pp. A1, A6; 'Fighting Molestation, And A Stigma, In Japan', *ibid.*, 15 July 2001, pp. A1, A10. James Brooke, 'Accelerating Decline In Japan Evokes Rust Belt Comparisons', *ibid.*, 31 August 2001, pp. A1, C2. Many of the comparisons come from Brown, *Britain and Japan, passim.*
6. Edmund L. Andrews, 'Germany Looks Like Europe's Weak Economic Link', *New York Times*, 28 April 2001, p. B2.
7. These judgements are based on the table in Middleton, *British Economy since 1945*, p. 86. However, Middleton organises his table according to the party in power; thus he blocks the whole period 1979–97 together. This grouping does not pay adequate due to the success of the Major government in getting the economy going again, the full benefits of which became more evident under the present Labour government. Thus, I assume a higher growth rate, lower inflation rate and lower average level of unemployment for the whole two decades than the numbers in his table.
8. Quoted in Ovendale, *Anglo-American Relations in the Twentieth Century*, p. 130.
9. *Ibid.*
10. Susanne Greenhalgh, 'Our Lady of Flowers: The Ambiguous Politics of Diana's Floral Revolution', in Kear and Steinberg, *Mourning Diana*, p. 42. Scott Wilson, 'The Misfortunes of Virtue: Diana, the Press and

the Politics of Emotion', in Richards, Wilson and Woodhead, *Diana, The Making of a Media Saint*, p. 48.

11. Richard Pells, *Not Like Us: How Europeans Have Loved, Hated, and Transformed American Culture since World War II* (New York: Basic Books, 1997), pp. 202–3.

12. Richards, Wilson and Woodhead, *Diana, The Making of a Media Saint*, p. 8.

13. Halsey, *Change in British Society*, p. 30.

14. Kumar, 'Social and Cultural Setting', in Ford, *The Present*, p. 58.

15. This is the argument of Adonis and Pollard, *A Class Act, passim.*

16. The journal the *Reasoner*, September 1956, quoted in Veldman, *Fantasy, the Bomb, and the Greening of Britain*, p. 181.

SELECT BIBLIOGRAPHY

Newspapers

Economist
Financial Times
Guardian
Guardian Weekly
Independent
New York Times
The Times (London)
Wall Street Journal

On-Line Newspapers

Guardian (News Unlimited)
Independent
Irish Times
Observer (News Unlimited)
Telegraph (Electronic Telegraph)
The Times (London)

Books

Abrams, Mark, Gerard, David and Timms, Noel, eds. *Values and Social Change in Britain*. Basingstoke: Macmillan, 1985

Acheson, James, ed. *British and Irish Drama since 1960*. Basingstoke: Macmillan; New York: St Martin's Press, 1993

Adeney, Martin, and Lloyd, John. *The Miners' Strike 1984–5: Loss without Limit*. London: Routledge, 1986

Adonis, Andrew, and Pollard, Stephen. *A Class Act: The Myth of Britain's Classless Society*. London: Hamish Hamilton, 1997

Aldcroft, Derek H. *Education, Training and Economic Performance, 1944–1990*. Manchester, New York: Manchester University Press, 1992

Alford, B. W. E. *British Economic Performance 1945–1975*. Cambridge: Cambridge University Press, 1995

Alibhai-Brown, Yasmin. *Imagining the New Britain*. New York: Routledge, 2001

Arnold, Matthew. *Culture and Anarchy*. Cambridge: Cambridge University Press, 1960

Arnstein, Walter L. *Recent Historians of Great Britain: Essays on the Post-1945 Generation*. Ames, Ia: Iowa State University Press, 1990

Arthur, Paul, and Jeffrey, Keith. *Northern Ireland since 1968*, 2nd edition. Oxford, Cambridge, MA: Blackwell, 1996

Artis, Michael, and Cobham, David, eds. *Labour's Economic Policies 1974–1979*. Manchester, New York: Manchester University Press, 1991

Bagehot, Walter. *The English Constitution*. Ithaca, NY: Cornell University Press, 1966

Ball, Michael, Gray, Fred, and McDowell, Linda. *The Transformation of Britain: Contemporary Social and Economic Change*. London: Fontana, 1989

Ball, Stuart, and Seldon, Anthony, eds. *The Heath Government, 1970–1974: A Reappraisal*. London, New York: Longman, 1996

Banfield, Stephen, ed. *Music in Britain:* Vol. 6, *The Twentieth Century*. Oxford, Cambridge, MA: Blackwell, 1995

Banks, Olive. *The Politics of British Feminism, 1918–1970*. Aldershot, Brookfield, VT: Edward Elgar, 1993

Barnett, Corelli. *The Audit of War: The Illusion and Reality of Britain as a Great Nation*. London: Macmillan, 1986

Barraclough, Geoffrey. *An Introduction to Contemporary History*. London: Penguin, 1967

Barry, Peter. *Beginning Theory: An Introduction to Literary and Cultural Theory*, 2nd edition. Manchester, New York: Manchester University Press, 2002

Bartlett, C. J. '*The Special Relationship': A Political History of Anglo-American Relations since 1945*. London, New York: Longman, 1992

Baylis, John. *Anglo-American Defence Relations, 1939–1984: The Special Relationship*. New York: St Martin's Press, 1984

Beer, Samuel H. *British Politics in the Collectivist Age*. New York: Vintage Books, 1969

Bernstein, George L. 'Liberals, the Irish Famine and the Role of the State', *Irish Historical Studies*, XXIX, 116 (November 1995), pp. 513–36

Bigsby, C. W. E., ed. *Contemporary English Drama*. London: Edward Arnold, 1981

Blackaby, F. T, ed. *British Economic Policy 1960–74*. Cambridge: Cambridge University Press, 1978

Blake, Andrew. *The Land without Music: Music, Culture and Society in Twentieth-Century Britain*. Manchester, New York: Manchester University Press, 1997

Bogdanor, Vernon, and Skidelsky, Robert, eds. *The Age of Affluence 1951–1964*. London, Basingstoke: Macmillan, 1970

Bouchier, David. *The Feminist Challenge: The Movement for Women's Liberation in Britain and the USA*. New York: Schocken, 1984

Bourke, Joanna. *Working-Class Cultures in Britain 1890–1960: Gender, Class, and Ethnicity*. London, New York: Routledge, 1994

Boyle, Kevin, and Hadden, Tom. *Northern Ireland: The Choice*. Harmondsworth: Penguin, 1994

Bradbury, Malcolm. *The Modern British Novel*. London: Secker & Warburg, 1993

Brake, Michael. *Comparative Youth Culture: The Sociology of Youth Cultures and Youth Subcultures in America, Britain, and Canada*. London, Boston, etc.: Routledge & Kegan Paul, 1985

The British Imagination: Twentieth-Century Paintings, Sculpture, and Drawings, with an Introduction by Edward Lucie-Smith. New York: Hirschl & Adler Galleries, 1990

Brown, Judith M., and Louis, Wm Roger, eds. *The Oxford History of the British Empire*, Vol. IV: *The Twentieth Century*. Oxford, New York: Oxford University Press, 1999

Brown, Kenneth D. *Britain and Japan: A Comparative Economic and Social History since 1900*. Manchester, New York: Manchester University Press, 1998

Bullock, Alan. *Ernest Bevin: Foreign Secretary, 1945–1951*. London: Heinemann, 1983

Burnett, John. *A Social History of Housing 1815–1985*, 2nd edition. London, New York: Methuen, 1986

Butler, David, and Butler, Gareth. *Twentieth-Century British Political Facts 1900–2000*, 8th edition. Basingstoke: Macmillan; New York: St Martin's Press, 2000

Butler, David, and Kavanagh, Dennis. *The British General Election of February 1974*. New York: St Martin's Press, 1974

—. *The British General Election of October 1974*. Basingstoke: Macmillan, 1975

—. *The British General Election of 1979*. Basingstoke: Macmillan, 1980

—. *The British General Election of 1983*. New York: St Martin's Press, 1984

—. *The British General Election of 1987*. New York: St Martin's Press, 1988

—. *The British General Election of 1997*. Basingstoke: Macmillan; New York: St Martin's Press, 1997

Byrd, Peter, ed. *British Foreign Policy under Thatcher*. Oxford: Philip Allan; New York: St Martin's Press, 1988

Cain, P. J., and Hopkins, A. G. *British Imperialism: Crisis and Deconstruction 1914–1990*. London, New York: Longman, 1993

Cairncross, Alec. *The British Economy since 1945: Economic Policy and Performance, 1945–1995*, 2nd edition. Oxford: Blackwell, 1995

Caldwell, John. *The Oxford History of English Music.* Vol. II: *From c. 1715 to the Present Day.* Oxford, New York: Oxford University Press, 1999

Campbell, Colin. *The Romantic Ethic and the Spirit of Modern Consumerism.* Oxford, Cambridge, MA: Blackwell, 1987

Campbell, John. *Aneurin Bevan and the Mirage of British Socialism.* New York, London: W. W. Norton, 1987

—. *Edward Heath: A Biography.* London: Jonathan Cape, 1993

Cannadine, David. *The Decline and Fall of the British Aristocracy.* New Haven, London: Yale University Press, 1990

—. *The Rise and Fall of Class in Britain.* New York: Columbia University Press, 1999

Carlton, David. *Anthony Eden: A Biography.* London: Allen Lane, 1981

—. *Britain and the Suez Crisis.* Oxford: Basil Blackwell, 1988

Cashmore, E. Ellis. *No Future: Youth and Society.* Aldershot: Gower, 1985

—. *United Kingdom?: Class, Race, and Gender since the War.* London, etc.: Unwin Hyman, 1989

Cashmore, Ernest. *Rastaman: The Rastafarian Movement in England.* London, Boston, Sydney: Unwin Paperbacks, 1979

Chalmers, Malcolm. *Paying for Defence: Military Spending and British Decline.* London, Sydney: Pluto Press, 1985

Charmley, John. *Churchill's Grand Alliance: The Anglo-American Special Relationship 1940–57.* New York, San Diego, London: Harcourt Brace, 1995

Childs, David. *Britain since 1945: A Political History*, 3rd edition. London, New York: Routledge, 1992

Churchill, Randolph S. *Winston S. Churchill*, Vol. II: *Young Statesman, 1901–1914.* Boston: Houghton Mifflin, 1967

Churchill, Winston S. *The Second World War*, Vol. 1: *The Gathering Storm;* Vol. 2: *Their Finest Hour.* Boston: Houghton Mifflin, 1948, 1949

Clark, David, ed. *Marriage, Domestic Life and Social Change: Writings for Jacqueline Burgoyne (1944–88).* London, New York: Routledge, 1991.

Clarke, J., Critcher, C. and Johnson, R., eds. *Working Class Culture: Studies in History and Theory.* New York: St Martin's Press, 1980

Clarke, Peter. *Hope and Glory: Britain 1900–1990.* Harmondsworth: Penguin, 1996

Clarke, Peter, and Treblicock, Clive, eds. *Understanding Decline: Perceptions and Realities of British Economic Performance.* Cambridge: Cambridge University Press, 1997

Coakley, Jerry, and Harris, Laurence. *The City of Capital: London's Role as a Financial Centre.* Oxford: Blackwell, 1983

Coates, David. *The Question of UK Decline: The Economy, State and Society.* Hemel Hempstead: Harvester Wheatsheaf, 1994

Cohen, Stanley. *Folk Devils and Moral Panics: The Creation of the Mods and Rockers*. New York: St Martin's Press, 1980

Colley, Linda. *Britons: Forging the Nation 1707–1837*. New Haven, London: Yale University Press, 1992

Collings, Matthew. *Blimey! From Bohemia to Britpop: The London Artworld from Francis Bacon to Damien Hirst*, 4th edition. London: 21 Publishing Ltd, 1998

Collins, Bruce, and Robbins, Keith, eds. *British Culture and Economic Decline*. London: Weidenfeld & Nicolson, 1990

Colls, Robert, and Dodd, Philip, eds. *Englishness: Politics and Culture 1880–1920*. London, Sydney, etc.: Croom Helm, 1986

Compton, Susan, ed. *British Art in the 20th Century: The Modern Movement*. Munich: Prestel-Verlag, 1986

Coopey, R., Fielding, S., and Tiratsoo, N., eds. *The Wilson Governments 1964–1970*. London, New York: Pinter, 1993

Coopey, Richard, and Woodward, Nicholas. *Britain in the 1970s: The Troubled Decade*. New York: St Martin's Press, 1996

Corcoran, Neil. *English Poetry since 1940*. London, New York: Longman, 1993

Coupland, Sir Reginald. *Welsh and Scottish Nationalism: A Study*. London: Collins, 1954

Crafts, N. F. R., and Woodward, Nicholas, eds. *The British Economy since 1945*. Oxford: Clarendon Press, 1991

Crafts, Nicholas. *Britain's Relative Economic Decline: 1870–1995: A Quantitative Perspective*. London: The Social Market Foundation, 1997

Crick, Bernard, ed. *National Identities: The Constitution of the United Kingdom*. Oxford, Cambridge, MA: Blackwell, 1991

Croft, Stuart, ed. *British Security Policy: The Thatcher Years and the End of the Cold War*. London: HarperCollins, 1991

Croft, Stuart, Dorman, Andrew, Rees, Win, and Uttley, Matthew. *Britain and Defence 1945–2000: A Policy Re-evaluation*. Harlow: Longman, 2001

Crowther, J. G. *Science in Modern Society*. New York: Schocken, 1968

Cunningham, Michael J. *British Government Policy in Northern Ireland 1969–89: Its Nature and Execution*. Manchester, New York: Manchester University Press, 1991

Curtis, Tony, ed. *Wales: The Imagined Nation. Studies in Cultural and National Identity*. Bridgend: Poetry Wales Press, 1986

Darby, Phillip. *British Defence Policy East of Suez 1947–1968*. London: Oxford University Press, 1973

Darwin, John. *Britain and Decolonisation: The Retreat from Empire in the Post-War World*. New York: St Martin's Press, 1988

—. *The End of the British Empire: The Historical Debate*. Oxford: Basil Blackwell, 1991

Davie, Grace. *Religion in Britain since 1945: Believing without Belonging.* Oxford, Cambridge, MA: Blackwell, 1994

Davies, Charlotte Aull. *Welsh Nationalism in the Twentieth Century: The Ethnic Option and the Modern State.* New York, Westport, London: Praeger, 1989

Davies, Christie. *Permissive Britain: Social Change in the Sixties and Seventies.* London: Pitman, 1975

Davies, John. *A History of Wales.* London: Allen Lane, The Penguin Press, 1993

Davis, John. *Youth and the Condition of Britain: Images of Adolescent Conflict.* London, Atlantic Highlands, NJ: Athlone Press, 1990

Davis, Lance E., and Huttenback, Robert A. *Mammon and the Pursuit of Empire: The Economics of British Imperialism,* abridged edition. Cambridge, etc.: Cambridge University Press, 1988

DePorte, A. W. *Europe between the Super-Powers: The Enduring Balance,* 2nd edition. New Haven, London: Yale University Press, 1986

Devine, Fiona. *Social Class in America and Britain.* Edinburgh: Edinburgh University Press, 1997.

Devine, T. M. *The Scottish Nation 1700–2000.* London: Penguin, 2000

Dintenfass, Michael. *The Decline of Industrial Britain 1870–1980.* London, New York: Routledge, 1992

Dobson, Alan P. *The Politics of the Anglo-American Economic Special Relationship, 1940–1987.* Brighton: Wheatsheaf; New York: St Martin's Press, 1988

Dockrill, Michael. *British Defence since 1945.* Oxford: Basil Blackwell, 1988

Dockrill, Michael, and Young, John W., eds. *British Foreign Policy, 1945–56.* New York: St Martin's Press, 1989

Dorey, Peter. *British Politics since 1945.* Oxford, Cambridge, MA: Blackwell, 1995

—, ed. *The Major Premiership: Politics and Policies under John Major, 1990–97.* London and Basingstoke: Macmillan; New York: St Martin's Press, 1999

Dormois, Jean-Pierre, and Dintenfass, Michael, eds. *The British Industrial Decline.* London, New York: Routledge, 1999

Doyle, Brian. *English and Englishness.* London, New York: Routledge, 1989

Drabble, Margaret. *The Ice Age.* London: Penguin, 1977

Driver, Stephen, and Martell, Luke. *New Labour: Politics after Thatcherism.* Cambridge: Polity Press, 1998

Dumbrell, John. *A Special Relationship: Anglo-American Relations in the Cold War and After.* Basingstoke: Macmillan; New York: St Martin's Press, 2001

Dutton, David. *British Politics since 1945: The Rise and Fall of Consensus.* Oxford: Basil Blackwell, 1991

—. *Anthony Eden: A Life and Reputation.* London, New York, etc.: Arnold, 1997

Edgerton, David. *Science, Technology and the British Industrial 'Decline', 1870–1970.* Cambridge: Cambridge University Press, 1996

Edmonds, Robin. *Setting the Mould: The United States and Britain, 1945–1950.* Oxford: Clarendon Press, 1986

Eksteins, Modris. *Rites of Spring: The Great War and the Birth of the Modern Age.* New York, London, etc.: Doubleday, 1989

Elbaum, Bernard, and Lazonick, William, eds. *The Decline of the British Economy.* Oxford: Clarendon Press, 1986

Eldridge, John, and Eldridge, Lizzie. *Raymond Williams: Making Connections.* London, New York: Routledge, 1994

Elsom, John. *Post-War British Theatre.* London, Boston: Routledge & Kegan Paul, 1976

English, Richard, and Kenny, Michael, eds. *Rethinking British Decline.* London: Macmillan; New York: St Martin's Press, 2000

Evans, Brendan. *Thatcherism and British Politics 1975–1999.* Stroud: Sutton Publishing, 1999

Evans, D. Gareth. *A History of Wales 1906–2000.* Cardiff: University of Wales Press, 2000

Evans, Eric J. *Thatcher and Thatcherism.* London, New York: Routledge, 1997

Evans, Neil, ed. *National Identity in the British Isles.* Coleg Harlech: 1989

Fairlie, Henry. *The Spoiled Child of the Western World: The Miscarriage of the American Idea in Our Time.* New York: Doubleday, 1976

Fevre, Ralph, and Thompson, Andrew, eds. *Nation, Identity and Social Theory: Perspectives from Wales.* Cardiff: University of Wales Press, 1999

Fielding, Steven, Thompson, Peter, and Tiratsoo, Nick. *'England Arise!' The Labour Party and Popular Politics in 1940s Britain.* Manchester, New York: Manchester University Press, 1995

Floud, Roderick, and McCloskey, Donald, eds. *The Economic History of Britain since 1700,* Vol. 2: *1860 to the 1970s.* Cambridge, etc.: Cambridge University Press, 1981

—. *The Economic History of Britain since 1700,* 2nd edition; Vol. 3: *1939–1992.* Cambridge: Cambridge University Press, 1994

Foner, Eric. *Reconstruction: America's Unfinished Revolution, 1863–1877.* New York: Harper & Row, 1988

Ford, Boris, ed. *The New Pelican Guide to English Literature,* Vol. 8: *The Present.* Harmondsworth: Penguin, 1983

Forrester, Tom. *The Labour Party and the Working Class.* London: Heinemann, 1976

Frankel, Joseph. *British Foreign Policy, 1945–73.* London, New York, Toronto: Oxford University Press, 1975

Freedman, Lawrence. *Britain and the Falklands War.* Oxford, New York: Basil Blackwell, 1988

Frith, Simon. *Sound Effects: Youth, Leisure, and the Politics of Rock 'n' Roll.* New York: Pantheon Books, 1981

Frith, Simon, and Horne, Howard. *Art into Pop*. London, New York: Methuen Books, 1987

Gaggi, Silvio. *Modern/Postmodern: A Study in Twentieth-Century Arts and Ideas*. Philadelphia: University of Pennsylvania Press, 1989

Gamble, A. M., and Walkland, S. A. *The British Party System and Economic Policy 1945–1983: Studies in Adversary Politics*. Oxford: Clarendon Press, 1984

Gamble, Andrew. *The Free Economy and the Strong State: The Politics of Thatcherism*, 2nd edition. London: Macmillan, 1994

Garlake, Margaret. *New Art New World: British Art in Postwar Society*. New Haven, London: Yale University Press, 1998

George, Stephen. *An Awkward Partner: Britain in the European Community*, 2nd edition. Oxford: Oxford University Press, 1994

Giddens, Anthony, and Stanworth, Philip, eds. *Elites and Power in British Society*. Cambridge: Cambridge University Press, 1974

Gilroy, Paul. *Against Race: Imagining Political Culture beyond the Color Line*. Cambridge, MA: Belknap Press of Harvard University Press, 2000

Gilroy, Paul. *'There Ain't No Black in the Union Jack': The Cultural Politics of Race and Nation*. Chicago: University of Chicago Press, 1991

Gissing, George. *New Grub Street*. London: Penguin, 1968

Glennerster, Howard. *British Social Policy since 1945*. Oxford: Basil Blackwell, 1995

Glennerster, Howard, and Hills, John. *The State of Welfare: The Economics of Social Spending*, 2nd edition. Oxford, New York: Oxford University Press, 1998

Glyn, Andrew, and Miliband, David, eds. *Paying for Inequality: The Economic Costs of Social Injustice*. London: Rivers Oram Press, 1994

Goodman, Geoffrey. *The Miners' Strike*. London, Sydney: Pluto Press, 1985

Gorst, Anthony, Johnman, Lewis, and Lucas, W. Scott. *Postwar Britain, 1945–64: Themes and Perspectives*. London, New York: Pinter Publishers, 1989

—. *Contemporary British History 1931–1961: Politics and the Limits of Policy*. London, New York: Pinter, 1991

Goulbourne, Harry. *Race Relations in Britain since 1945*. Basingstoke: Macmillan; New York: St Martin's Press, 1998

Grant, Alexander, and Stringer, Keith J. *Uniting the Kingdom? The Making of British History*. London, New York: Routledge, 1995

Hall, Kathleen D. *Lives in Translation: Sikh Youth as British Citizens*. Philadelphia: University of Pennsylvania Press, 2002

Hall, Lesley A. *Sex, Gender and Social Change in Britain since 1880*. New York: St Martin's Press, 2000

Halsey, A. H., ed. *British Social Trends since 1900: A Guide to the Changing Social Structure of Britain*, 2nd edition. Basingstoke, London: Macmillan, 1988

—. *The Decline of the Donnish Dominion: The British Academic Professions in the Twentieth Century*. Oxford: Clarendon Press, 1992

—. *Change in British Society, from 1900 to the Present Day*. Oxford, New York: Oxford University Press, 1995

Halsey, A. H., and Webb, Josephine, eds. *Twentieth-Century British Social Trends*, 3rd edition. Basingstoke: Macmillan; New York: St Martin's Press, 2000

Hamer, D. A. *Liberal Politics in the Age of Gladstone and Rosebery*. Oxford: Oxford University Press, 1972

Hanham, H. J. *Scottish Nationalism*. London: Faber and Faber, 1969

Hansen, Randall. *Citizenship and Immigration in Post-war Britain: The Institutional Origins of a Multicultural Nation*. Oxford: Oxford University Press, 2000

Hargreaves, John D. *Decolonization in Africa*. London, New York: Longman, 1988

Harris, Kenneth. *Attlee*. London: Weidenfeld & Nicolson, 1982

Harvey, David. *The Condition of Postmodernity: An Enquiry into the Origins of Cultural Change*. Oxford, Cambridge, MA: Blackwell, 1990

Harvie, Christopher. *Scotland and Nationalism: Scottish Society and Politics 1707–1994*, 2nd edition. London, New York: Routledge, 1994

—. *No Gods and Precious Few Heroes: Twentieth-Century Scotland*, 3rd edition. Edinburgh: Edinburgh University Press, 1998

Haseler, Stephen. *The Gaitskellites: Revisionism in the British Labour Party 1951–64*. London: Macmillan, 1969

—. *The English Tribe: Identity, Nation and Europe*. Basingstoke: Macmillan; New York: St Martin's Press, 1996

Hastings, Max, and Jenkins, Simon. *The Battle for the Falklands*. New York, London: W. W. Norton, 1983

Henwood, Melanie, Rimmer, Lesley, and Wicks, Malcolm. *Inside the Family: Changing Roles for Men and Women*. London: Family Policy Studies Centre, 1987

Herman, Arthur. *The Idea of Decline in Western History*. New York, etc.: The Free Press, 1997

Hewison, Robert. *In Anger: British Culture in the Cold War 1945–60*. New York: Oxford University Press, 1981

—. *Too Much: Art and Society in the Sixties 1960–75*. New York: Oxford University Press, 1987

—. *Culture and Consensus: England, Art and Politics since 1940*. London: Methuen, 1995

Hill, Michael. *The Welfare State in Britain: A Political History since 1945*. Aldershot, Brookfield, VT: Edward Elgar, 1993

Hinton, James. *Protests and Visions: Peace Politics in Twentieth-Century Britain*. London: Hutchinson Radius, 1989

Hitchens, Christopher. *Blood, Class, and Nostalgia: Anglo-American Ironies.* New York: Farrar, Straus & Giroux, 1990

Hobsbawm, E. J. *Industry and Empire: From 1750 to the Present Day.* Harmondsworth: Penguin, 1969.

Hobsbawm, Eric, and Ranger, Terence, eds. *The Invention of Tradition.* Cambridge, New York: Cambridge University Press, 1983

Hobson, J. A. *Imperialism: A Study.* Ann Arbor: University of Michigan Press, 1965

Hoggart, Richard. *The Uses of Literacy.* London, New Brunswick, NJ: Transaction Publishers, 1998 (reprint of 1957 edition)

Holmes, Colin. *John Bull's Island: Immigration and British Society, 1871–1971.* Basingstoke: Macmillan, 1988

—. *A Tolerant Country? Immigrants, Refugees and Minorities in Britain.* London, Boston: Faber and Faber, 1991

Holmes, Martin. *Political Pressure and Economic Policy: British Government 1970–1974.* London, etc.: Butterworths, 1982

—. *The Labour Government, 1974–79: Political Aims and Economic Reality.* New York: St Martin's Press, 1985

Holt, Richard. *Sport and the British: A Modern History.* Oxford: Clarendon Press, 1989

Holt, Richard, and Mason, Tony. *Sport in Britain 1945–2000.* Oxford, Malden, MA: Blackwell, 2000

Hopkins, Eric. *The Rise and Decline of the English Working Classes, 1918–1990: A Social History.* New York: St Martin's Press, 1991

Hoppen, K. Theodore. *The Mid-Victorian Generation 1846–1886.* Oxford: Oxford University Press, 1998

Horne, Alistair. *Macmillan, 1894–1956: Volume I of the Official Biography.* London: Macmillan, 1988

—. *Macmillan, 1957–1986: Volume II of the Official Biography.* London: Macmillan, 1989

Howard, Anthony. *RAB: The Life of R. A. Butler.* London: Jonathan Cape, 1987

Hughes, Meirion, and Stradling, Robert. *The English Musical Renaissance 1840–1940: Constructing a National Music,* 2nd edition. Manchester, New York: Manchester University Press, 2001

Ingham, Geoffrey. *Capitalism Divided? The City and Industry in British Social Development.* Basingstoke: Macmillan, 1984

Inglis, Fred. *Radical Earnestness: English Social Theory 1880–1980.* Oxford: Martin Robertson, 1982

—. *Raymond Williams.* London, New York: Routledge, 1995

Jackson, Alvin. *Ireland 1798–1998: Politics and War.* Oxford: Blackwell, 1999

Jacobson, Jessica. *Islam in Transition: Religion and Identity among British Pakistani Youth.* London, New York: Routledge, 1998

Jeffreys, Kevin. *Retreat from New Jerusalem: British Politics, 1951–64.* New York: St Martin's Press, 1997

Jenkins, Philip. *A History of Modern Wales 1536–1990.* London, New York: Longman, 1992

Jenkins, Simon. *Accountable to None: The Tory Nationalization of Britain.* Harmondsworth: Penguin, 1996

Jenkins, T. A. *The Liberal Ascendancy, 1830–1886.* New York: St Martin's Press, 1994

Johnson, Christopher. *The Economy under Mrs Thatcher 1979–1990.* Harmondsworth: Penguin, 1991

Johnson, Lesley. *The Cultural Critics: From Matthew Arnold to Raymond Williams.* London, Boston: Routledge & Kegan Paul, 1979

Joly, Danièle. *Britannia's Crescent: Making a Place for Muslims in British Society.* Aldershot, Brookfield, VT: Avebury, 1995

Jones, Harriet, and Kandiah, Michael D., eds. *The Myth of Consensus: New Views on British History, 1945–64.* Basingstoke: Macmillan; New York: St Martin's Press, 1996

Jones, Mervyn. *Michael Foot.* London: Victor Gollancz, 1994

Kahler, Miles. *Decolonization in Britain and France: The Domestic Consequences of International Relations.* Princeton: Princeton University Press, 1984

Kavanagh, Dennis. *Thatcherism and British Politics: The End of Consensus?,* 2nd edition. Oxford, New York, etc.: Oxford University Press, 1990

—. *The Reordering of British Politics: Politics after Thatcher.* Oxford, New York, etc.: Oxford University Press, 1997

Kavanagh, Dennis, and Morris, Peter. *Consensus Politics from Attlee to Major,* 2nd edition. Oxford, Cambridge, MA: Blackwell, 1994

Kavanagh, Dennis, and Seldon, Anthony, eds. *The Thatcher Effect.* Oxford, etc.: Clarendon Press, 1989

—. *The Major Effect.* London: Macmillan, 1994

Kay, William K., and Francis, Leslie J. *Drift from the Churches: Attitude toward Christianity during Childhood and Adolescence.* Cardiff: University of Wales Press, 1996

Kear, Adrian, and Steinberg, Deborah Lynn, eds. *Mourning Diana: Nation, Culture and the Performance of Grief.* London, New York: Routledge, 1999

Kellas, James G. *The Scottish Political System,* 4th edition. Cambridge, etc.: Cambridge University Press, 1989

Kennedy, Paul. *The Rise and Fall of the Great Powers: Economic Change and Military Conflict from 1500 to 2000.* New York: Random House, 1987

Keohane, Dan. *Labour Party Defence Policy since 1945.* Leicester: Leicester University Press, 1993

Kidson, Peter, Murray, Peter, and Thompson, Paul. *A History of English Architecture,* revised edition. Harmondsworth: Penguin, 1979

King, Anthony, Crewe, Ivor, *et al. Britain at the Polls 1992.* Chatham, NJ: Chatham House Publishers, 1992

Kramnick, Isaac, ed. *Is Britain Dying? Perspectives on the Current Crisis.* Ithaca, NY, London: Cornell University Press, 1979

Kyle, Keith. *Suez.* New York: St Martin's Press, 1991

Lamb, Richard. *The Failure of the Eden Government.* London: Sidgwick & Jackson, 1987

—. *The Macmillan Years 1957–1963: The Emerging Truth.* London: John Murray, 1995

Laqueur, Walter. *Europe since Hitler: The Rebirth of Europe,* revised edition. London: Penguin, 1982

Lawson, John, and Silver, Harold. *A Social History of Education in England.* London: Methuen, 1973

Layton-Henry, Zig. *The Politics of Race in Britain.* London, Boston: Allen & Unwin, 1984

—. *The Politics of Immigration: Immigration, 'Race' and 'Race' Relations in Post-war Britain.* Oxford, Cambridge, MA: Blackwell, 1992

LeMahieu, D. L. *A Culture for Democracy: Mass Communication and the Cultivated Mind in Britain between the Wars.* Oxford: Clarendon Press, 1988

Letwin, Shirley Robin. *The Anatomy of Thatcherism.* London: Fontana, 1992

Levy, Roger. *Scottish Nationalism at the Crossroads.* Edinburgh: Scottish Academic Press, 1990

Levy, Shawn. *Ready, Steady, Go! The Smashing Rise and Giddy Fall of Swinging London.* New York, London, etc.: Doubleday, 2002

Lewis, Jane. *Women in Britain since 1945: Women, Family, Work and the State in the Post-War Years.* Oxford, Cambridge, MA: Blackwell, 1992

Lewis, Peter. *The Fifties.* New York: J. B. Lippincott, 1978

Lewis, Philip. *Islamic Britain: Religion, Politics and Identity among British Muslims,* new edition. London, New York: I. B Tauris, 2002

Loughlin, James. *The Ulster Question since 1945.* New York: St Martin's Press, 1998

Louis, Wm Roger, and Bull, Hedley, eds. *The Special Relationship: Anglo-American Relations since 1945.* Oxford: Clarendon Press, 1986

Louis, Wm Roger, and Owen, Roger, eds. *Suez 1956: The Crisis and Its Consequences.* Oxford: Clarendon Press, 1989

Low, D. A. *Eclipse of Empire.* Cambridge, New York, etc.: Cambridge University Press, 1991

Lowe, Rodney. *The Welfare State in Britain since 1945,* 2nd edition. Basingstoke: Macmillan; New York: St Martin's Press, 1999

Lowe, Roy. *Schooling and Social Change, 1964–1990.* London, New York: Routledge, 1997

Lucie-Smith, Edward. *Art in the Seventies.* Ithaca, NY: Cornell University Press, 1980

—. *Art in the Eighties.* Oxford, New York: Phaidon, 1990

Ludlam, Steve, and Smith, Martin, eds. *Contemporary British Conservatism.* New York: St Martin's Press, 1996

McIntyre, W. David. *British Decolonization, 1946–1997: When, Why and How Did the British Empire Fall?* New York: St Martin's Press, 1998

McKibbon, Ross. *Classes and Cultures: England 1918–1951.* Oxford, New York: Oxford University Press, 1998

McSmith, Andy. *John Smith: A Life, 1938–1994.* London: Mandarin, 1994

Manser, W. A. P. *Britain in Balance.* London: Longman, 1971

Marquand, David. *The Unprincipled Society: New Demands and Old Politics.* London: Jonathan Cape, 1988

Marshall, Gordon. *Repositioning Class: Social Inequality in Industrial Societies.* London, Thousand Oaks, CA, New Delhi: Sage Publications, 1997

Marwick, Arthur. *British Society since 1945.* Harmondsworth: Penguin, 1982

—. *Culture in Britain since 1945.* Oxford, Cambridge, MA: Blackwell, 1991

Mason, Tony. *Sport in Britain.* London, Boston: Faber and Faber, 1988

—, ed. *Sport in Britain: A Social History.* Cambridge, New York: Cambridge University Press, 1989

Massey, Anne. *The Independent Group: Modernism and Mass Culture in Britain, 1945–59.* Manchester, New York: Manchester University Press, 1995

Maynard, Geoffrey. *The Economy under Mrs Thatcher.* Oxford, Cambridge, MA: Blackwell, 1988

Mellor, David. *A Paradise Lost: The Neo-Romantic Imagination in Britain 1935–55.* London: Lund Humphries, 1987

Mellor, David Alan, and Gervereau, Laurent, eds. *The Sixties – Britain and France, 1962–1973: The Utopian Years.* London: Philip Wilson, 1997

Michie, Ranald C. *The City of London: Continuity and Change, 1850–1990.* Basingstoke: Macmillan, 1992

Middlemas, Keith. *Power, Competition and the State,* Vol. 1: *Britain in Search of Balance, 1940–61.* Basingstoke: Macmillan, 1986

—. *Power, Competition and the State,* Vol. 2: *Threats to the Postwar Settlement: Britain, 1961–74.* Basingstoke: Macmillan, 1990

—. *Power, Competition and the State,* Vol. 3: *The End of the Postwar Era: Britain since 1974.* Basingstoke: Macmillan, 1991

Middleton, Roger. *The British Economy since 1945: Engaging with the Debate.* Basingstoke: Macmillan; New York, St Martin's Press, 2000

Minkin, Lewis. *The Contentious Alliance: Trade Unions and the Labour Party.* Edinburgh: Edinburgh University Press, 1991

Mitchell, B. R. *British Historical Statistics.* Cambridge, etc.: Cambridge University Press, 1988

Modood, Tariq, Beishon, Sharon, and Virdee, Satnam. *Changing Ethnic Identities.* London: Policy Studies Institute, 1994

Modood, Tariq, Berthoud, Richard, *et al. Ethnic Minorities in Britain: Diversity and Disadvantage*. London: Policy Studies Institute, 1997

Morgan, Kenneth O. *Rebirth of a Nation: Wales 1880–1980*. Oxford, New York: Oxford University Press, University of Wales Press, 1981

—. *Labour in Power 1945–1951*. Oxford, etc.: Oxford University Press, 1985

—. *The People's Peace: British History 1945–1989*. Oxford, etc.: Oxford University Press, 1990

—. *Callaghan: A Life*. Oxford, New York, etc.: Oxford University Press, 1997

Morley, David, and Robins, Kevin, eds. *British Cultural Studies: Geography, Nationality, and Identity*. Oxford, New York: Oxford University Press, 2001

Morris, Terence. *Crime and Criminal Justice since 1945*. Oxford, New York: Basil Blackwell, 1989

Morrison, Blake. *The Movement: English Poetry and Fiction of the 1950s*. Oxford, New York, etc.: Oxford University Press, 1980

Mulholland, Marc. *The Longest War: Northern Ireland's Troubled History*. Oxford, New York, etc.: Oxford University Press, 2002

Mungham, Geoff, and Pearson, Geoff. *Working Class Youth Culture*. London, Boston: Routledge & Kegan Paul, 1976

Murphy, Philip. *Party Politics and Decolonization: The Conservative Party and British Colonial Policy in Tropical Africa, 1951–1964*. Oxford: Clarendon Press, 1995

Nairn, Tom. *The Enchanted Glass: Britain and its Monarchy*. London: Radius, 1988

Nehring, Neil. *Flowers in the Dustbin: Culture, Anarchy, and Postwar England*. Ann Arbor: University of Michigan Press, 1993

Northedge, F. S. *Descent from Power: British Foreign Policy 1945–1973*. London: George Allen & Unwin, 1974

O'Brien, Patrick K. 'The costs and benefits of British imperialism 1846–1914', *Past and Present*, 120 (1988), pp. 163–200

O'Gorman, Frank. *British Conservatism: Conservative Thought from Burke to Thatcher*. London, New York: Longman, 1986

Orwell, George. *The Road to Wigan Pier*. New York, London: Harcourt Brace Jovanovich, 1958

Osmond, John. *The National Question Again: Welsh Political Identity in the 1980s*. Llandysul: Gomer Press, 1985

—. *The Divided Kingdom*. London: Constable, 1988

Ovendale, Ritchie. *Anglo-American Relations in the Twentieth Century*. New York: St Martin's Press, 1998

Panitch, Leo, and Leys, Colin. *The End of Parliamentary Socialism: From New Left to New Labour*. London, New York: Verso, 1997

Parsler, Ron, ed. *Capitalism, Class and Politics in Scotland*. Farnborough: Gower, 1980

Paxman, Jeremy. *The English: A Portrait of a People*. Woodstock, NY: The Overlook Press, 2000

Pells, Richard. *Not Like Us: How Europeans Have Loved, Hated, and Transformed American Culture since World War II*. New York: Basic Books, 1997

Penniman, Howard R., ed. *Britain at the Polls, 1979: A Study of the General Election*. Washington, DC, London: American Enterprise Institute, 1981

Perkin, Harold. *The Rise of Professional Society: England since 1880*. London, New York: Routledge, 1989

Pimlott, Ben. *Harold Wilson*. London: HarperCollins, 1992

Pollard, Sidney. *The Wasting of the British Economy: British Economic Policy 1945 to the Present*. London, Canberra: Croom Helm, 1982

—. *Britain's Prime and Britain's Decline: The British Economy 1870–1914*. London: Edward Arnold, 1989

—. *The Development of the British Economy, 1914–1990*, 4th edition. London: Edward Arnold, 1992

Ponting, Clive. *Breach of Promise: Labour in Power, 1964–1970*. London: Hamish Hamilton, 1989

Porter, Bernard. *The Lion's Share: A Short History of British Imperialism 1850–1995*, 3rd edition. London, New York: Longman, 1996

Porter, Dilwyn, and Newton, Scott. *Modernisation Frustrated: The Politics of Industrial Decline in Britain since 1900*. London, Boston, etc.: Unwin Hyman, 1988

Prais, S. J. *Productivity, Education and Training: An International Perspective*. Cambridge, New York, Melbourne: Cambridge University Press, 1995

Ramdin, Ron. *The Making of the Black Working Class in Britain*. Aldershot: Gower, 1987

Ramsden, John. *The Age of Churchill and Eden, 1940–57*. London, New York: Longman, 1995

—. *The Winds of Change: Macmillan to Heath, 1957–1975*. London, New York: Longman, 1996

Ravetz, Alison. *The Government of Space: Town Planning in Modern Society*. London, Boston: Faber and Faber, 1986

Reitan, Earl A. *Tory Radicalism: Margaret Thatcher, John Major, and the Transformation of Modern Britain, 1979–1997*. Lanham, MD, Oxford: Rowman & Littlefield, 1997

Reynolds, David. *Britannia Overruled: British Policy and World Power in the Twentieth Century*. London, New York: Longman, 1991

Richards, Jeffrey, Wilson, Scott, and Woodhead, Linda, eds. *Diana, The Making of a Media Saint*. London, New York: I. B. Tauris, 1999

Riddell, Peter. *The Thatcher Era – and its Legacy*, 2nd edition. Oxford, Cambridge, MA: Blackwell, 1991

Roberts, Robert. *The Classic Slum: Salford Life in the First Quarter of the Century*. Harmondsworth: Penguin, 1973

Rowbotham, Sheila. *The Past Is Before Us: Feminism in Action since the 1960s.* London, Boston: Pandora, 1989

—. *A Century of Women: The History of Women in Britain and the United States in the Twentieth Century.* Harmondsworth: Penguin, 1997

Rubinstein, W. D. *Wealth and Inequality in Britain.* London, Boston: Faber and Faber, 1986

—. *Capitalism, Culture, and Decline in Britain 1750–1990.* London, New York: Routledge, 1994

Sampson, Anthony. *Anatomy of Britain.* New York: Harper & Row, 1962

Samuel, Raphael, ed. *Patriotism: The Making and Unmaking of British National Identity.* Vol. I: *History and Politics*; Vol. II: *Minorities and Outsiders*; Vol. III: *National Fictions.* London, New York: Routledge, 1989

Sanders, Andrew. *The Short Oxford History of English Literature,* revised edition. Oxford: Clarendon Press, 1996

Sanderson, Michael. *Educational Opportunity and Social Change in England.* London, Boston: Faber and Faber, 1987

—. *The Missing Stratum: Technical School Education in England 1900–1990s.* London, Atlantic Highlands, NJ: Athlone Press, 1994

—. *Education and Economic Decline in Britain, 1870 to the 1990s.* Cambridge, New York: Cambridge University Press, 1999

Schneer, Jonathan. *Labour's Conscience: The Labour Left 1945–51.* Boston, London: Unwin Hyman, 1988

Schoen, Douglas E. *Enoch Powell and the Powellites.* New York: St Martin's Press, 1977

Scott, John. *The Upper Classes: Property and Privilege in Britain.* London, Basingstoke: Macmillan, 1982

Seldon, Anthony. *Churchill's Indian Summer: The Conservative Government, 1951–55.* London, Sydney, etc.: Hodder & Stoughton, 1981

—. *Major: A Political Life.* London: Weidenfeld & Nicolson, 1997

Seldon, Anthony, and Ball, Stuart, eds. *Conservative Century: The Conservative Party since 1900.* Oxford: Oxford University Press, 1994

Seldon, Anthony, and Collings, Daniel. *Britain under Thatcher.* Harlow, New York, etc.: Longman, 2000

Seyd, Patrick. *The Rise and Fall of the Labour Left.* Basingstoke, London: Macmillan Education, 1987

Sharp, Paul. *Thatcher's Diplomacy: The Revival of British Foreign Policy.* Basingstoke: Macmillan; New York: St Martin's Press, 1997

Shaw, Eric. *Discipline and Discord in the Labour Party: The Politics of Managerial Control in the Labour Party, 1951–87.* Manchester, New York: Manchester University Press, 1988

—. *The Labour Party since 1979: Crisis and Transformation.* London, New York: Routledge, 1994

—. *The Labour Party since 1945: Old Labour, New Labour*. Oxford, Cambridge, MA: Blackwell, 1996

Shepherd, Robert. *Enoch Powell*. London: Hutchinson, 1996

Silver, Harold. *Education as History: Interpreting Nineteenth- and Twentieth-Century Education*. London, New York: Methuen, 1983

Silver, Harold, and Silver, Pamela. *An Educational War on Poverty: American and British Policy-Making 1960–1980*. Cambridge, New York, etc.: Cambridge University Press, 1991

Simon, Brian. *Education and the Social Order 1940–1990*. London: Lawrence & Wishart, 1991

Sked, Alan. *Britain's Decline: Problems and Perspectives*. Oxford: Basil Blackwell, 1987

Sked, Alan and Cook, Chris. *Post-War Britain: A Political History*, 2nd edition. Harmondsworth: Penguin, 1984

Smith, Harold L., ed. *British Feminism in the Twentieth Century*. Amherst, MA: University of Massachusetts Press, 1990

Solomos, John. *Race and Racism in Britain*. Basingstoke: Macmillan, 1989

Spalding, Frances. *British Art since 1900*. London: Thames and Hudson, 1986

Spencer, Ian R. G. *British Immigration Policy since 1939: The Making of Multi-Racial Britain*. London, New York: Routledge, 1997

Stevenson, John. *Third Party Politics since 1945: Liberals, Alliance and Liberal Democrats*. Oxford: Basil Blackwell, 1993

Stevenson, Randall. *The British Novel since the Thirties: An Introduction*. London: Batsford, 1986

Stewart, W. A. C. *Higher Education in Postwar Britain*. Basingstoke: Macmillan, 1989

Stopes-Roe, Mary, and Cochrane, Raymond. *Citizens of this Country: The Asian-British*. Clevedon, Philadelphia: Multilingual Matters, 1990

Strange, Susan. *Sterling and British Policy: A Political Study of an International Currency in Decline*. London, New York, Toronto: Oxford University Press, 1971

Tanner, Duncan, Thane, Pat, and Tiratsoo, Nick. *Labour's First Century*. Cambridge: Cambridge University Press, 2000

Taylor, A. J. P. *The Origins of the Second World War*. New York: Touchstone, 1996 (reprint of 1961 edition)

Taylor, Bridget, and Thomson, Katarina, eds. *Scotland and Wales: Nations Again?* Cardiff: University of Wales Press, 1999

Taylor, Gerald R., ed. *The Impact of New Labour*. Basingstoke, London: Macmillan; New York: St Martin's Press, 1999

Taylor, Robert. *The Trade Union Question in British Politics: Government and Unions since 1945*. Oxford: Basil Blackwell, 1993

Thornton, Peter. *Decade of Decline: Civil Liberties in the Thatcher Years*. London: National Council for Civil Liberties, 1989

Thwaite, Anthony. *Poetry Today: A Critical Guide to British Poetry 1960–1995.* London, New York: Longman, 1996

Timmins, Nicholas. *The Five Giants: A Biography of the Welfare State*, revised edition. London: HarperCollins, 2001

Tiratsoo, Nick, ed. *The Attlee Years.* London, New York: Pinter, 1991

Tiratsoo, Nick, and Tomlinson, Jim. *The Conservatives and Industrial Efficiency, 1951–64: Thirteen Wasted Years?* London, New York: Routledge, 1998

Tomlinson, Jim. 'Inventing "Decline": The Falling Behind of the British Economy in the Postwar Years.' *Economic History Review*, New Series, XLIX, 4 (Nov. 1996), pp. 731–57

Townshend, Charles. *Ireland: The 20th Century.* London, Sydney, Auckland: Arnold, 1998

Turner, John. *Macmillan.* London, New York: Longman, 1994

Veldman, Meredith. *Fantasy, the Bomb, and the Greening of Britain: Romantic Protest, 1945–1980.* Cambridge, New York, Melbourne: Cambridge University Press, 1994

Vincent, John. *The Formation of the British Liberal Party.* New York: Charles Scribner's Sons, 1966

Walvin, James. *Football and the Decline of Britain.* Basingstoke: Macmillan, 1986

Watt, D. Cameron. *Succeeding John Bull: America in Britain's Place, 1900–75.* Cambridge, etc.: Cambridge University Press, 1984

Weeks, Jeffrey. *Sex, Politics and Society: The Regulation of Sexuality since 1800.* London, New York: Longman, 1981

Weight, Richard. *Patriots: National Identity in Britain 1940–2000.* London: Macmillan, 2002

Wiener, Martin J. *English Culture and the Decline of the Industrial Spirit 1850–1980.* Cambridge, etc.: Cambridge University Press, 1981

Williams, Philip M. *Hugh Gaitskell: A Political Biography.* London: Jonathan Cape, 1979

Wilson, Elizabeth. *Only Halfway to Paradise: Women in Postwar Britain 1945–1968.* London, New York: Tavistock Publications, 1980

Woods, Tim. *Beginning Postmodernism.* Manchester, New York: Manchester University Press, 1999

Young, Hugo. *One of Us: A Biography of Margaret Thatcher.* London: Macmillan, 1989

Young, John W. *Britain and European Unity, 1945–1999.* Basingstoke: Macmillan; New York: St Martin's Press, 2000

Young, Ken, and Rao, Nirmala. *Local Government since 1945.* Oxford, Malden, MA: Blackwell, 1997

Ziegler, Philip. *Wilson: The Authorised Life of Lord Wilson of Rievaulx.* London: Weidenfeld & Nicolson, 1993

INDEX

Numbers in italics refer to tables

INDEX

Channel 4, 405
Chariots of Fire, 403
Charles, Prince, 392, 518, 519, 677
Charlotte, Queen, 516
Chiang Kai-shek, 97, 137
Chicago, University of, 531
Chiefs of Staff, 90, 106
China, 8, 96, 97, 137, 138, 141, 585, 586
Chinese, 284, 285, 286
Christchurch, 655
Christians, 293, 448–52
Christie, Agatha, 399
Christie's, 393
Chrysler, 186, 187–8
Church of England *see* Anglican Church/Church of England
Church of Scotland, 453
Churchill, Randolph, 128
Churchill, Lord Randolph, 58
Churchill, Winston
    attacks leaders, 650
    and Attlee, 71, 72
    and coalition, 116, 117, 118–19
    and Cold War, 95–6
    creation of Wages Councils, 566
    economic policy, 57, 58, 59
    and Eden, 124, 125
    and general election (1945), 71, 119–20
    and India, 101, 122
    and labour mobilisation, 40
    Moscow visit, 76, 79
    and policy, 121
    and political parties, 116–17
    and Scotland, 472
    and Second World War, 68–9, 70–1, 73
    and 'special relationship' with United States, 66–71
    and Suez, 89
    tensions at end of career, 124
    and trade unions, 118, 124
    and Zionism, 106
    brief mentions, xxix, 47, 94, 129, 140
Citizen's Charter, 562, 656
City, 32, 32†, 35, 37, 178–9, 206, 258, 394, 477, 556, 561, 565, 615
City of Birmingham Orchestra, 374

Clapton, Eric, 407†
Clarke, Kenneth, 540, 563, 653, 664
Classic FM, 401
Clause IV, 46, 143, 145, 146, 151, 240, 639, 659
Clinton, President Bill, xxx, 507, 507*, 508, 598, 608, 615, 659
    administration, 609
Clydeside, 281*
Coal Industry Commission (1919), 47
Coates, Ken, 321
Cobden, Richard, 17
Coca-Cola, 396
Cold War, 20, 40, 74, 78, 81, 93, 95, 96, 103, 110, 136, 137, 138, 140, 146, 402, 590, 594–8, 610, 627–8, 646
Collings, Matthew, 392
Colonial Office, 110–11
Columbia University, 360
Commission for Racial Equality, 291, 434
Common Agricultural Policy (CAP), 220, 242–3, 244, 245, 598, 599, 600–1, 612, 615
Commons, House of *see* House of Commons
Commonwealth, 10, 35, 95, 102, 104, 111–14, 127, 131–2, 220, 240, 243, 244, 247, 285, 287, 580, 581, 586, 587, 593, 623, 675, 676
Commonwealth Immigrants Act (1962), 288
Communism
    and African National Congress, 587
    and China, 97, 137
    and colonial empires, 103
    and Czechoslovakia, 78, 137
    and Greece, 79
    and Korean War, 138
    and Labour Party, 72, 134, 136, 207
    and Malaya, 107
    and North Vietnam, 96
    and Russia/Soviet Union, 66, 68, 76, 78, 466
    as threat to Europe, 81
    and trade unions, 134, 216, 548
    and Truman Doctrine, 80
    brief mentions, 110, 120, 236